"MA`HEO`S CHILDREN"

Early History of the Cheyenne and Suhtaio Indians.

[Second edition, updated and expanded, Vols. 1 and 2 combined]

CHEYENNE CHIEF STONE-CALF AND WIFE. WASHINGTON D.C. 1873.
[SMITHSONIAN INSTITUTION. BUREAU OF ETHNOLOGY. WASHINGTON. D.C.]

MA`HEO`S CHILDREN

**A new perspective on the origins, early migrations
and intertribal relations of the Cheyenne and Suhtaio Indians.
From Prehistoric times to AD. 1800.**

**By
Brian [Spotted-Tail-Eagle] Keefe**

Also by Brian L. Keefe.

The Battle of Rainy Butte. *"The English Westerner`s Society."* 2006.

Red Was the Blood of Our Forefathers. *Caxton Press.* Idaho. 2010.

Making Pacts with Old Enemies. *"The English Westerner`s Society."* 2012.

A Double Defeat for the Atsina. *"The English Westerner`s Society."* 2014.

"Apsarokee." History of the Crow Indians. *"Choir Press."* Gloucester, England. 2014.

First Published by The Choir Press in 2018
ISBN 978-1-911589-98-3

Typesetting and Design by Brian Keefe.
Cover design by Cathouse Art. 2014.
Front cover; High-Back-Wolf, A Cheyenne / Suhtai Sweet Medicine Chief.
[Painted from life by George Catlin in 1832].
Original in the Smithsonian Institution, Washington D. C.

CONTENTS

TABLE OF CONTENTS.

Foreword.   ix
Acknowledgements.   xi
Introduction.   xv

PART 1.
THE ANCIENT TIME.

CHAPTER 1.   Nomads on the Arctic Tundra.   1
CHAPTER 2.   *"They Come Red."*   13
CHAPTER 3.   Early Neighbours and Cousins.   23
CHAPTER 4.   Cree Forefathers.   28
CHAPTER 5.   The Montagnais Element.   38
CHAPTER 6.   March of the Algonquians.   46
CHAPTER 7.   Into the Southland.   58
CHAPTER 8.   Proto-Cheyennes in the *"Great Falls"* Region.   69
CHAPTER 9.   Reappraising the Evidence.   80
CHAPTER 10.   *"When The People Became Orphans."*   88
CHAPTER 11.   Retreat from the St. Lawrence Country.   100
CHAPTER 12.   To the Upper Great Lakes and Beyond.   108
CHAPTER 13.   The Time of Starving.   122

PART 2.
THE TIME OF DOGS.

CHAPTER 14.   In the Marshlands of Minnesota.   133
CHAPTER 15.   The Coming of the *"Sacred Arrows."*   149
CHAPTER 16.   *"Grasshopper People."*   169
CHAPTER 17.   Dispersal of the Bands.   177
CHAPTER 18.   Last days in the Red Lake`s District.   184
CHAPTER 19.   In Terror of the *"Ho-Hay."*   195
CHAPTER 20.   Return of the Suhtaio.   208
CHAPTER 21.   Dog Men.   219
CHAPTER 22.   At War and Peace with the Suhtaio.   229
CHAPTER 23.   *"Issiwun"* is brought to the People.   240
CHAPTER 24.   The *Ve`ho* Commeth.   249

CONTENTS

PART 3.
THE TIME OF BUFFALO.

CHAPTER 25.   Of Missionaries, Myths and Maps.   267
CHAPTER 26.   In the Land of Blue Earth.   282
CHAPTER 27.   Of Pots and Sherds and Earthenware.   290
CHAPTER 28.   A Village on the Yellow Medicine.   300
CHAPTER 29.   Last Days along the Minnesota.   309
CHAPTER 30.   Early Days at the Sheyenne River Settlement.   318
CHAPTER 31.   Roamers in the Coteau Country.   329
CHAPTER 32.   Across the Wide Missouri and Trouble with the Mandans. 347
CHAPTER 33.   Horseback Raiders from the Western Plains.   361

PART 4.
THE TIME OF HORSES.

CHAPTER 34.   "People of the Bow."   375
CHAPTER 35.   On Porcupine Creek.   393
CHAPTER 36.   Wanderings of the Suhtaio.   404
CHAPTER 37.   Last Days at the Sheyenne River Settlement.   418
CHAPTER 38.   Cheyenne Villages Adjacent to, and West of the Missouri. 430
CHAPTER 39.   Into the Black Hills and the Coming of the Tetons.   446
CHAPTER 40.   Home at Last, and War and Peace with the Tetons.   463

APPENDIX A.   485
APPENDIX B.   486
NOTES AND SOURCES.   488
BIBLIOGRAPHY.   497
INDEX.   506

PHOTOGRAPHS AND LINE DRAWINGS

Front piece; photo of Stone-Calf and wife.   ii
Pretty-Nose.   xiv
Wooden-Leg.   xiv
Brave-Bear.   xiv
White-Hawk.   xiv

CONTENTS

Little-Wolf and Dull-Knife.	xxii
Ancient mammoth hunter`s camp.	10
Clovis points and use of Atlatl.	19
Cheyenne informant to Author, Bill Tall-Bull.	25
Cheyenne informant to Author, Clarence `Bisco` Spotted-Wolf.	27
Old-time Cheyenne-speaking informants.	35
Cheyenne informant to Author, James King.	42
Sacred stone `Turtle` monument in Outer Mongolia.	49
Algonquian chiefs and warriors, circa, 1590.	77
Algonquian stockade village, circa, 1590.	78
Battle of Soriel Island.	83
Cheyenne Okh`tsin lance.	93
Cheyenne drawing of people`s return to the north.	104
Spotted-Wolf and Crazy-Head.	130
Northern Cheyenne, Chief Two Moons.	132
Cheyenne informant American Horse.	143
Stands in Timber and Red Hat.	153
High-Backed-Wolf.	161
Cheyenne informant, Fire-Wolf.	179
Cheyenne Kit-Fox warrior.	188
Assiniboine warrior.	201
Cheyenne Red-Shield warrior.	205
Blackduck and Selkirk ceramic ware.	215
Cheyenne Crooked-Lance or Elk warrior.	217
Cheyenne Dog Soldier.	227
Cheyenne informant White-Bull.	237
The Suhtaio Sacred Buffalo Hat.	247
Cheyenne Contrary warrior.	254
Northern Suhtai, Elk River and wife.	266
Cheyenne pots from Sheyenne River site.	295
Plan of Sheyenne River village site.	322
Arial view of Sheyenne River site.	323
Old village site overlooking Maple River.	327
Cheyenne Chief, Three-Fingers.	374
Site of old Cheyenne Village overlooking Porcupine Creek.	397
1731 French model of Fort Beauharnois.	410
Plan of the Fort Lincoln Village site.	438
Baptiste-Goad`s Winter-Count entry, 1785 /`86.	468
Cloud-Shield`s Winter-Count 1790 /`91.	470
American-Horse Winter-Count, 1795 /`96.	471

CONTENTS

Sioux Winter-Count entries "Long-Haired enemy killed." 472

American-Horse Winter-Count entry, 1798 /`99. 478

Northern Cheyenne, Little-Chief, 1879. 484

MAPS

Distribution of Siberian Peoples circa, 2010. 3

Laurel and Blackduck culture areas. 55

Tribes of the St. Lawrence and Great Lakes region, c. 1350. 66

Algonquian migration routes in the North eastern Americas. 109

Archaeological sites in the study area. 117

Tribal distribution in the Upper Mississippi area, circa, 1600. 137

Louis Jolliet`s map of 1674. 218

Hennepin`s map of 1684. 221

Joseph LaFrance`s map of 1744. 263

Louis Franquelin`s map of 1699. 273

Belin`s map of the Upper Great Lakes, 1743. 280

Daniel Coxe`s map of 1722. 283

Cheyenne village sites adjacent to Minnesota River. 302

Map of villages in Coteau des Prairies. 340

Map of the Middle Missouri region and tribes thereof. 352

Portion of Victor Collett`s map of Cheyenne River. 445

FOREWORD

In early summer 1868 within the confines of Fort Larned, Kansas, a group of Indian chiefs looked on in silence, as the white man's Soldier General Phil Sheridan addressed them.

Questions had been posed by the Indians regarding a treaty-signing more than a year past. Where were the annuities promised then by the Great White Father? Where the promised guns and ammunition needed by the Indians to hunt? As agreed, the chiefs had stayed within the limits of their reservation and kept their young warriors at home. They were endeavouring to honour their part of the bargain - it was time the white man honoured his.

While an interpreter relayed the General's answer, an old Indian whose long white braids had weathered sixty-six winters, stood tall and erect in the forefront of his fellows in the adobe-walled conference room. His thin-lipped, broad nose countenance remained impassive, but in his eyes the pride and dignity of his being could clearly be discerned. Dressed in the frock coat of an army major, along with scalp-fringed leggings and beaded moccasins, he looked every inch a picture of Native splendour. Cradled in the crook of his left arm was a long-stemmed pipe, signifying his authority and the solemnity of the occasion. The wind wafting over the buffalo grass had been the very breath of his nostrils, and the hot blood of the equestrian Plains nomad still ran like wildfire through his veins. In his younger days he had been a great warrior, but now the humility and wisdom of years had earned him the office of chief; to guide and protect his people through the trials and calamities which lay before them.

He had come to hear the words of the Great White Father, not as bowing supplicant, but as an equal to those who presumed to dictate to his people, who though temporarily vanquished in war - were not so in their spirit.

The Agent Wynkoop turned to the General. He asked that the Indians be issued the promised guns and ammunition, to which the General replied with words to humiliate,

"Give them arms and if they go to war, our soldiers can kill them like men."

As these stinging words were relayed through an interpreter, he with the long-stemmed pipe struggled within himself to retain composure, and when the interpreter had finished, the old man replied, *"Then let your soldiers grow their hair long, so we can have some honour when killing them."*

Here was a man not to be cowed by the tone of his uniformed adversaries sitting across the table before him. Neither by the military might which the Soldier General represented. For this man's name was Stone-Calf; a chief of the Cheyennes.

The General and his aides must have started aback at Stone Calf's words. Perhaps, they thought, what kind of man was this standing unnerved before them, who had the gall to remain unawed by the white man's infinite power and resources? From where did such people come and along what devious path had they travelled to think they could contest the flood-tide of white expansion across tribal hunting grounds, and by so doing, halt the spread of the white man's infinite greed and alien culture? Was it by such men as Stone-Calf that the Cheyennes had become the people they were? Proud, resilient, tenacious; respected by friend and foe alike; their bravery renowned and the chastity of their women unequalled across the Plains.

No wonder a man when asked his tribal name held high his head and slapped his chest with pride, if he answered, *"Na-tsi`-hest-tai,"* meaning; *"I am Cheyenne."*

Who indeed were these people; and what then is their history?

$$-0-0-0-0-0-0-0-0-0-0-0-0-0-0-0-0-$$

ACKNOWLEDGEMENTS

Research for the present volume began in 1965 and has continued to the present day. It has involved the author consulting hundreds of published and unpublished works, along with a significant amount of personal correspondence and conducting interviews with Cheyenne tribal members themselves. The result is that what follows, is a history of the Cheyenne people from the perspective of their own traditions, which are corroborated and supplemented to a large degree by the traditions of other tribes once in contact with them. It is a premise contrary to the standard approach which has depended moreover, on written documented historical sources. In recent years, however, more interest has been shown regarding the pre-contact traditional period pertaining to Native American Indians in general. Consequently, much new information through the scientific disciplines of archaeology and philology is being amassed. This new material does not in any important way discredit the analysis and conclusions gleaned from the traditions themselves. Rather, it is corroborating and adding substance to them. As a result, the present author has been able to expand and clarify many episodes of Cheyenne traditional history by correlating the said traditions with the new information, gleaned from an analysis of finds which are constantly coming to light. It has, though, been necessary to ignore the modern-day Cheyenne dialectical pronunciation and spelling [which has evolved somewhat different to that once spoken by tribal members prior to the latter half of the twentieth century], in order to clarify certain old-time linguistic comparisons as explained in the present study.

When first I proposed the scenario of a specific migration of Algonquian-speaking peoples, across the North Atlantic from Western Europe to the eastern seaboard of North America, DNA technology and accompanying analysis was in its infancy. Since then, however, rapid advances in the same technology and analysis has tended to corroborate many of my earlier assertions and conclusions, and actually add substance to tribal oral history and traditions previously dismissed by academics of an earlier day. This should not be surprising, for as usual regarding the higher minded Institutions, their faculties are not prepared to question age-old assumptions or reappraise what they themselves have been taught and which they themselves continue to teach, if only because it is convenient to do so.

Owing to such narrow perspectives which often exclude disciplines outside its chosen field, resulting in a blinkered and prejudiced view which prevents taking into account comparisons with other cultures, oral traditions and age-old religious practices to allow a more objective understanding, my assertions and conclusions have, hitherto, been largely ignored by many die-hard conservative scholars, who, albeit in the face of overwhelming scientific evidence gleaned from most recent Mitochondrial Haplo-group analysis, rigidly cling to, what I believe, their original flawed premise that all Native Americans crossed to the Americas from Siberia via a Beringia land bridge.

ACKNOWLEDGEMENTS

Thus they continue to advocate only one route of migration by successive groups from Siberia to Alaska, while dismissing oral traditions from Native peoples themselves, even though such traditions fit with the aforesaid up-to-date analysis of Haplogroups and their subclades which actually indicate at least three separate migration routes, by three separate genetic groups during three widely separated periods in time.

Having said this, due to corroborating evidence constantly coming to light, there are, at last, a number of more enlightened scholars who are coming around to the same conclusions as I have earlier proposed, albeit that their progress appears slow, as they are still in the process of researching supporting evidence to confirm what I here offer in the guise of tribal traditions, oral history and theological and ceremonial comparisons to substantiate my claim.

Notwithstanding a most recent analysis of Haplogroup genetics which shows that the category Q-m242 [pertaining to most indigenous Native peoples of both North and South America], is strongly connected to the DNA of ancient peoples of Siberia, the particular sub-category designated R-m173, or simply R1, applies, specifically, to Algonquian-speaking peoples, including the Cree and Chippewa and their offshoots the Cheyenne, and is compatible with both Eurasian [Northern European] and some Southern Asiatic peoples as opposed to those of the previously noted Q-m242. This does suggest that there was indeed, more than one direction from where came mass migration to the Americas, albeit occurring during different periods by different genetic groups. Migrations both from west to east via Beringia and, what is most important to our present study, from east to west across the North Atlantic Ocean.

Undoubtedly then, some of the assertions throughout the following will prove controversial to hitherto accepted ideas. Hopefully, they will generate discussion and add to a more intimate understanding of the Algonquian-speaking Cheyenne [TsisTsisTsas] and Suhtaio during their prehistoric and proto-historic periods.

I do believe that what is here presented is the most acceptable scenario deduced from all the available evidence at hand, and although my conclusions have been arrived at independently from other contemporary scholars, among whom are included John H. Moore, James V. Wright, Ives Goddard and Karl Schlesier among others, the study here presented does supplement and greatly enhance their studious works. The present work, however, attempts to go much further into Cheyenne and Suhtaio origins and their early migrations, and the author takes full responsibility for the conclusions herein.

Many thanks are extended to several persons who have both encouraged and assisted me over the years, without which the present volume may not have seen the light of day. Among these are Ben Burt of the Museum of Mankind [London], along with Douglas Shelley and Peter McGregor both one-time active experts in the field, for their enduring faith in the project. Native American friends and informants are many, but particular thanks are here given to James [Jim] King, Bill Tall-Bull and Clarence "Bisco" Spotted-Wolf among the Northern Cheyennes of Montana. Wayne Medicine-Elk and Edward Red-Hat among the Southern Cheyennes of Oklahoma, and Joe Medicine-Crow and Winona Plenty-Hoops among others of the Crow Nation

ACKNOWLEDGEMENTS

of Montana. Other informants include tribal members among the Delaware, Pawnee, Sioux, Kiowa and Blackfoot tribes, albeit too many to mention here, but who are certainly not forgotten.

Much appreciated is the research material gathered by LaDona Brave Bull Allard of Fort Yates, North Dakota, and of Kingsley Bray of Greater Manchester, England, regarding data on Lakota Sioux bands and their construction. Thanks are also given to the staff of The British Library [London], The Braun Research Library of the Southwest Museum [Los Angeles], The New York Public Library [New York], The Big Horn College Library and Archives, Crow Agency [Montana], The Dull Knife College Library and Archives, Lame Deer [Montana], the National Archives [Washington DC.] and the Smithsonian Institution [Washington DC.]. Finally, full credit and acknowledgement must be accorded those illustrious scholars of an earlier period, among whom are included George Bird Grinnell, George A. Dorsey, Truman Michelson, James Mooney, George E. Hyde and George Bent among others, without who`s interest and painstaking research, no such work as the present would be possible.

$$-0-0-0-0-0-0-0-0-0-0-0-0-0-0-0-0-$$

Pretty-Nose. Southern Cheyenne. 1877.

Wooden-Leg. Northern Cheyenne.

Brave-Bear, Southern Cheyenne

White-Elk, Northern Cheyenne.

INTRODUCTION

The Cheyenne Nation is composed of two related tribes namely, the TsisTsisTsas [Cheyenne-proper] and Suhtaio. Although speaking varied dialects they have, since the mid-eighteen-thirties, been incorporated as one people. Centred in the town of Lame Deer on the Tongue River Reservation, Montana, and at various locations throughout western Oklahoma, the majority of the Nation reside. Together they constitute around fourteen thousand persons [as of the year 2013], known as the Northern Cheyenne and Southern Cheyenne respectively. Today they strive to retain their tribal identity as descendants of big-game-hunting equestrian nomads; clinging to their old religion and philosophy in an alien environment. Once their young men had raided far afield for horses, scalps and captives, and the vast herds and mixed blood in their veins had been testament to their ability in such pursuits.

Regrettably, yet inevitably, their assimilation into white American society dominated by its material values, has now become the greater part of their present existence, and soon, their age-old traditions will be as far removed from these people, as are now those of the legendary King Arthur to his British descendants.

It is, however, but a comparatively short time ago when Cheyennes were both feared and respected by Indian and White man alike and their condition typical of the Plains nomad, who hunted the shaggy buffalo for his subsistence and stretched its hide over a conical frame of poles for his shelter. During the nineteenth century Cheyennes were noted for their cleanliness; the virtue of their women; superb horsemanship and the indomitable will and pride of their warriors. Indeed, Cheyenne manhood bedecked in eagle-feathers and paint, had constantly exhibited their prowess in warfare with enemy tribes, and engaged themselves in a prolonged and bloody struggle against the unlimited resources of the American military machine. All those acquainted with them spoke highly of their valour and of the integrity of their chiefs.

Underlying these physical attributes was a deep sense of spiritual awareness, in which all tribal members were involved. Among the Cheyennes, as compared to most other nomadic Plains Tribes, their religious indulgence and sincerity was of a high degree, revolving around their concept of a Supreme Being known as *Ma`heo*, and their culture-hero prophets Sweet-Medicine and Erect-Horns.

At their height of power; circa, 1840, the Cheyennes were divided into ten proper bands, each of which had stemmed directly or indirectly from a common nucleus, having broken away from a parent band at different periods in favour of a particular hunting territory or preferred alliance with another tribe. Always, though, they considered themselves Cheyenne and one people, and at least once a year during midsummer, they reunited as a tribal body in order to conduct important religious ceremonies together. At other times they joined in communal war ventures against common foes, and at ten year intervals, came together to select the forty-four chiefs of their people, who were to lead them both in war and peace through the ensuing decade.

These separate bands grew larger or smaller depending upon importance and circumstance, so that whilst some became defunct, others rose to prominence. Subsequently band names were constantly changing, although all Cheyenne informants agreed that during the middle years of the nineteenth century, the bands in existence could be listed as follows.

Omissis.	(Eaters). The largest band and the Northern Cheyenne.	
Heviqsnipahis.	(Burnt Aorta).	The most important band.
Heviatanio.	(Hair-Rope-Men). Also the name for the southern Cheyennes.	
Oivimana.	(Scabby).	Offshoot of the Heviatanio.
Issiometanui.	(Ridge Men).	Mixture of Heviatanio and Suhtaio.
Oktouna.	(Jaws).	Offshoot of the Masikota.
Hofnowa.	(Poor People).	Offshoot of Oktouna and Oivimana.
Masikota.	(Prairie Men).	Later a part of the Dog-Soldier band.
Suhtaio.	(Buffalo Men?). Earlier known as "Dogs," an adopted tribe.	
Watapio.	(Those who eat with the Sioux). Half Sioux / Half Heviatanio.	

An eleventh band the Moiseo [pronounced *Mo-wee-see-o*] had, of old, been of paramount significance as one of the original Cheyenne-speaking components. But by the 1850s owing to a diminished population and admixture of foreign blood, they survived only as one of several small extended family groups among the tribe. During the period in question of circa, 1840, they had lost much of their earlier importance and had no precise place in the tribal camping circle, being attached to one or another band as circumstance dictated.

At times when the entire Nation united, the people pitched their tepees in the shape of a large horseshoe several ranks deep, it`s opening toward the east and the rising sun. If one faced the horseshoe from the east, the Heviqsnipahis or Burnt Aorta band occupied the opening of the circle on its south or left side, the other bands being positioned around the arc in their particular order of significance, now forgotten, but with the Omissis band occupying the north or right side of the opening opposite the Aorta.

In the centre of the circle stood two lone tepees, wherein were housed the Nation's most sacred tribal talismans, i.e., the four Sacred or Medicine Arrows *[Mahuts]* of the TsisTsisTsas, and the Sacred Buffalo Hat *[Issiwun]* of the Suhtaio. Around these talismans both the religious and cultural life of the people were inexplicably linked. The power from such objects ensured the continuation of the tribe both in hunting and in war, and in all other things pertaining to the well-being of the people. Such is still the belief today regarding these sacred icons, which having mythological origins, had been given long ago to the Cheyennes and Suhtaio at separate times by their respective culture heroes. They have been and yet remain the most important and revered objects among that Nation. Successful war-parties once made offerings to the "Arrows" or the" Hat" as tokens of gratitude and at times, both palladiums were carried against an enemy tribe to guarantee success. Such occasions were rare and occurred only when the whole fighting force of the Nation was involved.

This fighting force consisted of several military societies or clubs, each of which competed against the others for tribal prestige and renown. They were not age-graded in their makeup and any youth of fighting age was eligible to join. Although admittance was usually by invitation, few were turned away from their society of choice. As a rule, although by no means always, son or nephew followed father or uncle into a particular society and remained a member all his life.

Each society had its own songs, dances and regalia and took turn in policing the camp, organizing tribal hunts; camp movements and combined war ventures. There were four original societies later expanded to eight, and these have remained the only important ones throughout. Some were known by a variety of names and the list below gives the most commonly used terms.

Whkesh`hetaniu.	Kit-Fox; aka, Motsounetaniu, i.e. Flint Men.
Hi - mo`weyuhks.	Elks or Elk-Horn Scrapers; aka, Crooked-Lances.
Mahohe`was.	Red Shields, aka, Bull or Buffalo Soldiers.
Hota`mita`niu.	Dog or Dog Rope Soldiers.
Himatanohis.	Bowstrings; aka, "Bows" and Wolf Soldiers.
Whiiu`Nutkiu.	Chief Soldiers or Chief`s Band.
Hotami`-Massau.	Crazy-Dogs; aka, Northern Bowstrings.
Hohnuhk`e.	Contraries; aka, Clown Society.

The ten bravest younger warriors within the Kit-Fox Society [aka, Swift Hawks or simply Hawks.], regarded themselves as a subsidiary society. They were once well-known, but no longer extant by the latter years of the nineteenth century.

Together these tribal bands and warrior societies, [the last named at times being recognized as bands in their own right], were always included as integral participants in the Nation's two important religious ceremonies; that of the Sun Dance [also known as The Medicine Lodge or Willow Dance], adopted originally from the Suhtaio and held once a year in midsummer, and the `Massaum` [also called Animal or Crazy Dance], which was of ancient origin among the TsisTsisTsas or Cheyenne-proper, not usually held annually, but whenever the need arose, such as times of drought, famine, pestilence or migration. Both were Earth Renewal ceremonies, the performance of which guaranteed the continuity of creation, while at the same time, the participants sought the benevolence of the Great *Ma`heo* and subordinate unseen powers of the Above World and Below World, in order to ensure not only the personal well-being of the tribe, but for the whole of mankind in general and for all living things, including plants and animals, which the Great *Ma`heo* had created.

This, though, had not always been their state, but was of a comparatively recent date as regards their existence as a united people with a singular identity. Prior to this, the ancestors of the Cheyenne Nation had, for the most part, been a sedentary horticultural group of loosely knit bands and even earlier, timid, pedestrian, hunter-gatherers wandering as nomads throughout the year; impoverished without corn, horses and guns; spending nearly all their time in pursuit of game and wild growing food stuffs in a cold snowbound country of the north. They were then often harassed by other tribes, who`s more aggressive warriors drove them repeatedly from one hunting ground to

INTRODUCTION

another.

Before the late seventeenth century no white man had heard of the Cheyennes, and apart from fleeting references by contemporary traders and travellers, they remained obscure until the latter decade of the eighteenth, by which time much was already written and more known about tribes in contact with them. One must, therefore, when attempting a study of early Cheyenne history, resort to tribal tradition in order to obtain relevant information relating to that people's early locations and migrations. Also of important episodes such as when horses and guns were first introduced among them, two gifts from the Old World which proved decisive factors in Cheyenne cultural and military history. Indeed, revolutionizing our subjects from proto-historic pedestrian hunter-gatherers and sometimes agriculturists, to fierce equestrian nomadic warrior / hunters of the historic time.

How far tribal traditions can be accepted as factual evidence has always proved a difficult question to answer, and it is proper here that we evaluate their worth.

As it is with any people in a state of illiteracy, oral storytelling is held in high esteem. Such stories whether ethical or heroic in content, contain the history of their ancestors and through them; the tribe claims its individuality and right to exist. Stories are - and ever have been - told with the utmost care and exactitude, any discrepancy being quickly corrected by the listener, as might a child point out the slightest variation in the repeated recital of a favourite fairy-tale.

That these stories are in essence authentic, even though handed down over many generations by word of mouth, there can be little doubt, and distortions, if any, should not always be blamed upon recital from the Indians themselves, but upon their translation into other languages. Of course, the original source must be suspect to a degree, in so much as a lack of scientific knowledge and having a different perspective of reality to our own, caused the primitive raconteur to interpret phenomena of nature as being the responsibility of unseen powers, good or evil, depending upon the occurrence and its consequence. This sometimes confuses historical fact with fantasy, yet a more in depth perusal often enables the researcher to separate the two. The real problem facing the historian is that of chronology.

As a general rule the Cheyennes, in olden days, along with most other Indian peoples inhabiting the Continent north of Mexico, harboured a time concept different to that held by the white man. Cheyenne speech was often conducted in the present tense; even though referring to events of long ago. Their culture denied them a precise and detailed chronological perspective of the past and future. In Cheyenne ideology all was part of a continuous cycle bound up with the present and was not considered separate to their everyday actions. Thus, their history could only be perceived as a series of events free-floating in time and often interchangeable, as regards their belonging to an earlier or later period in whichever way the recipient chose to view them. This is not to say that specific past events and persons were not remembered, only that they were remembered in the present idiom. A man when dead did not remain in the past, his spirit went to the camp among the stars where his ancestors lived and where life continued as it did on earth. In short, his spirit remained part of the tribe for all time, only it resided in another camp.

On the other hand, the future deliberately would not be conceived beyond their immediate or seasonal needs; their environment would not allow it, and because a high mortality rate was a profound reality in their day to day existence, speculation upon the future was often a depressive and dangerous pastime. The lack of a more detailed expression of chronology was, in itself, a subtle instrument employed to instil the above philosophical ideology into future generations, without which, tribal rational may have collapsed.

Thinking constantly in the present idiom brought the deeds of ancestors into everyday life, so that heroics were not of history but current; to be imitated, rather than merely recounted as occurrences of a bygone age unconnected to contemporary values.

Fortunately, the Cheyennes have since become a little more precise; in so much as they now divide their past into four phases, i.e., the `Ancient Time,` the `Time of Dogs,` the `Time of Buffalo,` and the `Time of Horses.` These can be understood in much the same way as we might divide periods of European history into the Bronze Age, Iron Age, Renaissance and the Industrial Age. Each of these Cheyenne phases, though, are used only as guidelines and do not include any systematic order of events, other than a number of related anecdotes being lumped together into a particular time phase.

Stories had no real need to be chronicled, they being told at random; one following on from the other by some comparison of content, and the fact that one event should either precede or succeed another in its proper chronological order, was deemed of little if of any importance, as only the essence of the tale was heeded. For these reasons, not a few historians have dismissed tribal traditions as having little authenticity, yet upon close inspection one finds that such traditions abound with clues, which not only prove many of them explicitly, but also make it possible to fix a date.

It is worth noting that although many of the traditional events recorded by various Sioux Indians in their calendar histories or Winter-Counts, as they are more commonly known, cannot be borne out by documented evidence, where such evidence can be consulted it invariably corroborates them. These *"Counts"* had been set down as permanent records during the second half of the nineteenth century, entirely from oral tradition handed down through the years from father to son. Therefore, contrary to the general view, tribal traditions should be consulted; not only those in concurrence with documented evidence but also those that appear sound enough in their consistency to be acceptable when corroboration is no longer extant. Nonetheless, the importance of constantly bearing in mind the Indian concept of time when attempting to date traditional events, even tentatively, cannot be overemphasized.

In practice it is not the truth of these traditions that limit us, but the shortage of material. Over the centuries, many stories relating to any tribe's far-off days have been forgotten, for although interesting to the modern historian, they did not appear so to the Indian, who deemed them superfluous to the main theme of tribal history, and only those stories needed to keep the tribe's cultural, spiritual and military heritage in a semi-constant flow now remain. In short, the Cheyennes themselves have a meagre store of traditions, but of those that have survived, they are remembered in detail.

Definite historical knowledge pertaining to Cheyennes as a distinct tribal entity, is not forthcoming before the late eighteenth century, during which period they were at last positively identified as a tribe in their own right, inhabiting their historic position in the short-grass prairies between the middle course of the Missouri River on the east and the Black Hills of South Dakota on the west. Prior to this, all else is shrouded in oral tradition and myth. However, by correlating a mass of related material and much fragmentary data supplemented with archaeological findings, a clearer picture can now be had of the ancient and proto-historic time pertaining to the early migrations and intertribal relations of our subjects. This being so, the Cheyennes allow us to document the rise and decline of a typical Plains Indian people, tracing their emergence from a Palaeolithic, hunter-gatherer culture into present-day industrialism.

Predominantly then, this is the story of the origins, early migrations and intertribal relations both peaceful and hostile, of the three original Proto-Cheyenne component groups comprising the early Moiseo, Omissis and Suhtaio bands. These being the nucleus of early separatists from an Algonquian-speaking conglomerate which, subsequently, formed the basis for what has since become the Cheyenne Nation of today.

- 0 - 0 - 0 - 0 - 0 - 0 - 0 - 0 - 0 - 0 - 0 - 0 - 0- 0 - 0 - 0 - 0 – 0 -

PART 1.

"THE ANCIENT TIME."

**LEFT TO RIGHT, LITTLE-WOLF and DULL-KNIFE, NORTHERN CHEYENNES.
[SMITHSONIAN INSTITUTION. BUREAU OF ETHNOLOGY. WASHINGTON. D.C.]**

CHAPTER 1

NOMADS ON THE ARCTIC TUNDRA.

Philological comparisons show conclusively that the Cheyennes, including the Suhtaio component now absorbed within the tribe, belong to the great Algonquian linguistic family. Members of which include the Abenaki, Arapahoe, Blackfoot, Chippewa, Cree, Delaware, Fox, Menominee, Miami, Monsoni, Montagnais, Ottawa, Pottawatomi, Sauk, Shawnee and Wheskerinni among others. Along with the Arapahoe and Blackfoot, the Cheyenne tongue constitutes one of the three most aberrant variations of the stock language, their nearest linguistic relatives today being the Montagnais; Monsoni Cree and Fox.

As regards the racial ancestry of the Algonquian family, like most Amerinds inhabiting what are now the United States and Canada, indisputable evidence shows a close genetic relationship with north-eastern Asiatic peoples, whose origins lie in the early Cro-Magnon, Neanderthal and Denisovan Palaeo-Siberian societies of and north of the Altai Mountains between 50,000 and 40,000 years B. P. [i.e., before the present]. Such is apparent from compatible DNA genomes and `O` blood grouping which include Mongoloid `*types*` that are predominantly `O,` but with an infusion of blood group `B.` Paradoxically, present-day Cheyennes in conjunction with their linguistic cousins the Blackfoot, according to a study by A. E. Mourant, [1956] show that when compared to other Algonquian-speaking tribes, they have a high influx of blood group `A` which is the predominant trait of white Caucasians, particularly among Anglo Saxons of Western Europe. This anomaly among the Cheyennes and Blackfoot might suggest an ancient kinship with certain Caucasoid peoples, although it could also be explained by their absorption during the late historic time of white non-Indians within their respective tribes. More pertinent is that an even closer Algonquian connection with ancient Western Europeans, has been substantiated by a correlation of genetic testing through DNA sequences. The results of a recent investigation in which human DNA samples were compared across the Globe, has shown that a modern-day full-bloodied Greek of ancient Celtic ancestry and a modern-day full-blooded Cree Indian of Algonquian origin, shared common family ancestors from southern Siberia, with an estimated time scale of at least 20,000 years B. P. Having said this, the question of how and when and from which direction Algonquians first arrived on the North American Continent, has long been a breeding ground for assumption and conjecture.

The popular idea of the whole of North America having originally been inhabited by human groups crossing from west to east via the north-eastern tip of Siberia to Alaska over an ancient Bearing Strait land bridge known as Beringia, should not, I believe, apply to all Native North American linguistic groups. It can be argued that too many similarities and identical traits between ancient northern European societies and those of Algonquian-speaking peoples of North

NOMADS ON THE ARCTIC TUNDRA

America and Canada, contradict such a generalization for Native Americans as a whole, and that an *east* to *west* migration across the North Atlantic Ocean - certainly for Algonquian-speakers - is a more likely scenario. For many decades, however, without definite tangible evidence, this idea has remained largely unsupported, although due to additional research by like-minded enlightened scholars which include Dennis Stanford, Bruce Bradley and Michael R. Waters, others are now coming around to this way of thinking and are themselves, at last, questioning and reappraising the previously supposed early migration patterns to the New World from the Old. The discovery of distinct similarities between thin bi-facial knapped-flint tools belonging to what is termed the *Solutrean Culture* of Paleolithic south-western Europe [southern France, Spain and Portugal] with a starting date of at least 20,000 years B.P., and those of identical artefacts found in the Chesapeake Bay area of present-day Maryland, which are likely proto-types of the later-date Clovis [*Llano Culture*] fluted stone points of North America starting around 13,200 years B.P., suggest that what has previously been regarded merely as an informed hypothesis, will eventually be confirmed.

Genetic studies on ancient skeletal remains in Siberia and on those of more recent date pertaining to North American Indians, do indicate strongly that their ancestors had a common origin in northeast Asia. Nothing, though, resembling the unique Solutrean and Clovis point technology of North America has yet been found in Siberia, East Asia or Alaska, although Clovis tools and points do show their having been greatly influenced by proto-types found in south-western Europe. Clovis, in fact, seems to represent a progression of the same technology used by certain western European Paleolithic groups, albeit long after they had migrated out of Siberia and relocated in southwestern Europe. This suggests that a group or groups of the same people did migrate west from a point in Western Europe, and first settled permanently somewhere on the eastern seaboard of the North American Continent where Solutrean-like artefacts have been found. Consequently, as additional evidence of a western European and Native North American Paleolithic connection comes to light, through the finding of more comparable tools and artefacts and, not least, with the progression of DNA technology, the idea of an *east* to *west* route across the North Atlantic by some early groups of migrants to the Americas, having moved along the southern edge of the Late Pleistocene ice sheets, will be proved beyond doubt once and for all.

Notwithstanding that identical traits to those of certain Native American groups do occur in what remains of the archaic religion and ceremonial complexes among the Mongol-related Evenk [also known as Tungus], Yakut and Koryak peoples of north-eastern Siberia, more precise DNA testing techniques may further indicate an additional close ancient Native American relationship with north-western Caucasians of both Celtic and Germanic stock. These last-named peoples also show a predominance of `O` blood group types, and would then explain the close ties and parallels in mythology, theology, cultural attributes and linguistic structure between Native Americans of the New World and what we know of ancient north-western Europeans. Such comparisons are most profound in the ethnographic and mythological material relating to Algonquian-speaking groups on the one hand, and to ancient Gaelic and Scandinavian peoples on the other.

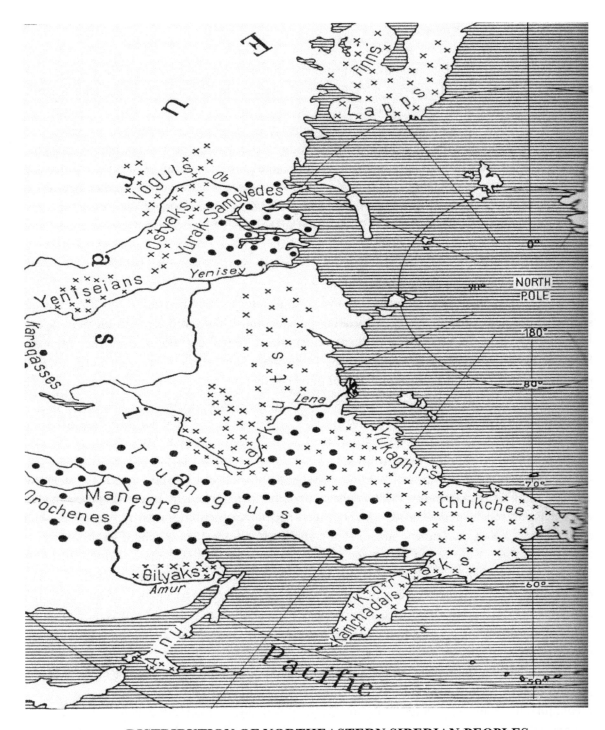

DISTRIBUTION OF NORTHEASTERN SIBERIAN PEOPLES.
[From "Man. God and Magic." By Ivar Lissner. P.161. Jonathan Cape. London. 1961

Certainly, the Archaeological evidence as recently interpreted by Dennis Sanford among others, suggests that the first Paleolithic migrations to North America [25,000 to 30,000 years before the present] were by Europid-Asiatic groups, who had occupied northern Siberia in an even earlier prehistoric time. However, later groups of prehistoric Siberian societies with a strong admixture of Mongolian blood in their veins, and collectively known as Palaeo-Asiatic, who probably included ancestral Algonquians [then closely consanguine with Giliyak peoples of the Amur River, coupled with Ainu groups of Sakhalin Island southwest of Kamchatka], evidently conducted a second western migration from Asia to North America during the Last Great Ice Age of between 14,500 and 12,000 years B.P. Yet a third Asiatic migration involving the ancestors of other Native American linguistic groups, seems to have taken place during the more recent period of between 11,500 and 10,000 years B.P., during what has since been termed "The Younger Dryas Period," when apart from the ice-free corridor of the Baring Straits, a significant part of the Northern Hemisphere embracing the North Atlantic and North Pacific Oceans, was once again locked in an environment of ice sheets and tundra.

This last migration conducted by other groups later to become Native North Americans, such as Athapaskan and Shoshonian-speaking peoples, most likely did cross to the New World from eastern Siberia to Alaska, across the aforementioned ice free corridor of Beringia. It appears, however, that Proto-Algonquians and, perhaps, Proto-Iroquoians, albeit even earlier and at different periods in time in the guise of small bands of hunter-gatherers; pedestrian and fully nomadic, had followed the herds of Mega–fauna such as woolly mammoth, giant caribou, elk and musk-ox, across the Northern Hemisphere from *east* to *west*; rather than *west* to *east*, encircling the globe over several millennia along the southern edge of the tundra and ice-bound regions.

Indeed, prior to the close of the Last Great Ice-Age around 12,000 years B.P., and again for a prolonged period of several hundred years beginning around 11,500 years B.P., to around 10,000 B. P., there had been several such glacial periods which locked up the Ocean waters in great ice sheets, drastically reducing sea levels so that accessible routes formed by staggered island chains covered with intermittent stretches of snowbound forest, shallow tundra swamplands and gigantic ice-floes, were extant over large areas between what is now Siberia, Northern Europe, Iceland, Greenland and Canada. During the time span of the people's continuous wandering, their route of travel would have been conducted from one hunting ground to another, travelling on foot and sometimes in dugout canoes, sealskin boats or other small craft across what was then a mixture of the aforesaid features, which in prehistoric times, reached many hundreds of miles further south than they do today.

Archaeological remains in the guise of midden pits relating to the peoples of those glacial and interglacial periods, and who were then roaming the northern tundra lands, suggest they fed predominantly on mussels, crabs, seals and the great Auk now extinct, but which then were extant in great number, and bird's eggs of many varieties while at night, they lured cormorants and other feathered species in close with blazing torches to enable the people to club them to death and eat them. Other bone deposits found in quantity at specific 'Kill-sites' with tool cut-marks on the bones themselves, and sometimes, hand-made flint points still embedded in the carcasses, indicate that Mega-fauna and other big-game land animals were hunted also; probably by means of a `surround,` in which all the people of an entire band might be involved employing atlatl-propelled spears with long-fluted blades. In addition, from the deep Arctic waters, seals, sea-lions and the occasional whale were dispatched with harpoons and gorged upon. Such food rich in oil and fat, would have provided the human body with much needed insulation against the unremitting cold of their environment, and thus, fire, too, was the essence of the people`s survival.

Traditionally, since ancient times, the spirit of fire among Algonquian-speakers has always been revered as an important deity and was often referred to as "Grandfather," being regarded as originating from – if not a personification of - the sun. The same word for fire among various Algonquian-speakers was sometimes applied to the Algonquian culture hero known as *Michabo* or *Mahabozo*, i.e. "The Great Hare," being the benevolent spirit personage of eastern Algonquian mythology and theology and which animal in its white winter coat, was also referred to as the "Great Light" or "Spirit of Light," symbolizing those aspects which are related to the sun and to the concept of creation itself. The term `Grandfather `when used in its reverential idiom by pertaining to the sun, fire and light, is also compatible with the sacred being of creation known as *Ma`heo* among our subjects the Cheyenne In ancient times, so we are told in Algonquin speaking Chippewa, TsisTsisTsas [Cheyenne-proper] and Suhtaio traditions, he who was delegated to be the "Keeper of the flame" was a holy man of high repute, who during the ancient past when the people had crossed the tundra lands and frozen waters, led them from the front, carrying about his person a piece of sacred flint and tinder wrapped in a water-proof skin bundle. During later times, the sacred fire was carried in a hollowed out horn, the bearer of which raised the first dwelling when the people stopped to rest, then offered forth the sacred flame from which the people kindled their hearth fires, along with oil lamps or blazing faggots for their respective needs. Such dwellings as then used by those Proto-Algonquians when camping on the frozen tundra, were composed either of small oval-shaped willow-frames covered with seal skins, or alternatively, of long Mammoth-tusk-framed hide-covered tents. When on the ice-floes, upturned skin boats likely sufficed as temporary shelters and in all, the people`s existence must have been that of the itinerant, constantly searching for the means of subsistence.

These same ancient Proto-Algonquians, although of a different race and origin to some others with whom they came in contact, shared through the passage of time, certain cultural traits with foreign peoples such as European `types` north of the Altai Mountains including Denisovans and Neanderthals perhaps, along with the Evenk of eastern Siberia and Ainu peoples now confined to islands southwest of Kamchatka, and with which peoples, ancient Algonquians seem to have shared a compatible theology, ceremonial affiliation and mythology, vestiges of which, were still apparent many thousands of years later among the Evenk and Ainu and Algonquian-speaking peoples during their historic periods.

During a more recent time in their ancient past, but whilst still roaming the wind-swept north lands of the late Pleistocene age and long after most other species of Mega-fauna had disappeared from Central and Southern Europe, there yet roamed giant game animals, such as buffalo, mastodon and moose, along with fierce predators; including the huge ferocious Cave Bear and Saber-Tooth Tiger; man-eaters both, which hunted the people and ate them.

As an emerging faction among their northern Asiatic cousins and northern Europid associates, the ancestors of our Algonquian-Cheyenne subjects must have traveled back and forth across the moss and lichen-covered Sub-Arctic terrain; through the stunted taiga of spruce and birch and over the rocky, frozen lands above and west of the Tunguska River. Always in an incessant search for food. The Archaeological record further shows that ancient peoples of those regions knew not the use of metals, but with primitive weapons tipped with stone and bone, they took fish from the icy rivers; small game from the forests and with the aid of the atlatl or spear-thrower and detachable-headed harpoon, hunted the big-game herds and sea-dwelling mammals upon which they mostly depended for their meat, their clothing and shelter. A primitive people in a primitive environment, whose daily life was filled with the harshness of reality, consuming them in constant battle against the uncompromising world around them. Perhaps, they thought, the spirits of their departed kinfolk believed to be dancing in the northern sky [*the Aurora Borealis*], were ever mocking them in their earnest endeavours to exist.

In that Sub-Arctic world of the ancient nomad, life would have been cruel and unrelenting; a struggle against not only the elements of nature, but also against their innate fear of the unknown which included a myriad of unseen powers; ever present; ever threatening. In all things there were good or evil spirits, constituting a host of potent forces and the people believed they were surrounded by them. According to the Cheyennes themselves, they then worshiped the `Blue Sky` which personified creation and also, they paid homage to the unseen spirits of the Above World associated with it, from whence came the thunder; the lightning; the four winds, and as the Cheyennes knew it, the malevolent destructive power of *"Ho-im-a-ha"* e.g. `Winter Man,` also known as the `Great Ice-Giant of the North.` These powerful forces had their abodes in the `Blue Sky` close to the mountain peaks, and so the people held the mountains and rocks in awe and in their wisdom, built sacred shrines on top of high places where they left offerings to appease the temper of their Gods. Indeed, the curious so-called Stone Medicine Wheels along with other stone configurations, still seen today atop high points dotted across the North American States and Canada and northern Europe, are, perhaps, ancient vestiges of such shrines and their prehistoric concepts.

The phenomena of Thunder, heralding spring and new grass, thus encouraging the game herds to emerge from their supposed underground confinement and allowing the cycle of seasons to continue, likewise needed to be placated. A special ritual was conducted in which the hibernating bear; the material manifestation of its celestial spirit seen in the night sky constellation of what we know as *Ursa Major* - representing the year cycle by its dormant time in winter and re-emergence in spring - was ceremoniously ensnared; sacrificially killed and given a message to take on its spiritual path to the Above World of the Gods. Reminding them to bestow their benevolence upon the people, who were observing the laws of nature and should not then, be forgotten.

Also, there were the fickle forces of the World Below, among whom resided the guardians of the game. These, too, had to be propitiated, that the animal spirits continue to be released from their underground refuge and rematerialize again in physical form, so that the people could hunt and fill their bellies with meat. Elaborate rituals were performed to entice the animals from their Below World confinement, and the people sacrificed their own bodies by enduring long periods of thirst and hunger along with self-inflicted wounds, all as overt expressions of gratitude to the animal spirits and their `Keepers.`

Everything animate and inanimate possessed a soul; the wild fowl of the waters and of the air and the beasts of the land. The trees; the grasses; the stones; the rocks, the running streams and the profound mystery of fire which kept the people warm and roasted their victuals. Each was recognized and their spirits conciliated to ensure the harmony of creation. All this and more to guarantee the continued existence of Mankind along with all living things. Failure to observe the proper rituals both in action and in thought, or a lack of respect for the spirit forces around them, would, it was also believed, inevitably bring more suffering upon the people and destroy the precarious balance of their world.

It was considered imperative therefore, that every adult male, being both hunter and at times a warrior when need arose to protect family and tribe, obtain power from some supernatural force. Without which no control could be had over one`s personal destiny, contributing to much distress and bad luck through life and premature demise due to some unfavorable circumstance. This power, or, as later-day Algonquians knew it, `*medicine,*` was thought to emanate from the Great Spirit of creation personified by the `Blue Sky.` Yet the transmittance of such power was only made possible through non-human forms and celestial bodies including the sun, moon and stars, along with natural phenomena such as thunder and lightning etc. Each of these manifestations were constituent parts of the Spirit or Other World which, it was supposed, presented a parallel dimension to that wherein Mankind in his more lowly state, was obliged to exist.

To obtain such power or *medicine*, it was necessary for the potential recipient to actually enter into the realm of the Other World, albeit temporarily, but which could only be achieved by undergoing a period of prolonged fasting or some other form of self-denial, in addition to; in many cases - a more tangible sacrifice such as self-mutilation of the body in order to show sincerity and a serious commitment to one's endeavor. When during such undertakings a state of incognizance had been attained, then in a vision or dream, one could communicate with the Other World and obtain the benevolence of a particular Spirit Being, along with harnessing for one`s own use the specific attributes associated with that Being, which the recipient could, thereafter, not only depend upon when in time of need, but be blessed with power to emulate that Beings specialties peculiar to itself. The ability to harness such attributes, ensured self-preservation in the hostile environment in which one struggled to survive. In certain cases, it allowed the recipient to receive additional power to cure sickness, heal wounds, prophesy forthcoming events, locate missing persons or belongings and bring forth the game when needed, along with other attributes too numerous to mention, but all of which were regarded as supernatural properties outside of one`s natural world and ability. Thus, when one proclaimed that a personal Spirit helper which had previously proved its worth, was dictating his actions, there was no room for indifference among one`s peers. They believed without reserve in the potency of such *medicine;* which should not be ignored and certainly not dismissed out of hand. For to do so would be to the detriment of all concerned.

Such then was the people`s condition for countless millennia, until the advent of more temperate climates and the melting of the ice sheets created a significant rise in sea level.

These Proto-Algonquians during their incessant wandering and probably in small number, then found themselves isolated on the North American Continent, where they most likely just happened to be at the time of the rising oceans. So we find vestiges of a common relationship with other diverse peoples of the Northern Hemisphere from whom the ancestral Algonquians were now irreparably separated. Facets of culture and theology which remained among the Algonquians in their isolation, could still be recognized as traits once common to their ancient Old World cousins, such as the conical skin or birch-bark tepee; the sweat lodge; shaking tent; comparable mythology and the cult of the `Celestial Bear.` Each are aspects of ancient Northern Asiatic and Northern European cultural manifestations, still extant today in North America, Northern Scandinavia and north-eastern Siberia. They are particularly apparent in what we know once related to the ancient culture and traditions of the Celtic and Nordic races of north-western Europe, while - not surprisingly - the Siberian and Mongol concepts of the `Everlasting Blue Sky` as representing the domain and personification of the Supreme Being, is in accord with the Cheyenne world view and theology, in which the same `Blue Sky` is likewise regarded as the domain of the Supreme Being, and as an actual manifestation of the latter who the Cheyennes know as `Ma`heo.`

Likewise we see in the mythology of the Algonquian Blackfoot, the personage and character of the Trickster Hero "Oki," the bringer of fire among other things. Such corresponds almost exactly to that of "Loki" in ancient Norse mythology and has its counterpart in the Cree term, "Oki," meaning a high chief of some sort or other, but, more specifically, pertaining to a deity or important spirit. Certainly the Algonquian Cree expression "Oki-Sikow" translates as something like "Spirit of the Above or Open Space," which when rendered in its English idiom would be analogous with the Christian concept of the "Place of Angels." i.e. Heaven. Likewise, the `Bear Spirit` warriors among the Cheyennes who, supposedly, were invulnerable to iron weapons and fire, are seemingly identical to the same concept attributed to the `Berserker` warriors among ancient Germanic and Scandinavian peoples, while the earlier mentioned "Mahabozo" or "Great Hare" along with "Glooskap," both of which are prominent mystic personages in Algonquian creation tales, are reminiscent of the God "Balder" in ancient Scandinavian versions of the same. The "Twin" aspect, so common a theme in Germanic and related people's legends and mythologies, is identical to the `Twin` symbolism in Algonquian mythology, and, more pertinently perhaps, in certain Cheyenne tales regarding their own origin and to some of their cultural acquisitions which relate to the buffalo and corn. Also in the Cheyenne pantheon of nature's powerful spirits and in their theology, it is a female spirit who has charge of the North and a male spirit in charge of the South. The same as in the ancient Celtic pantheon whose female spirit of the North was known as "Morgana." More relevant to our present study, however, is the "Yellow Haired Maiden," who personifies the underworld female spirit guardian of the animals and corn in traditional Celtic literature. Surely, she has her counterpart in *"E`hyoph`sta,"* the mystic "Yellow-Haired-Maiden" of Cheyenne accounts, who also, was the Underworld female keeper of the game and corn.

The famous Chauvet cave paintings and those of Lascaux in southern France, dated as between 11,000 and 40,000 years old, along with similar prehistoric depictions found in almost inaccessible underground caves in the Basque country of the Pyrenees and at Altamira in northern Spain, and pertaining to either Neanderthal or Cro-Magnon peoples of `O` type blood groups, seem to indicate, I believe, an ancient concept of an underground refuge for the animal spirits. Thus, the animals themselves have been portrayed in detailed and animated form so as to encourage their manifestation as perfect specimens, when, periodically, they were released by the "Yellow-Haired Maiden" into the people's world and allowed themselves to be killed. It is known that the people themselves did not, in that far off ancient time, actually live in the caves in question, but seem to have used the deep recesses in them for paintings and ceremonial purposes alone. Certainly the depictions of figures with animal heads and human bodies on some of the cave walls, do suggest an ancient belief in a spiritual transformation or interchange between animals and humans, as indeed, Algonquian and Cheyenne priests and shaman in recent time were believed to have had metamorphic abilities to do so. Particular prehistoric depictions of human female bodies with buffalo heads, suggesting a spiritual metamorphosis with some kind of fertility symbolism, are reminiscent of the "White Buffalo Woman" among the Lakota and Dakota Sioux, and also of the Cheyenne personage *E`hyoph`sta* [noted above], and of *Issiwun*, the metamorphic female buffalo-spirit of the Suhtaio.

There are many other comparisons between these Northern Asiatic, Northern Caucasians and Native Americans - especially among Algonquian speakers - which point to the fact that all were probably closely associated in the distant past, sharing, at least, a common theology and world view.

Owing to the lengthy time span of Algonquian isolation on the North American Continent, these existing traits must be of great antiquity, being so strong and deep-rooted, that they were yet a part of Algonquian thought and action several millennia later when, during the first half of the nineteenth century serious study was first undertaken to preserve their memory in the written word.

The Delaware tribes during the late historic period, are considered to have been a typical `group type` of the Algonquian-speaking family, and they do have traditions relating to a great migration of their people that commenced during their ancient time when once they had inhabited a very cold and desolate country in the far north which in Delaware tradition is referred to as "The Trembling" or "Burned Land," and might indicate an ancient place of residence for Proto-Algonquians in what today is known as the `Keronki Reserve` in the peninsular of Kamchatka of eastern Siberia, or, perhaps, during a more recent time, in the regions of either Iceland or Greenland where, it is known, volcanic eruptions have also been typical features for thousands of years, and during the very ancient past of around 12,000 years before the present, active volcanoes were in much greater profusion. An even later place of residence, however, as mentioned in the Delaware tradition is referred to as "The Old Turtle Land of the North, " which some scholars believe denotes either the Keewatin area west of Hudson's Bay in north-central Canada, where it is known powerful volcanic eruptions for many thousands of years were also a feature, and continued to be so as recently as the eleventh century AD., or even to the Yellowstone area in north-western North America, which environment was then of a similar nature.

As previously noted, there are strong connections between the religion and sacred rites and ceremonies among the Evenk and Ainu peoples [particularly that regarding the 'Celestial Bear`] with what we know was once practiced by the proto-historic and historic Algonquians of North-Eastern North America, and which include, of course, the Delaware and their related tribes.

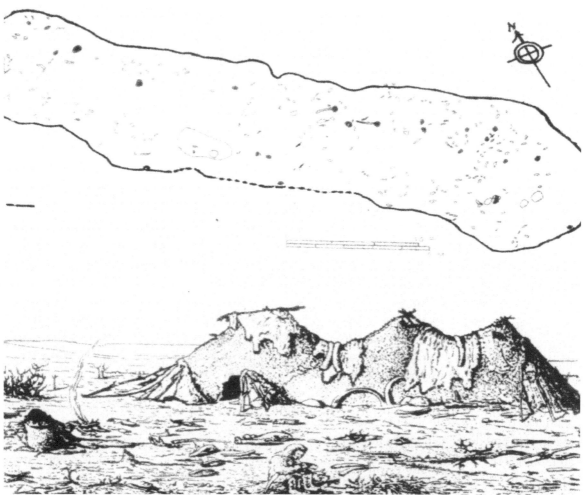

TOP; PLAN OF MAMMOTH HUNTER`S LONG HOUSE CONSTRUCTED FROM A MAMMOTH TUSK FRAME, COVERED WITH WATERPROOF SKINS. [FROM KORENSKI IV USSR].
**BOTTOM; RECONSTRUCTION OF A MAMMOTH HUNTER`S LONG HOUSE BASED ON FINDS AT PUSH KARI. THE HUT IS 12 METERS LONG AND 3.7 METERS WIDE IN A SHALLOW DEPRESSION.** *[From Brian M. Fagan`s "Men of the Earth. P. 140. Little Brown & Co; 74].*

These comparable traits are in addition to the Algonquian mythological comparisons previously mentioned, which are very close, if not identical to, a number of those pertaining to the ancient Norse, Celtic and Germanic peoples of Northern Europe.

The Delaware traditions of their own origin and migrations are contained in various stories, including a supposed concocted account known as the "Sacred Red Score" or *"Wallum Ollum,"* as it is more generally called. These various traditions, however, are important here, as the Delaware and their offshoots were always a prominent and populous Algonquian-speaking faction, and what then pertained to this group during their `Ancient time` of existence, is likely compatible for all Algonquian speakers, including that faction from which the Cheyennes at a much later date, evolved.

To say merely that the aforementioned Northern European comparisons; particularly in mythology and theology, came originally from a much later historic Algonquian intercourse with small parties of both Celtic and Norse visitors to Labrador and the Eastern Seaboard States, beginning, perhaps, with the legendary Saint Brendan`s voyage sometime in the sixth century A.D., and continuing with the arrival of Vikings around AD. 982, or with those of an even smaller number of Scandinavian settlers on St. John's Island, Newfoundland of circa, AD. 1342-1360 and, perhaps, some such sites even further west on the North American mainland, does not explain how Algonquians - who by the latter dates comprised a very numerous population, and had been in situ for an extensive period affording ample time to strengthen or modify their ancient beliefs and traditions - could have been so profoundly influenced to the dire detriment of all that had gone before. It is not really feasible that all older aboriginal Algonquian traditions, myths and theology, which surely must then have been extant, could have been so utterly obliterated in favor of so sudden an appearance of new innovations, brought to them by later-date Celtic and Norse visitors alone. The proposed contact period, must then, have been during a time of much greater antiquity.

The evidence needed to be amassed and analyzed in order to prove this as either being or not being the case would require a book in its own right, and this is not practical or even particularly relevant to our present study. In truth, such a connection would prove to be so far removed from what could be accepted as indisputable historical fact, that the people we now know as Cheyenne would not, in that far distant time long-prior to the beginning of the Christian era of circa, A.D.100, have been a separate recognizable entity distinguished from others of their linguistic stock. Neither could we be sure that the Algonquians themselves would have been recognizable as Algonquians as we know them from their historic period, as indeed, the inhabitants of Ancient Britain cannot in any way be compared to English-speaking peoples of today. However, by accepting Cheyenne tradition, which indicates their ancient lifestyle as being compatible with that of the ancient nomadic hunter of the Sub-Arctic tundra and taiga regions, it can be construed that the ancestors of the historic Algonquians and, therefore, of the Cheyennes, must once have been in contact and in close association with ancient Northern Asiatic peoples and Northern Europeans, to have embraced a similar culture and theology as was then current among other ancient Sub-Arctic peoples.

This being so, it was long after becoming isolated on the North American Continent, far removed from their Palaeo-Asiatic and Mongol forebears still roaming the wind-swept steppes of Northern and Central Asia, that these ancient Algonquian inhabitants increased in number and spread across the vastness of the land. Undoubtedly, they intermixed with indigenous peoples of an earlier migration, perhaps of Palaeo-Asiatic or of Palaeo-European stock, who were then already long-time Natives of the same country. Hence, the two diverse Native American skull shapes commonly known as `round-head` and `long-head. The amalgamation of these skull `types,` had likely caused the classic Asiatic physiography of these new Algonquian arrivals to alter somewhat, by their evolving a more prominent, aquiline- shaped nose of the Palaeo-European `type,` as compared to the smaller, inverted nasal bridge of their Asiatic Mongolian, Giliyak and Ainu cousins. [2] But still for a period of untold centuries, there is but little evidence of their existence which might definitely associate them with latter-day Algonquian peoples. All has been lost in time. We only know for certain that by AD.100, they had become a distinct Native grouping, distinguished by their peculiar styles of stone tools and artefacts and likely, in language, dress and culture from many other migratory peoples also of ancient Siberian origin and later known collectively as Native Americans. It is only from this time on that Algonquians as a separate people can be recognized as such. They then consisted of many small hunter / gatherer bands or extended family groups, the even older cultural remains of which covering the period 6,000 to 2,000 years before present, have since been found in the eastern Canadian provinces, and are classified by the Archaeologist under the collective heading of "Shield Archaic."

If the distribution of `Clovis` point culture material, coupled with Cheyenne traditions which describe their ancestor`s ancient places of habitat are indications, then it may be assumed that the earliest Algonquian arrivals in North America first traveled west from the Atlantic seaboard of that Continent, and, perhaps, as far inland to where today lie the Central Great Plains, before turning north, as warmer temperatures forced the tundra lands to retreat in that direction and the prairies and woodlands expanded in their wake. In such a way both the big-game herds and those Algonquians who depended upon them for their material needs and sustenance, were drawn ever farther north, until they reached what is now the Keewatin region of north-central Canada. Hereabouts, our subjects appear to have lingered for several lengthy, albeit staggered periods in time within the scale of two-thousand years or more, or, at least, as long as the warmer eras persisted due to alternating climatic variations which occurred over several millennia. Certainly, archaeological finds belonging to what is known as the above mentioned "Shield Archaic" culture [which can definitely be associated with ancient Algonquian peoples], show semi-continuous occupation in the Keewatin region by the same cultural groups, and which in total, cover an extensive period of years between 6,000 and 1,000 years B.P.

In this latter area; particularly embracing the Canadian Keewatin region, but also including the northern Manitoba district west of Hudson`s Bay, some small groups would likely have followed the migrating herds of caribou, upon which the people would have depended a large part not only for food, but for nearly all their domestic needs and clothing. Some other groups would, perhaps, have corralled small herds of that same animal, in much the same way as Scandinavian and Siberian nomads do today with the reindeer of their own regions.

We do find striking comparisons between the Northern European Sami reindeer herders of Scandinavia along with the Asiatic Mongol reindeer herders of the tundra and taiga lands of southern Siberia, whose lifestyle and culture have endured virtually unchanged for thousands of years, as was also the case with the old-time caribou hunters of northern Canada. Indicatively, even until the mid-twentieth century and later, certain groups of Inuit [Eskimo] and, more importantly, groups of Algonquian-speaking "Inniu" peoples [i.e. Montagnais and Naskapi most closely related to Cheyennes], were still in the habit in recent times of both herding and corralling caribou as a necessary part of their survival in the Sub-Arctic regions of north-eastern Canada. Perhaps these herding peoples offer a glimpse into the lifestyle, culture and theology as once pertained to our subjects the Cheyennes; albeit then one with all other ancestral Algonquians during the long ago "Ancient Time" of their traditions.

So begins the history of a number of nomadic kindred groups from which, many centuries later, emerged the Cheyenne Nation of the late historic time.

Throughout the foregoing, I have used the terms prehistoric and proto-historic in a lose sense, in order to refer collectively to those obscure millennia; shrouded in myth and tradition, that predate our first documented reference to Cheyennes as a distinct tribal entity by the French Canadian trader Jean Baptiste Trudeau in 1794. Today, as mentioned previously, the latter themselves divide their ancestral heritage into four phases, beginning with the "Ancient Time" and following with, the "Time of Dogs;" the "Time of Buffalo " and the "Time of Horses." Of these phases, the first two in their entirety correspond to our terms prehistoric and proto-historic. We are then at this point in our study concerned with the "Ancient Time," and by omitting the more obvious apocrypha, by which it is surrounded, we will endeavor to detail the early migrations, culture and general situation of our subjects at different periods in those far-off days, along with their relationships – both hostile and friendly – with neighbouring tribes. [1]

- 0 - 0 - 0 - 0 - 0 - 0 - 0 - 0 - 0 - 0 - 0 - 0- 0 - 0 - 0 - 0 – 0 -

CHAPTER 2.

"THEY COME RED."

As there is no reason to suggest that Cheyenne prehistory shows any significant traits to distinguish it from other Paleolithic Algonquian peoples, then sharing a similar hunter / gatherer culture and ancient environment, we might do well to start at the point where Cheyenne tradition itself opens the story and by following its course where substantiated by its consistency - if not positive corroboration - determine their transition from the prehistoric into the proto-historic period. What follows is a composite version of Cheyenne tradition pertaining to their "Ancient Time." It includes data from present-day tribal informants, interspersed with material collected by various Anthropologists early in the twentieth century, such as George Dorsey, James Mooney, George Grinnell, Truman Michelson and W. P. Clark among others.

In the beginning, say the Cheyennes, `Ma`heo;` the all-powerful who is the *Great Medicine* and giver of life and death to all things, created the water and all creatures that live therein and

13

upon its surface, and among whom, was the `Giant Turtle.` To the duck he commanded dive into the water's depths and bring forth mud, and with this mud, `Ma`heo` molded a ball which he then placed on the Turtle's back. The mud began to spread until the Turtle could not be seen and this became the Earth; upon which all things live; the plants, the trees, the grasses and every creature that breathes - all carried on the Turtle's back.

Next `Ma`heo` molded a figure from clay in the shape of a human being. Into its nostrils he blew air and put life into its body. After a while there were more people and at that time, it is said, Long before they had bows and arrows, the people lived in a `Beautiful Far North Country,` where it was always summer.

Every animal both large and small and many then of giant size; every bird, fish and insect could talk to and understand the people whom `Ma`heo` had put among them. For in that long, long ago time, human beings and all other creatures lived in harmony with one another, sharing a common language and like the other creatures; the people always went naked. The people then lived on honey, wild fruits and tubers and did not know the pangs of hunger. They wandered everywhere among the animals and when it was time to rest, they simply lay down on the grass and slept. During the day they talked to the animals for they were friends, and came together as one.

The Great Medicine had actually created three kinds of human beings and there was also a race which seemed like giants among them. There were Hairy People who had dark skins with hair all over their bodies, and others that had much lighter skins and long beards with hair covering their heads, arms and legs. Then there were the Indian People, who had very long hair, but only on their heads. The Hairy People were very strong and active, whilst the Light-skinned-Hairy People with their long beards, were the most tricky and cunning of all in that Beautiful Country.

After a time, the Great Medicine `Ma`heo` taught the human beings how to fashion weapons and hunt. Also how to make fire with which to cook their food and keep themselves warm. Thereupon, the human beings distanced themselves from those who were still without fire [e.g. the animals] and became separated from them. It then happened that the Hairy People left the `Beautiful Country` and went south where the land was barren. The Indian People followed the Hairy People into the `South Land` and the Light-skinned Hairy People also left the `Beautiful Country,` although no one knows where they went. It is sometimes said that they must have been the ancestors of today's white race, who have since taken for their own use all the lands which the great `Ma`heo` first gave to the Indian People.

When the Indian People left the `Beautiful Country` of the north and went south, they went in the same direction in which the Hairy People had gone. These Hairy People remained naked, but the Indian People had since learned to clothe themselves because `Ma`heo` had bid them do so. When the Indian People went south, the Hairy People scattered and fled to the hills where they made their homes in caves high in the sides of mountains. The Indian People seldom saw the Hairy People after this, for the Hairy People were afraid and always fled inside their caves when the Indian People went to see them. In their caves, these Hairy People had beds made from leaves and skins and also, pottery and flint tools fashioned like those of the Indian People. But the Hairy People did not increase. Instead, they decreased in number until finally, they disappeared completely and no one can say what became of them.

Sometime after the Indian People's arrival in the south, `Ma`heo` the all-powerful, warned them that a great deluge was coming, so the people returned to the north from whence they came. The Indian People, though, were now the only humans in the north, for the Light-skinned Hairy People had earlier left that country and even some of the giant animal species had also disappeared.

A long time passed and again the Indian People went south. But again there came a terrible flood which this time, scattered the People far and wide, creating many different bands as opposed to the previous periods when all Indian Peoples had been united, and by now the Giant people had disappeared. In due course, there followed a very lean and barren time, during which the earth often shook and the mountains threw out fire and smoke [ash?]. There followed intense cold and darkness across the land and yet again, recurring floods and violent storms, so the different bands of Indian People, including the parent group from whom the Cheyenne-speaking people of a later time evolved, were obliged to live in caves to protect themselves from the fierce elements outside.

Large rocks lay strewn around and game was scarce, so that the group including proto-Cheyennes, often went hungry. This was still before they had bows and arrows and were obliged to trap small fur-bearing animals for their food and clothe themselves in rabbit skins, cut into narrow strips and laced together at the edges. Still, though, there were certain giant creatures roaming the land.

Some among George Dorsey's old Cheyenne informants stated that a particular species of the giant animals of tradition, was similar to the domestic cow, although four times larger. By nature these Cow-like animals were tame and grazed disconcertedly along the river banks. The people milked them, while boys to the number of twenty could climb upon their backs without the animal being disturbed. Some other animal species, however, are said in tradition to have been as tall as present-day cottonwood trees, and these particular animals chased the people and ate them. Yet another resembled the horse in appearance, although twice as large, with horns and long, sharp teeth. This was the most dangerous animal in the country, it ate the people and would trail a person across the rivers and through the tall grasses by its power of smell alone. Of these terrible creatures there were few, but in the rivers there lived gigantic long snakes whose bodies were so large, that a man could not jump over them.

The people were thus obliged to live in caves; partly because of the severe cold and snow of that country, but also, for their own safety against the giant man-eating beasts, and in these dark, dreary caves, they lived for many years. After a long time, the people's population increased sufficiently for them to confront the man-eating beasts and soon after this, the people followed a light at the end of the cave, until they came out of the darkness and, it is said, the light hurt their eyes. It was then that the people once again began to roam across the land.

The tradition goes on to say that the next thing remembered while still without bows and arrows, is that the people were always travelling; constantly moving from one small island to another.

In a later time - how many centuries or millennia later the tradition does not say - the people came to the shores of great lakes and here, the people lived the year round; catching fish in long seines fashioned from twisted willow-shoots, while hunting Big-game animals by the employment of `Dead-Fall` traps.

Cheyenne informants of George Grinnell on the other hand, declared that in those far off days when in the vicinity of great watery expanses, they were a part of the Cree tribe and together, they lived in the cold and barren country far north-east of their late-historic High Plains habitat. At length, the faction which later became known as Cheyenne, separated from the Cree-speaking parent band and embarked upon another long and devious migration, which was to terminate only when they reached the buffalo prairies of the Western Great Plains.

Before this, so the tradition continues, between the people having broken away from the Cree and before reaching the Western Plains, it is said that from the cold lake country of the north, the people [early Cheyennes] traveled south through a great marsh land, and after wandering around for a number of years, finally settled on the shores of another large lake. This was close to an extensive stretch of prairie and here they again resided for a long time. Now they lived in lodges made by planting a number of saplings in the ground, bending them over so that their tops came together, then covering the whole with reed-matting, plastered over with mud mixed with powdered stones to keep out the wet and cold. They fished in the lake and hunted deer and buffalo in the adjacent prairie. Sometimes the entire band went out some way from the village, to a group of stony hills where large numbers of skunks could be found. Communal skunk hunts were then organized, in which all the men, women and children took part.

Next they moved further south to a `Blue River` running through a `Blue Earth Country,` and here the people built stronger, more permanent lodges of earth and timber; planted corn along with other crops, and hunted deer and buffalo in the prairies to the south.

Tradition does not say why they vacated this `Blue Earth` district, but eventually the people moved west, first to another large lake and thence, further west in stages, until after many years, they reached and crossed the Missouri River. By this time they had horses and soon after, they abandoned the sedentary village lifestyle altogether, to become mounted buffalo-hunting nomads of the western High Plains.

Thus in essence, runs the Cheyenne tradition of their "Ancient time," supplements to which will be given where appropriate. Recent archaeological findings, however, along with linguistic comparisons and ethnological studies in general, offer a more plausible, if not more graphic account of the origin of our subjects, although certain parts of the Cheyenne tradition now under consideration, are born out to some degree by what is regarded as more up to date and certainly, a more scientific knowledge of the past.

How far back in time the above Cheyenne oral tradition extends, one cannot say. It does, however, appear to reach into the prehistoric Pleistocene age, both prior to and after the time of the of the Last Great Ice Age between 14,500 and 12,000 years before present, and includes that period between the end of the Pleistocene and early Holocene of 12,500 and 11,500 years B.P., after which wide spread gasification returned covering a period of several hundred years, and also, that of a more recent inter-glacial warm period of between 6,500 and 5,900 years B.P., when the Thermal

Maximum of the Holocene period [present day] reached its highest temperatures to date. Such is evident by the mention in both Cheyenne and other tribal traditions of the existence of giant land mammals [*Mega-fauna*], in addition to extensive and excessive periods of cold, along with at least two occurrences of excessive inundation and prolonged periods of earthquakes and volcanic eruptions. All of these epochs are well-substantiated by present-day scientific data. In the Cheyenne traditional account related above, it is said that the Indian People moved south from the `Beautiful Country` of the north, and after an unspecified period, they returned from whence they came before migrating south for a second time. These supposed movements might well have coincided with the times of dramatic climatic shifts, creating cold and drought periods alternating with warm, wet periods over several millennia. Indeed, ice-core samples taken from Greenland not only verify such occurrences, but enable us to roughly date them in chronological sequence during the Holocene period with a starting date of circa, 12,500 years B.P.

Thus we know certainly, that around the time 11,500 B P., the climate in the North Atlantic region changed abruptly from a warm environment to one of excessive cold and drought [known scientifically as the "Younger Dryas Period," or alternatively, as "The Big Freeze"]. This lasted at least six-hundred years and probably longer, before returning again to a warmer and wetter environment. Such calculated dates compare favorably with the start period of Clovis culture on the North American Continent of around 12,800 years B.P., and might corroborate, therefore, the event of human migration - which likely included Proto-Algonquian peoples - across the Atlantic to the eastern and north-eastern parts of North America. These alternating climatic conditions must also be coupled to the later decline of Mega-fauna and the end of the Clovis culture around 10,000 B.P., and the beginning of the Folsom point culture period of around 9,000 years B.P. Separately, these events likely led to several movements by resident Algonquian peoples when actually on the North American mainland, forcing alternating migrations from north to south and south to north, as asserted in Cheyenne and other Algonquian traditions.

Most likely then, the above Cheyenne tradition reaches far back into the deep mists of the prehistoric era of human occupation in the Northern Hemisphere. It refers to subsequent movements of Algonquian-speaking peoples, as they were obliged to relocate back and forth within the confines of what today, likely embraces both Northern Europe and North America. The people referred to; evidently, migrated into one habitable environment after another in consequence of the sub-arctic ice sheets and tundra repeatedly advancing and retreating, and much of the land then being alternatively flooded or made barren by drought. In addition, the Hairy People of Cheyenne tradition may refer to either Cro-Magnon or Neanderthal groups, the Neanderthals specifically, having prehistorically occupied northern Europe, Portugal, the south-western part of Spain and the island of Gibraltar. It is now known that Neanderthal man did inter-breed with Homo-Sapiens of central and southern Europe, and, perhaps, the so-called Giant people included the humanoid species referred to in many traditions and mythologies around the Globe, and now associated with Denisovans of the Prehistoric time, whose skeletal remains indicate their having been between at least 7 and 8 feet tall. On the other hand, the ancestors of the so-called "Hairy" Ainu peoples of Yezo, South Sakhalin and some of the Kurile Islands southwest of the Kamchatka Peninsula of eastern Siberia, who, along with other comparisons, once practiced a near identical cult of the `Celestial Bear` as later found among Algonquians, may have been included among the `Light-skinned Hairy People` referred to in the same Algonquian traditions. Human skeletal remains known as `Kennewick Man` found in the state of Washington, USA. in 1998, and thought to be 9,000 years old, not only show a very close DNA affinity with the Ainu, but an Ainu-type stone spear point was found embedded in the pelvis bone of the `Kennewick` skeleton.

It is indicative to note here that the Cheyennes have a story entitled "The Great Race." This tells of a time during their very ancient past when the animals and people, it is said, agreed to race each other to decide if animals should kill and eat humans, or that humans should kill and eat animals. All the split-hoofed and other meat-giving beasts were on one side, whilst the eagle, the hawk and magpie were on the side of the humans. In the event the magpie won the race on behalf of the humans, and thereafter, the animals allowed themselves to be killed and eaten by the people. It is for this reason that the magpie plays such a prominent role in both Cheyenne and Suhtaio religious symbolism, while the story itself is an apology for the killing of `Ma`heo`s` creatures. Such a story seems to indicate an added ancient connection with early northern Asiatic peoples, as the same, or similar concept of mankind and animals being equal in the eyes of the creator, is apparent in oriental Buddhism which actually forbids the killing of animals. The same comparison can also be found among the Chang Tung nomads of Lakdah between present-day Pakistan and Tibet, and it is indicative that these last-named people are even more closely related both genetically and linguistically, to Northern Asiatic groups, especially to those of Mongol stock and thus, indirectly, to proto-Cheyennes of the ancient period.

It was long after this time in their mythological past, so the Cheyenne story continues, that their people became acquainted with the bow and arrow. Perhaps then, the story of "The Great Race" actually relates also to a so-called `happy time` when the people were able to the kill big-game at will. These animals would have included giant herbivores belonging to what is known as Mega-fauna such as the mastodon, mammoth, giant buffalo, giant sloth, giant elk, giant beaver and giant moose among other species, and were brought down by the employment of the long-bladed missiles mentioned above known as Clovis points along with their more recent counterparts known as Folsom. Anciently, such points were used as component parts of hand-held spears propelled with the aid of an atlatl or spear-thrower. Thus, in the allegorical sense, the people could then talk to the animals and consider them their friends, as the latter allowed themselves to be killed more easily, in order to both feed and clothe the people.

The advent, however, of climate change that both warmed and flooded the land, forced the tundra to retreat north and prairie grasses to encroach in that direction, thus reducing tundra food resources which likely heralded a drastic drop in Mega-fauna populations. Perhaps, this event created a good deal of inbreeding among those few giant beasts remaining, such as the buffalo and moose, whose metabolisms unlike the herbivore [plant-eating] mastodon and mammoth, allowed them to ruminate [cud-chewing] on the invading grasses, but which significantly reduced their size, although Mankind by employing both Clovis and Folsom point technology, likely contributed to

18

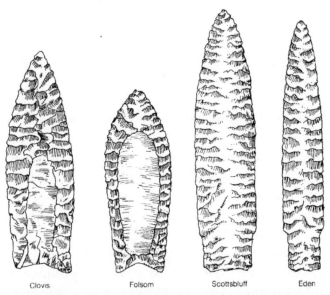

LONG-BLADED FLUTED STONE POINTS FROM THE PERIODS 13,200 B.P TO 8,000 B.P.
[Drawing by Author. Author`s collection]

DIAGRAM OF TECHNIQUE FOR USING AN ATLATL OR SPEAR-THROWER
[Drawing by Author. Author`s collection.]

the impact, and such, it seems, led to the extinction of Mega-fauna between 12,000 and 8,000 years B.P.

Subsequently, this event probably led to the explanation given in Cheyenne tribal tradition, that the giant big-game animals returned underground from whence they came, back into the safe keeping of *"E-hyop-sta,"* the `Yellow-Haired Maiden` who was `Keeper of the game` in the `World Below.`

So the people - having helped diminish the big-game beasts, who`s numbers were already declining due to a changing environment - no longer found enough animals to sustain their needs. As a result, the people inaugurated elaborate religious rites, such as the Cheyenne `*Massaum*` and `*Ox`htsin*` ceremonies, to encourage regeneration of the animals and to gain their permission to share the land; albeit still in the guise of hunter and hunted. Now also, there likely evolved a new human ideology regarding conservation, in order to sustain the smaller-sized beasts which took the place of Mega-fauna. Certainly according to the archaeological record, the manufacture and use of Clovis and Folsom points devised specifically to slay giant herbivores as once existed on the North American Continent, ceased around the same time as the disappearance of Mega-fauna from the Northern Hemisphere. This seems to coincide likewise, with a new bow and arrow technology being adopted in place of the atlatl and hand-held spear.

Having said this, the traditional account of the wanderings of our proto-Cheyenne subjects, only really enters the realm of proven historical content, from the point where it is stated that they were once a part of the Cree.

By treating the Cheyennes and Suhtaio as one group for the time being, the fact that several tribal informants indicate the Cree as being the parent tribe of the Cheyenne, rather than some other Algonquian-speaking people, is precisely what one should expect owing to the strong language affiliation existing between Cheyenne and Cree, which points to a closer linguistic relationship than with any other tribe. The Cree themselves having no more abundant memory of their "Ancient time," and hostile toward the Cheyenne for many years during the historic period, did, though, recognize a similarity of speech between them and always referred to the Cheyennes as either `*Ka-nea-hea-was-tsik,"* meaning "Those with a language somewhat like us," or simply, "Cree Talkers."

Additional evidence of a prolonged and close Cheyenne - Cree relationship, at least during the proto-historic time, is that the Siouan-speaking Dakota or Sioux tribes which linguistically, also include the Assiniboine, referred to the Cheyennes as *"Sha-hi-ela"* or *"Sha-hi-ena"* depending upon the dialect and meaning `red talkers.` This name, so certain Sioux declare, was dubbed on the Cheyennes by the fact that when the Sioux first contacted them, they, the Cheyennes, painted their bodies red and wore red-painted clothes and robes. The Sioux name for the Cree is the same and it is known from early document sources that during the early colonial period in the north-eastern United States [circa, 1634], the Cree were also painting themselves profusely with red paint and were accustomed to wearing red-painted clothes and robes. In corroboration of the above, the Northern Cheyenne historian John Stands-In-Timber, once stated that another early name for the Cheyennes was, indeed, "Red-Painted" or "Red-Coloured People," which he rendered in his tribal language as *"Hahemo-seah."*

However, this same informant also gave the alternative names of *"Watustahtah,"* meaning, "Created Men" or "From the Creator." [1]

On the other hand, there are Sioux informants who declare that the term *"Sha-hi-ena"* conveys `People who speak a foreign tongue,` which is also the Sioux idiom denoting `stranger` and is synonymous with `enemy.` The Sioux describe a people whom they understand, that is, those who speak the same or similar language, as *"Ska-e-a,"* i.e., `white talkers,` and for those who speak unintelligibly or a foreign tongue as *"Sha-e-a,"* i.e.,` red talkers,` the terminal `na` or `la` merely added as a suffix to denote `people` in the respective `n` and `l` dialects of the various Nakota and Lakota Sioux groups respectively Thus in the `n` dialect of the Yankton Sioux, this latter term is represented as *"Sha-hi-ena"* and from this came the French term `Chaiena,` corrupted to `Shayen` by the English and thence to `Cheyenne` by the Anglo-American. That the word should have derived from the French term `Chien` denoting `dog,` because of the Cheyenne warrior society of `Dog Men` or `Dog Soldiers` as some writers have asserted [including De B. Randolph Keim], remains unsubstantiated, although an early name given specifically to the Suhtaio was "Dog People" and will be discussed later in this study. It is worth noting here that in old Celtic languages; especially in Welsh, the same analogy was once used, whereas one was regarded as either a "red talker" or "white talker" depending upon whether one was considered an enemy or friend.

As it stands, such data is confusing if not seemingly superfluous to our present theme. Yet when analyzed, these Siouan appellations do give a clearer indication as to the parent tribe and help determine a period for their separation. The reality is that both appellations, albeit in their own way, are correct.

The Lakota or Teton Sioux division, those of the `l` dialect, had no significant contact with Cheyennes until the latter decades of the seventeenth century. At that time the majority of Cheyennes were living along or adjacent to the middle course of the Minnesota River and further west, in the vicinity of Lake Traverse and Big Stone Lake on the eastern edges of what are now the states of North and South Dakota. By then, they had abandoned their old tribal habit of daubing themselves and clothing profusely with red paint. The Yankton Sioux, however, being those of the `n` dialect and from which group the Assiniboine originated, had previously lived near Cheyenne-speaking peoples and also near the Cree in the headwaters country of the Upper Mississippi in northern Minnesota. This was at least as early as circa. A.D.1640 and they have no doubt whatever, that their name for the Cree, i.e. *"Sha-hi-ena,"* refers to the old Cree habit of applying red paint to themselves and their clothing as decoration. Not surprisingly, they give the same definition for the Cheyennes. Probably then, the Yankton and their relatives the Assiniboine, identified the Cheyenne and Cree as two factions of the same people, until that is, the Cheyennes moved away from the region, having become the victims of hostile incursions from both the Cree and Assiniboine armed with guns and later, from the Yankton themselves.

Throughout the early sixteen-fifties the Yankton then including the Assiniboine were at war with the Cree, and as Cheyenne-speaking groups at that time were still on friendly terms with certain Cree bands, they [the Cheyennes] no doubt also suffered accordingly. However, when separating from the Wazikute Yankton parent group around the date 1640, the Assiniboine went north and while continuing to war with the Cree, they were also at war with their own Yankton kinfolk. Because of this, the Assiniboine at first patched up their quarrel with the Cheyennes who themselves were then in fear of the Yankton. But soon after the Assiniboine arrival, hostilities broke out between the two and the Assiniboine then drove a wedge between the Cheyennes and Cree which, as a consequence, helped finalize the separation of our subjects from the parent Cree stock. Perhaps then, as alternative translations of both the Assiniboine and Yankton terms *"Sha-hi-ena"* are given as "They Come Red," the term implies more specifically, that both the Cheyenne and Cree were the latter`s foremost enemies at that time, for `red` in this sense, means `blood.` It is also indicative nonetheless, with regard to the Yankton specifically, that they were to some degree sedentary farmers and gatherers of wild rice with which they supplemented their diet, while both the Cree and Cheyennes for the most part, were conversely nomadic hunter-gatherers and thereby, predominantly meat eaters the year round. Because of this, the term *Sha-hi-ena* among the Yankton may have had a further connotation pertaining to the fact that the Cheyenne and Cree were habitual meat eaters, i.e. "The shedders of blood," rather than relying on horticultural produce and wild rice as did the neighbouring Yankton.

In the world of Cree and Cheyenne symbolism the colour red is sacred, and in a general way represents hunting, fighting and death. Together, they are related to the sunset and the west, in which direction the spirits of departed animals and humans reside. Paradoxically, however, the colour red also applies to the east and sunrise, whence comes the light and regeneration of all life and thus, the continuing cycle of creation itself.

Additionally, in a particular Cheyenne tale relating to the origin of the Aorta Cheyenne-proper band, it is mentioned that the people then used red mud or clay extensively as a body and clothing decoration and also, that they were then users of what was called "Cree Tobacco," rather than a variant type of weed which the Cheyennes later acquired in its stead. The Aorta, albeit under the somewhat earlier name of Moiseo, were the descendants of one of two component groups that originally constituted the Cheyenne-proper. As will be seen later in this study, the Aorta band represented the more nomadic hunter element of the tribe, as opposed to that other element which was more sedentary in its habits and raised a small amount of garden produce. The name of the culture hero or first ancestor of the hunter-gatherer element [i.e., the ancient Moiseo band or Aorta], is usually translated as "Red, Red, Red, Red," although a more precise meaning would be "Blood, Blood, Blood, Blood." Sometimes this connotation pertains to creation as in `new birth,` but it can also corroborate the Yankton and Assiniboine alternative meaning of their name for both the Cheyennes and Cree as, "Shedder`s of blood."

The Teton Sioux conversely, not being familiar with the red paint aspect any more than other tribes were accustomed to using the same colour upon their persons, naturally assumed in later years, that their appellation denoted foreign speech, and therefore, enemies, even though as they did not come into regular contact with Cheyennes until sometime after their Yankton cousins, they had most probably picked the name up from the Yankton in the first place.

If in truth the Sioux term for both the Cheyenne and Cree did originally convey "alien speech," which in the Eastern Sioux dialects of Yankton, Mdewankanton and Sisseton, is used moreover, as a synonym for `enemy,` then why was it not conferred upon all foreigners who spoke a different language? The fact is that the Sioux only used the term *"Sha-hi-ena"* as a general appellation when an enemy's proper tribal designation was unknown, and so were unlikely to have applied it to the Cheyennes or Cree for any prolonged period if its meaning was purely to denote foreign speech. However, after a part of the Cheyenne amalgamated with certain Teton Sioux bands along the Upper Minnesota [circa, 1700.], the name may have had an interchangeable meaning as either `People who paint themselves red` or, `People of alien speech,` the latter term being used as a somewhat derogatory nomenclature.

It is likely that at a later date, because some bands of Sioux, particularly the Teton, were more times than not amicable toward Cheyennes, their designation did signify `alien speech,` whilst those of the Yankton who were always hostile toward the Cree and at times toward the Cheyennes, employed their designation to denote the use of red clay or paint, in order to differentiate them from other enemies also speaking a foreign tongue.

As late as the eighteen-sixties certain Cheyennes persisted in styling their hair in the unique Cree fashion, which entailed cutting the hair straight across the forehead in line with the eyebrows and when during ceremonies or in combat, of plastering the front lock with clay causing it to stand upright while the rest was braided in multiple strands left hanging down the back. The Suhtaio likewise until a late date, continued to paint their clothes red, more so than did most other tribes around them, and together, both Cheyenne and Suhtaio holy men continued to use red clay or pigment profusely as a body-paint during religious ceremonies and on other important occasions. Perhaps then, each of these aspects were merely symbolic of the Cheyennes and Suhtaio ancient time, and of their ancient close affiliation with the Cree.

- 0 - 0 - 0 - 0 - 0 - 0 - 0 - 0 - 0 - 0 - 0 - 0- 0 - 0 - 0 - 0 – 0 – 0 –

CHAPTER 3.

EARLY NEIGHBOURS AND COUSINS.

It is interesting to note that the Fox tribe, which was once very closely related in dialect, social organization and religious beliefs to both the Cheyenne and Cree, and, therefore at one time in the past, undoubtedly connected with them, have a tradition of once residing in the cold forest country north of the Upper Great Lakes during their early days and of having used red pigment extensively as a personal body and clothing decoration, an old name for the Fox being *"Mesquakie"* meaning `Red-Earth People.` Likewise the `Kinah` or Blood band of Blackfoot, almost certainly an early offshoot from the Cree, often mentioned the term `Red Painters` as being one of their own ancient names. We might add that the Missouri River Hidatsa who spoke a Siouan language, called the Cree *"Scha-hi"* or *"Sha-i-ye,"* signifying like the Sioux, `red talkers,` although in this instance the term appears to have specifically denoted `enemy,` as indeed, the Cree were often the enemies of the Hidatsa. More important, however, is that anciently the Hidatsa applied the same name to the Cheyennes, but during a period when their two tribes were at peace with one another. It is also indicative that neither the Hidatsa, Sioux nor Assiniboine used the same term for the Chippewa, with whom they were often at war and who were very closely related in language, culture and habitat to the Cree. At a later date, the Chippewa were so infused with certain Swampy, Woods and East Cree bands, that there was little to immediately distinguish between them.

It should not then be surprising that the Hidatsa during one stage of their own migration history, roamed lands adjacent to the Red River of the North and east of that river about the headwaters of the Mississippi in the northern part of the state of Minnesota. In this same general territory, Cree, Cheyenne and Suhtaio bands once resided, at which time they were each in regular and harmonious contact with the Hidatsa.

By the time the Cheyennes reached the Black Hills west of the Missouri River in sufficient number to claim that country by force of arms around the date 1760, they were calling themselves collectively *"TsisTsisTsas,"* sometimes spelt with an initial `D.` This term can be freely translated as either `Similarly Bred,` `Our People,` `Like-Hearted People,` `Like Us` or simply, `Us.` It is noticeable; however, that none of these translations occur in the definitive, as would have been customary among most other Algonquian groups, and implies that the Cheyennes did not claim to be an original tribe, but a branch from it. John Stands-In-Timber, though, stated that this name was actually the old Suhtaio appellation for the Cheyenne tribe proper and conceivably, was only adopted by the Cheyenne Nation as a whole at a later date. Also deserving contemplation is that owing to the peculiar structure of the Cheyenne dialect, the term "TsisTsisTsas" can also mean `cut` or `gashed,` said to refer specifically to the tribal habit of cutting strips of skin from the forearms as offerings to their deities, or alternately, to the `coup de grace` given by Cheyenne warriors to slain enemies involving the amputation of the victim`s arm or fingers. [From `ehista,` i.e. `he is of the kind,` or `E-hista,` i.e. `he is cut or gashed`]. More to the point is that this expression can also denote their severance from the Cree by employing a slight inflection, so as to render its meaning as `cut off` or `torn apart.`

The Arapahoe, we know, were also offshoots from a Cree-speaking ancestral group closely related to the Algonquian Miami, and they, the Arapahoe, along with other Plains Algonquians such as the Atsina [Gros Ventre] and Blackfoot, when in their historic seats in the western High Plains both north and south of the Missouri, pointed to the far northeast as being their ancestral location, and from where the Blackfoot migrated west into Manitoba and Saskatchewan, whilst the Arapahoe and Atsina moved into the Lower Red River valley district in what is now north-western Minnesota and north-eastern North Dakota. The Arapahoe go further by declaring that they with the Atsina and Cheyenne, left the Lower Red River country together and moved west to the Missouri and then out onto the Plains beyond that river at about the same time. It is true that this was the case as regards the Arapahoe and Atsina, for these two were then one people. But the latter part of the Arapahoe statement which refers to the Cheyenne is not true, and here Arapahoe tradition has been confounded.

Indisputable evidence which will become apparent throughout, establishes Cheyennes in large number on a western tributary of the Upper part of Red River and at various other locations in the Coteau des Prairies northeast of the Missouri, at least a generation after the Arapahoe had settled in southern Saskatchewan and northern North Dakota, straddling both sides of that river. Certainly, no significant number of Cheyenne-speaking peoples ever lived permanently more than a few miles west of the Missouri until sometime after the Arapahoe had vacated the aforesaid country and relocated much further southwest, in what are now the states of South Dakota, Wyoming and Colorado.

NORTHERN CHEYENNE FRIEND AND INFORMANT, BILL TALL BULL.
[Photograph; Courtesy of the Fort Phil Kearney/Bozeman Trail Association]

Cheyenne oral tradition itself relates that they and the Arapahoe first came together on the west side of the Missouri, at which time the Arapahoe were in two bands and were raising corn near the Black Hills of South Dakota. Cheyenne tradition even recalls the names of the Arapahoe Head chiefs at that time as "The Wolf" and "Cedar-Tree" respectively, while Grinnell on the other hand, gives the alternative name of "Curly" as then being the overall Arapahoe Head chief. [1] It might be conceded, however, that if at some early period the Arapahoe were in close proximity to certain Cheyenne or Suhtaio groups in the Lower Red River valley - which we have no reason to doubt - then a small group of Cheyenne-speaking adventurers may well have accompanied the Arapahoe into the Plains west of the Missouri, and were in contact with Arapahoe bands out near the Black Hills at a much earlier date than has previously been supposed, although what became of them is conjecture.

The Anthropologist Truman Michelson was told by a Cheyenne-speaking informant, that the Suhtaio crossed the Missouri before the TsisTsisTsas, and further implied that both the Suhtaio and TsisTsisTsas when independent groups, had been in the habit of going back and forth, from east to west and west to east, long before deciding to remain permanently in the buffalo Plains on the Missouri`s west side, so that the Arapahoe statement most probably, refers specifically to a Suhtaio group. The associates of the migrating Arapahoe may thus have been that Cheyenne-speaking group of which the aged Cheyenne historian Black Moccasin spoke, when he told William

Philo Clark in 1880, that members of his tribe had been roaming far west of the Missouri as early as 1683.

The eminent historian and ethnologist George Bird Grinnell on the other hand, thought they could have been those designated *"Chienes"* by the Spanish Governor De Vargas in 1695, when referring to a band of Indians visiting the town of Santa Fe in that year, although these last named people appear moreover to have been a White Mountain Apache group from the southwestern part of the Southern Great Plains and known as *Chienes*, but of these events we will also speak later. What is important is that the first part of the Arapahoe statement infers that of old, Cheyennes once resided in an area close to the Cree and to other tribes, whose ancestry was also of Cree extraction.

Regarding the Blackfoot, there appears to be little room for doubt from a philological viewpoint that they, too, were originally a part of the Cree nucleus and in corroboration, we find that Blackfoot tradition and mythology contain many elements which are current among both the Cree and Cheyenne. Particular notice should be given to the stories common to all three groups relating to the "Rolling Head" and Blood-Clot Boy" and in addition, there are traces of Blackfoot migration from the area between the sources of the Upper Mississippi and eastern Manitoba.

Undoubtedly then, during the ancient time of their evolution, both the Arapahoe and Blackfoot must have been in close contact and perhaps closely affiliated with the Cheyenne and Cree, although whether all three were then factions of one specific tribe or separate tribal groups, is now impossible to determine. From such data, nonetheless, it can be deduced that during their proto-historic time, i.e., not long prior to circa, 1700, the Blackfoot, Arapahoe [including the Atsina], Cree, Cheyenne, Suhtaio and Fox, along with some other Algonquian-speaking bands which later became incorporated among the Chippewa and Cree, constituted one great branch of the Algonquian family inhabiting the most western outpost of their stock.

That the Cree are the nucleus of the above list of tribes is indicated by their numerical strength, once estimated by James Mooney as around twenty-thousand persons around AD. 1600, and that the Cree language in its East Cree and Montagnais-Naskapi dialect, seems to be the oldest among all present-day Algonquian speakers, and thus, it should likely be closest to that of the ancient Proto-Algonquian tongue.

What the circumstances would have been of sufficient importance to induce a rift within the Cree group, we can only surmise. In similar instances such as the separation of the Assiniboine from the Yankton, the Crow from the Hidatsa and the Arapahoe from Atsina, respective traditions invariably tell of a family feud or some comparatively trivial intra-tribal disagreement which occasioned their divorce. A comparable explanation may also apply to the Cheyenne split from the Cree, yet considering the latter's uncomfortable existence during those early years of their history - alternating between extreme cold on the one hand and starvation on the other - it would be more reasonable to suppose that the Cheyenne faction simply wandered off, so to speak, in search of more hospitable hunting grounds, thereby reducing the number of mouths to feed within a non-provident area.

There was at that period, unlikely to have been any hard and fast tribal organization among them. Each band probably acted as an independent unit throughout most of the year, essential to the hunting economy of those cold north woodland regions. The practice of separating from the main body during times of privation, was in vogue among all hunter-nomad tribes up until Reservation days late in the nineteenth century. That this was the case with the Cheyennes is enhanced by the fact that other Algonquian groups, also speaking close dialects of Cree and tracing their origins from them, apparently left the main body before or soon after the Cheyennes, and by

NORTHERN CHEYENNE FRIEND-INFORMANT, CLARENCE SPOTTED-WOLF.
[Photograph by the author. Lame Deer, 008, Montana. Author`s collection]

the middle of the eighteenth century, were recognized as independent Nations under such diverse names as Blackfoot, Arapahoe and Fox. To ascertain, however, a date as to when the Cheyenne became independent from the parent Cree group, cannot now be done with precision, yet it appears probable that it occurred as recently as the middle of the thirteenth century or a little earlier, around AD.1200.

Both the Arapahoe and Blackfoot tribes were already separate entities speaking diverse dialects, when resident about the Lower course of the Red River of the North and in southern Manitoba respectively. Certainly as early as the 1670s they were considered sufficiently distinct from their Cree cousins, so as to be harassed by certain Western or Plains Cree bands, joined later by the latter`s Assiniboine allies who along with the Cree were armed with guns and together, began terrorizing all the tribes around them.

Because of their close dialectical connections, the Cheyenne, Suhtaio, Arapahoe and Blackfoot were, evidently, very close cousins to one another during an early period of their evolution, but by the above mentioned date of circa, 1670, they each had evolved separate dialects, one from the other and certain tribal characteristics sufficient to immediately distinguish them as separate entities. Such distinguishing traits as became apparent would undoubtedly, have taken well over two hundred years to evolve. The Arapahoe are said to be very closely connected dialectically with the Algonquian Miami of the East Woodlands and if this is true, then the Arapahoe when residing in the northern parts of Michigan and Wisconsin of the eastern woodlands, had likely also been in contact, at least, with the Suhtaio then in the same region, and with Cheyenne-proper and Cree peoples further west in northern Minnesota until comparatively late during their proto-historic time. However, each of these tribes` divorce from the parent Cree group must have occurred several hundred years earlier than the opening of the seventeenth century. During the period of separation between the Northern Cheyennes and their Southern kinfolk from about 1826 until 1926, variations in language and dress were apparent, although easily recognized by each. But when, for example, the Cheyenne and Suhtaio came together again during the latter half of the seventeenth century after a prolonged period of separation, so Cheyenne tradition relates, both found it very difficult to understand the other, yet, notwithstanding Ives Goddard`s view to the contrary, the Suhtaio spoke a dialect of Cheyenne, not Cree.

The informant George Bent who lived among the Cheyennes for more than forty years and learned much of their history in detail, calculated that the tribe's earliest location was close to the headwaters district of the Upper Mississippi about the date 1600. That his tribal informants stated that this was their tribe's earliest remembered home would seem to imply their split from the Cree as having occurred about that time, and was the beginning of the Cheyenne people`s period of evolving into their separate identity. Bent, though, does not say that the Cheyenne divorce from the Cree occurred around the date 1600, only that their earliest home was during their time of residence in the Mississippi headwaters region.

We know that Cheyennes continued to live near the Cree with whom they initially carried on friendly relations, and one would be correct in supposing that each had regarded themselves as separate factions long before that time. This assumption when used as a starting point, will help to fix a rough date of separation as occurring about four-hundred years earlier, i.e. circa, AD 1200.

To simply declare, however, that our Cheyenne subjects were originally a part of the Cree, is too general a statement to afford any solid information regarding early Cheyenne history. Only if they can be associated with a particular Cree group whose own early situation can to some extent be determined, should we attempt to reach back further far beyond the late seventeenth century in order to shed some light on those dark ages, that witnessed the origin and evolution of Cheyenne-speaking peoples, before they eventually came together to create a Nation in its own right.

- 0 - 0 - 0 - 0 - 0 - 0 - 0 - 0 - 0 - 0 - 0 - 0- 0 - 0 - 0 - 0 – 0 – 0 –

CHAPTER 4.

CREE FOREFATHERS.

The numerous groups of peoples collectively known as Cree, constitute a populous and widely scattered Nation divided into four main cognate divisions. Each division comprises a number of sub-bands which, although practicing similar customs, taboos and religion, speak varied dialects peculiar to their respective territories. Earlier writers have generally treated these divisions as separate entities and classified them accordingly as the Montagnais-Naskapi [East Main or Eastern Cree], Muskegon [West Main or Swampy Cree], Christeneaux [Western; including Woods and Bush Cree] and Monsoni / Plains Cree.

As a `type,` the Sub-Arctic Cree groups are the nucleus of all Algonquian speakers as is evidenced by their language structure, which is clearly more closely connected to that of Proto-Algonquian, more so that is, than others of that linguistic family such as the Central and Western dialects. The Cree divisions themselves can be traced back through their own dialects to a common ancestry, namely that of an archaic Montagnais group.

It is apparent that each of the aforementioned Cree divisions arrived in their historic seats [circa, AD. 1700.] by diverse routes, so that if it can be deduced from which particular Cree group the Cheyennes evolved, we may then determine a comparable migration route for our subjects.

Certain Cheyenne informants of James Mooney declared, that an ancient name for their people was `Moiseo` [singular `Mois`], given as the nucleus of the tribe from whom all the later Cheyenne-proper [TsisTsisTsas] bands evolved. The term itself, according to the linguist Rudolph Petter, means `flint` and refers, he said, specifically to the old-time flint arrow heads manufactured by the tribe, before intercourse with white traders brought them iron points. Petter went further to assert that the term was synonymous with that of `Arrow Men,` which was recalled by Petter's tribal informants as a very old band name of the Cheyennes, among whom the Sacred Arrows or *"Mahuts"* cult was first introduced.

Conversely, in Frederick Hodge's *"Handbook of American Indians North of Mexico,"* [1905], the term `Moiseo` is translated to mean "Many Flies," [from the root word *"his"* = "fly,"], which according to one of Truman Michelson's Cheyenne informants in 1910, was a name once applied to the original Cheyenne-speaking nucleus, due to the fact that the chief of that band was considered scruffy and unclean and always surrounded by flies. However, the latter-day Northern Cheyenne informant James King, stated to the author that the name "Many flies" was but an old nomenclature for the TsisTsisTsas, who were once known colloquially among themselves as "Mosquitoes" and even `Dragonflies.` Of this we will speak later, although neither explanation is a correct interpretation of *Moiseo*. In reality, the term has several spelling variants such as *Moseu, Moisio, Moiseyu, Mowissiyu, Mowitsiu, Mosuni* and *Motsoni,* most of which, so Mooney further declared, are merely dialectical corruptions of the Cree divisional name Monsoni. In the several

Cree dialects the term *Monsoni* is comparable to `Moosh-wa,` meaning `Moose` or `Moose person` as in `Omo-so-[ni]-iw,` while both the Menominee and Chippewa whose dialects were once closely compatible with that of Cheyenne, use the term `Mons` to denote the moose, which with the added Central Algonquian suffix of `inni` or `iniu` meaning `People,` becomes `Mons-ini` or `Mons-iniu` which also translates as `Moose People.` Among the Cheyennes the word `Moiseo,` as noted above, supposedly means `flint` and today the two meanings of `moose` and `flint` are in no way interchangeable. This is not to say that Mooney was wrong in connecting Cheyennes with the Monsoni Cree, only that his analogy has yet to be explained. In order to do so, it is necessary to first determine wherefrom the name Moiseo is derived, and to dismiss what appear to be connections with other meanings which certain past authorities have erroneously accepted as fact.

In 1885 De. B. Randolph Keim gave the term `Mutes-ohue` meaning in Keim's translation `Flint Band` as an alternative name for the Southern Cheyennes as a whole, then also known colloquially as Hevitanio or `Hair-Rope People.` The term `Mutes-ohue,` Keim said, referred to the latter's residence along the Arkansas River which was known in the vernacular to the Cheyennes as `Flint River,` owing to extensive flint deposits and man-made flint points found within that river's vicinity. On the other hand, some later Cheyenne informants declared that this river actually derived its Cheyenne name from the fact that Cheyennes; during their late historic period, obtained their first flintlock guns from both Mexican and Anglo-American traders either along or adjacent to its course, The fact, however, that other tribes, such as the Kiowa, Comanche, Crow and Arapahoe who were much earlier residents of the Arkansas River district than were the Cheyennes, also knew the Arkansas as "Flint River" even before guns came among them, suggests that Keim's first explanation for the term must be accepted as the older and proper definition.

This discrepancy in definitions may be explained by the assertion from the Northern Cheyenne historian John Stands-In-Timber, who stated that he had been told by old tribal members, that the name *"Mutes-ohue"* should more properly be rendered as, "Striking flint` or `Making fire People.` Thus, there seems to have been a confusion among later-day Cheyennes as to whether the term applied to the trade of flintlock guns, or to a source from where they obtained flint with which to make fire. Here Stands-In-Timber was actually referring to a time when, since the ancient past of Cheyenne tradition, a well-respected holy man had kept the *sacred* flint and tinder needed to create fire for the people. The Algonquian-speaking Pottawatomi were recognized among the Chippewa host of tribes as the "Fire People" for this same reason, as their clan alone had been the "Keepers of the flame." In such a way the Moiseo had become the "Keepers of the flame" among all the later Cheyenne-speaking bands, as the Moiseo were then recognized as having been the first of those later known as TsisTsisTsas to separate from the parent Cree group, and later, under the collective band name of Aorta, were long regarded as the most important Cheyenne group because of that fact. Keim did not say that his rendering of the Native term *Mutes-ohue* is Cheyenne in its etymology and it might, therefore, have been a garbled version of an Arapahoe equivalent, from whom Keim likely obtained his information in the first place.

30

Coupled to this is the tribal group known as `Munsey,` they being a cognate division of the Delaware Nation who themselves, were once closely consanguine with the early Montagnais and so by definition, also with the early Moiseo, i. e., the proto-TsisTsisTsas.

The term `Munsey,` sometimes rendered `Moosuni,` is the modern equivalent of `Mins-iu,` being a contraction of the proper term `Minassin-iu` meaning "People of the stony country." It is now said to refer to the Munsey's historic habitat in the rugged area along the Upper Delaware River in the state of New Jersey, although earlier, it seems to have referred to the stony country of Ontario when during the ancient time of their traditions, the Munsey as a part of the great migrating Algonquian host, inhabited that region along with their Montagnais and Moiseo cousins. Whatever the case, here we have the terminal `iu` which corresponds to the archaic Cheyenne term `u` meaning `men` or `people.` During the historic period the Munsey constituted a major group of the Delaware Nation, but actually spoke a dialect distinct to that of other Delaware bands, being more akin to the Sub-Arctic Algonquian groups, particularly the Montagnais branch. Indeed, it is the Munsey Delaware group that was associated with the cult of the `Celestial Bear` and coupled with the Unami Delaware group, revered the turtle for its role in the Great Flood of tradition, more so that is, than did other Delaware tribes. On the other hand, the Monsoni Cree were both anciently and historically, resident in a very stony district of southern Ontario and we have already noted in Cheyenne tradition of their own origins and early wanderings, that the Moiseo, too, lived for a long period in a very stony country, ostensibly near the Monsoni Cree. One might then be justified in supposing that the term `Stony People,` in one form or another, should be the proper translation of the term `Monsoni` and subsequently, its variant form of `Moiseo.` But this analogy is confounded when we learn that the old Cheyenne word for `stone` was *"O-ho-na,"* [modern Cheyenne; H*o-ho-na-hke*] which bears no resemblance to that of `Mois.`

Alternatively, the Cheyenne term `Mois` when translated as `flint,` may appear to come from the same root from which `moose` is derived, perhaps pertaining to the peculiarities of that animal, in so much as the Algonquian term `mooshwa` of which `Monsoni` is a dialectical variation, actually means `wood cropper` in reference to the moose habit of lopping off branches with its widespread antlers, and that a flint in olden times, was probably used as a tool for cutting wood - hence a simile long since forgotten. Certainly, flint was a very important commodity among all tribes before the introduction of metal items among them. Flint tools were recognized as necessary artefacts in the people's day to day living, especially as superior cutting implements and as a means of making fire. Consequently, flint itself did warrant a more distinctive term, merely than being included under the general collective term for `stone.`

A more feasible hypothesis, however, is that the word Moiseo is derived from a compound term contracted from one or another Cheyenne word of either *"mo`i"* or *"mo`e,"* both meaning `elk` or `moose,` and this, coupled with *"is-se-eo"* meaning `root` or `medicine,` may relate to the Cheyenne's early affiliation with a people claiming some supposed affinity with the elk or moose. This compound term is also found among the Cree in its dialectic form of `Monsomin` which likewise, can be translated as "of the elk seed" [or "berry"]. Indeed, the historic habitat of the

Monsoni Cree abounded with elk and an old colloquial name for that people was "Moose Indians." Thinking along these lines, we find in the Cheyenne language that *"eo"* means `river` and thus, if coupled with *"mois"* to create `mois-eo,` we have the term `river elk,` which would be an apt description of the moose in its natural habitat and, of course, be compatible with the Cree name Monsoni, or more properly, "Moose people."

As recently as the mid-colonial period of North America [1680s.], the Monsoni Cree did reside in close proximity to one or another Cheyenne-speaking group, before the latter moved west and crossed the Missouri River, and are yet remembered in both Cheyenne and Suhtaio traditions as, *"a friendly tribe."* [1]

Even today there is yet extant among the Cheyennes a warrior society called Kit-Fox Men, an older name for whom was `Motsonitanio,` supposedly meaning `Flint men` and regarded by many Cheyennes as being the most ancient of their tribe's military fraternities. At some remote period, they seem to have been a band in their own right, as indeed to be explained later, was originally the case with the famous Cheyenne Dog-Soldier and Bowstring societies so prominent in late historic times. It is indicative also that the *Motsonitanio* or Kit-Fox Men were guardians of the tribe's Sacred Arrow talismans, and that a particular item of *Motsonitanio* regalia was an old-time flint arrow head worn suspended by a cord around the neck. This suggests their recognizing a more personal connection with the ancient Moiseo, or Arrow Men as Petter calls them, than did other Cheyenne societies.

An alternative hypothesis is that the first part of the society name, i.e. `Motsoni` [being a variant spelling of Moiseo noted above], is a corruption of `mo`e` or `motsi,` both of which terms were used by Cheyennes as a prefix denoting the male of any large ruminant especially that of the moose or elk and more specifically meaning, `Breeder` in the vernacular. The second part of the word `tanio` is merely a variant of `man` in its plural form, i.e. men or people. Thus, `Motsonitanio` may actually mean `Male Elk People` or more properly "Breeder People," and appears to be a variation of the term `Moi-is-se-eo,` possibly signifying that the latter were the original seed, that is, `Breeders` of the Cheyenne Nation. It is evident then, that the *Motsonitanio* Society originally stemmed from the ancient Moiseo and as will be seen, included in its later years the warrior society of Kit-Foxes then incorporated into the Masikota band, as by circa, 1840, the parent Moiseo band had become a small remnant of its original population and a conglomerate of both Cheyenne and Sioux extraction with little importance as a tribal unit.

Having said this, a more correct pronunciation of all these variations of the term Moiseo, appears to be that offered by George Bent in the guise of `Moiseyu` and *Mowissiyu,* as in this form the term can be positively identified with that of `elk` and `moose,` and subsequently, with the Monsoni Cree.

In the Monsoni / Plains Cree dialect the words for moose and elk are not synonymous, whilst the Cheyennes in contrast used the same word `mo`e` for both animals, merely adding a suitable prefix if the moose needed to be designated more specifically, such as adding the term `ma`hpe` meaning `water` or `poeh-poevese` meaning, `flat-horned.` Apparently, they had forgotten their ancient perceived filial association with the moose after abandoning the northern countries wherein the moose abounded, and after severing themselves from the parent Cree band, changed their tribal affiliation from *Monsoni* denoting the moose, to that of *Mowissiyu* denoting the elk, this being the animal they were next most acquainted with and in so doing, kept the original concept of their old tribal name alive. The Cheyenne term `mo`e` actually means `grass,` which when coupled to the Algonquian term `quissi` [Cheyenne; `messi*] meaning `to eat,` along with the contracted Cheyenne suffix `io` or `iu` denoting `men` or `people`, becomes *"Mo`issi`o"* or *"Mo`issi`u"* meaning "Grass-eating People," as indeed both the moose and elk are so designated in the Cheyenne idiom. Notwithstanding each of the above mentioned alternatives, the term in its pronounced form of `Mowissiyu` seems, moreover, to be a Cheyenne dialectical variant of the Cree term `Wawskasiu` also spelt `Ua-Ua-Skeh-Su,` which in the Monsoni / Plains Cree dialect specifically denotes the `elk,` and is also a variant form of the Algonquian-speaking tribal group of *"Wheski-rinni."* These latter named people were known to the early colonial French by the term *La Petite Nacion* and were actually the Algonkin-Proper from whom the linguistic family derives its name.

Today, the Algonkin-proper are usually classified as belonging to the Chippewa – Ottawa linguistic group speaking what is termed the "Middle Tier" of Algonquian dialects, while the Montagnais-Naskapi are classified as of the `East` or `Eastern` Cree` dialects, and constitute a separate grouping to those known as Central and Western Cree [albeit anciently originating from the same parent Proto-Algonquian tongue]. This distinction, however, is far from satisfactory, as it is clear that prior to white contact of circa, 1603, certain bands that later became component parts of the Wheskerinni or Algonkin-proper entity were of East Cree, Montagnais-Naskapi and even of Huron extraction. While it is true that Algonkin-proper speech like that of Chippewa includes both `l` and `r` dialects depending upon band location, the `l` dialect is thought to be a late innovation. It is likely that the `r` dialect had been predominant during an earlier period, but even before that time, both consonants had been completely absent. In fact, the Algonkin-proper dialect during the earlier period had been more akin to that of archaic Montagnais-Naskapi. This is shown by the Montagnais example of `inniu` meaning `human being,` which predated the Montagnais of Tadoussac and Algonkin-proper later renderings for the same meaning in the guise of `liniiu` and `riniiu` respectively.

The Cheyenne language also lacks the consonants `l` and `r` and the original Montagnais-Naskapi term of `iniiu` meaning `human being,` is compatible with the archaic Cheyenne term of `iu` likewise meaning `human being,` and is merely a contracted variant of the Algonkin-proper terms *riniiu* and *liniiu*. It is, therefore, unwise to draw distinct lines between late-historic Algonkin-proper terminology and late-historic Montagnais-Naskapi, based solely on a study of modern-day phonetics and demographic considerations, as for over two centuries East Cree groups have become so infused with French, English, Chippewa and other ethnic influences, that not only dialects, but blood groupings and mythologies also have been altered somewhat from the original.

Certainly the Algonkin-proper – particularly the Wheskerinni bands – resided during the early historic time [circa, 1603] next to the Montagnais, with the St. Maurice River of south-eastern Quebec Province being the boundary between them. At an even earlier date [long prior to 1603] the Wheskerinni and Montagnais-Naskapi had been closely confederated and intermixed by marriage. As a result, both people's dialects have undergone significant changes since that time. This is particularly apparent regarding the Wheskerinni owing to the latter's additional later association with adjacent Chippewa-speaking groups, and when we learn that the Wheskerinni were just as closely confederated to the Monsoni Cree during their "Olden Time," inhabiting the same locale within the confines of the St. Maurice tributary of the Lower St. Lawrence, it follows that they were; most probably, also closely confederated to our Cheyenne-speaking subjects then known as Moiseo.

The last two syllables of the term *"Weske-rin-ni"* come from a corruption of the Proto-Algonquian term `inniu` meaning men or people, which was often used by the early French, albeit in its later Montagnais form of *rinii*, as an appendage to several tribal names. Thus we have the proper term *"Whe-ske,"* which if we add the older Montagnais suffix denoting people, gives us the term *"Whe-ske-innu"* or in its archaic Cheyenne form, *"Whe-ske-iu."* Here we see a remarkable similarity to the Lewis and Clark term *"Wee-hee-skeu,"* the name the explorers gave to one of two Cheyenne-speaking bands of the Cheyenne Nation then residing along or close to the Missouri River between 1804 and 1805. The word in each of its guises denotes a large ruminant, specifically the elk, and so the Algonkin-proper or *"Petite Nacion"* being a collection of related bands which included the Wheskerinni as the predominant faction, once likely also included among its number – if only as confederates during the so-called "Ancient time" of Cheyenne tradition - the forebears of both the Moiseo and Monsoni Cree. Although representing a very poor rendition of the Native term [as is typical of many names recorded by Lewis and Clark], it is nonetheless clear that the term *"Wee-hee-Skeu"* is the explorer's adulterated rendition of *"Mowissiyu."* Lewis and Clark have omitted the Cheyenne prefix `Mo` indicating the male species, but by retaining the terminal `u` they preserved; albeit unwittingly, the older and more proper Cheyenne form. It will be shown throughout the course of this study, how the Moiseo remained somewhat aloof from other Cheyenne bands until after their vacating the Missouri banks around the date 1806, and in addition, that this particular group had once been very closely associated with both the Wheskerinni and Monsoni Cree. Hence their retaining a dialectical affinity with both. Only after the Moiseo re-amalgamated with other Cheyenne-speaking groups west of the Missouri, was the suffix `iu` or `u` denoting `people dropped in favor of the modern colloquial suffix `io` denoting the same.

It is worth remembering here that the Montagnais-Naskapi tribal name for themselves as a collective of `Inii,` meaning `people,` is an elongated variant of the contracted archaic Cheyenne form of `u.` It appears that the early colonial French had difficulty with the letter `w` and in its stead, often used the term `oui` and sometimes `m` as in Ouisconsin and Misconsin respectively for what we know now as Wisconsin. Thus we see early map and document notations for `Ouissi,` `Ouissy` and` Omissi,` each of which terms are meant to denote the Moiseo Cheyenne-speaking people, albeit, then erroneously associated by early chroniclers with either a Cree or Chippewa group. If one applies `m` as a prefix to either of the above terms, we have the equivalent of `mouissi` and `moissy` [pronounced Mo-wissi] which with the appended archaic Cheyenne suffix `u` creates `Mowissiyu;` the very same as given by the half-Cheyenne informant George Bent as

CREE FOREFATHERS

CHEYENNE INFORMANTS OF THE LATE 19th AND EARLY 20th CENTURY.

CHEYENNE WARRIOR, WHITE-FROG.

[Smithsonian Institution. Washington D.C.]

MIXED RACE CHEYENNE, GEORGE BENT.

[Smithsonian Institution. Washington D.C.]

WHITE-BULL aka WHITE-BUFFALO

[Smithsonian Institution. Washington D.C.]

SHUTAIO WARRIOR, BULL-THIGH

[Smithsonian Institution. Washington D. C.]

being the name of an early Cheyenne-speaking group, notwithstanding that George Bent himself erroneously believed, that the Mowissiyu were of Sioux extraction merely adopted into the Cheyenne Nation at a later date as a component band. By the same reasoning, if one applies `w` as a prefix to either of the above terms, we have the equivalent of `Whee-see,` which with the appendage of the archaic Cheyenne-proper term `u` meaning `people,` becomes `Whee-see-u` and thence `Whee-hee-Skeu` as used by Lewis and Clark in 1805 to designate one of two Cheyenne-speaking groups encountered on the Missouri River.

In truth, there can be little doubt that the derivation of the terms `Moiseyu` and *Mowissiyu* are synonymous with the Monsoni Cree and Wheskerinni terms for `elk` and are the archaic forms of `Moiseo.` This fact strongly suggests that the Mowissiyu and, therefore, the original Cheyenne-speaking faction, was during some remote period confederated - if not actually amalgamated with - the ancient Wheskerinni and Monsoni Cree and definitely was not originally a Sioux band.

Having said this, at a later date the Moiseo did associate intimately with certain Teton Sioux groups and among whom they intermarried freely. They thus spoke Sioux as a second language in consequence of this liaison and imitated facets of Sioux dress and culture. But always they considered themselves first and foremost Cheyenne. We have the corroboration of Truman Michelson's tribal informant named Bull Thigh, a Suhtaio band member well versed in matters relating to early Cheyenne history, and who stated that in his opinion the Moiseo were originally a Cheyenne-proper speaking group. Indeed, the Aorta band descendants of the original Moiseo, unlike each of the other Cheyenne-proper bands [excluding the Omissis and Suhtaio who were not originally Cheyenne], did have their own seperate creation story, which indicates their being the original of all the later Cheyenne-speaking bands.

The name Mowissiyu, in fact, can be found on early colonial maps and in related documents in such diverse forms as `Ouissyloua` [Joliet map 1673], `Ouissycouseton` [Franquelin map of 1684], `Ouassy` [LaFrance 1739] and `Ouissy` [Trudeau 1796]. All these notations are from French renderings of tribal names and are pronounced with an initial `Oui` which, of course, is consistent with Lewis and Clark's `Whee.` That many Cheyenne informants late in the nineteenth and early twentieth century thought the word `Moiseo` a foreign term, derives from the fact that it was an archaic word from the Cheyenne / Monsoni / Montagnais dialect, unfamiliar to most other Cheyennes by the time the Moiseo albeit at much later date, reunited with the rest of the tribe after crossing the Missouri River.

I think it self-evident in the light of the foregoing analysis, that the term `Flint Men" as offered by some as a tentative translation of `Motsonitanio` and *Moiseo*, owes its derivation to an early nickname, so to speak, for the original Moiseo band, due both to that clan`s ancient importance as Keepers of the flame and to the flint arrow head pendent worn by its Warrior Society members representing their connection with the Sacred Arrow talismans of the tribe. The term `Moiseo` in its singular guise of `mois,` thus becoming the term for flint in the vernacular and once used interchangeably with that of `elk.` While it is possible that the `s` in `Moiseo` is a dialect contraction of the common Algonquian term `assini` meaning `stone` or `rock` etc. it is just as likely that it represents an abbreviated form of `Skee,` this being a part of the Cree and archaic Cheyenne term for `elk.`

That the Moiseo Cheyenne-proper speaking group was indeed, once resident in the far northeast above the Lower course of the St. Lawrence River and close to the Montagnais, is corroborated by a statement from the Jesuit Priest Father Allouez who in the year 1666, contacted what he believed to be a Cree group somewhere close to the north-western tip of Lake Superior. In truth, the people so designated by Allouez were, most likely, a mixed band of Moiseo and Suhtaio [as will be made clear in a later chapter], but of whom Allouez said,

".Concerning the Kilistenouc [Cree], they appear to be extremely docile, and show a kindness uncommon among these barbarians. They are much more nomadic than any of the other Nations, having no fixed abodes, no fields, no villages, and live wholly on game and a small quantity of oats [wild rice] which they gather in marshy places......They speak nearly the same tongue as do the people formally called Poisons Blancs [Whitefish], and as the savages of Tadoussac" [2]

The above statement is important, for the *Poison Blancs* as the Father calls them were an Algonquian people more commonly known as *Attigamiques*, who we know, comprised a predominant band among the Wheskerinni [Algonkin proper] confederacy that once inhabited the Upper reaches of St. Maurice River on the north side of the Lower St. Lawrence. The *Attigamiqus* by the time of the Allouez visit, however, had been almost entirely exterminated owing to attacks by the Iroquois, coupled with the ravages of smallpox during the late 1640s and early 1650s.

On the other hand and what is more pertinent, is that the so-called `savages` of the Allouez account mentioned as being inhabitants of Tadoussac, were actually the Wheskerinni, e.g. *"La Petite Nacion"* or Algonkin-proper themselves, then with an element of Montagnais-Naskapi included among their number, and were therefore, very close cousins to, if not indeed at one time confederated among both the Moiseo and Monsoni. Father Allouez does not actually say that the Kilistinouc with whom he met were the same tribe as those of the Upper St. Maurice and of Tadoussac, merely that they spoke a dialect peculiar to those particular Algonquian-speaking peoples and implies that although of different band affiliations, they were all very closely related to one another and at one time, long before the coming of the white man, they had been together in the same general locale far to the east in the Lower St. Lawrence country, and just such would fit well with the Moiseo.

An added connection between the proto-historic Moiseo and Monsoni Cree, even though tentative, is that the historic Plains Cree tribes who themselves were certainly more recent offshoots from the Monsoni, but in later years had far less contact with the Chippewa than had their East Cree cousins, continued to observe many cultural traits manifest in military custom, tribal government, law ways and mythology, along with some religious practices shared only with the Cheyennes and Fox. This indicates that these three peoples alone [including the Monsoni], had once constituted a single generic cultural group and retained vestiges of their ancient relationship down to the late historic period.

CHAPTER 5.

THE MONTAGNAIS ELEMENT.

As regards the Montagnais connection, profound similarities exist in certain stories current in both Montagnais and Cheyenne traditions and mythology, particularly those pertaining to the deeds and attributes of *"Nenimis,"* a fabulous hero of both the Montagnais and Naskapi. The story of *"Nenimis"* is almost identical to that among the Cheyennes which relates to a time when the people were starving and to the appearance of two similarly dressed young men, commonly known as "The Twins Story." Likewise, there are descriptions of `Great Man-eating Beasts` and even of `Hairy People,` who in the Montagnais-Naskapi tradition are defeated and destroyed by the aforesaid Nenimis. We see also profound comparisons between the Monsoni Cree "Earth Renewal" ceremony and the *Massaum* and *Sun Dance* ceremonies of the Cheyenne and Suhtaio respectively, each of which have a northern origin encouraging nature`s regeneration from winter to spring, whilst peculiarities pertaining to rituals connected with the Sacred Hat or *"Issiwun"* of the Suhtaio, have their counterpart [and probably their origin] among the Fox and Sauk.

It is not surprising that in later years, most Western Cree bands did not show many comparable traits with their cousins in the east, for the East Cree groups had by then, become virtually assimilated with northern Chippewa bands, adopting many facets of Chippewa religion and custom wholesale. In contrast, the Cheyenne, Plains Cree and Fox after splitting from the common Cree-speaking parent group, had gone their separate ways, becoming independent from the Eastern Cree and to a large extent from each other. For many years they were opposed to foreign influence which may eventually have diminished their singular identity and at a later date, although the Fox confederated with the Sauk, the Cheyenne with the Sioux and the Monsoni / Plains Cree with the Assiniboine, all managed to keep their ancient tribal peculiarities and individuality intact.

The previous analysis in this study had attempted to show that the Moiseo, and therefore, the original Cheyenne-speaking group, was very closely connected to the Monsoni, Wheskerinni and Montagnais and that sometime during their Prehistory, Cheyennes once inhabited a country much further east than that of the Mississippi headwaters where, so earlier scholars have assumed, the Cheyenne people first came into being.

We should not construe from this alone, however, that the Moiseo, Monsoni, Montagnais and Wheskerinni were one body. Only that in more distant times these related groups wandered over-lapping territories and as will become apparent throughout, were separate bands merely stemming from the same parent tribe. It has previously been mentioned that a variation of the tribal name Monsoni is `Monsomin,` which when translated means "of the elk seed" or "berry." The name today is applied to a botanical species, but may once have denoted "people evolving from a particular group who had once been commonly known as "Elks," in all likelihood, the original seed of all Algonquian offshoots. This would then substantiate the Cree collective name for themselves of *"Nehiyowuk,"* i.e. "The exact speaking People."

Prior to contact with white men above and northeast of the Mississippi headwaters, circa, AD.1634, the Monsoni Cree can be traced to a more eastern woodland seat above the St. Lawrence River in what is now the central part of Quebec Province. If the early proto Cheyenne group was then associated with them, then Monsoni country was close – if not actually shared with that of the Cheyennes.

Indeed, we find yet another clue to Cheyenne residence in territories further east than the Mississippi headwaters, in that Cheyenne informants told Lewis H. Morgan sometime during the year 1862 that their people,

> *"...had come from east of the Mississippi, having crossed two large rivers before reaching the Plains."* [1]

In corroboration of this, the unpublished field notes of Truman Michelson reveal several references in the form of information supplied by Cheyenne and Suhtaio tribal members, of an early habitat of both these peoples far east of the Mississippi, and will be discussed where appropriate in this study.

Other evidence, although circumstantial in content, but which also points to a more eastern location for our subjects, is that the shafts of the four Sacred Arrow talismans of the tribe, [originating among the Moiseo, i.e. *Arrow Men*], are fashioned from a type of wood peculiar to the eastern woodlands. The original shafts of these Arrows have been preserved within the tribe's `Arrow` bundle for many hundreds of years before inquiries were first made as to their age late in the nineteenth century. Furthermore, the feathered flights of these Sacred Arrows when being renewed, are always fixed to their shafts with a fish-based glue, which indicates that when the Arrows first came among them, the Cheyennes were living in the lake country of tradition, during which period they subsisted for the most part on fish. More can be said on this matter below. However, it may also be noted that a particular decoration used by members of the Cheyenne Kit-Fox or *Motsontanio* society was the scalp-lock, consisting of the head being shaved but for a narrow strip of hair extending from the forehead to the nape; a fashion once sported by most East Woodland tribes, but not apparently, by the Monsoni / Plains Cree or Cheyenne and Suhtaio when contacted by white men late in the eighteenth century, and was merely a reminder, perhaps, among the Motsonitanio of an old association with East Woodland peoples, being the continuance of an ancient fashion abandoned by the rest of the Cheyenne tribe after their relocation in the western High Plains. *

* The Sacred Arrows were once captured by the Pawnee. Two were later retrieved by dubious means and two still remain among the Pawnee. It was necessary, therefore, for the Cheyennes to make two new "Arrows" to replace those missing and, it is said, that the wood required for their shafts be obtained from somewhere east of the Missouri so as to be consistent with that used in the manufacture of the originals.

Corroboration can be had in Sauk tradition which places their tribe along with the Fox and other Algonquians, somewhere along the St. Lawrence River in Quebec Province above or just below where the city of Montreal now stands, and this at a time prior to the coming of the French with Jacques Cartier in 1534. The Fox especially, and the Sauk albeit to a less degree, were close dialectic cousins to the Cheyenne and also, to the Monsoni / Plains Cree. At an early date, all these tribes probably constituted one group of Algonquian bands hailing from a common nucleus and residing in close proximity to one another.

The profuse use of red earth or red clay pigment as a body decoration, coupled with certain religious observances; comparisons in mythology; tribal tradition and customs, in addition to their linguistic connections as mentioned in the previous chapter, appears to substantiate this by implying a close relation of habitat, which owing to each of the above mentioned tribe's later widely scattered geographical positioning when first noted in the early documents, could not have been much further west than the eastern outlet of Lake Superior at the Sault St. Marie.

It is comparatively recent that an in depth study of the Algonquian language has been made and the fact established, that the tribal group known historically as Montagnais should actually be classified as a proper Cree division. What is more important, is that it appears to be the root dialect of all variations spoken by the numerous and widely scattered Cree bands.

It must then be accepted, that all those peoples most closely related linguistically to the Cree and therefore, including the Wheskerinni along with the more populous Chippewa and Delaware groups, can claim ancestry directly or indirectly from the Montagnais.

The Fox tribe who we mentioned earlier as being dialectically connected to the Monsoni / Plains Cree, were, in truth, just as closely connected, it seems, to the Montagnais, having retained more of their compatibility in the late historic period than had the Chippewa, Delaware and even some other groups later classified as Cree. Now as the Cheyenne are known to have had very strong dialectic ties with both the Fox and Monsoni, it follows that they also must once have been intimately associated with the Montagnais. It should, though, be admitted here that there is little evidence in the traditional accounts to suggest all the aforesaid tribes were, proto-historically, one Nation, although there is evidence to support the idea that at one time during their more ancient past, they did comprise a particular Algonquian branch, and were then close neighbours and associates during early stages of a common migration to the south and southeast from the cold snowbound lands of the north.

Other evidence places proto-Cheyennes among the Montagnais during an early period, in so much as the particular ancient culture and environment of the Montagnais, compares exactly with that recalled in Cheyenne tradition regarding their own most ancient area of habitat and lifestyle. It is worth noting the existence of a Montagnais-Naskapi band known in historic times as `Moisie.` These people once lived about the mouth of the river of that name which flows south into the Gulf of the St. Lawrence. We cannot be sure if the name is of French derivation meaning either *musty* or *mouldy,* or alternatively, from a French or Anglo corruption of a Native term and as a consequence, has since been confused with the French definition. This we know was the case with the French term `chien` meaning `dog` which in the mid-nineteenth century was believed by some to have been the origin of the name Cheyenne.

Now the Huron who once claimed territory along both banks of the St. Lawrence and the shores of Lake Erie and Lake Ontario, at least as early as AD.1000, called the Montagnais Algonquians, `Chau-hague-ronon,` this being the early French rendering of the name, and with whom as early as circa, 1600, if not before, were militarily aligned against the Iroquois. In later years when the French trader Jean Baptiste Trudeau contacted Cheyennes in 1794/ `95 on the Missouri River, he called them `Cha-gui-ennes` which name is not too dissimilar to the Huron term for the Montagnais. This Huron term includes the tribal suffix *ronon,* appended to many tribal names in order to denote `men` or `people. 'The early French colonials between circa, 1550-1660 also adopted this appendage when referring to certain tribes, but later contracted it to the single syllable `ron. ` Thus there appears to be a compatibility between the terms *Chau-hague* and *Cha-gui*, and it is known that by the date 1650, the Huron had abandoned the St. Lawrence country completely and relocated along the southern shores of Lake Superior, and even further west along the east bank of the Mississippi in central Minnesota. Here they no doubt came into contact with Cheyenne-speaking peoples, either Cheyenne-proper or Suhtaio, and conceivably, regarded them as a part of the old Montagnais - Wheskerinni group that once lived north of the St. Lawrence in the St. Maurice River area adjacent to the old Huron country. [This last named area as we will see during the course of our study, being the same country where the Cheyenne nucleus, e. g. the Moiseo, most probably once resided.]. Not surprisingly then, the Huron may have also referred to the Moiseo by the Huron`s old name for the Montagnais and Wheskerinni. The French may have picked up the name from the Huron and applied it to, as they thought, a Cree group with whom at that time the Huron were in friendly contact, and not until Trudeau ascended the Missouri in 1794 /`95 and recognized the Cheyennes as a distinct Nation, was the mistake finally rectified.

Certainly, Trudeau employed Huron guides among his retinue during his numerous trading and exploratory expeditions, which he conducted both in the Upper Mississippi country and further west along the middle Missouri.

The two connotations then, as used by the Huron and later by Trudeau are very alike if not synonymous, the term being used as an early colloquial name for the Cheyennes, who throughout the early years of colonial exploration, were consistently mistaken because of their culture and style of dress as a Cree people. The Huron term in its old-time French pronunciation would render the `g` silent and thus, is reminiscent with that of `Chaa-ha` as noted on some early maps of the Great Lakes area and who the Chevalier de LaSalle mentioned under the name *Chaa.* These last being a band of strange Indians hailing from somewhere close to the Upper Mississippi, which visited LaSalle at his Fort Crevecoeur near the mouth of the Illinois in the early part of February, 1680, and the name `Chaa, ` as also will be demonstrated later in this study, can be definitely identified as designating an early Cheyenne-speaking group.

This would partly explain why, other than a few map references, early documentation regarding Cheyennes is not forthcoming, when French voyagers must have met with or at least heard of them, long before the latter date, and especially so, when we learn that the French were then in contact with tribes living near and allied to Cheyenne-speaking bands. It is obvious that throughout the early years of white exploration, our subjects were regarded as members of some other Nation, as indeed Cheyennes were later confused with the Sioux by both the Sieur de LaVerendrye in 1743, and by Jonathan Carver in 1766.

That the original Cheyenne-speaking Moiseo group were separatists from a Montagnais faction, might appear to be contradicted by the linguist Petter's remark in the preface to his compilation of a Cheyenne grammar, wherein it is stated that the Cheyenne dialect was, in his opinion, more closely related to `Natick` than to either Blackfoot or Cree. However, the peoples that constituted the *Natick* were Algonquian refugees from several tribes predominately of Delaware extraction, who founded a Christian colony in Massachusetts under the guidance of the Moravian Church. Included among their number was a strong Montagnais element, to the extent that the dialect of the colony was actually a mixture of Delaware and Montagnais tongues. Petter's name of `Natick` may also have included the `Nyack,` a Delaware band of the Unami division, they being the `Turtle` clan of the three cognate dialectic groups comprising the Delaware Nation.

We have previously noted that a fabulous turtle figures predominately in both the Delaware and Cheyenne creation myths, and there are further striking similarities in both people's traditions regarding their early existence, including a particular species of "Giant Beast" which ate the people, forcing them to live in caves for a long time.

Recollections from the Delaware themselves concerning their tribe's ancient and proto-historic habitat, compare exactly with that recalled in both Cheyenne and Montagnais accounts and coupled to this, is that the annual sacred rites pertaining to the Great Celestial Bear, which in a time past played such an important role in the religious life of the Delaware and their cognates, had a particularly relevant connection to similar rituals once practiced anciently among the Cheyennes and as recently as the late historic period, among the Monsoni and Montagnais also. From these facts and those mentioned earlier regarding the Munsey, it might justifiably be construed that the Munsey and even the Unami Delaware groups at least, were once connected closely with the original Cheyenne-speaking nucleus and that all were once involved in a common migration at an early date - along with other Algonquian-speaking groups - only that the Cheyenne were then members of a Montagnais-Cree faction.

It does appear that a major Algonquian movement from the northwest to the Lower Great Lakes and St. Lawrence River country in the southeast, was undertaken at around the same time by the Delaware and their offshoots, and also by the Chippewa tribes who; at the time in question, were very much akin to, although independent from the Cree. Because of this Chippewa - Cree relationship, it has often been suggested by earlier scholars, that the Cree and Chippewa were one body during the initial stages of their migration from the northland and later forcibly split into two groups by the event of enemy incursions; pinched out in fact from the St. Lawrence River country by such pressure, the Cree thence veering off toward the far northwest, the Chippewa more directly west to the Upper Great Lakes via the St. Lawrence itself. The available evidence, however, implies that the Cree and Chippewa were, of old, opposed to one another and that their respective migrations even though contemporaneous, were from the start completely separate, the Cree actually preceding the Chippewa in first settling and abandoning the St. Lawrence and Upper Great

THE AUTHOR`S NORTHERN CHEYENNE FRIEND AND INFORMANT, JAMES KING.
[Photograph from "Little Bighorn Remembered" by Herman J. Viola. Times Books New York. 1999.]

43

Lakes country. Indeed, the evidence points conclusively to the assumption that a migration of Chippewa groups from the Atlantic seaboard toward the northwest, to Lake Superior and beyond along both the north and south shores of that lake, was the much more recent of the two, and at a period when the Cheyenne and Monsoni / Plains Cree were already old occupants in territories far northwest of the St. Lawrence, having been in situ in these latter positions since before the time the Chippewa migration northwest from the Atlantic seaboard, had come to a temporary halt on the northern shore of Lake Huron around AD.1400.

Traditions from the Plains Cree concerning their tribe's ancestral home, prior that is, to entering the Canadian prairies of Manitoba and Saskatchewan in the early historic time, point to the far northeast as being their ancient seat of occupation, along the shores of a "Great Salt Water" which aptly describes Hudson's Bay, before occupying the region between Lake Winnipeg on the west and the Upper course of the St. Lawrence River to the south-east. Beyond this nothing is remembered and it is safe to assume that the Cree held this area a long time; several centuries no doubt, before Jacques Cartier sailed into the Gulf of that same river in 1534, although by that date, the Cree had gone from that region.

During those early days of their history the Plains Cree were one group with the Monsoni, and precisely the same ancestral location as indicated in Monsoni / Plains Cree tradition, is also indicated in that of both the Chippewa and Delaware regarding their respective tribal origins. The fact that these three peoples spoke very closely related dialects and the country north and northwest of the Upper Great Lakes was, prehistorically, occupied by Algonquians alone, make it more likely that the area between Lake Winnipeg and the Upper St. Lawrence is indeed, the same general area referred to in tradition. A more definite location cannot now be given from the traditions alone, but it can be asserted with confidence that the parent band from which spawned the proto Cheyennes, came originally from the tundra and forest country far north and northwest of the Upper Great Lakes.

It has also generally been accepted by earlier scholars, even though supporting evidence is lacking, that all Cree-speaking peoples came into their late historic seats from the coastal area of Labrador, having first taken a route due west into the cold barren lands adjoining the western shore of Hudson's Bay. The Montagnais, however, when first contacted by the French late in the sixteenth century were then occupying the north bank of the St. Lawrence. This suggests that their migration, at least, was toward the south and this is corroborated by Sauk tradition, previously mentioned, which avers that they, along with the Fox and other Algonquian groups then occupied a seat near the island upon which the town of Montreal now stands.

I believe it naive to suppose that the Cree, through preference, should first move due east from somewhere west of Hudson's Bay into lands as harsh, if not indeed, harsher than those they had apparently left, and where an inhospitable climate and environment would subject them to extreme cold and privation. Rather than attempt to better themselves by heading for the warmer, game-filled forest country to the south and southeast, as did their Delaware and Chippewa cousins.

We do know that prior to the date 1250, the climate west of Hudson`s Bay became decidedly colder and more uncomfortable for Human habitation. Thus it appears obvious that the later position of the Cree in the Sub-Arctic region was not initially claimed by choice. Most likely they were forced back into it and only after the *"Nonsuch"* sailed into that same Bay in 1670, heralding a regular English supply of iron artefacts and firearms, did the Cree gain any advantage from their state. We also know that certain Algonquian-speaking peoples which then included the Suhtaio, did in fact move southeast from northern Manitoba into the southern Ontario region after abandoning the far north country, and at a much later date, confederated with the old proto-Cheyenne group or groups [Moiseo], after these latter had re-entered that same area, having undertaken a second migration west from the St. Maurice River area in the east.

It is more likely then, that a large segment of Algonquian-speakers, particularly the Montagnais-Naskapi [then including the Monsoni, Wheskerinni and Moiseo], did initially migrate from the far north in a south-easterly direction to or near the Upper St. Lawrence as did both the Chippewa and Delaware groups of tribes, but for some reason were prevented from permanently occupying those lands.

Traditions from the Chippewa relating to their own proto-historic time, being more detailed than those of the Cree, mention early wars with the Iroquois and refer to other hostile encounters with neighbouring tribes whose names; though now unrecognizable, may well have been Delaware factions. It is indicative that after the Chippewa arrival on the Island of Montreal around the date or a short time after AD.1350, the Cree are not mentioned again in Chippewa tradition until some two hundred years later, and then as a foreign people occupying neighbouring lands both north and northwest of Lake Superior.

On the other hand, the Delaware, who of course are Algonquians, but of a different group to the Cree in their late historic time, have solid traditions of their peoples` heritage preserved in a number of sacred traditions, among which is included that of somewhat doubtful authenticity known as the *"Wallum Ollum"* or *"Red Score."* This latter is preserved as a pictographic mnemonic device purporting to record that tribe's migrations and conquests at least as far back as the opening of the tenth century AD. The first location recorded in this account for the Delaware tribes and their cognates, designates an area covered with snow and ice the year round. From this land, say the Delaware, they migrated towards the southeast until, eventually, after a period of prolonged and devious wandering; they arrived in the country immediately southeast of Lake Ontario, in what are now the northern and central parts of the states of New Jersey and Pennsylvania.

There yet remains a high degree of controversy regarding the authenticity of the *Wallum Ollum*. However, its transcribed content is compatible in many instances with separate alternative accounts from other Delaware and cognate tribal legends and traditions, so as to give it additional credibility. If indeed, the *Wallum Ollum* as it exists today in note book form, was, in fact, fraudently devised by one C. S. Rafinesque in the mid-1820s for spurious motives, as now appears to have been the case, it is also apparent that even though showing some mistranslations of the Delaware language along with pictograms debatable as to their veracity, it was nonetheless, compiled from a knowledge of authentic Delaware and other Algonquian traditions as existed at the time of its publication. For this reason, I suggest that after ignoring the respective pictograms, the verbal content should be taken as a serious historical record, albeit open to alternative interpretation based upon recent scientific data of both an archaeological and linguistic nature, but which – in most cases – actually compliments the essence of the *Wallum Ollum* and other Algonquian traditions of their people's migrations and ancient history as handed down in original Native forms.

The whole essence of the Delaware migration traditions is to record the heroic conquests of the `Lene-Lenape` - as the Delaware-proper called themselves - and shows that their southern advance from the north as members of a great Algonquian host was not a peaceful progress. In truth, they bludgeoned their way through foreign resident groups sometimes meeting determined opposition. But being victorious, all their enemies were ultimately compelled to retire before the Delaware line of advance.

Both the Fox and Sauk, undoubtedly, were involved in the initial stages of what may be termed the Delaware migration, and we have seen from the above discussion that these two groups; along with the Monsoni, Montagnais, Wheskerinni and Moiseo, shared similar dialects, traditions and religion, coupled with mythology, culture and habitat throughout their people's early years in the northeast. This being so, it can reasonably be conjectured that each of the aforementioned tribes had vacated their ancient far northern homelands at about the same time and for the same reason. Thus, they were included in a common migration of Algonquians from north to south and, particularly, that accorded to the Delaware Nation, accounts of which have been preserved in some detail and wherein, we find references albeit in obscure form, to the old-time original Moiseo Cheyennes.

- 0 - 0 - 0 - 0 - 0 - 0 - 0 - 0 - 0 - 0 - 0 - 0- 0 - 0 - 0 - 0 – 0 – 0 – 0 -

CHAPTER 6.

MARCH OF THE ALGONQUIANS.

It has been estimated that around the date 1,000 B.C., staggered groups of Proto-Algonquian-speakers of the *Shield Archaic* culture, which is defined by hunter / gatherer communities with a complete lack of pottery in its archaeological inventory, erupted out of the cold, Keewatin district of Northern Canada, and migrated in a southeast direction into central Ontario. Eventually, soon after A.D. 100, they moved into the state of Maine and other North Atlantic seaboard regions. In these last-named areas a continuation of Algonquian occupation – albeit of successive cultural focuses – persisted from that time forward into the historic period which begins around A.D.1534. It has also been asserted, that these particular groups represent the ancestors of those Algonquian-speaking tribes now known as Micmac, Maliseet and Abenaki. Doubtless other migrations now completely lost to memory had occurred in earlier times, to bring Indian peoples into the same Keewatin area in the first instance, and at various dates since then, one group and another divorced itself from the parent body; vacated that far north land and blazed new paths south and southeast. Paths which ultimately, became well-worn by moccasin feet.

Indeed, another more populous egress of Proto-Algonquian-speaking peoples occurred during the 6th century A.D. These later migrants also spread southeast from the Keewatin district, but lingered for a significant period in southeastern Manitoba and the central parts of Ontario and Quebec across what is known today as the Canadian Shield. These latter peoples comprised a conglomerate of closely related bands, predominant among whom were the forefathers of present-day Delaware tribal groups. These peoples were then a part of what in archaeological terms is known as the *Middle Laurel Cultural Tradition* of between A.D.500 and A.D.900, and is differentiated only from that of *Shield Archaic* by the introduction of ceramic wares among its artefacts. This last-named movement was the tail-end, so to speak, of a staggered Algonquian exodus from the Canadian tundra, bringing to conclusion a history of incessant wandering spanning thousands of years, ever since their Asiatic ancestors had crossed the frozen wastes of the Northern Hemisphere and became isolated on the North American Continent.

The advent of this last mass upheaval from the Keewatin district was occasioned, perhaps, by the necessity to find more provident hunting grounds for an expanding population, although hostile pressure from Eskimo and Chipewyan groups, who having a more sophisticated bow and arrow technology and thereby, holding the advantage over these early atlatl-using *Middle Laurel Culture* Algonquians, may have had a more direct influence [See Harp; 1978]. In addition, changing climatic conditions occurring around that same time creating a more inhospitable environment, must also have proved an important factor. However, traditions from the Delaware offer a more graphic if only apocryphal reason which serves to open the migration legend of that people. A legend in which we see a close affinity with other Algonquian groups, including our subjects the Cheyenne.

The Delaware migration tradition as preserved in that Nation's sacred oral history, traces their people's movement away from those cold lands of the Far North, southeast into their idyllic seats of more recent time in the mid-eastern and Atlantic Seaboard states. Tribes included in this account that were once a part of a great Algonquian-speaking host, evolved into separate entities during particular stages of migration, splitting from the main body as circumstance or preference demanded, whilst the nucleus of the host, i.e., the Delaware-proper and their cognates continued along the route. These offshoot groups became recognized in later years as tribes and Nations in their own right, under such names as Cree, Montagnais, Wheskerinni, Shawnee, Miami, Fox, Sauk, Abenaki and Nanticoke among others, and more important to our study, Cheyenne, Suhtaio and Monsoni.

This Delaware tradition is not lacking in detail or continuity, but still proves difficult for the student who, by using the few topographical details given, attempts to trace the actual route of travel on a modern day map. The course I have traced, therefore, is that which is most consistent with the existing evidence at hand and is either corroborated by, or correlates to an acceptable degree with traditions from related tribes, coupled with what might be considered more definite knowledge, such as dialectical comparisons and archaeological findings which relate to each of those people's prehistoric and proto-historic periods. This tradition as rendered by Brinton begins,

> "Long, long ago the Delaware and their cognate tribes were created beyond the Great Waters [i.e. The Great Lakes] far west of their historic homes along the Atlantic seaboard and adjacent territories. There arose a great flood, and the people were saved only by the arrival of a fabulous turtle upon whose back they took refuge until the waters subsided. The turtle remained with the people for many years, during which time they lived in caves, for outside roamed fierce man-eating beasts called `Great Naked,` or `Hairless Bear` in tradition. At last the people had to take to the water to escape them. In this country it was very cold; it froze, and often stormed, and from here, the Northern Plains, the people went south to possess milder lands abounding in game. [1]

The myth of a fabulous turtle carrying the world on its back, is current among the Mongolian, Giliyak and Evenk peoples of north-eastern Asia, and, of course, among various Algonquian-speaking tribes including the Cheyenne, who assert that the land in which they originally dwelt was formed on the back of a giant turtle, and like the Cheyennes, the Siberian Evenk further relate that a duck first brought up mud from beneath the waters and placed it on the turtle`s back. The `Giant Turtle` in reality, probably alludes to an expanse of land surrounded by water and thus, to a particular period of inundation that occurred in the northland. Such an event can well point to the southeastern part of Siberia known as Kamchatka, during one of the temperate climatic periods that area has been subjected to over past millennia. Indeed, the Cheyennes add that their own most ancient seat of occupation of which their traditions tell, was in the far north, where - as is also the assertion of the Delaware, – *It was extremely cold; giant animals roamed the land and ate Human Beings, forcing the people to live in caves for a long time.*" [2]

Regarding these man-eating beasts of tradition, a species of `Giant Bear` [i.e. *Ursus Spelaeus Blum*], three times larger than the present-day Grizzly, still roamed the Siberian tundra during the latter stages of the Last Great Ice-Age [12,000 to 11,500 years B P.] and is believed by some to have also been extant in certain remote areas on the North American Continent. In addition, Delaware tradition mentions the occurrence of a great battle between these `Giant Beasts` and humans, in which event the beasts were finally defeated, and this, apparently, is merely a variation of the Cheyenne story previously referred to, and known as "The Great Race."

On the other hand, it is indicative that in a supplementary Delaware tradition, there is a description of a giant horned animal, which ancient beast was known to the Delaware by the term `Yah Qua Whee` and was, they say, placed upon the earth as a beast of burden for the benefit of the people and to make itself useful to them in other ways. Such a description is consistent with the Cheyenne tradition of the `Giant Cow-like` animal upon which the people rode, and, supposedly, domesticated for its milk [See Chapter 2]. It should not be surprising then, that in Montagnais-

Naskapi tradition along with those of some other Eastern Algonquians including the Chippewa tribes, there are also references to similar `Giant Beasts,` which Dr. Frank G. Speck, the one-time leading authority on the Montagnais-Naskapi, believed as having some genuine historical basis.

For some reason C. A. Weslager asserted that the Delaware account referred to the ancient mammoth or mastodon, even though such animals were unlikely to have been tamed, let alone [as stated in Cheyenne tradition] to have been milked by humans. Although it must be conceded that if the mammoth possessed the temperament of the modern-day elephant and its long curling tusks have been remembered in tradition as teeth, then Weslager may not be completely wrong in his conclusion. There were indeed, mammoths existing in Siberia as recently as six-thousand years ago, the remains of which ancient species have also been found in the tundra region on the North

**A Sacred stone `Turtle` [or Tortoise] monument in the remote steppes of Outer Mongolia.
[Photograph by Ivor Monteagu in "Land of Blue Sky." Dobson Books Ltd; London1956.]**

American Continent harkening back to the same period, and which, conceivably, survived much later in this latter area than the extinction of their counterparts in Northern Europe. Perhaps, though, these Delaware and Cheyenne traditions actually refer to the Giant Stag-Moose, which animal did have conspicuous long front teeth and between eight and six-thousand years ago, still roamed the Northern Hemisphere in large number. Or indeed, it refers to the giant caribou of ancient time, of which the smaller modern reindeer equivalent; even today, is both milked and ridden by northern Siberian, Mongolian and Scandinavian nomads. Such similarities, however, in both Cheyenne and

Delaware mythology and in their traditions concerning their very early days of evolution, are compatible with the traditions of both the Montagnais and Chippewa tribes. This does imply that during some remote period, all these groups resided in the same general locality and if not actually congregated as one body, were certainly in contact with one another and closely aligned. Distortions and contradictions between the several independent traditions, such as differences pertaining to the exact role of these `Giant Beasts` as recalled by each of the aforementioned tribes in their historic time, have occurred only because of a prolonged period of separation at a later date, and with regard to the Cheyennes specifically, their own much later affiliation with foreign speaking peoples such as the Kiowa and Sioux among others, who had their own traditions pertaining to giant beasts and water monsters during their ancient time, so that the details have since become somewhat confused and corrupted from the original version.

The first part of the Delaware tradition as quoted above, concerning the original homeland of the Delaware and their cognate peoples, probably alludes to the Siberian and Northern European regions, whilst the migration from the *Northern Plains* as it is called, likely refers to a much later period, after the people had ensconced themselves on the North American Continent, ostensibly in the southern Keewatin district of Canada west of Hudson`s Bay. In its turn, the subsequent migration to the south or southeast, refers to the people`s entry into the central Ontario country.

The Delaware account states that the Shawnee, Potawatomi, Sauk, Fox, Chippewa, Miami, Kickapoo and Ottawa tribes, all once dwelt together in the "Cold land of the North," and further, that each of the aforementioned tribes called the Delaware their Grandfathers, while the Delaware referred to the Unami or Turtle faction among themselves, as their own Grandfathers, thus indicating the original Delaware-speaking group. This is consistent with a Sauk tradition once told by a Chief Masco to Major Marston in 1819, which stated that the Ottawa, Potawatomi, Fox, Kickapoo and Sauk originally came from a cold, snow-covered land north of the St. Lawrence River, and thence migrated south to a point just above or below where the city of Montreal now stands. In that distant place, Chief Masco continued, all were created and dwelt as one tribe. These statements are important, for the tribes mentioned by the Delaware and in Chief Masco`s account, represent at least two, perhaps three distinct dialects of the Algonquian tongue, and infers therefore, that all Algonquian-speakers once lived in the same northern area during their archaic period. What then was true for this particular branch of the Algonquian family, must be true also for our subjects the Moiseo, i.e., the proto-Cheyennes, as the Moiseo were very closely related in dialect and by their traditions to most of the aforesaid tribes, especially with the Shawnee, Menominee and Kickapoo, whilst the Chippewa state that their own ancestors also came from the north.

Supplementary fragments of tradition recounted by various Algonquian groups, recall that whilst living in the cold north land, i.e., the *Northern Plains* of Delaware tradition, the people were very poor and often hungry and did not know the use of the bow. This compares exactly with Cheyenne accounts relating to their own `Ancient Time` of tradition, which often start with the phrase "Before we had bows and arrows." It is indicative that throughout the many years of archaeological research north of the Upper Great Lakes, no evidence of a prehistoric use of the bow has yet been found. In fact, it was the later arrival of certain Eskimo peoples and others of Athapaskan stock around A.D. 1000, who first introduced the bow and arrow into the region. However, several items reminiscent of the atlatl or spear-thrower have been discovered, the inference being that the `no bow` statement is correct; the people of that time and place relying upon the spear-thrower in its stead, which in the hands of an expert becomes a formidable asset, adding velocity and accuracy to the hand-wielded missile. That this traditional anecdote is common to most Algonquians, also suggests the same period of ancient environment and culture for all.

Certainly, owing to the high concentration of Algonquian peoples in the north-eastern United States during the proto-historic and early historic periods, coupled with the lack of traditional and artefact evidence to associate them with either a more southern or western habitat at that time, while not forgetting their having evolved much earlier from a paleo-Asiatic group in the northeastern part of Siberia, I suggest that this part of the tradition refers specifically to Algonquians then inhabiting the north-central part of Canada, wherefrom; due to an increase in population and climate change, the people spread from the *Northern Plains* apparently from a point in the Sub-Arctic area immediately west and northwest of Hudson's Bay. This last-named area then contained tundra and boreal forest, the latter extending south and southeast to envelope the entire James Bay district, before merging with the hardwood and spruce-pine regions further south which cover the eastern part of southern Ontario and the whole of southern Quebec.

Having said this, it has been asserted by some scholars of the subject, solely from a correlation of a Proto-Algonquian word list, that the Proto-Algonquian homeland of 1200 to 900 BC., was the area between that of the Georgian Bay eastern spur of Lake Huron and the west bank of the Ottawa River. Some others view the occupation of this same area as one of Algonquian culture originating from the earlier *Shield Archaic,* but showing a progression into so-called *Lake Forest Archaic* and *Middle Woodland* culture periods, which include the introduction of horticultural pursuits and of pottery in their archaeological inventories of between 300 BC., and AD.100. Obviously, these opinions do not take into account the existence of other Algonquian cultural complexes comprising both *Shield Archaic* and that known as *Laurel,* which were then concurrent far northwest of the Upper Great Lakes. Neither do such opinions concur with most Algonquian tribal traditions, which attest to their peoples during their "Ancient Time," as residing in an area compatible with that of the southern Keewatin region during the same period. While it is true that Algonquians of the *Shield Archaic complex* were indeed, to be found in the above suggested more eastern area during the same calculated time span, such cultural remains must be associated with the earlier Algonquian migrants of Beothuk, Micmac and Naskapi affiliation, and did not include the Montagnais, Chippewa and Delaware conglomeration of tribes, which – according to their own traditions and archaeological inventories - only entered the eastern designated region after circa, AD. 1,000. Prior to this beginning around AD.100, there were in that vast territory embracing central Manitoba and Ontario immediately northwest of the Upper Great Lakes, several contemporary cultural complexes, termed *Lake Forest, Middle Laurel* and *Nakomis* respectively. These are known collectively as the *Middle Woodland tradition* in archaeological terms, each of which represent Algonquian groups, some of whom were then still in situ in the older *Shield Archaic* region west of Hudson's Bay, and likely included the ancestors of the Delaware, Chippewa, Cree and Moiseo [proto-Cheyenne] Algonquian groups.

The inference is, that the area between Georgian Bay and the Ottawa River so designated by scholars such as Frank Siebert [1967], does not appear feasible as being the earliest assumed homeland for the entire Algonquian-speaking family on the North American Continent. Rather, the area including the Keewatin district of north-central Canada is more acceptable, and is compatible with Algonquian tribal traditions which describe the environment during their *Ancient Time* as an area of very few trees, in addition to much snow and cold. The evidence does suggest that from a Keewatin central point, successive Algonquian migrations took place towards the south and southeast, instead of in a northwest direction from the Georgian Bay / Ottawa River region as Siebert's conclusions would have us believe. The *Northern Plains* of the Delaware account which is referred to alternatively in supplementary Delaware traditions as the "Great cold land," appears then, to have been in the Sub-Arctic region northwest of Hudson's Bay, and not the coast of Labrador as some earlier scholars have assumed, and where, of course, there is a great abundance of wood suitable for a variety of needs, including the manufacture of bows and arrows. To date no archaeological evidence has been uncovered either in Labrador or Newfoundland, to suggest a pre-circa, A.D.1., occupation of the Labrador area specifically by Algonquian peoples, while the Montagnais-Naskapi who were occupying the same territory during the early historic period of circa, AD.1603, have definite traditions of having earlier lived far to the northwest on the other side of a "Great Water." From there, they say, they migrated in a south-easterly direction into what is now the thickly timbered hinterland of the southeastern part of Quebec Province and the southern part of Labrador.

The *"Great Water"* here referred to, is, undoubtedly, either Hudson' Bay or James Bay, and as the Montagnais appear to have been the parent group of all Algonquian speakers, their ancestral home west of the *Great Water* of their tradition, must have been the same also for the Delaware and their associates. In the Keewatin Sub-Arctic region there is a lack of suitable wood available for the manufacture of bows, whilst the now extinct Great Cave Bear of those districts may, in reality, be the animal referred to by the Delaware and Cheyennes as the great man-eating beast sometimes called "Great Naked" or "Hairless Bear" in tradition. Perhaps the Thule Eskimo peoples, who were in the same area until the date circa, AD. 1,000 and who, prehistorically it seems, were associated with the Ainu of the Kamchatka Siberian shoreline and certain islands of Japan, are likely to be the `Hairy People` of both Cheyenne and Montagnais-Naskapi tradition [as mentioned in the previous chapter], whilst Viking visitors from Scandinavian communities in Greenland who we know from the archaeological record and manuscript sources, were during the same period [circa, A.D. 1,000], at least frequenting if not for short periods permanently residing in adjacent territory to the east in present-day Labrador, are, perhaps, the `White Hairy-Faced` people mentioned in the Cheyenne account.

It does appear, though, that other Algonquian migrations from the northwest occurred around the same time as this Delaware movement which, even though conducted by small groups in comparison, reached the Upper and Lower Great Lakes and much further south. These, too, have all the hall marks of having originated from the ancient cultural focus of the Canadian provinces of Manitoba, Ontario and the western part of Quebec and termed *"Middle Laurel"* by the archaeologist. This particular cultural focus period began around AD.100, and shows variations in its more recent southern and south-eastern areas under the names *"Late Laurel," "Blackduck"* and *"Late Point Peninsular."* These last named *phases,* continued well into the historic era of the seventeenth century. All these early Algonquian movements nonetheless, can be traced from the same rough starting point in the cultural area known as *Shield Archaic.* This area takes in the southern Keewatin district and embraces the northern half of Manitoba including Lake Winnipeg and its adjacent Lakes, before stretching east as far as Hudson's Bay. As mentioned earlier, the area covered is known as the Canadian Shield, which vast region consists predominantly of boreal forest, although the more northern area gives way to a tundra terrain.

From a correlation of the various Algonquian accounts regarding their ancient locations, coupled with certain archaeological findings later to be explained, it is thus inferred that the above mentioned area of Keewatin is indeed, the earliest seat recalled for the Algonquian family of which we can be certain, and here they had evidently remained in situ for many centuries. Most likely, the final movement toward the south and southeast was triggered by the occurrence of extreme climatic change in this northern area, which had its beginning around the date AD.400.

As regards dating this movement of the Delaware and their cognate groups from the *Northern Plains* as it is termed in the Delaware account, it is a comparatively recent innovation that enables us to differentiate climatic variations for the Northern Hemisphere over past millennia. Already it has shown to be indispensable in delineating the emergence of Ancient and proto-historic cultures and of human movement across the Globe. Accurate documented meteorological data are recorded only for the previous one hundred years or so, but an analysis of tree-ring growth rates; fluctuating lake levels; the growth and succession of vegetation types in both marsh and bog terrain and compatible studies in ice strata levels, can determine general periods for successive environmental changes. Particularly relevant to our study are the climatic variables apparent in the eastern parts of North America and Canada, from which a table of occurrence not only enables us to understand more fully the impetus for migration and cultural development of indigenous peoples in the north and northeast, but also bear out several traditional anecdotes from various tribes, hitherto virtually ignored by historians and ethnologists alike.

TABLE OF CLIMATIC VARIATIONS IN THE N. E. AMERICAS.

300 BC	to	AD. 300	=	Mild.
AD.400	to	AD. 600 or 700	=	Cold.
AD.800	to	AD. 1300.	=	Mild.
AD.1300	to	AD. 1450	=	Cool and Dry.
AD.1450	to	AD. 1550	=	Mild.
AD.1550	to	AD. 1880	=	Colder.

By consulting the table of climatic variations shown above, it can be seen that; generally speaking, during the period between 300 BC., and AD.300, the weather was mild in the aforesaid area and thus, could offer a relatively comfortable existence for the semi-nomadic hunter. From circa, AD.400, however, the climate began to change; the temperature became decidedly colder and more uncomfortable for the inhabitants both man and beast. This variation continued until about AD.600, probably reaching its severity around AD.500. The caribou herds upon which a number of Indian inhabitants of these northern lands depended so heavily for a great part of their subsistence during certain seasons, moved south, as the ice sheets and tundra expanded in that direction, and the people found it increasingly difficult to find enough large game animals to satisfy their needs. Undoubtedly, the majority of Algonquians suffered this gradual change for a while, and coincides with the period asserted in both Cheyenne and Delaware traditions of their living in a cold, inhospitable country of the far north, at a time when they were always hungry.

Earlier, however, between AD.100 and AD.300, a particular faction of Algonquian migrants – which, I suggest, likely included those peoples constituting what was known at a much later date as the Powhatan confederacy [who themselves were closely related linguistically to the Cree], had already advanced in a south-easterly direction from the Keewatin region; reached the Upper Great Lakes and remained in situ for a prolonged period around the western tip of Lake Superior. These, perhaps, were associated with that known archaeologically as the *Nakomis Complex*, before they set off again on their travels and over the course of many generations, finally found themselves in what are now the eastern seaboard states of Maryland, Virginia and North Carolina.

At the beginning of the historic period of circa, 1534 [the date of Jacques Cartier's first voyage on the Lower St. Lawrence], these eastern coastal Algonquians, who at that later date included the Abenaki, Powhatan and the several confederated Delaware tribes among others, had already become a sub-grouping of Algonquian language speakers; having long since been separated from their ancient proto-Cheyenne cousins by both time and geography. The Powhatan tribes being linguistically close to the Cree, are by definition, therefore, close relatives to the Moiseo proto-Cheyennes also. The Powhatan, though, must have left their parent body in the Canadian Shield area; earlier, that is, than others closely connected with the Cheyennes, as not only were the Powhatan in situ southeast of the Lower Great Lakes of Erie and Ontario prior to the coming of the Delaware and their confederates which then included the Moiseo and Monsoni Cree, but were forcibly pushed further south into the Virginia Tidewater district by these same intruding Algonquian Delaware migrants.

During the slightly later period of between A.D.300. and A.D.500, another Algonquian-speaking faction composed of ancestral Malecite, Passamaquoddy and Massachusetts groups, also moved southeast from the same Keewatin area to the east side of Lake Winnipeg. Thence southeast around the southern tip of James Bay and down the Ottawa River to the north bank of the St. Lawrence; then east along the southern coastline of Quebec Province before crossing the St. Lawrence itself near Tadoussac close to the mouth of Trois Riviere. Eventually, they settled in New Brunswick, Nova Scotia Island, the New England states and even later, on the island of

Newfoundland where at the time of their arrival around A.D. 1,000, the Micmac and Beothuk peoples were already entrenched as far flung branches of an even earlier group of Algonquian migrants.

A third conglomerate of Algonquian-speaking peoples among whom proto-Delaware bands were the predominant factions, had themselves left the snow-bound Keewatin district around AD. 540, and started upon a long and devious migration toward the south and southeast, which was to terminate several centuries later when reaching the Lower St. Lawrence region and

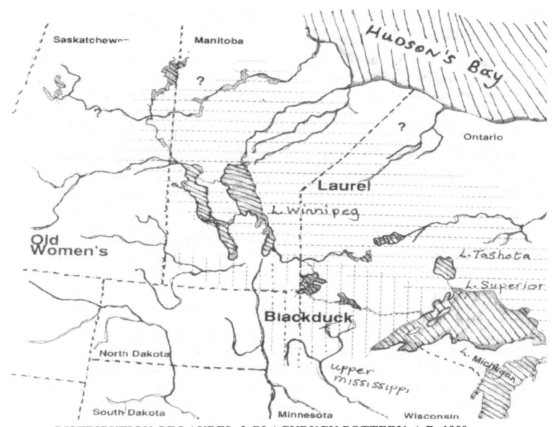

DISTRIBUTION OF LAUREL & BLACKDUCK POTTERY. A.D. 1000.
["Plains Indians A.D. 500- 1500." Ed; Karl Schlesier. University of Okl; Press P.113. 1994].

the Northeastern Atlantic seaboard. This particular period of migration beginning around A.D. 540 on the North American Continent is important here, as it coincides with the seemingly concurrent great volcanic eruptions on the island of Krakatoa, Indonesia, and where is now Lake Llopango in El Salvador of Central America. These explosions created catastrophic consequences to climates right across the Globe, so much ash being thrown into the atmosphere that for a significant time the sun was virtually blocked out. The overall world temperature dropped dramatically and with it, came both drought and famine on an unprecedented scale. This event effected all world regions for at least two decades, and, most likely, instigated human migration which included the Delaware group then incorporating the proto-Cheyenne, to search out more habitable regions conducive to their continued survival.

Following this Delaware movement from the northwest, there later occurred in the same Keewatin region between circa, AD.700 and AD. 800, yet another climatic shift. It then became much milder, creating a temperate zone which caused the tundra ice to melt somewhat, coupled with a more propitious rainfall, allowing existing water levels to rise significantly. This change in climatic environment forced the game herds and as a consequence, the remaining human populations of the region, to also search out more hospitable lands conducive to their continuing a hunter / gatherer culture. Thus another faction of Algonquian-speaking peoples, the fourth in its turn, advanced southeast from the Keewatin region and after splitting into two groups, moved due south into southern Manitoba and northern Minnesota respectively. Here they remained for several centuries, eventually becoming those peoples which included the ancestors of the historic Suhtaio, Arapahoe and Blackfoot. The Suhtaio group was part responsible for the later-date cultural focus known in the archaeological record as *"Blackduck,"* and the Arapahoe with that of *"Mero,"* whilst Blackfoot peoples were probably responsible for the complex known as *"Duck Bay,"* and even later, with that known as *"Old Woman Phase"* in southeastern Saskatchewan.

In its turn, *Blackduck* appears to have given way to that known as the *Arvilla Complex* in northwestern Minnesota of between AD. 800 and AD. 1600, as will become clear as we progress, and that during its later period of circa, A.D.1600, *Arvilla* was very closely connected with both proto-Cheyenne and proto-Suhtaio groups which then were inhabitants of the northwestern Minnesota region. [Ossenberg; 1974].

It is apparent, nonetheless, that each of the aforementioned Algonquian migrations from the Keewatin district of the northwest were not executed in a continuous manner, but in a series of forward and backward movements in accordance with the varying climatic conditions of the time. Thus a period of many centuries likely elapsed before those involved came to a final halt along the Atlantic seaboard and adjacent inland territories, and where indeed, the Delaware and several of their cognate tribes were found by the first European explorers including Jacques Cartier, during the first half of the sixteenth century.

The event of the Delaware migration from the *"Northern Plains"* of their traditions, and with which at this point we are primarily concerned, appears then, to have been the third great upheaval of Algonquians from the Keewatin region likewise alternating between a series of advances and retreats, along a route south and southeast from an original starting point somewhere west of Hudson's Bay as, of course, had been the general direction of those earlier migrating Algonquian groups noted above such as the Micmac, Beothuk and Naskapi. However, unlike their Powhatan cousins, before reaching the northern shores of the Upper Great Lakes the Delaware migration apparently turned east; crossed or rounded the southern tip of James Bay and continued on into central Quebec. Only then did it turn south, following the course of the Ottawa River downstream toward the Lower St. Lawrence. Hereabouts a part of the host including the Abenaki, Narraganset and Pequot among others, veered off from the route; crossed the St. Lawrence and traveled northeast along that river's southern shoreline as far as Tadoussac and even further to the

St. Lawrence Gulf at the Strait of Belle Isle. The remainder of the group which, evidently, comprised the Monsoni, Montagnais and Moiseo [proto-Cheyenne], along with those which later comprised the Delaware tribes proper of Munsey and Unami, each of whom was now completely separated from their Suhtaio, Arapahoe and Blackfoot cousins in the northwest, instead crossed the St. Lawrence near the mouth of the Ottawa where they remained in situ, until at length, the Delaware-proper and their cognate bands split from the Monsoni and Moiseo; turned west and traveled upstream along the south side of the St. Lawrence and eventually reached the southern shores of the Lower Great Lakes of Ontario and Erie.

Thus, leaving the Suhtaio for the present and treating the Moiseo as a separate entity as they now were as part of the migrating Delaware host, we see that the country through which the Moiseo must have traveled and occupied for an indefinite period during their initial stage of migration from the Keewatin region and before reaching the St. Lawrence, is impregnated with countless small lakes and inter-connecting streams. During the warmer days of the 10th and 11th centuries A.D., these lakes were in even more profusion than today, so that almost the entire area appeared flooded to a much greater degree. This description, of course, even if circumstantial, fits nicely with the statements in both Delaware and Cheyenne traditions that their people when roaming the far North Country, *"...were constantly sailing in their boats."* [3]

Further south toward the northern shores of the Lower Great Lakes and the St. Lawrence River, the timber is more abundant and varied with a plentiful supply of large game and small fur-bearing animals which would have sustained the people more comfortably, and this is precisely what Delaware tradition states as being the reason for their moving from the inhospitable *Northern Plains* in the first place, in order to seek out better, more provident lands.

Additional corroboration can be had in Cheyenne tradition, which recalls that the area into which they then moved after vacating the northland, was strewn with large and small rocks, which aptly describes the country of central Ontario and west central Quebec, where even today, the terrain is literally peppered with large rocks and stones of various size, being a vestige of the last Wisconsin glacial advance. It is worth noting here that a particular lake in west central Quebec bears the name `Wasinipi.` This term is of Algonquian derivation but from the Montagnais dialect and said to mean "far" or "distant water." It should, however, be more properly translated as "People of the far" or "distant water" and in olden times, was used specifically to denote a Montagnais band known as the Waswanipi. In addition, the area along the north shore of the St. Lawrence and immediately north of the Lower Great Lakes, was, of old, occupied by the Huron and their cognates [Iroquoian speaking groups] and later, by Chippewa Algonquian bands, both of whom have given their respective dialectical names to most other topographical features in that vast territory. Perhaps, then, the present-day place name of `Wasinipi` is derived from the fact that members of the migrating Delaware host may once have lingered in that lake's vicinity and that it was already so named from the Montagnais dialect, before the Huron and Chippewa themselves arrived in the same region.

- 0 - 0 - 0 - 0 - 0 - 0 - 0 - 0 - 0 - 0 - 0 - 0 - 0 - 0 - 0 - 0 – 0 – 0 – 0 -

CHAPTER 7.

INTO THE `SOUTHLAND.

We must continue with the Delaware account in order to ascertain the route of migration of the latter and their confederates, among whom were then included our subjects the Moiseo, and thus the succeeding passages in Delaware tradition tell us,

> "In the white or snow country, the north country, the Turtle land and the hunting country were the Turtle men or Linapawi. The Snake or evil men, the Akowini, afraid in their cabins. The Snake priest said to them "Let us go away". Then they went to the east, the Snake land sorrowfully leaving, thus escaped the Snake people, by the trembling and burned land to their strong island `Akomenaki`." [1]

It is important to determine who these `Snake people` were, lest they include the proto-Cheyennes and to further deduce the Delaware line of march, as it is obvious from the above statement that the `Snakes` or `Akowini` lived near, if not actually with the Delaware and so must have been Algonquians, as no peoples of other linguistic stocks were then roaming the Hudson's - James Bay and central Quebec areas between the years circa, AD. 1000 and AD. 1250.

The Thule Eskimo whose cultural remains have been discovered in these same areas, had already retreated from Quebec province and southern Labrador, having retired toward the far north and even northeast across the sea to Greenland before the beginning of the period in question [A.D. 1000]. On the other hand, the name itself of `Akowini,` does not actually mean `Snake` but, rather, something in the nature of `He is good at finding game.` The word for `snake` in the Delaware dialect is *"Shioni"* and was used as a synonym for `enemy.` The *"Akowini"* were snakes in this sense; that is, `enemies,` but are distinguished from other foes throughout Delaware history who are also called `Snakes.` This being so we read of the Sioux of Minnesota being called by the Delaware `Nadowa` meaning `Adders,` and the Iroquois being called in the same dialect `Adowa` or `Real Adders,` a more distinct appellation with the same meaning of `enemy.` During a later period than that covered by this tradition, the Delaware applied the term `Akowini` to the Chippewa tribes specifically, which probably stemmed from the fact that the latter were the descendants of, or at the least, offshoots from the original `Snakes` of Delaware tradition, viz. The `Akowini.` *

This assertion is corroborated by an entry in the fur trader Alexander Henry`s journal for August 18th 1800. At that time, Henry and his retinue had set up camp at the forks of the Assiniboine River where they were visited by a party of Indians on horseback. Apparently these Indians came

* In another Delaware dialect the name is rendered as Akonapi. It may be noted here that in late historic times, the Cheyenne called their Shoshoni enemies "Snakes," which word in the Cheyenne dialect is rendered `Shu-shu-ni,` this being merely a variant of the Delaware form.

from an area close to Portage la Prairie on the north side of the river, and Henry remarked,

> "They were of the tribe called Snakes, who formerly inhabited the Lake of the Woods [northern Minnesota]. They once were numerous, but at present cannot muster more than fifty men. They may be said to be of the same Nation as the Cree, but have a different dialect, something resembling the Saulteaux [Chippewa] language." [2]

I believe then, that the term *"Snakes"* as used in the Delaware tradition at this point, is meant to be a synonym for Chippewa-speaking peoples, particularly those known historically as Micmac who when first contacted by Europeans in the early part of the sixteenth century and perhaps, even earlier by Viking adventurers, were occupying parts of New Brunswick and Nova Scotia Island. All the tribes to the west and southwest of the Micmac have strong traditions of coming from the west and of pushing the Micmac into their historic eastern position. Indeed, the Micmac belong to the Chippewa group linguistically, whilst their western neighbours the Malecite, Passamaquoddy and Massachusetts are akin to the Delaware.

It is not feasible that the *"Snake* "people of Delaware tradition should have gone directly east from the Keewatin district into the northern or central part of Labrador to voluntarily suffer its harsh climate and environment, when the timbered warmer and in all other ways more favorable country to the south adjacent to the north shore of the Lower St. Lawrence, was virtually unoccupied during the same period.

It has been noted above that the Montagnais mentioned their own route of migration into their historic seats as being directly from west to east, although in their case, the time of this particular Montagnais movement, actually refers to a much later date than the period we have now reached as indicated in Delaware tradition of circa, A.D. 1100. In truth, it refers to a later time after circa, A.D. 1350, when the area adjacent to the northern shores of the Lower Great Lakes and St. Lawrence was being invaded by hostile Chippewa and Iroquois-proper groups, forcing the Montagnais and allied Naskapi to retreat east and northeast respectively to escape such hostile pressure. Coupled to this is the Delaware assertion in the account that they *"followed the `Snakes` into a "Beautiful pine country,"* [3] which must, therefore, lay towards the south, owing to the northern limit conducive to the growth of pine in the north-eastern United States and Canada. This infers that the Micmac, without doubt, also came originally from the Lower St. Lawrence country into their historic location, after having been pushed into the New Brunswick and Nova Scotia Island regions by other invading Algonquian peoples, among whom the Delaware and their cognates were predominant.

The route of migration taken by the `Snakes` was likely then, to have been followed in its` general direction by the Delaware groups and here an old-time Indian trait may prove a point, in so much as Indians invariably travelled predefined routes when possible, which often proved the most beneficial for camping sites, fresh water and directness from one place to another. Hence the well-known war roads in constant use in later years and particularly, the trading trails utilized by the early French and English traders, but previously blazed and worn smooth by the moccasin feet of various tribes over countless previous generations. Thus the route traveled by earlier Algonquian migrants was likely to have been followed by succeeding groups and ultimately, by the Delaware host itself.

The `Trembling` or `Burned Land` referred to in the account at this point, probably alludes to the Keewatin and Hudson's Bay region, which area was still prone to sporadic volcanic eruptions and earth tremors as recently as the tenth and eleventh centuries AD. Further migration may well have been brought about by another severe climatic change apparent in the Hudson`s Bay and Lake Winnipeg area during this period of circa, A. D. 1100. Such we know involved the overall rising of summer temperatures in the Northern Hemisphere to a significant degree, that it melted part of the ice sheets and unlocked the waters of the frozen tundra, thereby inundating the country.

The `Strong Island` on the other hand, is hard to locate, and it has been this particular reference in the tradition which has led a number of eminent scholars to suppose that the Delaware migration commenced originally from the North Atlantic seaboard, or more precisely, from a point along the Labrador coast and thence, continued south to the Gulf of the St. Lawrence and from there upstream to the Island of Montreal.

This view, however, of an east to west migration at this point in the account, is not consistent with the available evidence at hand, as will become apparent throughout the course of our study.

The *"Strong Island"* in this case, appears to have denoted a particular place of habitat of the *"Snakes"* somewhere north or northwest of the St. Lawrence River, as it is here referred to separately to that of a later reference in the same tradition, which mentions the *"Snake Island"* specifically, but then is referring to the Island of Montreal in its literal sense.

Now the predefined respective hunting territories of nomadic hunter / gatherer bands and family groups, which was a typical feature during colonial times among all Northern Algonquians, and survives today among the Cree, Montagnais-Naskapi and Chippewa of the Canadian Shield region, were often referred to by both Algonquians and Iroquoians alike as "Islands," being the Indian's poetic metaphor to describe a specific area bounded on all sides by the borders of foreign tribal hunting grounds. Thus the `Strong Island` of the account may not be an island in its proper sense, but merely an area of land claimed by a particular band or tribe, which then becomes an island – in the allegorical sense and no more. Certainly, in the Cheyenne idiom, the same word is used for both an `Island` in its proper context and a people's particular area of residence.

The Delaware tradition continues by stating that after the Snakes had left *"The white or Snow Country"* i.e. "The Northern Plains," the Delaware and remaining Algonquians or `Northerlings,` as they are called in the account,

"All went forth, free from opposers and separated in the land of snow....but by the open sea, the sea of fish, tarried the fathers of the White Eagle and of the White Wolf."
4

The above passage indicates the separation of different Algonquian factions from the main body, one of which, we have noted, without doubt included the Fox and Sauk along with the Monsoni and the proto-Cheyenne group of Moiseo. Another included those known historically as Malecite, Passamaquoddy and Massachusetts, while yet another comprised those later known as Miami and Shawnee. Those who remained by the "Open Sea" [which most likely refers to the ice-free expanse of James Bay on the Delaware line of march] are likely to have been the main Montagnais-Naskapi group - "The Fathers of the White Eagle" - who at a later date moved into the country of eastern Quebec and even further, into the southern hinterland of Labrador as far as the coast where the `white eagle` [the North American Osprey and Bald Eagle] once flew supreme in significant number.

The other group, those of the `White Wolf,` probably refers to a Cree faction, the Muskegon [Swampy Cree] which then included the Monsoni who eventually split from the Montagnais; moved northwest and were still occupying the country around the western shores of both James and Hudson's Bay when first contacted by Europeans not long prior to the middle years of the seventeenth century. Hereabouts, white wolves were then found in great abundance. Pierre Radisson, in fact, when referring to his sojourn in the Hudson's and James Bay regions in 1658, did mention two Indian groups ostensibly of Cree affiliation who at that date, frequented the same region and were known to surrounding tribes as "The People of the White Wolf" and "The People of the Long-horned Beast. This last name refers to the moose and, therefore, to the "Moose people," i.e. The Monsoni Cree. Indeed, the two last-mentioned peoples noted in Delaware tradition, and later, it seems, by Radisson, were of the same group whose cultural archaeological remains have since been classified as the "Selkirk" complex. This complex relates specifically to the ancestors of the Muskegon [Swampy] Cree and Monsoni / Plains Cree collectively. What is certainly apparent, however, during this particular stage of their migration, is that the Delaware and their cognates must then have been in the lake district of Quebec southeast of James Bay, for the account goes on to say,

"The people were rich and constantly sailing in their boats, they discovered to the east the `Snake` Island." Then said the Beaver and the Great Bird, "let us go to the Snake Island. "All responded, "Let us go and annihilate the Snakes. "All agreed, the Northerners, the Easterners, to pass the frozen waters; wonderful, they all went over the waters of the hard stony sea to the open Snake waters. In vast numbers, in a single night they went to the eastern or Snake Island, all of them marching by night in the darkness. The Northerlings, the Easterlings, the Southerlings, Beaver men, Wolf Men, the Hunters or the Best Men, the Priests, the Wiliwapi with their wives and daughters and their dogs." 5

In an additional statement in the same traditional account, it is further noted,

> "The Northerners were of one mind and the Easterners were of one mind; it would be good to live on the other side of the frozen water. Things turned out well for all those who stayed at the shore of the water frozen hard as rocks, and for those at the Great Hollow Well." [6]

The above statement that the people were constantly sailing in their boats, suggests an area interlaced with numerous streams and interconnecting lakes, and is compatible with the southern Ontario and central Quebec regions. If, however, the `Snake land` did in truth, lay toward the east, then it must be assumed that the Delaware host had migrated into identical terrain as they already possessed and by so doing, were risking aggression from the Snakes for no better reason than a Delaware wish to inaugurate a hostile confrontation. Only if the *Snake Land* was a more favorable habitat can such a move be justified, and Delaware tradition further asserts that the land of the Snakes was, *"A beautiful land covered with spruce pine."* [7]

The term "toward the east" is, in reality, a Delaware synonym for "toward the light" and was often used as a metaphor to denote prosperity etc.; and so, should actually be rendered as, "toward a better or richer land." Thus the `Snake Land` must, in effect, have been to the south or southeast. Likewise, the reference of going over *"...the hard stony sea to the open Snake waters,"* [8] probably applies not to a sea in the literal sense, but to the land north of the St. Lawrence where the lakes and streams freeze over for several months of the year, along with the St. Lawrence River itself, so that the whole country might be alluded to as *"...a hard stony sea,"* again in the allegorical idiom. The `stony` aspect would, in turn, denote the multitude of rocks and stones strewn all over the southern Ontario and Quebec regions.

As regards the march across to the *"Snake Island"* supposedly executed in the space of one night, again this is an allegorical phrase and unlike the Goths who we are told in the Roman Annals crossed the river Danube during the space of one night, in the case of the Delaware host it refers either to one year, or - and what is more likely in this respect - to some longer but unspecified period. It seems to imply moreover, to the length of time it took the Delaware host to migrate from the central Quebec area south, to and across the St. Lawrence. This is evidenced by other reliable Delaware traditions which state that the people crossed a broad stream rich in fish in order to get to the `Spruce Pine Land,` and there they met the Iroquois, who had struck the same river higher up. This is important, for the St. Lawrence was known as `Fish River` and sometimes even `Fish Country` to all Northern and Eastern Algonquians when first contacted by the French [circa,1603], and we know that Iroquois-speaking groups were settled along the Upper St. Lawrence and around the outlet of Lake Ontario, at least as early as AD. 1000.

The Delaware migration [ostensibly following the course of the Ottawa River downstream] must then have reached the St. Lawrence somewhere in the vicinity of Montreal Island and here, of course, we have corroboration in the guise of Chief Masco`s statement [previously referred to] that his tribe the Sauk, along with other Algonquian groups were created in the North, and after migrating south, settled for a while along the St. Lawrence a short distance from where the city of Montreal now stands.

The Sauk coupled with the Fox and Kickapoo are the `Wilipawi` of the Delaware account, the name signifying "Western Men," and which likely included at that time, the Moiseo proto-Cheyenne group, notwithstanding that the same term at a later date was extended by the Delaware-proper to include the Potawatomi, Menominee and most other Central Algonquian tribes west of the Lower Great Lakes. The `Northerlings,` I believe, denote the bulk of Monsoni and some other Cree groups known in late historic times as Muskegon and Bush Cree, who during the current period of Delaware migration from the *Northern Plains,* were then closely related to and aligned with the `Western Men.` The `Easterlings` represent the Abenaki; the `Southerlings` the Shawnee; the `Beaver Men` the Miami; and the `Wolf Men` the Munsey or, perhaps, the Mohegan [meaning `wolf`]. These last two names refer to Delaware offshoots, while the `Hunters` or `Best Men` refer to the Unami or Turtle clan of the Delaware-proper. The `Priests,` perhaps, denote a group of Shaman which constituted a sodality in their own right connected to the `Wilipawi` [Western Men], if indeed, they do not represent the Montagnais or even the Wheskerinni [Algonkin tribe proper] who although related to the Chippewa, were also closely connected to the Montagnais and thus by definition, to the Moiseo proto-Cheyenne group also. Certainly at a later date, both the Montagnais and their allies the Wheskerinni, were always noted for the profusion of magicians or "Shamen" among their number.

The added statement in this part of the tradition, that *"things turned out well for those who stayed along the shore"* applies, obviously, to those groups which did not cross the St. Lawrence, or more properly, did not remain permanently on its south side. On the other hand, those that continued on to "The Great Hollow Well," refers to the "Southerners" or Shawnee and also to the Delaware-proper group itself. The first named going as far as Lake Erie on its south side and even further into the area around Niagara Falls, whilst the Delaware-proper went due south from the mouth of the Ottawa, if that is, the term "Great Hollow Well" actually refers more specifically to the swamp country of Upper New York State. This region in a later passage in the same Delaware tradition is designated as "The Swampy Vales" which in its allegorical idiom can also be alluded to as a "Hollow Well."

Indeed, the account goes on to say that after the Delaware conglomerate of peoples had crossed `Fish River` [St. Lawrence] and reached the land of `Spruce Pines,`

> "They began searching; the `Great Fine Land,` the Island of the `Snakes,` but the `Snakes` were weak and hid themselves in the `Bear Hills,` or, as in the alternative Delaware account, "The Swampy Vales." [9]

Here the `Bear Hills` denote the present-day Adirondack Mountains in Upper New York State. This was the old colloquial Indian name for that region, the northern part of which is invested with swamps and Lower-lying water and, as noted above, may in fact be the "Great Hollow Well" of tradition. The term *"Snakes"* conversely, refers predominately in this case to the Iroquois-proper, particularly to the Mohawk and Seneca tribes, but evidently, also includes Chippewa groups which ostensibly, then resided to the east of the Iroquois.

Certainly the number of these foreign Algonquian peoples now intruding into the Lower St. Lawrence country at a point near the mouth of the Ottawa, is said in Iroquois tradition to have been small initially, and their presence did not immediately incur resentment from the indigenous populations. Here the Iroquoian tradition is likely referring to the Chippewa-speaking groups called *Snakes* in the tradition. However, as is also suggested in both the Delaware and Iroquois accounts, as the country began to fill up with these new Delaware-speaking arrivals - perhaps extending over a period of one or two generations, friction arose between the resident Iroquois and Delaware Algonquian immigrants, eventually reaching a climax which, to the Indian way of thinking, could only be resolved through war.

The Archaeological record corroborates this assumption by showing that a wave of Indians of a hunter / gatherer culture and among whom, the use of red ochre was a predominant trait, thus indicating Algonquian-speaking peoples [See Chapter 2.], intruded into the Upper part of New York State between circa, AD.1100 and 1200, having come originally from somewhere north of the Upper Great Lakes. This event appears eventually, to have inaugurated an era of chronic warfare in the region, resulting in the destruction of indigenous agrarian cultures along the St. Lawrence and in the northern parts of New York, Pennsylvania and northeastern Ohio. It is indicative that during the period AD.1100 / 1150, Iroquois-proper villages along and in the vicinity of the St. Lawrence [as opposed to Huron-speaking tribes], show the sudden introduction of defensive features, such as tighter groupings of previously more scattered living quarters of bark and timber long houses - creating a more compact area to defend - in addition to palisade perimeters and protective earthworks and ditches, and here we have the evidence of the French trader Nicholas Perrot; a man in close and prolonged contact with the indigenous peoples of the Great Lakes and surrounding area during the latter half of the seventeenth century. Perrot recorded details regarding this first outbreak of hostility ostensibly between these same Northern Delaware-speaking Algonquian groups and the Iroquois, having obtained his information from the Indians themselves. According to this valuable account,

"...The country of the Irroquois [sic] was formerly the district of Montreal and Three Rivers; they had as neighbours the Algonkins, who lived along the river of the Outaouas, at Nepissing, on the French River, and between this last and Taronto. The Irroquois were not hunters; they cultivated the soil...The Algonkins, on the contrary, supported themselves by their hunting alone, despising agriculture as a pursuit little suited to their ambitious pride, and regarding it as infinitely beneath them - so that the Iroquois were regarded in a certain sense as their vassals. That did not hinder them from trading together; the Iroquois carried to them grain, in exchange for the dried meat and skins which the former obtained from the Algonkins....Once it happened during the peace that reigned between these peoples, that the Algonkins sent word to the Irroquois that the latter should spend the winter among them; and that during the winter they would supply their guests with fresh meat, which made better soup than dried meat. The

Irroquois accepted the offer. When the season permitted they [all] set out on a hunting trip, and wandered far into the forests, where they succeeded in killing all the beasts that they encountered within the limits of the places where they could hunt in the vicinity; then they lacked provisions and were obliged to break camp and go further in search of game. But as the savages can accomplish only a very short march in a day - because they have to carry with them their cabins, their children, and whatever is necessary to them, when they shift their quarters for hunting. The Algonkins chose from their best hunters six young men to go to kill game for the coming of the people from both villages; and the Irroquois engaged to add to these six of their men who should share the game which all of them killed, and who should go ahead of the two tribes with their meat.....On the next day the [six] Algonkins, each with an Irroquois, went out in various directions; they found many moose, which they failed to secure and were obliged to return to camp without having obtained any game. They went again to that place the following day, but had no better success. But the Irroquois demanded their consent to go and hunt by themselves. The Algonkins replied very haughtily that they were astounded that the Irroquois should presume to expect that they could kill beasts, since the Algonkins themselves had not been able to do so. But the Irroquois without consulting them further on this point, set out on the morrow, to do their own hunting, without the Algonkins; and finally arrived at their camp laden with meat. The others who had accomplished nothing, when they saw those whom they had despised now had the advantage, resolved to take their lives, and did so; for one day when the Irroquois were asleep, the Algonkins murdered them, and covered up their bodies with snow. As for the meat, they dried it, that it might be less to carry, and went to meet their people. When they were asked what had become of their companions, they replied that the latter were all lost in the icy waters of a river which they had passed; and, in order to give more colour to this falsehood, they broke a hole in a large ice-field in order to show the place where these men had been drowned......they encamped all together in that locality, and spent the rest of the winter there in hunting, without any tidings of the murder which had been committed there. When the snows began to melt towards spring, the bodies of those dead men caused an unsupportable stench in the camp, which led to the discovery of the murders. The Irroquois made complaint of the crime to the chief of the Algonkins, who rendered them no justice therefore; but with a threatening countenance he told them that he was very near driving them out of their own country, and even entirely exterminating them, and that it was only through pity and compassion that he spared their lives. The Irroquois decided to retire quietly, without making any answer to this speech of the Algonkin chief; but they immediately sent information to the [other] Irroquois allied to some Algonkins whom they met in a lonely place. But, not being able to avert the consequences which this deed drew upon them from the Algonkins, those Irroquois departed and fled for refuge to Lake Erien [i.e. Erie], where the Chaouanons [Shawnee] dwelt; these made war on the Irroquois, and compelled them to go to settle along Lake Ontario, which is now Lake Frontenac. All these hostilities were very useful in accustoming the Irroquois to war, and rendering them able to fight the Algonkins, who before that time carried terror among them." [10]

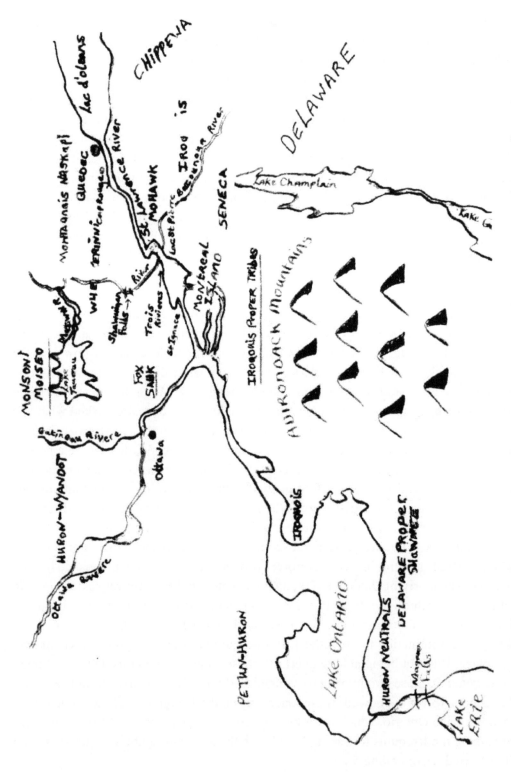

DISTRIBUTION OF TRIBES IN THE ST. LAWRENCE & LOWER GREAT LAKES REGION CIRCA; 1360. *[Map by Author].*

Apparently, after evicting the resident Iroquois groups, the Delaware host remained adjacent to the south shore of the Upper St. Lawrence for many years, during which time two of their chiefs passed away. The next chief, called `Snowbird` in the account, decided to go to *"Shawanki,"* the `Southland` while, *"...to the east went the Beaver."* [11] The inference here is that the Delaware group was rapidly expanding its population and as a consequence, after crossing to the south side of the St. Lawrence, a separation into different factions occurred. The `Beaver` in this sense refers not to the Miami, as in the earlier case, but to a chief of that name and in all probability, denotes those Algonquian peoples later known as Malecite, Passamaquoddy and Massachusetts, and including, perhaps, the Algonquian Abenaki tribes whose collective name actually translates as `People of the Sunrise` or simply `Easterners.` Allowing then for the life span of two chiefs as mentioned in the account, the date now reached in the Delaware tradition seems to be the period of circa, AD.1200.

The "Fish Land" referred to, evidently being east of the "Buffalo Land," was more precisely, the lake and swamp region of Upper New York State and the western part of Maine which, then as now, abounds with small lakes and streams and was always a favorite fishing ground for Algonquian peoples, when toleration from the Iroquois would permit.

In yet another Delaware account added as a supplement to the main tradition, it is asserted that the `Great Spruce Land` was toward the shore and the `Snake Land` toward the south. The shore in this instance is the south bank of the St. Lawrence, and so the `Snake Land,` most probably, was also the `Fish Land` which in addition, embraced the `Swampy Vales` and `Bear Hills` country mentioned previously.

The traditional histories of the Malecite and Passamaquoddy particularly, declare that before finally reaching their historic homes in what are now the states of Maine and New Brunswick, their people had resided to the west and southwest of those lands and in their advance east, they had pushed the Micmac Indians from their territory. So it would seem that the people with the `Beaver` as their chief, now favored a further pursuit of the `Snakes` who by fleeing east [or rather northeast], drew the Malecite and their allies in that direction. On the other hand, those Delaware-proper groups that went south with their chief `Snowbird,` must actually have moved southwest to a point somewhere along the Upper course of the St. Lawrence on its south side not far east of Lake Ontario, for reference is made to the `Shore Land` and toward the Lakes was the `Buffalo Land.` [12]

It is known that as late as the early colonial period of North America and Canada, buffalo still extended their range as far east as the country between Lake Michigan and Lake Huron and sometimes, even further east as far as the outlet of Lake Ontario, being found in no small number south of Lake Erie across the open meadow lands in what are now the states of Indiana and Ohio.

At this period between AD.1200 and 1250, the Delaware groups that moved west following the course of the Upper St. Lawrence along that river's south side, would have been encroaching into lands still held by Iroquois-proper tribes, these latter peoples having been in occupation of that country for generations prior to the Delaware's crossing that river. The Iroquois, however, were not then united in their later famous confederacy and were often fighting among themselves, so that these Algonquian invaders may well have had the advantage in numbers along with a more aggressive spirit. Even so, it is most unlikely that the Iroquois would have surrendered their homelands without a determined show of resistance, and the following passages in the Delaware tradition appear to allude to this fact,

> "After `Snowbird, ` `Great Warrior, ` was chief (or `Seizer` was chief)....All were killed....Then our fathers went to war against the `Robbers, ` the `Snakes, ` the `Bad Men` and the Assinapi. [13]

Having previously deduced that the `*Snakes*` of Delaware tradition are synonymous with the various proto-Chippewa tribes, and that the term in its later context included certain tribes of Iroquois-proper, the other three names in the above passage most likely represent Iroquoians also, for that people were the only inhabitants along the southern shores of the Lower Great Lakes and adjacent territory at that time. While it is true that both the `Robbers` and `Bad Men` of the account cannot be positively identified with any particular Iroquois tribe, the last named, the `Assinapi,` may well have been the Mohawks, who previously had retired to the shores of Lake Ontario due to an earlier spate of Algonquian pressure. The term `Assinapi` is Algonquian and means "Stone Men" which seems to have been applied as a distinct appellation, rather than a mere derogatory term as is the case with the other two names of `Robbers` and `Bad Men.`

Now an ancient name for the Mohawks according to themselves, was *"Caniengahakes,"* which translates as `People of the place of stones` or `flint,` and Mohawk tradition places their tribe along the south shore of the Lower St. Lawrence near the Island of Montreal from an early date, until eventually, they were evicted by Algonquian invaders from the north. Indeed, this same area opposite Montreal Island where the Mohawks once lived, was noted for its flint deposits and, perhaps, the Delaware term `*Stone Men*` alludes to that fact.

It appears to have been during the time of the Delaware chief *"Snowbird"* that the Iroquois-proper were driven from their villages, the latter then taking refuge in the lake and swamp region of central New York State. Archaeological findings show that, anciently, the Iroquois lived along the southern shores of the St. Lawrence, their villages extending downstream as far as the Island of Montreal. But later, they appear to have been overwhelmed by intruders from the north practicing a predominantly hunter / gatherer culture who dispersed the resident groups.

This fits in with reliable Iroquois tradition which relates how their villages were harassed at an early date by Algonquians who are called *"Ottawa"* in the accounts. Now the name *Ottawa* was at first used as a general term by the Iroquois-proper [the five confederated tribes] in order to designate specifically, those Algonquian-speakers with whom during this early period, the Iroquois were in contact. The name was not applied to the tribe known historically as Ottawa - who themselves were offshoots from the Chippewa Algonkin group - until the middle part of the colonial era of circa, AD.1700.

In the earlier case the name referred, moreover, to members of the Delaware host, which fact is further enhanced when we realize that the first group of peoples called Ottawa in Iroquois tradition held the Upper hand over the latter, whilst the Ottawa of the Chippewa group and of a later time, suffered diabolically from Iroquois harassment. The inference is clear; the name Ottawa was originally daubed upon the Delaware Algonquians, but later, after the Delaware and their cognates had left the St. Lawrence and Chippewa-speaking tribes had overrun their [the Delaware`s] old domain, by recognizing these newcomers also as Algonquians, the Iroquois naturally gave the Chippewa the same appellation as once had been applied to the Delaware.

Thus the "shore land abounding in tall firs" which is synonymous with the "Great Spruce Pine Land" and the "Beautiful Land" of the supplementary Delaware account, can be located with a fair degree of accuracy, as being somewhere between the south shore of the eastern outlet of Lake Ontario and as far west as the headwaters of the Susquehanna River. This assertion substantiates Cheyenne tradition [previously recounted in Chapter 2.], which relates to a time when the original nucleus of their Nation abandoned the "Northland" and moved south, before sometime later returning to the `Northland` from whence they came. For here in this new land; the `Beautiful Land` of both Delaware and Cheyenne traditions, these Algonquian invaders then came into close and regular contact with a people called in the Delaware account, "Tallegwi" and against whom, they engaged themselves in a prolonged and bloody war of attrition. Indeed, the Delaware tradition continues by asserting, *"...Then there were many wars east, west and south, spanning a period of ten chiefs before peace came at last into the "Beautiful Land."* [14]

- 0 – 0 – 0 – 0 – 0 – 0- - 0 – 0 – 0 – 0 – 0 – 0 – 0 - 0 – 0 -

CHAPTER 8.

PROTO-CHEYENNES IN THE *"GREAT FALLS"* REGION.

It is necessary again to continue with the Delaware account as contained in their migration traditions, in order to elucidate the position now reached by the Moiseo during their early period of migration across the Canadian Shield.

Since the time the Delaware host had first reached the St. Lawrence and made contact with the Huron, the latter had told them of a powerful Nation to the south and southwest, who were mighty warriors and enemies of the Huron. We know of these people in Indian tradition only by the name *"Tallegwi"* [or *"Allegwi"*], while John D. Heckewelder [1818] associated them with the Old Mound-Builder peoples of Ohio. Most other scholars since his time, however, are agreed that more specifically, the *Tallegwi* were the ancestors of the present-day Cherokee, whose indigenous tribal name for themselves of *"Tsalaki,"* is merely a variant form of *Tallegwi*. Certainly the Wyandots of Huron affiliation, have always stated that the *Tallegwi* were the same people as the Cherokee. Concerning the *Tallegwi* in Algonquian tradition, it is said that they built angular fortifications and protective enclosures composed of earthworks and ditches *"...from which they sallied forth to fight."* [1] One of these forts stood adjacent to the mouth of the Huron River near Lake St. Clair on its north side, and others were sited along that river itself near Sandusky about eight or nine miles east of Lake Erie. The remains of these earthworks were still to be seen early in the nineteenth century and nearby, were a number of flat-top mounds, where; so Indian tradition also relates, hundreds of slain *Tallegwi* lie buried.

According to the Delaware account coupled with fragments of supplementary Delaware traditions, after crossing *Fish River* [i.e., the St. Lawrence], the Delaware host wished to pass through *Tallegwi* country to settle lands on the far side of that people's domain and accordingly, they sent an embassy to ask permission to do so. The Delaware ambassadors were received in friendship and given to understand that permission had been granted. However, when half the Algonquian host had crossed the river, the *Tallegwi* reneged on their promise; cut the Delaware host in two, and either prevented the rest of the host from crossing, or actually drove them back across the river. In any event, a great battle was fought between them in which many Algonquians were killed. Furious at this act of perfidy on the part of the *Tallegwi*, those of the Delaware host still entrenched on the south side of the river, sought the assistance of certain Huron-speaking tribes called *"Tallamatans"* in the Delaware account, who resided above the Lower Lakes and who also, were enemies of the *Tallegwi* with whom they had been at war for many years. The Delaware and Huron formed an alliance; avenged themselves upon the common enemy and made a pact that when they finally defeated the foe, they would divide the *Tallegwi* country between them. *

Thereafter, numerous bloody battles were fought with the *Tallegwi* during a war that dragged on for several generations, although the Delaware and their Huron allies generally held the advantage. At length, another great battle took place in which a very large number of *Tallegwi* were slain at one time [some accounts say one thousand or more], and as a result, the latter finally abandoned their country and fled south into what is now the state of Kentucky. As agreed, the victors then divided the conquered land between them, the Huron claiming the area around the Lower Great Lakes, whilst the Delaware settled lands south of the lakes and as far west as the Wabash River in present day Indiana.

Some few years later, after a second war with the Delaware, the *Tallegwi* retreated even further south into Tennessee and West Virginia. It is evident that the first period of warfare against the *Tallegwi,* had continued for one hundred years before the latter were finally dispersed, which would bring us to the date circa, A.D. 1300. Furthermore, as the Delaware tribes were then fighting both the *Tallegwi* in the west and against Iroquois-proper tribes in the east, the "Bad Men" and "Robbers" of the account may, in truth, refer to members of either of these latter peoples, or more probably, to both. Returning to the Delaware tradition, the account continues,

> "They all arrived at "Shinaking," the land of firs where they tarried, but the `Western Men` hesitating, desired to return to the old "Turtle Land of the north." [2]

* Wyandot tradition collected in 1802, confirms this period of warfare with the Tallegwi and the latter`s expulsion south.

The above passage implies that the main group of Delaware was now firmly entrenched in the `Land of Firs,` south of Lake Erie about the headwaters of the Allegheny and Ohio rivers [circa, AD. 1300], but that another part of the Algonquian host had been left behind in the vicinity of the St. Lawrence.

Therefore, the `Western Men;` and likely the `Northerners` who were closely associated with them, and thus, comprising the Fox, Sauk, Monsoni, Montagnais and Moiseo along with the recently confederated Wheskerinni, apparently remained on that river's north bank, or having been prevented from settling permanently in the south, had actually re-crossed the St. Lawrence from south to north, which would then be compatible with both Fox and Sauk tradition that recalls how they, along with a number of other Algonquian groups, came into their historic seats in Wisconsin and Minnesota from north of the Upper Great Lakes via Sault St. Marie.

Evidently then, the "Western Men" are those tribes referred to above during the traditional war with the *Tallegwi,* and were those who were prevented by the latter from crossing permanently to the south side of the St. Lawrence. Here a supplementary Delaware tradition recorded by John D. Heckewelder explains more fully the situation at that time. This account states that the whole of the migrating Algonquian host did not reach the southern country,

> "Many remained behind, in order to assist that great body of their people which had not crossed the Namaesisipu [Fish River], but had retreated into the interior of the country on the other [north] side." [present author`s parenthesis]. [3]

That the `*Westerners*` of Delaware tradition had found it prudent to settle the St. Lawrence country on that river's north side, also makes it unreasonable to suppose that this was the *"Snake Land"* of Delaware tradition, or that the `Snakes` retreated downstream along that river following its northern shoreline. It is more feasible that the `Snakes` had, in fact, earlier crossed the river to its south side and settled in what is now the northern part of New York State [i.e. *"The Swampy Vales"*], before being driven further east.

More important to our study, however, is that as the Monsoni and Montagnais groups - who of course, were a part of the *"Western Men"* - were now ensconced on the north side of the St. Lawrence presumably around Trois Rivieres and Quebec, then the Moiseo [proto-Cheyenne] were sure to have been close by, having likely been caught up in the expulsion of these same Algonquian groups during the war with the *Tallegwi.*

So intimate did a number of these intruding Algonquians become with one or two neighbouring Huron groups, particularly during the course of the first *Tallegwi* war, that a significant degree of intermarriage took place, moreover between those of the Delaware-proper and Petun [Tobacco] Huron from the area of Notsawaga Bay, and also, with the Neutral Huron-speaking bands residing further south. At a later date, after 1649, the remnants of these same Huron groups made up the bulk of refugees forced west by Iroquois-proper tribes and thereafter, known collectively as Wyandot. They then became very closely aligned with other refugee Algonquians, although how long the earlier period of friendship had persisted, we cannot be sure.

Certainly by circa,1300, warfare had erupted between the same Delaware-proper groups and those Huron-speaking peoples of the Rock and Deer tribes, whose villages then stretched along the Upper reaches of the St. Lawrence and north of the Lower Great Lakes. Moreover, it was the Petun [Tobacco] Huron; later called Wyandot, who suffered most from Delaware harassment, and as a result were then forced north into the region between the north shore of present day Lake Huron and the southern shore of James Bay.

The Neutrals on the other hand, appear to have kept aloof from these hostilities with the Delaware, for they remained in situ in the Lake St. Clair area and actually began warring against their Petun cousins. At the same time, they continued in harmony with those Algonquian groups on the north side of the St. Lawrence - including our subjects the Moiseo - with whom they carried on an intertribal trade.

The Delaware tradition admits this by claiming that after their first war with the *Tallegwi,* they then drove the above-mentioned Huron groups out of a part of their [the Huron] country. This is consistent with Chippewa tradition, which states that the Huron were driven towards the north from the Lower Great Lake shores by Algonquians, although the Chippewa do not implicate themselves as then being involved. On the contrary, the Chippewa were pushed from the St. Lawrence by these same Huron at a later date, after the latter eventually reoccupied their old lands to the south early in the fifteenth century.

Huron tradition declares, that they themselves came into their early historic seats where they were first encountered by Europeans in 1534, from some place far north of the Upper St. Lawrence probably in the region abutting the southern tip of James Bay, and from where they migrated south to the St. Lawrence near the Island of Montreal.

At first view, when comparing this assertion in the light of recent archaeological and ethno-historical evidence, this part of Huron tradition seems to be in error, for they were, of course, Iroquoians and members of that stock have a southern and southwestern origin. However, when the Delaware pushed the resident Huron from the Upper St. Lawrence, some Huron groups at least, may well have fled north toward James Bay as both they and the Chippewa assert, and thus, after returning to the St. Lawrence which they evidently did after the Delaware migration had moved on, remembered only as far back as their enforced habitat north of that river. Another hypothesis is that as the Delaware now say that the Wyandot are their kinfolk, some informants going even further to assert that the Delaware are actually descended from them, it may be that the Wyandot, being descendants of the progeny of the earlier Delaware -Huron liaison, adopted the tradition of an ancient seat around James Bay from their Algonquian forebears, along with the Algonquian story of their migration south to the St. Lawrence and into their proto-historic homes around the Lower Great Lakes and the Island of Montreal.

By 1534, the date of Jacques Cartier's visit to the Huron near Montreal, the Huron then occupied most of the country from Tadoussac on the east to Georgian Bay towards the northwest, and their earlier vacation of the St. Lawrence because of pressure from the Delaware - long before Cartier's visit - offers a sound reason why the `Westerners` of Delaware tradition were allowed to occupy the north shore country of the St. Lawrence. It was then, the presence of Huron groups slightly northwest, that likely created a buffer against the *Westerners* going further north in order; as stated in the account, to return to the `Turtle Land` of their forefathers.

Now the old Cheyenne informant Black-Pipe told W. P. Clark in 1879, that during the "Ancient Time" of Cheyenne tradition, his people had once lived near a large lake, the river running from it, *",,,flowed east and fell to a great depth."* [4] This was beyond the `Big River,` Black-Pipe said, and before falling, the stream was narrow then suddenly wide. A great mist rose to the sky and a loud rumbling noise was heard. Clark himself associated the Falls with those of Mini-Ha-Ha in the east-central part of Minnesota, but as Black-Pipe was speaking from his home then far west of the Missouri, the river mentioned by Clark as being connected to Mini-Ha-Ha Falls cannot be said to be `beyond` the Mississippi, as it actually flows east into that river and neither is the height of Mini Ha-Ha Falls [only some fifty feet], sufficient to create such a mist and noise as asserted by Black- Pipe. James Mooney [1896], accepted Clark's location and added that the `Falls` were near a "River of Turtles," averring that this was an old Indian name for the St. Croix River that flows into the Upper Mississippi north of the aforesaid Falls. But this assumption is also in error, for the St. Croix flows southwest not east, and was formally known as "Tortoise River" not "Turtle."

It does appear that both Clark and Mooney supposed the "Big River" of Black-Pipe's statement to be synonymous with the Missouri, and took the phrase `beyond the Big River` to mean somewhere in the region of the Mississippi. The Cheyennes, though, called the Missouri *"Eo-mi-tai"* meaning "Greasy" or "Fat River," and used the term `Big River` specifically, to designate the Mississippi alone. This being so, "beyond the Big River" must mean either to the north or east of the Mississippi.

A likely location north of the Mississippi may have been that known as Rainy Lake and its connecting stream of Rainy River in the northern part of Minnesota. This river does, in fact, boast a water fall which owing to its profusion of spray and precipitous rainfall in the region, has given rise to the name `Rainy` for both that lake and river. Unfortunately, though, neither does this river flow "east;" but southwest and then north into Lake of the Woods. So likewise, it cannot really be considered, even though at a much later date than we are at present concerned, the Monsoni and perhaps one or more early Cheyenne-speaking band or bands, did reside in that general area. Logically then, the phrase *"beyond the Big River,"* must refer to somewhere east of the Mississippi, and the next compatible location is quite a distance from both the Mini-Ha-Ha Falls and Rainy River in the northern part of Minnesota.

With a stretch of the imagination, it may be construed that another likely early habitat of these proto-Cheyennes in accordance with the traditional description, is the area adjacent to Niagara Falls between Lakes Erie and Ontario. But again, the river of these `Falls` does not flow "east," but north, and all the country for a considerable distance around was occupied by Huron Iroquoian tribes from before AD. 1200, and continued to be so, until the middle years of the seventeenth century when hostile pressure finally drove them west. By the latter date, however, there certainly were no Cheyenne-speaking peoples residing permanently or otherwise that far east of the Mississippi.

It seems that the only site consistent with Cheyenne tradition and which, incidentally, would fit the location of tribes belonging to the Algonquian family, who if not then confederated with these proto-Cheyennes would certainly have been in close proximity to them, is the Mattawin River of east-central Quebec Province. This last named river issues from a Lake Taureau some seven miles broad and ten miles long, then flows due east into the St Maurice which in turn, flows south and enters the St. Lawrence northeast of Montreal Island at a place now called Trois Rivieres. Only a few miles from the mouth of the St. Maurice there is a great fall known as Shawanigan Falls, with a drop of at least one hundred and fifty feet.

The environment of the Lake Taureau district fits exactly with Cheyenne tradition, concerning their culture and habitat during this early period of their evolution, while the country north of the St. Lawrence at this point and for a considerable distance around Trois Rivieres, was for a long time, the recognized territory of the Montagnais Algonquians who were then the close neighbours and confederates of the Wheskerinni, Moiseo and Monsoni Cree. Certainly, for several centuries, Montagnais-speaking groups resided in this area prior to the early sixteen-thirties, when they were finally dispersed to the east by hostile Iroquois-proper tribes.

Indeed, it is only in recent time [1978] that stone implements and other artefacts, indicating a proto-historic occupation of this area by a people that used red ochre extensively and who show *Late Woodland* Algonquian traits in their archaeological inventory, have been discovered in the Mattawin River district, where, we might add, it was previously supposed that no aboriginal settlement had existed in the pre-colonial period.

The Cheyennes declared that during this time they wore little if any clothing which suggests that the climate was then rather mild to say the least. This certainly would not have been the case if they had resided any further north than just above the Lower Great Lakes. From the site of Quebec on the Lower St. Lawrence and as far west as Georgian Bay, the climate between the years circa, AD.10,00 and circa, AD.1350, was surprisingly mild as compared to surrounding areas, including those of the same latitude further west that embrace the Upper Mississippi country. Throughout most of the year the Lake Taureau district came well within this warm-clime belt, whereas, the Upper Mississippi country would not, at that period have permitted a near-naked existence. It is indicative to note that the Neutrals, then residing north of Lake Erie about Niagara Falls and claiming country even further east as far as the extreme Upper part of the St. Lawrence, are recorded in the early *"Jesuit Relations"* as wearing no clothes at all [during summer one assumes], in contrast, we might add, to others of their stock.

During this same period of their "Ancient Time," say the Cheyennes, whilst living near the Lake and nearby Falls, *"...our people first acquired corn."* [5]

We know that to the west and southwest of Lake Taureau there then lived the corn-growing Huron, and it is inconceivable that proto-Cheyennes did not adopt such a cultural asset from their neighbours as a welcome supplement to their usual meat and fish based diet; and particularly so, as the Delaware accounts also mention the introduction of corn among themselves, after entering the "Great spruce pine land" of tradition.

The Cheyennes assertion that they had corn, either obtained in trade or raising it themselves, also confounds the assumption that the `Lake` and `Falls` referred to by Black-Pipe, were in the Mini Ha-Ha Falls or Rainy Lake area of the Upper Mississippi. As we do know that the aboriginal corn-growing belt did not extend much further north than the area of present-day St. Paul [Minnesota] during the period of prehistoric and proto-historic Indian occupation.

As noted above, the climate of the Northeast on the other hand, beginning around AD.1200 [after a short interruption of colder weather between 1259 and 1260 due to a great volcanic eruption in faraway Indonesia], had again become decidedly more settled, with an overall warmer temperature including adequate rainfall conducive to agricultural pursuits. This climatic situation persisted in that part of the Continent well into the fourteenth century. It is evident then, that this welcome change in the environment induced a temporary halt of those Algonquian migrants comprising the Western Men of Delaware tradition, in their returning to the "Old Turtle Land of the North," and the early part of this period is consistent with the Delaware and their cognate bands occupying the south side of the Lower Great Lakes as far west as Wabash River in present-day Indiana. It also coincides with the period recalled in Cheyenne tradition when the latter had corn and wore little if any clothing, whilst more recent archaeological discoveries have since confirmed that the area around Lake Taureau was indeed, a recognized aboriginal corn-growing area during both the prehistoric and proto-historic eras.

It was also during this period, say the Cheyennes, whilst still residing somewhere near the `Great Fall` during their "Ancient Time" of tradition, that they made sugar from the sap of the maple tree and were introduced to vegetables, tobacco, smoking pipes and buffalo. All these things were new to them and the mention here of tobacco and pipes is particularly interesting. It suggests that the Moiseo were one time visitors, if not indeed occupants, of the Lower St. Lawrence River and its surrounding country including the St. Maurice and Mattawin river regions. Any distance further north - which would include the Upper Mississippi district - tobacco was not a viable crop, the tribes of that area relying upon a mixture of willow bark and dried leaves as a substitute.

It is indicative that not far southwest of Lake Taureau, the numerous Petun Huron villages were scattered around the northeastern shore of Nottawasaga Bay on the southern coast of Lake Huron. Now the word `Petun` comes from the Spanish word for tobacco, and these particular Huron were renowned among their neighbours for the superior quality tobacco they raised and traded to surrounding tribes. On the other hand the Mohawk [of Iroquois-proper stock], were noted manufacturers of smoking pipes which they likewise traded to their neighbours. The Mohawk, having since been forced back east into their original homelands by those Delaware groups once led by the chief, Snowbird, were at this time, positioned again on the south side of the St. Lawrence directly across from the mouth of the St. Maurice. Thus, they were only a comparatively short distance from Lake Taureau and the Mattawin River, where we have suggested, the proto-Cheyenne, i.e., Moiseo, once resided.

It has been explained in an earlier chapter, how the first part of the name Moiseo may once have been used interchangeably with that of `flint,` which adds substance to the conjecture that Cheyenne-speaking peoples did at one time, reside near Lake Taureau, in so much as the `Flint` definition of the term `Mois,` could have originated from an early Moiseo residence in close proximity to a particular flint deposit, or because of a possible relationship hostile or otherwise, with the Mohawks, whose own name for themselves translates as "People of the place of flint."

The Cheyenne tradition concerning this episode which relates to their receiving buffalo, corn and tobacco, is steeped in mythology, but its essence nonetheless, remains sound. The Cheyennes say that at this time they moved to the vicinity of a great waterfall. The whole tribe went along including the women, the children, the old folk and their dogs. Here they set up camp and waited for a certain people to visit them. The Cheyennes were filled with apprehension for they were not sure what to expect. Soon, however, they were visited by two similarly dressed young men [twins] in the company of a beautiful yellow-haired woman called *"E'hyoph'sta"* in the account, who, after performing some seemingly magical acts, brought forth the buffalo, whilst in their turn, the two young men gave the people corn, melons, squashes and other food stuffs and, more importantly, smoking pipes and tobacco, enough to accommodate the whole tribe. For a while after this, so the story continues, the people were happy and prospered. There is, it is true, another story in current Cheyenne tradition concerning two young men and the introduction of buffalo and corn among the tribe. But this later version, although similar to the earlier event, applies to the reuniting of the Cheyenne-proper [i.e. Moiseo or TsisTsisTsas] and the Suhtaio after a prolonged period of separation, and is said to have taken place when in the Upper Minnesota country, or alternatively, even further west near the Black Hills of South Dakota, and at a time after the coming among the Cheyennes of their sacred prophet and culture hero, Sweet-Medicine.

On the contrary, the alternative traditional account with which we are presently concerned, states emphatically that the first event occurred beyond the Missouri River, at a site near a Great Lake far northeast of their historic High Plains habitat and *before* the coming of Sweet-Medicine. This particular tradition also records that sometime after this episode, the Cheyennes *...lost the buffalo"* [6] and did not find them again until the people had migrated into a new country west of the Mississippi. This event is now only related in the context of mythology concerning the tribe's supernatural culture-heroes. But as implied above, fabulous myths; generally speaking, are based upon some historical occurrence long since forgotten and free-floating in time. The inference is, of course, that prior to their losing the buffalo, these early Cheyennes must have been familiar with that animal, which would not have been the case if the ancient Moiseo had not resided as far south as the St. Lawrence, and been acquainted with the southern shore country of Lakes Ontario and Erie, where buffalo could then still be found in sizeable number.

Now of the ten bands which later comprised the Cheyenne Nation during the nineteenth century, the Aorta and Omissis [or Omiss-io], were regarded as descendants of the two earliest component groups, that came together in order to interact as one in a political, social and religious manner. Prior to their amalgamation, or rather, confederation, both had been distinct tribes as is apparent by the fact pointed out by John H. Moore, that these two groups spoke different dialects of the Algonquian language. The original Aorta group which included the TsisTsisTsas element among them, was that same group earlier known as Moiseo, whilst the component group was known as Omissis which translates simply as `Eaters.` Only these two groups among all the later

Cheyenne-speaking bands [excluding the adopted Suhtaio], had in their traditions separate creation stories to account for their origins, which indicates further that these two early components were indeed, of different tribal affiliations before their unification.

ALGONQUIAN CHIEFS OF THE NORTHEASTERN WOODLANDS.
[From an engraving by Theodore DeBry, circa 1590.]

In reality, regarding the term Omissis or Omiss-io, if one omits the proper noun prefix `O` and changes `m` for `w,` while transposing the terminal `io` for the archaic `u,` as of old was common usage among eastern Algonquian-speakers, we have the term `*Wissi-u,*` which is but a variant of the Algonkin-proper tribal name for themselves of Whe-ske-u and also, of the Lewis and Clark term Whee-Skee-U as earlier explained [Chapter 3]. This term has the meaning of `elk` or, more precisely, `grass-eater,` and has merely been shortened in the vernacular of modern-day Cheyenne to mean `Eaters.` Thus, as the Omissis origin story mentions their early habitat as being *"the forest country east of the Mississippi,"* it might be supposed that the original Omissis people

AN ALGONQUIAN STOCKADE VILLAGE OF THE NORTHEASTERN WOODLANDS
[From an engraving by Theodore DeBry. Circa, 1590.]

included a part of the Algonkin-proper, i.e., the Wheskerinni tribe of the old colonial documents. This would explain how the Cheyenne language - when referring to those of Omissis ancestry - is considered by some to be closely compatible with the dialects of Fox, Sauk and Kickapoo of the eastern woodlands, as of old, the Omissis would have been associated more with the last-named tribes than with the Cree. Indeed, a more correct Cheyenne-proper term for `Omissis` is `H-mis-sis` [as given by Mooney 1907]. The `H` in this Cheyenne term being substituted in place of the initial `O, which is not Cheyenne but belongs decidedly to the eastern Algonquian dialects as in O-Tawa, O-Monsoni and O-Saki among other examples.

The idea of a separate ancient tribal affiliation for the Omissis, is further enhanced by the positioning of the respective bands in the Cheyenne tribal camp circle, whereas it is always the Aorta [originally known as Moiseo] and the Omissis that have the position on the two sides adjacent to the opening of the camp circle facing east, thus indicating their more ancient origins by being the first two component groups, and of their subsequent importance over the other bands.

One suspects then, as regards the supposed coming together of the two similarly dressed men of Cheyenne tradition, that the Moiseo had moved to a designated area of rendezvous in compliance to a previous agreement, and here they met with members of other tribes, if not to hold some kind of council, then to partake in a grand inter-tribal trading fair. The whole story probably represents the coming together of the Moiseo proto-Cheyenne group and a specific foreign people such as the Omissis, who hereafter, confederated with them. Thus the two component groups of this confederation are represented by the two similarly dressed men, while the fair-haired maiden *"E'hyoph'sta,"* merely represents the female underworld guardian of the game and corn.

In corroboration of this, we know that before the arrival of Europeans during the third decade of the sixteenth century [1534-35], Algonquians north of the St. Lawrence, and those Huron Iroquoians residing along that river's course and around the Lower Great Lakes, were in the habit of holding regular trading fairs at a place now called Tadoussac at the mouth of the Saguenay River near Trois Rivieres on the Lower St. Lawrence. This being near where the Wheskerinni once resided. At a later date, the same area became a favorite rendezvous point for the French and Indian trade that flourished after 1603, having perhaps been inaugurated even earlier by French explorers after Jacques Cartier first ascended that river in 1534, and contacted Huron peoples from their stockade towns of *Hochelga* and *Stadacona* near present day Quebec and Montreal respectively. The site itself at Tadoussac had been the gathering place of several tribes for many generations long prior to the coming of Cartier, whereat Algonquians from the north brought meat, furs, hides and even amulets supposed to have magical qualities, to exchange with the Huron for corn, squash, vegetables and tobacco. Thus, if the Moiseo did not actually raise corn themselves at this time, then without doubt, they were obtaining it from other peoples as participants in this intertribal commerce.It appears that as the Neutral and Petun Huron then lived to the north of Lakes Erie and Ontario, the area referred to in this part of Cheyenne tradition, is not the Shawanigan Falls, but the great cataract of Niagara between the aforesaid lakes, since several Cheyenne myths indicate a knowledge of that district. However, I strongly dispute the assumption that this particular area was ever a permanent location for Cheyenne-speaking peoples, even though the latter would have been acquainted with and occasional visitors to the Niagara Falls region. They would still also have been in contact with Delaware-proper groups which lingered in the country south and southwest of the Falls. But the Moiseo alone would not have been inclined to contest those Niagara Falls hunting grounds with formidable Huron tribes whose country it then was.

The above explanation does suggest that there were by now two groups, comprised of Moiseo and the confederated Omissis, the first named residing in the vicinity of Lake Taureau and the Upper St. Maurice River region; the second residing not far east of the Huron villages around Niagara Falls, and that the story recounted above is actually symbolic of these two original ancestral groups of the later-day Cheyenne Nation coming together at that time.

$$- 0 - 0 - 0 - 0 - 0 - 0 - 0 - 0 - 0 - 0 - 0 - 0 - 0 - 0 -$$

CHAPTER 9.

REAPRAISING THE EVIDENCE.

The previously recounted analysis and conclusions concerning Algonquian movements as recorded in both Delaware and related tribal traditions, might appear to be discredited by a variant account of the Delaware migration story written down in the early years of the nineteenth century. The Moravian missionary John Heckewelder obtained this alternative version from tribal sources which has since been published in part by C. A. Weslager in his recent work on the Delaware [1989]. According to Heckewelder's analytical translation, that part of the account which is relevant to our study at this point, runs as follows,

> "These [the Delaware], say that [at] an early period - many hundreds [of] years ago, they emigrated from a far country into this - That their number then was very great - a great many thousands - That they were on the journey into this country a good many years"....."That at length they reached the Namaessissipu [Mississippi] followed the same down according to its course, until they came within a hundred or more miles from where the Ohio river falls into the same where they made a halt in order to reconnoiter [sic] the country on the east side of the same - That while there they fell in with some of the Menque [Mengwe] Nation, who also had emigrated from a very distant country into this, and of whom they learnt that they had come in more to the north, and were about settling on large lakes [Erie and Ontario?] that were in that direction, where they would have not only both game and fish in abundance, but would be able to secure themselves against a might [sic] people inhabiting the country to the southward said to be great warriors." [1]

In a later passage from the same account, it is mentioned that the Delaware,

"...had first to defeat the powerful Tallegwi before they could occupy the south side of the Lower Great Lakes." [2]

These enemies, as previously noted, had strong fortifications built around their villages, which likely relate to the remains of such structures of a similar nature still to be seen near the headwaters of the Scioto River in central Ohio and further north. These ancient structures are, however, a long way from the mouth of the Ohio, but very close to the Lower Great Lakes in which area the Delaware by their own and Huron admission, were fighting a war of conquest against a foreign people [*Tallegwi*], who then held that same country which extended from west to east along the south shore of Lake Erie. This fact also suggests that the Delaware line of advance from north to south from the James Bay region was via the Ottawa River and then across the St. Lawrence, and not across the Mississippi so much further west.

The non-confederated Huron Iroquoians, among whom the Neutral and Petun [Tobacco] Nation were predominant factions, were then entrenched along the St. Lawrence as far east as Montreal Island and as far west as the north side of Lake Erie in the Lake Simco district. They even extended their habitat north around Georgian Bay, this being a northeastern spur of Lake Huron. The route of Algonquian migration from the north must, therefore, have led them in a south-easterly direction from central Ontario towards the St. Lawrence, and not directly south to the Mississippi, or these migrants would not then have been in such close proximity to, and in such close physical contact with the *Menque* at that time.

Not far from Lake Erie's southern shoreline are the sources of the Scioto and Allegheny rivers which flow into the Ohio near that river's head. The Delaware themselves and most other Algonquians did not apparently differentiate these rivers with separate names, but applied the same name *"Allegwi-Sipu,"* i.e. *"The River of the Allegwi"* to all three. It should be noted that the Heckewelder account does actually state that the Delaware reconnoitered the country east of the Ohio, which statement if we take it to mean the head of that river, would place them in an area not far south of the Lower Great Lake shores. In truth, it appears that the Delaware host crossed the St. Lawrence near the Island of Montreal and reached the southern shores of Lakes Ontario and Erie, ostensibly by the date circa, A.D.1200, as the various Huron and Iroquois-proper tribes seem not to have been in those lake shoreline positions much earlier, but rather, further north and still along the St. Lawrence River itself. The Archaeological record goes some way in substantiating the above conclusions. Having previously deduced that the center of prehistoric-Algonquian population - termed *"Shield Archaic"* by the archaeologist with a starting date of around 100 BC.,- was in the far north between Hudson's Bay on the east and the western shores of Lakes Winnipeg and Winnibigosis on the west in north-central Manitoba, by circa, A.D. 800 or A.D. 900 [then known by the term *"Middle Laurel complex"*], it had extended south and southeast as far as southern Ontario on the one side and the western tip of Lake Superior on the other. This last-named *complex* actually manifested itself in variant form during an even later period further east as far as the northern shore of the St. Lawrence, and is known in the archaeological record as *"Point Peninsular."* Yet another very close manifestation of the same, is also found in areas immediately south of the St. Lawrence, and without doubt, all are of Algonquian origin. However, although the greater part of the original *Shield Archaic* cultural population had, evidently, left its northern area of habitat by circa A.D.1000 during the *"Middle Laurel"* period, small groups must still have remained in situ, because a few original *Shield Archaic* sites continued to be occupied in that region as late as circa, A.D.1400.

There does appear to have been two main routes of initial movement from the north by *Middle Laurel* peoples, beginning between A.D. 800 and 900. One of these movements included those peoples later responsible for *"Point Peninsular"* found in the vicinity of the Upper and middle course of the St. Lawrence, and thus conceivably, involved the Delaware and their associates then including among others, the Montagnais, Monsoni Cree and Moiseo [proto-Cheyenne]. The other predominant route of migration from the north, led due south into southern Ontario and even farther, into both the northern and central parts of Minnesota below the international boundary. The cultural remains of this last group of peoples, then likely including proto-Arapahoe bands and their Suhtaio associates, are recognized in the archaeological record as the *"Mero"* and *"Blackduck* complexes respectively."* Specific traits regarding *"Blackduck"* show that it was very closely associated with that of *Middle Laurel* and must have grown out of it, beginning around A.D.800 and lasting as late as circa, A.D.1650. In its middle phase of between A.D. 1300 and 1400, some *"Blackduck"* peoples are shown to have spread east along the northern edge of Lake Superior as far as that lake's outlet at Sault St. Marie, which owing to the later geographical positioning of the Suhtaio along with one or two Bush and Swampy Cree bands, strongly suggests that in or around this same area close to the aforesaid Sault, the ancestors of these last named groups once resided, representing the eastern branch of *"Blackduck"* peoples.

Having said this, and continuing with the Delaware account as recorded in that people's traditions, we are told that after the separation of the "Western Men" [which included the Moiseo, Fox, Monsoni and a part of the Wheskerinni later known as Omissis], the Delaware-proper and their cognates; the Unami and Munsey and others, continued their travels and from the `Southland` *["Shawanki"]*, they moved southwest, evidently close to the Ohio headwaters and here in this new land recently wrested from the *Tallegwi*, they remained for many years, planting corn, which practice they had obviously picked up from Huron-Iroquoian peoples during an earlier time. Then came a drought of severe proportion and with it a great contagion which together, forced the Delaware to leave their fields and migrate *east*, where *"They found food on a pleasant Plain."* [3]

Here the term *"east"* is again used in its metaphorical sense, indicating a movement to a better or richer land. [4]

The next location given in the Delaware account is the `Yellow River,` which may be the river of that name that forms a branch of the Kanakee in the northwestern part of Indiana, yet if this is so, then there must still have been a large Delaware-speaking group east of that point, for soon after this move, war broke out between the Delaware on the one side and the *"Akowini"* [Snakes], the *"Lowanski"* [Northern enemies] and the *"Tawa-kons"* [Aka Father Snakes] on the other. The *"Akowini"* are surely the same people as mentioned earlier near the beginning of the

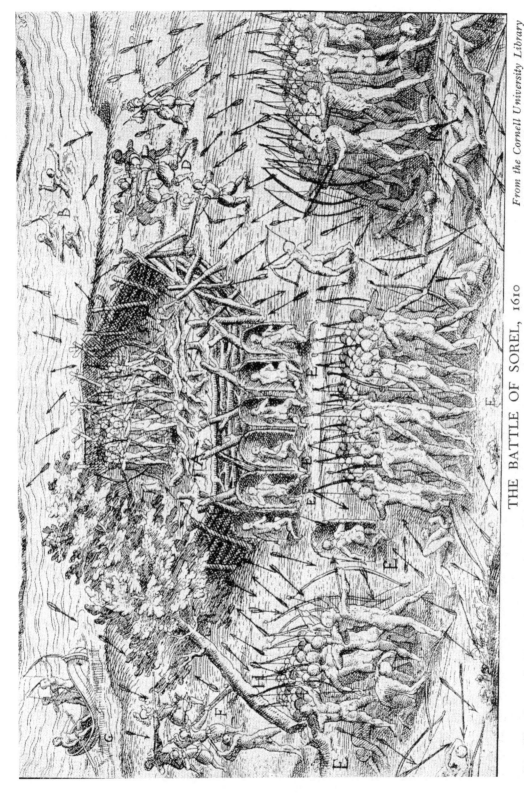

THE BATTLE OF SOREL, 1610

From the Cornell University Library

"A. The Iroquois Fort. B. Iroquois jumping into the river to escape, pursued by Montagnais and Algonquins, jumping in after to kill them. E. All our savage friends. F. The Sieur des Prairies of St. Malo with his companions. G. The Sieur des Prairies' shallop. H. Great trees cut down to demolish the Iroquois' fort."

account who we have averred, are synonymous with the Micmac and their relatives and therefore, Chippewa factions. The *"Lowanski"* likely refer to another Chippewa group or to one of their allies such as the Potawatomi, who during this early period were an integral part of the Chippewa host. The last named, the *"Tawa-kons"* are important, for they without doubt, refer specifically to the Ottawa of the historic Chippewa confederation of tribes. The expression `Tawa` or `Taway,` was the colloquial Delaware term for `trader` and applied singularly to the Ottawa tribe along with the added Algonquian suffix of *"Kon,"* said by some to denote `people,` but more probably meaning `snow` and implying, "Traders from the Snow" [i.e. Snow Land]. Their other designation of *"Father Snakes"* merely denotes the Ottawa position in Algonquian ancestral hierarchy, indicating that anciently, they were more important members of the Chippewa, perhaps the parent group; the `Fathers,` in fact, of the *"Akowini"* [or *"Snake"* people] and of the *"Lowanski."*

Certainly in the related Montagnais-Naskapi dialect, the comparable term *"Notawa"* means "Father," or more literally, "My Generator."

In a later passage from the same Delaware tradition, the *"Tawa-kons"* are again mentioned as Delaware enemies, but then as one tribe in a group of three, the other two being the *"Sinako"* and *"Lowako."* I believe the *"Sinako"* to be synonymous with the *Sinago* band of Ottawa and the *"Lowako"* merely a variant of *"Lowanski"* or `Northern Enemies` noted earlier, who obviously were close allies and confederated with the Ottawa. Perhaps this latter name again included those known as Potawatomi, but more likely, here it refers specifically to the Chippewa-proper themselves, who at the later date of circa, 1650, generally resided northwest of the Delaware about the western shores of the Upper Great Lakes. Thus, we have the historic Ottawa making their entrance into the Delaware account and must, therefore, relate to the period when the Chippewa group of tribes [i.e., the *"Snakes"* of the tradition], were then roaming lands to the east of Lake Huron and the Lower Great Lakes.

The Delaware account further relates that soon after reaching the *"Yellow River"* and their war with the *"Tawa-kons"* and with others noted above, some of their people [the Delaware] became tired of war and, *"...went off to the sun rising."* [5]

En route they again came into contact with the *Tallegwi* upon whom they warred for a second time until, eventually, the Delaware once more evicted them from their lands and drove them even further south.

Now the phrase *"to the Sun rising"* means in this context, towards the east in its proper sense and, as explained previously, the *Tallegwi* appear to have been the ancestors of the present-day Cherokee, rather than a part of the old Mound-Builder peoples as suggested by Heckewelder. The date circa, 1350 when Chippewa groups most likely resided in the Montreal district, must then coincide with this same period in the tradition, after the Delaware and their cognate tribes had moved further west and occupied the *"Land of the Yellow River,"* before moving southeast into the land of the now vanquished *Tallegwi* and here, Cherokee tradition lends its corroboration.

We know that the Cherokee - who themselves were of Iroquoian stock - were living in the southern Ohio valley around the date A.D.1300 and that close to the opening of the fifteenth century, were dispersed by enemies, who drove them toward the south and south east into the states of Tennessee and West Virginia. Suffice to say, this second Delaware - Cherokee *[Tallegwi]* war, probably began in earnest around the date A.D.1375 and saw the eviction of the Cherokee from the Ohio valley around A.D.1400. This then places the Delaware group of tribes in the Yellow River country between these same dates [circa, 1375-1400], so they must have been resident in the *"Buffalo Land"* of tradition west of the Ohio headwaters country before this, that is, sometime during the period A.D.1350 to 1375.

The current situation surrounding the St. Lawrence country during the period of Moiseo [proto-Cheyenne] occupation, can be deduced from the traditional histories of both the Huron and Chippewa, which also corroborate the chronological sequence of events as determined in the previous chapter.

Archaeological research has established that Huron-speaking tribes were again entrenched along both shores of the St. Lawrence near the Island of Montreal, around the date A.D.1400 and that people's traditions state, that when they themselves reached the north bank of the St. Lawrence, presumably after their return from the southern James Bay district, the Seneca, an Iroquois-proper tribe, was then living south of the river, but still claimed the Island of Montreal as a part of their territory. This suggests that the Seneca had previously been driven from the Island and owing to constant hostile pressure, were reluctant to reoccupy their old seat.

The Seneca traditions confirm this by declaring that between circa. 1350 and 1400, their tribe and their relatives the Mohawk, then in situ south of the St. Lawrence, were once again beset by Algonquians also called *"Ottawa"* in tradition, who then claimed lands to the southeast and from which position, they invaded the Seneca country. The result was that the latter and their relatives were eventually driven away, most of the Seneca taking refuge in the hill and swamp area in the west-central part of New York state, whilst the Mohawks - by their own assertion - fled west of Lake Ontario where they sought succor among their kinfolk the Neutrals.

The event of Huron peoples returning to the St. Lawrence from the north, must have occurred after the bulk of Delaware migrants had abandoned the Lake Erie district and moved west into the Ohio headwaters country. For the Huron would not, and indeed, could not, have positioned themselves along the St. Lawrence at that point if Delaware proper groups, being the same people that had evicted them in the first place, remained nearby in force.

Huron tradition goes further by asserting that when they arrived to commence this second period of occupation near Montreal Island, the Ottawa then lived to the west and the Delaware to the east. By this assertion we can see that here the name Ottawa refers to those of the Chippewa group specifically, and so alludes to a much later date than the expulsion of the Seneca and Mohawk Iroquois by Delaware factions. It refers, in fact, to a time after the Chippewa themselves had vacated the Upper St. Lawrence country in their own advance from east to west, probably around the date A.D.1390.

The Chippewa have detailed traditions concerning this period in their history, which wholly corroborate the Delaware traditions at this point.

The Chippewa assert that it was nine generations before 1852 when the statement was first recorded, that the Chippewa, including their later offshoots the Ottawa, Potawatomi and Nipissing, reached their early historic seat on the island of La Point at the head of Chequamegon [now Keweenaw] Bay at the western tip of Lake Superior. Long prior to this, one of their locations had been on a large island in the St. Lawrence, which they themselves declare, was the island upon which the city of Montreal now stands.

The Chippewa historian William Warren who obtained this information, estimated forty years as being the average extent of a generation among the Chippewa, before disease and restricted living conditions brought upon them by the white man drastically reduced the Indian's life expectancy. Working from Warren's estimate, therefore, the date given for the arrival of the Chippewa at La Point, can be reckoned as occurring at about the same time as Christopher Columbus was making his famous discovery in A.D.1492. Allowing for a period of roving between the Island of Montreal and that of La Point, the Chippewa may have been in situ on Montreal Island sometime around the date A.D.1360.

The Chippewa tradition continues by claiming that their people did not reside long on the island, being constantly beset by a new enemy of Iroquoian stock [Huron], whose savage inroads caused a prolonged residence untenable and finally, compelled the Chippewa and their cognates to migrate northwest, skirting the Upper eastern and northern shores of Lake Huron as they did so and from where, after a few short stops via Sault St. Marie, they continued on to the Island of La Point.

On the other hand, traditions from the Huron-Wyandot as related to Rev. Joseph Badger about the year 1845, declared that after a long residence along the north bank of the St. Lawrence near the Island of Montreal, their tribe [Huron] and the Seneca - with whom they had earlier been on good terms, - engaged in a war with each other lasting fully one hundred years before the French came to Quebec, by which time, the Huron had been forced to retire northwest of the St. Lawrence in favor of the lake that today bears their name.

Presumably, the French here referred to are those that came with Samuel Champlain and built a fort on the present day site of Quebec City, rather than Jacques Cartier, who had found the Huron firmly entrenched on and around Montreal Island in 1534.

The Huron tradition also states, that when the French came to Quebec, they began supplying the tribes with guns and iron implements.

Cartier we know, did trade for furs and slaves, but did not include firearms in any significant quantity in his dealings with the Indians. Whereas, Champlain supplied guns to both the Huron and Algonquians in order to assist those tribes in their ongoing war with the Iroquois. Champlain built his fort at Quebec in 1608, so that the Huron - Seneca war, evidently, began at or around the date A.D.1508, and Cartier speaks of this war then going on when he visited the great Huron town of *Hochehelga* in 1535.

By the time Champlain came to Quebec, however, the country along both sides of the St. Lawrence was deserted; *Hochehelga* and its fields abandoned and in an advanced state of decay. The area had in fact become a *"no-man's land"* for war-parties going against one tribe or another, and both Huron and Chippewa traditions concur in asserting that the Chippewa were driven west of the Island of Montreal by the Huron.

It was only after the Huron themselves had been whipped and totally demoralized by Iroquois-proper tribes after 1649 and forced to retreat northwest due to warfare initiated by the Colonial beaver trade in the 1640s, that the Huron and Chippewa finally patched up their quarrel and thereafter, joined as allies against the common foe.

Thus the Chippewa must have vacated the Upper St. Lawrence region at a much earlier period, i.e., when the Huron did not need an Algonquian alliance in order to check their Iroquois-proper foes, and which time was prior to the outbreak of the aforementioned Huron - Seneca war.

As a consequence, whilst some Chippewa-speaking groups retreated west along the north shore of Lake Huron, and those like the Nipissing settled around the lake which today bears their name, others, particularly the Ottawa, broke from the main Chippewa group; retraced their steps down the east coast of Lake Huron, crossed its southern peninsular or rounded it and moved west into what is now the state of Michigan. Thence they moved north along Lake Huron`s western shoreline, during the course of which, they met and confederated with the Sauk and Kickapoo then in the vicinity of Saginaw Bay. *.

This expulsion of Chippewa groups from the St. Lawrence district, probably then, occurred at about the same time as certain Huron tribes were attempting to reclaim their old territory along the north shore of Lake Ontario and the St. Lawrence after their enforced sojourn in the area around the southern tip of James Bay, and thus, the Chippewa were barred from a more direct route of migration west via the Upper St. Lawrence and Lower Great Lakes. Instead, they were obliged to take a northwesterly route which carried them to the northern shore of Lake Huron. This must substantiate the calculated date of Chippewa removal as being circa, A.D.1390 or thereabout, as we know that the Huron were again firmly entrenched in the aforementioned districts of Lake Ontario and along the north shore of the St. Lawrence a decade later. Obviously, this was long after the Delaware-proper groups had left.

What though, had happened to the *"Western Men"?* Those remnants of the Delaware host and their allies who had lingered in the country immediately north of the St. Lawrence during the first *Tallegwi* war, and among which the Moiseo [proto-Cheyenne], Fox, Wheskerinni [Omissis] and Monsoni were then included.

$$- 0 - 0 - 0 - 0 - 0 - 0 - 0 - 0 - 0 - 0 - 0 - 0 - 0 - 0 - 0 - 0 -$$

* Warren's estimate of the average time span covered by a generation appears far too high. However, it is not impossible and was probably offered as corroboration to the Chippewa dating when no actual documentary proof was available, save the verbal tradition. Between twenty-five and at the most, thirty-three years would be more in line with a generation as we know it in most other human social groups.

87

CHAPTER. 10.

"WHEN THE PEOPLE BECAME ORPHANS."

There is no reason to suppose that the Moiseo were ever personally in conflict with Huron-speaking peoples either before or after AD.1300, although as we have seen, Delaware-proper factions were then engaged in chronic warfare with most Iroquoian groups. On the contrary, the Moiseo and their close associates the Monsoni, Montagnais, Wheskerinni and Fox, appear to have derived no small benefit from these same foreign contacts. From Huron-Iroquoian peoples directly or indirectly, these particular Algonquian groups acquired a knowledge of crop growing, tobacco smoking and, most probably, the art of making pottery. [1]

It is indicative that throughout the virulent wars then being waged between Huron and Delaware groups, the Moiseo and their allies, along with certain other Northern Algonquians [the *"Western Men"* of Delaware tradition], were generally regarded as the Huron`s friends. Even later, around AD.1600, both Huron and Montagnais-Naskapi bands along with the Chippewa-speaking Weskerinni north of the St. Lawrence, were joined together as allies in their fierce fighting against the five tribes of the Iroquois-proper confederacy.

Regarding the Moiseo specifically, neither is there evidence that they ever occupied permanent villages the year round at this period in their past, although by raising a small amount of garden produce their lifestyle; in the main, was substantially different to that of their "Ancient Time," which had been that of the wandering hunter / gatherer, moving from one foraging ground to another as dictated by the seasons. While it is true that a certain group of the *Western Men* [i.e. Muskegon Cree] did attempt to return to the old " Turtle Land of the North," as asserted in Delaware tradition, after they, as members of the migrating Delaware host had first reached the *"Great Spruce Land,"* their Moiseo, Monsoni, Fox, Montagnais and Wheskerinni confederates appear to have remained in the south, preferring the region close to the north shore of the St. Lawrence. But the Wheskerinni and Montagnais and, in all probability, their Moiseo confederates, were soon to suffer disaster at the hands of invading Chippewa-proper groups infiltrating the middle St. Lawrence region.

We have seen how the Trois Riviere, Mattawin and St. Maurice River country during the period in question, was conducive to a semi-agrarian economy, which would have helped in no small way in keeping these remaining Algonquian groups in and around those districts. Their villages, though, would have been no more than semi-permanent, as indeed, were those of other Algonquian tribes residing in these same areas at a slightly later date, and which was still the Cheyenne habit during a later century when resident in northern Minnesota. Certainly among the Huron it was necessary to rotate their crop-growing, and because of a diminishing game supply caused through over-hunting, to abandon their villages after certain periods and relocate them in order to allow the soil to rejuvenate and the game in the surrounding district to repopulate.

Modern studies estimate an occupation period for the average permanent village community among proto-historic peoples along the St. Lawrence and in adjacent areas as around twelve years owing to the need for field rotation, although during the early sixteen-hundreds, Samuel Champlain said of the Huron and others from personnel observation, that some villages remained occupied as long as thirty years. However, in the case of these earlier pre-Champlain Algonquian groups, among whom were the Moiseo proto-Cheyennes, horticulture was practiced only on a small scale, the people still relying moreover, upon the products of the chase. Their villages therefore, being semi-permanent habitations and occupied for short periods during times of planting and harvesting, or when important events such as the election of chiefs and religious ceremonies took place, probably sufficed for a much smaller number of years before they fell into total disrepair and were abandoned completely.

It is also unlikely that the Moiseo, Monsoni, Fox and Montagnais comprised one body at the time of their settlement in southern Quebec. Rather, they had previously separated into their respective entities sometime during the course of their migration southeast from the "Old Turtle Land of the North." These separations were not necessarily due to internal rift or undertaken by large cohesive bodies, but were occasioned by the preference of particular family groups to accommodate more fully their hunting needs, entailing divorce from the parent tribe. Even so, it is evident that these separatist groups, certainly whilst located in that region abutting the north shore of the St. Lawrence, remained in practical proximity to one another and were in some kind of loose alliance with neighbouring Wheskerinni and Huron peoples. They nonetheless constituted separate villages and hunted specific designated areas, which was the condition of most if not all semi-nomadic groups that depended predominately on fish and game for their subsistence. Such would be comparable to the system of family hunting territories, still extant today among the Indians of northern and eastern Canada.

Thus, we can be sure that several groups closely akin to the breakaway Muskegon Cree, did not favor returning to the cold harsh lands in the north; from where incidentally, they had not too many generations before, so happily left.

This is additionally acceptable when we realize that the country north of the St. Lawrence, both east and west of Montreal Island between the dates AD.1300 -1350, was then virtually unoccupied and that an adequate supply of food and fuel was readily available.

We know that the Montagnais and Weskerinni or *"Petite Nation,"* as they were often called, were entrenched along the north side of the St. Lawrence in the Lower St. Maurice River country and around Trois Riviere including the present day site of Quebec, before Champlain reached that point on the same river in 1608. These two groups had been very closely aligned to the Moiseo and Monsoni during their earlier period of residence. At the later date of circa, 1620, a combined band of Montagnais and Weskerinni were yet together, having established themselves in adjacent semi-permanent villages still near the mouth of the St. Maurice.

The earliest colonial narratives relating to this area and to the tribes thereof, suggest a peaceful co-existence between these particular Algonquian bands and neighbouring Huron-speaking peoples of the St. Lawrence, along with one or two Iroquois-proper tribes across that river to the south. This harmonious situation is said in the traditional accounts, to pre-date the coming of Jacques Cartier and other Europeans early in the sixteenth century.

We learn from several tribal traditions, that with no serious enemies to contend with, the above mentioned peoples north of the St. Lawrence grew in strength, so that further divisions took place within the bands, as a particular faction or family group sought new hunting grounds for its expanding population. Among the Montagnais, divisions had undoubtedly already taken place, the splinter groups becoming known in historic times as Moiseo, Monsoni and Fox. Perhaps they had separated from the parent body at the same time as the Muskegon Cree decided to return to the "Old Turtle Land of the North." Either way, each of these separatist groups at a much later time, became recognized as independent tribes in their own right, albeit speaking varied dialects of Montagnais Cree, but with their own religious practices and style of dress peculiar to themselves.

As a result, all those bands that remained north of the St. Lawrence including the Moiseo, Fox and Monsoni, who evidently, still retained a cursory amount of contact with the Muskegon and Montagnais, became all but isolated from their Delaware-proper cousins. At times, one or another of the latter's cognate tribes may have been met accidentally or by design, in order to keep up a degree of amicability. Each group, nevertheless, was left to evolve along its own path and generate its own peculiarities, not least of which became evident in language. Thus at a much later date, we hear of all the above mentioned tribes as separate entities, in every apparent trait to the layman's eye.

It might be taken then, that the inhabitants of the above mentioned areas during the period AD. 1300, did exercise a degree of tolerance and were at peace with their neighbours; trading with each other at the great intertribal fairs at Tadoussac, and exchanging aspects of individual craftwork and culture. This may be another of those times which are indicated in Cheyenne tradition, whereby it is asserted that of old, there were no wars and the people were happy and prospered.

How long this situation continued we cannot say. Certainly it was no longer than the appearance of Chippewa-proper peoples from the east, whose intrusion into the Lower St. Lawrence district about the date AD.1350, upset the stability of the country and inaugurated a prolonged period of bloody internecine strife. It would appear that at the time of this Chippewa encroachment, there began a general war between the Chippewa factions on one side and most other Algonquians on the other.

The event of this foreign hostile advance from the east along both sides of the St. Lawrence, split the resident Algonquians like a wedge; the Montagnais and Naskapi on the east; the Fox, Monsoni and Moiseo along with the Sauk and cognate Kickapoo on the west, whilst the several bands of Wheskerinni [*Algonkin-proper*], attempted to hold on to lands embracing Trois Riviere and the south side of the St. Lawrence near the mouth of the Beccancouer River.

While it is evident that at a later date, both the Sauk and Kickapoo, at least, were treated with more tolerance by the Chippewa - for then all three were joined in a league as allies, - during the particular time whilst inhabiting the area around the Island of Montreal, most resident tribes suffered harassment from Chippewa factions, to the extent that finally, the Montagnais and Naskapi along with the main Wheskerinni group, retired further east as far as the site of Quebec and beyond, while the Moiseo, Fox, Monsoni and a part of the Wheskerinni, i. e. Omissis, migrated north and northwest in an endeavor to extricate themselves from their foes. But as will be seen, although the last mentioned group of tribes traced similar routes of retreat, they did so as separate bodies.

An episode in the Chippewa migration legend typifies the aggressive situation along the St. Lawrence north shore country during this period, and may well explain the reason for the Moiseo's upheaval at this time.

In brief, the Chippewa tradition recalls that whilst en route through the St. Lawrence country from east to west, they came into hostile contact with a people called in the account, *"Mundua,"* the exact meaning of which has now been lost. Apparently, the *Mundua* lived in one great town on the edge of a large lake and often attacked the invading Chippewa, who considered them a risk to further expansion. As a result, the Chippewa collected together a formidable force and after a long march, attacked the enemy town on three sides where it was not bounded by the lake shore. It is said that the *Mundua* men-folk were absent on the hunt when first the Chippewa attacked, so that on the first day of battle, only boys came out from the town to fight. [Although this is probably meant as a slur on the *Mundua's* fighting ability]. On the second day the *Mundua* men-folk did join the fray, having evidently crossed the adjoining lake so as to enter the village at a point where it was not besieged by the enemy. By nightfall, however, the Chippewa host had driven the enemy back and was in possession of half the town.

The third day saw the *Mundua* warriors in full force, augmented by old men and young boys, all arrayed to face their attacker's onslaughts and now much of the fighting was hand to hand. After a hot contest the Chippewa again proved the stronger and finally, the defenders were dispersed in great confusion.

It is said that many of the *Mundua* women and children threw themselves into the adjacent lake to avoid capture and in such a way perished. The survivors led by an old medicine man, fled into the surrounding forest and there hid a number of women and children under the thick ferns and fallen boughs and even in the forest floor, leaving each a small hole in the earth through which to breathe. The remaining *Mundua* warriors then turned back and engaged the enemy in yet another fierce battle, but once more the Chippewa force was too strong. After a short melee the *Mundua* turned and fled, in the opposite direction from where they had concealed their kinfolk, in an attempt to draw the pursuing enemy away from their hidden families.

Very few *Mundua* warriors escaped, yet of those who did, they later returned to the battle ground area and recovered their surviving wives and children hidden safe in the forest floor. The tradition adds that sometime during the following year, the remnants of the once powerful *Mundua* were again attacked by the Chippewa, who this time took many captives whom they absorbed into the Chippewa tribe.

The above event is said in tradition to have taken place during the Chippewa residence in the east, at an early stage of their western migration, and so must have occurred somewhere between the present day site of Quebec and the Island of Montreal.

The tradition continues by relating that the *Mundua* survivors adopted into the Chippewa tribe, eventually became a clan in their own right, taking the Martin as their totem. Not only did they become one of the leading Chippewa factions, but many centuries later, were famous for the several renowned chiefs and warriors which that clan produced.

An important fact concerning Chippewa clans is that those known as Martin, Reindeer and Moose, traditionally all stem from a common nucleus, termed *"Mous-oneeg"* in the latter`s dialect and meaning `Moose.` Chippewa tradition has it that whilst still inhabiting the eastern country towards the rising sun, the family of "Moosoneeg" lived in one large village and was powerful and warlike. A war erupted between these people and their relatives the *"Martin"* clan, during the course of which, the latter were generally beaten in the contest. As a result the Martin clan gained assistance from some other Chippewa groups and by a treacherous act, exterminated most of the Moosoneeg men-folk by burning them alive and adopted the women and children among their own, so that today, these two clans consider themselves related.

As regards the Reindeer [caribou?] people mentioned above, they also are an offshoot from the Moosoneeg, and so belong to the same ancestral family group.

From this it is clearly seen that the Moosoneeg and Martin clans were once separate groups, albeit at a later date than the *Mundua* massacre, and one cannot help but notice, the obvious relationship the former must have had with the Monsoni Cree, or indeed, with one or another of the Monsoni`s close relations, including the Moiseo proto-Cheyennes.

It would not be improbable that the original *Mundua* captives had soon `settled down` as it were, among their foster tribe, whilst the Monsoni-proper and their close relatives, continued feuding with the invading Chippewa and soon began raiding their own *Mundua* kinfolk who under the clan names of *Martin* and *Reindeer* were now aligned with the Chippewa enemies of the Monsoni. This is likely if the *Mundua* had been further removed from the Monsoni than just a family clan and might suggest, that they were in effect at the time of the war, a separatist faction that for some time previous to their dire defeat and dispersal, had dissented from co-habiting with their Monsoni relatives on a regular basis.

Such a situation would fit well with the Moiseo and, of course, with any other Algonquian group claiming direct ancestry from the Monsoni. But who at the time of this Chippewa intrusion, was already a separate tribe.

Now when the aged Cheyenne informant Black-Pipe told W. P. Clark in 1879, that his tribe's ancient seat of occupation was near or on the edge of a large lake, which we have averred, refers to Lake Taureau or in its vicinity at the head of the Mattawin and St. Maurice rivers, Black-Pipe further stated that whilst occupying this seat, a disaster of severe proportion visited the tribe and almost exterminated them, reducing their number to three or four lodges. In yet another Cheyenne account obtained by George Dorsey from tribal informants, details of a similar calamity that had occurred during the tribe's "Ancient Time" of tradition are also recalled.

**CHEYENNE SACRED "OKH`TSIN" OR "WHEEL-LANCE" AS CARRIED BY THE MOISEO
SHAMAN "WHEN THE PEOPLE BECAME ORPHANS."**
[Photo from Peter Powell`s "Sweet Medicine," Vol. 2. P. 451. Univ; of Okla Press, 1969.]

In this latter version, even though mythological in much of its content, the Cheyennes are said to have then lived across a great body of water and for two or three years, were overpowered by a fierce enemy people who greatly outnumbered them. The Cheyennes were about to become slaves when a medicine man with the aid of a magical hoop, saved the remnants of the tribe from complete annihilation and led them toward the west and safety. The period of this disaster is known among the Cheyenne as, *"When the People became Orphans"* and is placed in their traditional chronology as a supplement to the "Ancient Time."

Added to this, the ethnologist James Mooney, notwithstanding his assertion that in his opinion, the Cheyennes originated somewhere about the headwaters of the Mississippi, did refer briefly to another tradition which recalled their being defeated by a stronger, more aggressive tribe and further stated that this event apparently, took place in a more easterly location than the Upper Mississippi. Also, the Cheyennes themselves refer to having *"...lost the corn and the buffalo"* at about this time. However, whilst resident along the Minnesota River [a western branch of the Mississippi below its Upper forks], the Cheyenne and Suhtaio were fully acquainted with buffalo and at the same time practiced a good deal of agriculture, raising corn, squash and other vegetables and continued to do so albeit to a less degree when along the Little Missouri and Platte rivers, until they finally abandoned the Black Hills district of South Dakota about the date 1851.

In the version obtained by Dorsey, concerning the magical hoop-like object carried by the Cheyenne medicine man who led the people to safety, one is reminded of a sacred *"Okh`tsin"* or "Wheel-Lance" owned by certain Cheyenne shamans and which, supposedly, had power to protect the people from harm. This item which was of ancient origin [and compatiable symbolically in many ways with the ancient Northern European encircled *Pentagon* motif], consisted of a slender willow stick about five feet long with a small carved human face at one end [representing the owner's chosen spirit helper] and a blue painted stone point at the other. About three-quarters distance along its length near the carved end, was attached a braided willow hoop, supporting eleven pendent eagle or magpie feathers. The hoop itself was believed to have power to ensnare the owner's specific spirit helper and when held upright, - the be-feathered meshed hoop and carved image facing toward the enemy - then the latter were blinded by the power of the ensnared Spirit, while at the same time, all those behind were rendered invisible, thus protecting them from harm.

The owner of such a lance was thought to possess certain magical abilities, such as prophecy and discovering the whereabouts of objects lost or stolen. He could also determine the fortunes of missing persons, such as a war-party which had not returned within a given time and whether its members were alive or dead. These powers were related to those of the tribe's Sacred Arrow talismans of a later date and also, to the "Spirit Lodge" common to all Northern Algonquians along with eastern Siberian and Mongol peoples of the Russian Steppes. The "Wheel-Lance" itself, appears to have been unique to the TsisTsisTsas or Cheyenne-proper during their people's late historic period, although it had its counterpart in the shamanistic rites of the northern Siberian nomads and, perhaps, its origin can be traced back to a more ancient Siberian cult.

It is indicative that when the Cheyennes traveled as a tribal body from one hunting ground to another, and especially so during the course of migratory movements into a new country of habitat, a renowned medicine man [shaman], walked in front of the people carrying a "Wheel-Lance" held horizontally in his right hand, the carved head and hoop pointing the way forward. In his left hand he held a staff symbolizing his holy office and in so doing, all those who followed including the men, women and children and their dogs, would be protected from both human and animal predator alike. This reminds one of the events pertaining to the *Mundua* massacre cited above, and is what the Chippewa account is actually referring to by its mention of the *Mundua* medicine man who had led the survivors into the forest and hid them from view in the undergrowth, thereby, symbolizing their being rendered invisible and which, of course, would be consistent with Dorsey's version of the people being led away to safety, evidently into another land.

On the other hand, the statement from Black-Pipe [Clark's informant] that only three or four lodges survived the disaster spoken of in Cheyenne tradition, should not be taken as referring to the average population of a buffalo-hide tepee when on the Western Plains, which generally contained from five to eight persons, but to the larger willow-framed bark-covered oval structures common among the Fox, Sauk and other East Woodland tribes, and still in use as late as the end of the nineteenth century wherein several families comprising any number between twenty to thirty persons were housed. Cheyenne tradition itself declares, that such was a style of shelter at a late period during their people's "Ancient Time."

This being so, although Cheyenne tradition asserts that during that period, their people did live in semi-permanent or temporary villages sometimes referred to as towns, it is unlikely that their construction was in anyway comparable to the formidable impregnated timber 'forts' as built by the Huron and other Iroquoian-speaking peoples. I suggest that these early Cheyenne towns of tradition were not primarily defensive structures at all, being merely a collection of rude bark and willow shelters covered with grass mats or birch bark, as was typical of Algonquians north of the St. Lawrence when first contacted by Europeans early in the seventeenth century.

Archaeological excavations of Huron-Iroquoian towns between circa. AD.1350 and 1400, show the profuse introduction of timber stockades and other defensive features, indicating an increase in warfare during that period and this, incidentally, coincides with the time of hostile Chippewa infiltration along the St. Lawrence River. Those Algonquian groups that included the Moiseo, Wheskerinni and a part of the Monsoni, all of whom were enemies of the Chippewa, were then in close contact with Huron-speaking bands, and in all probability, they would have adopted similar defences as a necessary precaution against attack if, that is, they had resided in villages of any permanency longer than a season.

Indeed, the Chippewa account as recorded by William Warren, makes no mention of the *Mundua* town sporting a stockade or protective breastwork, which if the town was of a permanent nature, it would undoubtedly have had.

So it does appear that the *Mundua* site was, in reality, a temporary village incorporating a large cluster of predominately willow and bark shelters, sufficing for a short sojourn and during which time religious ceremonies may have been performed, the several bands and clans being congregated as a united body only for the duration of the rites. It might alternatively be conjectured that the people had come together in order to hold some kind of trading fair between the various allied Algonquian and Huron groups, intending to remain in situ only as long as an adequate supply of game could be had in order to support such a gathering. At the close of festivities the village would have been abandoned; its once mixed population then scattering throughout their respective hunting grounds so as to prepare food stocks to sustain them through the impending winter.

Such was the habitual practice among all northeastern Algonquian tribes until the Reservation period kicked in - so to speak - and was typical at a later date among Great Plains equestrian groups west of the Missouri River.

Indicatively the name *"Mundua"* in the Chippewa dialect has something to do with `corn;` although its exact meaning remains obscure. Quite probably it denotes that the enemy to whom the term was applied, were corn-growers or traders in corn, both occupations held in contempt by the semi-nomadic, meat-eating Chippewa hunters of that time.

We have noted previously how the Delaware tribes succumbed to corn planting after reaching the "Great Spruce Land" of their tradition, [i.e. south of the St. Lawrence], having no doubt picked up the practice from neighbouring Huron tribes. The Chippewa, however, knew the Delaware too well and by a different name, so as not to associate them with the *Mundua* and a similar reasoning is true also regarding the Huron and Iroquois-proper tribes, these latter peoples likewise, being designated with distinctive appellations in Chippewa tradition. The *Mundua*, therefore, were certainly Algonquians, but were considered by the Chippewa as being separate from the Delaware, and so must have been those people or peoples residing on the north side of the St. Lawrence about Trois Rivieres and adjacent to the course of the St. Maurice River.

From our previous analysis and deductions, coupled with inferences from Cheyenne tradition itself, we know that these early Cheyenne-speaking groups [i.e. Moiseo and their confederates including the Wheskerinni], were either growing or using corn at this time and most likely, residing in an area close to if not indeed a part of that district then being invaded by the Chippewa. The implication is, that both the Moiseo and their kindred were undoubtedly effected by the fortunes of the *Mundua*, either because of a very close blood kinship, or simply as allies against a common foe. Certainly, the arrival of these hostile Chippewa groups along the St. Lawrence close to the above mentioned points, upset the stability of the country and inaugurated a period of warfare with all the resident tribes. First on a small scale perhaps, becoming more intense until reaching a climax between circa, AD.1350 and AD.1360.

Traditions from the Micmac mention this early period of warfare with the St. Lawrence Algonquians and also with the Huron, and the Micmac we know, during the proto-historic era were closely confederated with, if not then a kindred part of the Chippewa host.

Having thus deduced that the Mundua were Algonquians, but of a faction separate to both the Delaware and Chippewa, the Cheyennes appear to be the only group among tribes such as the Fox, Sauk, Kickapoo and Montagnais - each of whom were then living in close proximity to one another during this period of Chippewa invasion - who have preserved in their traditions similar details of such a defeat as attended the *Mundua*. Certainly, the supposed destruction of the Moiseo at this time, would explain the Cheyenne's comparatively small population as compared to those of the Arapahoe and Blackfoot in a later century, and especially so when we remember that these two last named tribes also stemmed originally from the Cree and, in all likelihood, were once compatible in population during their ancient time to their Cheyenne-speaking cousins.

It has been mentioned above that several bands or tribes of northern Algonquians were likely involved in this war, including the Algonkin-proper who are designated the *"Petite Nacion"* in early French documents of the seventeenth century. We have also previously noted that their personal name as rendered by the French, and who as usual added what they themselves thought was a suitable appendage, is recorded as *"Whe-Ske-Rinni."*

They once inhabited the same locale within the confines of the St. Maurice River and must, therefore, have once been very close confederates of the early Moiseo. They may then have been a part of the *Mundua* element of the Chippewa account and here a Wheskerinni tradition narrated to the Jesuit Priest Charlevoix around the date 1744, seems to allude to this assumption.

The Charlevoix account tells how the power of the Wheskerinni had once been destroyed and their fighting force decimated, during a great battle on the Beccancouer River on the south side of the St. Lawrence opposite Trois Rivieres, not far, in fact, from the intertribal trading fair site at Tadoussac. Charlevoix was further told that this event took place many years before white men came up the St. Lawrence [circa, 1534 ?] and was, they explained, why they had received their name of the *"Petite Nacion"* [*"Little Nation"*], they being the small remnant of a once much larger group. Whether this episode in Weskerinni tradition refers specifically to the massacre of the *Mundua* or to a separate occurrence, cannot be definitely determined, although it is highly probable that both events belong in chronology to this same period of Chippewa aggression. Consequently, the two episodes are in some way likely connected.

It might reasonably be supposed that the Wheskerinni or *"Petite Nacion"* and their allies - which then included all the above mentioned *"Western Men"* tribes or bands of the Delaware account - were in a league against the common enemy. That is, during the time of the Chippewa invasion from the east into the Lower St. Lawrence country. They, the Wheskerinni, may even have been a component part of our Moiseo proto-Cheyenne subjects, which would add credence to our earlier coupling of a Wheskerinni faction later known by the name *Omissis* as being confederated with the Moiseo when residing in adjacent territory during the same period in time. Although whether the main Wheskerinni group was then more closely associated with the Fox and Kickapoo than with the Moiseo, is perhaps impossible to say.

The event, however, of the Chippewa crowding up the St. Lawrence along both the south and north sides of that river, was in opposition not only to the *Mundua* [i.e. Moiseo / Wheskerinni as we have averred], but was in direct opposition to all resident Algonquians of that district. This fact is corroborated by the Chippewa statement that it took the combined strength of all their people, along with a number of auxiliaries in order to destroy the power of the *Mundua*, whilst the Cheyenne tradition, previously referred to, recalls the feud as being of a two or three year duration. The Moiseo could not have been in so large a number themselves at this period to have opposed the Chippewa force alone, neither, it may be said, could any of their Algonquian neighbours without bringing their forces together in some kind of loose confederation.

At this stage in their history, so Cheyenne tradition asserts, their people were not particularly warlike and in all likelihood, were often beaten in the contest. Thus, it must be construed that they and their allies were eventually driven from the country. Conversely, though, Cheyenne tradition itself also states that their people`s continued migration at this point in their history was a voluntary move made on their own volition. But this does not explain their motive for relocating in a much harsher and less provident environment compared to that which they had previously occupied.

That most other resident Algonquian groups of the St. Lawrence country, ostensibly in a league with the Moiseo and Wheskerinni during the same period, did not at a later date, apparently, mention such a catastrophic defeat upon their people, should not be surprising when we learn that, generally speaking, Indians of the olden-days were often reluctant to recall in detail unfavorable episodes of their people's past, such as ignominious defeats and expulsions by an enemy tribe unless pressed to do so, or if deemed necessary to explain or excuse a subsequent response on their part. It sometimes happens, therefore, that what is given in tribal tradition as a voluntary movement from one permanent area of habitat to another, in reality, can refer to their having been evicted, or at the least, obliged to move because of pressure exerted upon them by a more powerful force. This is likely the case concerning these Algonquian peoples such as the Moiseo proto-Cheyennes, along with the Monsoni and Fox and a part of the Wheskerinni [i.e. *Omissis*], whose real reason for vacating the St. Lawrence country was, most probably, a desire to extricate themselves from hostile aggression if not complete annihilation at the hands of the Chippewa host.

Where severe defeats or expulsions are recalled in various tribal traditions, the Indians often tell of some uncontrollable circumstance that initiated the derogatory event in the first place. A case in point is the Hidatsa tradition of having been forced to migrate to the Missouri River from a land in the Northeast due to the event of a "Great Flood," when the real reason for their being evicted was through hostile pressure directed against them by the Yankton Sioux. In another case, a massacre by the Kiowa of forty-two Cheyenne Bowstring warriors in 1837, was, according to the Cheyenne account, due to the slaughtered party having earlier committed an act of dire sacrilege upon the tribes` Sacred Arrow talismans and their keeper, which thereby, led directly to the party`s demise. The Kiowa have similar excuses and few indeed, were times when a tribe on the receiving end of a catastrophe would admit that its own fighting ability had been inferior.

To the Indian, all events were controlled by the spirit forces around them; good or bad depending upon the outcome. Thus, there could be no recriminations on their personal warrior prowess, but rather, they were at the mercy of much more powerful elements, made manifest in either spirit or monster form against which the people themselves had no chance of defeating. The people may, however, commiserate themselves by incorporating some exemplary attribute such as a particular heroic deed on their own part, which would then allow them to think themselves on a par with; if not in some way better than those by whom they had been vanquished or had forced them from their homes.

So we see in the Cheyenne account of their people's much earlier deliverance from a catastrophic defeat - as recorded in the Dorsey version - the escape of the Cheyenne survivors is facilitated only through the exceptional powers of an old-time medicine man or shaman, who leads the remnants of the people to safety aided by his sacred *"Okh`tsin"* lance and personal Spirit-helper. In such a way the Cheyenne shaman is thought of as being spiritually superior to his counterpart among the enemy, whose own powers were not, in effect, strong enough to match those protecting the Cheyennes, and so the enemy in this respect, is seen as inferior as they could not completely destroy the people.

Likewise, in the mythological account of *"E`hyoph`sta"* the Yellow-Haired Maiden who supposedly, first brought the Cheyennes buffalo and corn, it is further stated that owing to the Cheyenne's breaking of a certain taboo concerning a buffalo calf, she took the buffalo away from the people as a punishment. This analogy merely represents the migration of the proto-Cheyenne-speaking people or peoples back into the North Country where buffalo could not be found and conveniently, may well disguise what the Cheyennes at a later date considered was an embarrassing moment in their history, when they themselves had been defeated and actually driven from their idyllic seats by another more aggressive tribe. Suffice to say, the Moiseo`s traditional voluntary migration towards the northwest at this time between circa, 1350 and 1360, seems, in truth, to have been an expulsion due to hostile pressure, and is compatible with the destruction of the *Mundua* around the same date by invading Chippewa groups.

The above circumstance would fit well with the Cheyenne tradition earlier cited, wherein it is stated that the tribe's *"Ancient Ones"* were, at length, forced to return to the *"Cold Northland"* from whence they came, after having lived for some prolonged period in a *"Beautiful Land"* [i.e. *"The Great Spruce Land"* of Delaware tradition?] in the south.

As to dating this episode, the *Mundua* massacre must have taken place either during or just prior to the Chippewa stay on Montreal Island, which event working from Warren's estimates, apparently occurred during the middle of the fourteenth century or, perhaps, a little later around AD.1360. The Chippewa admit that they themselves did not reside long either on or around the Island of Montreal, for the re-occupation by Huron peoples in the same area was the prime factor in expelling the Chippewa from their seats, and we know from Huron-Wyandot traditions coupled with certain archaeological evidence, that several Huron groups arrived for the second time on or near Montreal Island about the date A.D.1400, or a few years earlier around AD.1390.

The attack on the *Mundua* town, no doubt, was then only one such episode in a prolonged struggle for supremacy, yet was the crucial factor in finally dispelling resident groups from the area. Indeed, whether the Moiseo were a part of the *Mundua* or not, it should be accepted that they - along with other Algonquian bands - vacated the St. Lawrence country during the same period as occurred this Chippewa intrusion.

CHAPTER. 11.

RETREAT FROM THE ST. LAWRENCE COUNTRY.

Today the Cheyennes repeat a legend, that may have originated from a distorted memory concerning their eviction from the St. Lawrence region, and of the subsequent separation of their people during the "Ancient Time" of tradition. Referring to this earlier time, it is stated,

> "The people originally moved away from the cold North Country where there was snow and ice the year round. After wandering for some time, they made a new home in the east, where the sun then warmed the land." [1]

The story goes on to relate how some time later, the people were crossing on the ice over a long stretch of water. The whole tribe was involved, including every man, woman and child with all their belongings and domestic equipment. A large group of people had already crossed and were positioned on the far bank waiting for the rest of the tribe to join them. Some others were actually on the ice in the process of crossing, while still others were bringing up the rear but had not yet started over. Among those in the process of crossing was a young girl. She spied what looked like an animal's horn protruding from the ice and attempted to pry it loose. Others soon joined her in her task, all curious to see what it was and as they pulled and tugged at the horn, a loud rumbling noise was heard and suddenly, a huge snake-like water monster rose up from the depths, throwing up great blocks of ice as it did so. There was much panic and confusion among the people and those who were on the ice were plunged into the freezing waters, regardless of age or sex and all were drowned. That group which had already reached the far bank and those still on the opposite bank waiting to cross, were seized with great fear. As a result, both groups fled the scene; the first going in one direction, the second in another, and thus the tribe became irretrievably separated one part from the other. For those who had not crossed over, were never seen again.

Such a story would afford a convenient explanation to describe how a part of any particular tribe became separated from its parent stock. It may, in truth, apply to an event that had in fact taken place, but which many years later remained only as a fragmentary memory of an episode free-floating in time. Certainly, the fur trader Alexander Henry`s journal for April 1st 1801, mentions the regular occurrence of buffalo becoming trapped in the ice and at times, breaking free in a like manner as had the water monster of Cheyenne tradition.

As regards the Cheyennes, however, the story is likely to have some firm historical basis. In so much that it may well be a disguised recollection of the dispersal of the Moiseo and Monsoni from the St. Lawrence country and of their enforced separation from the bulk of their Wheskerinni and Montagnais confederates. In the aftermath of which, the Moiseo and that Wheskerinni faction - later known as Omissis when a division of the later-date Cheyenne Nation - migrated in a northwest direction, while the main Wheskerinni and Montagnais groups migrated towards the northeast.

It is true that the Cheyennes have another story very similar to the above, which also concerns a separation within the tribe, at a time when the ice broke up while the people were in the act of crossing a frozen river. But in this second tale, there is no mention of a protruding horn or fabulous water-monster and the actual river is specified as the Missouri. The people involved are even designated as to their tribal band affiliations and in this latter tale, it is also said that those who did not cross over were never seen again, although they are named as a band of the Suhtaio and are said to have gone north and joined the Cree. The period when this particular event occurred, can even be calculated with a fair degree of certainty as sometime during the latter half of the eighteenth century. This being said, it should not be doubted that the story does refer to a proper historical event, but one not to be confused with the earlier protruding horn version recounted above, and which the Cheyennes themselves definitely place as occurring during the "Ancient Time" of their traditions.

It is interesting to note that the Arapahoe, likewise, have a story telling of a division between their own people, which compares very closely to the earlier Cheyenne tale. This Arapahoe story also makes mention of a frozen river; a protruding horn and the water-monster which caused the ice to break up. But here again the event has some strong historical significance, in that it actually refers to the Arapahoe crossing of the Missouri River to its south bank, in the event of which, they became separated from their Atsina kinfolk who remained on that river's north side.

It would seem, therefore, that as the Arapahoe supposedly crossed the Missouri some time before the Cheyenne, the latter's version may have come originally from the Arapahoe and was merely adopted at a later date by Cheyennes as a part of their own traditional lore. This is not to say that a split within the Cheyenne tribe had not occurred during the "Ancient time" of their traditions, but rather, because the Cheyennes could recall that such an event had indeed once taken place, albeit the exact details long since forgotten, the Cheyennes later incorporated the Arapahoe tale into their own repertoire in order to supply some supernatural reason for, what the people supposed, had been a derogatory event in their history, when a number of generations earlier, they had been dispersed from the St. Lawrence country by a stronger enemy force.

Returning to the old-time Indian trait of conveniently glossing over past episodes deemed derogatory to themselves, or which might minimize their perceived personal prowess and standing as a warrior people, the accepted explanation of becoming divided and dispersed, is here rendered as that of a powerful god-like creature or divine force made manifest as some kind of fabulous underwater monster [against whom the people could not have hoped to compete with any chance of success] which had created the situation in the first place while the people were in the process of crossing a river. Such an apocryphal event, no doubt, has since been adopted to explain how of old, the tribe became split from their old-time confederated groups and migrated in a different direction, rather than their having been defeated in battle by a stronger tribe and forced to flee into uncompromising lands, due to their inferiority against their enemies.

101

The first Cheyenne story which tells of a separation of the people while crossing a river, is said to have taken place somewhere in the east country during the "Ancient time" of their traditions, but at a time long after the tribe had left the far "North Land" where there was perpetual snow and ice the year round, and from where they had earlier migrated in a south-easterly direction toward warmer climes. This southern area could not have been too far south because, it is said, the main rivers and tributaries were still apt to freeze over during the winter months, which would be compatible with the St. Lawrence, St. Maurice and Ottawa rivers in the Canadian Province of Quebec. The story then, could well be a reference to the time of Chippewa intrusion into the Lower St. Lawrence country and the destruction of the *Mundua*. Certainly, it would make some sense of the Cheyenne tale regarding the so-called under-water monster, notwithstanding that the story came to be believed by the Cheyennes themselves to represent an actual event in their people's history.

Albeit that the mention of under-water monsters in one form or another occur in other tribes` traditions across the whole of the North American Continent. I suggest that the alleged water-monster in the particular Cheyenne tale above cited, is merely used as being symbolic of the Chippewa enemy who, in truth, had instigated the dispersal of the Moiseo and the associated Omissis in a northwest direction, and the latter`s subsequent separation from the main Wheskerinni and Montagnais groups in the east, with whom never again did they unite as a confederated people. So it is that the explanation given by present-day Cheyennes that during the "Ancient Time" of their history *"The People became Orphans,"* not only refers to their having suffered decimation at the hands of a powerful enemy, but also that they had been irrevocably separated from the main Wheskerinni group and from the Montagnais after being driven north from their idyllic seats in the "Beautiful Land" of tradition. It will be recalled from an earlier chapter that in the Cheyenne account which pertains to their "Ancient Time," it is said that the people, *"First lived in a beautiful land of the north, in that land it was always summer and the people went naked."* [2] *

This statement then, is also most likely used in a metaphorical sense to mean that in those far-off days, the ancestors of the historic Cheyennes then existed in an idyllic state of mind and environment, having an abundance of game along with other food stuffs, and no enemies to fear or contend with. It seems to apply, moreover, to the period covering several centuries, when the ancestors of the present-day Cheyennes were a part of the great Delaware Algonquian host, traveling slowly across a vast territory lying between the Keewatin district of the northern part of Manitoba in the northwest, and the Lower course of the St. Lawrence in the southern part of Quebec Province in the southeast, as the aforesaid tradition adds,

> "...From the Beautiful Land of the North, the people went south into a land that was barren and here they stayed for some time...At length, they returned to the north into the "Beautiful Land" of their fathers. But now they found this land was no longer a nice place to live, having since become cold and desolate in their absence." [3]

* The Sarsi and Nez Pearce tribes of the Northern Plains as do the Teton Sioux, have identical stories to account for ancient divisions among their own peoples.

Again, it seems, the latter part of the above statement should also only be taken metaphorically, and refers to the advent of the proto-Cheyennes [i.e. Moiseo and Omissis] after crossing to the south side of the St. Lawrence, or at least, having reached its northern shoreline, became involved in a series of bloody conflicts with numerous enemy groups.

First against the *Tallegwi* perhaps; as mentioned in an earlier chapter, and later against the Chippewa. These last named Chippewa foes had gained the Upper hand and in the process, utterly destroyed the people's one-time idyllic existence and cultural situation. As a consequence, the "Southland" [i.e., abutting the shores of the St. Lawrence] is said to have been "barren," inferring that the country became at length, too dangerous to allow the Moiseo a prolonged occupation, while at the same time the so- called "North Land" itself was no longer regarded as "beautiful" for the same reason. The people hereafter, having been forced through expediency if not actual decimation to reside in a country uncomfortable for human occupation. Now they were obliged to move around constantly as in their "Ancient Time;" from one hunting ground to another in search of subsistence and in order to evade their foes.

Thus it represents the end in tradition of a second *"Golden Age"* of the people's existence, as from that time on, the Moiseo and Omissis and their descendants who later came together to create the Cheyenne Nation, were forever at war with one or another of the more powerful enemy tribes around them.

What the compelling factors had been to inaugurate this particular phase of strife and aggression among all the East Woodland Indians and with it the subsequent and consequential event of mass tribal movement, was perhaps, more than just an inclination on the part of Chippewa groups to antagonize their neighbours. Rather, it was the result of some uncontrollable circumstance that pressured various peoples to seek out new locations, crucial to their survival and continued existence as cohesive tribal units.

From circa, A.D.1350 onward, conditions in the northeastern United States and southeastern Canada, changed perceptibly from a mild, temperate climate with adequate rainfall for horticultural pursuits, to that of a colder, excessively dry period, heralding the beginning of what is generally referred to as "The Little Ice-Age," with precipitation locked up in the expanding ice sheets of the Arctic. This condition in its severity, persisted intermittently between the dates circa,1350 and circa,1450, and continued in alternating lesser and greater degrees until the 1850s. Its early effect upon the local ecology in northeastern North America was profound and dire to many of the Native cultures. During that time there were prolonged periods of drought; crops failed; corn could not mature and fruit did not ripen. The grass yellowed and died forcing larger game animals to move away from the country, whilst a substantial drop in lake and river levels drastically reduced the fishing potential. The populations of whole villages began succumbing to malnutrition if not actual starvation and this, coupled with disease, which a deficiency of vitamins among the people helped merely to encourage in its ravages, the survivors were soon obliged through necessity to migrate in search of better subsistence.

It was surely this period of recurring drought coupled with disease, that had spurred the Delaware movement into the `Buffalo Land` southwest of the Lower Great Lakes between the dates

THE CHEYENNES' RETURN JOURNEY TO THE NORTH.
[From George Dorsey's "The Cheyenne." Field Columbian Museum. 1905. Plate XII.]

1350/1360 as referred to in their traditions, while in another area, the same reasons instigated the Chippewa movement from somewhere close to the Eastern Seaboard towards the west into the Lower St. Lawrence country, where food sources, although likewise diminished, were still more readily available, as is attested in the Chippewa migration tradition.

Other Algonquian-speaking groups far south of the St. Lawrence, who having much earlier migrated from the northern boreal forests of Keewatin perhaps just prior to the Delaware advance, also undertook further migrations around this time to the eastern coastal areas and towards the south and southwest owing to similar conditions, caused by the same current period of climatic shift that diminished food resources in their own country, causing both famine and pestilence to spread across the land. These latter groups included among others, those of the historic Powhatan confederacy and further north, the various Abenaki tribes. Indeed, there are extant several traditional accounts from Algonquian groups of Maryland and the Virginia tidewater districts respectively, which relate how their people migrated into their historic seats [i.e. where they were found during the early days of European contact, circa, 1607-1620] from other more remote districts around the date AD.1350.

The Abenaki, of course, are the *"Easterners"* in the Delaware traditional account, while the populous Algonquian-speaking Illini tribes, historically entrenched along the east side of the Mississippi in what is now the state of Illinois, arrived there sometime during this same era, that is, during the early part of the second half of the fourteenth century. No doubt, this movement was occasioned through pressure exerted upon them by other migrating Algonquians and some Siouan-speaking tribes. Certainly Siouan peoples of the southern Ohio valley and southeastern states also suffered accordingly during this period, both from climatic variation which disrupted their age-old agrarian culture, coupled with a sudden explosion of enemy aggression directed against them by numerous foreign tribes.

This is also assigned by modern archaeologists as being the period when the great, centuries-old culture and population center of *Cahokia* suddenly broke up and disintegrated and disappeared completely save its earthen mounds, which today, instill wonder and constant speculation as to their construction.

Cheyenne tradition itself clearly recalls a period of severe drought and disease, resulting in a drastic population decrease within the tribe. This event, traditionally, occurred during a late period during their *Ancient time*, and compares with both the Delaware and Chippewa traditions of famine and pestilence noted above.

Indeed, a correlation of tribal movement seems to suggest a general uprooting of peoples during the middle decade of the fourteenth century; most likely undertaken for similar or connected reasons. Connected in so much as hostile pressure from one group effected by climatic change, would force a neighbouring group to move before it and in turn, the pressured group then press upon its neighbour, creating a domino effect. The area of study needed to detail such movements during this period alone, is far too extensive and involved for our present theme, although the above statements, terse as may be, do I believe, offer sufficient corroboration for our analysis of the Delaware migration account as recorded in that people's traditions and its concurrence with Cheyenne myth and tradition regarding these early days of their history. This change of environment due to a variable climate, must have had more than a little bearing upon what pressure or pressures induced the Monsoni and Moiseo, along with the now confederated Omissis faction, to move at this time, and upon which direction of further migration they chose to take.

Such a disastrous economic situation would have been a prime factor in compelling the Moiseo and their cognate tribes, to give up any small fields of squash and corn they may once have raised in the Lake Taureau and St. Maurice districts, and after a number of severe reversals suffered at the hands of Chippewa invaders [i.e. the massacre of the *Mundua*], to disappear into the hinterland to the north and northwest, where they could fend for themselves more comfortably by fishing in the Upper Great Lakes and hunting and gathering in the northern forests.

The fact that the traditional histories of several tribes recall a pandemic disease of catastrophic proportion during this same period of between circa, 1350 and 1360, is particularly relevant. The occurrence coincides with a specific period of Scandinavian visits to the north - eastern coastal area of North America, at a time we might add, just after a most virulent contagion had ravaged the whole of Europe, carrying away in its wake, an estimated one third of the entire European population of that time.

It is evident from the numerous Icelandic Sagas and related Norse Legends, that Scandinavian adventurers had begun frequenting the northeastern shores of North America as early as AD.982, and additional evidence that in AD.1342 or 1343, a number of Scandinavian families abandoned their homesteads in western Greenland and actually relocated on the North American Continent, apparently just south of Gaspe Bay on the south side of the Gulf of the St. Lawrence.

The reason for this move from the Greenland settlements, is variously given as either the consequences of a spate of vicious Eskimo attacks upon their homesteads; a pestilence of severe magnitude, or a drastic deterioration in climate. Probably it had been a combination of all three factors, in so much as once their population had been sufficiently reduced by disease, they could not then ward off the constant Eskimo attacks effectively. Neither could they disperse into the treeless, barren ground of the interior without adequate protection against the increasingly harsher weather and with the loss of their domestic animals, while finding it difficult to sustain themselves by utilizing the natural food resources both on land and sea, they were obliged to seek new lands conducive to their agrarian lifestyle, and where an abundant supply of timber would afford ample material for both shelter and fuel to enable them to survive. It is not improbable, and in reality it is highly likely, that some form of pestilence was thus carried to the Mainland of Northeastern North America by European migrants and as a result, infected the indigenous Native populations who with no immunity, suffered it to spread like wild fire through their respective tribes. Perhaps the disease was smallpox, then prevalent within all European communities. However, the severity of the contagion, as indicated in tribal tradition, might relate more specifically to the "Black Death," a Bubonic plague that decimated Europe between the years 1348 and 1351. Likely this contagion that stemmed from the bites of rat-carried fleas, was somehow transported to the shores of Greenland and to the Scandinavian settlers thereof by merchant vessels sailing back and forth from Northern Europe, and thus was eventually carried, albeit unwittingly, to the north-eastern shores of North America during the early 1350s. Certainly, Bubonic plague occurred as far west as Iceland even as late as 1402 and again in 1494. *

The drought period of tribal tradition referred to, with its attendant cooler temperatures, would have created an ideal environment for the propagation of such a disease, whilst the presence of Europeans on the Continent at that time [1350s] would explain the source, and offer some confirmatory evidence for dating this important episode in Native traditional history.

I suggest that a combination of circumstances most likely instigated mass tribal movement over the whole eastern part of North America during the fifth and sixth decades of the fourteenth century. An event which overnight, as it were, changed the status quo of respective tribal communities, owing to severe decimation on the one side through disease, resulting in their inability to repel a numerically stronger invading group; and on the other, a need to find more provident hunting or farming grounds in order to sustain their populations.

* The archaeological record suggests the abandonment of the Cahokia Mound builder centers in the present-day state of Illinois, as occurring around the middle of the fourteenth century, while further evidence has since been uncovered, to indicate that hunter-gatherer types from the north and east, then infested the area and superimposed their own culture over that which they likely destroyed.

The period between AD.1350 and AD.1360 must then, coincide with the dispersal of the Moiseo and Monsoni from the St. Lawrence country. From here on, only Iroquoian and Chippewa tribes remained, the former extending their territory from Lake Simco on the west and as far as where Quebec City now stands on the east. This situation by the later date of AD.1400, caused the Chippewa-proper themselves to retire from the St. Lawrence in a northwest direction, and relocate on a stretch of land in the northeastern part of Lake Huron, now called Manutoulin Island. *

It seems to have been during the same period of upheaval, and at the same time as the destruction of the *Mundua*, that the Moiseo either divorced themselves completely from the Fox, Wheskerinni and Monsoni, or having become irreparably separated from their kinfolk for other reasons, started upon their own independent migration toward the northwest. Certainly, the Moiseo proto-Cheyennes now severed all kinship ties with the Montagnais parent band and, as will be seen in a later chapter, in association with a remnant group of mixed Montagnais and Wheskerinni later known as Omissis, they evidently not only aligned themselves at a later date with the Dakota Sioux, who were mortal enemies of most other Algonquian peoples, but also came to blows with their Plains Cree relatives. The Cheyennes even went on the warpath against their long lost Suhtaio brethren, until, that is, after several battles it was discovered by accident that their two tribes spoke mutually intelligible languages, and upon which knowledge they ceased hostilities against each other and thereafter, acted as allies before eventually uniting as a single tribe.

From all this involved analysis throughout the foregoing chapters, in order to describe the situation of Algonquian peoples north of the St. Lawrence prior to the coming of Europeans, it can be seen that the above mentioned tribes, between the dates circa, AD.800 and AD.1400, were one section of Montagnais offshoots and seceders from the Delaware route of migration from north to south. During some remote period, all spoke intelligible dialects stemming from a common language, but which, owing to prolonged separation over the centuries, became even more diverse and virtually unintelligible to each other. After the destruction of the *Mundua* [i.e. The Moiseo and their allies] these tribes became widely dispersed in their respective isolated groups; all but the Sauk and Kickapoo fleeing independently towards the northwest as the result of enemy pressure in their rear. The Fox, evidently, retreated along the same route as taken by the Monsoni, while the Moiseo, being the original Cheyenne-proper group, appear to have followed as a detached branch, but as the predominant faction among what had likely become a conglomerate body, composed of both related and confederated refugee peoples, including a part of those both of Wheskerinni and Montagnais blood.

The fact, however, that in their late historic time, the main bodies of all these aforementioned tribal groups for the most part, had no recollection of a common prehistory, suggests that their separation into independent entities had occurred during the "Ancient Time" of

* In 1960, the site of a Scandinavian settlement of circa, A. D. 1000, was unearthed at L`Anse aux Meadows on the northernmost tip of Newfoundland.

their traditions. Later in this study, we will note both the Monsoni and Moiseo as residing in the same country above the headwaters of the Mississippi west of Lake Superior. But of these later positions there are retained more definite memories in their traditions, whilst some contemporary documentation shows that, by then, they were separate tribal bodies; each with their distinguishing dialects and individual peculiarities.

– 0 - 0 - 0 - 0 - 0 - 0 - 0 - 0 - 0 - 0 - 0 - 0 - 0 - 0 - 0 - 0 - 0 - 0 - 0 –

CHAPTER 12.

TO THE UPPER GREAT LAKES AND BEYOND.

We have seen how the invasion of Chippewa groups into the Lower and Upper St. Lawrence country between AD.1350/ 1360, created a great upheaval of resident Algonquians, who subsequently, abandoned their old territories completely in an endeavor to extricate themselves from Chippewa aggression. The kindred Delaware who may have offered succor if not a degree of physical assistance against the Chippewa invaders, were by this time, too far removed from the St. Lawrence to prove practical allies, and besides, other more powerful enemies namely Iroquois-proper peoples, lay between the two.

Certainly by the early decades of the fifteenth century, only Huron and a few small straggling Chippewa-speaking bands remained in that vast region extending from the site of Quebec in the east, to Lake Huron on the west, bounded by the Lower Great Lakes and St. Lawrence in the south and on the north, by the Upper reaches of the St. Maurice and Ottawa rivers, thence continuing in a rough line west toward Lake Nipissing, around the shores of which the Chippewa group Nipissing resided.

It is important to determine the route of migration taken by these refugee Algonquians, in order to deduce the neighbours and general situation of our Cheyenne subjects then known as Moiseo, who continued in a loose alliance with the Fox, Sauk, Monsoni and a part of the Wheskerinni. These refugee Algonquians, although obviously in some kind of contact with one another, did not migrate as a body. Rather they moved as individual groups and at varied intervals one from the other, merely traveling a common route in a northwest direction.

The Fox made up one group; the Monsoni Cree a second, and the Moiseo in conjunction with the Omissis-Wheskerinni remnant a third, while the Sauk; albeit at a later date in association with the Kickapoo, comprised a fourth. There appears, in fact, to have been two main routes of retreat from the St. Lawrence valley. The Montagnais element being to the east of the intruding Chippewa, and having previously claimed the area along both sides of the St. Lawrence between Trois Riviere and the site where the city of Quebec now stands, chose to move further east along the St. Lawrence as far as its Gulf. They then turned north into the cold, sparsely occupied eastern part of Quebec Province and the southern part of Labrador.

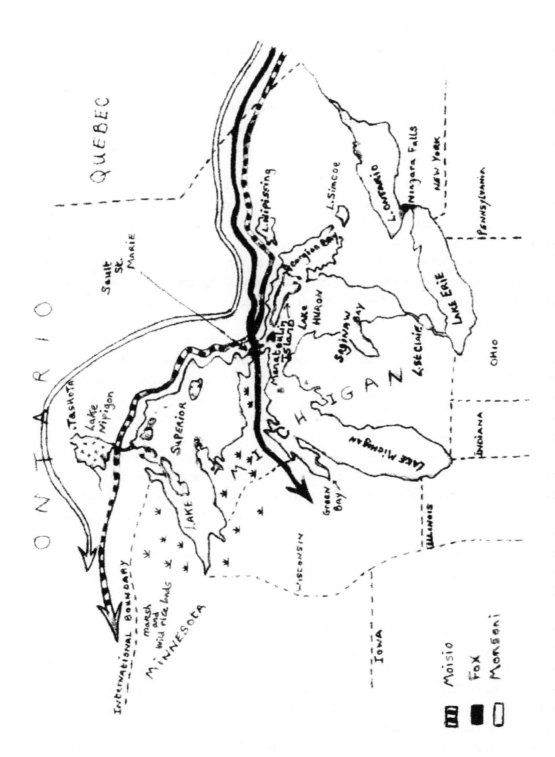

MAP OF PROPOSED MIGRATION ROUTES OF THE MOISEO, MONSONI AND FOX.

[From an original map by the Author].

109

Here in this inhospitable country they spread and populated and were found by the first white explorers into that region early in the sixteenth century. By the latter date, however, the Chippewa had all but gone from the St. Lawrence valley and as a result, the Montagnais - among which was the main group of Wheskerinni - soon after wandered back and reoccupied their old seats. They were then protected somewhat by their new role as middlemen in the white man's trade with more westerly Huron tribes on the Upper part of that river near present-day Montreal, and with Algonquians both from the Ottawa River country and north of the Upper Great Lakes. These same Montagnais-Wheskerinni bands even later, aligned themselves to the Huron and together, counterattacked the powerful Iroquois of the south who were the inveterate enemies of both. Long prior to this, around the date 1360, the situation was somewhat different. Of those Algonquian groups of Moiseo, Fox and Monsoni - likewise pushed out from the St. Lawrence country by the Chippewa - each appear to have retired towards the northwest above Georgian Bay into lands abutting Lake Huron's northern shore. This being the only route left open if they were to escape not only the Chippewa, but other enemies also.

Immediately southwest of the St. Lawrence roamed the several Iroquois-proper groups of Cayuga, Oneida, Onondaga, Mohawk and Seneca, fierce and defiant at this date towards all Algonquians. To the west along the Upper course of the St. Lawrence and adjacent to the northern shores of the Lower Great Lakes, stood the stockade towns of various Huron-speaking tribes including the Erie [Cat Nation], the Neutrals, Petun [Tobacco Nation] and others, who owing to their enmity with both the Chippewa and Delaware, were then also intermittently hostile to all Algonquian speakers and jealously guarded their frontiers against any foreign encroachment. To the north around Georgian Bay itself and parallel to the west bank of the Ottawa River, were the Huron-Wyandot, whilst in the south and southeast, of course, were entrenched the powerful and aggressive Chippewa invaders.

The Sauk and Kickapoo were the exception, in so much as they appear to have remained for a while in the vicinity of Montreal Island and actually aligned themselves with the incoming Chippewa, before that is, undertaking their own migration in the footsteps of their Fox cousins.

Traditions of the Fox state explicitly, that their tribe came into its historic seat in the area of Green Bay and Fox River in what is now the state of Wisconsin, from somewhere north of the Upper Great Lakes. Their near relatives the Sauk, recall only that sometime after their stay near Montreal Island, they [the Sauk] lived in the region of Saginaw Bay on the west coast of Lake Huron, and here the Ottawa found them shortly before the opening of the sixteenth century. Then, however, the Sauk were in a league with the Potawatomi - a Chippewa offshoot - who not only lived close by, but were then at odds with their Ottawa brethren.

This Sauk movement to Saginaw Bay must have been after the Fox, Moiseo and others had themselves been expelled from Lake Huron's northern shore. It postdated therefore, the Chippewa`s own advance northwest from the St. Lawrence and the latter`s arrival on Manitoulin Island in the northern waters of Lake Huron around AD.1400, as prior to this, the Ottawa, Potawatomi and Chippewa-proper were still confederated as allies, according to their traditional accounts.

It is likely then, that the Sauk met and allied with the Potawatomi somewhere on the north side of the Upper Great Lakes, probably in the area around Sault St. Marie. Together, these two tribes then migrated south from that point to the vicinity of Saginaw Bay in the present-day state of Michigan, in an endeavour to remove themselves from an influx of other Chippewa peoples into the Sault area itself.

Indeed, the only safe route for the Sauk from the St. Lawrence region lay north, into lands ostensibly uninhabited at this period and thus, into the cold, timbered country above Lake Huron the Sauk fled, albeit where from but a few centuries earlier, they had so eagerly left when members of the Delaware migration from the old *"Turtle Land"* in the southern Keewatin district of the Northwest. This is the logical conclusion gleaned from the fact that at the time of Sauk dispersal from the St. Lawrence when near the Island of Montreal, i.e. circa, 1390, Huron peoples then held lands around the southern shores of the lake of that name and the adjoining Lake Simcoe district. The Huron at this latter date, were then hostile to all peoples of the Chippewa dialect and with tribes in alliance with them. Surely then, the Huron would not have been obliged by force of arms or expediency, to allow the comparatively weak and hated Sauk to pass unopposed through their then hunting grounds en route to the western shores of Lake Huron, from where, incidentally, the Sauk could have established themselves in the Huron's rear.

Such a move directly through Huron controlled lands, would also mean that the Sauk were isolated from their Fox cousins for a period of at least two centuries prior to their two tribe's re-alignment as a confederated body. But this would not be compatible with the close dialectical and cultural ties as later existed between them, which alone indicates a far shorter period of separation than would otherwise be proposed if the Fox had migrated in a northwest direction from the St. Lawrence, and the Sauk as a separate group, had themselves moved directly west across the waters or around the southern shoreline of Lake Huron.

When at last the Sauk and Fox did reunite, it was after the Sauk had been evicted from Saginaw Bay and forced by pressure from the Iroquois, to migrate further west to the far side of Lake Michigan in present-day Wisconsin around the date 1400, and where they then found the Fox already entrenched. Obviously then, the Sauk also retired from the St. Lawrence in a northwesterly direction, albeit at a slightly later date than the Fox and thus, these two tribes remained in relatively close contact with one another for a prolonged period, even though moving as separate bodies and during successive periods in time. There is evidence to suggest that the Sauk if not actually confederated with the invading Chippewa, were at least in harmony with one or another Chippewa group and initially, tolerated by them. The statement by Chief Masco earlier referred to stating how the Sauk and Chippewa etc. once lived together near the Island of Montreal, appears to imply just that. Indeed, the Sauk may even have been the auxiliaries mentioned as being among the Chippewa forces during the attack on the *Mundua* town, and it is conceivable that the migration of the Sauk from the vicinity of Montreal Island was the advance guard, so to speak, of a later movement conducted by most Chippewa-speaking bands from the St. Lawrence country. This movement we know from reliable Chippewa tradition was, likewise, in a northwesterly direction so as to reach Georgian Bay, before continuing west along the north shore of Lake Huron and settling for a while in one great village on Manitoulin Island in the northern waters of that lake.

111

On the other hand, the Monsoni Cree certainly retreated from the St. Lawrence in a northwesterly direction, for we know from Monsoni Cree tradition cited in mid-seventeenth century manuscript sources, that they were nomadic hunters and gatherers, roaming the wooded area north of Lakes Huron and Superior at a much earlier date than when the statement was made, and perhaps, at least two centuries prior to being contacted by Europeans above Lake Superior in 1634.

It cannot be determined from Cheyenne tradition alone, what the precise route of Moiseo migration was, or exactly where they next settled after vacating the St. Lawrence district. Yet what was true of the Fox and Monsoni was, I believe, true initially for the Moiseo also. That Cheyenne tradition recalls the Monsoni as a *"Friendly tribe"* whilst living in the cold Great Lake country far northeast of their historic High Plains habitat, appears to substantiate this assumption. Certainly, there was no need for either of these groups to go further north than was necessary in order to reach Lake Huron`s northern shores. For the surrounding hunting grounds abutting those waters were virtually uninhabited during the period AD.1360.

Only the Sault St. Marie further west which flows east from the outlet of Lake Superior, sometimes played host to a few Siouan-speaking bands from the south that went there during certain seasons to fish, and these often improvident more timid groups at that time, posed little if indeed, any threat to the taller more aggressive Algonquians. Likely it is that there were by then other Algonquian-speaking groups situated west of the Sault St. Marie north of Lake Superior, composed of members responsible for the *"Blackduck"* archaeological complex of southern Ontario and northern Minnesota, who although not welcoming these Algonquian newcomers from the east with open arms, they did nonetheless, regard them as distant cousins and so tolerated their presence.

Conversely, if the Moiseo route of retreat from the St. Lawrence had been in a southwest direction, around the southern shores of Lakes Ontario and Erie into the Michigan peninsular, then we may assume that the lifestyle and intertribal relationships of our subjects would have been consistent with what we know of contemporary inhabitants of that country below the Great Lakes, whose culture and relationships were markedly different to those peoples in the north. The southern people were predominantly sedentary agriculturists residing in stockade towns and dwellings of some permanency, whilst the northern peoples were nomadic hunters, foragers and fishermen, residing in makeshift - or at the best - portable bark or reed mat shelters.

Archaeology has not to date brought to light any important village sites of the proto-historic period, which might definitely be attributed to either the Moiseo or their Monsoni cousins south of the Great Lakes. The absence of such sites; along with accompanying artefacts, suggests that the aforementioned tribes were nomadic hunters, inhabiting temporary bark or hide shelters for comparatively short periods, which was the habit of those peoples residing north of the said lakes during the historic time. Other than a few pottery shards and related artefacts such as stone arrow points and fleshers, along with remains of domestic refuse, little sign of their culture and even of their occupation would have survived into the present day.

This strongly implies that the Moiseo and their associates did, in truth, roam north of the Lakes, and traditions from the Cheyennes themselves along with those of some other northern

Algonquians, concur with this view. Of course, the fact previously noted that the Cheyennes "lost the buffalo and corn" during this period of roving, infers that they were in the north where buffalo were not found and the growing seasons too short of frost-free days to allow corn to mature.

South of the Lakes there was abundant game - including buffalo - and year round facilities for sustained agricultural pursuits, complementary to sedentary occupation in villages of permanent, or at the least, semi-permanent construction. Such dwellings were then composed of more durable material and have left traces of their existence for the discerning eye of the archaeologist. In the north, on the other hand, the environment and harsh winters compelled a nomadic existence, conducive to the people's continual search for subsistence. Thus we can be certain that the Cheyenne nucleus, i.e., the Moiseo in common with others among their northern Algonquian relatives, did retreat to remote areas north of the Upper Great Lakes where, they likely supposed, they could rid themselves of Chippewa harassment.

Cheyenne tradition which relates to their people's customs and style of dress during this early period does, it is true, include striking similarities with what anthropologists regard as the *"Central Algonquian type,"* typified in the historic period by tribes such as Fox, Sauk, Ottawa, Illinois, Miami and Shawnee, each of whom then resided south of the Upper Great Lakes. Yet this alone does not mean that the Moiseo traced their western route of migration via the country south of these lakes. Such peculiarities as were common to all would have been ancient traits, continued from the time when all these peoples had resided in the same general area embracing the middle course of the St. Lawrence, and had continued in superficial contact with one another during their circuitous wanderings after leaving that river's vicinity. Wanderings that finally terminated in the vicinity of Sault St. Marie at the junction of the three Upper Great Lakes of Superior, Michigan and Huron. There could also be found as many similarities between the historic Cheyenne, Northern Chippewa and Eastern Cree groups, and these two last-named peoples during their historic periods, were indigenous to the northern forests above the Upper Great Lakes in question.

In those days - Cheyenne tradition asserts - the people usually dressed themselves in rabbit skins and deer hide shirts and leggings which were without seams, being laced together with cords passing through holes cut into the front and back pieces of the garment. It was sometime after this that the Cheyennes learned the art of sewing [The Suhtaio, it may be said, continued to lace their garment pieces together late into the nineteenth century]. Other tribes, which were then neighbours of these early Moiseo Cheyennes, wore moccasins made from a single piece of leather in the manner of those Central Algonquians residing below the Upper Great Lakes, and only after reaching the Western Plains was a separate sole piece added to reinforce the tread. The Cheyennes on the other hand, according to their own accounts, from a very early stage in their evolution were unique, in so much as they alone fashioned their foot gear from two separate pieces of leather. However, the same Cheyenne informants did assert also, that in common with the Central Algonquian fashion, their people in those days often shaved their heads leaving only a small tuft of hair on the crown. At other times the hair was cut straight across the forehead level with the eyebrows, the rest hanging loose or braided in multiple stands. This last was always the recognized style among the Cree north of the Upper Great Lakes, presenting a novel appearance which distinguished them from other tribes.

How long the Moiseo and their cognates roamed the forest country abutting the northern shore of Lake Huron, was probably no longer than Chippewa absence would permit. In so much as the successive moves of these refugee Algonquians, seem to have been determined by the sporadic advances of the Chippewa. When the Chippewa migration came within a certain distance the resident Algonquians simply `packed up` and left, perhaps even before contact could be made.

In this way, the moves of the Moiseo were almost certainly conducted in a series of leaps and bounds, which coincide in time to the sporadic advances of the Chippewa host.

Thus about the date 1400, when the Chippewa suddenly re-appeared spreading along the northern shore of Georgian Bay, within striking distance again of those erstwhile refugees who had thought themselves free from their enemies inroads, these latter then including the Moiseo, moved further west as far as the rapids of Sault St. Marie and the northeastern shore of Lake Superior.

Chippewa tradition concerning their people's movements after leaving the St. Lawrence country, records their progress from the east as far as the western extremity of Lake Superior. This tradition enables us to calculate a rough date for each Chippewa halt along their migration route and by so doing, allows us to estimate a general date for the earlier vacation of these `halts` by the Moiseo and others of their ilk.

The Chippewa account which has survived the rigors of modern scrutiny, declares that after leaving the Island of Montreal, their tribe and its cognates journeyed in a northwest direction by way of the Ottawa River; thence by canoe and portage to Georgian Bay and then to the northern coast of Lake Huron. Here they remained for a few years before moving further west, first occupying Manitoulin Island in the northern waters of Lake Huron, then going on to the rapids of Sault St. Marie. From this last named area they eventually moved over to the island of La Point in the southwestern corner of Lake Superior, where they lived in one great village for a number of years. Then yet again, they continued west, now in a two pronged advance into territory both north and south beyond the western tip of the aforesaid lake.

By their own calculations the Chippewa date their arrival at Sault St. Marie as around AD.1450, and the fact that the Chippewa vacation of Montreal Island had occurred around the date AD.1390, owing to Huron infiltration into the area, suggests that the Chippewa appearance along the north shore of Lake Huron was sometime between the latter date and AD.1450. Perhaps then, they were entrenched on Manitoulin Island between circa, 1400 and circa, 1430.

It is indicative that the average length of stay in one village was between twelve to thirty years, as has been deduced in the previous chapter. It seems likely then, that these Chippewa movements were dictated by a need to relocate their villages. Especially as the tradition make no mention of the Chippewa being harassed by enemies once they removed themselves from the St. Lawrence, and along which river the Huron were again firmly entrenched, but satisfied to leave their erstwhile Chippewa enemies alone.

It becomes clear from the above, that it was the arrival of the Chippewa on Manitoulin Island in the northwestern part of Lake Huron about the date AD. 1400, which obliged the Moiseo and their neighbours to abandon the area above Lake Huron and flee west. This time into the country north of Sault St. Marie where, it was supposed, the Chippewa host would be reluctant to follow.

This is consistent with Cheyenne tradition which states that after their people left the country where the climate was cold and harsh [ostensibly north of Lake Huron], they moved towards the west in boats and for a long time, resided along the shores of a large lake the year round, which evidently, refers specifically to the area embracing the northeastern shore of Lake Superior adjacent to Sault St. Marie, known as the *"Fish Country"* in Cheyenne tradition.. Here they subsisted mainly on small fur-bearing animals, supplemented at times by some larger ruminants such as deer which they hunted by the employment of a *"Surround,"* and in which event, all the people; men, women and children took part. Other large game such as moose and bear were lured into `dead-fall` traps, and small game obtained by the use of snares. In this country; the Cheyennes say, they were happy and free from enemy harassment.

This northern country stretching from Sault St. Marie to the western tip of Lake Superior on its north side and beyond, was known to the colonial French as the *"Bois de Forts"* or `Strong Woods,` being a densely packed mass of forest and muskeg swamp with large and small lakes peppering the terrain. It was an ideal place of habitat, in direct line of advance for any people moving west from the Lake Nipissing district and hugging the northern shores of Lake Huron, as the Moiseo and their cousins evidently did. Deer and moose were plentiful in the surrounding woods of birch, spruce and maple; the birch offering its bark for the manufacture of lodges, canoes and domestic implements; the boughs of the spruce for roof and floor coverings etc., whilst the groves of maple trees were tapped when the sap flowed in February, providing the Moiseo with a welcome source of nourishment. This syrupy liquid was sometimes stirred with a wooden spade until it took the form of granulated sugar; at other times poured into birch bark containers in the shape of small scoops and left to harden, and in winter boiled; tipped onto the snow to solidify or spread over sheets of bark and left to crystallize in the heat of a lodge fire. Certainly, the Cheyennes alone, among all other tribes around them when inhabiting the High Plains country far west of the Mississippi, were still in the habit of collecting sap; albeit from Box elder trees, which they then still prepared in the various guises noted above.

Fish were also abundant and easily caught in the fast-flowing waters of Sault St. Marie, offering a welcome addition to vary one`s diet of venison and berries, and sustaining the people throughout the starvation months prior to the coming of spring. Included in the many streams and small lakes of the surrounding country were fish of many varieties; pike, pickerel, trout, sturgeon, whitefish, bass and others and these were taken in great quantity either by spearing, netting or with a simple rod and line. Trout were of a very large type often in excess of fifty pounds, while sturgeon weighing one hundred and fifty pounds were not at all uncommon and were so large, as to be driven from the shallows onto the sand banks before being dispatched with arrows, spears or large wooden clubs. The whole band, women and children included often joined in these seasonal fish hunts, after which the haul was either boiled or roasted and the surplus dried and smoked to be laid away in grass-lined pits ready for winter use.

There appears to be no specific mention in the "Ancient Time" of Cheyenne tradition regarding the peoples use of pottery, although the manufacture of clay pots is referred to in other stories and, of course, the archaeological record shows that virtually all Algonquians, whether north or south of the Great Lakes, were well-acquainted with the art, albeit that the more northern groups also manufactured domestic utensils from birch bark or woven reeds instead.

The memoir of Antoine Denis Raudot written in the year 1709, but referring to the condition of tribes prior to that century, records a brief description of those peoples then residing north of the Great Lakes, and among whom he included the Monsoni and their neighbours,

"..........The manner in which these savages shelter themselves is very easy : The shelter consists of several birch barks three feet high, sewn together, and eight feet long, with which they surround a circle of several poles that, fastened together at the top, form a large circle belowe [sic] to enclose the persons who are inside. Broken pine branches serve them as mattresses on which they spread several skins of bear or deer as a pad, and they wrap themselves in the beaver robes or covers to sleep........`

`As these savages of the northern regions are deprived of the convenience of having wheat by the poor quality of the soil and the coldness of the climate and are deprived of the different animals to the south that inhabit this part of the land, finding the climate more pleasing and more temperate, so God for compensation has given them the skill of being better hunters than those who have abundance in their country and whom this abundance renders indolent and lazy while necessity gives skill to the others...Their principle hunting is of caribou [Moose] which they kill in the summer in its tracks with arrows or guns...`

`They also use snares stretched in the customary passages of these animals to take them......in winter, snow-shoes are used to hunt caribou as well as other animals. These other animals are sometimes taken in traps and sometimes killed with arrows or gunshots.

`They are as skillful at fishing as at hunting; They make their nets of nettles or wild hemp, of which there is much in moist places, and the women and girls spin and twist these on their bare thighs. The cords used to draw these nets are made of the bark or Basswood or of leather and are very strong and difficult to break...As they know at what time the fishes pass by in the rivers, they make barriers there, leaving only one exit where they place some nets which they draw up full of fish when they have need of them......." [Raudot`s memoir. 1709]. [1]

The similarity of the above memoir with that offered in Cheyenne tradition cannot be denied, and was peculiar to Algonquian-speaking bands roaming country on the north side of Lake Superior between that lake and Hudson's Bay.

At the time of Raudot`s writing, however, the condition of these peoples had changed somewhat, in so much as they had then become reliant to a degree upon the white man's trade goods. Not least among which, was the firearm; the black *"Thunder-stick"* which gave its Indian owner the confidence and superior prowess to enable him to foray further afield than previously dared. Thus to encroach upon the hunting territories of neighbouring tribes with impunity.

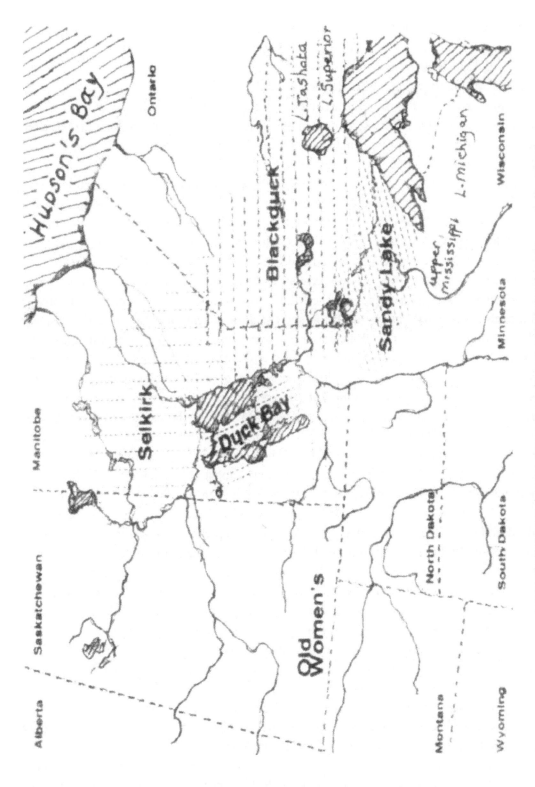

DISTRIBUTION OF ARCHAEOLOGICAL COMPLEXES Circa, A.D. 1250.

[After; "Plains Indians." Edited by Karl Schlesier. University of Oklahoma Press. P. 118. 1994]

117

Even so, every day hunting must still have been conducted in a similar manner as had been practiced for centuries prior to Raudot's time, that is, by means of the surround and the bow and arrow. Surely, one loud bark from an early trade musket would have sent all the game in the immediate area scurrying for cover before the first animal had fallen.

Tribes further west not personally involved in trade with the white man and having little contact with those who did, must have remained in a like state if not the same as they had endured for hundreds of years previously. Only that during Raudot's time of writing, they, too, suffered chronically in warfare from enemies armed with guns.

The Moiseo and with them at a later date the Suhtaio, Blackfoot and Arapahoe groups were included in this latter category, and each eventually, were forced to retire from several locations in order to escape such terrible weapons.

Before this, so Cheyenne tradition continues, when residing in a country *"close to a great lake,"* there were no wars and the people hunted and wandered as they pleased.

This statement, though, is likely apocryphal, as is the phrase, *"Before we had bows and arrows,"* which merely serves to emphasize the tribe's primitive state and extent of time lapsing between that of the "Ancient Time" of tradition and the more recent past. Having said this, war itself was hardly likely to have played an important part in their culture during this particular period of roving. The search for subsistence was probably so constant and grueling an employment, that there would have been little spare time or even the inclination to involve themselves in hostile activities, unless obliged to do so by some foreign invading group. While it is true that there is abundant archaeological evidence to support the existence of inter-tribal warfare throughout the whole of the archaic *Woodland* and *Mississippian* culture periods, perhaps as far back as several thousand years before the present, if such was also the case in the Sub-Arctic area and north of the Upper Great Lakes, then it must have been on a much reduced scale, amounting to little more than intermittent feuding between one group of inhabitants and another.

Indeed, sometime later, after the Chippewa themselves reached the northern shores of Sault St. Marie and like the Moiseo and Monsoni and the latter's neighbours before them, divided their number, those Chippewa who chose to inhabit lands abutting the north side of Lake Superior spent much of their time fending for their families, and it is relevant to note that the Southern Chippewa, i.e., those residing south of that lake, regarded their northern brethren as un-warlike and inferior; dubbing them *"Rabbits"* because of their clothing made from the skins of that animal, and also because of their supposed timidity. It is perhaps indicative that according to Clark [1881], the Assiniboine likewise used the sign language gesture for `rabbit` in order to denote the more northern bands of Chippewa, and used the same sign as a collective designation for the Cree.

No wonder then, that upon each stage of Chippewa encroachment into their hunting grounds, the Moiseo and Monsoni along with most other Algonquian groups of the country, simply withdrew from the Chippewa sphere of contact, rather than oppose them.

Unfortunately then, this aforesaid period of respite enjoyed by the Moiseo whilst resident around Sault St. Marie, is unlikely to have lasted more than a generation before the Chippewa host advanced yet again. This time the Chippewa crowded into the Sault area itself, and the Moiseo and Omissis, along with some other resident Algonquians, were obliged once more to pull up stakes and move away. Some groups which included the Fox, fled south and west into what is now the state of Wisconsin; whilst others, among whom were the Moiseo and the cognate Omissis, fled directly west and northwest into the less hospitable district of southwestern Ontario.

We should not construe from this that there was no hostile contact between the resident Algonquians and these Chippewa invaders, for undoubtedly there was. This on a small scale perhaps, but sufficient to induce the Moiseo and their neighbours to retire from the Chippewa line of advance. It does seem also that it was during this particular period of expansion, according to the Chippewa, that the Martin clan of the invading host almost destroyed the remainder of the Moosoneeg [i.e. Monsoni], as mentioned in the previous chapter, and which event likely involved to a great or less degree, the Monsoni`s Moiseo allies.

Probably then, as a consequence of continued Chippewa migration, the Moiseo and others with whom they were then in contact, had first left the Lake Huron shores in favor of Sault St. Marie just prior to the Chippewa arrival, i.e. AD.1400 /1410, and later - again because of Chippewa encroachment - abandoned the Sault area around the date AD.1450, or perhaps, a decade later. The Sault St. Marie now became a natural staging post, as it were, for the division of these numerous Algonquian groups. It was at this point that successive migrant Indian peoples invariably split, some continuing west along the north shore of Lake Superior, others crossing the Sault and moving southwest adjacent to Lake Superior`s southern shoreline. Such at a later date, was the case with the Chippewa host and before them, those Algonquian refugees whom they followed.

As previously mentioned, the Fox, evidently, crossed the rapids of the Sault from north to south and wandered off toward the southwest away from the Chippewa line of march. By following the course of the Fox River upstream, they allowed themselves to be led into the heart of present day Wisconsin, where they were found firmly entrenched by the first white explorers into that region during the mid- sixteen-hundreds.

The Sauk along with the Kickapoo also crossed the rapids of Sault St. Marie, but lingered on the south side of the Sault in northern Michigan; met some incoming Chippewa groups and after aligning themselves with the Potawatomi, moved further south to the vicinity of Saginaw Bay. The Monsoni, then including factions later known collectively as Swampy and Bush Cree, chose to stay on the north side of the rapids, before eventually spreading north and northwest as if to make room for the advancing Chippewa rather than oppose them. Hereafter, they hovered tentatively in the snowbound forest country between James Bay and the northwestern tip of Lake Superior and in all probability, were those responsible for the so-called *Selkirk* complex in the archaeological record.

The Moiseo and Omissis on the other hand, apparently traveled due west, initially following a route parallel to the undulating northeastern shoreline of Lake Superior, and then turned northwest into the country of west-central Ontario. Here they met with other Algonquians of the *Blackduck* cultural complex who, by that date, had extended their territory from central Minnesota toward the northeast above Lake Superior and among whom, one or more Suhtaio bands were likely included.

119

It is indicative that by A.D. 1300, the warm period covering north-eastern North America which had remained comparatively stable since A.D.1000, thereby allowing a sustainable agrarian culture in the St. Lawrence River and Lake Taureau districts, had begun to change perceptibly. The north-eastern region was in the throes of entering what is known as the Little-Ice-Age, this being a time of colder environments which persisted until 1850 if not later. However, during the first 150 years of the Little-Ice-Age period, weather patterns were somewhat erratic, alternating between extreme warm and then cold cycles sometimes lasting as long as a decade and more. The result on the one hand, caused crop failure due to prolonged drought, along with a dwindling number of large ruminants in certain areas owing to parched grazing lands, and also a diminished fishing potential as the result of drastic drops in lake and river levels. On the other, excessive precipitation which ruined crops before they could be harvested, along with accompanying storms and regular periods of North Atlantic oscillation, severely restricted sustainable offshore fishing along the north-eastern coast. This last coupled with a reduction of large animals to support even a semi-hunting economy, had probably been the major factor that actually caused the Chippewa–speaking tribes to move further inland in the first place around 1350, and especially into the St. Lawrence River region where fish stocks and large ruminants were then still in plentiful supply. The influx of Chippewa tribes into the St. Lawrence country obviously initiated greater competition regarding who controlled certain hunting and fishing grounds in the region, and this in turn, had led to warfare between indigenous residents and the Chippewa new-comers which had culminated in the destruction of the *Mundua,* as noted in the previous chapter.

Now, a full century later, owing to continued belligerence on the part of the Chippewa, the Moiseo and their allies – these being remnants of Monsoni, Montagnais and Wheskerinni offshoots - had once more evacuated their homes. This time from the vicinity of Sault St. Marie in order to distance themselves again from the Chippewa advance. Additionally, having previously seen their populations decimated by disease, may have dissuaded the Moiseo from encroaching upon lands already held by more populous tribes to the south and southwest, while the advent of a coincidental warm period during the varying climatic cycles at this time, likely not only help encourage the Moiseo to move from the Sault St. Marie region, but caused them to take a route west above Lake Superior, rather than crossing the Sault itself and moving along the south side of the lake en route to the rice and buffalo lands of Wisconsin as did their Fox, Kickapoo and Sauk cousins.

From the previous analysis, there can be no dispute that the early Cheyenne-speaking bands of Moiseo and Omissis came into the Upper Mississippi country in the northern part of present-day Minnesota directly from the north, rather than from the east below the southern shoreline of Lake Superior. The topography and tribal culture as described in Cheyenne tradition certainly indicates a northern route, when we compare such data with documented descriptions of other tribes residing above the Upper Great Lakes during their early historic periods, as observed by the first white men to enter that region. If, conversely, the Moiseo had crossed the Sault St. Marie to the south then taken a route west adjacent to the southern shoreline of Lake Superior, they would, without doubt, have been familiar with - if they did not take advantage of - the vast amount of wild rice growing so abundantly south of that lake; especially in the vicinity of Lake Michigan, and upon which abundant food source both the Menominee Algonquians and Eastern Dakota tribes relied so heavily for a great part of their diet.

The ethnologist James Mooney [1907], stated that his Cheyenne informants were adamant that their tribe had never harvested that plant, which statement might appear to be wrong considering a recent analysis by John Moore [1996]. But Mooney's observation might merely have been used by his Cheyenne informants to indicate that rice was not abundantly available along the particular route of Moiseo migration at that time, and therefore, was not included in traditional accounts as a regular food source. We might add that the tribe's emphasis in tradition concerning this period of their existence, i.e., that the people were often hungry prior to their moving south and entering the northern part of present-day Minnesota, makes it naive to suppose that they would not have taken full advantage of any food stock, so readily available and acquired as was this wild-growing rice in order to alleviate their hunger. Coupled to this, we know that at this same period, Dakota Sioux bands were roaming the length of the St. Croix River from its head to its mouth as early as circa, 1400, which would, of course, have positioned them in direct line of the Cheyenne advance if indeed, the latter had moved south of Lake Superior and west into the north-eastern part of Minnesota. Both the Sioux and Cheyennes, however, always emphatically declared that they did not meet each other until about two-hundred years later around the date 1640 or 1650, and at which time, the Cheyennes then resided in the Upper part of Minnesota State and the Sioux on the headwaters of the eastern branches of the Upper Mississippi.

It seems, however, that it was only the Suhtaio who, before amalgamating with the Cheyenne-proper, utilized wild rice as a regular food source. Cheyenne tradition recalls that when the Cheyenne-proper and Suhtaio again came together after a prolonged period of separation, the latter were in the habit of eating grass, which statement, conceivably, refers to the Suhtaio harvesting and subsisting on the wild rice of the region. We know also from cultural remains of those peoples once belonging to the *"Blackduck"* cultural complex and among whom, most likely, were included the Suhtaio, that they certainly utilized this food stock as an important part of their diet.

Having said this, we must leave the Suhtaio for the present and by treating the Moiseo and the cognate Omissis as a separate group, as they still were after vacating the area around Sault St. Marie, will attempt to trace the latter's wanderings and subsequent history before returning to the Suhtaio where appropriate, lest our narrative becomes more confused than necessary.

- 0 - 0 - 0 - 0 - 0 - 0 - 0 - 0 - 0 - 0 - 0 - 0 - 0 - 0 - 0 - 0 -

CHAPTER 13.

THE TIME OF STARVING.

The Cheyennes say that after leaving the *"Fish Country,"* [i.e. within the vicinity of Sault St. Marie] where they had been happy and content, they next entered *"a more sparsely wooded land"* which lay slightly northwest of a *"great lake."* [1]

In this new place of habitat, which evidently embraced the southwestern part of Ontario, small lakes are numerous and the land itself interspersed with outcrops of black, blue and grey pre-Cambrian granite and gneiss. Game both of the large and small variety is only slightly more plentiful than in the far north, but in the more southern area, deciduous forests take over; small fur-bearing animals are prolific and lakes of various size and shape can be counted in their thousands. As mentioned earlier, the climate in this area, certainly between AD. 1450 and AD. 1550, was that of alternating warm and cold periods so that although winters were harsh and game scarce throughout that season's duration, it was conceivably, the event of a particular warm period which most likely encouraged the migration of the Moiseo and their Omissis confederates into this part of the country, rather, that is, than crossing to the south side of Sault St. Marie as had other Algonquian groups.

Cheyenne tradition seems to indicate that here in the southwestern part of Ontario, peppered with innumerable silver lakes during this particular period of their history, the Moiseo and their cousins wandered for many years, perhaps several generations, beginning around the date AD.1450. Alone and unnoticed they subsisted mainly on fish and such animals as they could take with their stone-tipped arrows and spears. They evidently moved from lake to lake as the preference took them and according to their own account, the people were once again left to themselves and to a degree were content, at least throughout most of the year, being free from enemy harassment. But even this period of isolation and peace was not destined to last.

Unfortunately by the date circa, AD.1500, the Chippewa had again spread their deadly tentacles, this time further west along both the northern and southern shorelines of Lake Superior. So it was that early in the sixteenth century, the Moiseo; along with any other Algonquian bands of the region, were once more forced through expediency to vacate their hunting grounds and extricate themselves from the enemy's line of advance. This time our subjects retired further north, deep into the Upper west-central part of Ontario; into a colder, less hospitable area where life again became a continual search for subsistence. This period is remembered in Cheyenne tradition as a prolonged time of cold, privation and hunger.

In that land, say the Cheyennes, it was very stony with numerous small lakes and little suitable timber with which to construct dwellings in the style to which they had previously been accustomed. Instead, they built crude temporary willow-framed shelters, plastered over with a mixture of small stones and mud to protect themselves from the elements. In addition, the people now only occasionally managed to kill animals such as elk, bear and moose by the use of `dead-

fall` traps, for these larger animals were not so great in number as in the country the Cheyennes had left. Still, however, as in the old country, their main diet was fish, caught in large quantity in the shallows of the many lakes of various size which dotted the land. When only a few fish were caught and other game scarce, the women boiled and pounded down the fish bones, extracting pure white oil which they then ate for added nourishment.

At the same time all kinds of small game were trapped and eaten; - rabbits are especially mentioned. These were skinned and dried then pounded up with the bones into a powder which was mixed with fat and eaten raw. Come the summer months, berries were plentiful, including cranberries, blueberries, June berries, strawberries, raspberries and a particular variety of red berry known as *"Poire."* The surplus was dried; mixed with grease or maple sugar and compressed dried meat to make a kind of pemmican, then put in store for leaner times. In addition, the people ate the flowers of the milkweed; the roots of bulrushes; the sap of the aspen and basswood and withal, the sweet pith beneath the bark of the woodbine. Even the moss on pine trees was considered worthy nourishment during times when food became scarce and the people in dire need. In reality, this land is composed predominately of granite rock with very little soil for the profuse growth of trees and other vegetation and where trees are found, they are widely scattered and usually of stunted growth. The climatic environment is subject to contrasts; in summer warm and balmy, creating a provident subsistence, but throughout the winter months and early spring, it becomes a cruel and frozen habitat where temperatures are minus forty degrees Celsius. Game, such as it is, then becomes elusive to the hunter or, when caught, animals such as rabbits and thin-bellied moose prove too lean a quarry to adequately sustain the people, as a quantity of fat is indispensable to keep one from starvation and help insulate the body from the intense and continuous cold of the season. Informants among those who lived in similar environments used to say that if a hibernating bear was found in its den, then the people rejoiced, for there would then be a quantity of much needed fat and we have noted earlier, how the ancient Cheyennes pounded and boiled the bones of fish, in order to extract the pure white oil which was often their only sustenance during times of famine. Hunters needed to start out long before dawn in their constant and grueling search for game; no distance being considered too far to travel in its pursuit. Three or four days journey from the home camp was common place before a successful hunt might be made and then, one had to laboriously haul the carcass home through ever deepening snow and across ice bound streams and swamplands. If by chance the hunter himself succumbed to fatigue or frozen limbs, then with fatalistic resolution, he would merely sit down in some sheltered spot and wait patiently for the end.

Often through necessity, the people were obliged to eat their dogs, then to chew old leather garments and moccasins for added nourishment and when these were exhausted, they concocted a repugnant broth composed of moss and lichen scraped from the slimy rocks, called *"tripe des roches"* by the early French voyageurs who sometimes themselves, were forced to consume the same in order to survive. At other times, old fish bones were boiled to provide a fearful smelling soup which the stomach could barely keep down, and in dire times of need, they dug up the remains of earlier feasts and even those of human relatives and by boiling the bones, extracted from them what little nourishment they could, in order to sustain themselves and their families for yet one more miserable day of existence. One of the earliest written accounts, which relates to this same region embracing the north country above the Upper Great Lakes, graphically describes the sufferings of its Indian inhabitants during times of extreme privation during the latter part of winter and early spring. This account comes from the pen of Pierre Radisson, who himself, was obliged to suffer a similar experience during the winter of 1660 /´61 or thereabouts. His words are as follows,

"There did fall such a quantity of snow and frost, and with such a thick mist, that all the snow stuck to the trees that are there so rough, being deal trees, pousse cedars, and thorns.[It] caused darkness upon the earth; it is to be believed that the sun was eclipsed two months. After, the trees were so laden with snow that was as if it had been sifted. By that means [it was] very light and not able to bear us, albeit we made rackets [snowshoes] six foot long and a foot and a half broad. Often thinking to turn ourselves, we felled over and over again in the snow, and if we were alone we should have difficulty enough to rise again. By the noise we made the beasts heard us a great way off. So the famine was among [a] great many that had not provided beforehand and [who] live upon what they get that day, never thinking for the next..."[2]

The account goes on to report the arrival of one-hundred Ottawa Indians with their families,

"[They] are worst provided than we...Everyone cries out for hunger. The women become barren and dry like wood. You men must eat the cord, being you have no more strength to make use of the bow. Children you must die....here comes a new family of those poor people daily to us - half dead, for they have but the skins and bones. How shall we have strength to make a hole in the snow to lay us down? - seeing we have it not to haul our rackets after us, nor to cut a little wood to make a fire to keep us from the rigor of the cold, which is extreme in those countries in its season......in the morning the husband looks upon his wife, the brother, his sister, the cousin, the uncle the nephew, that were for the most part found dead......those that have any life seeketh out for roots, which could not be done without great difficulty, the earth being frozen two or three foot deep, and the snow five or six above it. The greatest subsistence that we can have is of rind tree, which grows like ivy about the trees. To swallow it, we cut the stick some two foot long, tying it [into] a fagot, and boil it, and when it boils one hour or two the rind or skin come off with ease, which we take and dry it in the smoke, and then reduce it into powder betwixt two grain stones, and putting the kettle with the same water upon the fire, we make it a kind of broth, which nourished us....But [we] became thirstier and drier than the wood we eat....The first week we did eat our dogs. As we went back upon our step for to get anything to fill our bellies, we were glad to get the bones and carcasses of the beats

124

that we [had] killed, and happy was he that could get what the other did throw away, after it had been boiled three or four times to get the substance out of it....We contrived another plot; to reduce the powder those bones, the rest of crows and dogs, so put all that together half-foot within [the] ground, and so make a fire upon it. We covered all that very well with earth, so feeling the heat, and boiled them again, and [that] gave more froth than before....in the next place [we ate] the skins that were reserved to make us shoes, cloth and stockings; yea, most of the skins of our cottages [lodges], the castors` skins where the children beshit them above a hundred times. We burned the hair on the coals. The rest goes down throats, eating heartily these things most abhorred. We went so eagerly to it that our gums did bleed like one newly wounded. The wood was our food the rest of [that] sorrowful time. Finally we became the very image of death,....we wanted strength to draw the dead out of the cabins.....here are above five hundred dead - men, women and children....here comes a wind and rain that puts a new life in us. The snow falls; the forest clears itself; at which sight those that had strings left in their bows take courage to see...The weather continued so for three days; we need no rackets more, for the snow hardened much. The small stags are [as] if they were stakes in it. After they made seven or eight capers it`s an easy matter for us to take them and cut their throats with our knives...” [3]

The above excerpt was penned at a time when firearms were of a primitive nature compared to their more sophisticated manufacture and performance of a later age. But even as late as the turn of the eighteenth century a captive white man named John Tanner then living with a Northern Chippewa family, often found himself roaming this same snow-filled country and he later recorded in his *"memoirs"* a number of episodes, when he and his Indian companions had suffered chronic starvation during the latter part of the hoary season. The following abstract is but one example of several occasions which he speaks,

“One of my dogs died, and we ate him. We were traveling on the old trail of some Indians, but a deep snow had fallen since they passed. Under this snow we found several dead dogs and other things thrown away or left by the Indians, such as bones, worn out moccasins, and pieces of leather. With these we were able to sustain life.” [4]

The coming of spring did not always bring an immediate end to suffering. Often an early thaw was quickly followed by a severe cold snap, that formed a hard crust atop the semi-melted snow and thus, gave the moose fair warning of a hunter's approach whilst enabling the rabbit to skip across the crust, rather than keeping to its usual trails in the drifts along which the Indian invariably set his snares. Spring, in fact, was more often the starvation time which may force the people into cannibalism in order to survive. And so the *"Wendigo,"* the Northern Algonquian`s spiritual personification of this abhorred; but sometimes necessary trait of human character, was a constant and much feared companion to these impoverished nomads. A particular story familiar to the Cheyennes and some other Algonquian tribes that include the Arapahoe and Blackfoot, each of whom once inhabited these same northern lands during the "Ancient Time" of their traditions, is that commonly known as "The Rolling Head."

The story tells how a man once murdered his wife and after cutting off her head, gave the rest of her body to his children - a young boy and his sister - saying it was from a deer he had recently killed, and that they should roast the meat and eat it. In their ignorance the children did as they were told while the man went off again to hunt. As the children were doing so, the mother's head came rolling up to the lodge and began vigorously banging against the door. It was intending to avenge itself upon the children. But the children escaped from the lodge and thereupon, a prolonged chase ensued, the brother and sister running in front, the head rolling after them at great speed. As the chase continued, the sister - who had magical powers - caused several natural barriers to spring up at intervals behind them as they ran and these retarded the head's progress somewhat, although always it overcame such obstacles and continued in pursuit of the children. At length, the sister created a deep chasm in the path behind them, at the bottom of which she conjured up a fast-flowing river and across the gaping chasm; she placed her digging stick to act as a bridge. Soon the rolling head appeared again and attempted to cross the chasm by rolling along the stick, but when the head was only halfway across, the girl suddenly flipped the stick over and the head was hurled into the chasm to be drowned in the waters below.

This story has all the hallmarks of being a disguised memory, relating to periods of extreme privation and starvation during each of these tribe's olden days when in southern Ontario and northern Minnesota, and likely pertains to the people then having to regularly resort to cannibalism in order to survive. In addition, the story symbolizes among the Cheyennes, at least, of a migration undertaken by their tribe into more provident lands, although the initial event that had caused the people to starve, does appear in this instance, to represent a period in their history when such a condition was not uncommon and, in reality, was more often the norm between the latter days of winter and early spring. Certainly, cannibalism was not unknown among many Indian groups and both the Chippewa and various Iroquois-proper tribes particularly, have strong traditions that tell of their people once indulging in such a practice - moreover out of necessity, rather than a mere ritualized partaking of human flesh, so as to absorb the power of a respected slain enemy.

At the same time, paradoxically, even the Indian regarded the act with a certain amount of ambivalence, in that the practice was readily resorted to in times of dire need, but generally frowned upon by the people, including those who had been obliged to participate in order to survive. In short, it was a practice regarded as being indicative of their people's savage state, before they became more enlightened culturally, or had moved into a more provident area and no longer subjected to the severity of an environment in which they had once been forced to exist, owing to more belligerent and powerful tribes around them. Late in the 1740s, a Cree Indian with his wife and children, started out from their winter quarters intending to reach a distant Hudson`s Bay post. In the words of the chronicler,

126

"They had the misfortune to meet with very little game on the way and in a short while, the man, his wife and children, were reduced to the last distress. In these circumstances, they plucked the fur from their clothes and preserved life as long as they were able by feeding on the skins they wore. But even this wretched resource failed them, and horrible to relate, these poor creatures sustained themselves by feeding on the flesh of their children. On arrival at the factory [Hudson's Bay post], the distracted Indian whose heart overflowed with grief, told this melancholy affair to the English Governor with all its effecting circumstances, which was received with a loud laugh. The poor savage, with a look of amazement, said in his broken English, This is no laughing talk, and went his way…" [5] *

For the Moiseo as with their northern Algonquian kinfolk, along with any other Indian groups including one or two Siouan-speaking bands [such as the Assiniboine who at the later date of circa, 1660 were also roaming this harsh, stony, country of the north], this was for the present, the reality of their miserable existence. Indeed, there are several stories in Upper Great Lake's Algonquian traditional lore, which tell of abandoning their own children in order that the parents could survive during the severest time of winter, and even today the Cheyennes recall that whilst inhabiting this inhospitable north Land, "…*The people were always cold and hungry.*" [6]

Some scholars might argue that the previous analysis and conclusions concerning these early periods of Cheyenne migration, have been misconstrued from the start, and that the regions referred to in tradition cannot really be located any further east or north than southwestern Ontario and northern Minnesota. As a consequence, it has often been assumed that the lake around which the Cheyennes once resided for a prolonged period is that of Rainy Lake and its associated Falls, and not Lake Taureau; the Mattawin River, or the more famous cataract at Niagara. We know, however, that the Cheyenne Nation is composed of at least four original linguistically related tribes, the TsisTsisTsas [Cheyenne-proper], Omissis, Pipe-Stem-Men and Suhtaio. It must be accepted then, that at one time there also existed four separate migration stories relating to the period when these same groups were independent of each other. The obvious scenario is that since their amalgamation into a united body sometime during the early eighteen-thirties, their separate traditions have become fused into one, the resulting conglomerate version now sufficing for the Nation as a whole. Once again the archaeological record appears to substantiate this assumption.

* Both Cree and Chippewa traditions have several stories of practicing cannibals among their peoples, which refer to this same period in their respective histories, whilst the Iroquois-proper tribes were forever feasting upon slain enemies; according to the early "Jesuit" accounts. The Shawnee on the other hand, had among them a society known as "Man-eaters" who ritually ate the flesh of their dead enemies, and the Shawnee were close cousins to the Moiseo, Omissis and Suhtaio. In addition, during the Russian famine of Samara in the winter of 1921, it was not uncommon for starving parents among the Tartar, Kazakh and Bashkir northern Asiatic peoples, to eat their own children in order to survive.

It has been noted in an earlier chapter that the people responsible for the so-called *"Middle Laurel complex,"* which had its origins in northeastern Manitoba and northern Ontario beginning around the date AD.800, evidently spread south and southeast, though still above the Upper Great Lakes. By the date AD.1100, a large segment of these peoples had reached the St. Lawrence valley, whereabouts a new cultural complex emerged termed *"Point Peninsular"* in the archaeological record. This latter complex shows only slight variations to that of *Middle Laurel*, which suggests that both complexes are very closely related and likely belonged to the same cultural group, ostensibly of Algonquian stock.

Earlier, at the same time as *Middle Laurel* had been expanding outward from its source in northeastern Manitoba and northern Ontario, other groups from the same ethnic origin, rather than join the main route of movement southeast above the Upper Great Lakes, instead spread directly south into southern Ontario and into northern Minnesota, where we find pottery shards and artifacts belonging to what the archaeologist has since referred to as the *"Blackduck complex."* Thus *Blackduck* is also a branch of *Middle Laurel* with but slight variations, although distinguishable from that of *Point Peninsular*. This should not be surprising, for such distinguishing features as are apparent, merely represent influence from other ethnic groups, i.e. Iroquoian and Siouan with whom both *Point Peninsular* and *Blackduck* peoples respectively later came in contact. The importance here is that the three complexes mentioned above, all are of Algonquian origin.

By circa, AD.1300, *Blackduck* peoples had expanded east, abutting the northern shore of Lake Superior and evidently, to some degree merged with those of *Point Peninsular*, for here the cultural remains show many mixed traits attributable to both complexes. This, of course, is what one would expect if peoples including the proto-historic Monsoni and Cheyenne [Moiseo] who must have been included among *Point Peninsular* peoples, had at a later date, traced a second route of migration, this time backtracking along a route compatible with their earlier line of march from the northwest, and in so doing, re-located somewhere in the vicinity of Sault St. Marie at the northeastern outlet of Lake Superior, and therefore, then in close proximity to the most eastern outposts of their *Blackduck* cousins.

Soon after the last mentioned date of circa, 1300, there suddenly appeared yet another cultural complex now termed *Selkirk* in the archaeological record. This seems to have been a progressive form of *Laurel,* having likewise originated in central Ontario, but with as many traits of *Point Peninsular* and *Blackduck* to be associated with these two complexes also. The current dates for *Selkirk* begin around AD.1300, and extend well into the historic period of around AD.1650. As with its counterparts, *Selkirk* is of Algonquian origin.

This seems to suggest that *Selkirk* was, in fact, the result of an amalgamation of slightly different cultures brought both by Algonquian newcomers from the east above the Upper Great Lakes, and certain *Blackduck* peoples from the central and northern regions of Minnesota. Together they enjoined with small remnants of the old original *Laurel* group, that had remained in situ in northern and central Ontario, long after the vast majority of their ancient kinfolk had left.

These *Selkirk* peoples included in their late historic time, those known as Swampy Cree [Muskegon], Plains Cree and Bush Cree, but during an earlier period between circa, A.D. 1450 and

1500, included among their number if only peripherally, the Monsoni and, of course, our subjects, the latter's Moiseo cousins. *Blackduck* peoples on the other hand, seem, initially, to have included those several Algonquian-speaking bands which, at a much later date, came together under the name Suhtaio who were then closely associated with the several proto-Arapahoe bands and thus, together, were responsible for the most eastern branch of the *Blackduck* complex.

Having said this, one should bear in mind that when Cheyenne informants related what they supposed was their people's migration tradition to white anthropologists and missionaries late in the nineteenth and early twentieth century, it depended upon whether the informants were of Suhtaio or TsisTsisTsas ancestry with regard to what version they related, and in what order of sequence they gave their people's various locations during their migration history. The fact that both people's ancient and proto-historic environments were similar - if not seemingly identical - has erroneously been interpreted as referring to one continuous sequence of location for all Cheyenne-speaking peoples, when the truth of the matter is, that whilst the Cheyenne-proper were residing in one place, their close cousins the Suhtaio were residing in another.

A pertinent example of this can be found at a later date, during which time the TsisTsisTsas or Cheyenne-proper were positioned in west-central Minnesota, at the same time as the Suhtaio were entrenched on the edge of, or near the northeastern shore of Lake Nipigon in east central Ontario north of Lake Superior. The respective environments and lifestyle of both groups at that time, were similar, as had been the case in earlier years. But as each group retained separate traditions regarding their respective places of habitat along their separate migration routes, then the TsisTsisTsas account is referring specifically to locations of an earlier or later period, when compared to the traditional locations of the Suhtaio.

So it is, that although fragments of various tribal traditions indicate a very early Cheyenne residence in the far northeast, ostensibly, somewhere on the north side of the St. Lawrence, that country's topography and the people's cultural description of that time, is also compatible with the people's later period of residence when in central and southern Ontario and in northern Minnesota. Because of this, these different areas of habitat - if not indeed other locations also - have since become confused, and as a result, after the amalgamation of the four original component groups which later comprised the Cheyenne Nation of historic time, they have since come to infer only one prolonged period of habitation in lands immediately north of the headwaters of the Upper Mississippi.

The whole essence of our study has shown this to be the case, as other much more easterly locations are indicated in Cheyenne tradition, which sugest that our previous deductions and conclusions are most consistent with the evidence at hand.

- 0 - 0 - 0 - 0 - 0 - 0 - 0 - 0 - 0 - 0 - 0 - 0 - 0 - 0 - 0 - 0 - 0 - 0 - 0 -

LEFT TO RIGHT, CHEYENNE CHIEFS SPOTTED-WOLF AND CRAZY-HEAD.
[SMITHSONIAN INSTITUTION. BUREAU OF ETHNOLOGY. WASHINGTON. D.C.]

PART 2.

"THE TIME OF DOGS."

NORTHERN CHEYENNE, CHIEF TWO MOONS. [1878].
[Courtesy; Bureau of Ethnology, Washington D. C.]

CHAPTER 14.

IN THE MARSHLANDS OF MINNESOTA.

How long the Moiseo roamed the lake-infested country of central Ontario we cannot be sure, although tribal tradition recalls, *"...It was a very long time."* [1]

As mentioned earlier, most present-day Cheyennes regard the district about the headwaters of the Upper Mississippi in northern Minnesota as being their earliest home. An assumption which has been taken to mean that the TsisTsisTsas and even the Suhtaio people, actually originated in that area. But this is not so, and after more careful inquiry into that Nation's traditions, coupled with certain archaeological evidence, it is clearly seen that this was merely the earliest habitat remembered by Cheyennes, after becoming a distinct tribal unit independent from all other Algonquians.

Before this, the Cheyenne-proper, i.e. Moiseo, had evidently regarded themselves as an Algonquian conglomerate including remnants of Monsoni, Wheskerinni and Montagnais affiliation, even though for many years previously as a scattered yet allied group, the Moiseo had followed their own whims of fortune and direction.

This period of prolonged Moiseo independence whilst in central Ontario, certainly finalized the divorce of the latter from any parent Cree and Chippewa relatives and from any confederation they may once have recognized with old-time allies in the east. So in later years when the Moiseo met with other Algonquian-speakers, they initially regarded them as alien.

It is then self-evident that the Moiseo must have roamed the aforesaid cold, inhospitable lake country for an extensive period – in excess of one hundred years. Long enough to abandon virtually everything concerning their people's earlier alliances and history save the few terse statements already referred to in present-day Cheyenne tradition.

Perhaps before becoming a separate entity, the Cheyennes considered their history as not being that of the Nation itself. It is just as likely, though, that whilst inhabiting this northern country prior to the middle of the sixteenth century, few if any important events had occurred to be considered worth remembering in their traditions, other than the people's day to day life-style. Indeed, only after the period in question do we at last have information in their own and other tribe's traditions, which is more precise and detailed.

Of one thing we can be sure, these early Cheyennes were not influenced by the new religious concepts and cultural traits which, during the late sixteenth and early seventeenth centuries, were being adopted by other Algonquian tribes to the south and east, or surely they would have retained much stronger historic Algonquian elements in their religious expression than were observed at a later date when roaming the Great Plains west of the Missouri. Elements reminiscent of the *"Midewiwin"* religion, perhaps, so important a ceremony in Eastern Cree, Chippewa and some other Central Algonquian cultures, and vestiges of which could still be found at a late date in certain Suhtaio ceremonies such as those connected to the Sun-Dance and Sacred

Hat. But the Suhtaio, as will be seen below, remained in close contact with a number of Eastern and Central Algonquian groups for many years after the Moiseo had become isolated and totally independent.

Religious beliefs and sacred rites do not change dramatically over night, so to speak, but like language change slowly, unless contact with revolutionary theology and concepts propel them. The Moiseo whilst in central Ontario were in virtual isolation, and even after more than one-hundred years since disassociating from others of their stock, i.e., after leaving the area around Sault St. Marie, they still held rigidly to their distinct old-time beliefs along with attendant ceremonies, while at the same time they evolved a dialect diverse to all other Algonquian-speakers.

It will become evident as our study progresses that some foreign influence [albeit at a later date than the people's residence in Ontario and northern Minnesota], did play an important part in the later-day fundamentals of Cheyenne sacred rituals and culture. We know, for instance, that the Moiseo along with any breakaway band or bands there may have been when residing in the vicinity of the Upper Mississippi, were then in close harmonious contact with several Siouan-speaking peoples from whom certain innovations were most likely adopted. This was not, however, until after circa. AD.1540, and before that date the Moiseo as a distinct tribal group, still retained strong elements of their archaic theology and continued to do so, even after their embracing the new cults of the Sacred Arrows and Sacred Hat. Even a century later, when their Central and Eastern Algonquian cousins were in the process of modifying their own religious practices by the absorption of new ideas, originating from a somewhat misconstrued interpretation of what white European missionaries were then teaching them, the Moiseo and their offshoots continued still, to adhere to their ancient beliefs and ceremonies.

When in central and southern Ontario the lifestyle of the Moiseo, as with all other Algonquian bands north and northwest of Lake Superior, was likely to have been one of routine; traveling about in canoes or dugouts during the summer months and hibernating in small family groups throughout the harsh winters in order to survive on the meager food supply. The finding of which was so constant and grueling a task, that there was probably little time, or indeed the incentive to inaugurate elaborate religious ceremonies, or even to contemplate the dubious pleasures of going to war.

In that *"Northern Land"* of tradition, the small Moiseo associated bands which, at a later date, came together to create the single entity known as *Cheyenne,* then included several remnants of related but different peoples. It will be recalled that since fleeing the Lower St. Lawrence country almost two centuries earlier, they then comprised a conglomerate of refugees from the main tribal groups of Wheskerinni, Montagnais, Monsoni and Moiseo, the last named, of course, being the predominant faction. Generally, these small remnants had remained in close association with each other to form a collective intermixed by marriage and blood, and whilst residing in central and southern Ontario far from other Algonquian-speaking groups who were thought to be alien, the Moiseo and their refugee associates became all but isolated in their existence save some little contact with the Monsoni, However, over the course of time, ties between the Moiseo and Monsoni which had originally joined them together as confederates when starting their journey toward the northwest, became progressively weakened and the Moiseo became more distinct to others of their Algonquian stock relatives. Of these other Algonquian-speaking groups inhabiting adjacent territory to the Moiseo during that same period, the forebears of the historic Plains Cree, Blackfoot and Arapahoe must be included.

The Plains Cree who were later offshoots from a conglomerate of Monsoni and Muskegon [Swampy Cree] ancestors, recalled that when they themselves reached the western limits of central Ontario, seemingly during the early decades of the seventeenth century, the Blackfoot and with them the latter's later confederated tribes of Bloods and Piegan, were entrenched near where the city of Winnipeg now stands in east-central Manitoba about the junction of the Red and Assiniboine rivers, while the Arapahoe for their part, recalled their people as once having resided in southeastern Manitoba, southern Ontario and the northwestern region of Minnesota adjoining the Red River of the North at around the same period, and thus were within easy contact distance of the Blackfoot. The Arapahoe were then one group with the Atsina and they further declare that Cheyennes were close by. Eventually, say the Arapahoe, they and the Cheyennes left this district together moving west, until they entered the short-grass buffalo Plains across the Missouri River.

Cheyenne tradition does not dispute that their tribe or a part of it, was once in close proximity to the Arapahoe prior to their crossing the Missouri, but are adamant that they and the Arapahoe moved as separate bodies and at different periods in time. Furthermore, say the Cheyennes, their two peoples did not become confederates until after the Cheyennes had entered the Coteau des Prairies of present-day North Dakota west of the Red River of the North. It does appear, though, from the archaeological record, that the Arapahoe may have had a degree of friendly contact with Cheyenne-speaking peoples during the early years of their proto-historic period of circa, 1600. But it is not feasible that they ever constituted a confederated body when residing immediately west and northwest of the Upper Great Lakes. Diversity of dialect and conflicting traditions of early culture tend to confound such an assumption by indicating a far longer period of separation. If indeed, these early Cheyennes and Arapahoe had been in such close and harmonious contact as Arapahoe tradition asserts during the later period of both tribes' evolution, then how was it after only a little more than forty years of separation, that is, between the period of supposed Cheyenne and Arapahoe interaction about the Lower course of Red River [circa, 1700] and their confederation as allies in the Plains west of the Missouri [circa, 1740], neither Cheyenne or Arapahoe could understand each other's dialect? The Suhtaio who were separated from all Cheyenne-proper bands for at least four centuries [during which time they only made superficial contact in battle], did have some difficulty understanding each other when at last they came together as friends. They could, nonetheless, communicate verbally with tolerable success, even though both groups pronounced many words differently.

It must be that the Arapahoe and the several Blackfoot tribes also, had disassociated themselves from the Moiseo group at a very early date. Probably during the initial time of their migration from the Keewatin district of northern Saskatchewan and northwestern Manitoba, out of what was then the center of occupation for the ancient peoples of the *Shield Archaic* and *Middle Laurel* complex areas, which in tradition is referred to as "The Old Turtle Land of the North." In

135

reality, the Arapahoe although closely connected dialectically to the Algonquian Miami of the Delaware conglomerate of peoples [Goddard;1978], and who in their early proto-historic time of circa, 1500 were likely resident in the Green Bay area of central Wisconsin, appear to be descendants of those Algonquian groups - including the Suhtaio - which together went southeast from the Keewatin district in the north and left their cultural traits in southern Ontario and northeastern Minnesota. These remains are known to the archaeologist as the *Mero* and *Blackduck* complexes respectively of the so-called *Early Woodland* era, with a starting date between AD. 600 and 800.

The *Mero* complex found predominately in the aforesaid Green Bay Wisconsin region, includes cord-wrapped, grit-tempered ceramics as in early Suhtaio ware – in contrast to shell-tempered ceramics of adjacent areas during the same *Early Woodland* period - and also include sites that are intermixed with those of *Blackduck* indicating a harmonious relationship between the people of both complexes. Here in the northeastern Minnesota region, *Blackduck,* I believe, represents ancestral Suhtaio, while those of the associated *Mero* complex of northwestern Wisconsin likely represent early Arapahoe and Miami groups. It will be shown in a later chapter how *Blackduck* was later connected to the archaeological complex known as *South Arvilla* of central and western Minnesota, which dates between 200 B.C. and A.D. 1700, and in its late period seems to indicate proto-Cheyennes as having been jointly responsible. The proto-Arapahoe for their part, gradually moved in a northwestern direction from the Wisconsin country and into southwestern Ontario and south-eastern Manitoba, away from their old-time Miami and Suhtaio associates. At an earlier date, however, owing to their location in northeastern Minnesota and western Wisconsin, the ancestral Suhtaio and Arapahoe in association with the Miami, would have had but little if any contact with Moiseo Cheyenne-proper speaking peoples, who then were already far to the northwest in central Ontario.

The late proto-historic Blackfoot were, in all likelihood, the descendants of another group from the *Middle Laurel* complex of Algonquian-speakers. They were later responsible for *Duck Bay* cultural remains, found in the vicinity of Lake Winnipeg and Lake Winnibigosis in east-central Manitoba which have a starting date of between AD 1400 and 1500. *Duck Bay* in fact, appears to be the precursor of the later-date cultural aspect known as *Old Woman Phase* in southeastern Saskatchewan which is associated with proto-historic Blackfoot-speaking peoples.

The truth is, that these three northwestern Algonquian-speaking groups of Moiseo, Arapahoe and Blackfoot in their proto-historic times, merely constituted the most western manifestation of their stock, while at the same time their linguistic kinfolk such as the Suhtaio, Fox and Sauk, were spreading southwest from Sault St. Marie into the woodlands of Wisconsin, Ohio and Michigan south of the Upper Great Lakes.

Evidently then, whilst in west-central Ontario and southeastern Manitoba, the Moiseo, Arapahoe and Blackfoot took individual routes of migration toward the Western Great Plains during various periods in time. It is not surprising that all three groups should have temporarily halted their advances on the peripheries of the open treeless lands stretching west from the southern

SOUTHERN ONTARIO & MISSISSIPPI HEADWATERS REGION. Circa, A.D. 1600.
[From an original map by the Author].

part of Ontario and the Lower course of Red River. As at that time the horse was unknown among them so the people as pedestrian hunters, were not able to follow as nomads in pursuit of the buffalo herds. Certainly these pedestrian bands which then had only the bow and arrow and stone-headed spears and clubs, would have been reluctant to leave completely the comparative safety and shelter of the wooded country with its fish-filled lakes and streams, unless compelled to do so.

As a result, after many years of wandering with most of their time taken up in an incessant search for subsistence, these peoples found themselves again in close proximity to one another. Although when in central and southern Ontario contact would have been at best of a superficial nature, as neither tribe today has any recollection in their traditions of an inter-action with one another during that period, albeit they must have been fully aware of each other's existence. It would appear that whilst in eastern Manitoba and the central and southern parts of Ontario, the only things these groups had in common - other than being of the Algonquian family - was that all were poor pedestrian foragers; hunting small game and fishing in the myriad of lakes which surrounded them. During the winter months their camps were probably "snowed in;" the occupants suffering from extreme cold and privation throughout that season's duration. As a consequence these remote peoples, who at that period constituted a number of very small, widely scattered extended family groups or clans which, in later years, formed the basis for their separate autonomous tribes of the late historic time, remained virtually isolated from each other, and each on their own volition spread forth along their separate chosen migration routes, while at the same time they evolved even more distinct dialects and tribal peculiarities one from the other.

The Arapahoe statement therefore, regarding an alleged early inter-action with Cheyenne-proper peoples either in central and southern Ontario or northern Minnesota, most likely refers to a much later date when both peoples occupied the rolling, treeless prairies in the Coteau district of the eastern Dakotas west of Red River. Indeed, all the available evidence suggests that the people actually referred to in this Arapahoe tradition were Suhtaio, who during an earlier century had been in the company of some proto-Arapahoe bands after migrating south from the old *Middle Laurel* complex center in the north. The Suhtaio had then travelled southeast from the southern Ontario district and finally, settled in mid-eastern Minnesota and mid-western Wisconsin, and where indeed, are found the archaeological complexes of *Blackduck* and *Mero* respectively. Their Moiseo cousins conversely, had migrated southeast from the Keewatin region to the James Bay area and thence, as previously explained in earlier chapters, into the St. Lawrence River valley as members of the great Delaware host of Algonquian peoples.

What, though, now induced these scattered camps of Moiseo Cheyenne-proper peoples to migrate south from the Ontario lakes district during the early 1540s; when to all intent and purpose, they had been happy to traverse the whole of the central and southern parts of that province without fear of harassment for a century or more? We might suspect that one or more specific circumstance had occurred beyond their control and which in turn, effected the people's condition and lifestyle sufficiently to propel them into yet another - albeit sudden - phase of migration.

Hostile pressure there may have been, although unlikely in their remote environment. Even if these proto-Cheyennes had already separated from their Cree forebears at that date - as their traditions imply - and become subject to attacks from a belligerent group of mixed Bush and Muskegon Cree seceders later known as Plains Cree, then it would have been natural for these Cheyennes, being comparatively weak in number and not recognized for their fighting ability, to have retreated due west into the Lake Winnipeg region. This region, ostensibly, was sparsely occupied at that period save certain Blackfoot-speaking bands who themselves, owing to Cree attacks, did migrate west at or just prior to this same time of Cheyenne upheaval, and thus they may have welcomed their Cheyenne cousins into the area to help resist the common enemy. Instead, the Cheyennes migrated south into the northern and central Minnesota country still within easy reach of the Cree, and where foreign peoples such as Hidatsa, Sioux and Suhtaio; all of whom potentially hostile, were already entrenched.

The Moiseo must then have continued in harmonious relationship with the Monsoni Cree, which would be consistent with the oft-time repeated assertion in Cheyenne tradition, that during the Cheyenne's early days of their evolution, the Monsoni were always regarded as *"a friendly tribe."*

The Cheyennes own explanation for this particular movement from the north, is, however, that they vacated their hearths in favor of more provident and environmentally hospitable lands to the south.

This statement is corroborated somewhat by the event of yet another severe climatic change, which occurred in the North Country during the first half of the sixteenth century.

It has been noted in an earlier chapter how, from the date 1350 or thereabouts, a comparatively warm period which persisted until circa, 1450, had allowed the Moiseo and others of their Algonquian relatives such as the Monsoni and Swampy Cree, to claim new hunting grounds in territory northwest of Lake Superior after abandoning the area around Sault St. Marie, and thus encouraged the Moiseo to move even further northwest into the central Ontario region. Since circa, 1450, however, the climate in the latter area had already altered appreciably; having become much dryer and decidedly colder. This episode which persisted for another hundred years, was the severest period of cold during what is known as the Neo-Atlantic or Little-Ice-Age and which continues in milder form to the present day.

As a consequence during the severest cold period, game in the central and southern Ontario country became scarce as animals migrated to warmer climes, and the environment could no longer support its human inhabitants in the manner to which they had become accustomed. Such an event must have been very closely connected with any major population shift; not only in the northern areas of both the eastern and Midwest states, but certainly, in the eastern and central Canadian provinces also. Indeed, there is strong evidence to suggest that the Arapahoe group of peoples, who we know from the archaeological record were then roaming western Ontario after having recently migrated in a north-westerly direction from western Wisconsin, undertook a further migration around this date. Only that their route of exit led southwest, which took them into what are the southern parklands of Manitoba and the northern part of North Dakota. In their turn, the Blackfoot-speaking groups also moved, they going in a south-westerly direction from the area around Lake Winnipeg and into the southeastern Saskatchewan region.

So it was, no doubt, the same reason which spurred the Arapahoe and Blackfoot movements away from the eastern Manitoba and central Ontario country, that initiated a further Moiseo Cheyenne migration, albeit that they themselves moved due south.

The above given date of circa, 1550 is but an estimation for the severest period of this particular occurrence of climatic and environmental variation in the *"Northland."* Several years - perhaps a decade - predated its most profound phase, so that the Moiseo Cheyennes and others may well have started their respective migrations a number of years before the middle of the aforesaid century. Thus by the early 1540s the Moiseo, along with any offshoot bands there may then have been, were likely settled with a degree of permanency in northern Minnesota, somewhere not far south or southwest of the marsh and lakes district just above the headwaters of the Upper Mississippi and known today as "Big Bog."

It is regrettable that other than our earlier deductions in this and the previous chapter, we have no information in contemporary documented sources regarding Cheyenne-speaking peoples in central and southern Ontario, and the archaeological record only tentatively associates any people belonging to a particular cultural complex with those of a recognized tribe of the late-historic period. Neither can we properly calculate a specific length of residence for Cheyenne-speaking bands in northern Minnesota until further phases of that Nation's traditional migration history have been determined and analyzed. So once again we must turn to the traditional account from the Cheyennes themselves, coupled with fragments of information from various foreign tribes then in contact with them.

In essence, Cheyenne tradition states that when finally their people moved away from the aforesaid cold, stony, lake-infested area of the far north, they migrated south or southwest in canoes. At length, they came to a very flat land which appeared to be flooded, for trees were standing in the water and the water itself was filled with very tall grass and reeds. On the border of this "flooded land,"

"The people came to a halt and went into camp where they remained for a short while." [2]

Eventually, so the story continues, some young men were selected by the chiefs to go ahead in their canoes, further into the marsh and swamp land to the south, for such it was, in order to discover what lay beyond. The reeds and grasses were so tall and abundant and the area so large that before the scouts started out they loaded their canoes with many long poles. Later, as they plied their way cautiously across the waters in and out among the clumps of reeds, every so often they would plant one of the poles upright in the soft mud bottom, in order to mark their route and enable them to find their way back. For several days the scouts meandered through the marshlands until at last, they came to a large, open lake with a great expanse of prairie on its far side. Hereupon, the scouts retraced their route and by following the line of poles, safely returned to their people.

When the chiefs were told of the large lake and its adjacent prairie, they decreed that all the people should move toward that place. The very next day, everybody loaded their belongings and other paraphernalia into their dugouts and canoes and started out in a body across the marshes guided by the line of poles. Upon reaching the lake shore, the people set up a permanent camp and thereabouts they lived for many years.

The Cheyennes recall that they were happy when living around this lake and far more comfortable than they had been in earlier years. Most of their time was spent either fishing in the lake or hunting coon, skunk, deer and sometimes moose in the adjacent prairies. Wild fowl was plentiful, including cranes, geese and various varieties of duck, while during the autumn large flocks alighted on the lake where they remained throughout the winter months, and come spring, the birds flew over the Cheyenne lodges on their return flight to the north. Before the flight north, however, the people would gather large quantities of birds` eggs, and in summer, they caught many fledglings too young to fly and older birds which having lost their feathers in the annual molt, could not escape by flight and so also were taken in great number.

Tribal tradition at this point does not mention buffalo as being an important food source, although small herds did frequent the area and were regularly killed for food, clothing and domestic utensils. Deer, it is said, were much more abundant and during the winter, the Cheyennes would go on foot far out into the adjacent prairie in order to hunt. At such times the women and children would surround small herds of antelope, deer or elk and drive them into deep snow drifts, whereupon, the men-folk would come up and kill the animals one by one with bone or stone-tipped arrows, stone-headed clubs and spears. Some distance from this Cheyenne village by the lake, so tradition continues, there stood a group of stony hills jutting up from the prairie floor and here, skunks abounded in great number. This place was named appropriately "Skunk Hill" by the Cheyennes, and the great skunk hunts which took place around these hills are yet remembered in their stories. On such occasions the whole tribe took part and as the animals were killed, the carcasses were heaped together to form a huge pile. Afterwards the dead skunks were laid out in rows and counted then divided equally among the people, and several centuries later, the Cheyennes were still using the phrase *"To make a Skunk"* as a simile for making a pile of anything.

The people during that period were entirely pedestrian and packed what game they killed along with their little lodges, on the backs of their women and their dogs. Wood was scarce in this prairie land so for fuel when on extended hunting expeditions, the womenfolk would often use dried buffalo chips instead, or gather up armfuls of very long grass peculiar to the region; bind it tightly into a twisted bundle like a faggot, so that when lit at one end it would take a long time to burn down.

Having previously deduced that before crossing the extensive marshland, the Cheyennes had roamed the cold, stony, lake country northwest of Lake Superior and north of the present-day state of Minnesota, then the *"large lake"* and adjacent prairie referred to in tradition - even though vague in description - can nonetheless, be pinpointed with a fair degree of accuracy.

Certainly, the only sizable expanse of marshland comparable to that mentioned by the Cheyennes and located south of or on the peripheries of the southern part of the Ontario Lake district, is the extensive marsh area of northwestern Minnesota known as "Big Bog." Within this area and to the immediate southeast are numerous lakes of varying size, which include those known today as Lake Winnibigoshish [previously known to the Indians as Little-Muddy-Water-Lake], Leech Lake and Bowstring Lake among others. Each of these expanses connect with the headwater branches of the Upper Mississippi and by canoe route with Rainy Lake and Lake of the Woods to the north and northwest respectively. It is indicative that Lake Winnibigosis was once called *Rush Lake* and was very marsh-like in its appearance. In places the rushes and rice-grass extended clear across it and was a typical feature of the whole country in that lake's vicinity, which during earlier times, was literally covered with very tall reeds, marsh rice and grass. The nineteenth century historian and traveler Henry Schoolcraft, after exploring the area in 1820 wrote, *"Sitting in a canoe you can see nothing but the waving grasses; the sky and the birds, and you have the feeling of being lost in a great sea."* [3]

Only the double expanse of Upper and Lower Red Lake, however, actually fits the description of the people's place of habitat next to a large lake and adjacent prairie, by boasting a vast prairie land abutting the Red River of the North on the west, then stretching east before giving way to the thickly-timbered and lake and marsh lands of the Upper Mississippi region in the central and northern parts of present-day Minnesota. In corroboration of the Cheyenne traditional account regarding this period in the early 1540s, we know that buffalo were not in any great number in the prairie lands east of Red River in the northern part of Minnesota, although small herds could frequently be found during certain seasons in the west-central part of that state. Certainly, this same prairie land at a later date was known to white colonials as "The Sioux buffalo prairies," owing to the habit of various Dakota bands to hunt such animals in the region. Generally, though, it is a country of sandy soil and rank grass with groves of timber here and there, while the grass, it was said, was so tall one could, *"…approach buffalo very near before firing on them."* [4]

Deer and antelope on the other hand were particularly numerous, supplying not only food but hides for clothing, along with bone and sinew for the manufacture of tools, weapons and domestic utensils and appliances. Many varieties of small game were also in great abundance, whilst in the country immediately west of Red River during the period in question; the land was teeming with buffalo. Pedestrian hunters with stone-tipped arrows and spears - could and did - cross the aforesaid river and subsist for lengthy sojourns entirely on that animal's meat alone.

It is unlikely then, that the aforesaid lake referred to in this part of Cheyenne tradition, could actually imply a point any further south or east of that known today as Lower Red Lake. To the south in the valley of the Minnesota River and prairie country across that stream to the south and east, buffalo were plentiful and we know that as early as circa, 1500 if not before, various Sioux or Dakota bands in large number, were already firmly entrenched on the east side of the Upper Mississippi and along most of that river's eastern tributaries; particularly from a point just south of the Upper forks of that river and extending as far north as the Falls of St. Anthony near the mouth of the Minnesota, where the twin towns of St. Paul and Minneapolis now stand.

Both the Sioux and Cheyennes state emphatically, that their two peoples did not meet each other until after the Sioux had undertaken a further migration north into the Mississippi headwaters country. This event, traditionally, was after at least a part of the Cheyenne people had already moved further south to the middle course of the Minnesota River, and which latter movement was

TRUMAN MICHELSON`S NORTHERN CHEYENNE INFORMANT, AMERICAN HORSE.
[Photograph from Julia E. Tuell in "Women and Warriors of the Plains." Macmillan. 1996.]

143

certainly after the date 1640. We must not forget that Cheyenne tradition clearly states [as noted in an earlier chapter] that the people's habitat close to the large lake with its adjoining prairie, was occupied before the people moved south to a *Blue River* flowing through a *Blue Earth Country,* which aptly describes the district about the Great Elbow Bend of the Minnesota River. The lake referred to in tradition is not intended to be consistent with either Lake of the Woods or Rainy Lake in the far northern part of the state, as both these watery expanses are respectively, to the north and northeast of "Big Bog." Added to this, there is no great stretch of prairie land anywhere near their shores. Also during the time in question, certain Cree peoples were then resident around both those lakes, and the Cheyennes assert that they themselves were then independent from all other tribal groups, having by that time become separated from the Cree. There are a few additional clues in the guise of comparisons, which also help to establish Cheyenne-speaking peoples as once residing in the vicinity of Lower Red Lake.

At first, say the Cheyennes, when in the country about this lake, they constructed their lodges in a similar fashion as had been employed in the north, i.e., an oval, sapling, framework, plastered with a mixture of stones and clay with a central smoke hole. But soon after their arrival as the climate proved warmer than in the northern country, the people built lighter lodges also in the form of a frame of bent poles, but with the gaps covered instead with grass, sheets of birch bark or mats of woven rushes, although sometimes, the roof was still covered with a stone-based clay being reminiscent of a *"swallow's nest."* In general, though, most of these early Cheyenne lodges resembled the small elliptical structures composed of bark and saplings once employed profusely by all Eastern Dakota bands. In other instances, they were constructed of tightly inter-woven twigs and saplings with a polished clay or dried mud oval roof, [29] as indeed, was the style of dwelling employed by old-time Hidatsa peoples who once resided in adjoining areas in the same northern Minnesota country. These were the lodges used in winter and were grouped together to form small villages. Come summer the Cheyennes usually left these lodges and in their stead, constructed less durable shelters fashioned from woven willow shoots which were left un-plastered to allow ventilation. When the people went off on their occasional extended hunting expeditions far out into the adjacent prairie, they made much smaller, temporary lodges of bent poles covered with reed mats or animal skins. These summer lodges, it is said, were so light and small that they were easily built and dismantled; packed on a dog's back and transported. [30] Tradition also recalls the type of dogs the people owned during this period, of which the late Northern Cheyenne historian, John Stands-in-Timber said,

> "..That was the time when our people first acquired dogs....These animals were more wolf than dog, and were semi-wild with exceptionally long bellies unlike any breed seen since, but in appearance were somewhat similar to the present-day Irish wolf hound...These were the first of such animals that the Cheyennes ever possessed and properly domesticated as working beasts." [5]

Thus this second phase of Cheyenne traditional history is referred to as, "The Time of Dogs." It applies to that people's period of residence south of the Ontario Lake country, ostensibly, in the vicinity of both Upper and Lower Red Lake. In corroboration of the early styles of dwelling then employed by Cheyennes, we have the Southern Cheyenne "Sacred Arrow" priest Red-Hat's assertion, which describes these old-time habitations as follows;

"In the old, old times, even before they [Cheyennes], had dogs, the houses were built of the shoots of a kind of willow, the twigs of which are reddish and very tough. These houses must have been tightly built, for it is said, they used to moisten clay and mix it with pounded stone, with which they plastered the whole outside, leaving a round hole at the top. The Lower walls leaned in, and the roof leaned in still more and was rounded over." [6]

This description by Red-Hat is important, as it conforms exactly to an account in the "Jesuit Relations," penned from a verbal report from the explorers Pierre Radisson and his companion Des Grossillers in 1658 / 59 or thereabouts. Here the Jesuit account mentions that they,

"... visited the country of the "Nadwechiwec," [Sioux] and finally the "Poualak" [warriors], who with bows and arrows alone, make themselves as terrible to the western tribes, as the Iroquois with guns do to the eastern; The wood in their country is scarce and small in size, so they burn carbon de terre [buffalo chips or the like], and build lodges of skins; The more industrious make lodges of loam, like `swallow nests`.... " [7]

The account further mentions that there were 30 villages of *Poualaks* and that the explorers then visited the *Assinipoulak* - warriors of the rock - who lived beyond the *Nadouechiouek* [Sioux] 35 leagues from Lake *Alimibeg* [Nipigon]. The number of 30 Poualack villages in the above account, may well be a misprint for `three` and they could not have been either Sioux or Assiniboine, as both those peoples are mentioned separately. The *"Poualaks"* by implication, were then living near the Sioux in an open or sparsely wooded country; they were hunters of buffalo and were the same people who Radisson himself later referred to as the *"Nacion du Boeuf."* They utilized both skin lodges and earth-lodges and were found to be so closely aligned to the neighbouring Sioux [which would not have been the case if they were Assiniboine or Hidatsa, who during the second half of the seventeenth century, were at war with all Sioux groups.] that even Radisson sometimes called them *"sedentary Sioux."* From the above passage it does appear that the explorers, unwittingly, were most likely referring to Cheyenne-speaking peoples.

Further corroboration of an early habitat of our Cheyenne subjects along the shoreline of or in close proximity to Lower Red Lake, can also be had in both Hidatsa and Chippewa traditions.

Between the period circa, 1500 and circa, 1620, the Hidatsa-Crow group of Siouan stock, then occupied the Upper part of Minnesota state, predominantly in the Sandy Lake and White Earth areas and along certain western tributaries of the Upper Mississippi above the Crow Wing branch on that river's west side. These people then resided in permanent earth or mud-roofed timber-framed lodges, similar in appearance to those mentioned in Cheyenne tradition regarding their own style of shelter during their period of occupation in the same area.

In the late eighteenth century, the English explorer David Thompson then employed by the Hudson's Bay Company, was told by a resident in an Awaxawi Hidatsa village situated on the bank of the Knife River branch of the Upper Missouri, that during the days of the Awaxawi`s great, great grandfathers, their people,

> "....had possessed all the streams of the Red River, and head of the Mississippi, where the Wild Rice, and the Deer were plenty, but then the Bison and the Horse were not known to them. They lived many years this way how many they do not know, at length the Indians of the woods armed with guns which killed and frightened them, and iron weapons, frequently attacked them, and against those they had no defense...." [8]

Surely if these early Cheyennes had resided in the Red Lake's region for any significant length of time, then they must have been in contact with this Awaxawi-Hidatsa group and may, in fact, have adopted the idea of their new style of dwelling from them. Chippewa informants when relating their traditions to the mid-nineteenth century Chippewa historian Reverend William Warren, remembered well these old-time Hidatsa lodges in northern Minnesota, although it is not improbable that these traditions were also referring, again unwittingly, to the same style of lodges once constructed by Cheyennes when the latter resided in adjacent territory to the Hidatsa. The Chippewa account describes these old-time Hidatsa as follows,

> ".....a tribe who are known to the Ojibways [Chippewa], by the name of Gi-aucth-in-in-e-wug, signifying, "men of the olden time," and named by the French, Gros Ventre, [Hidatsa], claim to have been formerly possessors of the country from which the Mississippi takes its rise. Their old men relate [that] they were forced or driven from this country by the powerful Dakotas, who have in turn given way to the Ojibways, now its present possessors....." [9]

Further on Warren writes,

> "Wa-won-je-quon, the chief of the Red Lake Ojibways, relates that several years since [i.e., prior to 1853], while on a visit to the earthen wigwams of the Gi-aucth-in-in-wug or Gross Ventres [Hidatsa], he was informed by their old men that the smoke from their village once arose in the vicinity of Sandy Lake,. They showed him a piece of bark on which was very correctly marked the principal streams and lakes on the Upper Mississippi, and pointed him out, as the site of their former village, the entry of East Savannah river into the St. Louis, where the remains of their earthen lodges, now

covered by a forest of trees, are still discernible.... Groups of these mounds are to be seen on all the principal lakes in the Upper Mississippi country...." [10]

We also have the testimony of Joseph Medicine-Crow, present-day tribal historian of the Crow tribe [1999], who related a tale to the present author once told him by an old Crow warrior of the buffalo days named, Cold-Wind.

It was in 1932, Joe Medicine Crow said, that the old man Cold-Wind, then over ninety years of age, told him that when he, Cold-Wind was a much younger man, he had visited his relatives the Hidatsa and whilst there, met with a Chippewa Indian who took him much further east to his own place of residence in the northern part of Minnesota. Joe could not be sure, but he thought this place must have been one of the Chippewa reservations either at White Earth, Red Lake or Leech Lake. Whilst in the east, another old Chippewa who was recognized as the tribal historian, took Cold-Wind both north and east and pointed out to him Hidatsa village sites where, in olden times, the latter had built their permanent lodges made of earth and wood. This same Chippewa historian also showed Cold-Wind certain ridge tops, along which, he said, some of the old-time Hidatsa had sited their tepees, for not all their people preferred to live in permanent lodges.

Here the Chippewa historian was, perhaps, repeating a tradition which originally was also meant to include the close neighbours and friends of these old-time Hidatsa. Such as the early Cheyennes of that region who, in conjunction with Hidatsa testimony, state that their forefathers were then in friendly contact with each other and further, as is here suggested, they hunted the prairie lands adjacent to the Lakes and during which period, they lived in portable skin shelters as indeed, the Radisson account previously cited makes clear. Only many years later, after all Cheyenne-speaking groups had left the northern Minnesota country completely and the Chippewa met the Hidatsa in the latter`s earth-lodge villages along Knife River on the Upper Missouri, did the Chippewa assume that all old village ruins in the Mississippi headwaters district must be the remains of Hidatsa sites, not remembering that Cheyennes once inhabited the same region.

More substantial evidence than the above, however, is to be had in the archaeological record of the Lower Red Lakes and Mississippi headwaters country.

Slightly southeast of Lower Red Lake stands the township of *Black Duck*. This is important to our study, as the town has since lent its name to a particular type of pottery recently excavated in its vicinity, and as a consequence, termed the *"Blackduck"* focus by the archaeologist. Upon this pottery's peculiar traits and possible connections we will discourse later, yet it is relevant to note here that its peculiarities are decidedly of Algonquian origin and at a date, prior to both Cree and Chippewa infiltration into the northern Minnesota country. Much of this pottery's unique characteristics match another focus type found in an authenticated old Cheyenne settlement located on the Lower Bend of the Sheyenne River which rises in the northwest and flows south and east before emptying into the Red River of the North in the southeastern part of what is now the state of North Dakota. In addition, pottery shards from both these focuses show very strong similarities with yet another type known as *Sandy Lake,* the pottery shards of which, have been unearthed in old village sites once likely occupied by Cheyenne-speaking peoples along the Minnesota River.

147

These are compatible with shards pertaining to later sites of Cheyenne occupation in the Coteau des Prairies and even further west along the middle Missouri, where albeit at a much later date, Cheyenne peoples were entrenched in several permanent earth-lodge villages.

There are two recognized types of *Blackduck* pottery known as *North Blackduck* and *South Blackduck* respectively. Examples of the southern variation which also include aspects of the *Mero* complex, might be attributable to earlier Algonquian residents, such as proto-Arapahoe groups and the Suhtaio, while northern examples albeit of a later date but before circa, 1650 and which include aspects from the *Selkirk* [Cree] *complex,* should unquestionably be associated with early Cheyenne-proper manufacture. The Cheyennes themselves always declared that after leaving the cold, northern lake country and their entering the headwaters region of the Upper Mississippi, they acquired the art of making pottery. The Hidatsa were adept pottery makers from an early date and it was probably through contact with these latter, that the Cheyennes picked up the art. No doubt the Moiseo had fashioned a more primitive ware during an earlier time as members of the great Delaware Algonquian host, but had since either abandoned the practice whilst roaming the Ontario lakes country, or that the Hidatsa now introduced them to a more sophisticated technique. Certainly, as would appear from the scarcity of pottery fragments found in the Ontario regions, the old-time peoples thereof, customarily, manufactured their domestic vessels from birch bark, a recognized peculiarity still practiced among the northern Cree, Chippewa and Montagnais-Naskapi until recent times.

The area east of Red River of the North, including the Upper and Lower Red Lakes where, by circa, 1540 roamed those early Cheyenne-speaking bands, comprises that same area in which the cultural complexes known as *North Arvilla* and *South Arvilla* have been so designated by the archaeologist. These complexes taken together, span a lengthy period of between 300 BC., and A.D. 1700, with *South Arvilla* showing the later phase of the two. In essence, *Arvilla* includes interment burials and pottery and is cognate with the adjoining complexes of northern Minnesota and southern Ontario known as *Selkirk* and *North Blackduck* respectively. These last-named archaeological complexes are closely related to each other and represent, in the first instance, the ancestors of certain Cree groups, and in the second, combined Cheyenne and Suhtaio. With regard to *Arvilla* specifically, in 1974 the Osteologist Nancy Ossenberg, published a paper which compared the size of crania obtained from a number of archaeological sites in central and northern Minnesota, with individual crania of Native Americans belonging to the late historic period. Her findings were most convincing when attributing *Arvilla* skeletal remains to those people ancestral to late historic Cheyennes. This adds scientific substance to that tribe`s own oral traditions, which attest to their one-time residence in northern Minnesota. At the same time, such findings corroborate the assertion in this study that of old, Cheyennes resided in the Red Lakes region and the headwaters district of the Upper Mississippi, beginning around A.D. 1540.

The two separate *Arvilla* complexes designated as *North* and *South*, can easily be explained by the high probability that the first represents an amalgamation of Cree [Monsoni] and Cheyenne [Moiseo] by showing a close relationship to the adjacent *Selkirk* complex, while the second represents Cheyennes predominantly, but with an admixture of Suhtaio derivation originating from the *South Blackduck* cultural complex, although both *Blackduck* complexes also show themselves very close with *Arvilla*. This, however, can likewise be explained by *North Blackduck* representing a mixture of ancestral Cree, Chippewa and Suhtaio of northeast Minnesota, while that of *South Blackduck* surely represents combined ancestral Cheyenne and Suhtaio, albeit probably including components from neighbouring Hidatsa and Dakota Sioux archaeological inventories.

As noted earlier in this chapter, the so-called archaeological *Mero* complex of Green Bay, Wisconsin, probably represents an early Arapahoe - Suhtaio association, and we see that *Mero* is closely connected to *Blackduck* which must, therefore by definition, be related to *Arvilla* also. This does, though, indicate superficial contact at least, between Arapahoees and Cheyennes during their proto-historic periods of circa, 1600, when the Arapahoe were in southwestern Ontario and the Cheyennes in northwestern Minnesota.

- 0 - 0 - 0 - 0 - 0 - 0 - 0 - 0 - 0 - 0 - 0 - 0 - 0 - 0 - 0 - 0 -

CHAPTER. 15.

THE COMING OF THE *"SACRED ARROWS."*

The beginning of the period of Cheyenne residence in northern Minnesota, coincides with that given by Cheyenne informants for the supposed coming of their Sacred Arrow talismans. When, according to tribal tradition, *"There was famine and pestilence in all the northland."* [1]

This event - certainly as far as the Cheyennes are concerned - is the most important episode in their history. It appears to have occurred out of necessity, following a movement of the Moiseo and associated bands of proto-Cheyennes, south from the southern Ontario region and into the area around Lower Red Lake of west-central Minnesota.

It is not within the scope of the present study to give a detailed analysis of Cheyenne religion, although the coming of the Sacred Arrows is relevant here. Not only does their appearance corroborate the positioning of Cheyenne peoples in the Upper Mississippi country in the mid-sixteenth century, but they embody all that pertains to the Cheyenne people as a Nation. They have also been instrumental in subsequent Cheyenne migration and social organization since that time, and therefore, warrant a brief synopsis at this point.

It was during the mid-1540s ostensibly; plus or minus a few years, when the revered prophet and culture hero, Sweet-Medicine, brought the Sacred Arrows to the people wrapped in a kit-fox skin. Before this event, tribal tradition relates, the Cheyennes had no hard and fast laws and no elected chiefs to lead them. Only those who proved themselves the strongest ruled the people according to their own whims, which were often selfish and cruel. These Sacred Arrows [*Mahuts*] being four in number were, and still are, considered the most holy of objects the Cheyennes have ever possessed. They are still held in great reverence and awe, both as a symbol of the Nation's unity and of the people's continuance as a separate cohesive entity in an alien environment. The shafts of two of these 'Arrows' are painted black, and are regarded as mediums through which the great Ma'heo; the all-powerful Creator along with its associated supernatural powers of the "Above World" and "Below World," bestow their benevolence upon the people. These black painted shafts are commonly called "Buffalo Arrows," for by the enactment of appropriate rituals in the Sacred Arrow ceremony itself, they supposedly, have power to bring forth the buffalo and other game in order to provide both material and physical sustenance to the people.

The second pair of 'Arrows' have their shafts painted red and, likewise, are regarded as the receptacles of those same unseen powers abovementioned, whereby, they protect the people from their enemies and, if the attendant 'Arrow' rituals are observed correctly, ensure that the Cheyennes achieve victory in battle. At the same time, it is thought that the powers of the omnipotent unseen spirits which are transmitted through the medium of the 'Arrows,' can preserve the people from disease and all other natural and man-made calamities which might cause them to become extinct as an independent body. In short, the periodic enactment of the Sacred Arrow ceremony which lasts four days, guarantees the well-being of the people and their continued unity and strength. Failure to treat the 'Arrows' with due reverence, or by neglecting to hold the ceremonies connected with them, would, it is believed, herald the destruction and subsequent demise of the Cheyennes, and thus these most revered of tribal talismans represent the very essence of the Nation; embracing all that is Cheyenne both in body and in spirit along with the people's very existence. Every so often it is necessary to renew the 'Arrows,' especially when an act of homicide occurs within the tribe, but also, in order to replace the feather flights which are of a perishable nature, along with the glue and sinews that bind the feathers to the shafts. The shafts themselves, though, cannot be renewed more than the sacred number four times throughout their existence. Today the 'Arrows' reside in the care of their present Keeper among the Southern Cheyenne tribe in Oklahoma.

In brief, the coming of the Arrows, this being the most sacred of Cheyenne stories, tells how the original prophet Sweet-Medicine during a violent altercation with a fellow tribesman, killed his opponent and thence, fled the camp in fear of retribution from his victim's relatives. He remained in exile several years, after which he returned to the tribe a reformed and transformed person, now possessing potent holy powers and bearing sacred instructions by which to organize the Cheyenne people into a *Nation* with a singular identity. During his period of enforced exile, it is said, Sweet-Medicine had journeyed alone to a sacred mountain called *"Novah-vus"* in the western part of what is now the state of South Dakota. Upon reaching the aforesaid mountain, he passed through an opening in the mountain-side, which previously had been obscured from view by a large rock covering the entrance. He thus entered into the mountain itself which resembled the interior of a large earth-lodge. Inside, several persons both male and female were seated in a circle, but these were actually Supernatural Beings or Spirits of the Underworld who were appearing to him in material form. Each of the male persons present represented a different tribe and each had a sacred bundle in their possession. There was one bundle, however, hanging from the wall of the lodge that belonged to no one. As Sweet - Medicine entered the lodge, the "Spirit" persons motioned him take a seat under this bundle which was wrapped in a kit-fox skin and contained a number of Sacred Arrows. He was then offered the option of claiming the bundle as his own; to which he agreed, and so became the possessor of the Sacred Arrow talismans that are still preserved and venerated among the tribe. After accepting the `Arrows` Sweet-Medicine remained among his hosts for a period of four years, during which time, he was taught the accompanying prayers and ceremonies connected with the bundle and its contents, and many other things which included a new set of laws by which his people, the Cheyennes, were to govern themselves after his return to the tribe. He was also instructed how to organize four warrior societies within the tribe, along with the particular regalia each society should wear. These societies would then take it in turns to uphold the tribal laws and, thereafter, protect the people from their enemies.

At length, when the four year period of teaching had expired, Sweet-Medicine returned to his own people. He told them all what had happened and accordingly, taught them all he had learned. In such a way, he gave them the knowledge and institutions which he had brought back from the "Sacred Mountain."

It is further mentioned that at the time of his return to the tribe, Sweet-Medicine * gave the people corn, and also brought back the buffalo from their underground refuge to alleviate the people`s hunger. He then showed them how to conduct communal buffalo drives with the help of an appropriate ceremony; along with teaching them new skills in both the method of skinning and of utilizing the hides of the animals killed. [9] In addition, he now had the ability to prophesy forthcoming events, which included the coming of horses among them; the appearance of cattle and of white-skinned people, each of which the Cheyennes would meet with in a future time.

Sweet-Medicine, it is said, had been given the Sacred Arrows personally by the Underworld Spirits that reside within *"Novah-vus,"* or `Bear Butte` as it is designated on modern-day maps. This being the "Holy Mountain" of the Cheyennes and hence, regarded as the center of their Universe. It stands in the western part of South Dakota northeast of the Black Hills near the present-day town of Sturgis. The site is a long way indeed, from the Mississippi headwaters country of northern Minnesota, and before the Cheyennes had horses of any description, it would have taken many months for Sweet-Medicine to reach there on foot. Other tribes, that include the Mandan, Kiowa-Apache, Kiowa and most important to our present theme, the Hidatsa, also regard Bear Butte as a very sacred place and the Hidatsa, we know, have a Sacred Arrow cult, which although not exactly the same as that practiced among the Cheyennes, does bear not a few remarkable similarities to it. Perhaps, then, the Cheyenne innovation to adopt such a cult came originally from the Hidatsa, who being sedentary hunters and agriculturists, and likely once connected with the old Mound-builder culture peoples of earlier times in Michigan and Wisconsin, no doubt had a more solid religious concept and ceremonial life before the less sophisticated Chey-

* Sweet-Medicine is also known as Eagle`s-Peak, Rustling-Corn-Leaf, Standing-Medicine, Standing-Sweet-Grass and Sweet-Root-Standing.

enne groups arrived in the Upper Mississippi country from the Ontario lakes district of the north.

That the Hidatsa were in contact with Cheyennes of the Red Lake's and headwaters district of the Upper Mississippi, is substantiated by the fact that in addition to assertions from both the Hidatsa and Cheyennes themselves, the Hidatsa anciently called the Cree *"Shahe"* or *"Scha-hi,"* which is but a variant of an old name for the Cheyennes of *Chaa*. This might serve to show that when Hidatsa and Cheyennes first met, the Hidatsa supposed the latter to have been a Cree faction, which because of the dialect and fashion of dress the Cheyennes then employed, would not have been surprising. Certainly, migrant Cheyennes from the southern Ontario region must then have been in reasonable proximity to the Cree and probably still associating; if only sporadically, with the Monsoni branch of that people [as Cheyenne tradition asserts], and also with the Hidatsa.

This indicates that the territory then inhabited by these early Cheyennes was far north of the Minnesota River, for when at a later date, Cheyennes did reside in the last named locality, they had very little in either dress or character to immediately identify them with the Cree. Neither were they then likely to have had much contact with the Hidatsa, who during the period of Cheyenne occupation along the Minnesota of circa, 1640 onward, were far northwest in the Devil's Lake district of the Coteau des Prairies in northeastern North Dakota.

That this was the case, does suggest that the *"lake and prairie"* country then claimed by Cheyenne-proper bands, did embrace both Upper and Lower Red Lake and the Mississippi headwaters district, ostensibly, in the vicinity of "Bowstring Lake." It will become clear later in this chapter, that the names Bowstring Lake and Bowstring River are derived from very old Algonquian terms, and that during the early period of Cheyenne occupation along the Minnesota River further south, the Cree were already referring to the Cheyennes as "Bowstring Men."

We can see also in the Hidatsa equivalent of the Cheyenne Sacred Arrows cult, that among the Hidatsa, their "Sacred Arrow" also has the power to protect one and all from harm and bestow benevolence upon the people as a whole. However, what is more important perhaps, is that the Hidatsa Sacred Arrow by its 13 component parts, represents the unification of thirteen clans that originally constituted the Hidatsa tribe. Perhaps as the Cheyennes then constituted a number of separate bands rather than specific clans, Sweet Medicine received a corresponding number of Sacred Arrows, rather than only one arrow to represent the whole group as was the case with the Hidatsa.

One of the most important attributes of the Cheyenne "Sacred Arrows," like that among the Hidatsa, is that they symbolize the unity of the Cheyenne people and in olden days, whenever the `Arrows` were to be ritually renewed or propitiated, the entire population was obliged upon pain of eternal ostracism from the rest of the tribe, to gather together as one body. In such a way, all the Cheyenne people congregated at regular intervals and by so doing, continued to be united in both a physical and spiritual manner.

It is indicative that as early as circa, AD.1400, according to the archaeological dating, the Awatixa-speaking Hidatsa group was already entrenched near the mouth of the Knife River branch

JOHN STANDS IN TIMBER.
Northern Cheyenne informant
And tribal Historian. 1960.
[Margot Liberty Collection].

RED HAT
Also known as
FAN MAN.
SouthernCheyenne"Sacred
Arrow" Priest and informant.
[R. Schukies photo. 1976].

of the Missouri, and even then they recognized the eminence of Bear Butte near the Black Hills as being a sacred place. Earlier they had recognized the butte known as "Dog Den" as being a similar holy site, where the same mythological events in the history of the Hidatsa were said to have taken place. This last-named site stands only a few miles west of the middle Missouri near the `Painted Woods` area across from the mouth of the Knife. In short, the same events said to have occurred at "Dog Den," were later transferred to that of Bear Butte after the Awatixa spread further west, and thus it is probable, that when earlier the Awatixa had themselves resided in the Minnesota country, then the Sacred Butte in Hidatsa mythology, had likely been associated with yet another such eminence in an even more eastern region. We know, of course, that the transference of one sacred site to another during the extent of a people's migration history, has been a common trait around the Globe among various races and peoples. Thus Sacred Mount Ida of the ancient Greeks, originally located in Greece, was later relocated in Anatolia of northwestern Turkey by Greek settlers in that area. A similar case is the biblical Mount Ararat upon the top of which Noah`s Ark supposedly came to rest after the Great Flood, the site of which has been moved to various places over millennia, while the sacred height known as Mount Sinai in the Sinai peninsula of eastern Egypt, where the biblical prophet Moses received the Ten Commandments, has at times also been transferred to the western part of Saudi Arabia, India and other, even more distant places. In addition, the various Sacred Hill sites in Northern Europe, relating to early Germanic and Celtic peoples respectively, likewise were re-designated in other areas during the course of those people's migrations and changing circumstances.

Having said this, it must be conceded that the Cheyenne culture hero Sweet-Medicine, may well have traveled to Bear Butte; perhaps through the persuasions or influence of Hidatsa-proper contacts, who even when in Minnesota, were likely making their own pilgrimages to that place, having adopted the idea from their Awatixa cousins already entrenched along the Knife.

Conversely, it may have been that the sacred butte known as "Dog Den," was the place where, originally, the Cheyennes obtained their Sacred Arrows, if not from yet another site far to the east of Bear Butte and much closer to the Red Lakes` district of northern Minnesota. Is it really feasible that certain persons who could then only travel on foot, would walk some 1,500 miles or more mostly over inhospitable terrain and back, when a similar much closer butte could fit the pattern just as well? It is worth noting that the shafts of the Sacred Arrows are fashioned from wood belonging to an East Woodland variety and two of these shafts, at least, are said to be originals brought to the tribe by Sweet-Medicine himself. It is also indicative that the feathered flights of these Sacred Arrows are always attached to the shafts with sinew and a fish-based glue, rather than the more common animal hoof glue as used when on the Western Plains. This seems to suggest that the talismans first arrived among the Cheyennes when they inhabited the lake country of northern Minnesota, at which time, unlike when in the buffalo country to the west, fish provided a great part of their diet.

It is indicative that the same Dog Den was also sacred to the Mandan, who state that one of their own traditional cultural heroes known as Okipa, released the buffalo from their underground refuge at that place. Here, of course, we see a comparison with the Cheyenne cultural hero Sweet- Medicine, who also brought the buffalo to the people, after the animals had likewise been released them from their underground confinement.

It seems that only after all Cheyenne-speaking groups had left the Minnesota regions and crossed the Missouri to become nomadic equestrian buffalo hunters of the Western Plains, that the mythological account of Sweet-Medicine`s holy journey to *"Novah-vus,"* the Sacred Mountain, was transferred from an original eastern location to that of a more convenient and perhaps, more relevant site in the west, such as that of present-day Bear Butte which same site was already regarded as a very holy place by the then resident tribes of that territory, including the Kiowa, Hidatsa, Mandan and Kiowa-Apache among other tribes.

It will be seen in a later chapter, how the Suhtaio did themselves transfer the original site of their own sacred mountain, - named `Timber Mountain` in the southwest corner of Minnesota - to that of Bear Butte in western South Dakota, where, it is said, their personal culture hero Erect-Horns first received *"Issiwun,"* the Sacred Buffalo Hat fetish of that tribe. Bear Butte being thus deemed a more convenient location to visit by the "Hat" Keeper and his wife when residing in the Western Plains, and undertaking their periodic pilgrimages to the site in order to express devotion to the sacred powers connected with it.

From a purely analytical viewpoint, alternative scenarios present themselves with regard to making historical sense out of the Sweet-Medicine cycle.

The first scenario assumes that a specific person, perhaps at the time in question a novice shaman, did indeed make the long and hazardous trek to the sacred mountain of Bear Butte. There he both fasted and prayed in order to receive a vision, the experience of which would enable him to become an important medium through which the powers of the Great Ma`heo - along with the spirit guardians of the Underworld who controlled the animals whose flesh gave sustenance to the people - would bestow their benevolence upon the Cheyenne tribe as a whole.

After suffering both thirst and hunger and likely, a loss of blood through the act of self-sacrifice, such as the lopping off of a finger joint [as was often the practice among Indians when on a vision quest], Sweet-Medicine`s desired vision was acquired, but in truth, was probably due more to the mind hallucinating, rather than the natural phenomena of a dream. Whatever the case, due to his vision, Sweet-Medicine would have fully believed that he had entered through a doorway into the very heart of the mountain, wherein, he was brought face to face with the supernatural Underworld personages made manifest to him in human form. In return for his personal suffering and reverence towards the Sacred Beings, the Underworld Spirits showed their compassion and as a reward, presented him with the sacred shafts.

They thereafter began instructing him in the ceremony and manner of devotion associated with them, which, he was told, he should then teach to his Cheyenne people in order that the Spirits themselves could ensure the welfare of his tribe.

That this is what actually happened, both Sweet-Medicine and the Cheyennes would have no doubt. From the Indian perspective there did indeed, exist parallel worlds, in one of which both humans and animals lived and thrived in material form; the other being that wherein dwelt the omnipotent powers, along with humans and animals in their spiritual state. One could, it was believed, albeit through the proper process of fasting and prayer and sometimes self-inflicted torture, cross over from one world into the next without difficulty and back again; for each was deemed merely an extension of the other.

In short, the whole of creation was regarded as an unbroken circle; everything pertaining to it being interconnected in one way or another. Life and death were but a part of this same continuous circle and enabled the inhabitants of the Spirit World to interact freely with each and all elements comprising its parallel counterpart, where life existed in its material form.

In the second scenario, again it is assumed that Sweet-Medicine embarked upon his pilgrimage in the hope of obtaining some kind of supernatural power, by which the current sufferings of the Cheyenne people through starvation and disease might be alleviated.

In this case, Sweet-Medicine does not actually reach the sacred mountain of Bear Butte. Instead, he visits the village of one or another Missouri River tribe, ostensibly one of Hidatsa affiliation, such as the aforementioned Awatixa group then located along Knife River.

Sweet-Medicine is invited into an Awatixa earth-lodge - one where resides specifically, a number of priests and holy men of the tribe - and here he receives the gift of the Sacred Arrows. The earth-lodge in question becomes through the process of mythological interpretation, analogous with the inside of the mountain wherein the holy spirits of the Underworld reside. At the same time, Sweet-Medicine's human hosts in the earth-lodge who give him the `Arrow` bundle and initiate him in the rites connected with its contents, become in their turn personifications of the Underworld Spirits themselves.

Such an interpretation would certainly explain the analogy between a semi-subterranean dwelling and that of the abode of the Underworld Spirits inside the so-called Sacred Mountain. The inside of which, one will recall in the Sweet-Medicine story, is likened to the interior of an earth-lodge as used by humans in the material world. Obviously, this indicates that the coming of the `Arrows` among the Cheyennes, did occur during a time before the latter employed buffalo hide tepees as their common means of shelter, and therefore, during an early phase of Cheyenne residence in northern Minnesota. Perhaps also, as we are told elsewhere that the original name of Sweet-Medicine before he received the `Arrows,` was Eagle's-Nest, his later names of Sweet-Root-Standing, Rustling-Corn-Leaf and that of Standing-Sweet-Grass, do in fact reflect his prolonged sojourn among some corn growing people; as the Awatixa-Hidatsa were, and of bringing corn seeds to his people, thereby re-introducing this food source among the Cheyennes when in their Minnesota habitat.

On the other hand, the aforementioned Cheyenne assertion that at the time Sweet-Medicine brought the Sacred Arrows to the people,...*"there was famine and pestilence over all the Northland,"* seems to refer to a period soon after the residence of Cheyennes in the southern Ontario country. As it was probably the event of these double catastrophes, which actually occasioned a Cheyenne migration south into the Mississippi headwaters country of northern

Minnesota and created the impetus to adopt some other, new medium, through which the people could counter the dire situation they were then in the process of suffering. Certainly the Sacred Arrows are also a medium through which the cosmic order of the Universe and of Nature itself can, at intervals, be re-connected to the world of the Cheyennes and to all mankind in general. Thereby eradicating chaos and preventing future disorder such as created by any climatic shift or pandemic, which likely effected the Cheyennes and their environment during the period under consideration.

Now we have previously noted how a severe climatic change did effect the aforesaid Ontario area during the time in question [circa, 1535 - 1540], and it is indicative that in 1534 and again throughout the succeeding years until 1543, far to the east on the Lower St. Lawrence, the French explorer Jacques Cartier made contact and traded with certain Algonquian and Huron groups in the latter's great towns of Hochelga and Stadacona, which then stood on the present-day city sites of Quebec and Montreal respectively. There had been much intimacy between the Indians and white men at those times, and it is not unlikely that some type of European disease such as smallpox or even a common strain of influenza, was thus passed on by these Frenchmen to their Native customers, who having no natural immunity and lacking even a basic knowledge of the process of contamination, could not prevent its deadly effects from sweeping through their populations, carrying off many thousands in its wake.

This appears to have been the case, for soon after 1543, the Huron apparently had abandoned their towns completely and disappeared from where Cartier had previously found them.

Any such contagion, undoubtedly, would have been transmitted by the infected Huron and their Algonquian allies to neighbouring peoples, causing it to spread far and wide from one tribe to another. Eventually, even Cheyennes in their remote Ontario habitat would likely have suffered the same decimation to their numbers; though they remained far removed from the original source of contagion.

Prior to this period, the several groups of refugee Algonquian-speaking peoples which, together, comprised the Cheyenne Nation of late historic times, probably constituted a significant population. They were then scattered throughout specific areas in their several autonomous, but closely associated bands, each of which had little adversity to contend with from enemies whilst in their remote Ontario habitat. Now, however, as appears to have been the case with other tribal groups to the north and east, their numbers suffered dire loss, which in turn, upset and destroyed any age-old social structure and tribal organization there may then have been among them. Indeed, it was probably around this same time of catastrophe and upheaval among virtually all tribes of the northeastern states and eastern Canadian provinces, that occasioned the subsequent coming of the legendary Dekanawida and Hiawatha, who sometime around the date 1560, reorganized the five Iroquois-proper tribes into their famous league, and introduced new laws by which they thereafter governed themselves.

As a result of the Moiseo and their cognate bands experiencing similar catastrophic events, it is likely that their people scattered into many, much smaller family camps in an endeavor to escape the same silent enemy of disease.

If there had existed any earlier sacred tribal talismans believed to have power to safeguard the people from harm, then it must have seemed that they had lost their potency. Probably the people would not have recalled suffering a similar devastating calamity within living memory and there would have been an urgent need to obtain some other form of medium, through which, by the enactment of certain newly devised rituals, the great Ma`heo and its associated benevolent spirits of the "Above World" and "Below," would again bestow their blessings upon the people; to preserve them from yet another similar catastrophe and in some way, unify the Moiseo and their cognate groups, to make them strong and independent and a complete tribal entity in their own right.

This becomes evident by the fact that long before the Sacred Arrows came among them, the Cheyennes had indulged in an elaborate religious ritual known as the *"Massaum"* [also known as the "Animal" or "Crazy" Dance"]. This was, predominantly, a ceremony of regeneration, the enactment of which persisted into the early years of the twentieth century. During the performance of the *Massaum* rites, a number of participants disguised themselves as various species of animals in order to propitiate the spirits of all living things. According to some, it was also a ceremony which gave the practitioners both power and guardianship over a certain area of land and over all living things that dwelt thereon. The actual concept surrounding the *Massaum,* appears to be of ancient origin and had its counterpart among the Siberian nomads of Kamchatka, in which region it had likely originated during a past millennium.

After the Cheyennes adopted the Sacred Arrows, along with the cult associated with them, the *Massaum* lost a good deal of its earlier importance, as the newly inaugurated ceremony of the Sacred Arrows now achieved a similar end. The *Massaum* continued to be performed, although not on a regular basis. The last occasion was in 1927, and then in association with the *New Life Lodge* ceremony more commonly known as the Sun Dance, which was adopted by Cheyennes from the Suhtaio at a late date. It seems, however, that in olden times; before the introduction of the Sacred Arrows and the Sun-Dance, the *Massaum* had been regarded as the most important ceremony then practiced by the Cheyenne-proper, and - albeit in varied form - by the latter`s closely related Cree kinfolk. The time of *"...famine and pestilence in all the northland"* as mentioned in Cheyenne tradition, which had caused the people to pull up stakes and migrate south into northern Minnesota in the first place, had probably decimated the Moiseo and other bands associated with them, as indeed, it did with their Algonquian cousins to the north and east, and threw any age-old social organization and religious observances associated with pre-existing sacred objects into disarray. Perhaps, then, this was the event or events, that diminished the earlier importance of the *Massaum* within the tribe, and when in a later century, the Cheyennes as a Nation adopted the Sun-Dance as a regeneration ceremony, the relegation of the *Massaum* to a much lesser position in the Nation's religious life became complete. Although it is true to say that in a later century, the then small remaining remnant of the original Moiseo band did alone persist in the importance of the *Massaum,* as an alternative to their adopting the Sun-Dance in its stead.

Certain holy objects of the olden time, evidently, did survive into the new era of the Sacred Arrows, such as those termed *"Okhtsin"* or `Wheel Lances` as they are sometimes called, which seem also to have evolved from an ancient northern Siberian concept. Supposedly, these Wheel-Lances had power to protect its owner and followers from harm in much the same way as did the Sacred Arrows, i.e., by causing those behind the lance to become invisible to their enemies. These objects, although not requiring a hereditary chain of custodians as did the Sacred Arrows, became intimately associated with the `Arrows` and had to be renewed at the same time as were the `Arrows` themselves. In one sense, though, the Wheel-Lances also became somewhat superfluous by their having very similar properties to the `Arrows,` and thus; as was the case with the *Massaum* rites, they eventually lost much of their earlier importance within the tribe as a whole.

According to Cheyenne testimony collected by George A. Dorsey during the early nineteen-hundreds, the Cheyennes first acquired their Sacred Arrow talismans between eighteen and twenty generations prior to 1905, when the statement was made.

There are several versions in current Cheyenne oral tradition of what might be termed "The Sweet-Medicine cycle," much of the contents of which tend to border on the mythological. Hence, Sweet-Medicine is reputed to have lived for an extensive period - "445 winters" to be precise, and in the ilk of the "Green Man" of ancient Celtic mythology, every winter he would grow old and haggard, but come spring, would rejuvenate into a much younger man. It must be remembered, however, that two of our conventional years correspond with three winters in the Indian idiom, so that the statement "445 winters" in reality, refers to 286 of our conventional years.

Of course, no human being can be said to have lived 286 years by our way of reckoning, and the original Sweet-Medicine of Cheyenne tradition is not regarded as anything other than a mortal human being, albeit, one who showed a remarkable ability to both create and innovate and possessed the power to prophesy important forthcoming events. Indeed, Sweet-Medicine is not only said to have given the Sacred Arrow bundle to the Cheyennes, but in addition, is attributed to having given the tribe its four original warrior societies and also, the "Chief's" society, along with many of the tribe's later cultural assets that since the time of Cheyenne residence in the Mississippi headwaters country, have been adopted during various periods by the people throughout their subsequent history.

We should not doubt from this that Sweet-Medicine was not at one time a real historical figure, only that since his demise at an advanced age, a successor had taken the name and embraced the same role as a symbolic personification of the original Sweet-Medicine himself, so that even today, there exists the position in current Cheyenne hierarchy and tribal government of a Sweet-Medicine-Chief. This being one who still personifies in spirit his illustrious namesake of olden times.

In truth, the alleged extensive life-span attributed to Sweet-Medicine, merely represents any given number of persons, who in succession, took on the mantle of their predecessors, both as the paramount religious shaman and as guardian of the sacred knowledge.

Each in turn became the personification of those who had gone before, as even today, the Pope is regarded symbolically as the personification - if not the reincarnation of St. Peter - the original founding father of the Holy Church of Rome.

This is substantiated by a Cheyenne informant of Truman Michelson, who stated in 1910, that it was about ninety years before that date, when Sweet-Medicine died.

Obviously, this particular Cheyenne informant was not referring to the original person of that name, but rather, to a personification of him endowed with the title Sweet-Medicine-Chief, and whose demise coincided with the end-phase of what we should call the "Traditional time" in Cheyenne history which ends around circa, 1820. Hereafter, the Nation's oral history takes on a much more definite format with precise names, dates and events, and which are recounted in their proper chronological sequence. Thus we know, that a man named High-Backed-Wolf was elected to the position of Sweet-Medicine-Chief either in, or just after the year 1820.

If we accept, therefore, that the number *"445 winters"* given as the extent of the original Sweet-Medicine`s life span, actually includes those personages who came after him until the end of the traditional era [e.g. 1820], whilst remembering that three winters in the Cheyenne idiom compares with only two conventional years in our modern reckoning, then by subtracting 286 years from 1820, i.e., when the last of the successive Sweet-Medicine Chiefs of the traditional era expired, as Michelson`s informant asserted, we have a working date for the period of the original Sweet-Medicine`s coming of around AD.1534.

Having said this, we know that Dorsey calculated a period of only twenty years as representing the average length of a generation, and which by counting back 18 generations as mentioned by his Cheyenne informants in 1905, gives us a date of around 1545 as being the time when the `Arrows` were first brought to the people, or perhaps, more precisely, when the first Arrow Keeper was inaugurated into that office by Sweet-Medicine himself.

In corroboration of these dates, the Cheyenne informant Ralph White-Tail, a noted Sacred Arrow and Sun-Dance priest during the early 1960s, listed 12 keepers of the Sacred Arrows prior to and including Chief Little-Man, who, in 1908, was the last of the long-serving Arrow Keepers from the time of the old buffalo days.

In 1838, the then Arrow Keeper named Grey-Thunder, was killed during a big fight between allied Cheyennes and Arapahoe on one side and the Kiowa, Kiowa-Apache and Comanche on the other. Grey-Thunder is noted as number nine on Ralph White-Tail`s list of Arrow Keepers. Thus if one calculates thirty years as being a more realistic period corresponding to the average length of a generation and as being the average length of time of any one Keeper's term of office, then deducts the time span of nine Keepers prior to and including the office of Grey-Thunder [which totals a period of 270 years], one arrives at the date of the first Arrow Keeper's inauguration as circa, 1568.

Assuming then that in this case, the time span covering each successive Arrow Keeper when in office; after taking account of probable premature deaths of one or more keeper [such as one who is said to have frozen to death around the date 1810], and of possible disqualification from the role, also corresponds on average to a period of thirty years, then once again we have the working date of 1545 for the inauguration of the first Keeper of the Arrows.

Taken together, these four proposed dates give a mean of A.D. 1548, which fits nicely with the period of Cheyenne residence in the Red Lake's district, and with the time of their close association with the Hidatsa. It also coincides with the particular period of famine due to climatic variation and possible pestilence which we know from tribal tradition and corroborating scientific data, enveloped the whole of the *"North Country"* close to the middle years of the sixteenth century.

THE SWEET MEDICINE CHIEF, HIGH-BACKED-WOLF.
[After an original line drawing from life by George Catlin in 1832.]

This proposed period also corresponds with the assertion, previously mentioned, that Sweet-Medicine on his return from the Sacred Mountain, foretold the future coming of horses among the people, which, coincidently, match the dates 1540 and 1541, when the Spanish Conquistadors Francisco Coronado and Hernando DeSoto respectively on their separate expeditions, brought the first horses since Prehistoric times onto the Southern Plains. Additionally, the mention by Sweet-Medicine of the future appearance of the white man's cattle, coincides with the first such animals which, having earlier been deposited on Sable Island by Baron de Lery in 1518 but long since abandoned by their owners and left to their own devices, by 1545 had multiplied into a significant number. Indeed, parties of French and Basque fishermen both visited and explored the Gulf of St. Lawrence several times during the first half of the sixteenth century, and had made intermittent contact with Natives on the Labrador coast. These events, surely, were known to Algonquians belonging to Montagnais and Naskapi peoples of that region, and transmitted by word of mouth further inland so that Sweet-Medicine, who, according to the Cheyenne informant John Stands-in-Timber had been a great traveler south, east, west and north, was made aware of these hitherto unknown newcomers, such as white men, horses and cattle.

In 1910, another of Michelson's Cheyenne informants named American-Horse, stated that during the early days of Cheyenne residence in the north [here referring to the Headwaters country of the Upper Mississippi before the people crossed to the west side of the Missouri], there were only two Cheyenne-speaking bands, although Michelson did not designate them by specific names.

One assumes therefore, that one of these two original bands was that known as Moiseo or Arrow Men as they were also called, and among whom so we are told in Cheyenne testimony previously cited, the Sacred Arrows were first introduced. It does not appear that American-Horse was implying that the Suhtaio should be included as one of the two bands of which he spoke, for he mentioned the Suhtaio as a separate tribe when giving additional information regarding this early period in Cheyenne history. Neither, however, does it appear that he was referring directly to the small remnant of Moiseo, but to an old-time breakaway band from them known as Masikota and among whom the Arrow Men faction of the original Moiseo parent band had since amalgamated. The other Cheyenne-speaking group then resident in the Mississippi headwaters country was that of the Omissis also known as Bowstrings, and both names of Masikota and Bowstrings; albeit during different periods in time, were each used as collective terms to include under their respective headings all the later-date Cheyenne-speaking bands.

As regards the Bowstrings group, it is mentioned in present-day Cheyenne tradition, how Sweet-Medicine was also recognized as something of a miracle worker, and certainly, some of the magical acts he is alleged to have performed are truly remarkable to say the least. One of these feats is particularly interesting at this point and will be included here from George A. Dorsey's description.

"........When the boy [Sweet-Medicine], was about ten years old he desired to go and take part in one of the magic dances given by the great medicine men and gain for him admission to the dance.......When the boy's turn to perform came he told the people what he was going to do. With sweet-grass he burned incense. Through the incense he passed his buffalo sinew bowstring, east, south, west and north. Then he asked two men to assist him while he performed. First he had them tie his bowstring around his neck, then cover his body with his robe, then pulls at the ends of the string. They pulled with all their might, but they could not move him. He told them to pull harder, and as they pulled at the string again, his head was cut off and rolled from under his robe.... They took his head and placed it under the robe with his body. Next they removed the robe, and there sat a very old man in place of the boy. They covered the old man with the robe, and when they removed the robe again, there was a pile of human bones with a skull. They spread the robe over the bones, and when it was removed there was nothing there. Again they spread the robe, and when they removed it, there was the boy again..." [2]

162

THE COMING OF THE "SACRED ARROWS"

The traditional account surrounding the culture hero Sweet-Medicine, declares that it was he also, who brought the four original warrior societies to the Cheyennes, and we know that one of these military fraternities was known as Bowstrings. However, Suhtaio statements given to Michelson in 1910, specifically state that the societies of Elks, Red-Shields and Dogs were originally inaugurated among the Suhtaio, while present-day informants state that only the societies of Kit-Fox and Bowstrings actually originated among the Cheyennes.

Perhaps then, both the band and warrior society of Bowstrings were so named, in memory of Sweet-Medicine`s remarkable feat with his buffalo sinew bowstring as recounted above, and it is highly indicative that the Southern Cheyenne Sacred Arrow priest named Red-Hat [also known as Fan-Man], asserted that, traditionally, the Arrow Keepers had always belonged to the Bowstring warrior society.

This particular fraternity of Bowstrings having originally been founded among the Cheyennes, was later adopted by other tribes in contact with them, eventually becoming a pan-tribal society on the Western Great Plains. By this it might be deduced that one of the two early Cheyenne-speaking groups as mentioned by the informant American-Horse, was indeed that of Bowstrings, which offers a clue as to where exactly these particular Cheyennes were then positioned in the northern Minnesota country.

It is no coincidence that slightly southeast of Lower Red Lake - just above the headwaters of the Mississippi - we find a Bowstring Lake and Bowstring River. These names are derived from translations of very old Algonquian Indian place names and are indicative that long ago, a group of people who evidently were Algonquian speakers and ostensibly Cheyenne, were known by the name Bowstrings who once resided in the aforementioned localities.

It seems to be also that in 1742, when the LaVerendrye brothers met a band of "Horse Indians" in the Great Plains west of the Missouri and called them *Gens L`Arc,* i.e. "People of the Bow," they were merely employing an old Algonquian name for that tribe, which should more properly have been rendered; "People of the Bowstring." Certainly an alternative name given for the *Gens L`Arc* of *Atchapeivinioque* in the Bourgainville report of 1757, is a Cree term for the Cheyennes, which translates as *Bowstrings,* not *Bow.*

The logical conclusion then, deduced from the American-Horse statement, is that those known as Omissis, who during these early years were also known as Bowstrings, represented one of the two bands of which he spoke. Thus the two original Cheyenne component bands of the American Horse statement quoted above, most likely comprised on the one hand the Arrow Men - later incorporated among the Masikota, and the Omissis, later known as Bowstrings, on the other.

As regards the Arrow Men component group, they likely represented a breakaway part of the old-time Moiseo which some time later, joined the Cheyenne-speaking group known as Masikota. These Arrow Men separates thereafter, adopted the Kit-Fox as their personal warrior Society owing to a kit-fox skin being connected to the Sacred Arrows, and became the most important Cheyenne-speaking faction paramount to all other bands. This is apparent by the fact that the proper name of the Masikota in the guise of `Grasshopper`

163

and among whom the aforementioned Arrow Men amalgamated, was adopted as a collective term for the Cheyenne Nation as a whole, while the specific role of the Kit-Fox society itself, was to protect the Sacred Arrow Keeper and his priestly retinue.

It will be shown later in this study that as the Masikota Kit-Fox Society during this early period, was regarded as the fighting element among the combined Cheyenne-speaking bands, they were thus represented by the *"Man"* arrows in the Sacred Arrow bundle. The Bowstrings Society on the other hand, which included descendants of Wheskerinni extraction comprising the more horticultural element of the tribe in addition to their semi–sedentary habits which, in some ways, caused them to become practitioners of a more regulated and less belligerent lifestyle as opposed to the more erratic and nomadic habits of the Masikota, were represented by the *"Buffalo"* arrows. Hence the successive Keepers of the Sacred Arrow bundle itself belonged to the more settled and industrious Bowstrings, while the original Kit-Fox Society represented the Arrow Men of tradition and, after associating with the Masikota, became the specific protectors of the Arrow Keeper and his priests. This is why Kit-Fox Warrior Society members of a later date, wore an old-time flint arrowhead along with a kit-fox stole as part of their fraternity regalia, in recognition of their being included among the first two bands that received the original Sacred Arrows brought them by the revered prophet Sweet-Medicine.

However, as the Moiseo or Arrow Men are said to have been the original recipients of the Sacred Arrows, it must be construed that the Masikota were then already separated as an independent group from the Moiseo, and as the Moiseo strengthened their ties with the Monsoni Cree in the north, the Masikota moved southeast into the headwaters district of the Upper Mississippi, whereupon the Arrow Keeper and his adherents later known as the Kit-Fox band, left the parent Moiseo group and joined the Masikota so as to remain independent of the Cree. *

At an even later date, this newly formed separatist group of mixed Arrow Men and Masikota; by including the Arrow Keeper and his priests, caused the Masikota population to increase substantially by further secessions from the parent Moiseo, and the main Masikota village thus became the focal point whenever the Cheyenne people gathered as a united body. At the same time, the much smaller Moiseo remnant although aligning themselves with the Sioux, still represented a separate Cheyenne-speaking band, albeit of greatly diminished importance after the Sacred Arrow people among them had joined the Masikota.

The fact that the Moiseo are said to have been the nucleus of all later Cheyenne- proper speaking bands, also suggests that the Arrow Men must have separated from the Moiseo parent band after migrating south into the Lower Red Lake region of Minnesota. At that time this break-

* Although the Sweet-Medicine cycle states that the prophet appeared at different times to the people, alternatively dressed in the regalia of each of the four original warrior societies of Kit-Fox, Elks, Bowstrings and Red-Shields before his pilgrimage to the Sacred Mountain to receive the Sacred Arrows, it is nevertheless made clear in the account, that these military fraternities were not actually inaugurated into the tribe until many years after Sweet Medicine`s return to the people.

away faction would still have retained the name Moiseo, thus creating two separate camps of that group, but soon after amalgamating with the Masikota, the Arrow Men faction adopted the name of Kit-Fox Men and even later, were known as the Tsis-Tsis-Tsas-proper in order to distinguish themselves as a separate entity. Together with the Masikota, they then moved closer to their Omissis-Bowstring cousins in the Mississippi headwaters country, and thus, unlike the successive Sweet Medicine Chiefs whose status and commitments debarred them from belonging to any warrior elite, the serving Keepers of the Sacred Arrows have all been members of the Bowstrings fraternity, as the informant Red-Hat asserted. At the same time, the protectors of the Arrow Keeper and his priests have always been members of the Kit-Fox Society and separate to the other later-formed Cheyenne societies of Elks, Dogs and Red Shields, each of which were originally adopted from the Suhtaio.

If, of course, both locations of Lower Red Lake and Bowstring Lake were simultaneously occupied by Cheyenne peoples, then there must indeed have been two main groups of Cheyennes at that time, as American-Horse stated. Probably these two main groups of Masikota and Omissis comprised several villages each, and this much is evidenced by the mention in certain Cheyenne stories which relate to the people's occupation in northern Minnesota when, it is said, they were being attacked by enemies from the north and northeast. Such stories often refer to the existence of several separate Cheyenne villages within reasonable traveling distance of each other. This would also explain how pottery shards of the so-called *"Black Duck"* focus which was predominantly Suhtaio, but which includes an abundance of early Cheyenne ware, are found in both the Lower Red Lake and Bowstring Lake areas.

Certainly for a prolonged period, each of the three Cheyenne groups then in existence [i.e. The Moiseo, Omissis and Masikota], remained in contact with one another, merely preferring to camp apart due to economic considerations. But by the early 1700s, the remnant of the Moiseo parent band had lost its prominence and prestige and eventually, by the opening of the nineteenth century, had become a small hybrid conglomerate, being an admixture of Cheyenne-proper, Suhtaio and even of Teton Sioux extraction.

It seems therefore, that originally, there would have been only two Sacred Arrows brought by Sweet-Medicine; one each for those two early Cheyenne-speaking groups of Arrow Men and Omissis, and that a part of the Arrow Men [i.e. the Kit-Fox band] then separated from the Moiseo parent group and amalgamated with the by then, first breakaway group from the Moiseo, later known as the Masikota.

This is corroborated by the Suhtaio statement given to Michelson in 1910, that when the Suhtaio first crossed into the Upper Mississippi country from the east, they met with the Sioux and Cree and three [bands] of Cheyenne. Obviously this Suhtaio statement was referring to those Cheyenne bands in existence during the time in question, and which must have comprised the then three separate bands of Masikota, Kit-Fox Moiseo and Omissis-Bowstrings.

At the much later date of circa, 1740, as inferred by Truman Michelson`s Suhtaio informant Bull-Thigh, the Cheyenne component groups of Masikota [including the Kit-Fox band] and Omissis had amalgamated with the related Pipe-Stem-Men [then enjoined with the Ridge Men], and also with the Watapio [a mixed band of Masikota remnants and Sioux known as *Sheo*], and thus the Nation then comprised four confederated groups from which all the later Cheyenne bands are said to have evolved. Because of this, two additional Sacred Arrows must then have been added to the `Arrow` bundle which, thereafter, contained two *Buffalo Arrows* and two *Man Arrows* making four in total. These in turn represented the unification of the above-mentioned four Cheyenne groups which during the late historic time [circa, 1830s], included the Aorta [originally known as the Kit-Fox band], the Omissis, Masikota, and Pipe-Stem Men / Ridge Men band. Together they were then known by the collective term of Hevietanio, and had the totemic names of four separate warrior societies which included the Kit-Fox, Bowstrings, Elks and Red-Shields respectively. Suffice to say, the earlier four separate Cheyenne groups after amalgamating with the Suhtaio among whom the Dog soldier Society was predominant, formed the basis for the ten bands and five warrior societies of the Cheyenne Nation of more recent time. [3]

All this indicates that the culture hero Sweet-Medicine must have returned to the people at intervals as the tradition asserts, but during specific widely separated periods in Cheyenne history, rather than during the course of one man's lifetime. As it was Sweet-Medicine himself, supposedly, who gave the people many of their later-day cultural and religious innovations and even the so-called Chief's Society embracing the forty-four council chiefs of the Nation, which, however, was also actually adopted among the Cheyennes at a much later date than the time of the original Sweet-Medicine himself. It is more likely then, that it was one or another of Sweet-Medicine's successors - in the role of Sweet-Medicine-Chief, - who by acting as the official inaugurator of successive cultural acquisitions, even though the idea for them may have derived originally from some other persons or tribe, became the symbolic innovator in his role as the personification of the first Sweet-Medicine prophet.

The importance of the coming of the Sacred Arrows is that previously, when in central and southern Ontario, the Moiseo and their cognates had likely been scattered across the region in numerous separate camps, in order to facilitate in a more practical manner their hunting and gathering potential. They then included among their number a hybrid admixture of Moiseo, Monsoni, Montagnais and Wheskerinni extraction, whose commonality was that all were refugees, having fled from Chippewa-speaking enemies in the east and that they spoke intelligible dialects one to the other. The predominant dialect of the collective group and its characteristics in general would, though, have been overwhelmingly Moiseo, e.g. proto-Cheyenne, albeit altered somewhat from the dialect spoken by the Moiseo parent band, whose members continued to use the more archaic and proper form.

Having said this, other than one or more archaic institutions such as the *Massaum* ceremony among them, which at times would have served to bring the scattered people together as a collective, there had probably been no hard and fast tribal organization or any serious bond of unity between the separate bands, albeit they would have considered themselves close cousins. These refugee peoples when residing in reasonably close proximity to one another, could have united in a common purpose, be it a communal hunt or when defending themselves against enemy attack. Yet each band would have been free to act in whichever way it chose without regard to any perceived inter-band responsibility. Without a tangible focal point to consolidate the separate bands into a united tribal entity with a common resolve and commitment, there must have been fear that one band or another might eventually wander off and become lost from the group, whereby, the overall strength among those remaining would be seriously undermined, along with the real possibility that the people would lose their social cohesion; sparse as it may have been, and thus become disintegrated and their extinction assured.

The coming of the Sacred Arrows and their associated rites, offered the means by which the Cheyennes could alleviate their recent period of suffering and restore a connection with the cosmic and natural order of things, temporarily disrupted so as to cause chaos and discord among the people and to their environment. In addition, the unity symbolized by the "Arrows," thereafter allowed the people in their separate groups, to wander further afield than previously dared, and to follow their own whims of fortune without fear of becoming irretrievably separated one from the other. From this time on, the various Cheyenne-speaking bands always regarded themselves as a united people; protected by the benevolence of the unseen powers through the medium of the Sacred Arrows, and which obliged each of the bands to keep in contact and assist each other in times of need. Certainly, the unification of the Arrow Keeper`s Arrow Men band with the cognate Omissis [Bowstrings] and Masikota, created the foundation by which that known as the Cheyenne Nation came into being. Through the people's collective devotion to the Sacred Arrows, the powers emanating from them even today, allow the Cheyennes to resist all oppressors and - notwithstanding that the current Northern and Southern divisions now have their own respective governments and separate political agendas - they yet regard themselves as a singular people, who through the medium of the `Arrows` will always be Cheyenne.

So it is that this period in the people's evolution; when the Sacred Arrows came among them, is regarded as the most important. It symbolizes the beginning of their history as an independent entity, and starts at the time of their residence in the Headwaters country of the Upper Mississippi. This explains why the informant George Bent asserted that the earliest home of the Cheyennes was in the aforesaid area. We need only then to tie up the loose ends, so to speak, in order to conclude this particular chapter in Cheyenne tribal evolution, when the people were resident in the area around Lower Red Lake and about the Mississippi heads.

By the Cheyenne's own account, they lived about the large lake of tradition with its adjoining prairie for many years. How many, we can only surmise. Certainly, by the later date of 1640 or thereabout, one Cheyenne-speaking band, at least, was in permanent residence much further south, either along or very near the Minnesota River. Tribal tradition recalls that the people's residence about the aforesaid Lake with its adjacent prairie, preceded any Cheyenne settlement along the Minnesota and therefore, from the time the Moiseo had been pushed from, or in any event, obliged to leave the district adjacent to the Sault St. Marie around A.D. 1450, to that of the first Cheyenne settlement along the Minnesota of circa, 1640, two-hundred years had elapsed and somewhere between these two dates, the Moiseo had roamed the lake country of central and southern Ontario and the northern part of Minnesota. In the interim, they had occupied a position of some permanency within the vicinity of Lower Red Lake.

The assertions made by Cheyenne informants to James Mooney [1907], previously cited, that the Cheyenne people had actually been created in the cold, lake-filled *"Northland"* above the Mississippi heads, leads one to suppose that by far the longest period of residence in these two areas, [that is, the Province of Ontario and of northern Minnesota], was in effect the Ontario country. Whilst inhabiting this latter region according to tradition, the Moiseo were almost constantly on the move in their never-ending quest for food and a more comfortable lifestyle. Accordingly, the people generally moved in a southwest direction and it may not have taken many years before the Moiseo reached the Red Lake's district of northern Minnesota, although during that period of wandering, they apparently forgot many details regarding their ancestry, along with their earlier cultural and historical affiliations with more eastern Algonquian groups.

Evidently then, the time span of Cheyenne residence in the *"Northland"* of tradition, was not a short period in their history. But as the traditional accounts recall clear descriptions regarding the people's residence and lifestyle when in the vicinity of the *"large lake and adjoining prairie"* [e.g. the Lower Red Lake], it does suggest a long period of residence in this latter area also. It is more likely that the assertion by Cheyenne informants that their tribe originated somewhere above the Mississippi heads, in reality applies merely to the time of their becoming completely separate from the Cree and their having a singular identity, which may be thought of as evolving in the aforesaid region as a separate tribe.

Before this, as previously stated, the component groups which comprised the Cheyenne Nation of late historic time, had originally constituted an admixture of peoples claiming Moiseo, Montagnais and adopted Wheskerinni ancestry, albeit sharing a common culture and history with only slight variations in dialect. Now, however, these once small autonomous bands had at last, come together as a united people, made manifest by their collective adherence to the Sacred Arrows and the new innovative cult connected with them which bound the people together as one. As a result, the coming of the Sacred Arrows became in time, to be thought of as being the origin of the Cheyennes as an independent entity, and which, of course, in an indirect way - it was.

On the other hand, the vacation by Cheyennes of the Red Lake's district can be calculated with far more precision. It will be seen later in this study that it seems to have occurred sometime between 1640 and 1650. Thus, it might reasonably be assumed that the original Cheyenne settlement about Lower Red Lake, began around the middle years of the sixteenth century - perhaps as early as 1540 - so as to allow ample time for a significant increase in Moiseo-Masikota and Omissis populations, which in turn, caused them to divide into the separatist Kit-Fox [Aorta], Masikota, Omissis [Bowstrings] and Pipe-Stem-Men factions, occupying specific individual hunting territories scattered throughout the Upper half of Minnesota. Indeed, at a later date than the time of Cheyenne residence around the shores of Lower Red Lake, the three separate Cheyenne-speaking groups of Moiseo, Masikota and Bowstrings, still resided in the headwaters country above the Crow Wing Fork of the Upper Mississippi, while the fourth group known as Pipe-Stem Men resided much further south along the Minnesota near that river's Great Elbow Bend and along one of its southern tributaries known as the Yellow Medicine. But here we are concerned with that early group among the Cheyenne confederacy still in the Upper Mississippi region, and known specifically as "Masikota."

- 0 - 0 - 0 - 0 - 0 - 0 - 0 - 0 - 0 - 0 - 0 - 0 - 0 - 0 - 0 - 0 –

CHAPTER 16.

"GRASSHOPPER" PEOPLE.

In the Mississippi headwaters country *"The land of stumps,"* as it is sometimes called in tradition, the Cheyennes could fend for themselves more easily and if threatened by enemies, could disperse at a moment's notice into the uncompromising swamp terrain, whereby they might better elude their foes. The division of the Moiseo into several scattered bands had occurred whilst residing in the lakes district of southern Ontario, and certainly, by the middle of the seventeenth century, there were four Cheyenne-proper groups dispersed over the Upper half of present-day Minnesota.

Regarding these Minnesota Cheyenne-speaking groups, certain Cheyenne informants of Grinnell [1923] mentioned the *TsisTsisTsas, Suhtaio* and *"Hetsisiomeistane"* as being three tribal groups related by blood and culture which, during these early years of their history, constituted the main components of what later became the Cheyenne Nation.

The first of these names represent a tribal collective term for the Cheyennes as a whole, which Grinnell inferred, was an ancient name and therefore would apply to the Moiseo faction specifically; in short, the Cheyenne-proper. The second refers, of course, to the Suhtaio, whilst the third which Grinnell actually calls *"a tribe,"* represents another closely related group whose name translates as "Pipe-Stem-Men."

On the other hand, George A. Dorsey [1905] also quoting from Cheyenne informants, listed the *"Arrow Men"* who are synonymous with the Moiseo; the *"Sutayo"* which is merely a variant spelling of Suhtaio, and a third group known in olden-times as *"Grasshoppers,"* which some Cheyennes declared, was sometimes used as an alternative collective name for the Cheyennes in their entirety.

Conversely, a Northern Cheyenne informant of the tribal historian John Stands in Timber, named Fire Wolf, stated that another early name for the tribe was that of *"Sand hill Men,"* while John Stands In Timber himself [1967] gave the term *"Nioh-ma-ale-a-ninya"* meaning *"Desert"* or *"Prairie People,"* and merely adding to the confusion is the term *"Masikota,"* a Cheyenne band name of late historic time, but thought by some scholars to have originally been applied to a foreign people presumed to have been of Teton Sioux stock and who of old, became so closely confederated with Cheyennes whilst residing about the headwaters of the Upper Minnesota River, that they were finally adopted by the latter and absorbed by them.

169

By differentiating these band names and deducing their respective territories, we are able to understand a little more the situation of our subjects during the period of these mist-shrouded years. It enables us also to follow in closer detail their respective wanderings and relationship with other tribes - hostile or friendly - as the case may be.

Now it has been shown earlier in our study that the Moiseo; or `Arrow Men` as Dorsey calls them, were the nucleus of the Cheyenne-speaking Nation, so that all Cheyenne-proper bands must have descended directly or indirectly from them. It is unlikely, however, that the Moiseo themselves represent Grinnell`s *"TsisTsisTsas."* Rather, these latter were breakaways from the Moiseo parent band who afterwards, not only came to greatly outnumber the Moiseo, but took charge of the tribe's traditions; sacred talismans and other features uniquely Cheyenne. The probability is that the term TsisTsisTsas which Stands in Timber stated was actually a Suhtaio term, belongs to a later date than Grinnell supposed and that those Cheyenne bands which adopted its usage as a collective name, were, at an earlier date whilst still in close contact with the Moiseo in southern Ontario and the northern part of Minnesota, known by other names of which only a faint memory remained within the tribe by the time both Grinnell and Dorsey were collecting their material.

The *"Sutayo"* as rendered by Dorsey need little explanation at this point, for as previously determined in an earlier chapter, they were an ancient and, in truth, the first separatist group from the Moiseo parent band when in the "Old Turtle Land of the North." This is implied in Cheyenne tradition which relates to the initial period of their people's "Ancient Time," and that the Suhtaio spoke a dialect of Cheyenne rather than some other Algonquian tongue. Since then the Suhtaio had pursued a separate migration from the old *Middle Laurel Complex* area, south and southeast into southern Ontario and northeastern Minnesota. They were thus distanced from the Moiseo for several centuries as is apparent by their diversity of dialect, but by the second half of the sixteenth century, the Suhtaio had entered the headwaters country of the Upper Mississippi and made contact again with their long-lost Cheyenne-speaking cousins.

The *"Grasshoppers"* of Dorsey`s list are particularly important and as I will endeavor to show, this term was but another early collective name for the bulk of Cheyenne offshoots from the Moiseo; synonymous with the original Masikota band and also, with John Stands in Timber's *"Desert"* or *"Prairie Men."*

There appears to have been disagreement among Cheyenne informants of a later date, regarding whether the Masikota were actually Algonquian speakers or Siouan. Sometimes they have even been confused with the Moiseo under the spelling *"Mowisiyu,"* which, so George Bent was told, was a foreign group that migrated with Cheyennes from the Upper Mississippi country and divided upon reaching the Missouri. Some of their number thence returned east from whence they came; whilst others amalgamated with various Cheyenne-speaking factions.

Of course, the term *Mowisiyu* is clearly a variant of Moiseo, the former rendition being the archaic and more correct form. This confusion, though, will become untangled as we progress, although the Masikota are most relevant at this stage.

It is known that the term *"Masikota"* was the name given to a famous Cheyenne band during the historic period of the nineteenth century. Around the date 1849, after a severe cholera outbreak in that year which decimated the tribe's population, they joined the Dog-Soldier warrior society amass that had since become a separate band in its own right, and were absorbed by them. Yet some Cheyenne informants were of the opinion that like the Moiseo, the Masikota were not originally Cheyenne-speakers at all, but a foreign people who co-habited with Cheyenne-proper bands when in the headwaters district of the Minnesota River. They further stated that the Masikota, again in the ilk of the Moiseo, migrated with Cheyennes to the Missouri and upon reaching which, a part of the Masikota returned east, while those who were left crossed the Missouri and remained with the Cheyennes as a component group of the tribal camping circle.

Even late in the nineteenth century the name Masikota was of doubtful meaning among the Cheyennes themselves, being variously translated as either "corpse from a scaffold," grey hair," "ghost head," "wrinkled" and even "drawn up." The word, in fact, is similar to the Cheyenne term for the cricket, i.e. *"masis-kot,"* supposed by Rudolph Petter [1907] the eminent scholar of the Cheyenne language, as being derived from the same root which pertains to the `doubling up` of that insect's legs. More likely, though, it derives from *"misi"* or *"misis,"* meaning "eaters," and *"kota,"* meaning "prairie" as in "prairie eaters," although the proper Cheyenne term for the cricket is *"HesKosema."* Thus Petter`s translation appears to have been used as a colloquialism for any of the various translations given above. Conversely, the Cheyenne word for grasshopper is `ha`kota.` Here the prefix `Ha,` denotes `much,` `intense,` `very,` etc. and the terminal `a` indicates something animate as opposed to anything which is inanimate. Thus *"masiskot"* must refer to something inanimate by lacking this suffix. The inference is that the term *masiskot* when and if applied to the insect, should actually be rendered *"Masiskota,"* and that the derivation of the word, therefore, will be the same as that of the Cheyenne band name of Masikota.

The Cheyennes themselves have long since forgotten the true derivation of the word and today, know only that it is a term applied to the cricket. Neither from Petter`s spelling can the term be broken down satisfactorily into component parts to represent any other Cheyenne words which, when joined together, would make sense. This suggests that its present form is either a poor corruption of an archaic Cheyenne word or words, or that it is not a Cheyenne word at all. There are, in truth, several spellings of the same term in the guise of Masiskota, Mashikota, Masikota and Matsishkota and these actually give us a clue as to its origin and true meaning.

As an alternative to the name being a Cheyenne term or even an original Cheyenne band, at first glance, it looks decidedly Siouan, and some scholars have translated it from the Sioux as meaning "allies" or "friends with guns," literally, *"mazi"* – iron, i.e., `gun` and *"kota"* - ally or friend. The late George E. Hyde [1956] gave the alternative rendition of its translation from the Sioux as "Iron shooters," that is *"mazi"* – iron and *"kute"* - to shoot. Today, however, the Sioux themselves have no recollection of one of their bands having had the name Masikota, but use the term Wazikute for that Dakota Sioux division known as "Shooters among the Pines."

George Hyde further postulated that the name Masikota, was once applied by the Sioux in reference to the Cheyenne's early use of guns. But all the evidence points to the fact that the Sioux were already well-equipped with firearms long before the Cheyennes, and therefore, the Sioux had no logical reason to pick the use of guns as being something peculiar by which to name the Cheyennes.

Indeed, a more convincing argument might be that the word derives from the Sioux term *"istahota,"* pronounced *"e-shtah-kho-tah"* and given to mean "grey eyes," which is one of the alternative meanings in the list of translations noted above. One might conject that the word Masikota is then, a Cheyenne corruption of this Sioux form and that "grey eyes" refers to the misty colorless pupils of a very old person when close to death, and is a synonym for "grey hair" which also denotes a very old person. Hence the reason why some Cheyenne informants thought the word was Sioux and why, in later years, it came to be used as a descriptive analogy for a corpse and analogous with its related terms of "wrinkled," "drawn up" and "ghost head."

It seems a pity that such erudite scholars such as Hyde and Grinnell, did not delve deeper into tribal groups closely related to the Cheyennes linguistically. As they may then have found the correct answer.

Both the Cree and Chippewa, of course, were very close stock relatives to the Cheyennes and in the Chippewa tongue we find the word *"mashkoda,"* meaning "prairie" or "expanse of grass." In the Plains Cree dialect this becomes *"muskota,"* in another Cree dialect, *"maskotay,"* and in yet another, *"maskute."* The word in all cases is commonly used as a compound noun in order to denote a connection with the buffalo specifically, but also to describe anything either to do with or living on the prairie. Therefore, the term can readily be applied to any creature both man and beast which is indigenous to grass expanses, and includes such insects as the cricket, grasshopper and even the mosquito. In a similar way the generic term M*ascouten,* which in colonial times included buffalo-hunting prairie tribes of the Wisconsin and Minnesota regions such as the Iowa, Illini and Potawatomi among others, who were long-time friends of early Cheyenne-speaking groups, also translates as "Prairie People" as opposed to those non-prairie tribes residing in more wooded regions to the east.

It is interesting to note Ben Clark's spelling of the Cheyenne band name Masikota which he rendered *"Matsishkota,"* for this is probably the nearest to the original form as we can now get. It can be seen at once the similarity of this Cheyenne term with that of the Cree and Chippewa versions. In addition, this Cheyenne term as given in Clark's rendering, can be divided into separate words which when put together, offer a plausible and sensible translation.

If we were to split the term as *"ma-tsi-shkota,"* then we have "grass like prairie" and by adding `s` to the second syllable so as to read *"ma-tsis-h-kota,"* it becomes "grass very like prairie" or in its English idiom, "very like the prairie grass." The `h` in this case is used as an indication of `much,` `very,` etc.; being a contraction of the proper Cheyenne form of `ha,` as in *"ha`kota"* meaning *"grasshopper."* We then have a logical reason for the derivation of the Cheyenne name for both the cricket and grasshopper. Referring, no doubt, to the camouflage colouring of such insects.

It is not inconceivable, in truth, highly likely, that Cheyennes whilst living about Lower Red Lake, and during which time they were accustomed to venture regularly into prairie lands to the south on prolonged tribal hunts more so than did the Iowa, Potawatomi and Illini, that they likened themselves to; or were thought of by others such as the neighbouring Dakota and Cree, as crickets or grasshoppers. They thus adopted the name which has since become corrupted into its variant form to mean "Prairie people," as indeed, grasshoppers particularly were often referred to by the Cheyennes.

The Cheyenne tribal name for `prairie` when used as part of a person's name is *"Tuktue,"* but when used as part of the term for buffalo is rendered as *"hotue."* Obviously, the form `ktue,` pronounced *"koot-to-a,"* represents `prairie` and comes from the same root as both the Cree and Chippewa terms of *"kota"* and *"kute."* Subsequently, this Cheyenne term needs only the appropriate prefix to qualify it.

Why the linguist Rudolph Petter offered his, as I believe, misleading definition, may have been because the women of a certain Cheyenne band in the nineteenth century, were in the habit of sitting with their legs `drawn up.` Other bands in their poetic wisdom referred to them as `crickets,` using the term *"Masikota"* which in the vernacular came to mean "legs flexed." In due course, the same name came to mean anything shriveled-looking, such as a body with its legs drawn up and which incidentally, is the posture a corpse is apt to take after having been left atop an open burial scaffold for a specific length of time. Hence the term's definition in the vernacular to denote any person either dead or in old age, in the guise of grey head, grey eyes, grey hair, wrinkled etc.

Taken further, the peculiar arrangement of syllables in the Cheyenne language, can also render the word with Clark's spelling as "Prairie Breeders" if one were to translate the first part of the word `matsi` as being a corruption of `motsi` meaning `breeder,` and the second part `shkota` as `prairie.` This would then offer a more meaningful name for these early Cheyennes if they referred to themselves as "Prairie breeders" or "Breeders of the prairie." One should remember that a similar appellation may well have been the origin of the name Moiseo. [See Chapter 3.]. If on the other hand we take Grinnell`s spelling of the name, which he rendered as `Masiskota,` then we may have the compound term `Prairie eater," c.f. *"mese"* = "eat" and *"kota"* = "prairie." Although if we accept the Cree translation of this same spelling, we have "Prairie master," cf. *"masis"* i.e. "master" and *"kota"* i.e. "prairie" in its contracted Cree form. Each of these supposed translations can be seen as merely variations of one another, but surely it explains the Cheyenne assertion previously mentioned, that one of their people's early names was "Prairie Men," applied as a collective designation by the fact that they once compared themselves to Grasshoppers or the "Prairie People" as they called them.

Probably the Chippewa once knew the Cheyenne by the name Masikota, or by some similar sounding term when the latter resided in the Upper Mississippi district. They, the Chippewa, knew the Suhtaio who during the same period, were in very close contact and likely confederated with certain Cheyenne-speaking groups. Either way, the actual name of Masikota appears to have been a remnant from the archaic Cheyenne dialect; closer to Chippewa and Cree than to modern-day Cheyenne. This would explain why the latter had forgotten its true derivation when inquiries were made among them late in the nineteenth century.

173

A comparative table of these numerous dialectical variations shows a profound connection not easy to dismiss.

Cheyenne and Suhtaio.	Chippewa.	Cree.
MasiKota.	Mashkoda	MasKotay.
MaTsiShkota.	----------------------	MasKute
TaShota		
Shuta	----------------------	Shota
Sohta	----------------------	
S`oh-tah	So` tah	Soto.

It was once reported that another ancient name for the Cheyennes was that of "Mosquitoes," while in the *"Handbook of the American Indian [1910],"* an attempt has been made to translate the term `Moiseo` to mean "many flies," from *"his,"* = "fly," and this itself, has also been averred as having been yet another of that people's ancient names. Of course, as we have earlier deduced, this is not the correct interpretation of the word Moiseo. The names "Mosquitoes" and "Many Flies" are, though, synonymous; even analogous with that of Grasshopper or Masikota, and this perhaps, is indicative that in the lake and swamp country of southern Ontario and northern Minnesota throughout which area the several Cheyenne-speaking bands once roamed, mosquitoes are to be found in great abundance. At a later date, however, the term Mosquitoes seems to have had a different connotation. Then referring to Cheyenne-speaking peoples going constantly to war; hitting their enemies [e.g., biting their enemies] consistently and aggressively.

It has been mentioned in an earlier chapter that Cheyenne-speaking peoples in southern Ontario and northern Minnesota, together once comprised a very large population [according to one account ten-thousand persons]. This was prior to the early 1540s, when a pandemic of gigantic proportion most likely swept away vast numbers of indigenous peoples across the whole of the Eastern and Midwest States. Perhaps, then, it was before the latter event that the Cheyennes being then a part of the Cree, had referred to themselves as "Many Flies," having supposed that their numbers were as populous as mosquitoes which swarmed in great multitudes over the lake and muskeg [i.e., swampy] lands of central and southern Ontario, or alternatively, merely because the proto-Cheyennes were then associated with that region.

The Cheyennes did not apply the term `many flies` to any particular insect species, but moreover, as a collective term to include under its general heading the grasshopper, cricket, mosquito, horsefly and dragonfly. Yet all these creatures did also have their individual names. The appellation of "Grasshopper" appears then, to have been substituted for that of "Mosquito" after the people had moved away from the aforesaid districts, and relocated in more open grassland areas where the grasshopper was predominant instead. By so doing, the original concept of the name `Many Flies` may have been kept alive in the guise of Masikota. Thus it was probably applied as an alternative to that of both "Many Flies" and "Mosquitoes." An alternative explanation of the term "many flies" is given as referring to a one-time chief who`s person and clothes were so dirty, that he was constantly surrounded by flies. This is indicative, as the chief in question is said to have been the head man of the Aorta Cheyenne band, who`s members, of course, were the later descendants of the original `Arrow Men` band, also known as Moiseo.

We further see in the Cree / Chippewa Algonquian dialects the word *"quissi,"* meaning `eaters,` or when rendered with the suffix `n` as in *"quissin,"* meaning `to eat.` *"Quissi"* is a contracted form of Moiseo and of its variant term of Mowisiyu, which in addition to referring to the grass-eating elk as in the Algonkin-proper name of Wheskerinni, it may once have denoted the eating propensity of the grasshopper, if not the biting habits of the mosquito.

Be this as it may, the fact that Cheyenne informants declared that the name "Grasshoppers" was once conferred upon the Cheyenne tribe as a whole, indicates that all other Cheyenne-speaking bands, which came into being during this early period of residence around Lower Red Lake and the Mississippi headwaters district [between circa, 1550 and 1640], had actually split from the Masikota group rather than the parent Moiseo or that of the Bowstrings.

Only after that remnant Cheyenne-speaking group which retained the name Moiseo, had become an independent body and more closely aligned to the Monsoni Cree and Upper Mississippi Sioux, did other Cheyennes adopt the name Masikota as their singular, collective appellation. Because the Masikota [among whom were the Arrow Men or Kit-Fox band with the Sacred Arrow talismans and their Keeper], were a separatist faction from the Moiseo parent band rather than from the Bowstrings, some later Cheyenne informants of both Hyde and Bent, likely confused the Masikota with the Moiseo. As originally both were merely kindred factions of the same group and once shared the name Moiseo.

Now the Kiowa tribe always called the Cheyennes *"SaKota"* [pronounced, *Sha-kota*], even though their two peoples did not meet each other until long after Cheyennes had left the Minnesota country and crossed the Missouri River. This name is not of Kiowa origin; neither could the Kiowa themselves give a satisfactory explanation for it. James Mooney [1892] was of the opinion that the word had something to do with the act of `biting,` perhaps even `Biters` and in this, albeit unknowingly, he was probably correct.

It is apparent that the first Cheyenne-speaking group to come into close contact with the Kiowa west of the Missouri, was, in fact, a large Masikota Cheyenne faction. What then a more appropriate alternative translation of the term Masikota than `Biters?` pertaining, moreover, to the "Grasshopper People" with the same connotation as `cricket,` `many flies` and `mosquitoes.`

It is true that the Kiowa also called the Missouri River Arickara "Biters.*"* But in this case they used the Kiowa term *"ka-a-ta"* which specifically refers to the action of biting corn from the cob. The Kiowa informants of James Mooney made no connection apparently, between this latter word and that of *"SaKota,"* implying therefore, that the two designations had separate origins and meanings. No doubt, the name *"Sakota"* is derived from a Kiowa rendition of *"Masikota"* having omitted the prefix `Ma,` and seems to have been adopted by the Kiowa from the Cheyenne language. This being the name by which the particular Cheyenne-speaking group with whom the Kiowa were then in contact, were employing as a personal collective name for themselves and their immediate offshoots.

In corroboration of this, the Northern Cheyenne band name of more recent time known as Omissis, which group in its earlier days appears to have evolved from a conglomerate composed from original Moiseo and Wheskerinni ancestors and among whom the Bowstrings had been the predominant faction, is also commonly translated as "Eaters." Thus they, too, can readily be associated with the old tribal collective name of Masikota or Grasshopper, in so much as a component group of the latter wishing to preserve a concept of their collective name, albeit using a distinguishing appellation from the existing Masikota band-proper, referred to themselves simply as "Eaters." Such would have been in reference to their own ancient name for themselves of Wheskerinni or Elks i.e., "grass eaters" and to the particular avidness of the grasshopper, for as we have seen in a previous chapter, the name Moiseo in its root form also has the connotation meaning "eaters of grass."

As a final piece of corroboration, there was until the great cholera epidemic of 1849, a Cheyenne band called *"Ohk-tu-unna,"* sometimes spelt *"Oqtoguna"* which as translated by Grinnell means "Jaws." A more precise translation, though, is "Lower jaw protruding" and is meant to convey the idea of eating so voraciously that the Lower jaw actually sticks out from the face. This, of course, is reminiscent of the habit of the grasshopper and its cousins the cricket and locust [this last named insect also included under the collective name of "Many Flies"], and we know that the *Ohktunna* were originally breakaways, albeit at a later date, from the Masikota parent band.

Why all this had apparently been forgotten by Cheyennes when inquiries were being made late in the nineteenth and early twentieth century, was, perhaps, that the populations of both the Masikota and the offshoot *Ohktunna* had been decimated during the aforesaid cholera outbreak of 1849. The result being that their few survivors were absorbed into other Cheyenne bands and soon after, not only lost their singular identity but save a few fragments, had also forgotten much of their personal band history and traditions.

On the other hand, the term "Desert people" as mentioned by the tribal historian John Stands in Timber, is also given as being an old Cheyenne collective name for themselves, and appears to be somewhat interchangeable with that of "Prairie Men," as he gives only one word for both meanings. This infers that unless otherwise stated, the same word sufficed in Cheyenne for any large open tract of land and if this be so, then the "Desert People" were synonymous with the "Prairie Men," i.e., the "Grasshoppers."

Similarly, the old Cheyenne collective name of "Sand hill Men" mentioned at the beginning of this chapter, no doubt referred to the habitat of the Masikota when in northern Minnesota.

This is substantiated by the account of Fire Wolf, the old Cheyenne-Suhtaio informant of Stands in Timber who declared that anciently, the TsisTsisTsas called themselves "Desert" or "Sand hill People." At the time referred to by Fire Wolf, the Cheyennes, he said, were then living near the Pipe-Stone Quarries in a land of lakes and were in the habit of heading north during a certain season when the birds shed their feathers. This, unquestionably places Cheyennes in either the central or northern part of the Minnesota country, far indeed from any desert or large expanse of sand. Fire-Wolf may have been referring to the Suhtaio alone, although sand dunes are a particular feature of the country immediately east of the Upper Mississippi and in the tall-grass prairie regions west and south of Lower Red Lake. These latter areas are composed of sandy soil interspersed with dunes and in which regions we know from both Cheyenne and Sioux tradition and some contemporary maps of the late 17th century, both Cheyennes and Suhtaio once roamed during the period in question. It was in this same area, incidentally, that the Masikota were principal occupants for many years and thus the term "Desert" or "Prairie Men," no doubt, was once applied to the Masikota and their immediate offshoots.

Certainly sand dunes are also to be found near the Pipe-Stone Quarries in the southwestern part of Minnesota and it is true, that some Cheyennes did frequent that region in order to obtain red sand stone [which was thought to contain sacred properties] for the manufacture of smoking-pipe bowls. Consequently, the term "Sand Hill People" or "Sand Hill Men" may have once been used colloquially in order to designate a particular Cheyenne-speaking band, some members of which often visited the said quarry so that in time, the name became analogous with that of "Desert Men."

No Cheyenne or Suhtaio bands, however, as far as our present knowledge extends, were ever permanent residents of the Pipe-Stone Quarry district, which was some distance south of the Minnesota River and the "land of lakes" mentioned in tradition. The informant Fire Wolf was not, though, actually referring specifically to the quarry area itself, but merely indicating the Minnesota Country as opposed to where he himself was then positioned when making his statement, which was the far-western High Plains country of southeastern Montana.

– 0 - 0 - 0 - 0 - 0 - 0 - 0 - 0 - 0 - 0 - 0 - 0 - 0 - 0 - 0 - 0 - 0 - 0 - 0 –

CHAPTER 17.

DISPERSAL OF THE BANDS.

The previous assertions gleaned from reliable sources, demonstrate that "TsisTsisTsas" was not an ancient collective term for the Cheyennes. Rather, it is a name of comparatively recent origin for the people or groups of peoples earlier known as Moiseo, Bowstrings and Masikota, but collectively, as Grasshoppers or Prairie People. We must not forget the statement from John Stands in Timber mentioned in the previous chapter, that the term "TsisTsisTsas" was the Suhtaio name by which they originally called the Cheyenne-proper, and which translates as "like us," "similarly bred" or something of that ilk, owing to the fact that the Suhtaio recognized themselves as sharing a close affinity in language, theology and religious observances with the early Cheyennes.

The TsisTsisTsas as a small, albeit important group, evidently broke away from the parent Moiseo band to associate more closely with the Masikota, as this separatist group of

TsisTsisTsas was the same which was connected to the tribe's "Sacred Arrow" talismans and were guardians of the tribe`s traditions. They were then a part of those known earlier as Arrow Men or the Kit-Fox band, and in later years, became an important component of the Cheyenne Nation; albeit generally included under the collective name of Masikota or Grasshoppers. They were also known at a later date as "Smoky Lodges" and even later, as the Burnt Aorta band and among whom the Sacred Arrows and their Keeper still reside. The Masikota band certainly included the Motsonitanio or Arrow Men element from among the united Cheyenne-speaking groups, which likewise, was closely associated with the Sacred Arrow talismans. Hence why members of the warrior society later known as the Woksihitanio or Kit-Fox Men whose alternative name was Motsonitanio, wore a kit-fox stole as part of their personal regalia in recognition of the sacred kit-fox skin bundle in which the said `Arrows` had been wrapped when first brought among the people by the prophet Sweet Medicine. In addition, they wore a flint arrowhead depending from a cord around the neck representing the Sacred Arrows themselves.[2] On the other hand, the Pipe-Stem Men appear to have been an early breakaway band from the Omissis-Bowstrings, rather from either the Moiseo or Masikota. This band was listed by Grinnell as an original component group which, eventually, amalgamated with the TsisTsisTsas and Suhtaio to create the Cheyenne Nation of more recent time. But of this we will speak later.

The one-time position of the Masikota as being the most populous and important Cheyenne-speaking group, or at least, the predominant element within the united tribe, can be construed at this period in their history by their personal name of "Grasshoppers" once being used as a collective term for the Cheyennes in their entirety, and also, by the subsequent situation of the Moiseo after the date circa, 1650. In so much as the parent Moiseo`s tribal role from that time on became greatly diminished. Thereafter the Moiseo became a small remnant of the larger Cheyenne-speaking body, choosing to be somewhat independent from the rest of the tribe. Indeed, from the date circa, 1700 on, they appear to have virtually confederated with the Teton Sioux of the Upper Mississippi region and among whom, a large proportion of the once independent Moiseo were later absorbed. Even the style of abode then employed by the Moiseo probably originated through their contact with the Sioux, who themselves, were scattered throughout the Upper Mississippi country on that river's east side between the mouth of the Minnesota and the Upper Mississippi Forks. They then resided in small villages composed of elongated oval-roofed bark wigwams. Grinnell`s informants told him that Cheyenne [Moiseo?] villages during the period between circa, 1650 and 1700 were more permanent than when residing in the far north, although the lodges themselves were generally of a flimsy nature, being composed of an elongated wattle frame with oval roof and the whole covered with birch-bark sheeting just as described for the Sioux. Such dwellings had the advantage, however, of being easily constructed and after the ravages of wind, snow and rain, they were just as easily repaired.

Withal, these Moiseo remnants intermarried among the neighbouring Sioux; changing their customs and dialect somewhat by their adoption of Sioux traits and phrases, thereby disguising to a large extent their own ancestry. In later years [circa, 1814 -`16] when a part of the Moiseo did rejoin Cheyenne-proper bands west of the Missouri River, the latter themselves could not make up their minds whether the Moiseo were of Sioux, Cree or of Cheyenne extraction.

Of those few Moiseo remnants who many years later rejoined the Cheyennes on the Missouri, they thereafter achieved but little significance. They were by far the smallest entity among all Cheyenne-speaking bands in the late historic period.

As suggested previously, the initial separation of the main Masikota faction from the parent Moiseo, had probably occurred whilst inhabiting the Lower Red Lake area, merely becoming finalized upon the abandonment of that region. Both the Moiseo breakaways known as the Kit-Fox band and the main Masikota group, moved at around the same time into the district of lakes about

NORTHERN CHEYENNE INFORMANT, FIRE WOLF.
[Photograph from "Photographer on an Army Mule." University of Oklahoma Press. 1965.]

the headwaters of the Mississippi. Only that the Masikota by then, were the predominant group which thereafter, became widely scattered throughout the northern half of the state of Minnesota.

Generally, though, it appears that the Masikota - compared to all other Cheyenne-speaking bands of that date - resided for the greater part of the year in the more open prairie country available on the west side of the Upper Mississippi, and employed light willow-framed skin or brush shelters as previously referred to, and hence, adopted the singular appellation of "Prairie Men" or "Grasshoppers" in recognition of their preferred habitat.

Whether the Masikota had come into being as a separate band through the advent of enemy pressure; overpopulation; internal dissension within the parent Moiseo group, or through a simple preference to seek out individual hunting grounds in order to accommodate an expanding population, we cannot know. However, an important factor was probably one of expediency.

The country surrounding the Upper Mississippi district was, predominantly, a marshy, lake and timbered country, not conducive to large villages of any permanency longer than a few months at most. The available supply of game would have soon become exhausted through over hunting, while the area needed to accommodate their numerous lodges, would have proved too extensive and of an irregular disposition for the villages to be successfully defended against assault. Smaller, more compact villages had the advantage in that the occupants could acquire sufficient food the year round, by moving from one hunting ground to another. At the same time, they could protect themselves more adequately by having a smaller, more compact perimeter to defend, yet, if need arose, the populous could disperse itself quickly into the marsh and forest terrain and hide until the danger was past. Such considerations became real concerns during the middle years of the seventeenth century, which was a period of much strife in Cheyenne history when they, along with most of their neighbours, were in constant expectation of attack from more powerful enemies armed with guns.

Having deduced that during this period of their evolution, the various breakaway Cheyenne bands referred to themselves collectively as Masikota or "Grasshoppers," each did, nonetheless, have individual names and were themselves divided into several smaller family groups dispersed over specific individual hunting grounds. Throughout the year these small camps for the most part, probably remained independent of one another. Although at certain times during the year, the inhabitants would have come together as a united body for tribal social gatherings; religious ceremonies and even for the common defense of the people, if not to conduct their own combined war ventures against one or another enemy tribe. It had been the adoption of the tribe`s Sacred Arrows that had made such gatherings imperative; even compulsory, and so kept the various bands united as a Nation.

In ancient times there may have existed some semblance of a clan system among the proto-Cheyennes, as indeed, was common among most other tribes including a number of Algonquian stock. Although no trace of such was extant among Cheyennes at the close of the nineteenth century when inquiries were first made concerning this point. It seems to be that these various Cheyenne-speaking groups when inhabiting the Minnesota country, should more properly be regarded as separate tribal divisions, each composed of several extended family camps and speaking slightly different dialects one from the other. Linear descent was not matrilineal, but Cheyenne society was certainly matrilocal, as a man upon marrying went to live with his wife's people. If there had once been a clan system at an earlier date, then the clans had since become so intermixed and having grown larger or smaller with successive generations, that prior to the latter decades of the seventeenth century, the particular totemic designations of "Kit-Fox," "Dog" "Elk" and "Bowstring" had come to denote separate tribal divisions, associated with the original groups of Moiseo [TsisTsisTsas], Suhtaio, Masikota and Omissis in that order, and only at a later date were the band names of Kit-Fox, Elk, Dog and Bowstring transferred to denote the Nation's respective warrior societies instead. By the early 1680s these breakaway bands in such a way, had adopted their different names in order to distinguish themselves from the old Moiseo parent group, and from each other.

From what can be gleaned from tribal tradition coupled with certain contemporary ethno-historical documentation, it is possible to corroborate the above assertion and to further designate five confederated groups, which when united at a later date, constituted what became known as the Cheyenne Nation. Each of these groups during the period covering the second half of the seventeenth century, were residing in their own particular territories in widely scattered locations throughout the Upper half of Minnesota, and can be listed as follows; i.e. Moiseo, Masikota, Bowstrings, Suhtaio and Pipe-Stem Men.

By circa, 1740, the Masikota had themselves divided into two groups, one large, the other small, although both retained the collective name Masikota. The smaller group, however, later became known by the Sioux appellation of *Sheo,* and - over the course of succeeding years - became an even smaller group in population with much less tribal prestige. At a later date, they lingered in the country close to the headwaters of the Minnesota River in the vicinity of Big Stone Lake, and like their Moiseo cousins before them, mingled with Teton Sioux bands of that district, ultimately losing their importance and independence by foreign amalgamation. When at last this remnant *Sheo* band of Masikota did reunite with other Cheyenne-speaking peoples west of the Missouri between the dates 1814 -`16, they were already a hybrid people composed of Masikota, some Cheyenne-proper [Moiseo] and a large strain of Teton Sioux blood. They then formed their own tribal band and although still regarding themselves as Cheyenne, all other Cheyennes referred to them by the term *"Watapio,"* i.e., "Eaters with the Sioux." Their old connection with the original Masikota group had become virtually obsolete, as did the true meaning of their old-time designation of "Grasshoppers." Like the remnant of Moiseo who in a similar manner had evolved by the same date into a mixed conglomerate of Cheyenne, Suhtaio and Sioux, these Watapio Masikota offshoots were often confused by Indians and white men alike as belonging to the Sioux, simply because of their strong affiliation with certain Sioux bands.

How is it then, in light of the preceding conclusions, that no mention of Cheyenne-speaking peoples, it seems, other than one or two late seventeenth century map references, are to be had in contemporary documentation of the period of Cheyenne occupation in either the Mississippi headwaters region, or in the vicinity of the Minnesota River ?

Perhaps, though, Cheyenne-speaking peoples are mentioned, but in obscure form, some of which appellations may or may not eventually come to light. It is, though, worth noting that the Cheyenne group Masikota - whose name we have deduced actually translates as "Grasshoppers" or more precisely, "Prairie People." - had by circa, 1640 become allied to the Iowa and Oto. They may then, in truth, have been incorporated within the generic Algonquian term of Mascouten, which was used by the colonial French to designate several `prairie` tribes and under which heading, the Miami, Illini, Potawatomi, Iowa and Oto were once included. Certainly the

Algonquian terms of *"Maskoutec" and "Mascouten"* along with numerous variations of the same, also mean "Prairie People," although they are often presented with a customary garbled French ending. The Mascouten-proper, however, were additionally known by the term "Fire people" and we must not forget the Cheyenne informant John Stands-in-Timber's assertion, previously cited [Chapter 3.], which states that an alternative translation of the late-historic Cheyenne band name of "Mutes-ohue" [i.e. Moiseo], was indeed, "Making fire people." Most likely then, included under this generic term were those Cheyennes of both the Bowstring and Masikota groups, along with their close offshoots which together, were also known to most other tribes at that time and to themselves, by the collective name of "Prairie People" or "Grasshoppers."

Cheyennes, it seems, went unrecognized by the colonial French map makers of the day as comprising a separate tribal group and, certainly, the early French reports often confused the *"Mascoutens,"* by sometimes applying the term to the Siouan-speaking Iowa and Oto; sometimes to the Teton Sioux and at other times to any group Siouan or Algonquian-speaking which was apt to roam the grasslands adjacent to the south side of the Minnesota or in the open prairie country east and west of the middle and Upper courses of the Mississippi. So in the case of these early Cheyenne- groups, their people were most likely included under the French collective heading of *Mascouten.* We know that an old Osage name for the Cheyenne was *"Tois Mois,"* which appears to substantiate the above assumption by meaning "Prairie Walkers" and surely, this is but a variant of the term *Mascouten.* The Osage themselves were offshoots from the Iowa - Oto Siouan group of tribes, and we also know that the explorer Pierre Radisson met the Iowa east of the Mississippi in 1658/59 or thereabouts. Radisson was told by neighbouring Algonquians that their name for the Iowa was *Mascouten,* but was actually a term used as a colloquial name for any peoples roaming the prairie country west of the Mississippi, no matter to which linguistic family they belonged.

It may be therefore, that the Minnesota River Cheyenne group or groups, were originally called *Mascouten,* being a dialectical form of Masikota. When the Iowa crossed the Mississippi along with some Central Algonquian tribes after the date 1693, and in the process occupied the old Cheyenne lands about the mouth of Blue Earth River, which the latter had since abandoned, the name was likely transferred from these particular Cheyenne-speaking groups and conferred upon the Iowa and Oto in their stead.

If this was the case, then the elusive *"Tartaga"* and *"Tartanga"* of Pierre Radisson's journal of 1660 / 61 which represents the Dakota or Sioux word for `buffalo,` and seemingly, applied by Radisson to the Algonquian-speaking Illinois tribes, may merely have been an alternative Sioux name for those peoples designated collectively as *Mascouten,* but which, moreover, included Cheyenne-speaking bands in the Upper Mississippi prairie country and those along the south side of the Minnesota River. If this be so, then it would be the earliest documented reference to our Cheyenne-speaking subjects.

The above deductions are corroborated by the late seventeenth century writings of the French trader Nicholas Perrot, at which time he reported that the Indian group known as *"Maskoutec,"* a name he translated as `Walkers` and with whom he met sometime during the early 1660s, were Algonquian-speakers of the prairies. They were, he said, practitioners of the Calumet ceremony and hunted buffalo for their domestic needs. Perrot went on to note certain customs among the *Maskoutecs* which were very similar to those still in vogue among the Cheyennes two centuries later. Even his account of the introduction of firearms among them; the first such weapons the *Mascoutecs* had seen, is so similar to the Cheyenne oral tradition concerning their own initial encounter with guns, as related by the Northern Cheyenne historian John Stands-In-Timber, that one wonders at the obvious connection.

At the time of his visit, Perrot's *Mascoutecs* were then in a league with the Potawatomi and Miami. This is consistent with the historical fact that by 1665, the Iroquois-proper had driven the Miami, Potawatomi and some Illinois bands from their eastern country; forcing them to flee to the west side of Lake Michigan and as far as the Mississippi and beyond. These refugee tribes crossed the Mississippi at a point near Lake Pepin, and as a result, placed themselves in close proximity to Cheyenne-proper groups, then residing near the mouth of the Blue Earth on the Minnesota and in the headwaters region of the Upper Mississippi.

This was the period immediately following the introduction of the Calumet ceremony among these particular Central Algonquian tribes, that is, sometime between circa, 1650 and 1665. It includes the time of Radisson's several visits to the west, which would explain how the Cheyennes - included under the generic name of *Mascoutec* - may well have been present among those peoples met by Perrot sometime during the mid-1660s. It would also add credence to the assumption that one Cheyenne-speaking group, at least, was entrenched along the middle course of the Minnesota River long prior to the 1680s.

The term *"Mascoutec"* as used by Perrot includes the Algonquian term for `prairie,` and like the Osage term more properly means "Prairie Walkers." This is not to say that *"Mascoutec"* refers singularly to the Cheyenne, only that they were likely to have been included under its collective heading. There would have been little significant difference between the dress and culture of all the above designated tribes at that time, and the French chroniclers of the day merely lumped them together, as it were, classifying them all as one people. The French themselves thus adopted the Algonquian custom of employing the name *"Mascoutec"* or a variant of the same, as a generic term for any tribal group inhabiting the prairie country.

Suffice to say that after the Masikota and the Moiseo Kit-Fox band had separated from the parent Moiseo, the small Moiseo remnant faction remained in north-eastern Minnesota in close proximity to the Suhtaio [i.e. Chongaskitons on early colonial maps]. They were then, it seems, from contemporary map references and French reports, positioned sometimes east and sometimes west of the headwaters of the Upper Mississippi, and always close to the Sioux. Indeed, the name Moiseo can be found on these early French maps, but in the guise of diverse spellings such as *"Quissy,"* *"Ouissi,"* *"Quissiloua"* and *"Quafsi."*

To the southeast of Lower Red Lake but still close to the Mississippi heads, evidently in the vicinity of Bowstring Lake and Bowstring River, resided yet another Cheyenne-speaking group noted by Louis Joliet on his map of 1674. Joliet designated this group as *"Chaiena"* which appellation, no doubt, is of Sioux derivation and seems to have been applied by Joliet to incorporate both the Masikota and Bowstrings [i.e. Omissis] Cheyenne groups combined. South of Joliet's

"Chaiena," although not shown by him or indeed, on any map of the period, it is likely that Grinnell`s *"Hetsiomisitane"* or Pipe-Stem Men resided.

This last mentioned group seem to have occupied territory somewhat distant from their Moiseo, Masikota and Bowstring cousins in the north. They cannot satisfactorily be associated with any definite place or tribal name on the early maps and documents which relate to that general area of occupation. The name, nonetheless, suggests they were the owners of pipes; perhaps supplying northern tribes with the sacred pipe stems as used in the "Hako" or "Wan-Wan" ceremony. They were, therefore, probably occupants of the old Cheyenne village site either on Yellow Medicine River [a southern tributary of the Minnesota], or adjacent to the shores of Lake Lac Qui Parle higher up the Minnesota. Both these sites, so Sioux tradition declares, were once occupied by one or another Cheyenne-speaking group, long before the opening of the eighteenth century. [See Chapter 2.].

Even earlier, these same Pipe-Stem Men appear to have been positioned near the Great Elbow Bend of the Minnesota near where the town of Mankato now stands. Presumably they had seceded from the Omissis-Bowstrings group and as will be shown, they included, albeit at a much later date, the historic Cheyenne band of *"Hissiometanio"* or "Hill Men" also known as Ridge Men, and which; so some of Grinnell`s Cheyenne informants declared, was an alternative name for the Pipe-Stem Men. All this, however, also belongs to a later chapter and here we are concerned moreover, with those Cheyenne-speaking groups then collectively known to themselves as "Grasshoppers" [i.e., the Masikota and Bowstrings], residing in the northern part of what is now the state of Minnesota within the vicinity of the Mississippi heads.

- 0 - 0 - 0 - 0 - 0 - 0 - 0 - 0 - 0 - 0 - 0 - 0 - 0 - 0 - 0 - 0 - 0 - 0 - 0 –

CHAPTER 18.

LAST DAYS IN THE RED LAKES DISTRICT.

Tribal tradition according to the Northern Cheyenne James King, recalls that while still roaming the southern Ontario lakes country, the Cheyennes knew no enemies, being all but isolated from other peoples and when later these same Cheyenne-speaking bands moved south, they lived about the lake with its adjoining prairie - ostensibly that of Lower Red Lake - for many years. The Cheyennes were happy during that time, James King said, and for a long period they were in harmonious contact with all the tribes around them.

This is an acceptable assertion when one remembers that when in southern Ontario, the Moiseo were then remote from the hunting grounds of more formidable and aggressive tribes to the east. No doubt the Moiseo had some degree of contact with one or more Arapahoe and Blackfoot bands inhabiting adjoining territories during that same period, for these former were close cousins to the Moiseo and practiced a near identical lifestyle and culture. Yet such meetings were likely to have occurred by chance rather than design, in the accidental coming together of their respective groups during the incessant wanderings of each. For the most part, these three tribal groups remained independent of each other, practically hibernating throughout the winter months; secluded and minding no one but themselves.

Rarely would there have been sufficient excuse to initiate hostilities with their neighbours. Certainly not on the grounds of protecting one's tribe from expulsion or extermination. Although there was always the economic necessity to safeguard against foreign trespass into one's tribal hunting grounds, in order to preserve the supply of game needed to adequately sustain the people. It seems to be just such a situation that at a later date, brought the Cheyennes into conflict with their long-lost Suhtaio cousins.

Perhaps, though, it was this period of virtual isolation from the outside world, which saw what my informant James King described as another of his people`s *"Golden Age"* periods. These being times when warfare, supposedly, was non-existent and there was no cause for fear.

An apocryphal statement maybe, although other than periodic internal feuds within the tribe itself, or the rare occurrence of economic pressure caused by environmental change due to climatic variation which, as we have seen, had incurred mass movement and inevitable clashes between resident and encroacher in earlier times, there was now no such thing as total war when the complete extermination of the enemy was the prime objective.

Prior to the middle years of the seventeenth century, before the beginnings of recurrent diseases which thereafter, spread west from European contacts along the Atlantic seaboard, the indigenous Indian population was, no doubt, much greater than it subsequently became. After circa. 1650, the proto-historic Indian population ratio of an average horticultural community has been estimated at around forty persons per 100 square miles, while in the forest and lake country of Ontario and northern Minnesota, whereabouts the Cheyennes, Blackfoot and Arapahoe resided during the period in question, an even sparser density of population was probably the norm. Thus the incentive to inaugurate and conduct wars of conquest was not there and; generally speaking, intertribal relations - certainly in the Upper Mississippi valley and further north - were more likely to have been cordial no matter to what linguistic stock a particular tribe and its neighbours belonged. This is evident also from the wide intertribal trading networks and cross-cultural contact and adoption, which at and long prior to this same time, extended across the whole of the northeastern and mid-west states, that is, during both the late pre-historic and proto-historic periods as recent archaeological findings in those areas suggest.

Sporadic internal friction within the tribe there undoubtedly was, as would be the case in any human social group and sometimes, such friction may have extended to neighbouring tribes. Intertribal feuding, though, would have been small-scale in extent, perhaps creating an atmosphere of excitement when the tedium of village life became excessive. Even the aforementioned period of Cheyenne conflict with the Suhtaio from what is recalled in the traditional accounts, can really only be regarded as a somewhat trivial affair.

As far as these early Cheyenne-speaking groups were concerned, their comparatively peaceable condition seems to have persisted throughout their period of residence in southern Ontario. In truth, all those hunter / gatherer peoples which included the Cheyennes, Arapahoe,

Suhtaio and Blackfoot while residing either in Ontario or northern Minnesota far above the aboriginal corn-growing belt, were probably too preoccupied in eking out a subsistence to allow themselves to contemplate serious thoughts of inaugurating internecine strife, merely to occupy their spare time.

On the other hand, the then horticultural groups of the Upper Mississippi area such as the Hidatsa and various Sioux tribes, albeit well-off economically in comparison to their hunter / gatherer neighbours, were during this same period, often too engrossed in complex religious activities and connected ceremonies to actually bother with all-out war for its own sake, other than conducting the sporadic hostile crusade against a protagonist tribe if it was thought necessary to do so. This is not to say that intertribal warfare was not by then already an important facet of the culture pertaining to all these northwestern tribes. The recently discovered Crow Creek massacre site adjacent to the Missouri River which dates between A.D.1325 and A.D.1350, tends on its own to contradict such a view. Only that war as the incessant, unrelenting occupation it later became, certainly after the arrival of Europeans and the opening of the fur trade and its ramifications in the early decades of the seventeenth century, had not as yet effected the southern Ontario and northern Minnesota tribes to any serious degree.

Having said this, at a later date while still in the Upper and Lower Red Lake's district, the fact that there was an adequate food supply and friendly neighbours nearby, make it unlikely that the then resident Cheyenne-speaking groups eventually vacated the region completely due to a restless spirit. More feasible is the assumption that the people were obliged to move owing to a sudden outbreak of hostilities with one or another foreign group. This we know was certainly the reason why the Hidatsa along with the Cheyenne's linguistic cousins the Arapahoe and Blackfoot, were forced to move west from their seats in adjoining areas at around the same time as did the Cheyennes.

One singular event which did help breach the general congeniality once harbored among those peoples of the Upper Mississippi country, occurred, traditionally, just prior to the middle years of the seventeenth century. This event, initially, was an internal affair specifically within the populous Dakota or Sioux Nation. The result being, that the Yankton Wazikute Sioux division split into two factions, one of which disassociated itself from the parent band and moved north above the headwaters of the Mississippi. This particular group of seceders became known in historic times by a corruption of their Algonquian name of "Stone Boilers," commonly rendered as *"Assiniboine,"* although Sioux groups knew them by the derogatory term of *"Ho-He"* or *"Ho-Hay"* meaning in the Sioux vernacular, "Rebels," albeit that a proper translation is "Fish Netters." The Cheyennes themselves often referred to these same people by the Sioux name *"Ho-Hay,"* but also knew them as the *"Hoehmehoheeoee,"* which was a Cheyenne-proper term meaning "Cradle people." Indeed, another Dakota name for the Assiniboine translates as "childish," said to refer to the unsophisticated or childish dialect spoken by the latter [indicating the Assiniboine as being breakaways from the parent stock]. But in truth, this was merely a term adopted by the Dakota from the Cree and Chippewa word *boin* or *bwan* meaning "weaklings" or "incapable ones," and from which the latter part of the name Assiniboine is actually derived.

This term was used by the more western or Teton Sioux because the Assiniboine were thought to compare unfavorably with other Sioux groups, and thus was also originally employed as an alternative derogatory term. It is then, this Cree and Chippewa concept that was adopted by the Cheyennes in its Cheyenne form of `Cradle People,` and might add substance to the idea that these early Cheyenne-speaking groups were then still in close friendly association with the Monsoni Cree, and so used the same Cree term to denote the Assiniboine specifically.

An even earlier Cheyenne name for the Assiniboine, however, seems to have been *Hoztova-Hotacea,* which translates into something like, "On two sides different Star People." The term itself "Star People" was, of old, used by Cheyennes to designate the Teton Sioux as opposed to other Sioux groups, and hence, the Oglala people of that Nation were known to the Cheyennes as "Little Star People. " The Assiniboine; being of Sioux extraction and at this early date, friends with the Cheyennes before becoming their enemies, were therefore considered as having two faces, i.e., one of which the Cheyennes recognized as belonging by blood kinship to the Teton Sioux - with whom the Cheyennes were then friends; the other, representing the ambiguity of the Assiniboine by their being enemies of the Yankton Sioux and later, of their becoming enemies of the Cheyennes themselves.

We are not told in Sioux tradition the true reason why the Assiniboine first split from the Yankton. But it induced the Assiniboine to move into the country of northern Minnesota, between the western tip of Lake Superior on the east and Lake of the Woods on the west.

The Assiniboine say that they left the Sioux [Yankton] on or near the headwaters of the Upper Mississippi, whilst the Chippewa; whose memories appear to have been more precise on matters concerning tribal movements, added that after breaking from the parent group, the Assiniboine went northwest and occupied the rocky country about Lake of the Woods. Hence, other Algonquian names for that people of "Stone Indians," "Stony Sioux" or simply, "Sioux of the Rocks" as the Algonquian prefix `assini` means rock or stone etc.;. Hereabouts, the Assiniboine remained for a few years, in close association with the Monsoni Cree around Rainy Lake and with Cheyennes in the vicinity of Lower Red Lake. At first these refugee Assiniboine had come into the country as supplicants, perhaps begging protection against their Yankton Sioux kinfolk with who they were then at loggerheads, as it does appear that they were then tolerated by both the Cree and Cheyennes and allowed to pass through those tribe's hunting grounds at will, even into the tall-grass prairies west of the Upper Mississippi Forks south of Lower Red Lake, in order to hunt buffalo and deer in what was then regarded as Cheyenne territory.

This overall congenial situation in the Upper Mississippi region as regards the already established inhabitants was, though, soon to alter somewhat, which was the consequence of contemporary events attending the fortunes of tribes east of the Mississippi between the years 1630 and 1650, of which a brief summery will make clear.

. During the latter days of Cheyenne occupation about Lower Red Lake [circa. 1620 - 1640.], drastic changes were already taking place among all tribes of the Lower Great Lakes region in the east. These were changes in culture, location and age-old values which, directly or indirectly, were to affect other peoples hundreds of miles distant from their sphere of contact. Such changes as came

187

upon the eastern tribes in many an instance heralded their eventual ruin and in some cases, were the cause of their oblivion from the face of the earth. Such events had their origins in the early years of the sixteenth century, after European fishermen began frequenting the North Atlantic seaboard and initiated a small trade in furs with the resident coastal tribes. By the beginning of the seventeenth century this trade in furs had grown sufficiently to become important commerce. Indeed, from the time Samuel Champlain founded his trading post on the St. Lawrence near present day Quebec in 1608, Natives in their thousands thereafter, flocked to that river with large quantities of pelts and beaver skins, eager to barter for the white man's iron arrow heads, hatchets, needles, awls, knives, liquor and, not least, firearms, which trade with these newcomers offered. Tribes nearest the white trader and his wares zealously guarded their position and to such extent, that tribes further inland were prevented from trading directly with the white man. It was a situation the coastal Indians could only have achieved by their acquisition and employment of superior arms.

MEMBER OF THE CHEYENNE MOTSONITANIO OR KIT-FOX WARRIOR SOCIETY.
[From an original drawing by the author. Author`s collection]

188

European trade items thus obtained, were in turn bartered to distant tribes for more skins and furs at exorbitant rates of exchange and within only two decades of Champlain establishing his post, several tribes notably the Ottawa and Nipissing, had become professional middlemen who spent all their time either undertaking trading trips or conducting war ventures against their enemies and competitors. They did little to support themselves; nearly all their food, weapons, clothing and domestic utensils being acquired through trade or as the spoils of war. At the same time, these Indian middle-men to the more western tribes became intensely jealous of competition and by the late 1630s, when the supply of fur had been over exploited and thus exhausted in the coastal Indian's own country nearest the white man, the inhabitants, in order to obtain furs in sufficient quantity to satisfy the requirements of the traders, began invading neighbouring tribe's hunting grounds in order to replenish their stocks The coastal Indians, of course, now had the advantage of being equipped with firearms and superior metal-bladed weapons obtained in such commerce, and as a result, they instigated hostilities and ongoing bloody intertribal feuds with neighbouring peoples which soon became endemic. It was this situation which exasperated the already entrenched war culture of the North American Indian, with its attendant peculiarities of captive-taking and avenging the spirits of the dead, along with the amassing of wealth - which at a later date manifested itself in stolen horses and domestic equipment - and a new incessant quest for war honours and trophies that by the late 1690s, had spread universally across the Continent.

No other reason than this appears to have led to the rise of the Ottawa and Iroquois and of their becoming the predominant tribal powers in the East Woodland States. A situation that brought them into conflict with other Algonquians and the Siouan-speaking Omaha along with the latter`s cognates tribes, and even extended to an outbreak of hostilities between the Ottawa and their own closely related Potawatomi kinfolk. Each of the beleaguered western tribes without access to the white man's goods, were no match with their stone-headed weapons and missiles and thus, being at a great disadvantage, they fell back in terror and confusion before Ottawa and Iroquois onslaughts. Finally, these discomfited peoples fled their age-old hunting grounds altogether, and dispersed into the country south of Lake Superior west of Lake Michigan in what are the present day states of Wisconsin, Iowa and the southern part of Minnesota in an effort to escape their foes.

This upheaval and dispersal of the once resident more western tribes began in earnest after the date 1640.

Initial blame for this state of affairs can be placed squarely upon the shoulders of the white man, including the French, English and Dutch in the guise of trader, explorer, missionary and settler. It must be conceded, however, that without the Indian's inability to unite with his brethren and act in concert - coupled with his incessant craving to prove his prowess and valor against tribal enemies, and a desire to take by force that which he coveted from his weaker neighbour if not freely given - then the subsequent tragic situation of the North American Indian might not have been realized. Certainly not in so short a space of time.

The Cheyennes were also destined to suffer. By their own accounts they were rather timid and unwarlike at this time, and the advent of firearms coming among tribes such as the Assiniboine and Cree to the north and east respectively, both of whom were obtaining such weapons and other

189

articles of European manufacture from various white trading establishments in the northeast and east, destroyed any concept there may once have been of a *"Golden Age."* This was especially true regarding all tribes then inhabiting the southern part of Ontario and northern Minnesota, and hereafter, the whole country was set aflame by war.

Having previously left the comparative safety of the snowbound, timbered, lake country of the north for more provident lands to the south in northern Minnesota, the Cheyennes, perhaps more so than their cousins the Arapahoe and Blackfoot, had unwittingly, placed themselves in a vulnerable position. Their camps were now much more accessible and wide open to attack from enemy war-parties, so that very soon they, too, began to suffer accordingly. Further south the territory bordered by Green Bay on the east and the Mississippi River on the west, was then held exclusively by certain Siouan-speaking peoples including the Iowa, Oto, Winnebago and Dakota.

From the available archaeological evidence coupled with certain tribal traditions, it can be averred that the Siouan group known to early French explorers as *"Nadouwessi"* and later by the name *Dakota* or *Sioux* [which included the divisions of Yankton, Yankton, Sisseton, Mdewankton and Teton], had been entrenched in the state of Wisconsin predominantly along the courses of the St. Croix, Black and Chippewa rivers on the east side of the Upper Mississippi, certainly as early as A.D.1400 if not two-hundred years before.

At times, they resided in sedentary villages of birch bark wigwams; sowed a few meager crops and harvested the abundant wild rice of that country. At other times, they wandered throughout the territory on foot or in birch-bark canoes, hunting deer and buffalo as they went and during such excursions, they made use of small, portable bark or skin shelters. They were not then regarded by other Nations as a particularly aggressive people and along with the Iowa, Oto and Omaha, indulged themselves in a complex religious culture which necessitated among other things, the building of large earthen burial mounds in various shapes and sizes. These mounds dotted the aforesaid country, and the Siouan-speaking people's northwestern routes of migration from southern Wisconsin and western Indiana, can be traced by the remains of such mounds which their forefathers had built in times gone by. Their mode of life was politically and economically stable in the pristine forests and lakes surrounding them, and if sporadic skirmishes had in earlier years occurred from time to time between one band and another or against some foreign tribe, there had probably been no such thing as total war.

The opening of the third decade of the seventeenth century, however, drastically changed the situation. In fact, destroyed it utterly, with the advent of refugee Algonquians including Fox, Sauk, Illini and Potawatomi along with a few small Chippewa-proper groups, fleeing west from eastern foes. These latter peoples now contested the same lands long held by the resident Siouans who being obliged to resist this foreign onslaught, quickly evolved into a warrior society and soon after were themselves regarded as ferocious opponents.

In truth, these particular Algonquian invaders brought nothing but destruction to the Native Siouan culture since first they appeared in the Wisconsin country. But by circa, 1650, they were themselves then suffering diabolically from enemy groups in their rear. Often these latter were Ottawa and Delaware Algonquians in league with Iroquois-proper allies, who having secured

190

French, Dutch and English trade goods including a quantity of guns, were antagonizing their weaker and inferiorly armed neighbours. In turn, pressure from the fleeing Fox, Sauk and others split the Siouan population as if an invisible wedge had been driven between it. The result being that the Winnebago and Dhegiha Siouan groups [those incorporating the Omaha, Kansa, Quapaw and Osage] remained in the south, while the Chiwere group [including the Oto and Iowa] retired west and northwest respectively, and the Dakota or Sioux [Yankton, Sisseton and Teton] were pushed north along the eastern and western flood plains of the Upper tributaries of the Mississippi. This latter country although heavily timbered, was composed predominantly of numerous small lakes and marshlands - familiar to the Sioux - and in which terrain they could disperse into dozens of small camps either to avoid contact with the invaders, or to counter-attack from ambush.

A report by the Jesuit Priest Father Allouez in 1666 / `67, stated that the Sioux then resided in the prairies near the Upper Mississippi; that they had skin tents instead of bark huts and harvested the abundant wild rice of the region. He went on to say that although they did not own guns, they were fine arrow shots; very warlike and generally feared by all their neighbours. Living to the west of these people, he said, were the *Kerezi* [as Allouez calls them and probably meaning the Western or Plains Cree if not Chipewayans], *"...beyond whom the world ends - is cut off."* [1] Father Allouez further commented, *"The Crees live to the east [of the Sioux] and to the north are a people who eat their meat raw [Eskimo]."* [2]

Most likely, the Sioux bands primarily involved during the initial years of conflict with these Algonquian invaders were of the Yankton - Assiniboine group, as they appear to have been the first of the Dakotas to have been forced to move and who, during this period, became the most northern of their stock. These were also the people so Hidatsa tradition declares, who drove the Hidatsa from the headwaters country of the Upper Mississippi and from that river's western tributaries between the dates circa, 1620 and 1640. As a result, the Hidatsa retired further west; crossed the Red River of the North and built new permanent villages along the Upper stretches of that river's western branches. The Yankton themselves, rather than occupy the Hidatsa`s old seats, first crossed the Mississippi at a point near that river's Upper forks about where the Crow Wing branch enters the main stream, and thence a few years later, moved northwest to Upper and Lower Red Lake. In this last-named region they were certainly entrenched by the date 1640, when a Jesuit report for that year first mentioned the *Nedouwessi* as being in the Upper Mississippi area.

In the meantime, the Assiniboine had moved further north into the country between Lake Nipigon on the east and Lake of the Woods on the west. On the one hand to distance themselves further from their Yankton kinfolk, but on the other, in order to be closer to itinerant English and French traders who, by then, were visiting Hudson's Bay and the northern shores of the Upper Great Lakes respectively.

This movement of the Assiniboine north into Cree country, even if at first a peaceable intrusion, inevitably brought their two peoples into hostility with each other, and as the Assiniboine population increased, they encroached ever deeper into the Cree domain, pushing the latter further north and northeast from their old haunt around Rainy Lake. At the same time the Cheyennes, being themselves of Algonquian stock and close friends to the Monsoni Cree, were likely brought into the conflict and subsequently, were pushed south and southwest from Lower Red Lake.by the Assiniboine.

Of equal importance is that the Cheyennes hereafter, were forcibly separated from the Monsoni by intervening hostile Assiniboine bands. They thus became ever more detached both in dialect and culture to their parent Cree stock.

It was, though, other Cree-speaking groups along with the latter`s Chippewa allies, who prevented the Assiniboine and Yankton from occupying territory even further north. These particular Algonquian groups were formidable and aggressive and being armed with European guns, they clashed with the encroaching Assiniboine and also with the Yankton in the vicinity of Upper and Lower Red Lake, from which region the Cheyennes, or at least, one of their important groups, had only recently left.

Regarding the Cree bands initially involved in successful offensives against the Assiniboine and Yankton, most belonged to the Muskegon [Swampy Cree] group, in company with a small number of Monsoni separatists who together, were later known collectively as "Plains Cree." They are thus distinguished from the Monsoni-proper who, the Cheyennes declare, were always *"...a friendly tribe"* living near them [Cheyennes] when resident in the lake country of the northeast, and which refers to the southern Ontario and northern Minnesota area.

Earlier, about the date 1350, the Muskegon had moved west as a separate body from the country immediately north of the middle course of the St. Lawrence; crossed the northern neck of James Bay and finally settled in the swampy, stunted timber country west of Hudson's Bay. Whilst in this position the Muskegon after circa, 1620, came into contact with Chippewa groups, the latter then moving west along the northern shoreline of Lake Superior and northwest from Sault St. Marie at the junction of the Upper Great Lakes.

Later, it seems, after consolidating their position around Sault St. Marie, the Chippewa grew tolerant towards those same northern Algonquians they had previously displaced, such as the Monsoni, Muskegon and even the Cheyenne-speaking Suhtaio. Each of whom had earlier fled from the Sault and ever since, had been hovering tentatively in the snowbound forest regions to the north and northwest.

By the early sixteen-thirties, however, these same refugees began sauntering slowly back to the Sault during the fishing season, and thus made friendly contact with the newly arrived Chippewa clans of that area. No doubt this peaceful interaction was due in part to both people's similar economic conditions and that the Chippewa now had little pressure in their rear, which had once obliged them to harass and evict neighbouring tribes in order to secure a foothold further removed from powerful Iroquois enemies to the east.

Together, they and the Muskegon Cree formed an alliance and as a consequence, the Muskegon themselves soon began obtaining European trade goods from their Chippewa contacts and even directly, from French and English traders as far east as Albany and along the Lower St. Lawrence now that the Chippewa allowed unobstructed access to and from the trading centers in the east. It does appear that from this time on, the Cree were actually supplying the Ottawa and

192

French trade with both furs and slaves at a common rendezvous point on the shores of Lake Nipigon above Lake Superior. This was made possible by interconnecting canoe routes, which both the Ottawa and French then utilized when travelling to and fro between the St. Lawrence and the North Country above the Lower and Upper Great Lakes.

Perhaps it had been the Reindeer clan of Chippewa who were related to the Monsoni Cree and in a time past, had been absorbed by the former after the destruction of the Mundua, [See Chapter 8.] who acted as intermediaries in inaugurating this pact between the Chippewa and Muskegon. In such a way it brought their two peoples together and so had come the invitation to other Cree bands to accompany the Chippewa to the French and Algonquian trading fairs, now held annually on the Lower St. Lawrence both at Tadoussac and at the mouth of the Ottawa River.

Such trade items as acquired by the Muskegon were, in turn, bartered to some other Cree-speaking groups; particularly those Monsoni - Muskegon separatists later known as Plains Cree, and hereafter, the Plains Cree moved west into the prairies of southern Manitoba to harass the peoples of that district, in order to obtain more slaves and booty with which to trade to white men in the east. It is evident then, that these Cree and Chippewa Algonquian groups residing north of Lake Superior did so in harmony with each other, whilst at the same time those Algonquians south of the Upper Great Lakes which included the Fox and Illinois, were still regarded as Chippewa enemies.

It was not long after this, ostensibly around the date 1640 if not a few years before, that these same Cree groups started raiding south into Minnesota in an endeavor to procure more pelts and captives as trade items. They were being aided in this enterprise - though not as allies - by the Assiniboine, and notwithstanding that the Assiniboine and Cree were still fighting each other at that date, both tribes found ample time separately to beset all the tribes in the northern half of Minnesota. They assaulted not only the Yankton and Hidatsa, but also the Moiseo, Masikota and Bowstring Cheyenne groups, and indeed, any other foreign-speaking bands there may have been during that period.

This unleashing of Plains Cree and Assiniboine aggression towards their erstwhile neighbours, was, of course, only made possible by firearms secured in their intertribal commerce with their Eastern Cree cousins and Chippewa allies, and although regarded as inferior fighters to the Sioux, it was the warrior element of these same Cree peoples belonging to this particular group of mixed Muskegon and Monsoni, that suddenly appeared in northern Minnesota between 1635 and 1640, aggressive and formidable with their superior weapons. With the aid of the Chippewa, the Cree succeeded in checking the northern advance of the Assiniboine and even turned the Yankton back from above the Mississippi headwaters, forcing the latter to make a stand around Upper and Lower Red Lake.

From this new position the Yankton; along with some of their Eastern Dakota cousins, counter-attacked the Cree and Assiniboine and even continued their harassment of the Hidatsa, now relocated along the western tributaries of the Red River of the North. At the same time, albeit unwittingly, the Yankton did protect the Cheyennes somewhat, by creating a buffer to the expansion of enemy groups from the north into the Minnesota valley, and managed to hold back the southward advance of the Chippewa for another forty years.

Obviously, the Cheyennes had already left the Red Lakes district before the arrival of the Yankton, or surely they, too, would have ran afoul of Yankton encroachment and being themselves Algonquian, would have been subjected to Yankton aggression also. However, the abandonment of the Red Lakes country by Cheyennes does not appear to have predated the arrival of the Yankton by many years, albeit that the contrary view has often been accepted by historians, solely, it would seem, from a statement by William Philo Clark expressed late in the nineteenth century.

According to Clark [1882], his Sioux informants told him that Cheyennes preceded the Sioux into the Upper Mississippi region and that when the Sioux themselves first entered that country, they found the Cheyennes firmly entrenched along the Minnesota River.[3]

Although there is no reason to doubt the first part of this statement, the second part is almost certainly in error, or has been taken out of its proper context.

Perhaps Clark, unwittingly, misconstrued what he was told and its real meaning, but it has since been taken by successive scholars to mean that the Cheyennes and Sioux either did not meet each other until the latter moved to the Minnesota, or alternatively, that Cheyennes were already resident along that river when the Sioux first entered the Upper Mississippi country.

Neither of these conclusions are correct.

As our study progresses, it will be shown that the Sioux and Cheyennes were in close contact with one another in the Mississippi headwaters district long before any Sioux settled along the Minnesota. Also, when the Sioux did find Cheyennes entrenched along that river, it was after a second Sioux migration, this time south from the Upper Mississippi sometime between the years 1685 and 1690. At a time, in fact, when the Yankton and some other Sioux groups known as Yanktonais and Teton, were being severely pressed by Cree and Chippewa groups and were forced to retire south and southwest, first to the Elbow Bend of the Minnesota and thence, further west as far as that river's source.

Additional Sioux testimony relating to their people's early migrations and their meeting with Cheyennes, declares that when they themselves first reached the Falls of St. Anthony on the Upper Mississippi near the mouth of the Minnesota, they found the Iowa, [another Siouan-speaking tribe], higher up the Minnesota and Cheyennes along the same river but above the Iowa. The Oto, they said, were then south and southeast of the Cheyennes. This statement is corroborated by early map references which show that these two Siouan groups, the Iowa and Oto, were not in these locations before circa, 1650, but rather, far southeast of those points. For these reasons, the movement of Cheyennes from Lower Red Lake must have occurred prior to that decade. Iowa tradition and contemporary French reports indicate that the Iowa were driven west by enemies to the mouth of the Minnesota about the date 1650 and did not go as far as the Elbow Bend of that river whereabouts Cheyennes were already entrenched, until the mid-1650s at the earliest.

The statement then as given to Clark must refer to a later date, which would co-respond with the second migration of the Teton and Yankton Sioux, this time from north to south.

This being said, all Cheyenne-speaking bands resident in the Upper Mississippi country north of the Minnesota River, were then fully engaged in defending themselves against hostile forays from the north and northeast. Often the Cheyennes were at a disadvantage by not themselves having firearms or even a compatible arsenal of iron-bladed weapons with which to match their foes. Cheyenne tradition admits that their people at that time suffered diabolically, and were in constant fear and expectation of being attacked and slaughtered.

- 0 - 0 - 0 - 0 - 0 - 0 - 0 - 0 - 0 - 0 - 0 - 0 - 0 - 0 - 0 - 0 - 0 - 0 - 0 –

CHAPTER. 19.

IN TERROR OF THE *"HO-HAY."*

We are not told in Cheyenne tradition why their people eventually left the Red Lakes region, yet the suffering of the Hidatsa at Yankton hands may have created some incentive to move, before the Cheyennes themselves became embroiled in the same hostilities.

It appears, however, that the Cheyennes already had other enemies to contend with, even prior to the coming of the Yankton. Enemies who came against them sometimes on foot and sometimes in fleets of canoes from the north and northeast; confident and terrifying with their iron-tipped arrows, spears and hatchets and withal; their deadly Thunder-sticks, never before experienced by these stone-axe wielding Cheyennes.

The Cheyennes do recall that whilst inhabiting the "Flat country" of tradition, this being the marshland and prairie regions adjacent to Lower Red Lake, they were suddenly attacked by enemies armed with guns. The first of such weapons the Cheyennes had seen. These enemies are termed *"Ho-Hay"* in tradition, which as noted previously, was the name used by Cheyennes in a later century to designate the Assiniboine specifically. But during these early years when in northern Minnesota, the designation was more often, used as a collective term to include the Cree and Chippewa as well.

The Assiniboine, so it is also said in Cheyenne tradition, were the most consistent and aggressive of all the enemies they had to contend with at that time. The Assiniboine alone had been the first of their *"Ho-Hay"* foes to actually attack them. This was after an Assiniboine party encroached upon Cheyenne hunting grounds somewhere in the prairie land south of Lower Red Lake, and even at the time of this first attack, the Assiniboine were armed with guns.

Now we have already noted that when first the Assiniboine entered the country north of the Mississippi headwaters, they were likely to have been tolerated by the then adjacent Cree and Cheyennes. But after moving further north deep into Cree country, the Assiniboine and Cree became embroiled in a war which, no doubt, also involved Cheyennes. The Cree at that time were already being supplied with guns, which although few in number, were sufficient for the Cree to better their foes. As a result, around the date 1666, the Assiniboine actually sued for peace with the

195

Cree and an alliance between their two peoples was effected. The prime reason for this was in order that the Assiniboine could have access to the white man`s guns and iron-bladed weapons and because the Assiniboine were then fighting their Yankton cousins and most other Sioux bands who were also the enemies of the Cree. On the other hand, the Cree while fighting the Sioux were pleased to have an ally with whom they could join in a common cause.

The M. Le Chevalier de Beaurain writing in the year 1702, reported from Indian sources, that the Assiniboine had separated from the Sioux at the time or soon after, the establishment of the English Hudson's Bay Company in 1670. That Company's traders, he said,

> ".....were at that time supplying the Cree with firearms, which gave the latter the Upper hand over their Sioux and Assiniboine foes. The Assiniboine however, found it expedient to sue for peace with the Cree, and because of this, other Sioux bands regarded them as traitors." [1]

While De Beaurain was correct in his reasoning, it was not the time of the establishment of the Hudson`s Bay Company when the Cree first obtained guns and that the Assiniboine split from the Yankton, but at a prior date when unlicensed free traders had begun visiting the Sault St. Marie at the junction of the Upper Great Lakes as early perhaps as 1640 if not before. Either way, by 1650 the Assiniboine and Yankton although related by blood, were already at war with each other and subsequently, the Assiniboine later joined the Cree as allies in order to attack the Yankton and other Sioux groups together.

Indeed, the Cree proved themselves an important ally to the Assiniboine, as it was the Cree who actually controlled the distribution of European goods from the north and western tip of Lake Superior. Thus, the Assiniboine now had regular access to the white man`s trade particularly with the English, who with the establishment of the first permanent trading post on Hudson`s Bay by Pierre Radisson`s partner Medard Groseillers at the mouth of Rupert`s River in 1668, began supplying all those who visited the post with as many guns and iron weapons as were needed.

It was also around this time that those Cree peoples who earlier, had been pushed out from the Rainy Lake district toward the north and northeast by these same - now recently acquired - Assiniboine allies, moved back into their old haunts around that lake and placed themselves within easy travelling distance to all Cheyenne and Sioux villages in the northern half of Minnesota. As a result, both the Cree and Assiniboine often combined their hostile operations and together, they assaulted not only all the Minnesota and North Dakota tribes which their war-parties could reach, but also those tribes to the northwest in both central and southern Manitoba, and even further west, as far as the province of Saskatchewan. Many years later the Hudson's Bay Company employee David Thompson recorded in 1797,

> "The Fall Indians [Thompson`s name for the Arapahoe-Atsina] are now removed far from their original country, which was the rapids of the Saskatchewan river, northward of the eagle Hill; A feud arose between them and their then neighbours the

Nahathaways [Cree] and the Stone Indians confederates [Assiniboine] and they were too powerful for them..." [2]

The reason, however, why the Cheyennes themselves were now regarded as legitimate targets by the Assiniboine and also by the Cree, was that by 1666, these same Cheyennes had become close friends and confederates of certain Teton Sioux groups in the Upper Mississippi district, and whether they wished it or not, Cheyennes were soon caught up in the bloody conflicts then going on around them.

The date 1666 when the Cree-Assiniboine alliance was effected, does not, though, necessarily mark the start of hostilities between the Assiniboine and Cheyennes, or even suggest a date for the abandonment of the Lower Red Lake area by our subjects. The Assiniboine had been accustomed to wander as far east as the Sault St. Marie, certainly since the date 1641 when Jesuit Priests recorded meeting them at that place. Most probably, these same Indians had been meeting with white traders at the Sault and even further east on the Lower St Lawrence some years prior to that date. They may well then, have picked up a few firearms much earlier than 1666, perhaps as early as when Jean Nicolet a French Canadian trader, had met with eastern Dakota Sioux peoples among others at the western end of Lake Superior in 1634. Thus the Assiniboine had been a terror to the Cheyennes and to their own Yankton Sioux kinfolk from the very start of hostilities between them. Certainly we know that English traders were already regularly visiting Hudson`s Bay and trading with tribes who came to meet them at that point, for a number of years before King Charles 2nd of England granted that Company its royal charter in 1670. It is also probable that it were the Assiniboine who actually drew the Cree into their war with the Cheyennes. Although the testimony of Plains Cree tradition suggests that the Cree had taken the initiative themselves as they certainly did against the Blackfoot, Arapahoe and Hidatsa, each of whom then resided only slightly north and northwest of the Cheyennes and Sioux.

The French trader Pierre Charles LeSueur reported in 1695, that it had been after the Assiniboine fled from the Sioux that they first met the Cree. Evidently then, it was soon after that time that their two peoples were at war with each other. LeSueur went on to say that the Cree were the first to obtain guns and soon subdued the Assiniboine, after which their two peoples made peace. The Cree, LeSueur said, then began providing their new friends with firearms and iron-bladed weapons and thereafter, induced the Assiniboine to join them in attacking other Sioux groups who had been the Cree`s long-time enemies. Here LeSueur is at first referring to events which had occurred some years prior to the sixteen-nineties and, as mentioned above, European traders had been visiting Sault St. Marie in order to supply their Indian customers with guns in the late 1650s and perhaps as early as the mid-1640s.

The serious escalation of hostilities between the Cree and Sioux beginning around the date 1650, probably then, coincides with the beginning of serious Cree offensives against the Cheyennes when in northern Minnesota. At the same time, it offers a corroborating date as to when the Cheyennes actually vacated the Red Lakes country.

According to a Plains Cree tradition, as narrated by Chief Masqua of the Piapot band to Buffalo Child Long Lance in 1922, it was two-hundred and ninety years before that date when in the company of a band of Chippewa, a group of mixed Muskegon and Monsoni Cree, later known as Plains Cree, met a party of white men from a trading vessel then lying at anchor somewhere near the Island of Montreal in the Lower St. Lawrence. Chief Masqua`s great, great, great, grandfather was with this party and had declared that these were the first white men he had seen. The traders came ashore and gave the Indians presents of knives, matches and a few guns, for which they received furs in return. These guns, Chief Masqua said, were the first of such weapons to be introduced among the Cree. At first the Indians were very frightened of the powder flash and ensuing explosion; they would discharge the piece, throw it to the ground and run.

There must, however, have been much friendly intercourse during this meeting, for the account goes on to say that after a short while the white men left, but returned again within a year, at about the time half-breed children were being born in the Indian villages. On this second visit the white men brought with them large quantities of iron weapons and other implements, and also tea, tobacco, many guns, powder and shot. When again they departed, both the Cree and Chippewa, Chief Masqua concluded, had acquired enough guns to *"...kill any Indian fort."*

The story continues by saying it was soon after this, when white men began settling the country, that the Cree started moving west in an endeavor to keep a satisfactory distance from them. Thus in essence runs Chief Masqua`s tradition as is relevant to our study. An analysis of which will substantiate our earlier assertions and conclusions, and present a clearer picture of the situation regarding the Cheyennes and lands they were then inhabiting during this period in their history.

From the documented evidence we learn that in the year 1633, a fleet of Ottawa canoes came to Quebec from the Upper Great Lakes in order to trade with the French. These were the first among that people to be seen by the French so far down the St. Lawrence for nearly twenty years.

Now the name Ottawa during these early years, was used by the French merely as a general term meaning, *"Trader."* It was often applied by the early colonials to any Algonquian group coming from the interior, northwest of the St. Lawrence River. Thus, visitors called Ottawa in these early documents, in reality, often included Cree, Chippewa and any other Algonquian-speaking band or tribe residing above the Upper Great Lakes and beyond.

Before 1633, the date when Samuel Champlain regained his authority along the St. Lawrence and debarred the English and all other illicit traders from that river, unscrupulous merchants had annually contacted various Indian groups from the Upper Great Lakes, trading guns, knives and liquor in exchange for large quantities of animal skins, slaves and furs. Certainly such traders were in action along the St. Lawrence below Quebec in the years 1632 and early 1633, as Champlain`s own memoirs report.

The Jesuit Priest Charles L`Allemant when referring to the pre-1630s, wrote the following concerning this earlier trade in furs between the northern Indians and white men along the St. Lawrence,

"The savages were visited by many people, to such an extent that an old man told me
he had seen as many as twenty ships in the port of Tadoussac [sic]." [3]

The aforementioned assertion by Chief Masqua that after the second visit to the traders the
Indians had enough guns to *"kill any Indian fort,"* appears rather exaggerated when compared to
the testimony of contemporary white traders and official documents, which attest to the lack of
firearms among the tribes at that time, even among those trading regularly with the white man. A
small number of guns were obtained by the Indians through such means at this date; enough to
alarm the enemies of both the Cree and Chippewa, but certainly, not in such quantity to create the
terror and destruction necessary for their users to actually evict neighbouring tribes by their
employment alone. In addition, not until a decade later did flintlock firearms begin to appear
regularly as trade items, whereas, prior to the 1650s, only the cumbersome [and often unreliable]
match-lock Harquebus had been available, and then in small number. By the mid-1660s, however,
the situation had changed.

Champlain died on Christmas Day 1635 and with his passing went any hope of realizing a
French-Indian Utopia in the New World. Since that time Dutch, English and independent French
traders had re-emerged in force and operated with impunity in an illicit and irresponsible trade in
both firearms and liquor. They lured the inland tribes to their trading fairs along the entire length
of the St. Lawrence, poisoning the Indian's spirit and his body with alcohol, while supplying all the
firearms their Native customers needed to enable them to indeed, *"kill any Indian fort."*

At the same time, the resettlement of the French around Montreal and Quebec, coupled
with an influx of other Europeans into the St. Lawrence valley, obliged most resident Algonquian
bands of that country to move, although no populous Cree or Chippewa group was residing
permanently in the immediate area at that time. More likely, it was the acquisition of guns and other
European tools of war, which created the incentive for these latter tribes to even up old scores and
venture into foreign, long-coveted hunting grounds, now they were better militarily equipped than
their enemies and neighbours and, without doubt, this was the actual period in time referred to in
Chief Masqua`s statement quoted above.

Writing of the years 1658 through to 1661, the trader Pierre Radisson recorded from
personal observation, that the Cree were then at war with the Nadourononons [i.e. Sioux] and at
peace with the Chippewa of Sault St. Marie, of whom he said,

" They calle [sic] themselves Christinoes [Cree], and their confederats [Chippewa]
from all times, by reason of their speech, which is the same, and often have joyned
together and have had companys of souldiers to warre against that great Nation
[Sioux]." [4]

In a later passage, Radisson added,

"Not many years since, they [Chippewa] had a cruell warre against the Nadoueseronons [Sioux]. Although much inferior in numbers, nevertheless that small number of the salt [Sault] was a terror unto them, since they had trade with the French. They never have seene such instruments as the French furnished them withall. It is a proud Nation, therefore would not submitt, although they had to doe with a bigger Nation 30 times then they weare, because that they weare called enemy by all those that have the accent of the Algonquin language, that the wild men call Nadou.......Now seeing that the Christinoes [Crees] had hatchets and knives, for that they resolved to make peace with those of the sault, that durst not have gon hundred of leagues uppon that Upper lake with assurance. They would not hearken to anything because their general resolved to make peace with those of the Christinoes and another Nation that gott gunns, the noise of which had frighted them more then the bulletts that weare in them. The time approached, there came about 100 of the Nation of the Sault to those that lived towards the north. The Christinoes gott a bigger company and fought a batail. Some weare slaine on both side. The Captayne of those of the sault lost his eye by an arrow. The batail being over he made a speech, and said that he lost his sight of one side, and of the other he foresee what he would doe; his courage being abject to that losse, that he himselfe should be ambassador and conclude the peace." [5]

The above excerpts appear ambiguous with regard to their true meaning. The implication seems to be that separately, both the Cree and Chippewa were at war with the Sioux during the time Pierre Radisson was in their country, and that the Chippewa by having guns obtained from the French, were generally holding their own against the numerically stronger Sioux. As a result, the Sioux proposed to make peace with the Chippewa in order to obtain guns for themselves with which to fight the Cree. The Chippewa, however, were then intending to ally themselves with the Cree and so refused the Sioux offer. Instead, the Chippewa and Cree formed a big war-party and fought a great battle with the Sioux. Only after the Chippewa chief had been wounded in the eye did he change his mind and accept the Sioux proposal. Later on in the Radisson account, we are told that the Chippewa did conclude a truce with the Sioux, albeit of temporary duration, while the Cree according to a later passage in the same journal, were still fighting the Sioux one year later. Indeed, Radisson later commented that,

"...We did what we could to have correspondence with that warlike Nation [Sioux] and reconcile them to the Christinoes [Cree]. We went not there that winter. Many weare slained of both sides the summer last. The wound was yett fresh, wherfore it was hard to conclude peace between them. We could doe nothing, for we intended to turne back to the French the summer following." [6]

One can see from these brief excepts that certainly by the late sixteen-fifties, the Cree were already in a league with several Chippewa groups and trading with them for French goods. They were then involved in a most virulent war against the Sioux and also against the Assiniboine who even though themselves at war with the Sioux, were at this time, being terrorized by Cree and Chippewa guns. Now of the Cree mentioned in Chief Masqua`s statement who, supposedly, were engaged in a trade for guns even prior to Radisson`s visit, those separatists from the Monsoni and Muskegon divisions now forming a conglomerate band of their own, soon abandoned the country north of Lake Superior and moved west. In 1666 the Jesuit Priest Father Allouez reported the Cree as being east of the Assiniboine, the latter then entrenched around Lake of the Woods in northern Minnesota. We know that the next location of this Cree conglomerate, famous in a later century by the name Plains Cree, was somewhere in the western part of Ontario and by then, they were already aggressive and adventurous and soon after moved into southern Manitoba and the Lake Winnipeg district. Around the date 1680 they set about vigorously assaulting the Blackfoot tribes of that region, who had fled in earlier years into the Lake Winnipeg country from southwestern Ontario because of a previous spate of harassment from the same Cree peoples, and without doubt, the adjacent Arapahoe groups at that time also suffered with them.

ASSINIBOINE WARRIOR OF THE GREAT LAKES REGION. Circa, 1700.
[From an original drawing by the author. Author`s collection]

According to Arapahoe tradition, it was between 1680 and 1690 when their people retreated west and the Atsina separated from them, owing to hostile pressure from gun-toting Cree and Assiniboine foes. It does not appear to be acceptable then, that the same conglomerate of belligerent Cree, who were then allied to the Chippewa during their bloody progress west from Lake Superior, did not assault those tribes that remained in northern Minnesota and especially so, as the Chippewa always coveted the Minnesota hunting grounds for their own. We must not forget also that the Assiniboine against whom the Cree and Chippewa were at war before 1666, were then still roaming the northern part of that state.

As previously noted, it was around 1640 when the Plains Cree reached the southeastern part of Ontario in their progression west. As a consequence, this event saw the beginnings of determined Cree and Chippewa aggression against most, if not all Cheyenne-speaking bands and against the Sioux of the Upper Mississippi region. The acquisition of guns and metal-bladed weapons by the Cree and their allies, coupled with a desire to hunt the country of northern and central Minnesota; rich in furs and potential slaves with which to sate the voracious appetite of French and English traders, present an obvious reason for the resulting Cree and Chippewa offensives; and for the latter`s enthusiasm in such pursuits.

Before the middle years of the seventeenth century, the Chippewa had not been inclined to trace across the cold, lake and swampy marshland terrain of southern Ontario and northern Minnesota searching for enemies to raid. Their quarry, it was thought, might easily elude them and were so poor, that if only their abandoned camp sites were found, there would be little worth taking home as booty.

By the late 1660s, however, this attitude had changed completely. Now with an adequate supply of guns, the Chippewa followed the example of their Cree allies and began raiding all neighbouring tribes with a vengeance. By so doing, they acquired both slaves and furs in abundance. Both these prizes could be obtained with relative ease from people remote from the trading routes and without guns and metal weapons of any kind, not to mention a lack of experience in what might be regarded as a condition of *"total war."* Such peoples would probably have stood transfixed in mute horror, as they were forced to witness the barbaric sadism their enemies inflicted upon their dead and dying relatives. People like the Cheyennes - lately refugees from the Red Lakes region - who by repeated suffering, would soon learn to retaliate in kind and ultimately, excel their foes in techniques of savagery when the opportunity presented itself to do so.

The eminent historian George Bird Grinnell obtained accounts of those terrible days, when the Cheyennes were at the mercy of the *Ho-Hay*. He had been given the information from Cheyennes whose great, great, great grandparents had been on the receiving end of *Ho-Hay* assaults. Some of his informants told him that the initial events of this war had occurred after the Cheyennes had made peace with the Suhtaio, but before the Cheyenne settlement on the Lower bend of Sheyenne River in the Coteau des Prairies west of Red River, which dates from around 1690. [18] These initial *Ho-Hay* attacks must then have occurred before that time.

When first they were attacked by the *Ho-Hay*, say the Cheyennes, their people had not seen any white men and had only stone-headed weapons such as bows and arrows, stone-headed lances

202

or sharpened sticks and clubs with which to defend themselves. Their *Ho-Hay* enemies on the other hand, had metal-tipped arrows, iron axes, and as the author's Cheyenne informant James King graphically put it,

> *"...a number of terrible Black Sticks that flashed fire and barked like thunder, creating much panic among the people and inflicting wounds of death."* [7]

The assertion that Cheyennes at that time were armed only with stone-headed weapons and wooden clubs, indicates that the start of these hostilities must have occurred when the Cheyennes lived in the northern region of Minnesota for two reasons.

(1) That all Cheyenne villages were then in close proximity to both the Cree and Assiniboine.
(2) That when resident along the Minnesota River and in the vicinity of the Upper Forks of the Mississippi, circa, 1670, they were themselves obtaining iron implements in trade with the Oto and Eastern Dakota, who were then in contact with French traders around the Upper Great Lakes and in the Ohio country east of the Mississippi.

In addition, traditions from the Assiniboine corroborate this Cheyenne statement, by saying that when they and the Cheyennes first came into conflict, both were endeavouring to surround the same herd of buffalo in the prairie country of northern Minnesota. A quarrel ensued and a fight started. The Cheyennes, it is said, had only clubs and sharpened sticks, whilst the Assiniboine had a few guns and in the ensuing melee, a number of Cheyennes were killed.

Cheyenne tradition also mentions this first hostile meeting with the Assiniboine whilst on a buffalo hunt. But add that the Assiniboine afterwards came at night to the Cheyenne village and attacked it, killing many of its occupants. This was, say the Cheyennes, the first time they had been confronted with firearms and in great fear and haste, they fled their village and hid themselves until the enemy had left the district and returned to their own country further north.

At one time when a group of surviving Cheyennes had returned to one of their smoldering, corpse-littered villages after an attack by the Ho-Hay, they found that the dead had their hair cut off - scalped - and according to James King, this was the first time they were made aware of this particular mode of mutilation.

Cheyenne informants of Grinnell told him that after the first defeat by the Ho-Hay, a young Cheyenne warrior harangued the people saying,

> *"Now we have been attacked, let us fight with all people we meet, and in this way we too will become great warriors."* [8]

This does not, though, seem to have been the case until several more years had passed. For from this time on, the Assiniboine on one hand and the Cree on the other came against the Cheyennes many times. Always they came at night and always the Cheyennes were defeated. The people were much afraid and lost many of their kinfolk killed or taken captive by these enemies, either to be traded to the French and English slavers, or to endure a life of drudgery among the lodges of their captors.

The Assiniboine themselves added that initially, the Cheyennes had no idea how to react to firearms, the Cheyennes would run up close to the Assiniboine warriors to use their stone-headed clubs and sharpened sticks effectively, and as a consequence, the Assiniboine managed to kill many Cheyennes with ease.

Usually the Assiniboine came against their Minnesota enemies in late summer and autumn after they, the Assiniboine, had held their annual religious ceremonies. They would then easily ply their way to their enemy's camps in birch bark canoes, before the waters of the interconnecting streams and marshlands froze over and prevented a quick escape. Winter raids would have forced a returning war-party to trudge laboriously through deep snow with prisoners in tow who would likely slow them down, and thus threaten their being overtaken by a pursuing Sioux or Cheyenne party intent on revenge.

So rare during these dark and fearful days did the Cheyennes manage to kill an enemy *Ho-Hay*, that when they were fortunate enough to do so, the whole village danced and sang in celebration for weeks and sometimes for months after the event.

Some of Grinnell`s Cheyenne informants also declared, that the Chippewa were not among their *Ho-Hay* enemies during the initial period of this bloody time of strife. Although it does appear from other evidence, that one or another Chippewa band at least was involved. Certainly by the date1670, as a result of the earlier Cree alliance with the Assiniboine, large war-parties composed of warriors from the three Nations of Cree, Chippewa and Assiniboine were organized on a regular basis in order to assault not only Cheyenne villages, but moreover, each of the scattered Dakota or Sioux camps in the Upper Mississippi country. As the Cheyennes were then closely confederated with the Teton and certain bands of Eastern Sioux, they obviously suffered accordingly, for the Chippewa and their allies made little or indeed, no distinction between them.

There is documented proof, albeit at a much later date, of a lone Chippewa force assaulting and destroying an important Cheyenne earth-lodge town in the Coteau des Prairies west of Red River. But be this as it may, by far the most consistent and aggressive foes with whom these poor Cheyennes had to contend during the second half of the seventeenth century, were the Assiniboine first and foremost and next to them the Cree.

Informants of Grinnell when narrating anecdotes pertaining to this early period of Cheyenne warfare with the *Ho-Hay*, repeatedly mentioned the people's familiarity with buffalo and of the Assiniboine trick of imitating buffalo mating calls when talking to each other before an attack. This should not be taken to mean that this bloody and important period in Cheyenne history, commenced only after the Cheyennes had left the marsh and lake country of northern Minnesota and settled in the buffalo prairies of the Coteau west of the Red River of the north. Buffalo were then also to be found in no small number in the open meadow lands south of Lower Red Lake and west of the Upper Mississippi in the northern half of Minnesota. It is just as likely, however, that it was the mating call of the moose that these *Ho-Hay* enemies employed and only in later years after the Cheyennes had abandoned completely the country wherein, moose were to be found in abundance, was the buffalo call substituted in the tradition for that of the moose. Even today Cree hunters of the Canadian forests, use the hollow stems of a certain plant or a rolled-up piece of birch bark to make the mating sound of a moose, in order to entice that animal close in for the kill.

CHEYENNE RED-SHIELD WARRIOR IN SOCIETY REGALIA. Circa, 1700.
[From a water colour by the author. Author`s collection.]

It is said by the Cheyennes that so constant did these *Ho-Hay* attacks become, that as darkness drew near, the haranguing of the camp crier resounded through all Cheyenne villages, telling the mothers to put moccasins on their children's feet and be ready to flee, lest they were taken by surprise and attacked in their sleep by their merciless foes, to be either killed or carried into bondage. Places of concealment had previously been prepared where the people could hide in case of attack and withal, at strategic points around the camp breastworks were erected along with other positions for defense. Young warriors armed with bows and arrows and lances guarded the villages both night and day, and if a sound was heard like that of the mating call of buffalo or moose in the rutting season, it was a sign to pack up and take flight. For in reality, it would mean that the dreaded *Ho-Hay* were in the vicinity, signaling to each other with the aid of hollow stems fashioned from a certain plant. There would be no argument as to whether the call be that of buffalo or the *Ho-Hay*; it had proved itself the latter too many times before. At one time, so Grinnell`s Cheyenne informants also recalled, some villagers had heard a sound like the mating call of buffalo. In response, they packed up their belongings and prepared to flee to the safety of another Cheyenne village further downstream, believing that the *Ho-Hay* were coming to slay their men-folk and carry off the women and children into captivity. The rest of the villagers scoffed at their concern and declared that it was merely the sound of buffalo they could hear and if they remained in the village that night, they would be able to fill their bellies with meat come morning. The others, though, would not be deterred. After gathering their close relatives around them, they took leave of the village in order to find a secure place to hide and those who remained were left to their fate. Sometime later, after having reached the safety of the other Cheyenne village, some of those who had fled lay down to drink from a nearby stream. The water, they thought, tasted strange and upon a closer look, they noticed it was red in colour. They spat it out as to their horror they realized they had been drinking the blood of their own people, lately shed in the village they had vacated the night before.

It is indicative to note, that the actual names Upper and Lower Red Lake, Red Lake River and that of the Red River of the North itself, are all from translations of Indian terms, originally applied by resident Algonquians to these places. More precise translations of these names, however, do not actually mean `Red,` but `Blood` and were meant to imply that prior to the coming of white men into the country, there had been much human slaughter in those areas.

There are several other stories in Cheyenne tradition that relate to conflicts specifically with the Assiniboine. One of which tells how a dog saved the Cheyennes from an Assiniboine attack and another, telling how the Suhtaio obtained a large quantity of guns after an old woman tricked an Assiniboine war-party into stumbling over a cliff edge and in the event of which, the whole Assiniboine party was destroyed. These episodes, though, belong to a much later date. Nevertheless, we have seen that by the earlier period of 1655 or thereabouts, the Moiseo, along with all other Cheyenne-speaking groups in northern Minnesota, were being vigorously raided by the Assiniboine and Cree; the result being that the Cheyennes soon abandoned the Red Lakes area completely. This position was far too exposed offering no protection whatever against the massed onslaughts of their enemies. A part of the tribe, therefore, retreated deeper into the headwaters district of the Upper Mississippi in the vicinity of the swampy Lakes now known as Winnibigosis, Cass and Bowstring. This region by its treacherous marsh and bog terrain, was thought to help deter their enemy's inroads and offer better protection against attack upon Cheyenne camps.

One other Cheyenne-speaking group retired due south, first to the small range of hills south of Lower Red Lake and thence, through the *"tall-grass"* prairie country to the Elbow Bend of the Minnesota. Here they settled for a number of years near where the town of Mankato now stands. This latter group is likely to have been the *"Hetstiomisssstane"* or Pipe-Stem Men band of which the Cheyennes themselves declare, was another early division of their people.

By going so far south this last-named group freed itself from any future *serious* Assiniboine and Cree attacks upon their people. Certainly they were immune to the chronic warfare suffered at a slightly later date by their northern kinfolk at the hands of those same enemy tribes. Whilst resident along the Minnesota, the Pipe-Stem-Men lived comfortably at various points for many years, and after 1660 they allied themselves to the then incoming Iowa, Oto and Omaha and for several decades thereafter, had little to do with their Cheyenne-speaking cousins in the Upper Mississippi country save intermittent contact, so that the history and subsequent migrations of both are, from that time on, virtually separate for the next one-hundred years.

By the year 1673 at the latest, those Cheyenne groups which remained in the north comprised at least four distinct groups. One of these groups was an adopted tribe commonly known at a later date as Suhtaio, whilst the others included the Moiseo, Masikota and Bowstrings. The two last-named Cheyenne groups of Masikota and Bowstrings, had evolved separately several decades prior to 1673 when they were first documented on early maps of the region, and upon these groups the *Ho-Hay* continued their aggression and harassment. It is true to say, however, that the treacherous marsh terrain of the Mississippi headwaters country did protect the Cheyennes somewhat, by deterring the more cautious enemy war-parties that feared being ambushed or of floundering in the numerous deceiving bogs of that country.

Added to this deterrent, Dakota bands commonly known as the Eastern or Mdewankanton and Sisseton divisions, only a short time later settled the same Upper Mississippi area, though on the east side of that river particularly around present day Mille Lacs and its adjacent district. They were themselves then warring with the same belligerent Assiniboine, Cree and Chippewa Nation of the north. But being known as ferocious and resilient adversaries, these Sioux newcomers generally succeeded in holding their own in such conflicts.

Conversely, those refugee Cheyenne peoples still in the north having recently arrived from the Red Lake's region, were comparatively small in number as compared to their Dakota neighbours and posed little threat to Sioux expansion and settlement. The Cheyennes were also a weak tribe in other ways, who if we are to accept tribal tradition at face value, were not particularly warlike or even aggressive at this period in their history. It is not surprising then, that the Cheyennes did not contest the encroachment of Dakota peoples into their [the Cheyenne's] new Mississippi headwaters domain. On the contrary, these incoming Sioux groups took the resident Cheyennes under their protective wing as it were, seeing in them a potential ally against mutual foes. Consequently, the much beleaguered Cheyennes - for a while at least - gained some relief from the savage pressure directed against them by their dreaded *"Ho-Hay"* foes.

Only many years later after 1685, with the aid of their recently acquired Assiniboine and Cree allies, did the Chippewa after migrating further west along the northern shore of Lake Superior and conducting hostile forays toward the south into the rich beaver country of northern Minnesota, finally drive the Sioux out of that part of the country once and for all. Even the more populous Teton Sioux then found it expedient to retreat towards the south and southwest to and above the great Elbow Bend of the Minnesota, although by that time, the Masikota Cheyenne-speaking group having earlier retreated south, was already entrenched somewhere along the middle course of that same river.

Soon after the Masikota movement south, the same northern enemies forced the remaining Cheyennes [i.e. *Bowstrings*] to cede the last of their lands completely in the Upper Mississippi district. Likewise they retired south, albeit to the Upper course of the Minnesota and ultimately, further west across the Red River of the North. They then settled in a permanent village on the Lower Bend of Sheyenne River in the eastern part of what is known as the Coteau des Prairies in present-day North Dakota.

The Arapahoe, Blackfoot and Hidatsa for their part, were obliged by the same Assiniboine and Cree pressure to move, although in their case, they took a north-westerly route into the prairies of the central and southern parts of Saskatchewan Province, Canada.

Only the Suhtaio group of peoples and the small Moiseo Cheyenne-speaking remnant among those closely connected to the Cheyennes, remained in the Upper part of Minnesota at that time. They were, it seems, regarded then as a somewhat *"neutral"* element between the warring sides. However, the later fortunes of the Suhtaio did eventually cause them to move out of the country also because of similar hostile pressure from the Cree, Chippewa and Assiniboine. Both the Suhtaio and at a later date the Moiseo remnant were eventually obliged to align themselves more closely to their Cheyenne-speaking cousins, and in such a way, it enabled the Suhtaio to become an important component of the Cheyenne Nation in the latter's late historic time.

- 0 - 0 - 0 - 0 - 0 - 0 - 0 - 0 - 0 - 0 - 0 - 0 - 0 - 0 - 0 - 0 - 0 - 0 - 0 -

CHAPTER. 20.

RETURN OF THE SUHTAIO.

The Cheyenne-proper group of Masikota which had split from the Moiseo along with the confederated and linguistically related Omissis [Bowstrings], by vacating the Red Lakes region and relocating in the vicinity of the lakes Winnibigosis, Cass and Bowstring close to the Mississippi heads, unwittingly brought them into contact and subsequent conflict with the Suhtaio. The same who several centuries earlier, had disassociated from the nucleus of the Montagnais-Cree parent band in the ancient *"Laurel"* archaeological area of northeastern Manitoba and northwestern Ontario [the "Old Turtle Land" of Cheyenne tradition], and by the middle of the seventeenth century, had intruded into the north-central part of what is now the state of Minnesota, and in which region the aforesaid Cheyenne-proper speaking groups were then positioned.

Doubtless the Suhtaio had been in friendly contact with the Moiseo throughout the time of both people's ancient wanderings in the old-time *"Laurel"* regions, but after vacating that country around A.D. 500 and embarking upon individual routes of migration, they had no further friendly contact with each other until coming together again in northern Minnesota, many centuries after their two people's had traced separate and circuitous routes in order to reach the last-named area.

208

That the Suhtaio in ancient times were a part of the original Montagnais Algonquian-speaking faction there can be little doubt, although a recent analysis by Goddard [1978], shows that the Suhtaio dialect must have evolved separately from that of Cheyenne-proper and seems to be more closely connected to proto-Arapahoe and Miami. Certainly as late as the nineteen-hundreds, even the Cheyennes would argue between themselves whether the Suhtaio were of Arapahoe, Cree, or even of Blackfoot extraction.

The early archaeological connections of both the Arapahoe and Miami are classified under the term *Mero Complex,* found in west-central Wisconsin and east-central Minnesota. While the Suhtaio, I believe, should be associated with the archaeological complexes generally known as *Blackduck North* and *Blackduck South* respectively.

Among accepted criteria regarding the archaeological record of the Mississippi headwaters country and southern Ontario, known in academic terms as "The Boundary Waters Region," the archaeological complex designated *Blackduck* seems to have evolved its distinguishing features beginning around A.D. 600, from the earlier complex known as *"Middle Laurel"* of central and southern Ontario. The *Middle Laurel complex* persisted in its later *Blackduck* phase throughout northern Wisconsin and northern Minnesota until circa, 1650.

Blackduck both in its *North* and *South* variations, although here speaking predominantly of the *South* example, show strong connections with that of the then contemporary *Mero* complex of central Wisconsin, and without question, the collective characteristics of both complexes associate those peoples with Algonquian-speaking groups, although a number of later intrusive Siouan traits are also apparent in that of *Blackduck South.* The area covered, however, is compatible with the traditional locations during pre-white contact times for both the Suhtaio and Arapahoe, so that these two groups either together or in close contact with one another, having earlier migrated south from the *"Middle Laurel"* occupation area into the rich subsistence country of Wisconsin during a period of mild climatic conditions, spread and populated across the land, and at a later date along with the associated Miami and Sauk, constituted a culturally and perhaps confederated Central Algonquian faction.

Regarding *Blackduck* sites collectively, burial mounds are a prominent feature and contain skeletons usually placed in a sitting position, while artefacts include small triangular notched and un-notched projectile points; unilateral harpoon and socket points; both end and side scrapers; tubular pipes; copper beads and awls, along with some beaver incisor gouges and fragments of pottery. *Blackduck* ceramics are determined as being thin-walled and globular in shape with flared rims, while exterior surfaces and rims are usually decorated with cord-wrapped tool impressions. Punctuates and bosses are also displayed, along with outside surface applications of vertical textile impressions. Of *"Blackduck"* ceramics found south of Lake Superior, they are often mixed with *Mero* ware, and show very close connections with ceramics of the *Selkirk complex* in southern Ontario - which is attributed to the Cree. It is apparent from the distribution of *Blackduck* sites, that slightly before circa, AD.1250, *Blackduck* peoples began vacating the central Wisconsin region and moved north. Radiocarbon dates cluster around AD.1020 whilst spanning an overall period of plus and minus of 565 years for this particular complex in central and northern Wisconsin, which gives us a rough date of circa, 1585 as being the end phase of `Blackduck` in that area.

It appears from the archaeological record, that if once a part of the great Delaware conglomerate of bands, during the latter's initial trek from the Keewatin area of the northwest into the Lower St. Lawrence country, then the Suhtaio element en route in close association with those later known as Arapahoe, Menominee and Illinois, veered off from the Delaware line of march somewhere far north of the Mississippi heads, and around the date A.D.1020, moved southeast through the Upper part of Minnesota and as far east as Green Bay in central Wisconsin. Hence, the close association of *Blackduck* and *Mero* archaeological complexes in that region.

Around A.D. 1360 the Illinois and refugee Miami; owing to Chippewa harassment from the east, moved west into the present-day state of Illinois; then further west to the east bank of the Mississippi. The Menominee remained in situ in the Green Bay region, while the Suhtaio and probably the Arapahoe moved northwest back into their old haunts in northeastern Minnesota, where they remained for many generations before again being obliged to move.

Between circa, A.D.1360 and A.D.1450, the majority of *Blackduck* population then inhabited the Lake Winnibigosis and Leech Lake Basins of north-central Minnesota and extended, albeit sporadically, toward the west as far as the Red River of the North. By its cultural remains in that area, *Blackduck* strongly suggests that those responsible then depended upon an intensive hunting and wild-rice gathering subsistence economy. They resided in both perishable reed-mat and bark dwellings and semi-squared semi-subterranean houses, grouped together to form villages with defensive palisades. Ceramics show an admixture of *Blackduck* and *Mero* ware, indicating that the inhabitants were still in contact with other Algonquian tribal groups, which included the ancestral Arapahoe, and with whom they apparently traded and exchanged certain cultural innovations. Not until circa, A.D.1450, with the advent of hostile pressure from aggressive refugee Algonquian groups from the East; coupled with Dakota Sioux groups from the Southeast and the encroachment north of Hidatsa Siouans from the South, all moving into the western Wisconsin and east Minnesota regions, coupled, perhaps, with a drastic change of climatic conditions which severely reduced crop-growing and hunting potential in those areas, were the proto-Arapahoe and Suhtaio again inclined to move, and in due course, the Suhtaio faction became separated by distance and subsequently in dialect from their proto-Arapahoe cousins.

By the later distribution of *"Blackduck"* findings, which relate to the period between 1450 and 1550, we must take it that the Suhtaio by then, had spread northwest into the *Boundary Waters Region* and northeast to the western tip of Lake Superior, and it was whilst in this latter position that they first met and allied with certain Cree and Chippewa groups, and moreover, made contact and eventually came into conflict with the Moiseo, who by 1550, had moved south from southern Ontario and entrenched themselves in the Upper and Lower Red Lake's region of northwestern Minnesota. It appears that between 1550 and 1650 the Suhtaio moved further east and northeast, extending their wanderings as far as Sault St. Marie and the southern shore of Lake Nipigon, while in the west, they still occupied the peripheries of the wild rice marshlands of northeastern and north-central Minnesota. This area of residence is corroborated to some degree by the Cheyenne-proper statement that when first they met the Suhtaio, the latter were in the habit of eating grass [e.g. wild rice] and fashioned their houses and clothes from reeds and rushes. It was during this period of circa, 1550, whilst still sporadically frequenting the central part of Minnesota on their extended seasonal buffalo hunts, so Suhtaio tradition avers, that they became a tribe in their own right, ostensibly at a place called *"Black Mountain"* around the base of which were several small lakes close to the present-day Timber Mountains. This location is north of the Pipe-Stone Quarries of southwestern Minnesota and if the tradition is correct, then it would agree with the finding of contemporary *"Blackduck"* sites not far north of that region in the west-central part of the state.

The Arapahoe faction, meanwhile, relocated in what is now southern Manitoba, and have since been associated with the archaeological complex of that district known as *Duck Bay*. At a much later period, one particular Suhtaio group moved into the Qu`Appelle valley of southern Saskatchewan, where they again made contact with and allied themselves to their old-time Arapahoe neighbours. Thus we find *"Blackduck"* sites in all the aforementioned districts and even on James River in southeastern North Dakota at the so-called Hintz site, where a Suhtaio permanent village ostensibly once stood. Likewise, across the Missouri in western South Dakota *"Blackduck"* pottery ware and artefacts have been found, as also in the Fort Lincoln-Missouri River area of North Dakota, where Suhtaio peoples were also entrenched during the late 18th and early 19th centuries.

Without doubt then, the many and widely scattered *Blackduck* sites located in Wisconsin, Minnesota, southern Ontario and the Dakotas must represent, predominantly, the ancestral Suhtaio, and shows that at separate periods during their long and varied history they shared a close interaction with several foreign-speaking tribal groups, which in turn, were responsible for the archaeological complexes scattered throughout the study area, such as *Selkirk* [Cree], *Duck Bay* [Arapahoe], *Mero* [Arapahoe and Miami], *Arvilla* [Cheyenne] and *Sandy Lake* [Assiniboine] among others.

The term itself of Suhtaio [Singular; Suhta or Suhtai], has numerous alleged derivations and spellings. It has previously been described by some as referring to the grunting sound made by a buffalo bull during the rutting season, or as a term used to designate; "speech hard to understand," which in the vernacular becomes; "strange talkers.*"* Both these definitions appear to have been used by the Cheyennes in order to denote any incomprehensible language and subsequently, were applied to the Suhtaio; it is said, in derision of their peculiar dialect.

The Suhtaio, however, employed the same term as a personal appellation and as it is most unlikely that they should have deliberately wished to deride themselves, the above explanations cannot really be considered. More feasible, if not actually correct, is the suggestion made by some of George Bird Grinnell`s Cheyenne informants, that the name is derived from *"issuht,"* meaning `ridge` or `hill;` alluding to the fact that the Suhtaio, so tradition asserts, were once accustomed to position their villages along ridge tops. We have no definite evidence to indicate this as either being or not being the case, although one must not forget the Chippewa historian Warren's statement mentioned in a previous chapter, which averred that some bands belonging to the old-time inhabitants of the Mississippi headwaters country, but who were thought by the Chippewa to be Hidatsa, preferred to camp along ridge tops rather than reside in permanent earth and timber villages on Lower ground. It should also be noted that the Cheyenne band name of late historic times rendered as *"Hisiometanio,"* translates as "Hill Men," which is said to refer to the ridge or long sloping escarpment of a hill and were chosen places for this particular band to site their camps. The two spellings of ʻ*Suhtai*ʻ and ʻ*issuht,*ʻ as clearly seen, are compatible with one another. The Hisiometanio are further said to have originally been composed from Hevietanio Cheyenne band members who intermarried among the Pipe-Stem Men and Suhtaio, so that Grinnell's informants who gave the term *"issuht"* and its definition, probably supposed some connection between the word for ʻridgeʻ and ʻ*Suhta,*ʻ this latter being the singular of *Suhtaio.*

It will become evident in a later passage, how a part of the Suhtaio did inter-marry among several Cheyenne bands whilst still in Minnesota, which might explain how some of the following alternative definitions have become misconstrued. The problem is made more confusing by an assertion from the late Northern Cheyenne historian John-Stands-In-Timber, who stated that the name Suhtaio actually means, "People descended." This seems to infer that the Suhtaio were descendants from the original Cheyenne-proper nucleus. But this is not an accurate translation of the name, rather a later-day colloquialism for which the term ʻ*Suhtaio*ʻ became used as a synonym. It more likely comes from the idea of the Suhtaio being descended, i.e., generated from what the Suhtaio believed were the first people on earth. John Stands-In-Timber, incidentally, always referred to the Suhtaio in his written data as *"Suktai,"* which appears to be his rendering of the Lakota Sioux term "Skutani" which itself is a Sioux dialectical corruption of the term Suhtaio.

Yet another translation of the name Suhtaio was tentatively offered by Grinnell, the meaning of which, he said, was "people left behind" and in all probability, was another colloquial translation once used as a synonym for the Suhtaio people. At the same time, Rudolph Petter, the able scholar of the Cheyenne language, obtained information from one Willis Rowland, a half-White half-Cheyenne informant, that the word Suhtai implies the idea of being "backward" or "behind," and suggested that it might have some bearing upon the order in which the Cheyenne and Suhtaio crossed the Missouri River; that is, the Cheyennes first, the Suhtaio second. This assumption is tenable, but appears to be confounded by the well-known Cheyenne clan name of *"Totoimana"* which likewise, is translated as ʻbackward,ʻ even though in this instance the term is now used in conjunction with that of ʻshyʻ or ʻcoyʻ etc.: There is, however, strong evidence to show that Cheyennes did cross the Missouri before the Suhtaio, although this on its own does not confirm the above definition of the name, as the term *"Totoimana"* actually comes from the root word *"toto,"* denoting the crawfish and refers, moreover, to the curious backward movement of that creature. It is not clear if the ʻ*Totoimana*ʻ were an offshoot from the Masikota or the Suhtaio, or merely very closely associated with the Suhtaio, more so, that is, than were other Cheyenne bands. Yet it seems obvious that it was by this connection that the statements of Willis Rowland and his Cheyenne informants became confused on this point. The ʻ*Totoimana*ʻ band usually roamed side by side with the Suhtaio and in a later century, were sometimes found west of the Missouri and sometimes east of that river. No doubt other Cheyenne-speaking bands in their poetic wisdom gave the ʻ*Totoimana*ʻ their name as a consequence, and at times, frequently used it as a collective term for the ʻ*Totoimana*ʻ and *Suhtaio* together. It is dangerous to go further on this point, but there may indeed be a simile between the Cheyenne-proper word `Toto` and that of the late historic Plains Cree term of `Soto.` This latter being a name given by the Cree to an alien but confederated band which was likely of Suhtaio descent, and later absorbed completely by the Plains Cree.

Be this as it may, surely the most convincing contender for a proper translation of the name, is Father Peter Powell and his assertion that the name *"Sota"* [Plural; *Sotaeo*] means "Buffalo People" applied in relation to the "Buffalo" ceremonies of the Suhtaio and to their unique abilities both in calling and renewing the herds. Powell's spelling is probably the closest offered yet to the old dialectical form, the latter-day pronunciation of `Suhtaio` being its corruption into the Cheyenne language proper.

Now the Chippewa recalled an alien people called *"Shota-winniwug,"* as once having lived somewhere between the western tip of Lake Superior and Leech Lake near the headwaters of the Mississippi until the early 1700s. But they could not explain the name other than the last part of the term *"winniwug,"* meaning `men.` Neither had they any idea where that people went or what happened to them. One might suppose then, that the first part of the term *"Shota"* as given above, was a Native term used by the Suhtaio themselves and merely adopted by the Chippewa along with the latter's Cree associates. In corroboration, we are told by Grinnell that as late as the eighteen-nineties, one Cheyenne woman at least, always spoke of the Suhtaio as *"Soh-ta."* Today the original Suhtaio dialect is dead, and of those few words surviving among the various Cheyenne communities in Montana and Oklahoma, they have probably become corrupted from the original through their amalgamation with that of Cheyenne-proper. In the Cheyenne dialect the word for buffalo when used as a general term is `ho-tue` [pronounced ho-to-a], so that in the archaic Suhtaio dialect the same word may well have been `so-ho-ta.` Certainly, the `a` suffix of the form `Sohota` indicates an animate or Proper noun and cannot, therefore, satisfactorily refer to either a ridge or hill, which would then be rendered without the animate suffix.

Of course, there were no buffalo north of the Mississippi headwaters; Sault St. Marie and Upper Great Lakes regions, where the Suhtaio would have been in close contact with the Chippewa and Cree. Although it should be remembered that the word for buffalo in all these guises during the early days of Cheyenne residence in the Northeast, was interchangeable with that of any large ruminant and so, could have referred to the moose or elk, which would then have some bearing, perhaps, upon the relationship the Suhtaio once had with the Monsoni Cree, who we know, were also referred to colloquially as "Moose Men." The Suhtaio thus continuing to call themselves "Moose" or "Elk" people, even after breaking from their Cree cousins.

Why in the late nineteenth century the Chippewa had no recollection of the meaning of the name *Shota-winniwug,* might easily be explained by the fact previously noted, that perhaps it was not a proper Chippewa word at all, but rather, an adulterated form of an alien term and that the latter also knew the Suhtaio by another, more popular name, long since forgotten, yet once used alternatively with that of `Shota.` Likely, both names remained extant among the Cheyennes and Suhtaio themselves, but had been dropped by the Chippewa and Cree around the end of the eighteenth century, by which time the Suhtaio had disappeared completely from the sphere of Chippewa and Cree contact. However, a more recent explanation given by Henry Little Coyote who was the current Sacred Hat Keeper in 1958, stated that the term Suhtaio should actually be rendered as *"Issih`omih`tio,"* which, he said, translates as "People of the marsh waters that flow into the dark bushy country." [Quite a mouthful for such a short word?]. [1] Be this as it may, yet another name for the Suhtaio was given by Lewis and Clark in the account of their expedition of 1803 - 1806, during the course of which they were told of a people roaming west of the Missouri south of the Black Hills [South Dakota] who they called *"Staitan."* This, undoubtedly, is the explorer's incorrect rendering of *"Suh-tai-hetan,"* the answer a Suhtaio would have given when questioned as to his tribal identity and literally meaning, *"I am a man of the Suhtaio."*

This same source also mentions the *"Kite"* Indians in the context of an independent tribe and which, according to Ben Clark, another half-breed among the Cheyennes during the latter half of the nineteenth century, was but an early nickname along with that of `Flyers,` applied specifically to the Suhtaio, and dubbed upon them because when seen by other tribes they were invariably at a distance and in flight. Further corroboration can be found in the journal of Captain Bell who while a member of Major Stephen Long`s expedition across the southern Plains to the Rocky Mountains in 1819/`20, also mentioned a tribe then extant known as *"Staitans"* or *"Kites."*

Traditions of the Suhtaio which relate to their habitat during a period immediately prior to their entering the Upper Mississippi region, are compatible with those of the Cheyenne, in so much as they mention a *"very cold land"* and a long period of residence around or near *"a large lake."* This traditional area could have been in the vicinity of present-day Lake Nipigon, around which the Monsoni Cree and at a later date a remnant of the Moiseo Cheyenne-proper group then designated as the *Quissy* once resided, and hereabouts, immediately northeast of this lake is the small township of *"Tashota."* The name unquestionably is Indian in its etymology and Algonquian at that, yet how exactly the name came about or even its true meaning is not recorded. Could it denote that at one time in the past, a people with a similar sounding name resided in that lake's locality?

The Cheyenne language uses the appellative `ta` as a preposition to mean `at` and *"Tashota,"* therefore, may have inferred something like, "Buffalo people at," or in its English idiom, "Place of the Shota." [2]

Alternatively, the term may have derived from the Chippewa dialect, being formed from the compound term `tash,` meaning to `split` or `tear` and of `ta` referring to the third person of the future tense. `O` before a consonant, signifies `his,` `her,` `its` or `their` when preceding a substantive and thus, *"Tashota"* may actually have denoted something in the order of, "they split his" [her, its, etc.] which would be compatible with the Cheyenne-proper word `Ehista,` from whence is derived the later tribal designation of `TsisTsisTsas,"* referring to their being split or torn apart [See Chapter 2.]. Indicatively, the actual term TsisTsisTsas, so we are told by the tribal informant John Stands-In-Timber, was originally the Suhtai name applied to the Cheyenne-Proper.

Perhaps then, the term `Tashota` was an old colloquial name which had lingered on in the Lake Nipigon area where the Suhtaio group once resided, and so designated the actual place where the Suhtaio had finally broken away from their Chippewa and Cree confederates, i.e. "where the Sohta split." An alternative analogy is the comparison between the name `Sohta` and the Chippewa

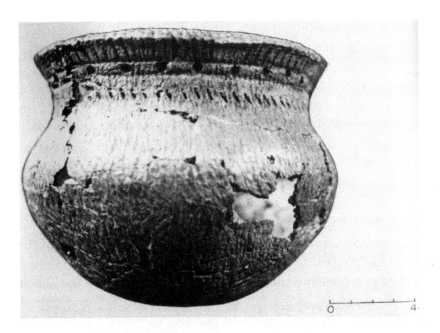

BLACKDUCK VESSEL. LAKEHEAD UNIV; THUNDER BAY, ONTARIO.

[From "Plains Indians. A.D. 500-1500. Ed; K. Schlesier. Univ; of Okla; Press.P.114.1994].

SELKIRK VESSEL FROM EAST-CENTRAL SASKETCHEWAN.

[Photo by T. Gibson. in "Plains Indians, A.D. 500-1500. Univ: Okla.: Press P.119. 1994].

expression *"Ma-sho-ta,"* meaning, `Prairie people` [i.e., being an analogy for `moose,` or more properly, `elk.`] and with that of the historic Cheyenne band name Masikota, which, as we have already noted, is the Cheyenne dialectical form of the Chippewa and Cree term `Ma`shota` with the same connotation as `Prairie People.`

In the case of the Cheyennes, the term `Prairie People` is synonymous with that of `Grasshoppers` in the guise of *Masikota*, but one cannot deny the strong similarity between the Chippewa terms `Mashota and `Sohta` if one omits the first syllable `Ma,` so that the latter term of `Sohta` may merely be a contracted form of the same, and a long-forgotten colloquialism formed from the same root as the Cheyenne-proper band name *"Masikota,"* but in the case of the Suhtaio denoting the "Prairie ruminant" or "Buffalo People."

Certainly, the Suhtaio were once in close and harmonious contact with both Cree and Chippewa groups while resident north of the Upper Great Lakes, and in all likelihood, they visited the big intertribal trading fairs at Sault St. Marie where they were sure to have had not a little intercourse with other Algonquian tribes of that region. So close were the Suhtaio to the Monsoni Cree both culturally and dialectically, that in later years many Cheyennes regarded the Suhtaio as being descended from the Cree, although what probably happened was this.

The Suhtaio whilst roaming the country above the Upper Great Lakes, were in contact with and allied to both the Cree and Chippewa who; as mentioned above, knew them as `Dog People` and in the vernacular as `Moose` or `Elk Men.` After the Suhtaio moved southwest into the headwater district of the Upper Mississippi, they became familiar with buffalo in the "tall-grass" prairie country to the west of that stream, and as a consequence, began dressing themselves in that animal's skins and robes. Subsequently, owing to the intertribal trading fairs at Sault St. Marie along with the continued Suhtaio friendship with the Monsoni, they, the Suhtaio, paid regular return visits to their old haunts in the Northeast. The Cree and Chippewa perceiving the Suhtaio buffalo-robe clothing continued to call them "Moose Men," but with the added appellative for `prairie` in order to differentiate the buffalo, e.g., the prairie ruminant, [with which the Chippewa were then hardly acquainted] from the Moose, e.g., the woodland ruminant.

The archaic word *"Suhta"* in the latter`s own dialect, does not appear to have originally applied to the buffalo specifically, but was used as a generic term for any large ruminating quadruped such as the buffalo, moose or elk and among the Cheyennes in more recent times, it was the Elk Warrior Society that was always composed predominantly of Suhtaio band members, having originally been organized among the Suhtaio, as Truman Michelson`s informant White Bull asserted, long before being adopted by the Cheyennes themselves.

Of course, the Monsoni Cree, as we have seen, were also known as "Moose" or "Elk People," and what more corroboration is needed to associate the Suhtaio as being an old-time Monsoni and Moiseo ally and closely confederated with them? Indeed, according to Michelson's informants, the Suhtaio came originally from somewhere northeast of the Mississippi, and here close to Lake Nipigon, the Monsoni Cree were positioned on the Father Creux map as late as A.D.1660.

Bearing in mind the above conclusions, the map of Louis Joliet drafted in 1674, which lists those tribes along and adjacent to the Upper Mississippi at that time, does, in fact, mention the three groups of Monsoni, Suhtaio and Moiseo, albeit in obscure form. The name Monsoni is rendered on Joliet`s map as *"Ali-mous-pigioak"* being a garbled version of an Algonquian term, but which certainly refers to a group known locally as "Moose" or "Elk People." The latter part of the word *"pigoiak"* merely denotes `people` or the like, whilst the second syllable of `mous` is Joliet`s rendering of the Algonquian term `moose."

MEMBER OF THE CHEYENNE CROOKED-LANCE OR ELK WARRIOR SOCIETY.
[From an original drawing by the author. Author`s collection.]

217

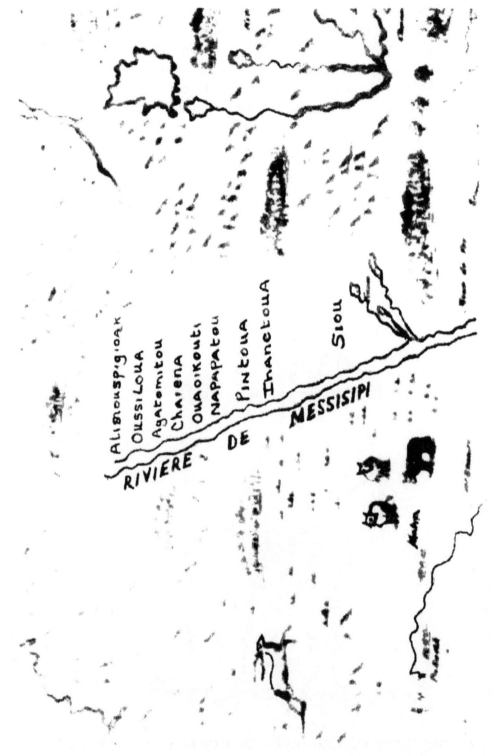

LOUIS JOLLIET'S MAP OF POSITION OF UPPER MISSISSIPPI TRIBES IN 1673.
[From a copy of the original in the Newberry Library. Chicago, U.S.A.]

218

The Monsoni, according to later map references were evidently, a small group closely aligned with the Suhtaio, both of whom were then in situ somewhere between Leech Lake and the western tip of Lake Superior. This being the same general area where Joliet had earlier positioned his "*Alimouspigioak*" and *Quissyloua* [Moiseo], and where also as Chippewa tradition asserts, once resided the *"Shota-winniwug."* Earlier, it seems, the name ʽ*Alimouspigioak*ʽ was originally applied to the Monsoni and associated Suhtaio without distinction. We know that Lake Nipigon was once called Lac Alimibegon, which term derives from a corrupted form of the Algonquian term *"Alimous,"* and was applied to that lake in reference to a people of a similar sounding name who once resided in its vicinity, before that is, they were pushed out of the country altogether by Assiniboine attacks on one hand, and the arrival of refugee Huron and Algonquian bands following 1653 on the other, who themselves, were fleeing west from Iroquois war-parties and European disease in their rear.

– 0 - 0 - 0 - 0 - 0 - 0 - 0 - 0 - 0 - 0 - 0 - 0 - 0 - 0 - 0 - 0 - 0 –

CHAPTER 21.

DOG MEN.

We are told by Michelsonʽs Cheyenne informant White-Bull, that another popular and early name for the Suhtaio was that of "Dogs," or "Dog People."

Some of the present author's own Cheyenne informants including James King and Bill Tall Bull, declared that this particular term had come into use after the Cheyennes themselves obtained horses, but while the Suhtaio were still pedestrian and used dogs as their only beast of burden. However, the Cheyennes, it seems, did not acquire horses in any significant number until sometime during the early decades of the eighteenth century [circa, 1730], and the term ʽDog Peopleʽ was definitely in vogue long before that time. Being the name applied to a specific group of people inhabiting the Upper Mississippi and Upper Great Lakes country certainly as early as 1660, when the Father Creux map showed a people by the name *"Agatomchien"* on the south side of the Sault St. Marie.

The name *"Agatomchien"* appears to be a conglomerate term, composed from a rendition of the Cree term for ʽdog,ʽ i.e., ʽatimʽ and the French word ʽchienʽ used for that same animal, or, perhaps, from the Sioux term *"Sha-en,"* indicating a close relationship of the *Agatomchien* with both the Cheyenne and Sioux.

On the map drafted by Joliet and previously referred to, we also note the tribal name *Agatomitou,* referring to a people who Joliet positioned somewhere between the headwaters region of the Upper Mississippi and the western tip of Lake Superior. In this instance, we have the appendage `tou,` which maybe a misspelling of the Sioux word `ton,` denoting `village,` although more likely, it is an attempt to render the Algonquian suffix `iu,` meaning `men,` as in the Cheyenne-Suhtaio word *"Hotamitan-iu"* meaning "Dog men." The first two syllables of Joliet`s rendering, evidently incorporate the Northern Algonquian word for `dog` of `atimita,` and this last is close to the Blackfoot contracted form of `mita` also meaning `dog,` whilst `atim` is merely the contracted form of the same word in Cree. The Cheyenne word for `dog` of *"hotam"* was then, in its archaic form, probably similar to the Cree version from whom Joliet`s name was probably obtained in the first place. Perhaps the first part of Joliet`s rendering, i.e. `Ag` represents the Cheyenne expression of emphasis, i.e. `Ho,` this being a variant of the more correct term `Ha,` which in the Cheyenne tongue expresses degree etc.; [See Chapter 13].

It would seem, therefore, that there was once a tribal group residing somewhere between the Upper Mississippi and Lake Superior during the middle years of the seventeenth century, who were known colloquially to the nearby Sioux and Algonquians by the name of "Dog Men" or "Dog People."

The position where Father Creux placed his `Agatomchien` within the vicinity of Sault St. Marie in 1660, shows they would have been in close proximity to and in contact with the Chippewa and other Central Algonquian tribes, such as Sauk, Fox, Menominee, Miami, Kickapoo and Maskouten, whilst Joliet`s later positioning and spelling of `Agatomitou,` indicates that by 1673 / 74, this same group had since moved west into the headwaters country of the Upper Mississippi, where they were then already in close and, one assumes, harmonious contact with both the Cheyennes and Sioux of that region. This fact is substantiated by one, Father Louis Hennepin, who wrote an account of his travels and experiences among the Upper Mississippi Sioux during the winter of 1680 / `81. Here we find clues regarding the situation of both the Cheyennes and Suhtaio at and around that time.

Father Louis Hennepin was a friar of the Recollect order who, in the year 1680, whilst a member of the Chevalier du LaSalle`s expedition from the mouth of the Wisconsin and down the length of the Mississippi to the Gulf of Mexico, ran afoul of Isanty Sioux somewhere along the Upper course of that river; was taken prisoner and forced to remain among his captors as their reluctant guest throughout the ensuing winter. The Isanty Sioux - more commonly known at a later date by the name Santee, - then resided, according to both Hennepin`s account and their own traditions, in the district around what today is known as Mille Lacs close to the Upper Mississippi, and Sioux tradition adds, that Cheyenne peoples were then living near them.

Unfortunately, Hennepin, who obviously obtained information from his captors concerning neighbouring tribes, did not mention any Indian group in his several narratives, instantly recognizable as a Cheyenne-speaking band by a name which was still in use during the late historic period. Nevertheless, when we consult his map, which shows the position of tribes about the Upper course of the Mississippi and surrounding country for the year 1680, we find the notation *"Nacion du Chien"* positioned just above a *"Changaskiton Lac"* to the northeast of the

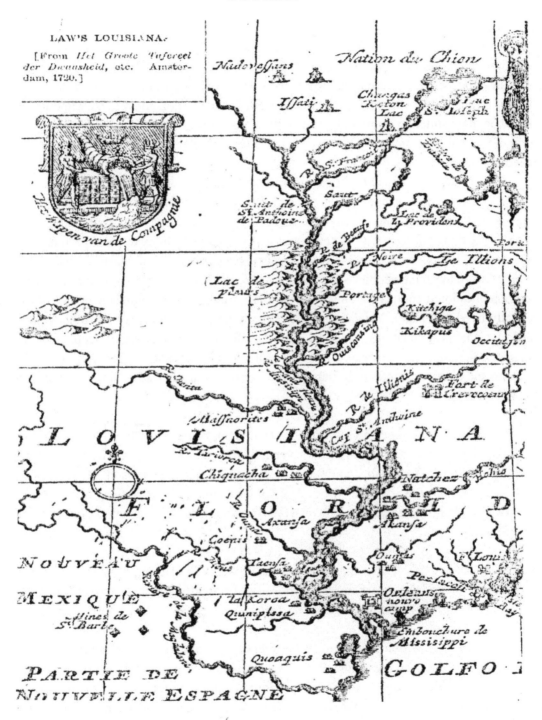

COPY OF LOUIS HENNEPIN MAP OF 1682, PUBLISHED IN AMSTERDAM, HOLLAND IN 1720.

[FROM JUSTIN WINSOR`S BOOK, "THE MISSISSIPPI BASIN." HERITAGE BOOKS INC; 2003.]

right-hand Fork of the Upper Mississippi.

Now we know that *"Chongaskiton Lac"* was the Father's name for a small expanse of water adjoining present-day Mille Lacs, and that the river he termed St. Francis connecting the said lake to the Mississippi, is present-day Rum River. Hennepin`s geographic scale is atrocious, in so much that Mille Lacs is shown as being due west of Lake Nipigon above Lake Superior and thus, seems to be more suited to Rainy Lake than Mille Lacs. However, Rainy Lake, of course, was then Cree and Assiniboine country and certainly, no Sioux was living that far north during the period of Hennepin`s sojourn among them.

The name *"Chongaskiton"* and its variant form of *Shongaskiton*, are derived from the Sioux word *"shonka,"* meaning `dog,` along with the added suffix `ton` meaning in the same language, `village.` It has since often been supposed that the name was once applied to the Eastern Dakota Sioux division known as Sisseton and was thought by some, to have been an alternative personal name for that tribe. From this erroneous concept, it has been construed that the *"Nacion du Chien"* were the same people as the *Chongaskitons*. This assumption, though, is not valid, for the map in question mentions not only a `Chongaskiton Lac,` whereabouts the people of that name apparently lived, but also a `Nacion du Chien` positioned above it. Was it the Friar's intention to record superfluous appellations, or did he wish to differentiate one group of people from another? The latter, I believe, was the case. It is not acceptable that the term `Chongaskiton` refers to the lake alone and not to a people of the same name, for the Friar's narrative also mentions a band by that name saying,

> "In the neighbourhood of Lake Buade, [Hennepin`s name for Mille Lacs] are many other lakes whence issue several rivers, on the banks of which live the Isanti, Nadouessons, Tinthonah, [which means Prairie Men] Ouadebathon; River people, Chongaskiton, Dog or Wolf tribe, [For Chonga among these Nations mean dog or wolf] and other tribes, all of which We comprise under the name Nadouessiou [Sioux?]." [1]

The fact that other tribal names in this list, as well as on Hennepin`s map, are given as one word and the `Chien` are designated as *"Nation of,"* suggests that even though allied to and in close contact with the Sioux, the *"Nacion du Chien"* were recognized by Hennepin as a separate people.

Hennepin`s positioning of this group infers they may have been Cree or Chippewa, who we know at that date; owing to the Daniel Duluth inspired peacemaking of 1679, were then allowed to hunt in the borderlands of Eastern Sioux territory, and it should be noted that at times, the Cree were referred to as "Dog eaters." However, the Cree had been contacted and well-documented by the time of Hennepin`s arrival and were widely known as *Kilistinons* and *Kilistinouc* or variants of the same.

Hennepin, unquestionably, knew of the Cree; having already a superficial knowledge of those tribes and their hunting grounds around the Upper Great Lakes even before his capture by the Sioux, and it would be naive, if not insulting, to suggest that he did not recognize the `Nacion du Chien` as *Kilistinoucs* if, in reality, they were one and the same as the Cree. This same conclusion must also apply to the false assumption that the *Nacion du Chien* could have been a Chippewa group.

It must follow, that Hennepin observed enough differences between the two, in order to give the `Nacion du Chien` a singular appellation.

Perhaps the term `Nacion du Chien` had been applied by Hennepin to a people known to the Sioux as *"Shahiena"* and which the Friar misconstrued as `chien` being a corruption of the earlier Joliet term of `Chaiena` for a group of people then residing in the Upper Mississippi country and who, undoubtedly, were synonymous with those later known as Cheyenne. By the same token, the term *Chongaskiton* meaning `dog village,` was probably applied to a people known by Hennepin to have been previously contacted by the Jesuit Priest Father Allouez more than fifteen years earlier, and from whom Father Hennepin may have adopted the name.

As early as 1666, Father Allouez had visited a people then living somewhere near the western tip of Lake Superior and reported,

"They pay idolatrous worship to the Sun, to which they are wont to sacrifice a dog by fastening a dog to the top of a pole and leaving it thus suspended until it rots." [2]

Allouez terms these people *"Kilistinouc,"* being a variant of *Kilistinou*, the name commonly applied to the numerous Cree bands in general. Yet these people are unlikely to have been Cree as such, for at this date, the Cree were all west and north of Lake Nipigon and where Allouez apparently found his `dog sacrificers,` was in the heart of what was then Sioux country when a most violent war of attrition was being conducted between most, if not all Cree bands and the Western or Teton Sioux. It is indicative, of course, as we have noted in a previous chapter, that Father Allouez also stated that these dog-sacrificing people were very closely connected dialectically with the Wheskerinni and other Algonkin-proper tribes [See Chapter.4.], that once inhabited the area adjacent to the St. Maurice River and at Tadoussac on the Lower St. Lawrence, including the country about the Upper reaches of the Saguenay where once the Moiseo and Omissis had also resided during their "Ancient Time."

They were then, probably Suhtaio who at this period of circa, 1666, according to their own testimony, still fashioned their hair and clothes in the Cree manner and, therefore, were likely to have been mistaken for Cree by the less discriminating observer. The Suhtaio at this date, were already confederated and co-habiting freely with not only the various Cheyenne-proper bands, but also with Eastern Sioux along with both Monsoni Cree and the Chippewa.

Indeed, the Sun worship all too briefly mentioned by Allouez, appears to have been similar to the Sun-Dance ceremony of the Plains Indians during a later century, as the pole to which a dog

223

was supposedly tied, reminds one of the center pole in the Cheyenne Sun-Dance Lodge to which a symbolic cut-out figure of a man was attached. There was a time previously, however, so George Dorsey`s Cheyenne informants told him, when human beings were captured and tied to the center pole as a sacrifice, in order to procure favor from the omnipotent unseen powers so that the tribe be blessed. Perhaps, then, when a captured enemy was not forthcoming, a dog was substituted in its place and we know that among many tribes, including the Cheyenne, the dog was regarded as a messenger to the Gods. Many Algonquian tribes, it is true, especially the Ottawa in common with various Iroquois-proper tribes, did also perform ceremonies in which a dog played an integral part and were similar to each other in the conducting of their rites, so that all such ceremonies had probably stemmed from an ancient common concept in the East Woodland regions.

The fact, however, that Father Allouez who, without doubt, was familiar with similar religious observances among the various tribes of his acquaintance, saw fit to mention what he witnessed near the western tip of Lake Superior, leads one to believe that this particular ceremony and accompanying rites, were peculiar to his `dog sacrificers` alone.

The Cheyennes; so we have noted elsewhere, always declared that the Sun-Dance - being one of their people's major religious observances when on the Western Plains - had originally come from the Suhtaio, who themselves had practiced a version of it at least since their early days in the Northeast. Probably the dance had continued in an older Northern or even Central Algonquian fashion until contact with the Sioux or Mandan caused other influences to creep in, for the Sioux had also worshiped a Sun deity since their early years in northern Minnesota. But Allouez was well-acquainted with the Sioux, and certainly, would not have confused them with the Cree.

Either then, the Suhtaio adopted the dance from the Sioux or - and what is more feasible - the Sioux adopted it from the Suhtaio, if indeed, not from one or another Cheyenne-proper speaking group such as the Moiseo, Masikota or Bowstrings, each of which were in a league with the Sioux at that date and also with the Suhtaio.

Of course, if the *"dog sacrificers"* of Father Allouez and Hennepin`s *"Nacion du Chien"* had, in reality, referred to a particular Cree-proper band, then why was it not recognized as such in later years ? The Cree remained in the northern Great Lake's country for some time after circa, 1680 and did not move in any large number from the area until the end of that same century. Several other educated white travelers did visit those wild tribes, both west and northwest of Lake Superior during the closing years of the seventeenth century. They contacted the very same peoples as had both Father Allouez and Friar Hennepin. Yet there remains no other reference other than copies of Hennepin`s data, to a `Nacion du Chien.`

Thus, Hennepin may merely have been alluding to the Allouez description when he dubbed the band in question `Nacion du Chien` when what he really meant was *"Nacion du Chaiena,"* i.e. Cheyenne. He would have known they were not Sioux, even though they cohabited with certain Sioux bands and used a number of Sioux words in their everyday speech. He would have realized also, that there was sufficient difference between them and the Cree to warrant a singular identity.

All this points to the conclusion that the `Nacion du Chien` was a Cheyenne-proper group, undoubtedly, those known as Moiseo, whilst the *Agatomitou* of Joliet, who were the *Agatomchien* of Father Creux and the *Songaskitons* of Hennepin, were a separate people generally known to other tribes as `Dog People` or something similar, and, therefore, the same as those later known as Suhtaio. Indeed, the people termed *Shongas-Hitan,"* noted east of the Mississippi above the Falls of St. Anthony on the Daniel Coxe map of 1722, has the specific Suhtaio-dialect ending of `hitan,` meaning, `man` or `men,` and thus the expression *Shongas-hitan* would have been the reply a Suhtai would have given if saying, "I am a man of the Dog tribe."

During the period of circa, 1680, so we are told in Cheyenne oral tradition as narrated by the aforementioned White Bull, the Suhtaio were an important tribal group consisting of four bands, then roaming the Upper Mississippi and western Upper Great Lakes region. They were then confederated with both the Sioux and the Chippewa on one hand, and with the Cheyenne and Cree on the other. They were, of course, the *"Shota-winniwug"* of Chippewa memory and the dog sacrificing people of the Allouez account.

Of one thing we can be sure, the name `Dog people` in one guise or another, was applied to the Suhtaio long before they became confederated among the Cheyenne-proper and some years prior to the latter obtaining horses. Having thus deduced that Friar Louis Hennepin's `Nacion du Chien,` were synonymous with the old-time Cheyenne-proper bands in northern Minnesota, and that the *Songaskitons* or `Dog people` were synonymous with the old-time Suhtaio, it should be possible to trace a migration route for the Suhtaio from somewhere north of Lake Superior, into the Minnesota country and the area around Leech Lake, where - so Chippewa tradition asserts - the *"Shota-winniwug"* once resided.

Now between the two locations mentioned above, we find a "Dog River" which enters Lake Superior's western shore in the region of Thunder Bay. The name `Dog River` is an old colonial term and includes along its course a `Dog Portage` and `Dog Lake.` This last named, during the period in question, yielded an abundance of white fish and is the source of Dog River itself. It was the custom of the early French explorers into the region, to apply names to rivers and lakes in accordance with the particular people found living nearby and as a consequence, the early maps are full of names such as Fox River, Assiniboine River, Ottawa River, Illinois Lake, Lake of the Christineux etc.: etc.

Thus `Dog Lake` is likely to have been a place of habitation for the Suhtaio, during that people's migration from Lake Nipigon to the Leech Lake district, and from the scant particulars given in the Allouez account as to the position of his `Dog sacrificers,` it would appear that present-day Dog Lake and its connecting river come well within the general area implied, and may have been so named owing to the fact, that a people known colloquially as "Dogs" by surrounding tribes, were once located in its vicinity.

Suhtaio traditions concerning their early days, like those of the Cheyenne-proper, mention their people's dependence upon large quantities of white fish during their years in the far northeast and even as late as the early eighteen-hundreds, Dog Lake was well-known for its abundance of white fish, particularly during the autumn months and for a long time - several centuries perhaps, - had been a favorite fishing ground for numerous Cree and other Algonquian-speaking bands.

In corroboration of the foregoing, George Dorsey [1905] was of the opinion that the Cheyenne band known during the late historic period as *"Hotamitanio"* or simply*,* "Dog Men" or "Dog Soldiers," was, originally, the name of an ancient Cheyenne band and was corroborated in this view by the able linguist Rudolph Petter, who inferred that the Dog Soldiers were an early-day separate dialectical group which at some remote time in the past, amalgamated with the Cheyenne-proper. As we have seen, the Suhtaio were known colloquially as "Dogs" and would explain Petter's analogy.

Indeed, the name `Chousa,` stated by Petter as being an old name for the Dog Soldiers, is the same term mentioned by the trader Jean Baptiste Trudeau in 1795, of which he said were, *"...One of the three hordes of the Chaguyenne Nation."* [3]

Undoubtedly then, the name applies to the Suhtaio; an old connection of whom was with the Masikota Cheyenne-proper group who themselves, albeit in a later century, chose to join the Dog Soldier Society band amass and were absorbed by them.

It has generally been erroneously supposed that the Cheyenne warrior societies of the late historic time, were fairly recent in origin; not in existence during the tribe's wanderings throughout the Northeast. However, the *"Whoksihitanio,"* more commonly known as "Kit-Fox Men," had the very early name of *"Motsonitanio"* denoting "Moose Men" or "Elk Men" and synonymous with the `Flint Men` which name alludes to the old-time flint arrowheads. This suggests that this particular society stemmed originally from the ancient original Moiseo Cheyenne-proper faction, an old name for whom was also "Flint" or "Arrow Men." Likewise, the "Bowstring" society was, according to Cheyenne testimony, a very old band name when in northern Minnesota, where it yet survives in the guise of `Bowstring River` and `Bowstring Lake; names which in all probability, were of old applied to the area whereabouts the `Bowstring` Cheyenne group once resided.

This being the case, one can reasonably conject that during the same period in time, there was a closely related band then known as `Dog People,` and from whom at a later date, came the warrior society name of Dog Soldiers or simply Dog-Men.

The Blackfoot, Arapahoe and Plains Cree all had a Dog Society, each of which likewise, claimed an ancient origin. These societies were prominent during those tribes` last years of freedom on the Great Western Plains, and were comparable in their regalia and singular peculiarities with that same society of "Dog Soldiers" or "Dog Men" among the Cheyennes. As regards the Arapahoe, their `Dog` society was also very closely connected with the Sun-Dance rites and like that among the Cheyennes, had the specific honour of erecting the center pole. The Arapahoe, however, declare that they were once in close contact with Cheyenne groups when in the far northeast and the northern Minnesota country, and also with the Blackfoot. So it would seem that when the concept for organizing warrior societies was fully adopted among the various tribes, the Dog Society was already common among several Cree offshoot tribes long prior to the opening of the eighteenth century, and during which latter period, all had since become inhabitants of the Great Plains west and north of the Missouri River.

We further learn from Cheyenne tradition, that the Dog Soldier Society was the fifth military fraternity to be adopted by the tribe, and unlike the original four societies that of the Dog Soldiers was brought to the Cheyenne at a later date and not by the tribe's culture hero Sweet-Medicine. The Dog Society then, was not originally Cheyenne, but was introduced among them by the Suhtaio, in fact; after their two peoples became joined as confederates. This is to say that the Cheyenne warrior or soldier societies of a later time, known as the Elks, Red-Shields, Kit-Fox Bowstrings and Dogs, had merely taken their singular names from which, earlier, had designated each of the original separate, but closely related five Algonquian-speaking groups which after the

CHEYENNE DOG SOLDIER WEARING DOG-ROPE and SOCIETY HEAD-RESS.
[From a pen and ink drawing by the author. Author`s collection.]

227

coming of the Prophet Sweet-Medicine, thereafter joined together to create the Cheyenne Nation of more recent time.

As mentioned earlier, Cheyenne tradition avers that at a much later date, during the third coming together of Cheyennes and Suhtaio west of the Missouri River, a part of the last named amalgamated with the Cheyennes, while the remainder went north and joined the Cree. Indeed, Truman Michelson`s informant White Bull stated in 1910, that four young Suhtaio families went north many years ago and did not come back, while as late as the nineteen-thirties, the Plains Cree informant Fine-Day remembered a small foreign Algonquian-speaking band as once roaming the prairies of southern Saskatchewan, Canada who were known by a variety of names, the most common of which was that of Cree-Stoney, owing to this particular band's singular friendship with a band of "Stony" Assiniboine. However, they were also known as the *"Soto"* or *"Sota"* and were closely confederated with a Chippewa group originally from the Sault St. Marie area of the Upper Great Lakes, and also with the Western or Plains Cree, who were off-shoots from a conglomerate of Muskegon [Swampy Cree] and Monsoni peoples and among whom the `Sota` were finally absorbed. More importantly, another name for the *Sota* was that of `Dogs,` or more properly, "The Dog Penis band," which seems to add substance to the possibility that they were originally Suhtaio who had long been known as "Dog People," and further, that they were that part of the Suhtaio which did indeed, move northwest and join the Plains Cree as the informant White Bull asserted. It is also indicative that during the late 1650s and early 1660s, the Suhtaio were not themselves at war with the Assiniboine, even though they were generally regarded as friends to the Cheyennes and Sioux and among which tribes, they appear to have constituted a neutral element in the northern Minnesota country, but of this we will speak later.

It is interesting to note that in later years, the Cree were known to have had a society called "Young Dogs," whose members performed a `Young Dog dance` supposedly deriving from an ancient origin and similar to the Sun-Dance of the Plains Indians in a later century. The Suhtaio, being the instigators of the Sun-Dance among the Cheyennes, show an added connection here, as they appear to be synonymous with the mixed Cree-Assiniboine band known as "Young Dogs." This particular Plains Cree band may well have included the same Suhtaio remnant which, according to tradition, had many years earlier separated from the rest of their tribe and gone north to join the Cree.

Could it be that the Plains Cree band known as *Pis-cha-kdw-a-kis* or `Magpies,` who the Fort Union trader Edwin Denig mentioned in 1855 as residing in earth-covered lodges near Tinder Mountain in south-eastern Saskatchewan and who hunted buffalo during the winter months, but also tilled the ground and raised a quantity of maize and potatoes among other crops, were actually of Suhtaio descent? Hence their adhering to a similar style of earth-lodge dwellings as once utilized by the old-time Suhtaio when resident west of the Red River of the North, while their name of `Magpies` may have been derived from the Suhtaio singular religious veneration for that species of bird. Certainly, the Magpie band was the only Cree group to reside in such dwellings and indulge themselves to a degree in horticultural pursuits.

CHAPTER. 22

AT WAR AND PEACE WITH THE SUHTAIO.

The aforementioned close relationship between the Suhtaio and Monsoni Cree, the latter including that faction later known as Plains Cree and with whom, a part of the Suhtaio are said in tribal tradition to have amalgamated at a later date, had probably induced the Suhtaio to advance southwest into northern Minnesota; having been caught up in the general momentum of the Monsoni - Plains Cree migration west from Sault St. Marie and the Lake Nipigon district. This event occurred after the Cree began obtaining firearms from their Chippewa allies and white traders along the Lower St. Lawrence, circa, 1640, and while they were still being harassed by powerful Iroquois enemies from the east. The Suhtaio on the contrary, probably did not have guns of any description and likely possessed only a few metal weapons if any, so that unlike their erstwhile Plains Cree associates, they did not risk venturing into unknown territory occupied by foreign peoples who might fervently resist their intrusion. Rather, they turned south and southwest into the marshlands on the east side of the Headwaters of the Mississippi, being unperturbed at the earlier Cheyenne movement into that same area.

Certainly, the Monsoni Cree were positioned next to the Suhtaio and Moiseo, [designated on Joliet's 1674 map as the *Alimouspigoiak, Agatomitou* and *Quissyloua* respectively] and very close to Sioux or Dakota bands, at a time we might recall, when most other Cree groups were conducting a vigorous offensive against both Sioux and Cheyennes alike. Furthermore, the map drafted by the Jesuit Priest Father Du Creux as early as 1660, definitely places the *Monsoomies* [sic] as then being entrenched around Rainy Lake, not far north of the Mississippi heads.

Thus by the late 1660s, the Suhtaio were in northern Minnesota, evidently somewhere northeast of Winnibigoshish Lake and close to Leech Lake – the same area, in fact, where the Chippewa account places the *Shota-winniwug* and therefore, in close proximity to the Moiseo and other Cheyenne-speaking groups.

Due to their lack of superior weapons necessary to gain the advantage over foreign forces who were sure to oppose their intrusion, this Suhtaio migration had hardly been undertaken on a voluntary basis, but as an act of expediency, in order to lose themselves in the dense marshlands of the area and, thereby, escape hostile pressure in their rear.

Such pressure as was then exerted upon them was instigated, once again, predominantly by the Iroquois, who in formidable war-parties now came regularly to the Sault St. Marie in order to pillage and destroy. No Algonquian or Siouan village was safe if within striking distance of their murderous war-parties, and the very name 'Iroquois' became synonymous with slaughter; causing stout hearts to tremble and set whole tribes to flight.

Until the middle years of the sixteenth century, the Iroquois had only just been holding their own against a determined Huron offensive, which was being supported by Algonquians of the Lower St. Lawrence country. The Iroquois were often too busy quarreling among themselves to enable them to concentrate fully upon stemming their enemy's inroads. But, at length, around the date 1550, the legendary Hiawatha and Dekanawida came among them; united the five Iroquois-proper tribes by founding a constitution, and thus brought them together which strengthened their prowess in war.

Later, from circa, 1630 onwards, both the Dutch and English began sending traders into the Iroquois country, supplying the latter with firearms and metal artefacts, and with such superior weapons coupled with a united resolve, the Iroquois commenced sending even larger war-parties against their foes; now engaging the enemy deep in the latter`s own territory.

No opposition could match that Nation's wrath, and none immune from the Iroquois goal of complete subjugation or annihilation.

The Huron - once proud and haughty - could not stand against these merciless onslaughts. After suffering severe reversals, they eventually withdrew across Lake Huron to the Straits of Michilmackinac, while their Algonquian neighbours, i.e., the Chippewa, Ottawa, Nipissing and Potawatomi, likewise reeled under the same deadly incursions and within only a short time after the Huron dispersal, had themselves scattered towards the west in confusion along both the northern and southern shorelines of Lake Superior.

So it was by the middle years of the seventeenth century, that the pristine forests, north, south and west of the Lower Great Lakes, writhed under internecine strife; as tribe began pushing tribe to accommodate a fleeing population on one hand; and a desire to inflict both death and carnage on the other.

It was indeed, a similar event as were the bloody *"Mfecane"* wars that were to rage over the whole of Southern Africa during the second and third decades of the nineteenth century, and which ultimately gave the powerful Zulu, Matabele and Swazi Nation their predominance. Six-thousand miles would separate this Southern African epoch from its North American counterpart, yet the rise of those Native African powers were, in essence, almost identical to that of the Iroquois in the coniferous forest and lake country of northeastern North America.

The aggression of these Iroquois war-parties had far-reaching consequences upon lands and peoples far removed from their line of advance. Peoples who had no knowledge of the Iroquois, were influenced by their actions, as those pressed by the Iroquois; pressed upon their neighbours; who in turn, pressed upon their neighbours in an endeavor to gain a foothold or refuge from attack. As a result, the virgin forests reverberated with the screams and agonies of combatants being slowly tortured to death, and the pitiful lamentations of those in mourning for kinfolk, carried into captivity to be forcibly conscripted to swell the Iroquois ranks.

.In 1649 the Huron suffered such a catastrophic defeat that thereafter, they could no longer regard themselves as a Nation, and as a consequence, both they and their Algonquian allies abandoned the Sault St. Marie and surrounding districts and fled west and southwest, in an effort to extricate themselves from the ever extending arm of their nemesis from the east.

We have no knowledge as to whether or not the Suhtaio and their Monsoni confederates actually engaged themselves in combat with the Iroquois during these dark and bloody years, although they obviously suffered because of them. Such was the fear and havoc now created in the eastern and central woodlands, that the mass upheaval and dispersal of numerous tribes around this date can be attributed directly or indirectly, to Iroquois aggression alone.

By 1660, bloodstained hatchets in the hands of the Iroquois had reached as far south as the Ohio; as far northwest as Chequamegon Bay at the western tip of Lake Superior, and even further west, to the very banks of the Mississippi.

Thus the Nipissing and by then, the already decimated Attigugamis along with some other smaller Algonquian-speaking groups, retreated north into the Lake Nipigon area and along the northwestern shore of Lake Superior in an effort to escape their foes. The Southern Chippewa bands for their part, fled west along the south shore of Lake Superior, whereabouts they allied themselves to the Fox, Sauk and Ottawa and in so doing, obliged the other resident peoples to either confederate with them, or vacate their hunting grounds altogether and move before them. If, like the Sioux, the beleaguered resident bands refused to leave, then they were obliged to defend their homelands armed only with inferior stone and bone-tipped weapons, while having to compete against the guns, steel hatchets and French and English sword blades and iron knives, which the Algonquian refugees from the East then possessed in abundance. It was an unequal contest and those like the Eastern Sioux and Suhtaio who were not prepared to capitulate, were soon forced west across the Mississippi, in order to put distance between themselves and their more formidable foes.

Cheyenne informants told Grinnell that it was before their wars with the Ho-Hay [Assiniboine], that the Cheyennes met the Suhtaio and came into conflict with them, whilst others among Grinnell`s informants said that the Assiniboine were the first foreign people with whom the Cheyennes fought, and that prior to this, the Cheyennes were unwarlike with no enemies to contend with. A dubious statement no doubt and both statements cannot be correct. It does, though, appear that the inconsistency has arisen owing to the importance of the Assiniboine as enemies at a later date, not only to the Cheyennes, but to the Suhtaio also.

It would appear that since the time proto-Cheyenne groups had moved into the region of the Upper Mississippi after abandoning the Lower Red Lake district, there occurred a general reduction of Assiniboine attacks upon their villages, due, moreover, to the latter`s unfamiliarity with the marsh terrain into which the Cheyennes had fled, coupled to the fact that the Assiniboine were now fully at war with their own Yankton and Yankton cousins – who in the wake of the Cheyennes, had by then moved into the Red Lake`s region and along with other Sioux groups, thereafter created a buffer which prevented the Assiniboine from having direct access to Cheyenne villages. Not until a later date, after most Cheyenne-speaking groups had moved southwest to the head of the Minnesota and further west across the Red River of the North, did the Assiniboine come again to attack them in large number; this time more heavily armed with guns and with a regularity not previously experienced by their victims. This was the start of a new offensive, which continued without interruption until the beleaguered Cheyennes finally deserted their permanent villages along the Missouri, some one-hundred and fifty years later.

It is the start of this second Assiniboine offensive which, I believe, is actually referred to in the above statement that the Assiniboine were the first enemies with whom the Cheyennes fought. In so much as preceding this, the Cheyennes themselves seldom went to war and when they did, their escapades usually took the form of small-scale contests, unimportant in outcome, as was likely the case also regarding Cheyenne conflicts with the Suhtaio.

Be this as it may, what event or events brought the Cheyennes and Suhtaio into conflict with each other in the first place, tradition does not recall, although the assertion noted in a previous chapter, that after first being attacked by the Assiniboine, the Cheyennes made the decision that thereafter, they would fight with every people they met, and thereby, become great warriors themselves, might seem to be the traditional explanation. The Cheyennes, however, did not, apparently, attempt opening a war with the powerful Sioux-speaking tribes with whom they certainly met when in the Upper Mississippi country, neither did they inaugurate hostilities with tribes such as the Hidatsa, Iowa and Oto whilst residing along the Minnesota, so the above statement must be taken as apocryphal, in order to fill a gap in tribal history.

Alternatively, one does not have to look far for a more convincing reason likely to have incurred hostilities between the Cheyenne and Suhtaio, when one remembers that the Suhtaio were very closely aligned to both the Plains Cree and Chippewa; those ferocious marauders who had so often swept down upon Cheyenne villages, burning, killing and mutilating, before carrying off the women and children into captivity.

Perhaps Suhtaio warriors had sometimes been in company with these Plains Cree and Chippewa raiders, although what is more likely is that Cheyennes, when first discovering the Suhtaio in northern Minnesota, identified them as allies to the Cree and Chippewa and immediately regarded them as foes.

Today, Cheyenne tradition remembers but little regarding detailed events of this Cheyenne –Suhtaio war and alludes only to the fact, that they fought each other many times before a chance encounter brought them together in peace. The lack of detail in itself, is an indication of the war`s insignificance and that the actual battles were of little consequence to the participating tribe`s on-going circumstances. War then, by its proper definition, it was not. Rather, an ongoing feud, during which small parties from both sides came to blows when they were apt to meet upon the trail. The wounding of one or more tribesmen would have been enough to bring the contest to an end and create a prolonged respite until the next time they just happened to meet. Of course, the actual slaying of a tribal member during such contests, may have occasioned a premeditated attack upon those responsible, solely to fulfill an obligation for revenge, but even so, it is unlikely that such occurrences were common.

Cheyenne testimony does assert that when they and the Suhtaio clashed, their two parties would form up in opposing lines, crouching behind large hide-covered shields, while shooting arrows at each other at close range amid torrents of verbal challenges and abuse. The usual procedure would be that a warrior champion from one side, would challenge a champion from the other and if the offer be accepted, the two contestants would battle it out in the no-man`s land between the two lines, whilst the onlookers shouted encouragement and insults until one of the champions was vanquished or driven from the field. The party who`s champion had been defeated, would then retire slowly from the scene and that would be an end to the affair.

Never was the extermination of the enemy during this Cheyenne – Suhtaio war seriously contemplated; the incentive was not there, if indeed, the Cheyennes and Suhtaio at that period, had the numerical strength and better arms to achieve such a design. As a result, the war proved indecisive and sufficed only to remind one to be respectful of the other`s hunting rights and continued existence.

Evidently, it was also a war of short duration. By 1673 according to the Joliet map pertaining to that year, the Suhtaio [*Agatomitou*] themselves were firmly entrenched just northeast of Leech Lake near the Mississippi heads, in which vicinity not only were there already Cheyenne-speaking groups [*Ouissyloua and Chaiena*], but several Sioux-speaking groups as well. The Suhtaio then, must at least have been at peace with the Cheyennes, or they could not have held such a precarious position.

It does appear, however, that the Cheyennes and Suhtaio had met earlier than the former`s movement into the Upper Mississippi area; the more adventurous Cheyenne parties from Lower Red Lake, having clashed with hunting parties of Suhtaio during the circuitous wanderings of both. Not until the sixteen-fifties were both the Cheyennes and Suhtaio in close enough proximity to engage in regular conflict and implies that the general theater of war was in the northeastern part of Minnesota State, which concurs with the opinion of several latter-day Cheyenne informants, who stated that the Cheyenne – Suhtaio war took place before the Cheyennes started their western migration to and beyond the Missouri. These same sources also declared that their two tribes, i.e. Cheyennes and Suhtaio, whilst still residing in the northeast about the Upper Mississippi, made a peace that has never since been broken.

The last fight between the Cheyennes and Suhtaio took place, according to Grinnell`s informants, when the Head chiefs of the opposing sides pitted their personal *medicine* powers against each other. The Suhtaio chief, it is said, could cause the rain to fall upon those opposing him, whilst the Cheyenne chief had somewhat stronger power which thwarted the Suhtaio chief`s design and instead, caused the snow to fall so thick upon the Suhtaio warriors, that one by one they succumbed to the freezing cold and died. It was after this, so the story continues, that the Suhtaio sued for peace with the victors and their overtures were accepted. The Cheyenne chief then went around among the dead Suhtaio warriors, who had frozen during the snow storm, and by employing some miraculous power brought them back to life.[9] This event is further said to have taken place during the time of the Cheyenne`s culture hero Sweet-Medicine, and so must predate that tribe`s initial conflicts with the Assiniboine.

AT WAR AND PEACE WITH THE SUHTAIO

According to the Northern Suhtaio tribal member and Sun-Dance priest named Fire-Wolf, the above mentioned peace-making took place when the Cheyennes lived near the Pipestone Quarries in southwestern Minnesota, Fire-Wolf stated,

"..In a land of many lakes the people were accustomed to travel north in a certain season, in order to gather birds eggs and feathers for ornaments. Whilst on such trips, they collided with the Suhtaio and the two tribes fought each other many times. At one time, however, the Cheyennes and Suhtaio stumbled across each other and at once a fight started. During the battle, a Cheyenne warrior named Wise-Buffalo, recognized the Suhtaio language as being similar to his own, and he called out something [now forgotten] to the Suhtaio from a distance. A Suhtaio answered back and a conversation ensued. After a while four Cheyennes and four Suhtaio came out from their respective lines, and in the open ground between them, they came together and spoke. The Cheyenne chief said to the Suhtaio, "We are the Desert People" and the Suhtaio chief answered; "We are the Suhtaio." The two parties then smoked a pipe together and made peace, after which they departed, and went their separate ways." [1]

Whether or not the Monsoni Cree had been involved in the Cheyenne-Suhtaio war, cannot be determined. But if they had been, then a Cheyenne peace with the Suhtaio would have meant peace with the Monsoni also, as at that time, the Suhtaio and Monsoni were close allies and confederates, and remained in close proximity to each other for many years thereafter.

Tradition relates that the Cheyennes and Suhtaio came together and separated three times before finally amalgamating as one Nation about the date 1834. It is evident, though, that one or more Suhtaio band had inter-mixed with one and another Cheyenne group long before the final union. Perhaps a number of Cheyenne bands had made separate pacts with the Suhtaio whilst other Cheyennes roaming more distant territories, continued in hostilities with them, and that the above account offered by Fire-Wolf, actually refers to a later date and concerns only the remnant Masikota band colloquially known as *Sheyo* then in residence around Big Stone Lake at the head of the Minnesota. These last were then somewhat aloof from their Cheyenne cousins then further west, and were close to the *Chongousceton* [Dog People i.e. Suhtaio] who themselves, in one or more bands, were then residing not far west of Big Stone Lake as the writings of the explorer Jonathan Carver make clear in his record of travels between the years 1766 and 1768.

Present-day tribal tradition even gives the names of the two Head chiefs at the time of peace making between the Cheyennes and Suhtaio, i.e., that of Wise-Buffalo for the Cheyennes and that of White-Dirt or Lime for the Suhtaio. The sparseness of the traditional account leaves much to be desired, although the essence of the event has been preserved and there remains some additional information from other Cheyenne sources.

One of Michelson`s informants named White-Bull [born 1846 and a Suhtai by birth] stated in 1910, that the Cheyennes and Suhtaio first met each other more than two-hundred years before that date. At that time there were only two bands of Cheyennes, White-Bull said, while the Suhtaio consisted of four bands, each of which took the name of its respective leader. The Suhtaio, White-Bull continued, originally came from somewhere northeast of the Mississippi and were still residing east of that river when they and the Cheyennes first met and fought each other as mortal foes. The Suhtaio chief was named White-Dirt [also known as Lime] and he told the Cheyenne chief whose name was Sweet- Medicine, that he knew the origin of the Cheyennes, to which Sweet-Medicine replied, that he knew better than that. By this it is inferred that the Suhtaio White-Dirt, had considered himself more powerful than Sweet-Medicine, as White-Dirt had killed many people belonging to other tribes [i.e. enemies], and had even tried to kill Sweet-Medicine himself. The Cheyenne chief, however, also had a powerful *medicine,* stronger than that of White-Dirt and had killed more people than he. At length, the Cheyennes got hold of the Suhtaio *medicine* bundles [defeated the Suhtaio?], after which they and the Cheyennes joined together under the auspices of the Sacred Arrows, and through the power of which mediums, the united Suhtaio and Cheyennes became great warriors. They then made war everywhere and were always victorious over their foes. This, said White-Bull, was the first time that the Cheyennes and Suhtaio came together, but after a while, the Suhtaio left the Cheyennes and returned east across the Mississippi and they and the Cheyennes went to war against each other for a second time. People were killed on both sides, but eventually, another truce was effected and the two came together again, and often camped side by side as friends.

The Suhtaio Chief White-Dirt, supposedly, then killed a woman within the tribe and was duly exiled from the people in accordance with new laws which the Cheyenne Sweet-Medicine had earlier inaugurated. White-Dirt and his personal followers thus again went east, and began avenging themselves upon the Cheyennes and also, upon those other bands of Suhtaio who had opted to remain with the latter as their confederates. At one time, the Cheyennes and their Suhtaio allies went to the Mississippi and confronted White Dirt and his adherents, who then lived on an island in that river and after a one to one personal contest between Sweet-Medicine and White-Dirt, during which neither could better the other, both chiefs surrendered and again made peace between their peoples. Not long after this, still according to White-Bull, the Suhtaio Chief White-Dirt once more returned east across the Mississippi, and was gone for a prolonged period [forty years in the account]. When White-Dirt did come back, it was at the same time as the Suhtaio prophet and culture hero Erect-Horns [also known as Standing-Horns and Red-Tassels] brought the buffalo and corn to the Suhtaio.

What this means, of course, is that this was the time when the Suhtaio migrated to the west side of the Mississippi and became confederated with the Cheyennes, among whom the Suhtaio introduced their Sacred Buffalo Head or *Issiwun* among the people. Conceivably, both the Cheyennes and Suhtaio must have then been resident in the buffalo country southwest of the Mississippi headwaters region and, perhaps, even west of the Red River, in order that the Cheyennes and Suhtaio could become regular buffalo hunters on the open prairies. This would tentatively date the period in question, as being sometime during the 1670s or early 1680s, at which period, we know, Cheyennes were in residence along the Minnesota River, and even west of that river's head. The above information does indicate also that the Suhtaio Chief White-Dirt, was but an earlier personification of the prophet and culture hero Erect-Horns, and we are told by the half white – half Cheyenne George Bent, that whilst residing in the Coteau des Prairies between Red River of the North and the Missouri, the Keeper of the Cheyenne's Sacred Arrows and the Keeper of the Suhtaio's Sacred Hat, became great friends with each other and that their two peoples along with a band of Moiseo, roamed and camped together throughout that region. This period, George Bent inferred, was after the Cheyennes had left the Upper Mississippi country, but before they crossed the Missouri. It thus belongs to a later period of history than that with which we are presently concerned, although as regards the coming together of the Cheyennes with Erect-Horns and the Sacred Hat of the Suhtaio, another informant of Michelson, named Wolf-Chief [a northern Cheyenne of the Omissis band, born 1851], related an ancient story which appears to commemorate the actual event.

In essence, Wolf-Chief said that a great many years ago when living east of the Mississippi [i.e. Missouri?], four separate people came at four separate times to the Omissis band. The first three persons soon went away, but the fourth man along with his wife, said that he and his wife had come from the big forest east of the Mississippi, that they had once been wild beasts and had come to the Omissis to tell them what they knew for the good of the people. This story is commonly known among the Cheyennes today as "The Holy Head of the Eaters," and refers of course, to the Sacred Buffalo Head [Hat] i.e. *Issiwun* of the Suhtaio being introduced and embraced among the Cheyennes who are represented in the story as the Omissis band, but which should really be applied to the early Masikota, then closely associated with that Moiseo Arrow Men faction that had the Sacred Arrows and Keeper among them. In fact, Fire-Chief was merely referring to the Northern Cheyennes who were known collectively as Omissis [i.e. eaters], and who, during Wolf-Chief's time, then included the bulk of Suhtaio descendants.

In yet another story regarding the coming together of the Cheyennes and Suhtaio, it is said that Red-Tassels [another name for Erect-Horns] brought corn to the people, whilst he who is called "Red, Red, Red, Red," brought them the buffalo. Now the word 'red' in Cheyenne is synonymous with the word for 'blood,' so that the latter name can just as well read "Blood, Blood, Blood, Blood," and refers to the hunting element of the two separate peoples mentioned as coming together. The name "Red, Red, Red, Red" must therefore, refer to the original Moiseo-Masikota Cheyenne group among whom were included the Sweet-Medicine people or "Arrow Men" faction [later known as the Burnt Aorta band], and who regularly hunted the buffalo and elk, as opposed to the more sedentary and somewhat horticultural Suhtaio led by Erect-Horns with the Sacred Buffalo Head or *Issiwun*. The story then, seems to apply to the time the Suhtaio crossed the Mississippi to become buffalo hunters in the open western country, in contrast to their previous semi-horticultural lifestyle in the forest and lake regions in the east and northeast.

It is worth noting here that again according to White-Bull, at the time the Suhtaio and Cheyennes were roaming on the east side of the Missouri, the Suhtaio were led by a chief named White-Buffalo-Tail while the Cheyenne chief was named Red-Paint. When finally most of the Cheyennes and Suhtaio decided to cross the Missouri to its west side, Chief Red-Paint refused to join them. Instead, he and his followers remained in the Coteau country and thus, probably represent the remnant band of original Moiseo, and of whom George Bent said, refused to cross the Missouri and instead returned to the northeast where they remained until circa, 1814-`16, before finally rejoining the Cheyennes and were absorbed among the different bands of that Nation.

NORTHERN CHEYENNE INFORMANT OF MICHELSON, WHITE BULL, aka ICE.
[Photo from "Photographer on an Army Mule." University of Oklahoma Press.1965.]

Alternatively, they may represent the remnant of the Masikota Cheyenne group known as *Sheyo,* who could still be found in the vicinity of Big Stone Lake at the head of the Red River of the North around the date 1800 and even later. This story, though, does serve to explain the change in culture of these early Cheyennes and Suhtaio when in the process of giving up their pedestrian lake and forest-dwelling lifestyle, for that of the nomadic, equestrian buffalo hunter of the Western Great Plains.

According to tribal informants of both Michelson and Mooney, it was after the Cheyennes and Suhtaio agreed for the last time to bury the hatchet between them, that the Suhtaio introduced the idea of warrior societies among the Cheyennes, and so was inaugurated the societies of Elk, Kit-Fox, Red-Shields and Bowstrings. However, the Kit-Fox and Bowstrings were originally Cheyenne, and must then, have been associated with the original component groups of Moiseo and Omissis, and as the Red-Shields are said to have been the first and oldest warrior society among the Suhtaio, so the Kit-Fox are said to have been the first and oldest among the Cheyennes.

We learn additionally from tribal tradition and early map references that the Suhtaio [i.e. Chongaskitons], originally comprised four separate bands, and these appear to have actually been the progenitors of the four later-date warrior societies of Elks, Red Shields, Kit-Fox and Dogs. Here, though, those referred to as Kit-Fox would have represented the mixed Suhtaio – Moiseo group [Chongaskiton and Quissy of early Colonial maps], and which presupposes that the Suhtaio adopted the name from the Moiseo breakaway band that had the Sacred Arrows in its care. This would explain how the Suhtaio claim to have been the inaugurators of the original four societies among the Cheyenne-Proper which included the Kit-Foxes, and at the same time, explains how originally, there were only two component bands of Cheyenne-proper [i.e. Moiseo and Omissis]. The Moiseo remnant when still in the Northeast along with their Suhtaio confederates, had both been known among themselves as Elks [i.e. Wheekeeu and Monsoni], while the Moiseo breakaway Sacred Arrow faction became known as the Kit-Fox band, and with whom the Suhtaio, - due to their close association with the Moiseo remnant and some Kit-Fox band members, - amalgamated and inter-married, thus adopting the band name of Kit-Fox among themselves.

Notwithstanding then, the tribal traditional account which states that Sweet-Medicine brought the warrior societies to the people, such should really only apply to the Kit-Fox and Bowstrings, and that the innovation for the inauguration of the four original warrior societies came originally from the names of each of the then newly-confederated bands of Masikota, Moiseo [Aorta], Suhtaio and Omissis, and later expanded to five with the inclusion of the Dog-Men warrior society. Thus the name Kit-Fox had once been associated with both the Moiseo breakaways [Aorta], and also with the mixed remnant Moiseo and Suhtaio band in the Northeast, while that of the Bowstrings belonged to the Omissis. On the other hand, the societies of Elks, Red-Shields and Dogs belonged to the Suhtaio, and only after the amalgamation and subsequent inter-mixing of the Cheyenne and Suhtaio, were the same band names applied to the warrior societies alone, members of which were then to be found among each of the bands which comprised the combined Cheyenne-Suhtaio Nation as a whole. In later years the Masikota became closely associated with the Elk and Dog societies, while the Red-Shields were embraced predominantly by the combined Suhtaio and Pipe-Stem Men / Ridge Men band.

From the evidence at hand, the time of the aforesaid confederation between the Cheyennes and Suhtaio when in the Black Hills of South Dakota, was the same time as the inauguration among the Cheyenne-proper of their warrior societies, an event which is said to have taken place at the sacred site of Bear Butte between circa; 1740 and 1750. But of this we will speak later.

Linguistic relationship alone, perhaps, was sufficient reason to warrant such a close affiliation between the Cheyennes and Suhtaio, although as the latter tribe was, at an earlier date when allied to the Cree, likely subjected to Assiniboine aggression also, it would have been expedient on the part of the Suhtaio to ally themselves with the Cheyennes and the latter`s Sioux confederates, whereby, not only would their united numbers afford better security, but their new-found Sioux neighbours would by their very presence, be instrumental in Suhtaio survival. Certainly, it was not until 1666, by which time the Cree were obtaining firearms in abundance from French and English traders on the Upper Great Lakes and Hudson`s Bay, that the Assiniboine made their pact with the Cree and confederated with them, and, subsequently, made peace with the Suhtaio also. Before that time, as we have seen, the Assiniboine and Cree had engaged each other in a virulent war and during which event, the Suhtaio along with their Monsoni Cree friends, would have been on the receiving end of Assiniboine attacks.

Once the Suhtaio had consolidated their friendship with the Cree and Assiniboine on one side, and with Cheyennes and Sioux on the other, the Suhtaio could wander with comparative impunity over the entire Upper half of Minnesota, and this they apparently did, for later we find the Suhtaio under the names *Shongaskiton* and *Chongaskiton* in company with the Cree, Assiniboine and Chippewa, and this at the same time as they were inter-marrying freely among both Cheyenne and Western Sioux [Teton] bands, and with whom in perfect harmony, some Suhtaio were already roaming the Coteau des Prairies west of the Red River of the North.

The return of the Suhtaio to the fold, as it were, thus at last, brought the entire Cheyenne-speaking conglomerate together, albeit scattered in several bands and in specific areas embracing northern Minnesota bounded on the east by the Upper Mississippi, and on the west by the Red River of the North. The Suhtaio were the most aloof of the now confederated bands, often camping apart from other Cheyenne groups, although hereafter, they always considered themselves a part of the larger Cheyenne entity and in common with the latter, they resisted whatever foreign influence neighbouring tribes might have exerted.

After the time of Cheyenne peace-making with the Suhtaio, ostensibly prior to 1666 when the Suhtaio and Cree made peace with the Assiniboine, the Cheyenne increased in population and prestige, while at the same time by their unification, they fast became a fighting force to be reckoned with. Certainly, owing to the collectiveness which the Sacred Arrow talismans had inaugurated, they were more than able to match their foes; if not with the white man`s guns, then by their own bravery and determination alone. By the latter decades of the seventeenth century, both the Cheyennes and confederated Suhtaio under a variety of designations, were familiar to all tribes in that vast area from the Upper Great Lakes in the east, and as far west as the Missouri River and beyond.

- 0 - 0 - 0 - 0 - 0 - 0 - 0 - 0 - 0 - 0 - 0 - 0 - 0 - 0 - 0 - 0 - 0 -

CHAPTER 23.

"*ISSIWUN*" IS BROUGHT TO THE PEOPLE.

Regarding the lifestyle of the early Suhtaio when in northern Minnesota and around the Upper Great Lakes, tribal tradition has preserved some details. Beginning about the year 1895, the eminent ethnologist and historian George Bird Grinnell began obtaining stories from several of his Cheyenne informants, which they in turn had heard from an old Suhtai named Standing-All-Night. This old Suhtai had died in 1867, reputedly more than one-hundred and forty years of age. He was, however, even during the years of his dotage, regarded as a very reliable tribal historian and often related how the Suhtaio and Cheyennes had once lived, before becoming permanent residents in the buffalo country west of the Missouri River. In essence, Standing-All-Night used to say that during those far off days when in the Northeast, the people would often travel to great lakes which were so vast, one could not see across to the other side. The Sioux, he said, were at that time close to the Mississippi and it was from that direction that the Arapahoe also came. The Suhtaio dialect was then quite different to that of Cheyenne-proper, but after many years of close association, the Suhtaio came to speak `broken Cheyenne.` Grinnell later described that time as follows,

"In these lakes there were many fish, some quite large. It was their practice to make nets of willow twigs tied together with strings of bark and sinew, strung close together on strings as backrests have been made in recent times, and to stretch such nets out diagonally from the shore into the shallow water. These nets were often very long. Men stationed along the net held it in place, and often men, with women and children, would go further along the shore of the lake and get into the water in a line, some of them going out as deep as they could go, and walked toward the net, driving the fishes before them. When they reached the outer end of the net it was slowly moved in toward the shore, enclosing a large space, and then was gradually dragged up into the shallow water, and men, women and children got within it and threw the fish out onto the shore. In this way they commonly caught many fishes, some of them of a very large size, probably sturgeons. After being secured, these fish were carried to the camp on the backs of the people, or packed on the dog travois. The larger fish were cut in pieces before they could be put on the travois. In the camp they were dried in the sun, the larger ones being cut into strips. The bones of the larger fish were pounded and boiled for grease, just as in later days, buffalo bones have been pounded and boiled. From the largest of these fish they got a white sinew which was useful for sewing. In his time [Standing-All-Night] the Indians at certain seasons used to make regular journeys to the breeding places of the water birds about these lakes to secure eggs and young, and at this season, these were their sole support." [1]

This old Suhtai historian also told how the people in those days made axes of stone and knives of flint. He mentioned the making of earthenware pots and dishes and described their process of manufacture. First, he said, fires were lit in holes in the ground and when the fires burned down, the ashes were partly raked out and the pots placed in the hole; then covered with ashes, the heat from which baked them hard. He even told of the old-style lodges the Suhtaio once used. These were not lodges in the proper sense, but merely small shelters covered with bark or grass. At times, he said, when the people went camping, they had short poles dragged by dogs, and these poles were stuck in the ground and bent over to form a framework over which they spread their robes or bundles of grass. Many would then crowd into one shelter for protection from the cold. It was a long time later, after they began hunting buffalo that they made better shelters, although they then took the form of willow frames covered with hides. These lodges did not have smoke flaps and when the occupants wished the smoke to escape from the hearth-fire within, they partly removed the hide coverings from the top of the rounded roof.

Standing-All-Night always said that the first time the Suhtaio and Cheyennes came together, was somewhere far to the northeast of the Missouri River, near the same Great Lakes that are often mentioned in tradition and that the second time their two peoples united, was on the south [west] side of the Missouri, a long time after the Cheyennes had already crossed that river.

Other references in present-day Cheyenne tradition regarding the early Suhtaio, recall that the Suhtaio then subsisted mainly on fish, birds and small animals. They also ate grass and supplemented their diet with wild turnips and potatoes, for at that time they did not have corn. Their houses, it is said, were built from straw [which probably means reeds and grass faggots] and the people themselves sometimes wore clothing woven from a special type of tall grass. They also had footwear made from the bark of trees. The above expression 'ate grass' applies, of course, to the wild rice that grew so abundantly in the Suhtaio area of habitat when first contacted by Cheyennes, and this entire description, perhaps, is merely used in that people's traditions to indicate how primitive the Suhtaio appeared to the Cheyennes when first met. The Cheyennes do recall, however, that during the period in question, the Suhtaio were conspicuous by their custom of binding their hair sometimes with otter skins and sometimes with buckskin, which was a singular peculiarity, and caused them to be known to the Cheyennes by the name of "Wrapped Hairs."

At a much later date, according to present-day tribal tradition, a large part of the Suhtaio allied themselves to the Cheyennes when west of the Missouri, whilst the remaining Suhtaio went north and joined the Cree. That group which opted to remain in the Western Plains, continued thereafter in close association with Cheyennes, although still as an independent tribe and were known as "No Colds," as opposed to those of their kinfolk that had retired to the north where winters were much more severe. Although the Suhtaio proved themselves important allies and associates of these early Cheyennes, it was not until around the date 1834, that the Suhtaio became a regular part of the Cheyenne camping circle and fully adopted members of the Cheyenne Nation.

Certainly, the Suhtaio were always a prominent component group when acting as confederates to the Cheyenne-proper and throughout their last years of freedom on the Great Plains, the Suhtaio produced not a few of the most outstanding chiefs and warriors among the so-called, *"Fighting Cheyennes;"* men such as Roman-Nose, High-Backed-Wolf, Sun`s-Road, Black-Shin, Little-Wolf, Black-Kettle, White-Bull [also known as Ice] and Gentle-Horse among others. They were also an important group as regards religion; both respected and honoured by the rest of the Nation. It was the Suhtaio who introduced the Sun-Dance or Medicine Lodge ceremony to the Cheyennes along with that of the "Sacred Buffalo Head" or Hat [*Issiwun*], both of which religious assets were embraced conscientiously by the Nation as a whole.

Issiwun, or the Sacred Buffalo Hat as it is more commonly called, is unique to the Suhtaio, being connected with the supernatural powers deemed necessary to renew the buffalo herds, in order that the people might continue to procure sufficient meat and material for both their physical and domestic needs. The Native name for this object *"Issiwun"* or *"Essevonuh* has been translated by Father Peter Powell as something to do with the female buffalo, being compatible in its analogy, he said, with that of "The bearer of new life." However, a more definite connotation of the term *Issiwun*, is derived from the much older ceremonial compound term of *Issi-whun*. The first part *Issi,* means "it is dark," and suggests the appearance of a herd of buffalo when covering the prairie. The term *whun* on the other hand, is said to pertain to the rhythmic grunting sound made by buffalo when on the run, which, incidentally, would explain how the name Suhtaio was misconstrued by some other informants, as referring to the grunting sound made by buffalo in the rutting season, and thus rendered in the vernacular as "speech hard to understand."

In essence, the Hat embodies all that was deemed essential to the Suhtaio, it being the integral object used during the performance of several sacred ceremonies, by which the spirits of the buffalo and other game animals when hidden away in their underground refuge, were enticed out into the open in material form to allow themselves to be hunted, and thereby, to continue sustaining the people`s requirements that enabled them to exist.

Even today, as a sacred icon the Buffalo Hat is still regarded as a powerful medium through which as in the case of the Arrows, the omnipotent supernatural forces of both the Above World and Below World can bestow their benevolence upon the Suhtaio, and when special attention and devotion is paid to the Hat by offering one's personal prayers and suitable gifts, then the powers embodied therein, can bring success against one's enemies and when actually carried to war as a tribal palladium before the people, it insures victory and the total destruction of the foe.

Unlike the Sacred Arrows, the `Hat` is composed of more durable material and so does not require its component parts to be periodically renewed, notwithstanding that the original porcupine-quill decoration on the brow band has, in all probability, been replaced with beadwork, as also deer horns on the original seem later to have been replaced with those of the buffalo.

Thus, as the Sacred Arrows are the most important holy talismans among the Cheyenne-proper, so *"Issiwun"* is the most revered ceremonial object among the Suhtaio, and as members of the Kit-Fox warrior society are the guardians of the Sacred Arrows, so members of the Elk warrior society are the special guardians of the Hat. It now resides in the care of its present keeper among the Northern Cheyennes at Busby, on the Tongue River Reservation, Montana.

One legend has it that the Suhtaio's own culture hero named *"Tomsivsi"* or "Erect-Horns," [with the alternative names of Standing Horns and Red-Tassels] was given the Hat by the powerful Spirit Beings of the Underworld and at the same sacred mountain of `Navah-hous` [Bear Butte], where the TsisTsisTsas or Cheyenne-proper had earlier received their Sacred Arrows. This was also at a time, so Suhtaio tradition asserts, *"When the people were starving and a great famine covered the land."* The Suhtaio, it is said, were unable to move to more provident hunting grounds because they were surrounded by fierce enemies. It was at that time, during the people's dire time of need, that a certain shaman came among them and made *medicine*, which induced the buffalo to come near the camp so that the people could hunt and fill their bellies with meat. After this the people again had sufficient food and warm robes to protect them from hunger and cold, and as a consequence the people survived. This statement refers in reality, not only to the inauguration of the *Issiwun* or Sacred Hat rites among the Suhtaio, but also to that people's migration west of the Mississippi into the buffalo and tall-grass prairie country, wherein Cheyenne-proper groups then already resided. Indeed, a prolonged period of warm temperatures with more than adequate rainfall, had existed in the Upper Mississippi and inland Canadian regions between circa, A.D. 800 and circa, A.D. 1250, known as the Neo-Atlantic period. The latter phase of this period had encouraged the Proto-Cheyennes and Proto-Suhtaio to practice agriculture on a more intensive scale. However, an era of drier summers between circa, 1250 and 1450; known as the Pacific period, likely instigated the initial Cheyenne and Suhtaio movement from their then less productive environments, and migrate deeper into the Upper part of Minnesota which country was more conducive to raising crops. At an even later date during what is termed the Neo-Boreal period [between circa, 1450 and 1880 intensifying around 1550], the growing season in the Upper Mississippi region was further shortened. The summers became much cooler and there were fewer frost-free days to allow crops such as beans and squash to mature. This event did not, though, effect the Native grasslands, so that grazing animals such as buffalo and antelope etc.; continued to flourish. This in turn induced a greater dependency by the now redundant crop-growing northern Minnesota peoples, to become, at least for the larger part of the year, traveling hunters following the herds for their subsistence.

Another account concerning the coming of *Issiwun,* was told by the Northern Cheyenne historian John Stands-In-Timber and runs as follows,

> "The Spirit [Ma`heo] had told a man that a Sacred head would start out from somewhere in the Black Hills by herself. This sacred head was a woman they said, and this man was a Suktai [sic] man who talked to a spirit. He always knew what

was going on and what was going to happen. The Cheyennes camped somewhere in South Dakota. The sacred head was right there. There were four different camps. The first camp was Sioux and the second camp was Arapahoe, then the Cheyennes and the last camp was Suktai. This man knew the sacred head was coming to look for the Suktais. She came first to the Sioux camp, then to the Arapahoe camp. She said they were not the ones she was looking for. Then she looked at the Cheyennes and went by them. Then she went up the hill again and sat looking down and saw these Indians. She said those are the ones I am looking for. She said she would tell them that she would be with them till the father comes again. The man who had talked to a spirit told them to look up and see the sacred head. He told the Suktais to look for a man to keep it for them, so they put up a teepee at the fron[t] of the other teepees and this man went up there and brought it down to this teepee. Everybody was using red paint on their bodies. That's why she was looking for the Suktais, and the man they chose had to take it. The spirit told this man that the sacred head was a woman, so the spirit said [that] women will never see it as long as it is with them, so the Indian women never knew what it looked like - just the men see it and they never open it unless they have a Sun-Dance. That is the only time that these dancers go in the teepee when a man who keeps it gets the scalps out for them. Sometimes when he is alone he looks at it. A Suktai man has to do that. Cheyennes are not allowed to do that because it did not belong to them. The Cheyennes and the Suktais never camped together. Sweet Medicine said whenever they prayed to the sacred head he would listen to them." [2]

Yet another version relates that Erect Horns actually received the Hat through his woman or wife, who had sexual relations with a *Mih`n,* i.e., an Underwater Monster, and during which event, the *Mih`n* had passed a small shell from its mouth into hers. The shell in the story represents the supernatural power attributed to the *Mih`n* in question and thus, the peculiar beaded inverted fret design above the brow band on the Hat symbolizes the aforesaid Underwater Monster. This same design was typically used as a representation of such a creature among other tribes of the Great Lakes region, among whom were once included the Sauk, Fox and Chippewa. The Hat itself also represents the personification of the Head chief of all the buffalo, which among the Suhtaio is regarded as having a female nature, and can be associated with the concept of *Eyhopsta*, the Yellow-Haired Maiden of the TsisTsisTsas [i.e. Cheyenne proper], who is the Keeper of the Game. Additionally, the Buffalo Hat is connected to the Northeast direction, which does, of course, point to the region of the Upper Great Lakes where the old-time Suhtaio once lived along with their then neighbours, the Fox, Sauk and Chippewa. Certainly, the inclusion of the shell element in the origin story of the Hat, suggests something compatible with the "Great Megis Shell," so prominent in Chippewa ceremonialism, so that the Hat of the Suhtaio may well have derived from an earlier Chippewa or other Upper Great Lakes tribe`s innovation. Indeed, although in the John Stands in

244

Timber account the "Sacred Head" [i.e. the Hat] is said to have been received somewhere in South Dakota, and which in other accounts is designated specifically as the same Bear Butte where the TsisTsisTsas received their Sacred Arrows, alternative accounts place the site of origin at either Black Mountain near the Pipestone Quarries in south-western Minnesota, or at a height known to the Suhtaio as Stone Hammer Mountain, close to the western districts of the Upper Great Lakes.

Whatever the case, the Suhtaio Hat is fashioned from the complete crown of a buffalo head with both hair and horns attached, albeit that the horns are shaved thin, tapered and flattened. The whole is designed to be worn on the head, although this has occurred only when taken into battle as a guarantee of success or during attendant ceremonies for war, which was the usual procedure to activate the Hat's specific protective properties.

The aforementioned decoration above the brow-band is composed of large blue and white `Pony` beads, once common trade items obtained from the white man during the 18th and first half of the 19th centuries, and one assumes that, originally, dyed, flattened porcupine quill-work had earlier served the same purpose. Certainly the Hat is regarded as being very old; some tribal informants having stated that it was first brought to the Suhtaio at the same time as the Sacred Arrows were introduced among the TsisTsisTsas between circa, A.D.1540 and 1560, and before the Suhtaio became confederated with the Cheyennes. This, though, is unlikely to have been the case regarding the Hat's original conception by the Suhtaio, although it does suggest that the Hat and its symbolism when inaugurated at Black Mountain in Minnesota, had merely been re-adopted by the Suhtaio as a later variation on an older theme, once founded upon the same fundamental innovation as was the "Medicine Dance" and *Midewiwin* ceremonies along with their associated rituals among other Central Algonquian tribes. Thus the earlier concept for the Suhtaio Sacred Hat ceremony of later times, may well have been associated with the time of the winter solstice and only when being reinstated among the Suhtaio, did it become a midsummer ceremony connected specifically with the buffalo when on the Western Plains. The Hat in its original form, would likely have been designed with deer horns or antlers, rather than buffalo horns as employed at the later date after the Suhtaio had become a fully-fledged Plains people, and certainly, the names of Erect Horns and Standing Horns would indicate deer antlers, rather than the curved horns of the buffalo.

It is indicative to note that the ceremonies connected with the "Hat" and also with that of the Sun-Dance with which the "Hat" is closely associated, resemble the Sauk and Fox "Medicine Lodge" ceremony in a number of its rites, whilst an apparent counterpart of the Sacred Hat itself, with its striking bead design, has since been discovered in the area of the Upper Great Lakes, only in this last-named version, deer horns take the place of those of the buffalo which adorn the Hat of the Suhtaio. It should not be surprising then, that Father Peter Powell further stated that *"Issiwun"* or *"Essevon,"* was a term once recognized by an old Sauk woman as being an archaic Sauk word meaning *"something coming out of the ground,"* and had been applied specifically to holy women involved in the "Medicine Lodge" and "Drum" ceremonies once practiced by both the Sauk and Fox. Additionally, the Sun-Dance ceremony of the Suhtaio also includes several important features that are identical to those performed in the `Midewiwin` ceremony of the Chippewa [A particular religious cult practiced albeit in slightly varied form by the Eastern Cree, Sauk, Fox and some other Central and Northern Algonquians]. One may construe from such similarities, that the Suhtaio had once been in a league with these last mentioned tribes, close enough to have shared a common theology and ceremonial complex. Thus it may be that the actual Sacred Hat ritual as later practiced by the Suhtaio, was not inaugurated among them until after the Suhtaio had left the Upper Great Lakes region, at which time they were no longer confederated, or perhaps, even in harmonious contact with Great Lakes Algonquians. The ceremony by then, was likely to have been merely a revival of an older religious expression, which the Suhtaio had modified to accommodate their new lifestyle and environment after entering the prairie country west of the Mississippi and at which time, buffalo became a more important dimension to Suhtaio existence as a food and utility source. Subsequently, the buffalo replaced the moose, elk and deer of the eastern woodlands and Great Lakes regions as their predominant asset for survival.

In short, the original concept that inaugurated the Suhtaio reverence for the Sacred Hat, had derived - in part at least - from either the Sauk, Fox or Chippewa, which must then place the early Suhtaio in the vicinity of Sault St. Marie at the junction of the Upper Great Lakes, where we know at one time, all the aforementioned tribes resided in close proximity to one another. Likewise, the Sun-Dance as introduced among the TsisTsisTsas by the Suhtaio, seems also to have had a northern origin, being a regeneration ceremony indispensable in an area where the seasons occur in the extreme, i.e., in winter ice-bound with deep snow and below freezing temperatures; in summer, as high as ninety degrees Fahrenheit, balmy, humid and wet. We do know from *Blackduck* archaeological remains that if they represent ancestral Suhtaio, then Suhtaio peoples were frequenting the area at the western tip of Lake Superior, if only sporadically, as early as the middle years of the thirteenth century, and as noted in the previous chapter, by circa.1450, the Suhtaio had moved further east along the northern shore of Lake Superior as far as Sault St. Marie. However, attacks from the Iroquois and perhaps from Ottawa bands [though not as allies] from the east and southeast during the early sixteen-hundreds, forced the Suhtaio west and not until circa, 1680, did the Suhtaio move back east between the western tip of Lake Superior and the Mille Lac region of the Upper Mississippi, as certain contemporary map references assert.

The influence of the Chippewa `*Midewiwin*` ceremony and its cult did not, apparently, permeate into the religious life of other tribes around the Upper Great Lakes until sometime later than A.D. 1660, when certain Cree and related Algonquian-speaking groups that included the Suhtaio, had thought it safe to return to their old haunts around Sault St. Marie, after the Iroquois and Ottawa menace had been removed. These returning refugees actually allied themselves to their erstwhile Chippewa foes, who were then the recognized occupants of the Sault region, and who already knew the Suhtaio by a variety of names.

Corroboration can be found in the form of an entry in the journal of Pierre Radisson, which documents his several trips into the country north of Lake Superior and west of Lake Michigan between the years 1658 and 1661. When referring to a group of Indians who Radisson supposed

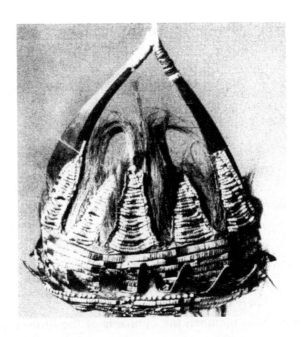

HORNED HEADDRESS FROM REGION OF THE GREAT LAKES C. 1750.
[MUSEE DE L`HOMME. PARIS.]

JAMES LITTLE BIRD WITH THE SACRED HAT.
[PHOTO BY FATHER PETER POWELL. HARPER AND ROW PUBLISHERS. 1981]

were Cree, and with whom he made contact somewhere between the northern coastline of Lake Superior and Hudson's Bay, ostensibly, along the course of Moose River, he reported,

"There is a Nation called among themselves Neuter; they speak the Beef and Christinoes speech, being friends to both." [3]

Earlier in the same journal Radisson mentioned the *"Nadouwsics,"* this being his rendering of the Chippewa name for the Sioux, but of whom, he said, *"we will call Beef Indians or the Nation of Beouf."* [4] Further on, however, Radisson speaks repeatedly of the incessant fighting then going on between the *Nadouwsics* and the *Christinoes.* Here Radisson`s *Christinoes* must, by elimination, refer specifically to a Monsoni Cree faction [hence their being encountered either along or very near Moose River, which stream was so-named in recognition that the Monsoni or Moose Indians were then often found along its banks.], while the *Beef Indians* must refer more specifically to a Sioux-proper group, rather than the Sioux-speaking Assiniboine who Radisson mentions separately as *Asenipoetes.*

Perhaps the *Neuters* also included the remnants of the Moiseo [after the Masikota and Kit-Fox elements or "Arrow Men" had split from them], but if not, then the *Neuters* were very closely confederated with the remnant of Moiseo at that time. Indeed, Cheyenne tradition mentions the close affiliation existing between the Moiseo and Monsoni Cree during that period and, undoubtedly, both the Moiseo and Monsoni were then in close harmonious contact with the Suhtaio. We are further told in tribal tradition - which is corroborated to some extent by early map references - that the Moiseo were then in friendly contact with the Cree, Chippewa, Sioux and Suhtaio. Thus it appears obvious that Radisson`s *Neuters* were, in fact, the Moiseo and Suhtaio combined. It is not known that the Cheyennes as a whole were ever particularly fluent in the Sioux language, although some Moiseo did speak Sioux owing to their close association with certain bands of the latter, and as neither Radisson nor the Algonquian Indians in his retinue were conversant with the Cheyenne dialect, which by then was somewhat diverse to all other Algonquian tongues, it is likely that Sioux was the common medium through which they conversed, and, we know, that both Radisson and some of his Indian companions did command a smattering of Sioux.

Obviously, the *Beef Indians* were close associates of the *Neutrals* by Radisson`s implication, and we are told in oral tribal traditions, that the early Masikota Cheyennes when in the Upper part of Minnesota State, were close friends and confederates of both the Sioux and Suhtaio, but at war with the Assiniboine and certain bands of Western [Plains] Cree. What is more important, perhaps, is that the Masikota were also in harmonious relationship with the Monsoni. They regularly hunted buffalo, while residing at times in portable skin tents or small willow-framed domed lodges plastered with loam, and thus described as resembling. *"...a swallow's nest"* in the Radisson account, and refers also to these same people as *"sedentary Sioux."* Although it is not said that these latter spoke the same language as the *Nadouwsics,* the remnant band of Moiseo, after the Arrow Men faction with the Sacred Arrows had joined the Masikota as mentioned in a previous chapter, intermarried among the Sioux and many band members spoke Sioux as a second language.

The Suhtaio on the other hand, spoke a dialect of Cheyenne, but some could converse adequately in Sioux. By 1655 they had confederated with both the Cheyennes and Sioux and also, importantly, were then in friendly contact with one or more Cree and Chippewa band. It would appear then, that while some of those peoples who Radisson noted as *Nadouwesic* were Cheyennes then in close alliance with certain Sioux groups, others were Suhtaio who like their allies the Moiseo, were wrongly classified by Radisson as being the same people as the *Christenoes* or Cree, owing to both people's similar life-style and close confederation with each other.

Cheyenne tradition further states that the Suhtaio and Cheyenne-proper [i.e. Moiseo, Masikota and Omissis], came together and separated three times before the Suhtaio were finally adopted as fully-fledged members of the Cheyenne Nation. The first time the Suhtaio became confederated with the Cheyennes, so it is also said in tradition, was during the time of the people's wandering in the Great Lakes and marsh country far northeast of their later High Plains habitat, which would fit well with the period during the first half of the seventeenth century, when both peoples were in the northern Minnesota country and in contact with the Sioux.

It must be then, that the Suhtaio during those early colonial days, were very closely associated with both the Moiseo and Monsoni Cree and at one time, were probably included under the heading *Alimouspigoiak.* By circa, 1660, i.e., around the same period as Radisson's visit, this particular Suhtaio branch of the *Alimouspigoiak* had already established itself in the marshlands of the Upper Mississippi. They were then allied to the Moiseo and Sioux of that region on the one hand, and to the Cree and Chippewa of the Upper Great Lakes on the other. All these aforementioned peoples at that time, knew the Suhtaio by the colloquial term of "Dogs" or "Dog Village People" [i.e. Chongaskiton], albeit that there were other designations, one of which was *Neutrals,* and it is likely therefore, that this was the time when the Suhtaio first embraced the original concept of the Sacred Hat and its religious significance. Having said this, it appears, though, that the 'Hat' keeper himself was not accorded the same reverence as was the keeper of the 'Sacred Arrows,' as the Suhtaio today recall that in a past time one 'Hat Keeper' when old and decrepit, had actually been abandoned by his people to die alone on the prairie, having been considered too much of a burden to warrant the people's continued support.

- 0 - 0 - 0 - 0 - 0 - 0 - 0 - 0 - 0 - 0 - 0 - 0 - 0 - 0 - 0 - 0 - 0 -

CHAPTER. 24.

THE *"VE'HOE"* COMMETH.

There were several Cheyenne and Suhtaio bands in northern Minnesota during the latter half of the seventeenth century. They then resided in the Upper Mississippi region, somewhere between the Sioux in the south along the St. Croix River above the Falls of St. Anthony, and the Monsoni Cree in the north between Rainy Lake and the western tip of Lake Superior.

Each of these Cheyenne and Suhtaio bands were semi-sedentary, some living in the lake and marsh area about the Mississippi heads; others preferring portable hide lodges in the tall-grass prairie lands west of the Upper tributaries of the main stream. For the most part, they subsisted on buffalo meat and venison obtained in some quantity, whilst during appropriate seasons the abundant wild fowl of the lakes was an important food source. Fish of many varieties were available year round and come winter, the people retreated into the thick forest regions, in order to seek protection from the deep snow and biting winds of the season.

Notwithstanding traditional assertions to the contrary, one or another Cheyenne-proper group must, at times, have exploited the wild rice so abundant around them, of which food source both neighbouring Sioux and even the Suhtaio took full advantage.

At this date, the Cheyennes were well disposed toward their neighbours and most other tribes, apart that is, toward the Assiniboine - the hated *"Ho-Hay"* enemies of the north. It does appear also that Cheyennes were then in the habit of wandering far abroad, east, west and south during periodic excursions from home, and there is strong evidence in traditional accounts and contemporary documentation of the period, to suggest a friendly association of Cheyenne and Suhtaio groups with various Algonquian tribes such as the Fox, Sauk, Illini and Menominee then inhabiting what are now the states of Wisconsin, Michigan and Illinois. In addition, there seems to have been some degree of friendly contact between the Cheyennes and Suhtaio and the Chippewa; at least with those of the latter residing adjacent to the northern shoreline of Lake Superior. But of all these foreign tribes it was the Menominee who had the closest affinity to our subjects, and especially so with the Suhtaio. The Menominee are usually classified as *"Central"* Algonquians and were occupants of the Wisconsin area, specifically in the wild rice country along that part of the Menominee River which flows immediately north of Green Bay.

The Menominee did comprise a somewhat distinct element among other *Central* Algonquian groups and had long been residents of the aforementioned area, several centuries before their Algonquian-speaking cousins of Fox, Sauk, Potawatomi and Kickapoo arrived in that region. Each of these later arrivals - apart from the Fox - showed marked differences to the Menominee particularly in dialect, but also in social structure and religious practices. The Menominee dialect, in fact, belongs to the same group as that of Fox, Cree and Cheyenne, although more closely related to Cheyenne by its lack of consonants `f,` `l` and `r.` Coupled to this, many old-time Menominee peculiarities regarding their culture and social organization were very close, if not in some cases seemingly identical with those of the Cheyennes. The inference is, that although a little too diverse to be considered one body later than the remote mists of both people's prehistory, Cheyennes and Menominee must still have been in regular contact with one another in the not too distant past.

It is reasonable to assume therefore, that Cheyennes during the second half of the seventeenth century, albeit in small number, were involved in events occurring east of the Upper

Mississippi, even though as a separate tribe they went virtually unnoticed by the colonial chroniclers of the day.

Of the numerous maps and volumes relating to the Upper Great Lakes and tribes thereof during the early period of French penetration into the interior west of Lake Huron, the name *Cheyenne* is nowhere to be found, not that is, until the 1670s and 1680s, when several corruptions of the term appear.

Material before that time is often of a geographic rather than demographic nature, and I believe it unreasonable to assume that Cheyenne-speaking peoples were not contacted, or were outside the sphere of white discovery during the period in question. More likely is the assumption that inadvertently, they were confused with other peoples; Algonquian or Siouan as the case may be, and as a consequence, included under one or another tribe's heading.

Now we know that the Moiseo, Omissis and Masikota Cheyennes by their own and Sioux traditions, were then closely aligned to Sioux bands of the Mille Lacs region above the Upper Mississippi Forks, and that the Suhtaio - then allied to both the Cheyenne and Sioux - were nearby around Leech Lake just north of Mille Lacs. Furthermore, all these groups after 1671 if not before, were in friendly contact with both the Monsoni Cree and certain Chippewa bands, owing to a recent French inspired truce having been effected between the Northern Chippewa and those Eastern Dakota Sioux peoples known as Santee and Sisseton. These Eastern Sioux groups thereafter, actually allowed certain Chippewa bands to roam with impunity in their hunting grounds, and thus these particular Sioux bands along with their Cheyenne and Suhtaio associates, must have been fully aware of events taking place east of their own country. Without doubt, Cheyennes were then acquainted with other peoples both red and white with whom the Monsoni Cree and Eastern Sioux, along with their newly acquired friends the Chippewa, were in contact.

As early as 1634, the French adventurer Jean Nicolet whilst trading at Chequamegon Bay at the western tip of Lake Superior, met with Sioux Indians from the Upper Mississippi and since then, Eastern Sioux bands had made intermittent contact with the French in the area around Green Bay and the western shore of Lake Superior.

At that same time, French *"Courier des Bois"* or *"Runners of the Woods"* as the more itinerant French-Canadian traders were known, had begun slowly edging their way into the interior both west and southwest of the Upper Great Lakes. However, some thirty years after the arrival of Nicolet, owing to a sudden intensifying of the ongoing Sioux - Assiniboine feud on one hand; and a serious outbreak of hostilities between the Eastern Sioux and a number of *Central* Algonquian tribes including the Sauk, Fox and Illini on the other, coupled with the advent of serious warfare of these same Sioux groups with Ottawa and Huron [Wyandot] refugees from the northeast, any further French encroachment west was brought to an abrupt halt, as both the Sioux and their respective antagonists, particularly the Fox, endeavoured to block the supply of French guns and ammunition from reaching their opponents. As a consequence, even the French traders themselves became vulnerable to attack from the warring tribes. But it was the Sioux who proved the fiercest and most desperate fighters when necessity demanded, and indeed, were regarded by the Jesuit chroniclers of the day as, *"The Iroquois of the West."*

Thus, even prior to the 1670s, the Sioux were often in enmity with most of their neighbours to the north, east and south with the exception of one or two Northern Chippewa bands and the Winnebago [a closely related Siouan group of Wisconsin], while only the Cheyennes and Suhtaio of northern Minnesota appear to have been Sioux allies.

Certainly by the above date, the country between the Upper Mississippi and Great Lakes of Superior and Michigan had become a bloody war-ground, through which small parties - whether of Indian or White men - travelled at their peril.

In the meantime, rumors were filtering through the forests to the ears of enterprising Frenchmen, hinting at the vast wealth in furs, slaves and minerals which, supposedly, lay untapped in the Sioux country, and what was deemed more important, was information regarding the true course of the Mississippi which, it was said, offered an unhindered route of travel to the Gulf of Mexico. All could be achieved with much profit, thought the French, if only the incorrigible Sioux and Fox who controlled the routes into the western interior could be appeased.

It was to this end that the French Intendant, Jean Baptiste Talon, acting on behalf of Pierre de Voyer Viscount d`Argenson the Governor of New France, ordered Sieur de St. Lusson; an intrepid soldier of fortune, to go west into the wilderness and invite a host of tribes from the interior to gather at Sault St. Marie in order to make pacts between each other and with the French. At the same time, it was intended that St. Lusson would take formal possession of all the uncharted *"Western Territory"* for his King Louis XIV, and thereby, pave the way for the propagation of French influence and interests in the western regions.

St. Lusson was successful in his mission and at least seventeen independent tribes responded to his call.

So it was on June 14th, 1671, a great multitude of Indians bedecked in all their gaudy finery, assembled at the Sault to hear the words of their Great French Father across the seas.

The scene was a myriad of colour which would have defied any artist to portray. Throughout the early days of the gathering, respective tribal chiefs and headmen smoked the Calumet of peace together and professed undying alliances between age-old friends and foes. Every face of those hundreds - perhaps thousands - of warriors present, was splashed with various painted designs in red, green, blue or yellow, some warriors having a red or black hand-print stamped across their mouths, indicating they had drank the lifeblood of an enemy. A profusion of feathers from the eagle, hawk, owl or turkey adorned almost every head, many of which were shaved but for a greased upright tuff rising from the crown. Others had heads shaved on one side only, while some sported high roaches stiffened with bear grease running from the forehead to the nape and painted in gaudy hues. Still others wore their hair long, cut straight across the forehead in line with the eyebrows with the side hair braided in two corresponding plaits or in multiple strands. And there were those who preferred their hair to hang loose and free-flowing, reaching to and below the waist.

Many of the men-folk were clad in deer-hide shirts decorated along the seams with dyed porcupine quills or brightly coloured beads, in addition to deerskin leggings and moccasins embroidered in similar fashion. Some warriors had wolf tails trailing from their heels signifying their prowess in battle, while still others went half-naked, wearing only breech-clout and moccasins. The bravest among them displayed bear claw necklaces or large marine shells around their necks, and withal, most sported brass earrings, along with copper or tin arm bands that glinted in the sunlight as they moved. Here were assembled Chippewa and Nipissings from above the eastern Great Lakes; Monsoni, Swampy Cree and Woods Cree from the northern forests; Shawnees from Ohio; Menominee and Potawatomies from the wild-rice country of northwestern Michigan; Winnebagos from Green Bay; Fox, Sauk, Kickapoo and Miamis from Wisconsin and numerous Mascoutens - The Prairie dwellers – from both east and west of the Mississippi. Even a number of Assiniboine were in attendance, having paddled their canoes to the Sault all the way from Lake of the Woods and even further, and withal, perhaps, small contingents of Eastern and Western Sioux, along with groups of Cheyennes and Suhtaio from the country about the Mississippi heads.

All had come together to meet with the white man`s emissaries, whose very presence the Indians supposed, promised an event of great significance and importance.

CHEYENNE CONTRARY WARRIOR. Circa, 1700.
[Pen and ink drawing by author. Author`s collection.]

Before the assembled host the Sieur de St. Lusson; looking resplendent in plumed fedora, frocked coat and with unsheathed sword in hand, proclaimed to his red audience through the various interpreters [among whom was the trader Nicolas Perrot], that the lands and peoples hereabout, were now subject to the Great French King their father, and henceforward they would be under the protection of the French sovereign ever more. A representation of the cross of the crucifixion, along with the coat of arms of King Louis XIV were raised upon crossed upright posts, much to the bewilderment, yet apparent delight of the Indian spectators.

The Jesuit priest Father Allouez, who could speak tolerably good Algonquian, then made a speech, in which he congratulated all those tribes present upon making their various pacts with one another and continued by expounding the greatness and virtue of his king. He went further in order to prepare his rude potential flock for their impending deliverance from damnation, if, that is, they were to accept the word of God, which he promised to impart among them when he visited their individual villages in the future.

A number of chiefs each in turn, then rose to their feet and made speeches of welcome to the Frenchmen, while professing their happiness at concluding pacts with the various tribes around them. It is unlikely that the Indians themselves understood for one moment the implications of the Frenchman`s address, as the idea of sovereign control was entirely alien to their natural concepts. But all appeared to be in good spirits by what was said and after the lighting of a great bonfire, the Grand Council; as far as the French officials were concerned, came to an end.

Doubtless, there then ensued much feasting, dancing and singing among the different tribes, as they cemented their renewed and newly-made pacts both with age-old friends and erstwhile foes, and declared mutual friendship between their respective tribes for time everlasting. There was also much visiting in each other`s lodges; the adopting of each other's children; smoking of pipes and the verbal exchange of adventures and anecdotes, predominantly concerning their valiant war deeds during past conflicts between their peoples. For several more days and nights the different bands remained together in perfect harmony. But at length, the tribal contingents one by one departed each for their own country, and the area around the Sault was once again duly left in peace, its natural serenity occupied only by its more permanent four-legged and winged inhabitants.

All in all, thought the Frenchmen, the council had been an astounding success and in truth, intertribal peace and goodwill among the tribes - for a short time at least - did reign in the northern wilderness. Although this was probably due more to the importance of the fishing season for some, and the need to procure supplies of meat for others in preparation for the onset of winter, rather than the persuasions of St. Lusson, or to the Indians being over-awed by the supposed prowess of the *Ancienne Regime.*

That Cheyennes had been present at the gathering; albeit in small number, is a feasible assumption, even most probable, for we know that the Suhtaio were still in harmonious and close contact with the Monsoni Cree, as well as being in friendly contact with the Menominee and western bands of Chippewa. The Cheyenne-proper bands as confederates of the Suhtaio, were included in these same relationships throughout the early 1670s, while at the same time, they were

254

in close and friendly liaison with the Mdewankanton Sioux and other Eastern Dakota-speaking groups. These latter were then in residence around Mille Lacs and along that lake's connecting stream of Rum River, an eastern tributary of the Upper Mississippi above the Falls of St. Anthony, and were militarily aligned with the Moiseo, Omissis and Masikota Cheyenne groups in their common war against the Assiniboine. This was in contrast to the Teton and Yankton Sioux, who were still in conflict with all so-called Central Algonquian tribes, including the Menominee, Mascouten, Fox, Sauk and Illini.

In truth, it cannot be determined whether or not Eastern Sioux bands were actually present at the aforesaid great intertribal gathering. Certainly, though, they were recipients to the articles of the resulting treaty and were party to the various intertribal pacts made at that time. Neither are Cheyennes or Suhtaio actually mentioned by name as being in attendance, although as we have seen, they were then at peace with the Menominee, Illinois and Eastern Sioux whom they often visited and co-habited with freely. Likewise, the Suhtaio were associating regularly with northern Chippewa bands at that date and so, most likely, had also been present at the Sault, if only as guests of any one of the above mentioned peoples. Probably then, Cheyennes and Suhtaio were included among either Cree, Chippewa or some other Algonquian-speaking group, or even misconstrued as being a Sioux faction depending upon whose company they were in at that time. It would, of course, have been a great advantage to the Cheyennes and Suhtaio to be included in the resulting intertribal pacts which then transpired, not to mention the benefit of their being able to open up new trade channels, whereby they could obtain the coveted items of European manufacture; not least of which were guns and ammunition.

In all probability, Cheyenne-speaking peoples had met with white men prior to 1671. Jean Nicolet and Pierre Radisson, we know, had contacted several tribes then in close contact with Cheyennes in 1634 and between 1658 and 1660 respectively. The arrival of the white men, initially, had a great effect upon all Natives west of the Upper Great Lakes who thought them "Mysterious Beings," owing to the wonderful objects such as guns and iron implements which the latter introduced among the tribes. Indeed, it was because the Cheyennes at first held the white men in awe, that they gave them the collective name *"Ve`hoe"* meaning "spider," as to the Cheyennes the spider is also a mysterious being which can do wondrous and remarkable things.

Following the aforesaid great council at Sault St. Marie and the way now clear of obstacles, the French lost little time in attempting to open up their newly acquired territory in order to exploit its resources; rich in furs for the financier; even richer in heathen souls to be baptized into the Catholic faith, and thus saved from the fiery torments of damnation.

Accordingly two years later in 1673, the enterprising young French fur-trader Louis Joliet, in company with the Jesuit priest Jacques Marquette and five French Canadian *"Courier des Bois,"* sailed down the Wisconsin River in two birch bark canoes as far as that river's mouth and entered on the waters of the *"Mighty Mississippi,"* the country abutting which and the extent of its course, being as yet unexplored by any white man.

Of the numerous Indian groups noted by Joliet, it is unlikely that many were actually met by him or his companions at that time. Rather, the expedition collected the names and positions of several tribes, especially those along the Upper Mississippi, from secondary sources gathered along the route. But be this as it may, if the explorers did not personally meet with Cheyenne-speaking peoples, they certainly heard of them, for the Joliet map drawn up in 1674, places the *"Chaiena"* as being fourth in a list of tribes, then residing along or near the Upper Mississippi in northern Minnesota.

The name *Chaiena* appears to be Joliet`s personal rendering of the Sioux appellation *"Sha-hi-ena."* It could not have denoted the Cree, for its position is placed too close to Sioux bands of both Teton and Yankton divisions who, unlike their Eastern Sioux cousins, were at that period, still engaged against all Cree groups in a most violent war of attrition.

The name must refer to Cheyennes, these being the only other foreign people so-called by the Sioux and who were in the area at that time. Thus, we have our first documented reference to our subjects, although where exactly the *Chaiena r*esided along the Mississippi, Joliet did not say.

Now in a line from north to south extending immediately below the *Chaiena,* there are listed on the same chart four Sioux groups, whose names are synonymous with those Dakota Sioux known in the late historic time as *Wazikute, Wahepeton, Teton* and *Yankton* respectively.

From later maps of the country and from Sioux tradition itself, it is known that during the period of Joliet`s sojourn, the *Wazikute* and *Wahepeton* lived about Mille Lacs at the head of Rum River, this last being an eastern tributary flowing north to south into the Upper Mississippi. As these two groups are placed by Joliet directly below the *Chaiena,* then the latter must have been somewhere north of Mille Lacs. It appears certain that Joliet obtained some of the names he listed from the Sioux and others from Algonquian-speakers who, in their turn, gave Joliet the names of tribes residing above the *Chaiena*, and listed by Joliet in succession from north to south as, *Alimouspigoiak, Quissiloua* and *Agatomitou.*

The *Alimouspigoiak* evidently refer to Algonquians, as the latter part of the name is the early French corruption of an Algonquian term denoting `*people.*` The prefix `*Ali*` cannot be definitely determined, but the following syllable of `*mous*` is clearly a rendition of the Algonquian word for *"moose"* and so refers specifically to the "Moose men" or "Moose people." Of course, the term `*Moose men*` was the common nomenclature applied by other tribes to the Monsoni Cree. However, at the date 1673, it may well have included one or more of the four old-time bands which then comprised the Suhtaio, for the Monsoni Cree, who were then also in enmity with the Teton and Yankton Sioux, were actually some distance to the northeast between Rainy Lake and Lake Nipigon, the area, in fact, where Joliet`s companion Father Jacques Marquette on his own map drawn from memory in the year 1674, positioned the *"Oumoomies"* [I.e. Monsoomies = Monsoni], and where in the same region the Suhtaio, under the names *Chongaskiton* and *Songaskiton*, were later positioned by Hennepin and Franquelin in 1682 and 1688 respectively.

Now on the Father Creux map of 1660, the Cree of the region north of the Mississippi heads are called *"Kilisalimibegkec,"* and are positioned just above a lake with the similar sounding name of *"Alimibegeon,"* which was the early French term for present-day Lake Nipigon. The *Kilisalimibegkec,* without doubt then, comprised those people called `Alimouspigoiak` by Joliet fourteen years later. The same Creux map also shows the `Monsoomies` placed above the Mississippi headwaters not far from Rainy Lake, either in what is now northern Minnesota or southern Ontario, and so implies that both groups were separate entities.

Creux himself was not personally acquainted with the Upper Great Lakes and Mississippi country, but obtained his information from secondary verbal sources. Perhaps then, these `Monsoomies` were actually the division later known as Plains Cree, which was a conglomerate of mixed Monsoni and Swampy Cree [Muskegon] seceders, although it is just as likely that the Monsoni-proper did move back and forth between Lake Nipigon in the east and Rainy Lake northwest of the Mississippi heads, so that both names are merely corruptions of dialectical forms, depending on which of Creux`s several informants gave the required data concerning these particular areas and peoples thereof. The term `Monsoomies` would have been a form of the Cree term for themselves; that is, "Moose People," while the name, `Kilisalimibegkec` was perhaps, the early French garbled form of another Native term for the Chippewa, or indeed, some other Algonquian-speaking tribe's synonymy. Most likely, this latter group comprised those people who having become separated from their Monsoni and Chippewa confederates, were later designated on colonial maps as *Shongaskiton* and who some two centuries later – became known as Suhtaio.

We have seen that the Suhtaio were then in close liaison with the Monsoni during these early years and have previously ascertained, that they were the same people met by Father Allouez in 1666 who he described as *"dog sacrificers."* The Suhtaio, who most certainly were once in residence around the shores of Lake Nipigon where the Monsoni-proper also once resided, seem to have migrated from that point in a south-westerly direction sometime after Creux`s notation in 1660, and by the time of the Joliet and Marquette expedition of 1673, had relocated somewhere near Leech Lake in northern Minnesota.

The Joliet name of `Alimouspigoak` is not too dissimilar to that of `Assinipouelac,` as used on later maps of the same country to designate the Assiniboine. However, on Joliet`s chart the Assiniboine are mentioned separately under the term `Assinibouls,` and are positioned just north of an `Assiniboul Lac` which applies either to present-day Lake Nipigon, Lake of the Woods, or even Lake Winnipeg in Manitoba, Canada. Either way, the name cannot be confused with that of Joliet`s `Alimouspigoiak.` The position of Joliet`s `Assinibouls` incidentally, does indicate that by 1673, the Assiniboine - having made their pact with the Cree - had already moved nearer their Cree allies so as to be in contact with English traders on Hudson's Bay and for this reason, the Suhtaio were now prevented from returning to their old hunting and fishing grounds north of Lake Superior due to Assiniboine penetration of that region. Thus the Suhtaio were obliged to remain within the vicinity of the headwaters of the Upper Mississippi, ostensibly in the Leech Lake district, where Chippewa tradition locates them by the name *Shotawinniwug* during the same period.

The next tribal name on Joliet`s list, i.e. `Quissiloua` has the suffix `loua,` which may be a misspelling or misinterpretation of the Sioux term `toua` from `ton` denoting `village,` as George E. Hyde postulated, although I think it more likely a corruption of the Algonquian suffix `iu` meaning `men` or `people.` However, as this term is unlikely to have denoted a Sioux band owing to their proximity to the Cree, then it obviously refers to a people in close relationship with both the Sioux and Cree respectively. By omitting the last part of the name *loua*, we are left with `quissi,` a word definitely of Algonquian derivation and identical with the term Quissy as used at a later date by the explorer and trader Jean Baptiste Trudeau in 1795 when designating in Trudeau`s words, *"...one of the three hordes of the Chaguanne Nation."* Furthermore, it is certainly a variation in contracted form of the Lewis and Clark rendition of *Whee-skee-u*, which name they also gave as a band of the Cheyenne Nation then residing on one side or the other of the Missouri River in 1803-`04. Notwithstanding that Joliet`s term *Quissiloua* appears at first glance, to represent the Cheyenne band name *Omissis*, it is a variation of the term *Moiseo* and therefore, most likely included both the Moiseo and Masikota Cheyenne groups together, while the Creux map of 1660 shows the *Quafsi* [i.e., an old spelling and corruption of *Quissi* and thus the *Moiseo*], as having earlier been positioned on the northwest side of Lake Superior.

On Joliet`s chart, the position of the `Alimouspigoiak` [i.e. Monsoni] being next to the *Quissiloua,* also leave little doubt that the last named were Cheyenne-speakers and synonymous with both the Moiseo and Masikota.

It has previously been mentioned how the French apparently, had difficulty rendering correct pronunciations and often substituted `qui` and even `m` as a substitute for `w,` as in `Ouisconsin` and `Misconsin` for both the river and state properly known as Wisconsin. Thus we have the term, `Quissi,` which in common Algonquian usage, pertains to the idea of `eating` or `eaters` [from the Algonquian root word `quissi,` or in another dialect `wheeskee.`]. In its Cheyenne dialectic form when referring to a group of people so-named, this becomes, `Mois-io,` which also noted earlier in this study, includes the Cheyenne prefix `M` sometimes pronounced in its archaic form of `Om.` This today is preserved in the modern Northern Cheyenne band name of Omissis, i.e. Eaters, which likewise has a connotation with grass as in `moi` which was an Algonquian colloquium for `elk,` the suffix `io` merely denoting `people.` On the other hand, the initial `O` of Omissis represents the word as being a proper noun, whilst like the early colonial French, the `m` of Omissis was interchangeable with `w` or its equivalent spelling of `oui.` Hence the archaic Cheyenne alternative name of Omissis being rendered by Lewis and Clark as `Whee-skee-u,` and synonymous with the Algonkin-proper tribal name *Wheske-rinni,* these being the ancestral group from which the Cheyenne Omissis group; also known as Bowstrings, had originally sprung.

The name *Quissiloua*, in fact, as it appears on the Joliet map of 1674, seems to position them just north of the headwaters of the Mississippi, not far from the two expanses of water now known respectively as Lake Winnibegoshish and Cass Lake and where - so we have previously deduced from Cheyenne, Suhtaio and some other tribal traditions - Cheyenne-speaking peoples certainly once resided.

258

The *Agatomitou* being third on Joliet`s list, have not to date been coupled with any known tribe other than conjectured affiliations; often having been classified as a Sioux group when no definite information was forthcoming. The word, however, as we have averred in an earlier chapter, is actually of mixed linguistic derivation and includes the suffix `tou,` which again is either a French corruption of the Sioux term `ton` meaning `village,` or from the Algonquian `iu` meaning `people.`

The people so named were then in close proximity with, or even allied to the Sioux of the region, although the first part of the name appears to come from the Algonquian / Cree term `atim` meaning `dog.` Thus the map name implies `Dog village` or `Dog people` and would have denoted the Suhtaio specifically, who we know of old, were familiar to surrounding tribes by the singular designation of `Dog Men.`

It may be taken from this, that those tribes on Joliet`s chart which have an Algonquian ending, were in league with Algonquians, if not themselves Algonquian-speakers, whilst those having a Sioux ending were in league with the Sioux.

It must be concluded from the above analysis that Joliet, who it may be said drew his map from memory and had himself, only a superficial knowledge of the Upper Mississippi and headwaters region, did not mean to imply that those tribes mentioned as residing in that country, did so in a straight line from north to south along the east bank of that river, but were merely roughly positioned as such, one from the other in relation to their neighbours either north, south, east or west of the main stream, whatever the case may be.

In fact, Joliet`s list of tribes should actually form an arc beginning in the north at a point northeast of the Mississippi heads, then curving in a south-westerly direction to Mille Lacs before continuing south along the main stream to and below the mouth of the Minnesota. This being so, the `Alimouspigoiak` [Monsoni] of Joliet`s chart, would have been in the northeastern Minnesota district near the southern Ontario border. Southwest of these would have been the `Quissiloua` [i.e. Moiseo and Masikota] and below them, both the `Agatomitou` and `Chaiena` [i.e. Suhtaio and Bowstrings-Omissis] would have been somewhere between Leech Lake and Lake Superior. Indeed, in the very district where, as also mentioned in an earlier chapter, Father Louis Hennepin only a few years later, placed both the *"Chongaskitons"* and the *"Nacion du Chien."*

It would appear that at the time of the Joliet and Marquette expedition, the Cheyenne and Suhtaio country included the area embracing Lake Cass, Lake Winnibigoshish, Leech Lake and the banks of Bowstring River and Bowstring Lake, all immediately northeast of the Mississippi heads. In corroboration of this, the stream known as Turtle [or Tortoise] River just to the west of Bowstring Lake is yet recalled in Cheyenne tradition, and a popular song during the *Ghost Dance* excitement in 1890, told of visiting the same Turtle River in the old Cheyenne homeland, in order to obtain sacred paints got from coloured clay deposits found along its banks.

Around Bowstring Lake and along Bowstring River itself, the *Chaiena* [Omissis] once resided and these people appear to have been the same who were known at a later date as *"People of the Bow."* This last name comes from an old Algonquian appellation and actually means *"People of the Bowstring,"* not *"Bow."* But this belongs to a later chapter. Close to these last were the *Quissiloua,* which as noted above, must by elimination have included those Cheyenne-speaking groups known as Moiseo and Masikota.

Notwithstanding the invaluable information subsequently added by both Joliet and Father Marquette to that already being amassed by visionaries in Montreal and Paris, the success of the French expedition of 1673 was not acted upon immediately. The result being, that the shadow of obscurity returned to the interior and again enveloped those Indian peoples residing west of the Upper Great Lakes.

The dreams of an Indian–white man Utopia under the guiding auspices of a French King were thus again frustrated, while it appeared that the sincerity of the Indians themselves when accepting the peace overtures of St. Lusson in `71, had also been short-lived. Intertribal war was, soon after, once more blighting the country and the pitiful wails of those in mourning for loved ones killed again resounded through Indian camps, including those of the Assiniboine and several Algonquian tribes along with the Sioux, notwithstanding that several of these peoples had actually attended the great peace-gathering at the Sault.

It was in truth, the English on Hudson's Bay and unscrupulous French traders out of Montreal, who by utilizing the then safe routes into the western interior which the aforesaid council of `71 had temporarily opened, inaugurated a nefarious trade in both guns and metal weapons to the tribes, and by so doing had rekindled the desire of their savage customers to reignite old feuds and force inroads into the country of the Sioux, who still lacking their enemy's advantage in weaponry, managed to hold their ground by their superior fighting ability and indomitable spirit alone. It does appear, that once a couple of seasons had elapsed after the gathering at the Sault, the warrior elements among those several tribes present had grown bored with inactivity, and longed to return to the warpath against all erstwhile foes. War belts were thus again passed around council fires and hatchets were soon stained red with the regeneration of nigh constant blood-letting through internecine strife. French exploration and further encroachment into the western country stagnated and in their impatience, the avaricious traders now badgered Government authorities to reopen the western sources of fur and slaves for their dwindling markets.

Subsequently, late in 1678, another expedition was organized in order to reverse this irritating obstruction to French expansion, before the rival English to the north and Spaniards to the south should take the initiative and exploit these unexplored regions for themselves.

This time it was the intrepid fur-trader Daniel Greysolon Sieur Duluth, who now invited the various Nations of the interior to come together again the following summer at a designated point at the western end of Lake Superior, where, it was intended, they would for a second time make peace among themselves, - especially between the Assiniboine and Sioux - and with all other Algonquian tribes with whom the Eastern Sioux were again at war.

During the ensuing winter, prior to the proposed second great gathering of tribes, Duluth stopped on the shore of Lake Superior at the site of what is now the township which bears his name.

There he held impromptu councils with several Sioux dignitaries who had assembled for that purpose.

The Sioux promised Duluth that they would adhere to their ongoing pact with the Chippewa and agreed to attend the proposed council later that year, so as to make peace again with all others among the Great Lakes and forest Nations. Duluth then accompanied these Sioux delegates on their return journey to their own country about the Upper branches of the Mississippi in the vicinity of Mille Lacs, and actually visited among the lodges of these ferocious denizens of the wilderness, among whom, Duluth believed, no white man had been before. He was apparently unaware of the earlier visits of Radisson and Grossiliers between 1658 and 1660.

The journal of Duluth records that he went to the, *"...great village of the Nadouecioux called Isaty"* [i.e. Isanti – later known as Santee], [1] and there he set up the royal coat of arms of his King in the ilk of his predecessor St. Lusson at Sault St. Marie. He then claimed all the Sioux country for France. It was during this same winter sojourn in the Eastern Sioux country, that Duluth visited the neighbouring villages of the *Houebatons* and *Songaskitons* before returning to the western end of Lake Superior, and where, in September 1679, he held council with the Sioux and Assiniboine and with some other tribes there assembled in response to his earlier invitation.

It is evident that Duluth fared somewhat better than his predecessor St. Lusson. At least, the Eastern Sioux bands and Assiniboine did make a truce which held for a significant number of years, whilst the several Central Algonquian tribes, with whom these Sioux had also been at war, likewise made their separate pacts which gave those such as the Fox and their allies enough respite from the Sioux, to allow them to concentrate more fully upon stemming hostile inroads upon their camps by powerful Iroquois-proper tribes from the east.

It is known that the Monsoni, Chippewa, Menominee and Sioux were represented in person at this gathering with Duluth and so, it is more than probable that contingents of Cheyenne-speaking peoples if not the whole bands themselves, were also in attendance at that time. Once again, however, as the Cheyenne-proper are not mentioned by any recognizable name, they may well have been confused with and thus included among either the Monsoni or Sioux or both, as befitted their respective band alliances. The *Shongaskitons* were, of course, synonymous with the Suhtaio and we know that they or a part of their tribe at least, were in attendance at the council, although erroneously inferred as being a Sioux band by DuLuth. This being so, then perhaps a temporary truce was also effected between the Assiniboine and Cheyenne-proper at this time. Although traditions from both tribes make no mention of such an event as ever having taken place between them, and surely if there had been a truce, then it must have been of very short duration and not deemed significant enough to remember in tribal tradition.

The Suhtaio [*Songaskitons*] on the other hand, did likely agree to a pact with the Assiniboine, a peace which may have endured for a decade or more, for it was about this time in their history, according to the later-day Suhtaio band member White Bull who was an informant of Truman Michelson early in the twentieth century, that the Suhtaio moved back east from the Upper Mississippi, while on French maps which relate to the same western country between the years circa, 1680 and 1700, the *Songaskitons* are shown as occupying the region between Lake Nipigon on the east and the Mississippi headwater country on the west; a region, we might add, then regularly frequented by both the Assiniboine and the latter`s Plains Cree confederates. Perhaps then, this event had its origins from the earlier date when Radisson referred to the Suhtaio as *Neutrals,* and was the reason why the Suhtaio split from the Cheyennes for a second time after their two tribe's initial coming together, as Cheyenne tradition asserts, and which would have been due to this temporary Suhtaio pact with the Assiniboine with whom the Cheyenne-proper continued to be at war.

Of one thing we can be sure, both the Cheyennes and Suhtaio were effected somewhat by consequences arising from the intertribal peace councils held by St. Lusson and Duluth respectively, and not least, by the changing situation those events initiated in the northern Minnesota country. Certainly, there was tribal movement which included the Cheyenne-proper in the years immediately following the more recent tribal gathering arranged by Duluth in 1679.

It was due to the Cheyennes losing their Eastern Sioux and Suhtaio allies against the Assiniboine, that some Cheyenne bands - particularly those incorporating the Omissis [Bowstring] and Masikota [Prairie People], suddenly found that they alone could not hold back the assaults made upon them by their northern enemies, and were soon obliged to move deeper into the hinterland of the central part of what is now the state of Minnesota, thereby putting distance between themselves and their foes.

Each of these Cheyenne groups were soon driven out of the northern part of Minnesota, the Omissis-Bowstring faction retreating southwest into the Glenwood district just below the Upper Mississippi Forks, and here groups of old Indian house sites have since been discovered which, Sioux tradition declares, were once the sites of old Cheyenne lodges during the period in question [1680 / 1690]. Likewise, that part of the *Alimouspigioak* which included a large part of the remnant band of Moiseo who no longer having the Eastern Sioux and Suhtaio as a protective barrier, also abandoned their territory at around the same time and for the same reason as did their brethren the Bowstrings due to Assiniboine and Plains Cree attacks. As a consequence, this second breakaway band of Moiseo at first fled west to and across the Red River of the North, but some years later, they returned east to their Moiseo relatives they had left behind, and relocated between the western tip of Lake Superior and Lake Nipigon, as is apparent from the map of Joseph LaFrance drafted in 1742, which notes the *Quassi Indians* [i.e. Quissy] as then residing in that region.

The Masikota Cheyenne group - designated by contemporary cartographers of the late 17th century by the name *Quissiloua* and alternatively, as *Quissecouseton,* - also finding themselves fully exposed, moved due south to be nearer the Yankton and Teton Sioux [these not being a party to the Duluth peacemaking among the tribes] and only a short time later moved even further south to the Elbow Bend of the Minnesota, having leap-frogged past the Omissis-Bowstrings Cheyenne-speaking group in the process. The Suhtaio [*Songaskiton*] conversely, chose to relocate in the region between Lake Nipigon on the east and the head of the St. Croix River on the west where they continued to associate freely with the Monsoni Cree, Assiniboine and Chippewa, and where they were positioned by Franquelin on his map of 1699. They later migrated in a south-westerly direction across the Red River of the North west of Lake Traverse, where the observations of Jonathan Carver positioned them in 1766-68. But of these movements we will also speak later.

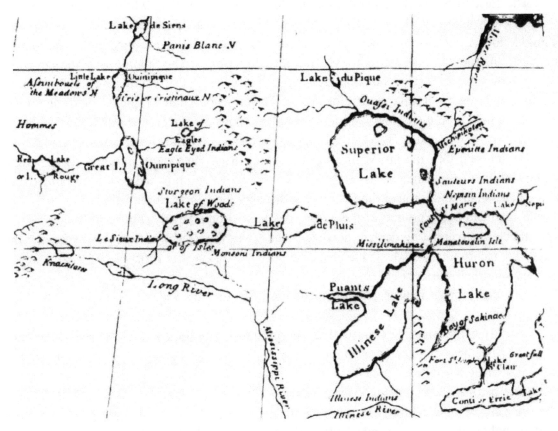

SECTION OF THE JOSEPH LAFRANCE MAP RELATING BETWEEN 1739 AND 1742.
[The Quassi Indians are here placed just above Superior Lake.]
[From Arthur J. Ray`s "Indians in the Fur Trade. University of Toronto Press. 1974.]

The dispersal of all Cheyenne-speaking groups from the Mississippi Headwaters country, was not peculiar to themselves. Other peoples both in the northwestern part of Minnesota and in western Ontario, i.e., the Arapahoe-Atsina, Blackfoot and Hidatsa-Crow, also vacated their hearths because of Assiniboine and Plains Cree pressure and fled west. The Blackfoot tribes for their part, went northwest, into what is now the Canadian province of Manitoba at a point along the Lower Saskatchewan River on the west side of Lake Winnipeg, whilst the Arapahoe-Atsina retired across the Red River of the North and into the northern part of the Coteau des Prairies, in what is now the eastern part of the state of North Dakota and the southern part of Manitoba.

The Hidatsa-Crow; having earlier left the Minnesota country owing to a previous spate of Assiniboine, Yankton and Cree aggression, at first fled north above Lake Winnipeg before returning south into the Coteau des Prairies and the Devil's Lake area of eastern North Dakota, and thereafter, moved further west in order to join their linguistic Awatixa cousins already entrenched along the Knife River branch of the Missouri in the Western Plains.

The Eastern Sioux, meanwhile, having lost most of their erstwhile enemies from the north and east owing to the Duluth peacemaking of 1679, by way of compensation, directed their own hostile incursions southeast against the Illinois tribes and also west; beyond the Red River of the North in order to reach the relocated Hidatsa-Crow camps. The Suhtaio who were in close liaison with these same Eastern Sioux bands were probably involved in raiding west of Red River, either upon their own initiative or as allies to the Eastern Sioux and Chippewa, and, therefore, their fierce enmity with the Crows - so pronounced and constant during the nineteenth century - actually had its origins in this early period of Suhtaio residence in north-eastern Minnesota.

Having said this, the important aspect resulting from the Duluth initiative as far as the French themselves were concerned, was that the Eastern Sioux and Fox had now been cajoled into allowing access into and through their countries, and that the course of the Mississippi; once the great war-road and battle ground of the tribes, was now comparatively quiet and free of risk to French travelers. It cannot be denied, however, that it was the French themselves by having the freedom and opportunity to trade with all tribes in this once disputed territory, who actually helped inaugurate intertribal warfare on an even grander scale, by supplying both guns and other weapons of European manufacture, indiscriminately to all those who had furs and slaves enough with which to barter in return.

From 1679 onward, Europeans in the guise of trader, missionary, explorer and adventurer, entered the wilderness country west and southwest of the Upper Great Lakes of Michigan and Superior. Slowly, but surely, the great Mississippi River and its connecting tributaries were mapped and the various tribes thereof, at last contacted and accounted for. And so begins the historic time of Cheyenne and Suhtaio evolution, as opposed to the previous Ancient and proto-historic periods steeped in mythology, apocrypha and tradition. We have followed our subject's journey as recalled in their own and other tribal traditions, from a distant time in their primeval past when roaming the tundra and taiga lands of the Far North, to their evolving a singular identity when inhabiting the pristine subsistence country of what is now the state of Minnesota.

- 0 - 0 - 0 - 0 - 0 - 0 - 0 - 0 - 0 - 0 - 0 - 0 - 0 - 0 - 0 - 0 - 0 -

PART 111

THE TIME OF BUFFALO

NORTHERN SHUTAIO ELK RIVER AND WIFE.
[From the book, "Photographer on an Army Mule," Uni; of Oklahoma Press, 1965]

266

CHAPTER 25.

OF MISSIONARIES, MYTHS AND MAPS.

In has been explained in preceding chapters how two confederated Algonquian-speaking peoples known as the Moiseo and Omissis, migrated back and forth across what is now Canada and the Eastern United States and by A.D. 1550, had settled in the Upper part of present-day Minnesota. They then expanded into four separate entities known as Moiseo, Masikota, Omissis [Bowstrings] and Pipe-Stem-Men, and after uniting at a later date with the linguistically related Suhtaio, they formed the basis of what became the Cheyenne Nation of more recent time. When in Minnesota their separate villages were widely scattered, and not until the late decades of the seventeenth century were Cheyenne-speaking peoples first noted on contemporary maps and in writings of the period, albeit confused with foreign groups and under a variety of names of mixed Algonquian and Siouan derivation.

Thus on the 1674 map drafted by the French Canadian Louis Joliet, the *Quissiloua, Agatomitou* and *Chaiena;* representing the Masikota, Suhtaio and Omissis in that order, are noted as residing in the Upper Mississippi region on that river's east side some distance above the mouth of the Wisconsin. Following this in 1683, the Recollect Friar Louis Hennepin in the first published account of his adventures, also included Cheyenne and Suhtaio groups, designated *Nacion du Chien* and *Chongaskitons* respectively, positioned north of Mille Lacs between the Upper Mississippi and the western tip of Lake Superior.

In 1699, however, the French Hydrographer Jean Baptiste Franquelin produced a more detailed map entitled *Nouvo Francais*. Franquelin included many additional tribal names clustered within the northern Minnesota region, having obtained his information predominantly from the trader and explorer Pierre Charles LeSueur when both were in Montreal in 1690. Unfortunately, by the time Franquelin's chart was actually completed and made available, a part of his information concerning tribal locations along the western tributaries of the Upper Mississippi was already out of date.

Franquelin did not include Hennepin's earlier notation of *Nacion des Chien*, but did note a tribal group with a similar name to Joliet's *Chaiena,* which Franquelin placed on a tributary stream adjoining the west bank of the Mississippi near the junction of its Upper branches, and which appears to be compatible with the 'Long Prairie' branch of Crow Wing Fork.

This group or band with a similar name to Joliet's *Chaiena*, Franquelin termed *Chaienaton,* which likewise, must have denoted Cheyennes. The name cannot be identified with any known Dakota or Sioux band and as Joliet did before him, Franquelin's term appears to have been an attempt to render the Sioux word *Shahiena,* but in Franquelin's case, with the added Sioux suffix 'ton' denoting 'village.' On a slightly later map of 1702/'03 drafted by the French cartographer Guillaume DeIsle, the *Chaieneton* are also noted, but with the additional term *Hommes Accomplis* [i,e. `Accomplished Men`]. It was the same Pierre Charles LeSueur when in Paris in 1701 -`02, who supplied such data to DeIsle and gave additional information to the compiler of the 1726 edition of the *"Dictionnaire Universel De La France Ancienne Et Moderne,"* wherein it is stated,

> "Chaienaton. One of the Nations of the Sioux of the west, situated to the west of the Mississippi, besides a small lake formed by a river which winds across the fine prairies where live the Sioux of the West. M. le Sueur explains their name as meaning those of the Accomplished Men. This people occupies itself in cultivation of the earth." [1]

This being said, earlier scholars have supposed that where the *Chaienaton* are positioned on the Franquelin and DeIsle charts, represents a point near the mouth of Sheyenne River which flows from the west into Red River of the North, while a *Lac des Assinipoils* shown on the same map represents; they believe, present-day Lake Winnipeg. Such assumptions are not, though, valid, when one analyses data gleaned from numerous tribal traditions and information found on alternative maps of the Upper Mississippi region relating to the period in question.

On the same Franquelin chart of 1699, we also find the *Ouaticouteton,* but which is spelt *Ouasicouseton* on the LeSueur-DeIsle map of 1702/`03, along with the added designation *N. du pein* positioned between two branches of the same river near the mouth of which the *Chaienaton* are located. Additionally, in a list of tribal bands which LeSueur himself designated collectively in his written manuscript as *"Sioux of the West,"* one finds the *Oasascouetons* with the sub-heading *"Villages dispersed in several little bands,"* [2] while another entry in the *Dictionaire Universel Ancienne et Modernne* includes the notation,

> *"Ouasicouteton, ou Nation du PinPerce, dans la Louisianne Suprentionale. C`est l`une des Nation des Sioux de L`Ouest, elle est fituee le long d`une Riviere qui communique a trais petit lacs, traverse les Belles prairies les arrose..."* [3]

Now if the term *PinPerce* in the above extract translates as "Pine Piercers," then it likely implies that the people designated were in the habit of piercing themselves with pine skewers, and might apply to an important element of the Sun-Dance ceremony then practiced by Cheyennes from a Suhtaio innovation. The Sioux, as far as known, did not adopt the Sun-Dance themselves until a much later date when west of the Missouri River.

It is also known that the colonial French had trouble with the consonant `w` and invariably substituted `oui` and sometimes `m` in its stead. Thus *Ouasicouseton* can also be pronounced either as *Wasicouseton* or *Masicouseton,* and which terms would then be of mixed Algonquian and Sioux derivation comprising the Algonquian words `wassi` or `massi,` i.e.`eats` or `eaters,` and ``kota` or `kute,` i.e. `prairie,` but with the additional Sioux suffix `ton` denoting `village.` Such therefore, would be consistent with the Cheyenne band name Masikota, and certainly, the Masikota were known as `Prairie People` and even `Prairie eaters` with the same connotation as the old Cheyenne collective name for themselves of Grasshoppers. During the period 1670-1680, the Masikota who were breakaways from the Moiseo Cheyenne-proper parent band, resided in the region of north-central Minnesota where they would have been close to another large Cheyenne-speaking component compatible with Franquelin`s *Chaienaton* and thus representing the Omissis Cheyenne group also known as Bowstrings. However, according to Cheyenne oral tradition, in 1685 or thereabout, the Bowstrings went southwest and thereafter, moved beyond the Red River of the North and relocated at a point overlooking the Lower bend of Sheyenne River in southeastern present-day North Dakota. They were soon followed in vacating the Upper Mississippi district by the Masikota, along with another breakaway group from the Moiseo then known as Kit-Fox Men, and among whom were the tribe`s Sacred Arrow talismans and their keeper. Together, the Masikota and Kit-Fox migrated southwest from the Upper Mississippi to the Blue Earth district of the Minnesota River.

The same recent scholars referred to above, have also assumed that the term *Ouasicouseton* translates from the Sioux as "Shooters among the Pines," [i.e. wazi or mazi = to shoot, and kute = pines], and applies to the Yankton Sioux band of Wazikute from whom the Assiniboine had earlier separated. But we know from Dakota Sioux tradition that the Wazikute were no longer in the Mississippi headwaters area in 1699, having moved south during the first half of the 1680s owing to constant Cree, Assiniboine and Chippewa attacks upon their villages. As a result, the Wazikute had first moved south to present-day Sauk Rapids adjacent to the Mississippi, then, around 1690, they moved southwest to the middle course of the Minnesota on that river`s north side.

If the term *Ouasicouseton* was meant to have been a variation of the name Wazikute, then what happened to the Masikota, who themselves were a large Cheyenne-speaking faction then residing in close proximity to several Sioux groups which are enumerated in detail by both Franquelin and LeSueur? It is most unlikely that the Masikota were not included on these last-named charts, rather they are noted by a name in varied form such as *Ouasicouseton* and confused as a Sioux group. This is especially likely, as a small remnant of Moiseo was still in the vicinity of the Upper Mississippi during the 1690s, while a small part of the Masikota was still around Big Stone Lake at the head of the Minnesota as late as circa, 1800, by which time that entire region had been overrun by Sioux.

It is true that the *Agatomitou* on Joliet`s chart of 1674 are not shown on later maps by that name, although this is explained by their being Suhtaio who, Cheyenne tradition asserts and which other late 17th century maps support, were still in northern Minnesota in the early 1700s north-east of the Mississippi heads and by1699, the *Agatomitou,* being at that time allies to both the Sioux and Chippewa, were designated by alternative names albeit of Sioux derivation rendered variously as *Nacion des Songaskiton* and alternatively as *Nacion des Chongaskiton.* Franquelin`s map of that year places a band known as *Shongatsquiton* between the Upper Mississippi and Lake Superior, and the term *Agatomitou* like the several variant spellings of *Chongaskiton* translates as `Dog People` or `Dog Village,` which were early names for the Suhtaio, not Sioux. One of the variant spellings of *Chongaskiton* as shown on a later map of the Upper Mississippi drafted by Daniel

Coxe in 1722, is *Shongashiton*, the suffix `hiton` here being a corruption of `hitan` which derives from the Suhtaio dialect specifically meaning `men` or `people,` so that the Daniel Coxe term in its etymology also translates as `Dog Men` or `Dog People. This same Coxe map shows the *Chongaskiton* on the east side of the Upper Mississippi and the *Shongashiton* on the west side, which is compatible with a statement made by the Cheyenne informant White-Bull to Truman Michelson early in the twentieth century, that originally there were several separate Suhtaio bands. LeSueur himself listed the *Songaiquitons* with the sub-heading *"Village of the Fort"* when designating bands which he included under the collective term, *"Sioux of the East."* In addition, when the Baron Lahontan listed a number of Siouan-speaking groups residing west of Lake Superior in 1688, he, too, included the *Songaskitons* of whom he said, *"...speak Algonquian."* [4]

Again in the 1726 *Dictionaire Universel Ancienne et Modernne,* we find the notation,

> *"Songatsquiton, Nation des hommes forts, l`une de celles des Sioux ou Issatis de L`Est, entre les lacs des Assinibouels, du Buade and les Montagnes qui separent tous les grands lacs."* [5]

The term `forts` in French means `strong.` So here the *Nation des hommes forts* translates as "Strong Men," while the latter part of the term Songatsquiton [i.e. *squiton*], is but an early variation on later-date names for the Suhtaio of *Squihitan and Staihitan* and its later-date Sioux equivalent of *Skutani.*

The Dakota Sioux group *Issatys* [i.e. Santee] noted in the Louis Hennepin data, are also shown on the Franquelin map of 1699, but under various headings of *Pinchaton, Psinchounaton* and *Isantiton.* Of these, Franquelin placed the first two names on the east side of the Upper Mississippi forks, in roughly the same location where the *Issatys* are positioned by Joliet and later by Duluth [1674 and 1679 respectively], but the third name *Isantiton,* Franquelin placed southwest of the Upper Mississippi just north of Minnesota River not far west from its Elbow Bend. This last named band, albeit by the variant name *Issatys,* Hennepin had also earlier located east of the Upper Mississippi, so by the time Franquelin`s 1699 map was drafted, they had already followed their Yankton cousins on the latter`s southwest migration.

Southwest of the *Isantiton* on Franquelin`s chart, is another Sioux group designated *Nacion des Tintons,* the same who Hennepin had earlier noted on the west side of the Upper Mississippi, but which Franquelin located around present-day Big Stone Lake at the head of the Minnesota, and the movement of both the Isantoton [i.e. Santee] and Tintons [i.e.Tetons] from the Upper Mississippi to Big Stone Lake, so we are told in Sioux tradition, had occurred more than a decade prior to 1700. The *Isantiton* then included that Dakota group later known as Saoni, which incorporated during the late historic period the Lakota Sioux bands of Hunkpapa, Two Kettle, Blackfoot, Sans-Arc and Miniconjou. The *Tintons* on the other hand, represent those Lakota groups later known as Oglala and Brule. This is important, as according to Sioux oral tradition, the Wazikute preceded the *Isantiton* south to the Minnesota River. We may conclude therefore, that

270

the Wazikute would have been a part of those Franquelin designated *Hinhancton,* which refers to the Yankton Sioux in general, and who Franquelin in 1699 correctly placed immediately north of the Elbow Bend of the Minnesota. The same position, in fact, where Sioux tradition locates both the Yankton and their Wazikute offshoots during the period between 1690 and 1700.

The Wahepeton Sioux who are said in tribal tradition to have vacated the area about the Upper Mississippi Forks around the same time as did the Wazikute, but as a separate body, are likewise noted by Franquelin who calls them *Ouacpeton.* He shows them still residing in the region of the Upper Mississippi, although by 1695 at the latest, they had actually relocated much further downstream just west of the Falls of St. Anthony above the mouth of the Minnesota.

On another map of the Upper Mississippi drafted by Connelli in 1688, and compiled mostly from Hennepin`s data, there is noted near a *"Lake du Buade ou des Issatis"* [present-day Mille Lacs], the *Oudebathon people du Gens de Riviere."* Just below these latter are noted the *Chongasketon* with the citation, *"Cest a dire Nation du chien ou du Loup."* While in a cartouche on the same chart it is noted,

> *"NADONESSION, grande Nation de 8000 sauvages... comprising the Issati, Nadouessans, Tinthonha, Oudebathon and Chongaskethons."* [6]

In other words, the *Chongaskethons,* due to the additional term of *Nation du chien* in the above extract, are recognized as being separate to the *Oudebathon,* but evidently, closely associated with them and other Sioux bands and hence, the trader Perrot`s statement in 1689 that, *"... the majority of Songaskitons dwell with the Menchoketon* [i.e. an Eastern Dakota Sioux group later a part of the Mdewankanton] *and with other Nadouessioux northeast of the Mississippi."* [7] The *Songaskithons* are, of course, synonymous with the Suhtaio, then known colloquially as "Dogs" and also as "Neutrals," being aligned to both the Eastern Sioux and Chippewa at that date.

At least one recent scholar has postulated that the *Oudebathons du Gens du Riviere* were Cheyennes, having assumed that the name is a variant rendition of the Cheyenne band name Watapio or Watapiu also known as "Eaters with the Sioux [i.e. the Sioux term `Watap` i.e.,`to eat` or `eaters,` and the Cheyenne suffix `io` or `iu,` meaning `men` or `people`]." However, the term *Oudebathon* is more likely derived from the Sioux word `wakpa` meaning `river,` along with the suffix `ton` denoting village, and hence the sub-heading given by LeSueur and others for this group of *Gens du Riviere.* Thus the Cheyenne band name Watapio has no connection with that of *Oudebathon,* although a remnant of the Moiseo Cheyenne-proper band did remain in the Mille Lacs region, and associated closely with several Eastern Sioux groups including the *Oudebathon* and *Mdewankanton* and inter-married among them, so that in later years this remnant of the original Moiseo was indeed, recognized as a hybrid band of Cheyenne and Sioux. It is also indicative that when at a much later date, the remnant of Moiseo did finally reunite with their long-estranged Cheyenne kindred on the west side of the Missouri, they chose to join the Watapio Cheyenne band, whose members by that time, also included a large admixture of Teton Sioux and Suhtaio.

As noted earlier, it was Pierre LeSueur, who having traded among the Sioux since 1679, and when in Montreal in 1690, gave Franquelin tribal positions of the Upper Mississippi region which Franquelin included on his 1699 chart, and at a later date, LeSueur also provided information to the cartographer DeIisle, who then incorporated such data on his own later-date map of 1702/'03.

However, although both Franquelin and DeIisle omitted the *Chaiena* from Joliet`s 1674 position and instead, under the name *Chaienaton*, placed them along the Long Prairie branch of the Mississippi`s Crow Wing Fork, from both tribal tradition and some archaeological evidence, it can be shown conclusively, that Cheyennes had already abandoned their positions near Crow Wing Fork some years prior to the drafting of the Franquelin and DeIisle charts.

That both Franquelin and DeIisle were a little out of date with their band locations, was not due to deliberate guess work on their part, for of all the late seventeenth century maps relating to the Upper Great Lakes and Upper Mississippi districts, the Franquelin and DeIisle charts are certainly the most lucid and detailed of all. There was, however, so much tribal movement during the time in question, and so little up to date authentic information to be had regarding tribal groups and bands of those regions, it was sometimes thought necessary to revert to earlier data in order to complete whatever map then under consideration.

In reality, Franquelin and DeIisle`s *Ouasicouseton* and *Chaienaton* are placed along a western tributary of the Upper Mississippi which enters the main stream near the present day town of Little Falls in central Minnesota, and is compatible with the region embracing Crow Wing Fork. Only a few miles southwest of this river are the Kettle Lakes close to the town of Glenwood [Minnesota], and hereabouts, fragments of pottery and human bones have since been excavated from a certain knoll which rises abruptly from one of the aforesaid Lakes and which Sioux tradition declares, was once the site of an old-time Cheyenne village.

Pottery shards discovered here match shards excavated from other old village sites, ostensibly once occupied by one or another Cheyenne-speaking group, and perhaps, this particular site rising out of the lake was occupied by either the *Ouasicouseton* or *Chaienaton,* albeit at a slightly later date than the mid-1680s. The small number of supposed house rings discovered so far, would suggest perishable bark or matted grass covered houses inhabited by a comparatively small group of people, or that the site actually represents a ceremonial center or even a cluster of earthen burial mounds, as no detailed examination has yet been undertaken. The site does nevertheless, indicate that the main body of those responsible, whatever the site's specific use, was likely residing elsewhere in the region, although the remains of their main seat of occupation have not to date been located.

More archaeological research is needed to verify actual positions of Cheyenne village sites in the Upper half of Minnesota, and one must remember that tribal locations as given on early colonial maps were meant only to be approximate, and as we have seen, were sometimes out of date by the time the maps were finally produced.

That the Glenwood site mentioned above is of Cheyenne origin, there can be little doubt, by the fact that the site has also yielded identical material and pottery fragments to those which can be positively identified as early Cheyenne ware from other sites further west overlooking the Missouri and that on the Lower bend of the Sheyenne tributary of the Red River of the North,. These sites to the west will be discussed in detail later in this study. They are relevant here as they suggest migration routes for those Cheyenne and Suhtaio groups once resident in the Mississippi headwaters country.

PORTION OF THE FRANQUELIN MAP OF THE UPPER MISSISSIPPI 1699.
[Courtesy of the Newbery Public Library, Chicago. U. S. A.]

Thus from the evidence at hand, the *Ouasioucseton* and *Chaienaton* were certainly synonymous with Cheyennes, and included both the Masikota [also known as Prairie Men and Grasshoppers] and the Omissis-Bowstring group respectively. It would seem from both Cheyenne and Dakota Sioux traditions that the *Chaienaton* [Bowstrings] had left the Mississippi headwaters country in the vicinity of Bowstring Lake no later than 1685, and moved southwest into the area now known as Kettle Lakes near the present-day town of Glenwood. Not long after this, the same group again pulled up stakes and moving west of the Red River of the North, entered the rolling grasslands of the Coteau des Prairies. Certainly a decade prior to the opening of the eighteenth century, according to both Cheyenne and Sioux traditions, they had built a permanent village of earth and timber lodges now known as the Biesterfeldt site, on the Lower Bend of Sheyenne River west of the Red River of the North.

Around the same time as the Bowstrings left the Upper Mississippi region [circa, 1685], the other Cheyenne-proper group of Masikota [Franquelin's *Quasicouseton*], abandoned their old habitat in the Little Falls district, and migrated due south to the Elbow Bend of the Minnesota on that river's south side. Later, around the date 1693, this same group migrated upriver to Big Stone Lake at the extreme head of the Minnesota, and at this point they divided, a large part of the Masikota which included the Sacred Arrows and their Keeper with the breakaway Kit-Fox faction from the parent Moiseo, moving west into the Coteau des Prairies, first to the head of Maple Creek near present-day Kulm and thence, further west, where the Kit-Fox element established themselves in a permanent earth-lodge village on the east side of the Missouri near what is now known as Long Lake.

The main Masikota group for its part, crossed the Missouri to its west bank and built a village overlooking the mouth of Porcupine Creek. A small remnant of Masikota like the remnant of Moiseo, likewise remained in the east and continued to occupy a semi-permanent village close to Big Stone Lake for a significant number of years. This Masikota remnant became closely associated with the Miniconjou Sioux and were later known by the Sioux term *Sheo*. But this belongs to a later chapter.

That none of the Franquelin or DeIisle maps show any tribal groups recognizable as Cheyenne or Suhtaio as resident along the course of the Minnesota River during the time their maps were drafted, adds substance to both Cheyenne and Sioux traditions, that the old Cheyenne occupants along the Minnesota had already moved west long prior to1699.

The reason for the earlier mass movement of Cheyennes from the Upper Mississippi region, had been due to a spate of nigh-constant hostile inroads from the Cree and Assiniboine; these being the dreaded Ho-Hay enemies of both Cheyenne and Suhtaio tradition.

It seems that after the Wazikute and Wahepeton Sioux bands vacated the Upper Mississippi for more favorable positions further south, all Cheyenne-speaking groups of that area, having earlier been protected somewhat by the presence of those same Sioux bands, suddenly found themselves exposed to the full brunt of aggression from the Cree and Assiniboine, and then stood alone in defending their hearth's against them.

The *Chaienaton* or Bowstrings were the first Cheyennes to move, they having been nearest the war-roads used by the Ho-Hay when resident in the Bowstring River and Bowstring Lake districts of the Upper Mississippi. Predominantly they belonged to the Omissis Cheyenne-speaking component, a part of whom much earlier, had already separated from them and moved south to the

Minnesota where they were known colloquially as Pipe-Stem-Men. Thus, from Joliet's positioning of his *Chaiena*, it might be reasoned that soon after 1674 [when Joliet's map was drafted], the Bowstrings had moved nearer their Teton Sioux allies and were soon followed by their Masikota cousins [Joliet's *Quisiloua*]. In the meantime, the remnant Moiseo under various name spellings of *Quissi, Ouissy* and *Quafis* and after the Kit-Fox element had separated from them, lingered in the northeast and remained in situ albeit intermittingly, between Lake Nipegon and the north shore of Lake Superior. Certainly as late as 1742, the Joseph LaFrance map drafted that year, shows the *Quassis* on the north side of the western tip of Lake Superior and thus, long after their Bowstring, Masikota and Moiseo Kit-Fox cousins had left the Minnesota country altogether in favor of the buffalo country west of the Red River of the North. By the mid-1740s this same Moiseo remnant were themselves at war with the Chippewa and Yankton Sioux who together, although not as allies, expelled the last of the Moiseo from their seat and forced them into the northwestern part of Minnesota. This Moiseo remnant then likewise crossed the Red River and re-joined their Moiseo Kit-Fox brethren on the Missouri, although thereafter, they continued to wander back and forth between the Missouri and the western peripheries of northern Minnesota.

Long before this, as previously mentioned, the Cheyenne-speaking group known as Pipe-Stem-Men had already vacated the Mississippi headwaters country, and which movement can be dated with a fair degree of accuracy.

It was in 1666 that the Assiniboine as an act of expediency, made their pact with the Cree, and four years later the Assiniboine themselves were in regular contact with English traders on Hudson's Bay, thereby acquiring all the coveted firearms needed to hold the advantage over their Minnesota foes. As a result of this Assiniboine - Cree alliance, coupled with Cheyennes then being confederated with the Teton and some other Sioux peoples of the region, all Cree groups excepting the Monsoni, suddenly also became fully embroiled in hostilities against Cheyennes wherever and whenever found. The Assiniboine and Cree then used a number of war-roads which from their own country in the north, led south into the marsh and lake districts of Minnesota where most Cheyenne bands resided, and if the routes of these war-roads can be determined, it should be possible to add substance to where Cheyenne villages were then located.

As earlier noted, the river along which Franquelin placed the *Chaienaton* appears to be that known today as Long Prairie, being a western branch of the Upper Mississippi's Crow Wing Fork. The right hand fork of this stretch of the Upper Mississippi above the Falls of St. Anthony, is designated on an earlier Franquelin map of 1688 as *Riviere des Assinibouels*, and is shown connected to a large expanse of water in north-western Minnesota known today as Lake of the Woods. This, though, is an error on Franquelin's part, for no river connects Lake of the Woods with the Upper Mississippi.

In truth, the right hand fork of the Upper Mississippi extends only as far as a point slightly northwest of Winnibigoshish Lake. However, not far north of this point are the headwaters of both the Big Fork and Little Fork southern tributaries of Rainy River, which latter stream flows west-northwest into Lake of the Woods.

So it would seem that unwittingly, Franquelin was actually referring to either the Big Fork or Little Fork when he designated the *Riviere des Assinibouels,* and this is substantiated by the DeIisle map of 1702/ `03 which shows a *Lac des Assenipoils* now known as Lake of the Woods, and a *Riviere des Assenipoils* marked as an eastern tributary of an unidentified river, but which flows into the southern shore of Lake of the Woods with its source near the head of the right hand Fork of the Upper Mississippi. Conversely, DeIisle`s *Riviere des Assenipoils* is shown emptying into the north-western shore of Lake Superior, and actually represents the chain of small intermittent lakes and streams now known as Long Lakes and Pigeon River between Lake Superior and Rainy Lake.

The Franquelin map of 1699 shows no such river or stretch of inter-connecting lakes compatible with DeIsle`s chain, but instead, supposes that the stream issuing north into Lake of the Woods [also called *Lac des Assinibouels* by Franquelin], connects with the Mississippi. This, however, as clearly seen on DeIsle`s map, really denotes either the Big Fork or Little Fork.

We also know that Lake of the Woods and north of that point, was held exclusively by the Assiniboine during the late seventeenth century, and therefore, Franquelin`s river of the same name indicates it being that tribe's path to enemy camps in the Upper Mississippi country. A well-travelled war-route, in fact, as indeed was the case with other chosen rivers employed specifically by war-parties of various Nations during their hostile ventures. Thus, the Red River of the North from Lake Winnipeg in Manitoba south to Lake Traverse in South Dakota, was constantly in use by both the Cree and Assiniboine and later, by the latter`s Chippewa allies. In turn, the St. Croix and Black River of eastern Upper Minnesota, along with the middle course of the Mississippi as far as Illinois River and further south, were likewise used as highways by Algonquian war-parties going against the Sioux, and by Sioux war-parties going against Algonquians. There were also well-defined canoe routes from Rainy Lake and Lake of the Woods which led to Bowstring Lake and from there, to Winnibigoshish Lake and thence to the Upper Mississippi itself.

By ascending the Little Fork stream, the Assiniboine would have reached the region embracing Bowstring Lake and Bowstring River, where, of course, the Bowstring Cheyenne group [Franquelin`s *Chaienaton*] then resided. On the other hand, by following the Big Fork and thence down the left hand branch of the Upper Mississippi, they would have found camps of Masikota [Franquelin`s *Ouasicouseton*], and it was for this reason that each of these Cheyenne-speaking groups suddenly found themselves in a very precarious position. Finally they deemed it prudent to remove their villages altogether from their enemy's line of attack, and thus retired towards the south and southwest.

Earlier scholars dealing with this period of French infiltration into the hinterland west of the Upper Great Lakes, have supposed that Franquelin`s *Lac des Assinibouels* refers to that known today as Lake Winnipeg in Manitoba, and further, that his *Riviere des Assinibouels* shown as connecting the lake of that name to the Upper Mississippi, refers to the Red River of the North. Both these assumptions are incorrect, and have led to countless misstatements by numerous historians and their ilk.

Until the early 1730s, the area now called Lake of the Woods was commonly known as *Lac des Assinibouels*, and on early maps is shown connected by a river designated *Riviere des Deux Lacs* to another lake called *Lac des Christinnaux,* but now known as Rainy Lake. The river in question connecting these two lakes is, without doubt, present-day Rainy River, the course of which flows west and is interspersed with numerous rapids and falls. Even so, by adhering to the old misconception, the *Lac des Assinibouels* is persistently associated by some scholars with that of Lake Winnipeg, and *Lac des Christenaux* with that of Lake of the Woods.

It can be seen on the Franquelin chart of 1699, that these two `Lacs` are connected by a river [designated as *Riviere des Deux Lacs*], whilst on the DeIsle map of 1702/`03, which has evidently been copied in part from Franquelin`s chart and updated, these same two *Lacs* and their connecting river are shown, but now with that river's intermittent falls and rapids marked in.

There are a number of reasons why these particular `Lacs` could not have applied originally to those of Lake Winnipeg and Lake of the Woods respectively. [1] That the *Riviere des deux Lacs* as shown on these maps, has only slight undulations as is the true course of Rainy River. [2] That the river shown as flowing north from Lake of the Woods and, supposedly, into Lake Winnipeg, traces a wide arc and is not snagged with numerous falls and rapids. [3] The fact that Lake Winnipeg and the Lower course of the Red River of the North were not known to French cartographers before 1733, when the explorer Du Sieur de LaVerendrye finally reached Lake Winnipeg`s eastern shore. The erroneous and sometimes fabulous information gathered by LaVerendrye from Indian sources prior to his personal discovery, corroborates this point.

In brief, when at Lake Nipigon in 1728, LaVerendrye was informed by a Cree Indian that a *Great Lake* lay towards the declining day, i.e., to the west; and poured its waters in three different directions; one outlet flowing north into Hudson's Bay; another southeast toward the Mississippi, and the last towards the west. LaVerendrye even produced an Indian map to corroborate his claim that the said river flowing west would lead to the much sought after *Western Sea*. This had long been thought as being the route across the Continent to the rich silk and spice markets of China and India. But this was not the case, and the *Great Lake* referred to by LaVerendrye`s Cree informant, was later found to be Lake of the Woods and its western outlet; a river which drains that lake southwest and then north into Lake Winnipeg.

Indeed, either of the two tributaries of Rainy River known as the Big Fork and Little Fork, actually represent that of the alleged river of LaVerendrye`s informant said to connect with the Mississippi, while any one of the Lake of the Woods several branches flowing north could, by employing the system of interlocking lakes, streams and portages, eventually lead one to Hudson's Bay. Again this could not apply to Lake Winnipeg, for of the three rivers purported to pour out from Lake Winnipeg, only that known today as Nelson River which flows northeast from that lake into Hudson`s Bay can be considered. The two other main rivers adjoining Lake Winnipeg actually pour into that lake; not out.

A detail which certainly would not have been misconstrued by LaVerendrye.

As early as 1692, the English on Hudson's Bay had at least some knowledge of Lake Winnipeg and its environs, owing to the perambulations of one Henry Kelsey, who accompanied a party of Assiniboine and Cree Indians during the latter`s wanderings throughout the previous year. Where exactly he and his Indian companions roamed, we cannot be sure, but from Kelsey's description, it was probably along the eastern shores of Lake Winnipeg and southwest of there in the open meadow lands and parks of southern Saskatchewan and, perhaps the northeastern part of North Dakota. Such would then place the Assiniboine in the country between Lake of the Woods and Lake Winnipeg, and would fit nicely with tribal tradition which affirms that the allied Assiniboine and Plains Cree evicted the Blackfoot tribes, along with the Arapahoe-Atsina and Hidatsa-Crow from the Lake Winnipeg district and south of there from the Devil`s Lake region of northeastern North Dakota around the date 1690.

Now we see on the Franquelin map of 1699 that a group designated as *Poulacs,* are clearly positioned to the west and northwest of his *Lac des Assinibouels*, and the term *Poualac* or *Les Pouls* as DeIsle calls them meaning, `warriors,` was a term adopted by the early Colonial French in order to designate specifically, the scattered bands of Assiniboine and, perhaps, the Plains Cree together. It was, no doubt, from English sources that French cartographers of the day heard of a Great Lake with a river issuing from it into Hudson's Bay. But the French before 1733 and the LaVerendrye visit, had supposed this lake to be Lake of the Woods - as yet unexplored - and thus they connected the said river to Lake of the Woods. This appears to have been the case, for this was also DeIsle`s contention on his map of 1702/ `03, on which he shows a river flowing from a *Lac des Assenipoils* [i.e. Lake of the Woods] northwards into Hudson's Bay.

On the aforementioned Franquelin map of 1699, a *Riviere des Assinbouels* is noted as flowing east and entering the north-western shore of Lake Superior. The actual source of this river was apparently then unknown, for Franquelin shows it starting abruptly somewhere between Lake Superior and the headwaters district of the Upper Mississippi. However, its entry into Lake Superior is shown by Franquelin as occurring at the same place where the chain of lakes and streams now known as Long Lakes connect with Lake Superior by way of present-day Pigeon River, and this is clearly shown on the later-date Bellin map of 1743. On an earlier Franquelin chart of 1688, there is shown yet another stream also called *Riviere des Assinibouels* connecting with his *Lac des Assinibouels* and the Upper Mississippi, and this has often been taken by earlier scholars to be consistent with the Red River of the North.

Obviously these two *Riveres des Assinibouels* as noted by Franquelin are not supposed to represent separate rivers with the same name; certainly not in so close proximity to one another, and so it must be concluded that a certain river, its exact course then unknown, was construed as adjoining the *Lac des Assinibouels* and used by that people as a route of travel which would, somewhere along its course, meet the second *Riviere des Assinibouels*, this being merely a continuation of the first so-named river before connecting with Lake Superior.

The chain of interconnecting lakes and rivulets between Rainy Lake and the western tip of Lake Superior was, in Franquelin`s day, the main highway for both Assiniboine and Plains Cree when visiting the fishing grounds and intertribal trading fairs at Sault St. Marie, and, of course, as a war-road to enemy camps.

The small fragments of additional information DeIsle managed to obtain by the time he compiled his chart of 1702/ `03, suggests that he was drawing near this same conclusion. For now he shows only one *Riviere des Assenipoils* connecting Lake Superior to a tributary running south-west from the *Lac des Assenipoils*, and which in this particular case can only be associated with Lake of the Woods.

Unlike Franquelin`s river shown in this same position, DeIsle`s *Riviere des Assenipoils* does not adjoin the Upper Mississippi; neither is it intended on DeIsle`s map to be Rainy River. This last named stream is noted separately by DeIsle with several of its numerous falls and rapids marked along its course, and is connected to Rainy Lake, or as DeIsle terms it, *Lac des Christinaux*.

As already noted, there is no such river issuing from Lake of the Woods and adjoining the Upper Mississippi, and it must therefore be accepted that it relates moreover, to either the Big Fork or Little Fork of Rainy River, which streams were also used as war-roads especially by the Assiniboine, and thus warranted the descriptive name *Riviere des Assenipoils* on Franquelin`s chart, and subsequently by DeIsle.

This is repeated by Bellin at a later date, even though he shows the canoe route of present-day Long Lakes connecting Lake Superior with Lake of the Woods as a separate course, and has it extended so as to connect with Lake Winnipeg. But as there was still no good reason to dismiss the earlier maps, Bellin merely included the existing mistakes with current, more up to date information.

The Bellin map of 1743 has at last got Lake of the Woods, Rainy River and Rainy Lake sorted out, along with their true connection to Lake Superior. But Bellin also shows above these features two lakes joined together by a *Riviere des Deux Lacs,* one of which is termed *Lac des Assinibouels,* the other, *Lac des Christinaux.* This last named `Lac` as on DeIsle`s 1702 chart, is actually shown as adjoined to Lake Nipigon [*Lake Alimibegon* on earlier maps] by a connecting river, and Bellin further shows a *Riviere Ou Petite Nord* issuing from his *Lac des Assinibouels* and entering *Lac des Bois* [Lake of the Woods]. He bisects the river called *"Petite Nord"* with an unnamed stream, purported as flowing northwest from Lake Superior, and which seems to correspond with DeIsle`s earlier *Riviere des Assenipoils.* More important, though, is that Bellin`s map now includes a *Lac Ouinnipeg,* shown as being west of *Lac des Assininboiels* and *Lac des Christenuax,* these two last-named lakes shown with the supposed inter-connecting river designated as *Riviere des Deux Lacs.*

By this we can see that the area north of Rainy River was, apparently, still unknown to French cartographers as late as 1743, even though Du Sieur de LaVerendrye had already reached Lake Winnipeg some years previously.

As early as 1666, Assiniboine and Cree contacts had given Father Allouez the impression that they lived near two large lakes to the north, and from this had originated the erroneous conception that there existed two great lakes in the area above Lake Nipigon, an error clearly shown on the DeIsle map of 1702. In truth, the Assiniboine and Cree had meant only that they resided around two large lakes to the northwest, i.e., about Lake of the Woods and Rainy Lake respectively. But the maps continued to show the two non-existent lakes above Lake Nipigon even after both Lake of the Woods and Rainy Lake were charted. It would appear that it was the practice of these early French map-makers to simply fit new information in with the old, rather than correct it.

The account of Father Allouez`s journey in 1666, implies that the Assiniboine then resided in a country northwest of Lake Superior, whilst a later narrative penned by Pierre Radisson, indicates that the Assiniboine and Cree who visited his trading post near the mouth of Hayes River on Hudson's Bay in 1668, came from the area between Lake of the Woods and above the western tip of Lake Superior, which in Joliet`s later topography [leaving much to be desired], is also probably intended to mean; northwest of Lake Superior.

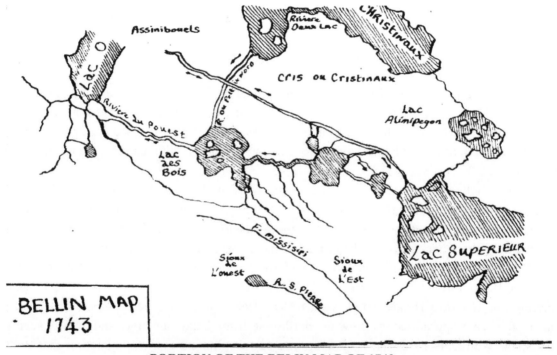

PORTION OF THE BELIN MAP OF 1743.
[Courtesy of the Newbery Public Library, Chicago. U. S. A.]

If both the Franquelin and DeIsle charts were in effect, meant to show present-day Lake Winnipeg as being the *Lac des Assinibouels*, then one must also accept that the Assiniboine Indians themselves resided north of that lake at such an early date. For the DeIsle map of 1702 notes that the country around the *Lac des Assinibouels* was then inhabited by *Les Pouls ou Assenipoils,* i.e. "warriors" or Assiniboine. This was an extremely cold and unproductive country, far too north for the hunting of buffalo, which pastime; so Assiniboine tradition tells us, always provided an important food source for their people. Such an assumption is also in opposition to historical,

280

traditional and even archaeological evidence, which does not place the Assiniboine permanently that far north during the period in question. Although at times, they did use both the Nelson and Hayes rivers as routes to and from the trading posts on Hudson's Bay.

It is not inconceivable that DeIsle merely lumped together, as it were, the intelligence he was obtaining concerning Lake Winnipeg, with that of Lake of the Woods and Rainy Lake, so as to make one great lake, and incorporated rivers from all three.

If, as some scholars believe, Franquelin's map of 1699 shows an important Cheyenne village which, we know, once stood on the Lower bend of Sheyenne River west of the Red River of the North, then it is nonetheless true, that he connected the aforesaid Red River with Lake of the Woods, rather than Lake Winnipeg, and into which last-named lake the waters of the Red actually flow from south to north.

The reason why these several maps became so confused is not hard to deduce, for after the Assiniboine and Cree began obtaining firearms in quantity from traders on Hudson's Bay, certainly by 1670, they began vigorously raiding other peoples to the west and northwest. These last included the Arapahoe - Atsina, Blackfoot and the Hidatsa – Crow and by 1690 / '95, the Cree and Assiniboine had encroached as far northwest as Lake Winnipeg. Plains Cree tradition remembers this, and asserts that their tribe drove the aforementioned resident tribes both south and west from the Lake Winnipeg area around that date.

When at last the French did reach Lake Winnipeg, which was not until the LaVerendrye visit of 1733, they found the Assiniboine and Plains Cree in control on both sides of that Lake, while other Cree bands were entrenched around Lake of the Woods, and the Chippewa then around Rainy Lake. It was only natural for the French to assume that both Lake Winnipeg and Lake of the Woods were the same as set down many years earlier by both Franquelin and DeIsle as *Lac des Assinibouels* and *Lac des Christinaux* respectively, not knowing that these latter tribes themselves, were comparatively recent arrivals into the Lake Winnipeg district.

Now we know from Sioux accounts concerning their people's own migrations and from fragments of documented evidence, that the Yankton Sioux and their immediate offshoots, abandoned the Mississippi headwaters and Upper and Lower Red Lakes region between 1685 and 1690, owing to hostile pressure from the Assiniboine, some Chippewa bands and the Cree. Thereafter, the Yankton retreated in a south and south-westerly direction to a point just north of the Elbow Bend of the Minnesota, and here the French trader LeSueur noted them residing in 1695.

The Cheyennes declare that they themselves were then also being raided by fierce enemies armed with guns, and that they fled south and southwest as a consequence to the middle course of the Minnesota River, leap-frogging the retreating Sioux groups in the process. The Cheyenne arrival along the Minnesota must then, pre-date the arrival of the Teton, and Santee.

The *Chaiena* of Joliet as we have seen were the same as the *Chaienaton* of Franquelin who on his map of 1699, are seemingly positioned near the Crow Wing Fork. This being so, then Joliet's name *Chaiena* must earlier have been applied to both the Masikota and Bowstrings Cheyenne groups without distinction, but who, by the time Franquelin's chart of 1699 was drafted, had already separated into two groups and had vacated the headwaters country; the Bowstrings in favor of the Glenwood district to the southwest, while perhaps even prior to the mid-1680s, the Masikota had established themselves near the mouth of Blue Earth River which enters the Minnesota on its south side where the town of Mankato now stands.

This being said, whatever the positions of Cheyenne-speaking groups whilst in the northern half of Minnesota, we can be certain that by 1685, having been constantly harassed by Assiniboine and Plains Cree, they first relocated in the marshland and tall-grass prairie country west of the Upper Mississippi Forks and from there, moved south as far as Minnesota River on its south side. Not long prior to the opening of the eighteenth century, they had been pushed by the same gun-toting enemies and some Central Algonquian tribes, to positions even further west beyond the Red River of the North and into the Coteau country of eastern North Dakota.

Before this, however, the previously mentioned Pipe-Stem-Men breakaways from the Omissis Bowstrings group, had already moved south to the Minnesota. Their lifestyle and relationships with neighbouring tribes were thus distinct to their more northern Masikota, Moiseo and Bowstrings kinfolk, and now warrant our attention.

- 0 - 0 - 0 - 0 - 0 - 0 - 0 - 0 - 0 - 0 - 0 - 0 - 0 - 0 - 0 - 0 - 0 -

CHAPTER 26.

IN THE LAND OF BLUE EARTH.

While Cheyenne and Suhtaio bands about the headwaters of the Mississippi had been associating with Teton Sioux of that region, and defending themselves against attacks from the Cree and Assiniboine, the Pipe-Stem-Men Cheyennes adjacent to the Minnesota River farther south, were themselves associating with other Siouan-speaking peoples such as the Iowa, Oto and Omaha, but who were enemies of the Tetons.

Numerous scholars have previously suggested that the first Cheyenne settlement on or close to the Minnesota, was either on the shore of Lake Mini-Tonka not far west from the mouth of the Minnesota; the Mini Ha-Ha Falls or near the mouth of the St. Croix River on the east side of the Mississippi, and even about the Falls of St. Anthony near where the twin cities of St. Paul and Minneapolis now stand.

The map drafted by Daniel Coxe in 1722, but showing tribal positions as they were between 1680 and 1700, shows two Suhtaio groups, i.e. the *Songashitons* in two villages on the west side of the Upper Mississippi, and the *Congaskiton* in four villages on that river`s east side. Importantly,

DANIEL COXE`S A MAP OF THE UPPER MISSISSIPPI COUNTRY, 1722.
[Courtesy of the Newbery Public Library, Chicago. U. S. A.]

Coxe also shows the *Schahas* along a stream north of another tributary designated *River des Tortoise,* which flows into the Upper Mississippi from the northeast. The name *River of Tortoise* was an early term for the tributary known today as St. Croix, and the term *Schahas* may be a variant form of *Shahiena* applied by the Sioux to Cheyenne-speaking groups. However, as late as the sixteen-nineties there were still Siouan-speaking Iowa and Oto bands located very near the mouth of the Minnesota not far south of the St. Croix, and Coxe`s term *Schahas,* more probably, derives from the Iowa and Oto name for the Cheyenne of *Shaha.*

In addition, the stream along which Coxe actually placed the *Schahas* represents present-day Rum River [known as St. Francis on early maps] and not the St. Croix. Coxe himself was not personally acquainted with the Upper Mississippi region or its peoples, and used information gleaned from the writings of both Hennepin and LaHontan and from data recorded by the Chevalier Du LaSalle, who had met Cheyennes at his post on the Illinois River in 1680.

It is true that any of the early colonial maps on their own, might be taken as giving credence to, or discrediting a point either way as one chooses, yet when analyzed and compared with other contemporary data, the location of tribes and tribal bands so designated, can really only be taken one way. Thus we find on the Raffix map drafted in 1692, Dakota Sioux bands are shown as being in complete control along both sides of the Upper Mississippi, both north and south of the mouth of the St. Croix and along the length of that river itself.

The *Schahas* as noted by Coxe could not have referred to either of Franquelin's two Cheyenne-proper groups of *Chaienaton* and *Quisicouseton* during the period 1680-1699, as these were then much further to the southwest high up the Minnesota and on the far side of Red River in the Coteau des Prairies of eastern North Dakota. It is more likely that the *Schahas* represent the remnant of Moiseo, or Mowiseyu as the informant George Bent always called them, after the Kit-Fox element had separated from them and joined the Masikota who Franquelin designated as *Quisicouseton*. Indeed, Cheyenne tradition declares that after the Kit-Fox element joined the Masikota, the Kit-Fox band became known as the Aorta, while the remnant of Moiseo; we have seen, lingered in the northeast before eventually reuniting with other Cheyennes along the west bank of the Missouri more than one-hundred years later.

Joliet's *Quisiloua* and *Chaiena* respectively had, earlier, resided in the Upper Mississippi region on that river's east side above the Falls of St. Anthony which includes the area embracing the St. Croix. They had, though, certainly left that region completely many years prior to Coxe's positioning of the *Schahas,* and at least eighteen years before the drafting of Franquelin's map of 1699.

During the spring of 1681 Duluth had sailed the length of the St. Croix to its mouth on the Mississippi, and did not mention any people who can be identified as a Cheyenne-proper group. Duluth did note the *Songaskitons,* but they were Suhtaio, not Cheyenne-proper.

It is indicative that of the great mass of archaeological remains since found in the Falls of St. Anthony, Mini Ha-Ha Falls, Lake Mini-Tonka and St. Croix districts, they suggest only Siouan occupation, and the profusion of effigy and linear burial mounds in the same region, in contrast to the Cheyenne type which are predominately round, infers that Siouan-speaking peoples had held those lands at least two-hundred years prior to archaeological study in the mid-nineteenth century. Likewise, both Hennepin and LaHontan, each of whom had knowledge of the Upper Mississippi country and its eastern tributaries during the 1680s when Cheyennes are alleged to have inhabited that vicinity, made no mention of Cheyenne-proper peoples by any discernible name as residing along the St. Croix or about the mouth of the Minnesota. On the contrary, tribal groups as noted by Hennepin and LaHontan by such names as *Nacion Du Chien* and *Songaskiton* [*Chongaskiton*] apply to the Suhtaio specifically, and are placed much further north and northeast of the St. Croix during that period.

Sioux traditions which are usually quite precise on such points, do not mention any large Cheyenne-proper group as ever residing permanently about the Falls of St. Anthony, Lake Mini Tonka or along the St. Croix, and further declare that they themselves [Sioux] were entrenched in those regions at least as early if not before 1634 when the Jesuit Priest Father Jean Nicolet met them at the western tip of Green Bay. These Sioux accounts are explicit in placing Cheyennes during the period 1680-1690 in several locations high up the Minnesota adjacent to the mouth of Blue Earth River and on the Yellow Medicine further west. This is not to say that Cheyenne-proper groups were not familiar with the St. Croix and other Upper Mississippi regions. Quite likely they passed through each of the aforementioned areas during periodic hunting, war and trading excursions. But it cannot be construed from this alone that with the exception of the small Moiseo remnant and the *Shonaskitons* [Suhtaio], any large Cheyenne-proper band ever held a *permanent* seat in either location when no corroborating evidence is extant, and such an assumption flies in the face of tribal tradition itself. Indeed, the later-day assertions by Cheyenne informants of both Grinnell and Mooney that their people once resided in the St. Croix region, only really applies to the small remnant band of Moiseo and the Suhtaio, and not to the larger Cheyenne groups of Masikota and Omissis. Now it is known that in 1680, a party of Cheyenne-speaking people visited LaSalle`s trading post Fort Crevecoeur on the Illinois River east of the Mississippi. LaSalle reported in February that year,

> *"D`autres, appeles Chaa, qui demeurent au haut de la Grand riviere arrivereant le*
> *24 Fevrier et nous inviterent a allrr chez eux, ou ils dissent avoir une grand quantite*
> *de castors et de pelletenes, et ester voisens de la mer de L`ouest."* [1]

The name *Chaa* in the above passage, is not said to have been the term by which the Indian visitors called themselves, but implies a foreign appellation dubbed upon them by others. The name, in fact, appears to be LaSalle`s rendering of the Siouan term *Shaha* as used by the Iowa, Oto and others to designate Cheyennes specifically. It is indicative that a party of *Matoutenas,* who can be positively identified as an Oto group, had arrived at the same post only seven days earlier, and it was probably from the Oto that LaSalle obtained the name which he rendered as *Chaa*. Certainly, both the Iowa and Oto and one or more Cheyenne group were allied at that date, and one suspects it had been the Oto who would have carried word to the Cheyennes of LaSalle`s invitation to visit his post in the first place.

When we learn that LaSalle`s post on the Illinois was only operated seasonally, it adds substance to the idea that Cheyennes visitors were in the vicinity for only a short time. This would be compatible with the short occupation period of a so-called Oneota archaeological site, since discovered in the Lake Pepin area on the Mississippi just south from the mouth of the Minnesota, and attributed to either the Iowa or Oto, but shows over-riding Algonquian connections in its inventory as would be compatible with the latter`s Cheyenne allies

The *Chaa* were also said by LaSalle to `dwell at the top of the Grande Riviere` which, no doubt, refers to the Mississippi, generally known to all surrounding tribes as `Big River.` However, this position did not include all Cheyenne-speaking bands, for LaSalle additionally stated that the *Chaa* came from somewhere further west by the phrase, *"et estre voisins de la Mer L`Ouest,"* i.e., *"...it is near the Sea of the West."* [2]

Albeit that the supposed existence of a nearby "Western Sea," providing access to the trading marts of Asia from the eastern part of North America was a fantasy, the idea was fully adopted by the Colonial powers of the day, and elaborated upon by Indian reports of a great watery expanse somewhere west of the Upper Great Lakes. Such claims, it was later learned, were spurious and had merely been references to the Great Salt Lake of Utah, the Gulf of Mexico or to Lake Winnipeg in the far north. Nevertheless, during the seventeenth and most of the eighteenth century such a sea was believed a reality, and in later years the term "Sea of the West" was still used by the French as a metaphor to designate all the country west of the Great Lakes and Upper Mississippi regions. It is unlikely that the *Chaa* who visited LaSalle were referring to any watery expanse of the Upper Mississippi country such as Mille Lacs, as LaSalle himself would already have had some knowledge of that region, and this reasoning must also apply to Lake Winnipeg to the northwest and also to Lake Mini Tonka and Leech Lake not far west of the Mississippi. More feasible in the light of traditional places of habitat for Cheyennes during the 1680s, is the expanse now known as Swan Lake in Nicollet County close to the Great Bend of the Minnesota. This is not a great a distance from the mouth of Blue Earth River on the south side of the Minnesota and where, so several tribal traditions state, Cheyennes once resided during the same period close to the Iowa and Oto.

This is not to doubt that members of a Cheyenne-proper or Suhtaio band from the higher reaches of the Mississippi were the *Chaa* referred to by LaSalle, as indeed, we are told in Cheyenne tradition that some of their people did visit several posts in the Upper Mississippi region during the early period of French infiltration west of Lake Superior.

These other early French posts would have included that of Nicholas Perrot's first trading establishment which he built in 1685 on the west shore of Lake Pepin. This he named Fort Antoine, although the single roomed cabin and crude picket fence of which it was composed hardly warranted the description of a fort, and was in use only until 1687 when finally abandoned. Perrot, though, did not mention Cheyennes by any recognizable name in any of his several reports, although he was visited by and made personal visits to a number of tribes in alliance with them, and when among the Iowa and Oto the previous year of 1686, Perrot had asked the latter to bring their furs and pelts to his fort the following spring. Cheyennes, then, probably went to the same post with their Oto allies from whom they had received word of the Frenchman's request.

Moreover, when in Montreal in late 1687, it was Perrot who gave Franquelin up to date information regarding tribal positions in the Upper Mississippi region, and which the cartographer then incorporated into his maps of 1688 and 1699. However, Franquelin did not include Cheyenne-proper groups by any discernable name in the St. Croix region on any of his charts, which suggests that no large Cheyenne-proper group was, during those years, permanently resident in that area. He did place the *Shongaskitons* [i.e. Suhtaio] on the east side of the Upper Mississippi which embraces the St. Croix region, and we must not forget Cheyenne tradition which pertains to the Suhtaio Chief White-Dirt [See Chapter. 22.], in which it is mentioned that White Dirt's band of Suhtaio did for a while, reside on an island in the Upper Mississippi.

In late 1688 or early `89 after his return from Montreal, Perrot built a second post on Lake Pepin also named Fort Antoine, but located on the east shore a little above his abandoned first post on the west side. We also know that a part of the Iowa and Oto were then in residence on the Mississippi`s west bank near the mouth of the Minnesota, and were trading guns obtained from Perrot to their relatives the Omaha and to other Iowa groups further west than themselves. Thus, most likely, they were also trading such items to those Cheyenne-speaking groups then in alliance with them. Certainly Omaha tradition places Cheyenne-speaking bands high up the Minnesota and along one of its connecting streams between 1660 and 1690, while the Cheyennes themselves declare, that some of their people did visit one and another French post during the same period both west and east of the Mississippi, and add that those Cheyenne visitors hailed not from the Mississippi headwaters, but from some point along the Upper course of the Minnesota. Conceivably then, only those Cheyennes from high up the Mississippi were those referred to by Coxe, and were known by the names *Shahas* and *Songaskiton* or variants of the same, while the term *Chaa* on the other hand*,* was used by LaSalle and the Omaha, Iowa and Oto, to designate not only the Moiseo and Suhtaio, but also those Cheyennes along the Minnesota.

There appears to be corroboration regarding this point, in the guise of notations on several early maps made in relation to the Joliet and Marquette expedition of 1673. These maps show two tribal groups designated *Kamissi* [also spelt *Kamasi*] and *Chaa* [also spelt *Chaha*], adjacent to each other west of the Mississippi, apparently along the middle course of either the Des Moines or on the Missouri`s east side. The name *Chaa*, of course, is compatible with the term *Chaa* as recorded by LaSalle and thus might also have referred to Cheyennes. The name *Kamissi* may have been another name for either the Omaha, Oto or Iowa who, during the 1670s, were positioned not far east of the Missouri on the Big Sioux, Little Sioux and near the Des Moines River in that order. However, the name could just as well have designated the Pipe-Stem Men breakaways from the Cheyenne Omissis parent group, as the names *Kamissi* and *Omissis* are very similar if not dialectical variations of the same and, as noted above, by the 1670s Cheyennes were then close allies and confederates to each of the aforementioned Siouan-speaking groups. They may even have been one of the original four bands of Suhtaio which, according to a Suhtaio informant of Michellson in 1913, *"drifted down the Missouri and were never heard of again."* [3]

All being said, those who probably visited Perrot would have been Cheyennes from villages near the mouth of the Blue Earth and on the Yellow Medicine [this last being a tributary flowing north into the Minnesota upstream from the Great Bend], while the *Chaa* who earlier had visited LaSalle on the Illinois, had likely also come from the Blue Earth and Yellow Medicine regions, but albeit perhaps, including Moiseo [Quisiloua] from high up the Mississippi, and who then collectively, were designated by the Oto, Iowa and Omaha as belonging to the same tribal stock which they knew as the *Shaha*. Of course, if Cheyennes did visit one or the other of Perrot`s posts, then we have the answer as to why and how the previously mentioned so-called Oneota site - which indicates serial short-term occupation with over-ridding Algonquian traits - occurs on the

Lake Pepin shore, for this would represent a Cheyenne-proper group in league with the Oto and Iowa, who's pottery type is included in the site's predominant Algonquian inventory.

The Cheyenne-proper group which visited LaSalle would not have given the site of a temporary village on Lake Pepin as their permanent home, and LaSalle's report that the Oto lived 100 leagues [300 miles] from Fort Crevcouer, is compatible with the traditional place of residence for the Oto at that period on the Upper course of the Des Moines west of the Mississippi, and who were then in alliance with Cheyennes along the middle course of the Minnesota. We know also from LaSalle's earlier writings, that the Oto had been visiting his Illinois post since 1679.

Thus the nearest and largest Cheyenne group to visit LaSalle's Fort Crevcouer, would have been the Masikota from the mouth of the Blue Earth who were then in close contact with the Oto, Iowa and Omaha and with one or more friendly Algonquian tribe whose hunting grounds did at that time, possess abundant stocks of beaver. The country adjacent to the Yellow Medicine on the other hand, was predominantly open prairie land, not recognized as a particularly rich area for fur-bearing animals, and certainly prior to the middle years of the1680s, Cheyenne-proper peoples were still involved in some kind of economic relationship with both the Illini and Menominee east of the Mississippi. So, no doubt, Cheyennes were familiar with the Mississippi and its environs for some distance along its course, and must have been acquainted one way or another with the posts of both LaSalle and Perrot. Indeed, at a much later date whilst roaming the Western Plains of South Dakota, according to the fur-trader Charles Mackenzie in 1806, Cheyennes were still traveling a great distance east in order to trade with their old-time friends the Illini and the latter's confederated tribes, then still in residence along the Mississippi.

It was not until Father Louis Hennepin and his rescuer Greyson Duluth returned to civilization from the Upper Mississippi country in 1682, that the existence of the Minnesota river was made known, and LaSalle, therefore, had likely assumed that the place of habitat of the *Chaa* about the higher reaches of the Mississippi, was the region where all Cheyenne peoples resided, not knowing that other Cheyenne groups also known as *Chaa* to the Iowa and Oto, were then resident adjacent to the middle and Upper course of the Minnesota.

By 1688 the Mississippi region embracing Lake Pepin, had become too dangerous for the Minnesota River Cheyennes and their Oto allies to enter. As by then they were at war with certain Algonquians east of the Mississippi including the Fox, Sauk and Kickapoo, who being better supplied with firearms, soon became the terror of the Western Tribes. Because of this, it would have been to the first of Perrot's forts that Cheyennes went to trade, before the outbreak of the aforementioned hostilities.

At a slightly later date than the existence of LaSalle and Perrot's Forts, the Iowa on the west side of the Mississippi also became the victims of attack from Eastern Algonquians and, eventually in 1690, they were evicted from their seats and driven further west. Even the Masikota Cheyennes in residence near the mouth of the Blue Earth who had usually been friends with most Eastern Algonquians, found it prudent to retire to and beyond the headwaters of the Minnesota and build new villages, so by the time Fancquelin completed his map in 1699, Cheyennes had already left the Blue Earth area. Earlier, in 1695, the trader LeSueur had arrived at the mouth of that same river, and was told by the Sioux that a part of the Iowa had joined the Omaha and Oto on the Missouri, and that the country of what is now western Minnesota including Big Stone Lake and the Pipestone Quarries, then belonged to the Teton and Yankton Sioux. LeSueur even called the newly arrived Yankton "Red-Rock Indians," because of their new habitat in the area of the aforesaid quarries. The conclusion must be that although Cheyennes did most likely visit the LaSalle and Perrot trading posts on Illinois River and Lake Pepin, no *permanent* settlements by the larger and more important Cheyenne groups of Masikota and Omissis were extant for any extensive period in the Falls of St. Anthony, Lake Mini-Tonka, Mini Ha-Ha Falls or St. Croix regions. Rather, Coxe`s *Schahas* refer to the remnant of Moiseo which, according to their own traditions, still resided near a *River of Turtles* as they knew it in the Upper Mississippi country, and were then close to the Suhtaio who are also noted on the Coxe map as residing in several small villages both east and west of the Upper Mississippi under the names *Chongastons* and *Songashiton.* In effect, this remnant Moiseo band being a part of the original Cheyenne-proper nucleus also known as *Quissy,* became so closely associated with the Sioux of that district, that not only did they speak Sioux as a second language and inter-marry freely, but were regarded as a proper Sioux group by some later-day informants among the Cheyennes themselves.

Of those Cheyenne villages in the vicinity of the middle course of the Minnesota, one position occupied for a prolonged period of which we have definite corroboration, was that near the present-day town of Mankato. This is probably the closest large and *permanent* Cheyenne village site to any of the above mentioned locations in the St. Croix area during the 1680s which can be accepted.

Traditionally, as related by the Cheyennes themselves, after vacating the lake and marsh districts of the north, a part of their people moved south until they came to *"...a clear blue water flowing through a country where the soil was composed of blue-coloured earth."* [4]

Now the actual name Minnesota is of Sioux derivation; a compound term literally meaning *"smokey-coloured water,"* and was applied by the Sioux specifically to the Minnesota River because of its exceptional smokey-blue appearance. The region about that river's Elbow Bend is noted for its blue and green clay deposits and hence, the tributary name of Blue Earth River at that point, although LeSueur originally referred to it as *"Riviere de Remy."*

During the early days of French penetration into the area, this earth was thought to be rich in copper ore and in 1695, LeSueur went so far as to build a small trading post at the mouth of the Blue Earth and mined two tonnes of clay which, after being transported to France incurring much cost and difficulty, was found to be worthless. On several old maps one can see the notation *Mines des cuivre* and *Fort de vert,* these being the sites of LeSueur`s old diggings and trading post near the mouth of the aforesaid river. The *"Blue Earth Country"* therefore, as mentioned in Cheyenne tradition, is undoubtedly, synonymous with that part of the course of the Minnesota in the Blue Earth River district, and this is further corroborated by other tribal traditions, each of which place Cheyenne-speaking groups in various positions along the middle course of the Minnesota both on its south and north side. Another Cheyenne village, it is said, stood slightly further west on a height overlooking the Yellow Medicine near its confluence with the Minnesota on that river`s south side.

Additionally, we are further informed by the Sioux that there were several Cheyenne groups along the Minnesota, and as late as the middle years of the nineteenth century, Sioux Indians pointed out to Dr. Williams and Riggs village sites once occupied by Cheyennes, including that near the mouth of the Blue Earth where, as late as 1871, could be seen a number of earthen mounds said by the Sioux to have been constructed by Cheyennes, along with the remains of cultivated fields which, the Sioux added, were where those old-time Cheyennes had raised their crops. [5]

There are, in fact, at least five identifiable sites relating to Cheyenne occupation along and adjacent to the Minnesota. These sites were not occupied successively by one band, neither necessarily, were they occupied concurrently. Although it will become apparent throughout the course of our study that the Cheyenne-speaking group about the Elbow Bend was divided in two factions, one of which remained in the latter district, the other moving upstream between Granite Falls and Lac Qui Parl closer to the head of the Minnesota. We are also told in Cheyenne, Sioux, Omaha and Iowa traditions, that lands bordering the south side of the Minnesota between Lac Qui Parl and Blue Earth River were, during the mid-seventeenth century, Cheyenne farming grounds.

Here then, we have corroboration that during their period of migration prior to entering the Great Plains west of the Missouri, the Cheyennes did not act as one body. For while the Joliet and Franquelin maps clearly show Cheyenne-speaking groups about the Upper reaches of the Mississippi during the period 1670 to 1699, reliable Omaha, Iowa, Oto and Dakota Sioux traditions locate several Cheyenne villages at that same time much further south, along and near the Minnesota close to its Elbow Bend and further west. In order, however, to ascertain more precise locations for our subjects; calculate periods of settlement at various points, and associate each site with a particular Cheyenne-speaking group, we must consult the archaeological record.

- 0 - 0 - 0 - 0 - 0 - 0 - 0 - 0 - 0 - 0 - 0 - 0 - 0 - 0 - 0 - 0 - 0 -

CHAPTER 27.

OF POTS AND SHERDS AND EARTHENWARE

Among the numerous archaeological "types" found in the southern half of Minnesota south of the river of that name, that termed Oneota is definitely Siouan in origin and can be associated with the ancestral Iowa, Oto and Omaha. Its artefact affiliations and style of ceramics have turned up in known historic Iowa and Oto sites found in northwestern Iowa, southern Minnesota and northeastern Nebraska, this last being a well-documented Omaha village site of the late eighteenth century. In archaeological jargon Oneota is of Late Woodland culture which, in effect, covers the period between circa, AD.1000 and AD. 1700. In its later phase [1640-1700], Oneota shows it to have been a progressive type of the earlier Aztalan culture of south-western Wisconsin and central Ohio, of which the Great Effigy Mounds are prominent features.

Near and along the Minnesota River, we find what archaeologists regard as several variants of Oneota, some of which, however, contain enough variation - especially in pottery styles - to warrant an independent classification with an occupancy period of between circa 1550 and 1700. These variations include an even earlier type known as Cambrian ware, which, I believe, relates specifically to ancestral Hidatsa-Crow peoples, who also were of Siouan stock once closely associated with the Iowa and Oto and during the middle of the 17th century resided in central Minnesota. It is also apparent by a comparison of pottery styles, that Cheyenne-speaking groups were later-day residents of one or more of the same Cambrian and so-called Oneota sites which suggest serial occupancy, albeit separated from Cambrian by significant periods in time. Be this as it may, all known Oneota sites both adjacent to and north of the Minnesota River have been attributed to either Iowa, Oto or Omaha groups, merely, it would seem, by the fact that these three tribes were long residents in the southern part of Minnesota, notwithstanding that a number of these sites occur along the Minnesota River about fifteen miles west of Mankato, and others in the neighbouring vicinity at the mouth of Blue Earth River. These last-mentioned sites fit the general location of Cheyenne groups during the period 1650-1700 as given in various tribal traditions and by the Cheyennes themselves, and what is more important, yet another so-called Oneota site is to be found higher up the Minnesota on that river's north side at Granite Falls, where Cheyennes are also located in tradition, but where no Iowa, Oto or Omaha group resided.

There is in addition a so-called Oneota site on the Mississippi at the southern outlet of Lake Pepin, which as noted in the previous chapter, indicates serial occupation for short durations and which likely, should also be associated with Cheyennes. Village sites in eastern South Dakota, specifically those of the Biesterfeldt village on the Lower bend of Sheyenne River west of Red River and that near the present day town of Kulm at the head of Maple Creek even further west, have also yielded so-called Oneota pottery, but are certainly connected with Cheyenne occupation during the first half of the eighteenth century.

The interesting thing about the last-named so-called Oneota sites, is that an overriding abundance of Algonquian woodland artefacts are included in their inventories, along with a fair amount of pottery shards which show clear Upper Mississippi traits, particularly of the so-called Black Duck focus of the Upper and Lower Red Lakes region. They also include other traits which are practically identical with those from the earlier Mille Lacs focus of the Upper Mississippi Forks, which generally come under the collective heading of *Psinomani* or Sandy Lake ware. Sandy Lake ware is predominantly of Assiniboine origin, mixed with that of an Algonquian type known as *Selkirk* which is attributed to the Cree. Some regions, however, where Mille Lacs and Sandy Lake ware are found, are also compatible with where the Cheyenne-speaking groups of Masikota, Moiseo, Bowstrings and Suhtaio were once located during the late Oneota and late Sandy Lake periods of between circa, 1550 and 1700. Thus, ancestral Cheyenne elements should likely be included regarding those sites with predominant Algonquian archaeological connections. No

Omaha, Iowa or Oto Siouan group ever occupied territory so far north, and the findings at these sites cannot be satisfactorily associated with the Teton or Yankton Sioux, or even with the Mdewankanton and other Eastern Sioux groups, whose pottery types are distinct again.

Several Iowa, Oto and Omaha sites have been determined in recent years southwest from the mouth of the Minnesota, and are grouped together under a polyglot of headings according to their location such as Orr, Silvernail and Blue Earth. Each of these are merely variants of Oneota-proper and none show enough Algonquian traits or artefacts, if indeed any, to enable them to be seriously considered as variants of the more northern so-called Oneota site inventories adjacent to and north of the Minnesota River which *do* show over-riding Algonquian traits. Even so, these northern sites, too, have consistently been associated with the Iowa, Oto and Omaha, even though no corroboratory evidence has been forthcoming.

Obviously, these more northern so-called Oneota sites were Algonquian with a strong influence of Dehighian [Iowa and Oto] Siouan, and to a much less degree, Chiwere [Omaha, Kansa and Missouri] Siouan styles. This would be consistent with what we know concerning those Cheyenne groups then residing along and adjacent to the Minnesota. In so much as they were then allied to and in close social contact with Oneota-proper peoples, such as the Omaha, Iowa and Oto.

It has been noted previously that one or another group of Cheyenne-speaking peoples visited LaSalle`s Fort Crevecoeur, and also, one or both of Perrot`s trading posts on Lake Pepin at various times during the sixteen-eighties, probably in the company of Oto or Iowa allies. These events would easily account for the remains of the serially occupied so-called Oneota site on Lake Pepin, and be consistent with the short length of stay of LaSalle`s and Perrot`s Cheyenne visitors, albeit at different periods in time.

At the present date, there is only one old Cheyenne village site east of the Missouri which can definitely be associated with our Cheyenne-proper subjects by contemporary documented evidence. This village known as the Biesterfeldt site once stood on a bluff overlooking the southern bend of the Lower Sheyenne River in the south-eastern part of what is now North Dakota, and is only a few miles from the present-day town of Lisbon. This site was extensively excavated in the summer of 1908 and again in 1968, and ceramics from which offer abundant examples of Cheyenne pottery. Thus it is easy to discern profound similarities between potsherds from this Sheyenne River site located west of the Red River of the North, with those from certain so-called Oneota sites along the Minnesota and with one and another so-called Sandy Lake site in more northern locations. Some aspects of style and manufacture are not only identical, but unique to these latter sites alone.

Unfortunately, no complete pots of Cheyenne manufacture have yet come to light from the Sheyenne River site, but from the three-thousand or more fragments unearthed, the original size, shape and peculiarities of Cheyenne pottery can be defined.

As a rule, Cheyenne ware is of a light buff colour, although tans, grey-black mottle and plain black occur in some quantity. Of the two-hundred and ninety-five shards examined apparently all from cooking utensils, the inner surfaces show the use of red `hematite` slips. Virtually all ceramics from this site are also grit tempered with either quartz or granite particles, ranging from very fine to coarse, and are unlike most Siouan ware, which is characteristically shell tempered.

Almost fifty-percent of Cheyenne pottery fragments have a heavily charred interior, indicating their use as cooking receptacles, while in shape, the most common is that of a Globular design, only one flat basal fragment having been found to date. The smaller pot samples have angular shoulders [as is the case of most Oneota ware]; triangular strap handles and horizontal Lugs. Decoration is varied, although the great majority show vertical Grass wiping of the neck and horizontal Paddle-marking on the body, this latter style being of either the grooved variety, or showing the use of thong-wrapped sticks. No examples of "twisted-cord" decoration - so common in Siouan ware - have yet been found among Sheyenne River fragments, some of which have no surface treatment at all other than rubbing or semi-polishing to give an even surface, although in rare cases, punch stamps or plaited matting also occur.

Shards from this site average a thickness of around 8mm; are of a flaky constituency, which tends to split into two layers, and is indicative of insufficient firing during original manufacture. Rim shards are of one type with only slight variations. These are characterized by slightly thickened, protruding, flat-top lips - again a common trait in Oneota ware - directed outward and downward at an angle of roughly forty-five degrees. These lips seem to be slightly everted, with either constricted or straight necks. Whilst some rim-shards show comparatively high necks, most are of a very Lower variety as if only the orifice had been turned back. In total, Cheyenne pots might thus be described as semi-constricted, that is, halfway between the constricted neck variety and that of bowl-shaped.

Decoration of the lips consist moreover, of vertical, horizontal and even diagonal lines, arranged in parallels. These features are made with cord-wrapped stick and single-cord impressions, while some shards are decorated on the inner lip with cord-wrapped stick impressions and a few others, with merely plain cord. Additional types with incision or punctuate markings also occur. A small number have necks decorated with cord-wrapped sticks and cord impressions in the form of horizontal parallel lines, while some fragments have shoulder decorations of either incised or opposed diagonal lines. Others are particularly noticeable by their sporting the roulette design, as is also found in certain Oneota ware, and a more noticeable feature is the occurrence of a herringbone design which was recognized by many tribes as uniquely Cheyenne. A Hidatsa informant of Colonel A. B. Welch named Bear-in-the-Water, stated in 1923 that of old, the various pottery styles of the River Tribes could be distinguished by the fact that in general, ceramics of the Mandan were black and very similar to those of the Hidatsa, whilst Arickara ware was lighter in colour and that Cheyenne ware was often decorated with a `herringbone` design. The clay used to manufacture such pots by the Mandan, Hidatsa and Arickara was, customarily, obtained from a point along Cannonball River not far west of the small hamlet of Solen in Sioux County, North Dakota now on the Standing Rock Reservation, so it was probably in this same area where of old Cheyennes also obtained their clay.

Regarding the `Roulette` design, it is almost identical with many shard samples from Mille Lacs cultural finds, while a number of shards from the Sheyenne River site show overhanging collars and embossed on the outside with small white beads; A singular fashion it would appear, of Cheyenne ceramics, albeit of a later date than that with which we are presently concerned.

Of other material unearthed from the Sheyenne River site, most important is the occurrence of Catlinite elbow pipes; several triangular knife blades and a number of stemmed arrow heads, albeit typically Siouan, but which suggests an amalgamation of both Algonquian and Siouan cultural styles. In comparison, there are several variations of so-called Oneota and of earlier Cambrian ceramics which in brief, can be described as follows,

Type A. Showing a good deal of Oneota-proper, i.e. Iowa and Oto influence.

Type B. A rare type distinguished by "S" shaped collar rims and Twisted-Cord decoration.

Type C. Being conspicuous by its angular shoulders; Rolled Rims and scroll designs.

Each of the above types show strong "Woodland" traits, particularly that of cord marking and all resemble those of the Mille Lacs focus, in so much as Mille Lacs pottery - which also is classified as Late Woodland Algonquian, albeit shell tempered as opposed to the usual Cheyenne grit tempering technique; are globular in body shape with round or semi-conidial bottoms, constricted necks and broad mouths. Rims are usually straight and surfaces either smooth or covered in cord-wrapped, paddle markings.

Many Sheyenne River shards although predominantly grit tempered, appear to be closely related to those of the Mille Lacs focus, specifically when bearing "Roulette" markings; a fashion which turns up regularly in other sites containing so-called Cambrian ware. Some Dakota Sioux traits are apparent in that of Mille Lacs to a greater or less degree according to their site of origin, so that those findings which show a high degree of Dakota style, would indicate Siouan manufacture, while those of a much less degree, would indicate Algonquian.

The Algonquians of the Mille Lacs district during the period of the Mille Lacs focus [circa, A.D.1500 to 1700], must have been predominantly Cheyenne-speaking peoples of Moiseo and Suhtaio affiliation, as these two groups were the only Algonquians residing permanently on the east side of the Upper Mississippi during that time span, and who then, were in harmonious contact with and in a position to be influenced by Dakota styles. Some Chippewa bands, it is true, albeit after the date 1695, were allowed freedom of movement by the Eastern Sioux close to this same area, but only for hunting purposes and for short periods, and it is unlikely that the Sioux in-between their prolonged outbursts of hostility with the Chippewa, ever gave the latter such concessions until after the main phase of the Mille Lacs focus had passed.

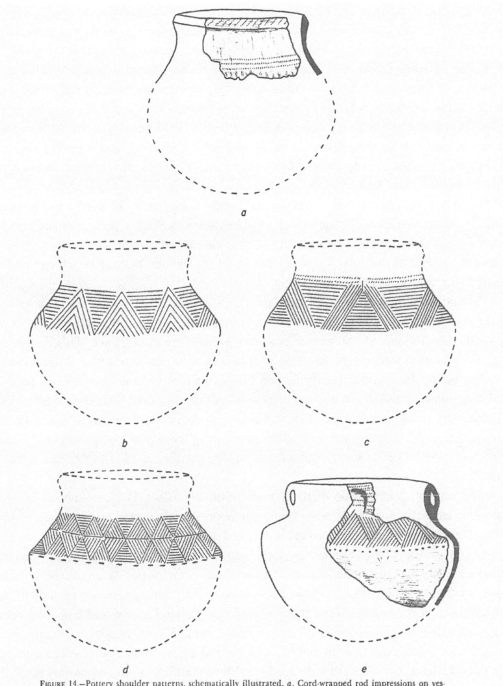

FIGURE 14.—Pottery shoulder patterns, schematically illustrated. *a*, Cord-wrapped rod impressions on vessel neck. *b*, Chevron-filled triangles with horizontally incised pendant triangles. *c*, Pattern similar to Pawnee examples. *d*, Complex pattern. *e*, Alternating triangle. Vessel outlines are hypothetical.

CHEYENNE POTTERY FROM THE BIESTERFELDT SHEYENNE RIVER SITE.
[Courtesy of the Smithsonian Institution Contributions to Anthropology. Number 15.]

It cannot be doubted that Cheyennes were once permanent occupants along and adjacent to the Minnesota, and whereabouts, they resided for many years in earth and timbered lodges; cultivated fields and produced hand-molded pottery in some quantity. It is not acceptable, therefore, that Cheyenne pottery fragments in the northern half of that State and along the Minnesota have not survived, or rather, that every archaeological find in both northern and central Minnesota should be attributed to other tribes, whether or not they actually occupied the sites in question. Yet still all so-called Oneota and all Sandy Lake sites in the Upper half of Minnesota are consistently classified as Siouan in origin, even though one so-called Oneota site, at least, and several so-called Sandy Lake sites are to be found in traditional Cheyenne locations where no Siouans are known to have resided during the late Oneota-proper and late Sandy Lake-proper periods of between 1650 and 1700. Added to this, some so-called Oneota and Sandy Lake pottery of northern Minnesota show as much, if indeed not more Algonquian connections than with Siouan, and certain aspects of Sandy Lake ware show conspicuous "grit" tempering, as is the case of ceramics from the Sheyenne River Biesterfeldt site and of that near Kulm in eastern South Dakota, both of which can definitely be associated with Cheyenne occupation.

Strong similarities also occur between the Sheyenne River aspect and that of the Black Duck focus of Upper and Lower Red Lake, similarities which appear regularly in Sandy Lake ware along with some variants of the more northern so-called Oneota ceramics. This is important, for neither Black Duck nor Sheyenne River traits appear in sufficient quantity in those other northern Minnesota focuses to warrant classifying them all as merely variant styles of one tribal group's work. Thus, some so-called Oneota ceramics although not identical with that of Sheyenne River ware, have very strong connections with it, along with connections to that of Black Duck and to some other Upper Mississippi sites, including a number of those previously attributed to the Sandy Lake and early Mille Lacs focuses, but which can also be associated with Cheyenne and Suhtaio peoples.

Our earlier identification of those responsible for Black Duck pottery as including the Suhtaio and some Cheyenne-Proper groups, corroborates our assertion expressed in preceding chapters, that Cheyenne-speaking groups once lived about Upper and Lower Red Lake, for other than Cheyennes, only the Siouan-speaking groups of Hidatsa, Yanktonai [including the Assiniboine], and perhaps some Mandan bands at an even earlier date, can be considered as possible candidates. In so much as these last-named groups during separate periods in time, had once been permanent residents of the area embracing Upper and Lower Red Lake. However, none of these latter tribe's various styles of pottery show enough comparisons to enable them to be associated with Black Duck or with that of Mille Lacs along with some other sites attributed to the Sandy Lake focus. On the contrary, Black Duck shows abundant Algonquian traits of the Lake Superior "type," which again, closely resemble sherds from certain Mille Lacs, Sandy Lake and so-called Oneota ware. Thus, as the Cheyenne and Suhtaio were the only Algonquian-speakers to reside permanently in the Upper Mississippi and Red Lakes districts during the period 1550 to 1700, Cheyenne and Suhtaio speaking peoples must have been responsible.

Certainly whilst in residence along the Minnesota, Cheyennes were in friendly contact with Oneota-proper culture groups south and southwest of that river, such as the Omaha, Iowa and Oto.

So it should not be surprising that Cheyenne pottery shows intrusive Siouan influences which, undoubtedly is also the case of pottery associated with more northern Cheyenne-speaking groups comprising the Moiseo and Suhtaio, and who themselves were then in close and harmonious contact with Dakota Siouans of the Upper Mississippi on that river's east side. As a result, both Woodland Algonquian and Siouan traits occur in the same sites, and this appears to be the case regarding so-called Oneota ceramics found adjacent to the middle and Upper course of the Minnesota, in so much as here we see a mixture of Cheyenne, Omaha, Iowa and Oto styles.

Why then, one may ask, do Algonquian variants of the Oneota-proper type turn up in certain village sites west of Minnesota in the Lake Andes region which are indisputably Siouan? The answer is simple, for as will be noted below, some Cheyennes, at least, continued in a league with the Omaha and the latter's allies even after abandoning the Minnesota country, and continued to remain in close and harmonious contact with each other until sometime after their crossing the Missouri River.

It was, according to Cheyenne tradition, during the latter decades of the seventeenth century after the Pipe-Stem Men Cheyennes had moved south, that an even larger Cheyenne group moved from the headwaters country of the Upper Mississippi, and arrived along the Minnesota at a point near the mouth of Blue Earth River. These, evidently, were the Masikota, an important and populous Cheyenne-proper group which in conjunction with their Omissis cousins [the *Chaienaton* or Bowstrings], comprised the largest concentration of Cheyenne-speaking peoples by far. It was the Masikota, of course, who would have brought Mille Lacs, Sandy Lake and Black Duck pottery styles to the Minnesota River.

This sudden movement of the Masikota south and of the Omissis [i.e. Bowstrings] towards the southwest, along with the later-date western movements of the Moiseo and Suhtaio, had been forced upon them owing to circumstances beyond their control.

To re-cap on our earlier deductions, by the date 1670 hostile incursions from Cree, Chippewa and Assiniboine each of whom were supplied with guns, began playing havoc with Western Sioux bands residing about the Upper Forks of the Mississippi and surrounding country. These Western Sioux groups which included the Yanktonai and Teton, reeled under such attacks, while their kinfolk the Eastern Sioux [i.e. the Santee and Sisseton], then living about Mille Lacs and the St. Croix were at the same time, generally tolerated by the Chippewa, although engaged in a bloody and protracted war with the Assiniboine and Algonquian tribes of the east including the Sauk, Fox and Illini. Indeed, in later years, the Eastern Sioux were constantly remonstrating with their western kinsmen the Teton and Yanktonai, accusing them of kicking up trouble with the Chippewa, thereby risking the latter's wrath being vented upon the more eastern Sioux bands.

By 1685, both the Teton and Yanktonai had suffered enough, and felt obliged by constant pressure to cede their territory and retire southwest into the region immediately north of the Upper course of the Minnesota.

Those Cheyenne bands about the Upper Mississippi were, evidently, not a little effected by this Sioux movement from the north, for not long after that same date, these Cheyennes also vacated their hunting grounds above the Mississippi Forks. Either they themselves were pushed out by the retreating Sioux, or, and what is more likely, after the Western Sioux had left the north country, these Cheyennes suddenly found themselves completely exposed to Cree and Assiniboine attacks and as an act of expediency, they, too, abandoned their territory and dispersed in several directions.

One large Cheyenne group thus migrated south from above the Crow Wing Fork, leap-frogging as it were, the retreating Western Sioux bands en-route, and finally established itself near the Elbow Bend of the Minnesota only a few years prior to the arrival of the Yanktonai. This, of course, explains the Sioux statement of a later date, in which it was averred that when the Sioux themselves reached the Great Bend of the Minnesota, they found Cheyennes already entrenched higher up that stream.

Cheyenne tradition states that it was during this particular period of upheaval in the Upper Mississippi region, that the Moiseo Kit-Fox element; among whom were the Sacred Arrows and their Keeper, joined the Masikota near the Minnesota`s Great Bend, although they continued to have a village of their own and at a later date, after moving west into the Coteau des Prairies, they often roamed as nomads with a Suhtaio band and with the Bowstring Cheyennes until, eventually, they moved across the Missouri to take up a semi-sedentary life-style. Before crossing the Missouri, the Kit-Fox Moiseo band had an earth-lodge village as a semi-permanent base not far from the Missouri`s east bank, and during which time, they became known as the Aorta band. It is further said in Cheyenne tradition, however, that a small remnant of Moiseo remained in the Upper Mississippi region somewhat aloof from all other Cheyenne bands, and close to the Eastern Sioux and Chongaskitons.

So it was, initially, after vacating the country about the Upper Mississippi Forks, that the Masikota, along with their Moiseo Kit-Fox associates, next settled on the south side of the Elbow Bend of the Minnesota and aligned themselves with neighbouring Cheyenne-speaking people of the Pipe-Stem-Men group. The Pipe-Stem-Men taught their newly arrived cousins how to hunt buffalo by the employment of a surround, and to build stronger more durable lodges from earth and timber. They even influenced existing Masikota pottery styles by introducing traits which the Pipe-Stem-Men had adopted from their Omaha, Iowa and Oto allies, while on the other hand, these Masikota migrants brought with them both Mille Lacs and discernible Black Duck and Sandy Lake cultural traits from the north. Thus we have the two so-called Oneota sites with predominant Algonquian traits near the mouth of Blue Earth River, indicating that these were either early Masikota and Aorta sites, or that one was of mixed Masikota and Aorta and the other, of the earlier Pipe-Stem-Men breakaways from the Omissis Bowstrings group.

The Great Elbow Bend of the Minnesota does appear to have been a natural dividing point for successive migrating groups, no matter to what tribal affiliation they belonged. A part of these migrating groups invariably crossed the Minnesota at its Elbow Bend and moved into the buffalo prairies on that river's south side, whilst the more cautious opted to remain on the north side of the river, preferring the protection and comfort of the lakes and forest region.

Certainly this was the case as regards the Teton Sioux, and after them the Yankton when at a slightly later date than the Cheyenne movement south, both these Sioux peoples reached the same Elbow Bend of the Minnesota. Something similar, no doubt, had happened earlier regarding the migrating Pipe-Stem-Men and Masikota groups, as here we find the previously mentioned so-called Oneota village site located high up the Minnesota on its north side near a place called Granite Falls, while nearby across the Minnesota on the southern tributary of the Yellow Medicine, stood another Cheyenne Earth-lodge village on a height overlooking the mouth of that stream. Those Cheyennes at the Yellow Medicine site may have been earlier residents of that at Granite Falls, which would make the inhabitants synonymous with the Pipe-Stem-Men division.

In addition, when we recall that Cheyenne bands generally remained aloof from one another throughout most of the year whilst in their respective hunting grounds, then perhaps it was one or another Masikota village near the mouth of Blue Earth River which was the actual focal point for the scattered bands of the tribe. Certainly, if the Nation's Sacred Arrows and their priests were closely associated with the Masikota at that time, as the latter`s absorption of the Kit-Fox faction [i.e. Aorta] suggests, then one of the Blue Earth River villages must have been the gathering place for the whole tribe whenever religious or important tribal functions were performed. It is a fact that one of the greatest dreads of these Cheyennes; as was the case with most other tribal groups during the early years of their history when on foot and prone to wandering far and wide in search of game, was that a part of the tribe might wander too far and become lost. In truth, one of the purposes of holding big annual religious ceremonies, was to unite the different bands of the Nation and bring them together as a tribal collective at least once a year.

Of one thing we can be sure, Cheyenne villages when along the Minnesota no longer consisted of numerous widely scattered temporary camps, the dwellings of which when in the North had been oval willow framed structures covered with matted grass or a loam-like mixture of white clay and small stones. The inhabitants had then often been impoverished and forced to flee in stark terror upon the approach of enemies. Now, while along and adjacent to the Minnesota, the people resided in strong, permanent lodges made from earth and timber grouped together in large concentrations protected with a defensive ditch and palisade. Game was plentiful and varied in the prairies south of the Minnesota, and the people supplemented their diet with garden and agricultural produce raised by their own industry. This enabled them to consider themselves somewhat affluent compared to previous expectations, while at the same time, the people now had time on their hands to concentrate more fully on creating a more stable and unified society, and of becoming a tenacious and adventurous people respected by friend and foe alike.

- 0 - 0 - 0 - 0 - 0 - 0 - 0 - 0 - 0 - 0 - 0 - 0 - 0 - 0 - 0 - 0 - 0 - 0 -

CHAPTER 28.

A VILLAGE ON THE YELLOW MEDICINE.

On the summit of a bluff overlooking Yellow Medicine River a few miles from its junction with the Minnesota, are the remains of an old Indian village which, Sioux tradition tells us, was built and occupied by Cheyennes who once claimed that part of the country as their own. During the second half of the nineteenth century, several brief descriptions concerning the site appeared in print. It was reported by a Dr. Comfort in 1877, that Indian fortifications resembling rifle pits were to be found on the Yellow Medicine near New Ulm where the Upper Sioux Agency once stood in 1863, and that arrowheads and certain domestic implements of bone and stone had been unearthed in the immediate vicinity. He further noted the existence of several small circular earthen mounds, which resident Sioux of the district declared, were also the work of old-time Cheyennes.

In another account penned by the same author, we are informed that the ruins on this site indicated an earthen enclosure,

> "...inside of which were noticed several very slight elevations which appeared to mark the places occupied by dwellings of those who were once entrenched there." [1]

Before this, a Dr. T. S. Williamson also referred briefly to this same site when he wrote in 1850,

> "The Cheyennes were then in the Upper part of the valley [i.e., of the Minnesota River] and near the Yellow Medicine, a fortification is still plainly visible which, it is said by the Sioux, was made by the Cheyennes near a good spring of water." [2]

When in 1853 the first ploughing was started in the region, large quantities of muscle shells were ploughed up, showing that the ground had previously been cultivated.

More important, however, is a reference to the site penned by Dr. Stephen R. Riggs, the one-time missionary to certain eastern Dakota Sioux tribes. Writing also in the year 1850, he recorded a reliable Sioux tradition which stated,

> "Two-hundred years ago or thereabouts, the Cheyennes had a village near the Yellow Medicine River in Minnesota." [3]

In a later work, he went on to describe the site in question,

> "The excavation [protective ditch] extends around three sides of a somewhat irregular square, the fourth side being protected by the slope of the hill [butte] which is now [1856] covered with timber. After the filling up of years, perhaps centuries, the ditch

is still about three feet deep. We found the east side in the middle of the ditch to measure thirty - eight paces, the south side by sixty-two and the west by fifty. The north side is considerably larger than the south. The area enclosed is not far from half an acre. On each of the three excavated sides, there was left a gateway of about two paces." [4]

From these, alas all too brief descriptions, it can be determined nonetheless, that this Cheyenne village on the Yellow Medicine once resembled other known permanent Cheyenne village sites, particularly that on the Lower bend of Sheyenne River in North Dakota, and it appears to have been a particular Cheyenne trait to build on high ground overlooking a stream.

Sioux statements further confirm that when they themselves reached the middle course of the Minnesota, after having left the Falls of St. Anthony district on the Mississippi, they found Cheyennes higher up the Minnesota near that river's Yellow Medicine tributary and formed an alliance with them. Here this Sioux statement is evidently referring to a date after 1690, by which time both Teton and Yankton Sioux groups had already migrated south from above the Upper forks of the Mississippi to the western part of the Minnesota valley on the Minnesota's north side. These Sioux accounts also corroborate the fact that the occupants of the Yellow Medicine village and of other sites along and near the Minnesota, then resided in permanent earth and timber lodges, not dissimilar to those used by the Mandan and Arickara along and west of the Missouri.

Both Iowa and Oto traditions which relate to Cheyenne occupation adjacent to the Minnesota prior to 1690, assert that they themselves were also building permanent timber-framed lodges covered with either turf or clay, and as both they and the Cheyennes of the region were then in contact with Skidi Pawnee, it might reasonably be assumed that Cheyennes and possibly the Iowa and Oto, had actually adopted the practice from the Skidi. Certainly, archaeological remains which can be attributed to the early years of Cheyenne, Iowa, Oto and even of Omaha residence in the southern half of Minnesota, suggest that a more flimsy type of abode had initially been employed, usually composed of bent saplings arranged in either a round or rectangular pattern with oval roofs covered with reed mats or grass. Such structures were always in need of repair and when abandoned, they soon collapsed and decomposed, leaving hardly any trace after a few years.

Other Cheyenne village sites when compared to that on the Yellow Medicine, seem to have been much larger, covering anything from two to three acres each. This being so, the number of Cheyennes in residence on the Yellow Medicine must have been a small group in comparison. Indeed, the Cheyenne village site on the Lower bend of Sheyenne River and that at the head of Maple Creek near the town of Kulm further west, evidently contained between sixty and seventy earth-lodges each with an average diameter of forty feet, so that the Yellow Medicine site probably contained only between ten and fifteen lodges at most. It should be remembered, though, that as many as three families constituting an extended family group would have resided in one lodge and, therefore, calculating a conservative estimate of six or seven persons per family, then the population of this village alone, may well have numbered between two-hundred and fifty and three-hundred and fifty souls.

The identity of those Cheyenne-speaking people once residing along the Minnesota, and particularly at the Yellow Medicine site, has often proved a poser to historians and anthropologists alike, but the answer is not hard to determine.

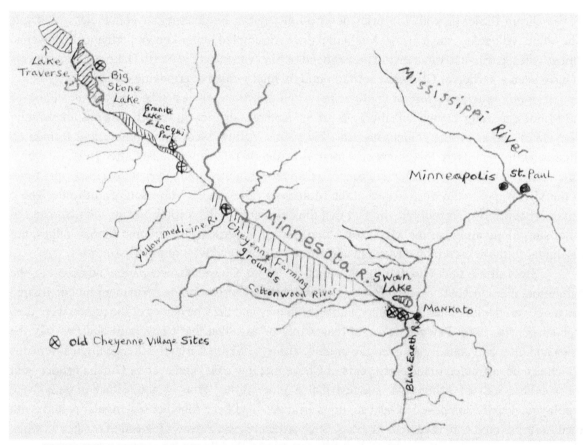

CHEYENNE VILLAGE SITES ADJACENT TO THE MINNESOTA RIVER. Circa. 1690.
[Author`s depiction]

In the late nineteenth century, George Bird Grinnell was told by Cheyenne informants that their Nation originally comprised three related tribes, namely the TsisTsisTsas [Cheyenne-proper] Suhtaio and the Hetsiomisitane or Pipe-Stem-Men. The first two names include those known as Moiseo, Masikota, Suhtaio and the main Omissis or Bowstrings groups, each of which have already been defined and located earlier in this study. The third name of Pipe-Stem-Men, however, now warrants our attention, and is that group as breakaways from the Omissis-Bowstrings who likewise spoke a dialect somewhat different to the Cheyenne-proper bands of Moiseo and Masikota.

The name Pipe-Stem Men is said by Cheyennes to have been an old-time appellation and thus, offers a clue to this group's early location and relationship with neighbouring tribes. Evidently they had some connection with pipes, although it is hardly likely that the pipes referred to represent the common smoking implements in almost universal use across the North American Continent. Rather, they were objects of some importance or peculiarity with a more specific use not originally shared by other Cheyenne-speaking groups. The possession of such pipes was, no doubt, the reason which earned the Pipe-Stem Men their name, and seems to have been applied because of certain pipe stems which they revered as ceremonial objects along with special rites connected to them.

The particular ceremony in question likely refers to that known as the *Hako*, which seems to have been adopted originally from the Caddoan-speaking Pawnee. Until late historic times, this ceremony was held whenever a binding peace was made between erstwhile warring tribes, and during which event, members of one tribe would be adopted into the other to cement the peace-making and the new intertribal relationship.

The integral objects of the *Hako* were two long ash wood pipe stems without smoking bowls, both richly ornamented with eagle, owl and duck feathers. A hole was bored through the stem centers from end to end, although the actual pipes were never used for smoking. At one end of each stem was stretched the head of a mallard duck, while from the stem centers themselves depended a fan of eagle feathers. The Omaha and their cognate tribes adopted such pipes and accompanying ceremony wholesale, which they retained until reservation days late in the nineteenth century. Among the Cheyenne, as was the case with certain other tribes, the ceremony appears to have lost its importance sometime during the course of their later wanderings, although Cheyenne informants declared, that the ceremony had once been considered important among them and of old, rigidly adhered to.

It appears that this particular Cheyenne group with the name Pipe-Stem-Men, was the first of their Nation to adopt such stems in their original form along with the attendant ceremony. Surely, if this Cheyenne group's name referred to the people's manufacture of common smoking pipes alone, then most likely the name would have merely been rendered "Pipe-Men." It seems, therefore, that they were devotees of the *Hako* ceremony, and were those who introduced the cult among other Cheyenne groups, which was reflected in their descriptive name of Pipe-Stem Men.

The subsequent loss of the ceremony among the Cheyenne should not be surprising, as in later years the Pipe-Stem-Men, who would have been the chief practitioners of the cult among their Cheyenne-speaking relatives, began to associate more closely with other Cheyenne and Suhtaio groups, and when taking to a nomadic, buffalo-hunting lifestyle after crossing the Missouri River, they slowly drifted out of their alliance with the Omaha, Iowa and Oto. Instead, the Pipe-Stem-Men chose to embrace the cult of the "Sacred Arrows," along with other religious observances such as the Massaum and Sun dance ceremonies as practiced by all other Cheyenne and Suhtaio bands, and in due course, the "Hako" and its ritualistic objects gradually fell into disuse among them.

Now we know from Sioux traditions that another Cheyenne group closely affiliated to those people on the Yellow Medicine, was positioned in a separate location further upstream along the Minnesota, and thus in Lac Qui Pal Township four round mounds are found on the summit of a bluff overlooking the south bank of the Minnesota, one quarter of a mile east from Lac Qui Parl River near the present-day town of that name.

These mounds are said by the Sioux to have been built by Cheyennes who, the Sioux declare, once had a permanent village in that vicinity. As yet no archaeological excavations have been undertaken at the site, if indeed, its exact position is now possible to locate. We cannot then be sure if the Sioux account refers to earthen burial mounds alone, or to the remains of collapsed earth and timber lodges which often give the appearance of Lower rises or mounds after the earthen roofs have fallen in. Of old, during the period in question, some Cheyenne-speaking peoples did bury their dead in conical mounds, and the Sioux statement concurs with Cheyenne tradition which states, that some of their people once resided in a permanent village in the same Lac Qui Pal locality.

Yet a third site alleged by the Sioux to have been an old-time permanent Cheyenne village, is located near Granite Falls on the Upper course of the Minnesota. Each of these sites, however, that is, on the Yellow Medicine, Lac Qui Parl and Granite Falls were small in size, which might indicate scattered groups of one particular Cheyenne-speaking division, rather than distinct tribal bands, and it is likely that these three villages together, may have housed the entire Pipe-Stem-Men population during contemporaneous periods of occupation.

There are other mounds which occur in the area of present day Big Stone City about one quarter of a mile north of Whetstone River further west at the head of the Minnesota, and also between the shores of Lake Traverse and Big Stone Lake in the same vicinity. Even more old village sites are mentioned in tribal tradition as being around Kettle Lakes near Fort Wardsworth not far west of the Red River of the North near where the town of Sisseton now stands, and in a few other places, all of which are attributed by both the Sioux and Cheyennes, as old-time locations of permanent Cheyenne villages.

One of the more important sites is that found at the head of Maple Creek near the modern day town of Kulm in North Dakota only some fifty miles west as the Crow flies from Big Stone Lake. It was, say the Sioux, to this location that the large Cheyenne group once entrenched near the mouth of Blue Earth River, and thus ostensibly of Masikota affiliation, next retired to before reaching the Missouri.

Suffice to say, Cheyenne burial mounds were probably the work of the old Pipe-Stem-Men group, whose more conservative members first occupied the village on Yellow Medicine; thence a village between Big Stone Lake and Lake Traverse, and after the majority of the population migrated to the Missouri in the wake of their Omaha, Oto and Iowa allies, they carried their mound building cult with them and to other Cheyenne bands with whom they later associated, and among whom they eventually became absorbed.

Of course, the building of earthen burial mounds was a predominantly southern Siouan trait, not Algonquian. But the fact that a number of Cheyenne-speaking groups were then in close alliance and contact with the Omaha, Iowa and Oto whilst along the Minnesota, and that these last named Siouans were then still practicing the old Mound Builder cult of their forefathers, it should

304

not be surprising if the Pipe-Stem-Men were so influenced by their allies. Thus they adopted the custom of mound building for themselves, albeit to a far less degree and lacking the sophisticated level of their Siouan contacts, but continued the practice for a number of years even after abandoning the Minnesota country. Perhaps when other Cheyenne groups began to associate more intimately with the Yellow Medicine Pipe-Stem-Men group and introduced their own, comparatively new religion obtained from the prophet Sweet Medicine, the Yellow Medicine people discarded mound building, and that those mounds said to be of Cheyenne work which stretch west from Minnesota into the eastern Dakotas and beyond in ever decreasing number, merely represent the last vestiges of the Pipe-Stem-Men`s Dehigian and Chiwere Siouan influence among them.

Certainly, as previously stated, Cheyennes occupying the town on the Yellow Medicine were in close and friendly contact with the Omaha, who *were* burial mound builders, and who after relocating from the Upper course of the Des Moines River about the date 1675, were occupying a new permanent village near the headwaters of the Big Sioux in eastern South Dakota, only slightly southwest from the Yellow Medicine Cheyennes.

We learn from separate Iowa, Oto and Omaha traditions, that when their three tribes first entered the southern Minnesota and northern Iowa regions, Cheyennes were already established along the middle course of the Minnesota, and that the sacred `Calumet` or `Hako` ceremony was introduced among the aforementioned Siouan tribes whilst living in the vicinity of the Big Sioux.

Historically, the Iowa and Oto had been driven west from the Ohio country by the Iroquois about the date 1649. They then fled to the banks of the Mississippi and settled for a time about the mouth of the Minnesota. However, they remained there only a few years before being evicted by Eastern Algonquians bands, who forced them to scatter south along both banks of the Mississippi and west of that river into the hinterland of the southern part of Minnesota. The Sioux account adds that the Iowa were already on the Minnesota below the Cheyenne when the Sioux themselves first reached the Falls of St. Anthony area near the mouth of the Minnesota around the date 1650.

The Omaha on the other hand, although also driven west from the Upper Ohio, did not enter the southern Minnesota country until sometime later about the date 1660 and their oral traditions are precise on this point. They state that upon reaching the south side of the Minnesota, they made peace with the resident Cheyennes into whose hunting grounds the Omaha were then encroaching. This Omaha movement had taken them into the west-central part of that state and farther west along what is now the Big Sioux River of eastern South Dakota, while their Iowa and Oto relatives remained both on the Little Sioux River and along the Des Moines throughout the duration of their stay in what are now the States of Minnesota and Iowa.

Corroborating evidence is to be found in contemporary French reports of the same period, which record the movements of the Omaha and their allies at that time, and with whom French traders were in regular contact. These traders followed their customers west and thus we are told that when about the date 1660, the Omaha flooded into the southern part of Minnesota from the east, they came as refugees fleeing from central Algonquian tribes who themselves, were fleeing from the Iroquois in their rear. The Omaha were a Dehigian Siouan folk with a slightly higher culture than the resident Minnesota tribes, and they encroached west across the southern Minnesota country as far as the Upper reaches of the Des Moines. Here, so Omaha tradition tells us, they met and formed an alliance with their kinsmen the Iowa and Oto, but at the same time got into a war with Cheyennes of the Minnesota River region.

This war, apparently, must have been of brief duration, for Omaha tradition recalls no details of it and on the contrary, they relate that a short time after their confederation with the Iowa and Oto, they also formed a league with the Cheyenne.

The fact that the Iowa were actually friends and allies to neighbouring Cheyennes during the same period was, perhaps, the initial factor which enabled the Omaha to come to terms with the Cheyennes and patch up their differences with them. At any rate, thereafter the particular Cheyenne-speaking group involved [the Pipe-Stem-Men] and the Omaha became close friends and allies, exchanging culture traits and ideas, and even inter-marrying to the extent that the Pipe-Stem-Men became a somewhat hybrid group of mixed Cheyenne and Omaha extraction.

As mentioned earlier, this close association between the Pipe-Stem Men and Omaha is perhaps, corroborated by the notation on several early Colonial maps of circa, 1700, which show a tribal group designated *Kamissi Chaa* adjacent to what appears to be the Lower Missouri [called River *Pimiteoui* or *Pekitanoui* on early charts].

It was from the Omaha, Iowa and Oto Siouans and likely the Pipe-Stem-Men, that the Masikota after moving south to the Blue Earth River, learned how to hunt buffalo by the employment of a surround, fashion buffalo hide tepees and how to build strong permanent timber and earth-lodge villages protected with defensive ditches and palisades. Pottery flourished among them, the resulting ware being a mixture of both Algonquian and Siouan styles, and of more importance, the Masikota rediscovered agriculture which, so the Cheyennes declare, was then picked up again from some neighbouring tribe. Evidently this neighbouring tribe was either the corn-growing Iowa, Oto or Omaha if not the Pipe-Stem Men themselves, and the Masikota soon became masters of farming techniques.

The particular Cheyenne group referred to in Omaha tradition, must also have been resident on the south side of the Minnesota to have initially opposed the Omaha intrusion from the east. This, of course, fits in with our earlier assertion that the large group of Omissis Cheyennes had divided somewhere in the north country, ostensibly about Upper and Lower Red Lake probably around the date 1640, and while the majority of Omissis moved east into the lake and marsh country of the Mississippi headwaters district around Bowstring Lake, the separatist group later known as Pipe-Stem-Men retired south, to and across the Minnesota River.

It was then, probably around the same period of peace-making with the Omaha in 1660, that the Pipe-Stem-Men adjacent to the middle course of the Minnesota on its south side, and who like the Omaha, were then subjected to attacks from the Eastern Sioux, deemed it expedient to relocate their population in a less vulnerable position. Thus the Pipe-Stem-Men re-established themselves in a stockade town on a height further upstream overlooking the Yellow Medicine near

306

its confluence with the Minnesota. To the immediate southwest of this point near a place now called Mill Creek the Omaha resided, and these became the close confederates and allies of the Yellow Medicine Cheyennes.

It happened then that the later Masikota Cheyenne arrivals, after establishing themselves near the mouth of the Blue Earth became allied to Siouans of the Chiwere group i.e., Iowa and Oto, whilst the separatist Pipe-Stem-Men on the Yellow Medicine further west, were already in a league with the Omaha and their offshoots the Ponca who were Siouans of the Dehighian group, and thus was the situation along the Minnesota between the dates 1660 and 1690.

A report penned by the Chevalier Du LaSalle in 1679, stated that the Oto were sending war-parties along and west of the Missouri River and beyond in order to raid the Panis and horse-riding Padouca tribes, and were bringing home Panis as slaves with which to trade to the French. LaSalle even noted one Oto warrior with a horse hoof tied to his waist-belt as a trophy. If then, the Oto were raiding so far west at that time, then their allies the Omaha, Iowa and even Pipe-Stem-Men Cheyennes were, in all likelihood, doing the same, and perhaps had been for several years prior to that date.

It would appear from this and other fragments of information, that the Yellow Medicine Cheyennes who, by definition, must refer to the Pipe-Stem-Men group, were raiding the Panis, Mandan and some other tribes along and west of the Missouri before other Cheyennes and Suhtaio did so, and who did not, apparently, do so until a much later date after moving west from the Minnesota country. Added to this, it was only the Yellow Medicine Cheyennes who after their peacemaking with the Omaha, would not have been considered trespassers in Omaha and Oto hunting grounds adjacent to the Big Sioux in eastern South Dakota, and through which country they would have to travel in order to reach the Lower course of the Missouri where the Panis and other foreign villages were then found. This fits nicely with a statement given to Lieutenant W. P. Clark in 1879 by an aged Cheyenne named Black-Moccasin that some Cheyennes had reached the Missouri as early as 1676 while the majority of Cheyennes were still in central Minnesota. At the same time, it adds substance to the suggestion that it was indeed, a Cheyenne-speaking group from a village close to the Minnesota and allied to the Omaha, who were the first of their Nation to adopt the *Hako* ceremony by which they received their name of Pipe-Stem-Men. However, the Pipe-Stem-Men; even though originally a separate part of the Omissis-Bowstrings, did at a later date amalgamate with other Cheyenne bands; particularly the Ridge Men and Suhtaio, and eventually were absorbed by them. So today there remains no discernible trace of the existence save the old name of Pipe-Stem Men.

It is interesting to note that the tradition among the Teton Sioux concerning the coming of the "White-Buffalo-Cow-Woman" among them with her own sacred catlinite pipe, and who supposedly, brought the buffalo and corn to the Sioux when residing in the Upper part of Minnesota, is dated by some as occurring around the middle of the seventeenth century. Now as we know that during this same period, certain Cheyenne and Suhtaio bands were in harmonious contact with various Sioux groups in the Upper Mississippi region, then perhaps the Pipe-Stem

Men Cheyennes had a degree of influence here in spreading a form of the *Hako* ceremony north, or at least, introducing a new sacred pipe cult among their Cheyenne-speaking relatives and who in turn, passed it on in variegated form to their friends the Sioux.

If calumet pipes in more primitive form were originally adopted by the Sioux from either the Omaha, Iowa or Oto, as some scholars believe, then it is nonetheless certain that the elaborate Calumet or Hako ceremony which undoubtedly came originally from the Panis, had previously been embraced wholeheartedly by the Pipe-Stem-Men, and if not actual manufacturers of the sacred pipe-stems themselves, they were without doubt, instrumental in the ceremony's diffusion among the Sioux and among other Cheyenne and Suhtaio bands.

According to Omaha tradition, after their tribe first entered the southern Minnesota country, they settled for a while on the Upper Des Moines near the Pipe Stone Quarries in the southwestern part of that state. But the Yanktonai Sioux attacked them there, and after a bloody battle drove the Omaha northwest to a place now called Sioux Falls on the middle course of the Big Sioux River. From this point, the Omaha moved further north to the vicinity of that river's head and from there, near the head of the Big Sioux, they and the Iowa and Oto began raiding toward the west as far as the Missouri and beyond. At such times, their war-parties often crossed that river in order to harass the Mandan and Pawnee-proper peoples, although they concentrated their attacks moreover, upon the so-called Pani villages, a number of which at that date, were still located on the east side of the Missouri. The Iowa and Oto by then had obtained a number of guns traded directly from the French or from tribes further east in regular contact with white traders, and for this reason, they generally held the advantage over their Missouri River foes who then [1680s], had very few European trade items of any sort, and only a few horses with which to balance the anomaly.

Those of the Missouri River peoples initially on the receiving end of attacks from the east, inhabited numerous earth-lodge villages below that river's Great Bend in South Dakota and north-eastern Nebraska, and appear on later maps under the designation Pani Blanc or White Pawnee. Thus, they were distinguished from the Pani Noir or Black Pawnee who lived further downstream to the south. The difference being that those Caddoan-speaking peoples with whom the French traded after circa, 1700, were termed `White, 'whilst those hostile or simply unfamiliar to the French, were termed `Black.` The Omaha and their allies concentrated their aggression upon the so-called White Pawnee or Pani Blanc, who as a result, suffered a period of chronic Siouan assaults.

Prior to the 1680s, the Pani Blanc had been a match for, if not actually getting the better of their Minnesota enemies. But then other foes had come against them from the Western Plains mounted on strange four-legged beasts [horses], and assailed the Pani Blanc with metal axes and Spanish sword blades. These mounted enemies, the like of which had not been seen before and generally called Padouca during these early years, soon became the terror of the river tribes, and the luckless Pani Blanc lost many tribe's people to their murderous, plundering raids.

The prime reason for this sudden upsurge of aggression on the part of tribes both west and east of the Missouri, was the insatiable appetite of the French, English and Spanish for slaves, in return for which the French and English for their part, bartered guns and ammunition, whilst the Spanish exchanged the usual assortment of beads, cloth, metal implements and utensils, all of which items were craved for by the Red Man. So much did the Pani Blanc suffer in these constant and merciless raids, that in the French colonies the very name *Pani* soon became synonymous for slave.

By the middle years of the sixteen-eighties, the Pani Nation was already diminishing rapidly and by the closing years of that decade, many of their people had been forced by enemy pressure to abandon their towns and flee higher up the Missouri to its Great Bend and the mouth of White River and even further west to the Elk Horn of eastern Nebraska. In each of these localities they built new villages protected with log palisades and defensive ditches. The French made contact with them in 1717 and called them Arickara, and which name has been carried down to the present day.

- 0 - 0 - 0 - 0 - 0 - 0 - 0 - 0 - 0 - 0 - 0 - 0 - 0 - 0 - 0 - 0 - 0 -

CHAPTER. 29.

LAST DAYS ALONG THE MINNESOTA.

By 1685, the Omaha were located near the head of the Big Sioux River not far south from Pipe-Stem-Men Cheyennes on the Yellow Medicine. We are told in both Dakota and Cheyenne tradition that Cheyenne-speaking peoples were by then, already roaming back and forth across the Missouri, which they had been in the habit of doing since 1683 if not a few years earlier. According to the Omaha the Cheyenne were then their allies, so it must have been that some Cheyennes in all likelihood Pipe-Stem-Men, were also engaged in raiding the Missouri tribes as were the Omaha.

Another Cheyenne informant of Clark named Black-Pipe, stated that it was as early as 1678 that Cheyennes first fought with the Mandan living along the Missouri banks, while on the other hand, Truman Michelson`s Suhtaio informant Bull-Thigh said that Cheyennes several times went as far west as the Black Hills of western South Dakota then back again to the Mississippi, and which statement probably relates to the same period in question.

Certainly by 1680, Cheyenne-speaking peoples along the middle reaches of the Minnesota and on the Yellow Medicine, were at war with Missouri River peoples which included the Arickara, Mandan and Skidi Pawnee, whilst these latter themselves were being raided by fierce so-called Padouca foes from the west. It does, though, appear from Omaha tradition, that it were they, the Omaha, along with their Siouan confederates who actually inaugurated their war with the river tribes, being the first to attack the Arickara villages both east and west of the Missouri. The chances are that the Omaha had always been doubtful friends of the Arickara since the western advance of the Omaha from the east into what is now the northwestern part of Iowa, and being persuaded by French contacts to procure slaves, while at the same time having the advantage of firearms and metal-bladed weapons, the Omaha discarded whatever tolerance they might once have had, and commenced raiding both the Arickara and Skidi Pawnee relentlessly.

Cheyennes, more especially of the Pipe-Stem-Men group would have become involved, if only because they were allied to the Omaha. Although the conduct of warfare during this period was such, that any tribal group in friendly contact with the enemy would have been considered "fair game" by the Arickara, and perhaps it was this fact, moreover, which likely caused the Pipe-Stem-Men to become embroiled. For their part the Omaha, Iowa, Oto and Cheyennes, had themselves lost tribal members to slave raiders from the eastern woodlands and Upper Great Lakes, whose human merchandise then passed into the hands of the French and English and thence - in a roundabout way - to the European tobacco and sugar plantations in the West Indies, and even further south to the tin and silver mines of Central Spanish America.

Conversely, it is unlikely that Cheyennes on the Yellow Medicine suffered a continuation of harassment from the Cree or Chippewa at that time, as this would mean that war-parties of those peoples were passing back and forth through the hunting grounds of warlike Teton Sioux groups, in order merely to reach the Yellow Medicine occupants. Other enemies of the Pipe-Stem-Men during the 1680s were the Yanktonai, at times allied to one or another Eastern Dakota and Teton band then resident east and north of the Minnesota, and Cheyenne tradition does imply that war-parties of Assiniboine continued to assault them, paddling their canoes from the vicinity of Lake of the Woods south along the course of Red River which stream they were apt to use as a war-road to Lake Traverse, and from there, travelled overland to reach their intended victims on the Yellow Medicine and those Cheyennes near the mouth of the Blue Earth. But such raids had become less frequent because of the difficulties and risks involved for the Assiniboine when traversing hostile country in between, and as far as the Pipe-Stem-Men themselves were concerned, more serious were attacks by Algonquian raiders from the east which included the Fox, Sauk and Kickapoo among others. Often the Fox either alone or with Sauk allies, would cross the Mississippi in their quest for Oto and Iowa slaves, and if these could not be found, then their war-parties assaulted those Cheyenne villages near the mouth of the Blue Earth and on the Yellow Medicine. As a consequence, lands immediately east of the Upper Mississippi soon became unattainable to tribes west of that river, particularly those entrenched adjacent to the Minnesota owing to the aggressive attitude of the Yanktonai, Eastern Sioux, Central Algonquians, and at times, even Iroquois wolf-packs from the Lower Great Lakes. Thus the Omaha and their Pipe-Stem Men allies in order to have something of value with which to trade to white men for much needed guns and ammunition, were obliged to get their slaves from the west.

The Oto we have noted, had been raiding one or another tribe of horse-using Indians west of the Missouri as early as 1679, as it will be recalled that one Oto warrior who visited LaSalle at

Fort Crevcouer in that year, had a horse's hoof tied to his waist belt as a trophy. In 1682, however, LaSalle further received a Padouca scalp from an Oto-Iowa war-party returning from a raid much father west.

It was the Arickara, though, who suffered most. They could not hope to endure for long the dreaded Padouca from the west, and Minnesota slave-raiders from the east, the first mentioned with horses, the other with guns, and accordingly, the Arickara sent runners to the Omaha and their confederates with proposals of peace.

As a direct result of this overture, so Omaha tradition informs us, a grand peace council was held with the Arickara near the Omaha village then located at the mouth of a canyon adjacent to the Loop of the Big Sioux. This site was the second Omaha village within the vicinity of the Big Sioux, their people having recently moved south from that river's headwaters region after a second disastrous attack by the Yanktonai who in 1685, had again massacred many of their people. Those Cheyennes in residence on the Yellow Medicine being allies and in close harmonious contact with the Omaha, and thus involved in the latter`s war with the Yanktonai, were fully aware of their own tentative position in southern Minnesota, and were, it seems, themselves desirous of a truce with the Arickara to gain allies against their own northern and eastern enemies, and, if needed, to secure a western refuge from the ever-encroaching Yankton and Teton Sioux.

It was then these serious offensives undertaken by the Yanktonai aided by some of their Teton cousins against the Omaha and the latter`s allies, which was the persuasive factor inducing all tribes of southern Minnesota to accept the olive branch held out by the Arickara.

Omaha tradition goes on to state that they along with the Oto, Iowa, Ponca and Cheyenne were present at the grand council with the Arickara. Alas, no details have been preserved concerning the gathering save that the ensuing pact was confirmed by the ceremony of the Calumet. The Omaha assert that this ceremony was first introduced among them at this meeting, but we know from the earlier narratives penned by Jacques Cartier, Pierre Radisson and Nicholas Perrot, that the Calumet and its attendant cult was then already widespread among Eastern tribes. We might suspect then that this part of Omaha tradition actually applies more specifically to the earlier mentioned "Hako" ceremony which, although similar to that already practiced by Eastern tribes, was different in certain aspects and had originated among the Arickara and their Pawnee-proper relatives west of the Missouri.

It is interesting to note that on the Marquette map of 1674, there is a notation for the Pana-Maha, which was an early colonial name for the Skidi Pawnee, then positioned near the head of the Des Moines River south of the Minnesota.

The Skidi have a tradition that their people came originally into the Nebraska Plains from the Allegheny country near the head of the Ohio much further east than the Missouri, while philological comparisons coupled with certain religious and cultural traits manifest in astrological theology and comparable pottery styles, link them to Iroquois stock, although to what degree and to which specific period in time, has yet to be positively determined. The Omaha remembered the Skidi as at first a friendly tribe living near them during their tribe's early days in southwestern Ohio and north-western Iowa around the date 1650, and on maps prior to 1700, there are notations for the "Maha" [i.e. Omaha] and near them, the Pana-Maha, while on the aforementioned Marquette map of 1674, the "Panas" are positioned slightly northeast of the "Mahas."

Now the name Pana prior to 1700, was used by the French as a generic term to designate those peoples of mixed Pawnee and other Caddoan-speaking groups which later became known collectively as Arickara, and the name Pana when coupled to that of Maha, was applied specifically and singularly to the Skidi Pawnee. The fact that one group of Pana during the early days of French contact was noted with the additional appellation of Maha, indicates that at one time the Skidi Pawnee were very closely associated with the Omaha, which indeed, is asserted in both Omaha and Skidi tradition.

Soon after Marquette`s notation, however, the Omaha and their Iowa and Oto confederates were at war with Arickara and Pawnee-proper peoples along and west of the Missouri, and soon forced the Pana-Maha [Skidi] out of the Minnesota country, pushing them west into the arms of their Arickara relatives. Not until some years later after patching up their quarrel with the Omaha, did the Pana-Maha return east to re-occupy their old seats and align themselves again with their erst-while Omaha foes. It is probable then, that the Pana-Maha, or Skidi as they should more properly be called, even at such an early date, were also in close and harmonious contact with those Cheyennes who were allies to the Omaha and thus, by definition, the Pipe-Stem Men. Indeed, this particular Cheyenne-speaking group being older residents of the Minnesota country than were the Omaha, had likely known the Arickara and their Skidi relatives much earlier than their Siouan allies; at a time, in fact, when these Cheyennes had first reached the Minnesota River about the date 1650 and perhaps even earlier, when small Cheyenne groups had been apt to cross the Red River of the North during periodic hunting trips west from the vicinity of Lower Red Lake, although at that time, there may not have been more than superficial contact between them.

Even so, it might reasonably be supposed that Cheyennes on the Yellow Medicine had earlier been acquainted with the ceremony of the "Hako," and were those who actually introduced the cult to their Omaha allies at the peace council on the Big Sioux.

Curiously then, it appears that this Skidi group after the aforesaid peace council, reentered into a harmonious relationship with the Pipe-Stem-Men and Omaha and after returning east into southern Minnesota, were included as a participating faction when the Pipe-Stem Men and their Siouan allies continued their raids west of the Missouri, the Skidi then acting as allies to the Minnesota tribes, rather than supporting their own Pawnee-proper relatives in the west.

A further report by Louis Hennepin when at LaSalle`s Fort Crevcouer on the Illinois River in 1682, mentions that the Gattacka Padouca [i.e. Plains Apaches] were allies to the Panas, and as it is known from Spanish records of that date that other Padouca Apaches were then at war with the Pawnee-proper, Hennepin`s "Panas" must be a reference to the Skidi group alone, and during a time of Skidi warfare with other Pawnee tribes.

This is explained in the Skidi story of the coming of Closed-Man, who albeit having since become a somewhat mythological figure, was at one time a real historical personage between the period 1680 and 1685. It was Closed-Man who; during a time of great strife between the Skidi and Pawnee-proper tribes which threatened to destroy the Skidi, brought the scattered Skidi bands together in more compact villages and, it is said, caused the people to build round, earth and timber lodges as opposed to the rectangular type as a better defense against their foes [although more likely to combat fierce winds of the region]. The scattered Skidi villages are said to have numbered seventeen at the time of Closed-Man`s coming, each of which is named and located individually in the story, and archaeologists have since uncovered the remains of all these village sites.

The Closed-Man story is important here, as it mentions that Closed-Man sent an invitation to all Skidi bands both west and east of the Missouri, requesting them to gather at a certain place and join as one in defeating the enemy which, in this case, were the three Pawnee-proper tribes of Chaui, Pitturahat and Kitahaki known collectively as the South Bands. They had recently invaded Skidi territory and in the event, most of the Skidi were defeated and subjugated by the victorious Pawnee. However, two Skidi factions said to have been living further east or northeast than the rest of their people, refused to accept Pawnee authority and subsequently, were driven further east from their fields and back into the southwestern part of Minnesota.

At a later date, these two independent Skidi bands joined the Arickara and were absorbed among them. The Arickara, though, actually comprised a conglomerate of peoples; being refugees from several Caddoan tribes who, at various times throughout the preceding one-hundred years or so, had divorced themselves from their parent groups and joining together, eventually constituted a separate Caddoan division. Their dialect and family connections were always closer to the Skidi than to other Pawnee-speaking groups, and it appears that it was the aforesaid Skidi faction composed of the two bands noted on the Marquette map of 1674 and also mentioned in the story of Closed-Man's coming, which were once resident in southern Minnesota and in regular contact with Siouans of that region along with the Pipe-Stem-Men Cheyennes. Probably then, it was the Pipe-Stem-Men who had acted as go-betweens if not the officiators in persuading the Omaha, Iowa and Oto into accepting the Arickara proposal for peace and for their coming together to hold a multi-tribal peace council on the Big Sioux. But whatever the case, the council did result in mutual friendships and alliances being forged against their common horse-ridding Pawnee and Padouca foes from the west.

As to dating this event, a French report in 1650 noted twenty-two separate Skidi villages, yet in 1684 the cartographer Franquelin counted only nineteen. Four years later [1688], a Father Douey gave the number as seventeen and in 1701 or thereabouts, an anonymous French map maker listed twelve. It would seem therefore, that somewhere between 1684 and 1688 was the time when the Skidi villages numbered seventeen, and was the period of subsequent retreat from the west of the two Pana Maha [i.e. Skidi] bands back east into the Minnesota country. The event of the aforesaid peace council is said to have occurred only a few years after the time of Closed-Man's coming during the Skidi war with the Pawnee, and must apply specifically to those Pana-Maha bands earlier noted on the Marquette map of 1674, before returning back east into Minnesota after having previously been evicted by the Omaha and their allies.

313

The Arickara peace council must have been a little later than 1684, at which time there were still nineteen Skidi villages, and the Omaha had moved south to the Loop of the Big Sioux because of the second Yanktonai attack, but before 1690, by which time the Skidi tribe had been reduced to seventeen villages and in which year, the Yanktonai in overwhelming number for a third time, attacked the Omaha then near the Loop of the Big Sioux and as a result, drove the Omaha from that position and towards the southwest.

This third and most serious assault by the Yanktonai upon the Omaha then near the Loop of the Big Sioux, was the worst catastrophe ever suffered by that tribe at the hands of an enemy. Tradition recalls that over one thousand Omaha, including men women and children lost their lives in this one attack alone. Be this an exaggerated figure or not, the Omaha along with their Ponca and Oto kinsmen then fled that river completely, and settled further southwest in the Lake Andes district on the east side of the Missouri in present-day Nebraska. Never again did the Omaha and their Ponca offshoots live permanently in the country of southern Minnesota, eastern South Dakota and northwestern Iowa.

Corroboration for the date of Omaha retreat from the Loop of the Big Sioux, can be found in the fact that a stone marker bearing the engraved date of 1691, was discovered over two centuries later near Lake Andes in a village site traditionally attributed to the Omaha. The engraved date is obviously the work of white men, and it is known from contemporary sources of the sixteen-nineties, that French traders followed the retreating Omaha and Oto to the Missouri in order to carry on their trade. In addition, Omaha tradition is explicit in stating that at the time of the great council with the Arickara, the Ponca were yet a part of the Omaha tribe, and we know from contemporary French reports that by 1690 when the latter moved to the Missouri, the Ponca had already separated from them.

After a brief stay in the Lake Andes district, the Omaha and their Ponca cognates travelled downstream to the mouth of the Big Sioux where they were located on the DeIsle map of 1702. They thence moved north, following the Missouri's east bank to a point across from the mouth of White River, which stream flows into the Missouri from the west in what is now the state of South Dakota. It was here according to both Omaha and Arickara accounts, that their two tribes again came together, and was the place where the Omaha and their Siouan allies actually first crossed the Missouri in order to settle permanently on the west side of that river.

With the Omaha and their Siouan allies gone from the country adjacent to the Big Sioux, the Pipe-Stem-Men on the Yellow Medicine suddenly found themselves alone in defending their hearths against the Yanktonai, Teton and Eastern Sioux. Evidently, they did not think it prudent to remain where they were, or indeed, at any point along the Minnesota. They could not have hoped to hold their seat indefinitely and they, too, abandoned their town and moved west, although instead of going straight to the Missouri as had their Siouan allies, Dakota Sioux tradition tells us that they first travelled up the Minnesota and not far beyond the head of that river, built a new village somewhere between Lake Traverse and Big Stone Lake. After a few years, the Pipe-Stem Men went southwest to the east bank of the Missouri across from the mouth of White River as their

Omaha allies had done before them, and where a number of years later, according to both Cheyenne and Arickara tradition, they were ferried over the Missouri to its west bank in the bull-boats of their recently acquired Arickara friends.

As a result of the intertribal peace making near the Loop of the Big Sioux, Arickara and Skidi bands became regular visitors and friends to the Omaha and Pipe-Stem Men Cheyennes and likely, as a consequence, with other Cheyenne groups in contact with them. * Certainly, there can be little doubt that from hereon, the Arickara were instrumental in the transition of both the Pipe-Stem Men and their Omaha allies in adapting from a Woodland mentality and culture, to that of the Plains-Riverine dweller. A separate piece of evidence which goes some way in substantiating the date of removal of the Pipe-Stem-Men from the Yellow Medicine, is found in an old Teton Sioux story of "The Lost Children." The famous Oglala war-chief of a much later date named Red Cloud, when telling the story to his friend Sam Deon sometime during the early eighteen-nineties included some snippets of information regarding this period of warfare between his people and the Cheyenne. In brief, Red Cloud declared that so many years ago when the Sioux lived far to the east, they had enemies to the south and southwest and were at war with the "Cut Fingers," who were also known to the Sioux as Shaiena, i.e., Cheyenne.

In reality the term `Cut-fingers` and its variant form of `Cut-Arms` were names later applied by the Sioux to all Cheyennes, but in earlier days it was daubed more specifically upon the Suhtaio and Pipe-Stem Men bands. The story continues by stating that after putting the Cut-fingers to flight, the Sioux followed them up, and every year their two peoples would have another big fight and the Cut-fingers be driven further west until, finally, they were pushed across the Missouri River. Red Cloud also mentioned that when first the Sioux drove the Cut-fingers out of Minnesota, a part of the Sioux then migrated southwest from the Upper Mississippi in order to occupy land recently vacated by their Cut-finger enemies.

The above actually refers to a time when the Teton [along with other Sioux groups] resided just west of the Mille Lacs district of the Upper Mississippi where they were contacted by Father Louis Hennepin in 1680. By the year 1695, however, when the French trader LeSueur reached the Elbow Bend of the Minnesota at the mouth of the Blue Earth, he found a large Teton group already entrenched around present-day Big Stone Lake and which because of its local inhabitants, LeSueur named "Lac Des Tintons" [sic]. The Yanktonai, he noted, had by then extended their range to include the Pipestone Quarries of southwestern Minnesota.

Now for the Sioux to occupy country adjacent to and southwest of the Upper Minnesota, they had first to expel the resident people, and these latter we have seen, included the Omaha, Oto, Iowa and Pipe-Stem Men Cheyennes. We also know from early French reports that around the date 1690 the Teton Sioux, wishing to extricate themselves from enemies coming against them from the north and northeast [Assiniboine and Chippewa], allied themselves to their Yankton cousins,

* In a variant version of Omaha tradition regarding this council, it is mentioned that the Yanktonai were also included.

315

and together, drove the Oto and a part of the Iowa from the Minnesota River and the Omaha from the Loop of the Big Sioux. The Sioux then followed their retreating enemies and forced them further southwest into the Lake Andes area and then even further down the Big Sioux as far as its junction with the Missouri. Of course, as allies and close confederates to the Omaha, the Pipe-Stem Men likewise, were driven from their hearths and so must have been those designated "Cut-fingers" in the Red-Cloud account.

The Reverend T. S. Williams gave the date 1693 as being the year the village on the Yellow Medicine was built, and further stated that this village was the most westerly site of Cheyenne occupation in the vicinity of the Minnesota. This date, though, appears to be in error, and more plausible is that it applies to the later Cheyenne village which, we are told, once stood somewhere between Big Stone Lake and Lake Traverse at the head of the Minnesota and which, according to the Sioux, was built next by those Cheyennes after the latter's move from the Yellow Medicine. The date 1693 in reality, refers to the vacation of the Yellow Medicine town and not its founding, which would then agree with the evidence at hand.

Cheyenne tradition as usual, has an apocryphal reason for their leaving the central Minnesota country, which avers that when they were away from their town on a buffalo hunt, a foreign people came and carried off the corn which the Cheyennes had stored for winter use. There was not left enough seed to plant more crops, and so the people abandoned their town and wandered south in order to follow the buffalo trails. This, the tradition continues, was a hard time for the people as they then had only dogs as beasts of burden. The people were slow-moving and had difficulty keeping up with the buffalo herds, so at times they kept themselves alive by eating their dogs until buffalo came again within reach.

Be this as it may, of one thing we can be sure, it was only a few years after the Omaha and their allies the Oto and Ponca left the Big Sioux, occasioned by the third disastrous attack by the Yanktonai in 1690, that the Cheyenne village on the Yellow Medicine was abandoned, its inhabitants at first retiring west between Big Stone Lake and Lake Traverse, and then southwest to the Missouri as had their Omaha allies before them. When the Pipe-Stem Men reached the Missouri, according to Cheyenne statements, they went to a point on that river's east side across from the mouth of White River where the Arickara were then entrenched on the Missouri's west bank being at that time the latter's most northern point of occupation, and where as noted above, the Omaha had earlier crossed. It must then be to this period which some Cheyenne and Sioux statements allude, when referring to the site of an old Cheyenne village on the east bank of the Missouri across from the mouth of White River, but which, unfortunately, the archaeology of the region has not located to date

While positioned on the east bank of the Missouri, the Pipe-Stem Men were within easy pedestrian traveling distance to tribes in the Great Plains west of that river, and hereafter, notwithstanding more powerful enemies to the east, their warriors began conducting regular forays far beyond the Missouri in order to attack the mounted Padouca [Plains Apache] and other equestrian peoples much further west.

It was some time after this that the Pipe-Stem-Men actually crossed the Missouri, and established themselves in another permanent earth-lodge village north of White River near the mouth of the Big Cheyenne not far from their Arickara friends, who earlier, had themselves relocated from the south into the same region. A part of the Pipe-Stem Men thereafter opted for the roving life, living for most of the year as tepee-dwelling nomads in the game-filled grasslands to the west, while at the same time, they confederated more closely with their Arickara allies.

Horses were few if not non-existent among most Cheyennes at that time, and by their own assertion, these western Cheyennes when wandering over the Plains then lived in small buffalo-hide tepees which they transported on crude forms of travois pulled by dogs. Nonetheless, this adventurous Pipe-Stem Men band soon became familiar with the Western Plains and, evidently, its members were crisscrossing the grasslands far west of the Missouri even as far as the Black Hills of western South Dakota in their raids upon enemy camps, long before other Cheyenne and Suhtaio bands attempted to do so.

The reason for this was simple. The Padouca and other western tribes had many horses, while even the Pawnee had begun obtaining a few such animals and the Pipe-Stem-Men wanted them more than anything else. The Chevalier LaSalle noted in 1683 that there were then many horses to be found among the Pana, Pancassa, Manrhout, Gatea, Panimaha and others, and further commented,

> "These Indians use them [horses] for war, the hunt, and in the transport of all things;
> are not accustomed to shoe them, let them sleep outdoors, even in the snow, and give
> them no nourishment except to let them pasture." [1]

By the mid-1730s the Pipe-Stem Men by raiding the Western Tribes and trading with the Arickara, began acquiring a sizable number of horses, and of these they traded a small number from their surplus stock to their cousins the Bowstrings at the latter`s earth-lodge village on Sheyenne River. From the Mandan, the Pipe-Stem-Men stole corn and other home-grown produce, thereby saving themselves the bother of raising their own, while the captives they might happen to take during their hostile ventures, were traded via the Bowstrings to the French and English or to other more eastern tribes acting as middlemen, in exchange for much sought after guns and ammunition.

I think it can be accepted from the previous analysis, that the Pipe-Stem-Men breakaway group from the Omissis, at one time lived in a permanent earth-lodge village on the Yellow Medicine. They were near the Omaha, Oto and Iowa with whom they were in a league against common foes, and by 1683; if not a few years earlier, were engaged in raiding the sedentary tribes along the Missouri. By 1693 the Pipe-Stem Men had relocated from the Yellow Medicine to a point between Big Stone Lake and Lake Traverse at the head of the Minnesota, but by 1695 at the latest, they had moved to the east bank of the Missouri across from the mouth of White River, and were roaming the short-grass buffalo prairies west of the Missouri as far as the western limits of present-day Nebraska and as far as the Black Hills of South Dakota. They had no fear of being opposed by the Arickara since the grand peace council near the Loop of the Big Sioux, and to whose lodges on the Missouri, so tradition asserts, these Cheyennes had arrived as supplicants rather than aggressors. At a later date, the Pipe-Stem Men amalgamated with the Ridge Men band of Cheyenne-proper and lost their old-time identity to them.

The circumstances then of the Pipe-Stem-Men, allow us to explain how Cheyenne tradition over the years has become confused regarding the Nation's wanderings. In so much as while some Cheyenne groups were sedentary, others were nomadic, and while some Cheyennes were confederated with Eastern Sioux bands, others were at war with the Tetons. It thus becomes obvious that the Cheyennes did not migrate as a single body, but rather, each component group moved on its own volition, one by-passing another whenever the fancy took them or when a particular circumstance demanded. The only thing these separate bands had in common as to vocational moves, was that all migrations were directed west, and for the same or similar reason of enemy pressure whether it be from the Tetons or from the Chippewa and Assiniboine in their rear.

- 0 - 0 - 0 - 0 - 0 - 0 - 0 - 0 - 0 - 0 - 0 - 0 - 0 - 0 - 0 – 0 -

CHAPTER 30.

EARLY DAYS AT THE SHEYENNE RIVER SETTLEMENT.

Around the date 1690, a short time before the migration west of the Pipe-Stem-Men from the Yellow Medicine, and Masikota from the mouth of the Blue Earth in central Minnesota, the main Omissis or Bowstring faction which had remained somewhat aloof from its kindred groups had likewise, already abandoned their old haunt in the timbered lake country just below the Upper forks of the Mississippi - ostensibly in the Glenwood district - and moved west into the open grasslands of the Coteau des Prairies in the eastern part of North Dakota. In this long-grass prairie country they built an earth-lodge village overlooking the southern bend of the Sheyenne branch of the Red River of the North, and here they remained for many years, during which time, it is said in tradition, they were sometimes obliged to drive back ferocious assaults upon their town.

One does not have to look far to determine the reason for this Bowstring movement west from the Minnesota lakes and wooded region, as it coincided with the Teton and Yanktonai Sioux retreat south from above the forks of the Upper Mississippi to the north side of the Elbow Bend of the Minnesota. It is obvious that when these Sioux groups abandoned their old districts, owing to increasing hostile pressure from the Cree and Assiniboine aided at times by the Chippewa, the Bowstrings in much the same way as had their Masikota cousins a few years earlier, suddenly found themselves wide open to the same hostile pressure, and could no longer count upon the Sioux who, previously, had acted as a buffer against attack from the north.

The Bowstring Cheyennes who at that time were without European trade of any sort; were far inferior in number to oppose their northern enemies effectively, and whilst still in northern Minnesota they could not site their villages in adequate positions for defense. Their only recourse was flight. To the immediate north were their foes the Plains Cree and Assiniboine, while to the east were the Sisseton and Santee Sioux - precarious neighbours at best, - and to the south lay the newly-claimed hunting grounds of the Teton and Yanktonai. Thus the Bowstrings moved southwest across Red River of the North and into the rolling prairie country of eastern North Dakota.

Overlooking the Great Bend of the Sheyenne River along its Lower course in what is now Ransom County, North Dakota, the Bowstrings selected a strong defensive position atop a prominent bluff. Here they erected a cluster of earth and timber lodges and fortified the whole with a surrounding ditch topped with a stout picket fence. From this position, the people could observe enemy war-parties coming from afar and could prepare to resist any attack on their town. They held a strategic advantage by occupying such a secure position, in a country which was generally devoid of comparable heights to that where the Bowstrings were entrenched.

The lifestyle of these Sheyenne River Bowstring people as recalled in tribal tradition, would also apply to other Cheyenne-speaking groups which, at various times and in various places, occupied the same prairie country between the Red River on the east and the Missouri on the west, prior, that is, to the event of horses and guns being introduced among them.

Both Sioux and Chippewa traditions remember well the period of Cheyenne residence on the Lower bend of the Sheyenne. The Chippewa imply that there were actually several Cheyenne villages situated at various points along that river, and even today the site of the village on the south bank of its southern bend is still visible. In 1908 the site was surveyed; some of its house-rings excavated and a cursory inspection made. Later, in the summer of 1967 a further examination was under taken and several more house-rings excavated. The results of these careful methodical examinations are impressive and have shed much light on this particular phase of Cheyenne history and culture. Certainly, the site offers a unique example of a permanent Indian village whose occupants during its early phase, were pedestrian agriculturists, but by the time of the town's later phase, had evolved into buffalo-hunting horsemen of the Western Plains.

Of the several good descriptions of the site which have appeared in print, I have chosen that of William Strong whose article was first published in the "North Dakota Historical Quarterly" in 1940.

"…The site is located on a river terrace with a steep bank on the north facing the former channel of the Sheyenne River. There are about seventy (actually sixty-two) house rings surrounded by a deep ditch or moat which surrounds the village except along the steep river bank. Our excavations tested the ditch, seven houses and numerous cache pits. The ditch proved to have a width of almost ten feet and a depth of almost five feet, there were no bastions. Extensive tests inside and outside of the ditch revealed no positive evidence of a stockade. A few irregular holes that may have been post molds were encountered, but there was no evidence of a regular palisade.

It is probable that earth embankments or some sort of temporary walls were used. The houses excavated were all circular earth lodges with four central posts set in an almost exact square and a central fireplace. With one exception the four central posts were oriented to the cardinal points. No definite cache pits were found inside any of the lodges. The lodges, aside from the above uniformity, were divided into three types. Three had only the four central posts, the rafters in one case leaning on an elevated border around the lodge. Three, in addition to the four central posts, had a second row of posts that ran round the outer edge of the floor. One house, the largest and best preserved, had four central posts, a row of intermediate posts, and a ditch or series of post holes around the outer circumference. This lodge conforms perfectly to the generalized Pawnee, Arickara, Mandan and Hidatsa earth-lodge pattern. From its location in the village, and from the nature of its artefacts, it may well have been a ceremonial center. In four of the houses covered entry passages were noted, in one no such evidence was found. (This house suggests a menstrual or old widowed woman's abode.). In two of the house sites the excavations were incomplete. All entry ways were to the Southeast except the largest one which opened Southwest upon an open area or plaza. Many of the post molds contained wood in good condition and were tamped in one place with bison or other large bones. Charred beams were particularly abundant in the largest houses. Characteristic furnishings of all the houses were numerous, large and small boulders some of which had well-used grinding surfaces. All houses that were excavated had been burned........Many of the numerous external cache pits gave indication of having served as refuse pits rather than storage places. Owing to the nature of the sandy soil, their outlines were usually irregular and although some represented dug pits, others appeared to be refuse-filled hollows. The cache pits averaged about four feet in depth and contained ashes, animal bones, especially bison and large numbers of stones and broken pottery and implements. No larger refuse heaps could be found and much refuse was probably thrown over the river bank and washed away..........Contact materials from this site include a few glass beads (Most of which were inset in pottery decoration) one piece of glass, a trigger guard ornament from a British or French gun of early eighteenth century manufacture and thirteen lance, arrow, and knife blades made of brass and iron. Horse bones were found in several parts of the site..........Other material from this site, although not particularly abundant or striking indicate that at this period the general framework of Cheyenne culture was very similar to that of sedentary Missouri River tribes. In addition there are traits that seem more distinctly woodland as is indicated by the pottery. In ground stone, elbow catlinite pipes occur but are rare; shaft polishers, rare; ground mauls (6) oval and discoidal hammer-stones, abundant; rubbing stones abundant; several flat grinding stones and mullers......five small sub rectangular scrapers chipped on all four sides. Permission to excavate a nearby field where burials were reported could not be obtained. However, a bundle burial and two skulls were found just outside one of the lodges....." [1]

    In actual fact the site stands on the highest part of the bluff; the land sloping away in every direction. The east slope is toward a shallow ravine; on the west toward a spring of water and on the south is a gradual slope to the prairie floor. The bluff on its north side abutting the old river bed, falls away at an angle of about forty-five degrees but with a height of only forty feet or so. A path leads down from the village on its west side to marshy ground and a spring, while other paths also lead down the bluff one of which goes only halfway down to a debris heap, and yet another, all the way down to the old river bed itself.

The site is on what was once the property of a Mr. Biesterfeldt and has become known in archaeological jargon as the Biesterfeldt site. It lies about seven miles to the southeast of the present- day town of Lisbon, and overlooks the Lower great bend of the river which rises in the northwest and flows south then northeast into the Red River of the North.

The village must once have covered an area of approximately three and one-half acres surrounded on three sides by a defensive ditch, and bounded on its open side by the steep slope of the bluff which runs down to what was, during the town's occupation, the river's course. The ditch when examined varied in width from sixteen to twenty-eight feet, and in places as much as thirty feet, while its depth even then, was some two and three-quarters feet deep with an opening on its west side. In no place was the ditch less than one and three-quarter feet deep, and if one takes into account the natural filling up of the ditch over the years, it can reasonably be assumed that its original depth was at least double or, perhaps, treble to that quoted above, and must have appeared an impressive obstacle to any enemy attempting to assault the town. It would, of course, have been no mean achievement on the part of the occupants to have constructed the ditch in the first place, given the primitive tools at their disposal.

In the center of the village is what appears to have been an open plaza, where we might suppose, religious and other tribal ceremonies were likely conducted. Most of the lodges had an overall diameter of around thirty feet and having long ago fallen in, they now give the impression of slightly sunken depressions in the ground. Some of the lodges were larger with only a few smaller, and even the small lodges would have been too large to have been merely cache pits. Probably they represent the small abodes as mentioned in Cheyenne tradition, wherein old couples sometimes lived out the remainder of their days if they were without kinfolk, or alternatively, where women retired during menstruation and which were common features in all Cheyenne villages whether of a permanent or temporary construction. Although no definite evidence of a palisade or picket fence was found during recent excavations, the fact that various traditional accounts concerning this particular village assert that it was often attacked and besieged by enemies, leads one to suppose that some form of defensive picket had once been employed, and probably stood atop the inner bank of the outer ditch in order to supplement its protection.

Certainly the village was occupied as a permanent base as early as 1724, for a Cheyenne tradition tells how once a Cheyenne war-party started out on foot from the town intending to attack foes along the Missouri. The party had not travelled far when the sky suddenly darkened and the sun completely blotted out, although previously it had been full daylight. The warriors took fright and giving up their original intention, they fled precipitately back to the village from whence they came.

This account refers to a total eclipse of the sun and by consulting "Oppelzer" 1962 in his "Canon of eclipses," we find that the only total eclipse visible on or near the Lower Sheyenne River during the period of Cheyenne occupation, occurred on May 22, 1724 and was discernible just north of the Biesterfeldt town. One can easy imagine how such a phenomena stuck in Cheyenne minds so that the event became enshrined in tradition, and corroborates our general dating for Cheyenne residence at the Biesterfeldt site.

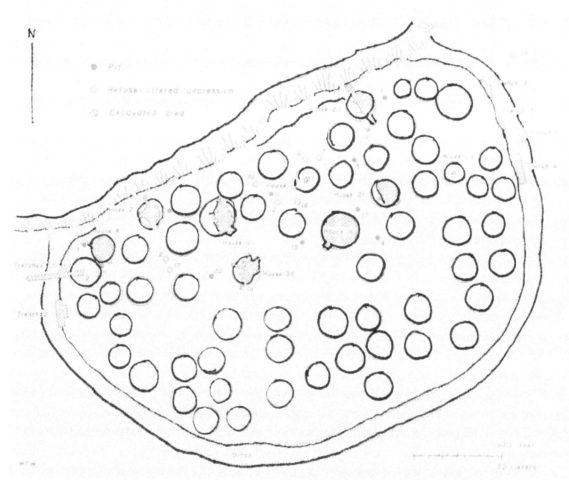

PLAN VIEW OF THE OLD CHEYENNE VILLAGE ON THE LOWER SHEYENNE RIVER.
[Courtesy of the Smithsonian Contributions to Anthropology. Number 15.]

The discovery of both French and British trade items, i.e., a metal trigger guard from an English or French trade gun of the mid seventeen-fifties, brass arrowheads, European glass beads and fragments of china ware, indicate that the village was still in use if only for short periods during the middle years of the eighteenth century and, seemingly, much later. Other evidence such as horse bones found within the living space of one of the lodges and tepee rings discovered in the ploughed-up area of the town on both sides of the ditch, along with contemporary documented evidence to be noted later, suggests that the site was visited at least seasonally long after the mid-1760s, at a time, in fact, after all Cheyennes including those from this Sheyenne River site, had already become fully nomadic horse Indians roaming the short-grass Plains west of the Missouri. Likely they returned to the old village in order to harvest a meagre amount of garden produce which continued to grow with little human intervention, although the earth-lodges themselves were then probably dilapidated if not caved in owing to a lack of maintenance, so that they were hardly if ever utilized again as permanent dwellings; portable hide tepees being employed instead.

It is indicative to note the existence of burial mounds in the Biesterfeldt town's immediate vicinity which, the Sioux assert, were made by Cheyennes who of old resided in the area. This must show conclusively that the specific band of Cheyennes occupying the site, once practiced a kind of Mound Builder cult as was current albeit to a far greater degree, among certain Siouans, particularly the Omaha and Oto and from whom, as has been opined in a previous chapter, the Cheyennes had probably picked up the custom, as no other Algonquian-speaking peoples are known to have employed such a practice.

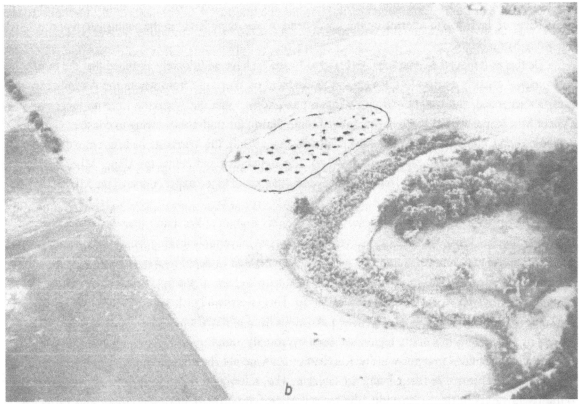

ENHANCED ARIAL VIEW OF THE BIESTERFELDT SHEYENNE RIVER VILLAGE SITE.
[Courtesy of the Smithsonian Contributions to Anthropology. Number 15.]

The Cheyenne Priest Chief, Flying-Thunder-Eagle, declared to William Strong in 1940, that Cheyennes had been residing permanently in the Valley of Sheyenne River as early as circa, 1600, and that their last village in the valley was still occupied until late in the eighteenth century.

The first date given by Flying-Thunder-Eagle does appear far too early for the Biesterfeldt site given the evidence on hand, although his second date would fit well with the general period of abandonment by a particular Cheyenne-speaking group of a permanent earth-lodge town, ostensibly sited along the course of the Lower Sheyenne, and of which we have documented evidence for its destruction, although not an exact date or even of the town's true position. Flying-Thunder-Eagle`s statement does infer, however, that there was more than one Cheyenne village along that river, which might give credence to his proposed early date for original Cheyenne settlement – even if occupied only sporadically - in the vicinity.

Dakota Sioux traditions on the other hand, seem to imply that they themselves knew of only one Cheyenne town actually sited on the Lower Sheyenne, and this they say was known as *"Shaiena- Wojubi"* which translates from the Sioux as, *"Where the Cheyennes plant,"* although Sioux traditions also refer to other Cheyenne-speaking groups which may have included one or more Suhtaio band, which likewise of old, resided in various earth-lodge villages located at unspecified sites in the same Coteau district. Added to this, the informant Flying-Thunder-Eagle further stated that the last permanent village to be occupied by Cheyennes in the Sheyenne River valley, was called by the Cheyennes themselves, *"Mo-om-sta-sha"* meaning "River of Reeds," and that the people sometimes ate the roots of such reeds for sustenance. It is indicative that this same name was later given to a later-date permanent earth-lodge town belonging to a Cheyenne group then positioned along the Missouri on that river`s west side known archaeologically as the "Farm School Site," and of which there has survived in both Cheyenne and Sioux traditions a few fragments of information to be discussed in a later chapter.

What is also important is that the eminent Ethnologist George Bird Grinnell stated in 1927 that of old, some Cheyennes fashioned the strings of their bows from a certain tall reed called `Milkwood.` This they twisted or braided to give it strength, and were unique among others of their Nation by employing this material in such a manner. What then more likely a name to dub upon this band whose peculiar habit it was to utilize these reeds in such a way than "Bowstrings," when all other Cheyenne-speaking bands used animal sinew to serve the same purpose? Indeed, this fact only adds substance to our previous assertion, that the Biesterfeldt site on the Lower Sheyenne was occupied by that Cheyenne group known as "Bowstrings," and that other tribes in their wisdom dubbed all Cheyenne-speaking bands "People of the Bowstrings" [later contracted by the French to *"Gens de Arc"* or "People of the Bow"] as a consequence.

It is not unlikely that Cheyenne-speaking peoples belonging to one group or another, had entered the Coteau des Prairies west of Red River at a much earlier date than even our present study has supposed, as early, in fact, as when Cheyenne hunting grounds proper were in close proximity to the Headwaters of the Mississippi and even earlier, whilst resident in the Upper and Lower Red Lakes district during the latter decades of the sixteenth century. The people then had only to follow

324

the course of a connecting river flowing almost due west from Lower Red Lake in order to reach the Red River itself. Whereupon, they could easily cross over into the tall-grass Coteau country on that river's west side. This is not to suggest that Cheyennes ever took up permanent residence in the Coteau des Prairies at such an early date, merely that they, or rather one or more of their bands, sporadically frequented that country during extended buffalo hunts and when conducting war ventures against tribes already hunting those prairies, such as the Arickara and Mandan whose villages stood further west on both sides of the Missouri.

Traditions from the Cheyennes relating to their early wanderings and lifestyle after migrating south from the Ontario lakes country, indicate as much, and perhaps they built several villages west of the Red and along the Lower course of the Sheyenne prior to circa, 1690. One or more such villages may have comprised a cluster of earth and timber-framed lodges, albeit of a more primitive construction than apparent during a later period, whilst other sites may have consisted merely of temporary shelters fashioned from brush and hides sufficing for short visits, or at the most, a season`s occupation, and this only when a particular Cheyenne-speaking band conducted communal buffalo or skunk hunts in the game lands of the Coteau.

About thirty miles almost due north of the Biesterfeldt site is the middle course of another waterway known as Maple River, not to be confused with the previously mentioned Maple Creek further west near the town of Kulm. This eastern Maple River flows south then northeast before entering the Sheyenne River only a few miles from that river`s mouth, and hereabouts on the Lower bend of Maple River, another old village site - smaller than that of Biesterfeldt - has since been discovered and partially excavated by the archaeologist.

This latter site is also situated on a bluff and overlooks the aforesaid Maple River on its north bank. The remains of what appears to have been a defensive inner ditch is clearly visible, although now almost completely filled in, but which, evidently, had been constructed at a time when the site contained only a small group of people. There is also an outer ditch with a raised embankment which encompasses a much larger living area likely constructed at a later date of occupancy after the population of the site had expanded to a significant degree. This outer ditch shows a consistent line of post-molds atop its bank which indicates that the expanded site was threatened with assault, and thus was additionally fortified with a stockade or picket fence. The village during its second phase, must have housed a fairly large population and is known as the Shea site, from the name of he who first located its position.

No strong evidence of earth and timber lodges or even house-rings have yet been observed at the Shea site, although several fire hearths; floor plans and some post-molds have been uncovered, albeit of irregular shape and size. Fragments of elbow catlinite pipes, the material of which originates from the Pipe Stone Quarries of southwestern Minnesota, along with Pottery shards showing very close if not identical associations with "Sandy Lake" ware from northern Minnesota and mixed with both "Oneota" and "Black Duck," have been found throughout the enclosed area and in debris strata in the site's outer ditch. Most bone finds indicate a dependence upon buffalo as a source for both food and implements, while numerous skunk bones suggest that animal supplemented the diet of the occupants. Small amounts of seed particles were also found, indicating some degree of planting and harvesting in close proximity to the village, but owing to the site's elevated and exposed position, it has been assumed that the site was only occupied for short periods, perhaps seasonally during the warm-weather months and abandoned periodically, in order to escape the extreme cold and severe winter winds and blizzards of the region.

Radio-carbon dates gleaned from fragments of charcoal and other debris within the site, suggest a period of occupancy between 1400 and 1643 with a mean date of circa, 1448. These dates are much too early, one might think, for the site to have been related to, or in some other way connected with the Biesterfeldt site on the Lower Sheyenne. But all these dates are probably too early, and the last date of 1643 could be much later, which was the calibrator's own opinion due to the unreliability of samples tested.

In total, there are five such sites discovered to date which compare favorably with that of Shea. All have been found in the area of the Lower Sheyenne River valley; are of similar size and each is situated atop a bluff or high point. Each site is surrounded by a ditch with evidence of a picket fence or stockade atop its bank. These sites also show comparable cultural aspects to that known as "Middle Missouri," examples of which are found along the middle course of the river of that name, and this fact, coupled with the presence of "Sandy Lake" ware, leads one to suppose that the Shea village site and those sites related to it found elsewhere in the Lower Sheyenne valley, [but not including the Biesterfeldt site], had originally belonged to the old-time Hidatsa who, for an extensive period between circa, 1550 and 1740, were in harmonious and close contact with Cheyenne and Suhtaio groups then east of and in the Coteau country.

I think there can be little doubt that the original occupants of the Shea site were the forefathers of historic Hidatsa, as according to that people's own traditions, they had once resided in the Sandy Lake area of the Upper Mississippi and as late as the middle years of the nineteenth century, the Chippewa could still point out old sites of permanent villages of earth and timber lodges where, the Chippewa declared, the old-time Hidatsa once resided. Both Hidatsa and Chippewa traditions also mention the existence of a number of scattered Hidatsa villages in the region of both the Lower and Upper stretches of Sheyenne River, and we have already noted how pottery types found in the region and designated Sandy Lake, as well as at the Shea and other sites west of Red River, are also found in the ruins of so-called "Middle Missouri" villages along the river of that name, in locations where also the Hidatsa at a later date resided. This, of course, indicates a western movement by a single cultural group, and concurs with what we know regarding the migrations of the Hidatsa from central Minnesota west to the Missouri River and beyond.

In brief, Hidatsa tradition indicates their people's residence in the Coteau country between the Missouri on the west and the Red River on the east, as occurring between circa, 1640 and 1740, although prior to the latter date, the Hidatsa-proper group which then included that faction later known as River Crow, was located near the headwaters of the Sheyenne and in the vicinity of present day Devil's Lake. Even earlier sites of Hidatsa occupation south in the Sheyenne River valley, had been abandoned one-hundred and fifty years before that time.

Certain Cheyenne and Suhtaio bands were once closely associated with the Hidatsa when in northern and central Minnesota, and also whilst in the Coteau country west of the Red. Thus, Cheyenne groups were probably well-acquainted with the so-called Shea site and its related villages even prior to Cheyennes themselves entering the Coteau district as permanent residents. However, as Shea site pottery shards show some "Black Duck" pieces which, we have averred in an earlier chapter, should mostly be associated with the old-time Suhtaio in conjunction with one or more Cheyenne-proper groups of northern Minnesota, then Cheyennes or Suhtaio may indeed, albeit at a later date than the original Hidatsa residents, have taken over some of the old abandoned Hidatsa sites such as that of Shea, and utilized their strategic positions for short periods when roaming the adjoining districts. By so doing, other tribes, especially the Sioux after the date 1650, began to associate the Cheyenne and Suhtaio with these same sites. The fact that the Shea site stands so close to that of Biesterfeldt, suggests that either it was abandoned by the Hidatsa long before circa 1600 when Cheyennes first arrived in the Lower Sheyenne River valley as Flying-Thunder-Eagle asserted, or that the later occupants of Shea who, incidentally, most likely navigated the outer perimeter ditch thereby extending the original living area of the village, belonged to either the Pipe-Stem Men or, at a later date to the Masikota/Aorta, and at an even later date to a Suhtaio band, and thus including the Cheyenne-speaking group referred to by Alexander Henry in 1801, as having abandoned their village in the Lower Sheyenne region around the date 1740.

THE OLD VILLAGE SITE OVERLOOKING THE NORTH BANK OF MAPLE RIVER.
[Arial photo courtesy of "The Shea Site."]

Certainly, the Shea site has definite connections with old village sites of the late seventeenth century in the Big Stone Lake and Lake Traverse districts of the Upper reaches of the Minnesota, and also shows close contact with Omaha and Oto sites in which Oneota-proper ceramics are found. Most important is that the Shea site by its numerous broken remains of catlinite pipes, appears to have been a place where such pipes were manufactured and this, together with the foregoing, would fit well with what we know regarding the Pipe-Stem-Men who, at a later date, were closely associated with the Suhtaio and were not only allies and close confederates of Oneota peoples such as the Omaha and Oto, but had been the advance guard, so to speak, of all other Cheyenne-speaking bands in their various migrations west.

Perhaps then, as the Shea site shows intermediate periods of occupation, this site, although likely earlier occupied by the Hidatsa, was at the later period beginning around 1650, being sporadically utilized by either the Pipe-Stem-Men, Masikota/Aorta or the Suhtaio and, as a consequence, was remembered by both the Sioux and Chippewa as being another old-time Cheyenne village. Such would corroborate Flying-Thunder-Eagle`s statement, that there had once been several permanent Cheyenne villages in the region.

Returning to the Bowstrings Cheyenne group, we can be sure from tribal traditions and documented evidence, that the particular earth-lodge village known as the Biesterfeldt site overlooking the southern bend of the Sheyenne, was utilized for a very long time; certainly longer than the thirty or so years asserted by Hyde [1915], supposedly from oral tradition. I think it likely that Hyde, albeit one of the most perceptive and informed scholars in his field, assumed a period of occupancy for this and other earth-lodge villages, by calculating the usual time it would take the lodges to succumb to a state of being considered beyond repair, and of how many years it would usually take on average, before adjoining fields became over worked and sterile, not to mention the implications deduced from Sioux traditions concerning the length of occupancy for the same site, coupled with the above mentioned account of Alexander Henry, who recorded a version of the destruction of a Cheyenne village somewhere in the Coteau des Prairies, and which he supposed, once stood overlooking a point on the Lower Sheyenne. In reality, these references may not apply to the Biesterfeldt site specifically, but to one or another permanent Cheyenne or Suhtaio village positioned further west in the Coteau, but of which during the times of both Henry and Hyde, there was no discernable evidence to prove their existence.

More recent studies indicate that the Biesterfeldt site housed in excess of one-thousand persons, suggesting a fighting force of some three-hundred warriors. House remains show both early and late examples of earth-lodge construction, extending over a period of at least seventy years, while the town itself was long known as a well-recognized feature of the country. A land mark for many years; its inhabitant's right to remain in such a position having been upheld not a few times, it is said, by bloody battles fought outside its walls.

In all fairness to Hyde, it will be noted in a later chapter how the Cheyenne inhabitants around the date 1771, were forced to abandon the Biesterfeldt village as a year-round seat of occupation, and having taken to a predominantly nomadic existence far into the Coteau country, they only returned to the village for short periods thereafter, in order to plant and harvest certain crops, and which they continued to do until late into the eighteenth century when the village was finally destroyed by enemies. But this also belongs to a later chapter.

In the meantime, let us continue with those other Cheyenne and Suhtaio groups later wandering the same Coteau des Prairies, and determine their subsequent movements and connections both friendly and hostile, with foreign peoples west of the Minnesota and beyond.

- 0 - 0 - 0 - 0 - 0 - 0 - 0 - 0 - 0 - 0 - 0 - 0 - 0 - 0 - 0 - 0 – 0 -

CHAPTER 31.

ROAMERS IN THE COTEAU COUNTRY.

The Coteau country consists of two distinct topographical features. On the east it is known as the Coteau des Prairies, composed of a rolling hill-invested plateau, stretching from eastern South Dakota in the north, to northwestern Iowa in the south, a distance of some two-hundred miles. Its broad uplands slope gently down to the Red River on the east and to the valley of James River on the west. A corridor covered with a carpet of lush green which, but for thick growths of timber along the courses of numerous rivers and streams flowing south and east, the central area is mostly devoid of trees and only a few rocky heights and shallow ravines break the monotony of the hilly landscape. Standing atop such rolling heights, one can see for miles in every direction until the prairie horizon merges with the vast blue sky. In summer there is oppressive heat - sultry and sticky, whilst in winter the snow is deep and drifting, and severe northern winds cut like a knife through one`s clothing and chills to the bone.

To the west lies the Coteau des Missouri, stretching from the southern branch of the Saskatchewan River of south-eastern Alberta in the north, to north-central South Dakota in the south where it abuts James River and the Coteau des Prairie on the east, thence extending west to and across the Missouri. This latter region consists of Lower undulating hills interspersed by numerous small kettle lakes, although other than a few streams flowing west into the Missouri, it is a land of scant waterways.

In such an environment, however, game was abundant. Herds of bison, deer, elk and antelope roamed the length and breadth of the Coteau, along with numerous small animals such as fox, wolf, skunk and prairie-dog which were also found in quantity.

During the latter half of the seventeenth century and the first half of the eighteenth, several tribal groups inhabited the Coteau, each having spilled over at one time or another from the timbered lake country of the east, and here they had settled, hemmed in by the Red and Missouri rivers on either side.

At that time, Hidatsa [then including their offshoots later known as River Crow], could be found entrenched in several earth-lodge villages in the Devil's Lake area and along the Upper branches of the Sheyenne River, while three or four Arapahoe bands incorporating those later known as Atsina or Gros Ventre of the Prairies, occupied lands north and northeast of the Hidatsa. Some Caddoan groups, predominately Arickara from the Missouri banks, often roamed east far into the Coteau, while Cheyenne and Suhtaio could be found in the central area and along the Lower course of the Sheyenne itself. Across the whole, war-parties from various Nations including Assiniboine, Cree, Chippewa and Sioux, crisscrossed the rolling grasslands en-route to and from their enemy's villages.

No documentation exists before circa, 1740 regarding the condition and more precise locations of those resident peoples, and we must again resort to tribal tradition, in order to piece together the history of this period of roving which relates to the early days of Cheyenne occupation west of the Minnesota River.

The Sioux traditions are important here, as they contain more exact information concerning not only their own people, but also of those with whom they were then in contact. Certainly this is true as far as the Cheyenne and Suhtaio are concerned, perhaps because in later years, the latter were more closely aligned with certain Sioux bands than were other tribes of the Coteau.

The well-known "Winter-Counts" of the respective Sioux bands, although sometimes contradictory in content when referring to early events, do nonetheless corroborate Cheyenne tradition in some respects and occasionally, actually add important details long since forgotten by the Cheyennes themselves. This is because the Sioux remained in the Coteau district long after the Cheyenne and Suhtaio had moved far to the west, and as a result, lost much of their memory relating to this period in their history.

It is not unlikely that of old, Cheyennes could also recall their history in a more precise and detailed form than was evident in a later century, and this much is suggested by certain terms of phraseology used by several Cheyenne informants, which indicate their having once calculated years by remembering important events and episodes identical in style to that of the various Sioux Winter-Counts. Examples of this are given throughout this study, but alas, no continuous record which might once have been kept by Cheyennes with the use of a similar calendar system to the Sioux has come down to us. It would appear that knowledge of these "counts" if in truth they did exist among the Cheyenne, simply died out with the demise of the "Keeper," or if ever committed to more permanent form such as pictographs painted on hide or cloth as was the case with the calendar records of the Sioux and Kiowa among others, then among the Cheyennes they no longer exist - perhaps buried with their owners or destroyed. One should remember that the Cheyenne among all tribes which did keep such records, suffered far worse in their later-day wars with the white man; many of their villages being destroyed by fire and countless numbers of their population either killed or scattered. Sometime during the course of this latter period of almost constant conflict and dispersal, the Cheyenne may have lost their `counts,` and only those events recalled to mind from fragmentary traditions survive among them.

Having said this, the Sioux `counts` often err by a few years either way when relating to events in which they were not personally involved. They do, however, offer a general dating for certain historical episodes, and more than once corroboration from an independent source enables the researcher to be more precise.

Thus even as late as the eighteen-nineties, certain Sioux Indians could locate with a degree of accuracy, the various village sites once occupied by Cheyenne-speaking groups along the Minnesota, and could trace their movements thereafter with appropriate dates, across the Coteau des Prairies to the Missouri and beyond, merely by using a particular winter-count as an aid to memory.

In later years Blue-Thunder, a Yankton Sioux historian, could determine the extent of residence of particular Cheyenne-speaking bands along the Missouri, simply by counting the number of years back or forward from a recognized event such as "The year the stars fell," which we know from documented and scientific evidence, relates to a Leonid meteoric shower which occurred in the night sky across the North American Continent in November 1833.

As mentioned above, the dating of these Cheyenne movements are not intended to be exact, although the actual positions of the various Cheyenne village sites reported by the Sioux are, for the most part, substantiated by present-day archaeology and by what remains of Cheyenne tradition itself. The migration of the Masikota Cheyennes from the Minnesota country being a case in point.

The situation of the Masikota was, that while the Pipe-Stem-Men had been defending their hearths on the Yellow Medicine against various enemies and conducting their own hostile forays west in their quest for horses, scalps and captives, the Masikota Cheyennes, having moved south from the Upper Mississippi forks, were still in residence near the mouth of Blue Earth River, and remained so as late as the early 1690s.

Each of the then existing Cheyenne groups would have been in contact with one another to a greater or less degree, and the migration of one group would not have gone entirely unnoticed by the others, even though in later years, Cheyenne informants could only recall their own particular groups migrations, and gave confused information when attempting to trace a common route for the Nation as a whole.

There was indeed, a general upheaval of all Cheyenne-speaking peoples during the last decade of the seventeenth century, and although each Cheyenne faction moved separately, the underlying incentive was the same for all.

It is evident that soon after the Pipe-Stem Men abandoned their village on the Yellow Medicine and moved southwest in the wake of the Omaha and Iowa, the Masikota Cheyennes near the mouth of the Blue Earth did not themselves remain long in that area, but likewise moved west, and according to both Cheyenne and Sioux tradition, while a part of that group settled between Big Stone Lake and Lake Traverse, the majority went farther west and built a new village in the prairies of south-central North Dakota. This Masikota movement from the Blue Earth must have occurred prior to 1695, at which date the French trader LeSueur reached the mouth of that same river and found the whole central Minnesota country overrun with Sioux.

It had been the guns and ammunition traded by Perrot to the Yanktonai and other Sioux groups, which had enabled the latter to expel the Omaha, Iowa, Oto and Pipe-Stem Men from their seats, and subsequently, the Yanktonai and their Teton allies then took possession of all the territory for many miles north and south of the Minnesota. It was obviously this shift in the balance of power which inaugurated the migration of all Cheyenne and even Suhtaio groups from the region, although today, the Cheyennes attribute this upheaval and the abandonment of their hearths and fields along the Minnesota, to their personal preference of isolating themselves from foreign influences as were then crowding upon them, rather, that is, than the result of actual conflict. However, although the Masikota Cheyennes had earlier been friends and allies to most Eastern [Dakota] Sioux bands when resident about the headwaters of the Upper Mississippi, and later, when entrenched in the vicinity of the Blue Earth they had been in a league with a number of Teton bands, particularly those later known as Oglala and Brule and among whom, traditionally, the Cheyennes are said to have introduced their Kit-Fox Warrior Society, there is abundant evidence to suggest that before the close of the century, most if not all Cheyennes were being vigorously raided by Eastern Sioux, moreover the Santee and Sisseton, and perhaps William P. Clark's Cheyenne informant Black-Moccasin was referring to this particular period of warfare between his people and the Sioux, when he stated in 1880,

> "For many years we were at war with the Sioux, particularly the Wychayelas. (All those with the `n` and `d` dialects.). [1]

These dialects refer to the Assiniboine, Yanktonai and Santee Sioux specifically, and hostilities of these three against the Cheyenne and Suhtaio, continued in earnest as late as the opening of the nineteenth century.

Initially, the principle aggressors appear to have been the Assiniboine, often in company with Cree and Chippewa allies and generally referred to in Cheyenne tradition by the collective term of "Ho-Hay." Since a few years prior to 1690, Ho-Hay enemies had been assaulting all Sioux bands with a relentless vigor, and it was the involvement of Cheyennes as allies to the Teton which finally induced most Cheyenne peoples of the Upper Mississippi to abandon that area and retire towards the south and southwest. Certainly as late as 1741, a combined Cree and Assiniboine war-band at the instigation of the French, executed a devastating raid on the Prairie [i.e. Western or Teton] Sioux, which likely included Cheyennes, when it was reported that at least 160 Prairie Sioux were killed including men, women and children, and so many captives taken and sold to the French as slaves, that when later paraded through the streets of Montreal, the captives created a line some 250 yards in length. [2]

Meanwhile, the Bowstrings of the Mississippi Headwaters region, had also been forced out of the district completely, perhaps in part by a sudden influx of Teton refugees, but more likely by the guns of the Assiniboine and Cree alone, and, as noted in the previous chapter, the Bowstrings then migrated west beyond Red River and into the long-grass rolling country of the Coteau des

Prairies. In this land close to the date 1690 on a bluff-top overlooking the Lower bend of Sheyenne River, they built a large stockade earth-lodge village now referred to as the Biesterfeldt site.

In 1695 the Frenchman LeSueur in the interest of trade, persuaded the Dakota Sioux on one side and the Chippewa and Cree on the other, to put aside their tomahawks and make peace, and as a result, the weight of Chippewa and Cree harassment directed against the Cheyenne was, for a while at least, lifted from them. This fact corroborates the assertion that the expulsion of the Bowstrings had occurred prior to the date of LeSueur's peacemaking of 1695.

Now, though, the Eastern Sioux [Santee and Sisseton] upon securing all the firearms they needed from both French and English traders, either on a direct basis or indirectly through their new-found Chippewa and Cree allies, suddenly turned savagely upon their own relatives the Teton and Yanktonai [Prairie or Western Sioux] and shortly thereafter, drove them from the prairies and woodlands about the Upper Mississippi forks south towards the Great Bend of the Minnesota and west, as far as Big Stone Lake at that river's head.

During the later date of the early 1740s –long after the eviction of the Teton and Yanktonai - the latter's one-time Moiseo remnant neighbours about the Mississippi headwaters, also fled west beyond the Red River as their relatives the Masikota, Aorta and Bowstrings had done one half-century earlier, although in the case of this Moiseo remnant, it was to escape the Santee and Sisseton Sioux specifically. This Moiseo remnant, thereafter, roamed back and forth over the Coteau des Prairies, at first living in small brush or skin shelters transported on the backs of their women and their dogs, although periodically they did return to the lake country of northern Minnesota in order to fish, and if the Assiniboine and other enemies allowed respite, they hunted moose and exploited the gatherings of wild fowl which flocked to the lakes in great multitudes during the nesting and molting season. Likewise, around the same date of 1740, the Suhtaio [i.e. *Chongaskitons*] of the Mississippi Headwaters district, although initially ignored by the Yanktonai and Tetons who had evicted the Pipe-Stem-Men from the Yellow Medicine - were themselves soon after the expulsion of the Moiseo remnant, also beset by the Santee and Sisseton, and were obliged by direct hostile pressure to abandon their homes and migrate in a southwest direction.

Travelling west along the course of the Upper Minnesota, the Suhtaio by-passed Big Stone Lake and relocated further west in the Coteau at a place called Kettle Lakes near the present-day town of Sisseton in what is now South Dakota, and where they were still entrenched when noted under the name *Chongaskiton* by Johnathan Carver in 1766 /`68.

It is unlikely then, that any Cheyenne-speaking band was a permanent fixture in the Minnesota country after the date 1741 at the latest, and only the sporadic excursions of Moiseo remnants into the northern lake district of that state, bore testimony to a former Cheyenne and Suhtaio residence and of that people's ancient right of occupancy.

The Santee and Sisseton on the other hand, once having established themselves along the Lower course of the Minnesota, appeared content for a while, and so those Cheyenne and Teton groups at the head of that river were allowed to remain in situ, even though they generally preferred to hunt west and southwest of their villages, rather than aggravate the situation with the Eastern

Sioux by re-entering their old lands downstream near the Minnesota's Elbow Bend unless compelled to do so, or during such times when the Eastern Dakota felt congenial enough to allow them to pass through their newly acquired territory unmolested.

A tentative peace then prevailed, during which trading relations were revived. But such gatherings as took place at the head of the Minnesota and which soon became annual events, were always on a precarious footing with neither side trusting the other, and such "Trading Fairs" as they became known, were likely to erupt into bloody melees upon the slightest pretext.

Yet with all this, the Cheyennes with their hearth-fires extinguished in the Minnesota country, had moved into the Coteau; never again to claim a permanent seat of residence east of the Red River of the North.

Dakota Sioux tradition tells us that the Cheyenne group once in residence in one or more villages near the mouth of the Blue Earth, left the Minnesota country a short time before 1695, and settled for a time between Lake Traverse and Big Stone Lake at the head of the Minnesota. Cheyenne tradition verifies this statement and further declares that most of this group then left the latter area and moved west into the Coteau des Missouri, where they built a new earth-lodge village situated on a flat at the head of Maple Creek, a stream flowing into the Missouri from the east. This particular village stood slightly southwest of the present-day town of Kulm, and not far from this site are several earthen burial mounds, said by the Sioux of the district to have also been built by Cheyennes who of old, lived in that vicinity, and as late as the middle of the nineteenth century, the remains of permanent house sites were still visible.

Continuing with Sioux tradition, it is said that these Cheyennes on Maple Creek near Kulm, lived there for a number of years before moving further west to the Missouri River, and after a short stay on the east side, eventually crossed to the Missouri's west bank and built another earth-lodge town overlooking the mouth of Porcupine Creek only a few miles north of where Fort Yates later stood near the North–South Dakota state line. This last-named village on Porcupine Creek stood at a point in almost direct line from that of the old site near Kulm, which; so the same informants told George Hyde, had been occupied for thirty years or so before the people's move across the Missouri to the Porcupine.

We have in the Sioux accounts a few dim clues as to the identity of this Cheyenne group on Maple Creek. They stated that those Cheyennes once living near the mouth of the Blue Earth, were in friendly intercourse with Teton Sioux of that region, and in contact with all other Cheyenne-speaking bands of the Minnesota country and with those beyond that river in the west.

Only the Masikota with their Aorta associates once in residence in the Blue Earth district, had actually been in alliance with the Teton during those early years, whilst their kinsmen the Pipe-Stem-Men and Bowstrings were then generally at loggerheads with all Sioux-speaking bands, or at least, were reluctant to have much contact with them. Only the Masikota, therefore, would have felt at ease near the head of the Minnesota amid a host of Sioux groups, and likely to have been tolerated by the Sioux themselves.

Corroborating the above is that a number of Miniconjou Sioux informants of Josephine Waggoner early in the 1920s, stated that soon after the date 1740, when the Miniconjou first settled around Big Stone Lake, the old fields and fences of the previous Cheyenne tenants were still to be seen. They further said that a part of the Masikota remained in that area and inter-married among the Miniconjou. Perhaps then, these Cheyenne stragglers from the main Masikota and Aorta group belonged to either the *Oqutuna* or *Hofnowa* Cheyenne sub-bands, both of which were off-shoots from the parent Masikota. Indeed, at the later date of 1825, the Masikota were still visiting and camping on the west bank of the Missouri, close to and in harmony with a large Miniconjou Sioux band, the latter then residing in a permanent earth-lodge village on the Missouri`s west bank. Among the Masikota at that time was the Suhtaio-born Sweet Medicine Chief, High-Backed-Wolf, who earlier had joined the main Masikota band and among whom was the old Moiseo Kit-Fox faction [i.e. Aorta] with the Sacred Arrows and their keeper.

That those Cheyennes remaining in situ about the head of the Minnesota were indeed a part of the Masikota division, is evidenced by the fact that a small band by that name, was still located near Big Stone Lake and confederated with Teton bands of that area many years later. However, by then they were generally known by the colloquial term *Sheyo,* and under which name are documented as residing in the aforesaid area as late as circa, 1800, albeit as a band small in size. Usually they have been classified as Teton Sioux, although their precise tribal affiliation has always been in doubt. The name itself of *Sheyo* is a Sioux term interpreted as referring to the "Forked-tailed-grouse," but has a more definite connotation of "Legs Flexed," and it is this name which seems to bear more than a little relationship with the Cheyenne proper designation of Masikota, a variant translation of which, as noted in an earlier chapter, is also "Legs Flexed." It is apparent that in reality, the *Sheyo* by circa, 1800, had become a mixed band of Cheyenne and Teton Sioux whose mutual association could be traced back through the years to their earlier period of residence near the mouth of the Blue Earth River.

From this brief analysis, it can nonetheless be ascertained with a degree of certainty, that the Cheyenne group later entrenched in a permanent earth-lodge village at the head of Maple Creek near Kulm, and even later at a site overlooking the mouth of Porcupine Creek on the west side of the Missouri, belonged to the Masikota division.

Much is recalled in Cheyenne tradition concerning their people's period of occupancy in the Coteau des Prairies, particularly of the Masikota whilst inhabiting the Maple Creek site near Kulm, and of the Bowstrings at the Biesterfeldt site on the Lower Sheyenne. Most of these recollections refer specifically to the people's lifestyle at that time.

In late spring or early summer, corn, squash, beans and other food stuffs along with a little tobacco were planted outside the town in small fields on the adjoining flats, after which the whole band, including men, women and children and their dogs, would move out on foot into the very heart of the prairie in search of buffalo, deer and antelope. Such animals would supply them with meat and with robes and hides for clothing and most all their domestic needs. In early August, the people would return to their town and harvest their crops, during which time they resided in earth-

335

lodges, but if the weather was still warm, they often camped in small brush and deer hide shelters outside the town. Here they would stay for several weeks making leather garments and moccasins, all elaborately embroidered with either flattened dyed porcupine quills, elk teeth or an assortment of furs. They also made pottery as described in an earlier chapter along with other domestic items and utensils, and come late autumn or early winter, the band would go again far out into the prairie on its winter hunt, at which time the buffalo robes were thick, although then the old people, the infirm and very young would remain behind at the town in their earth-lodges.

Buffalo were usually hunted in a manner which has since become known as the "surround." When a herd was sighted the whole band would form a circle encompassing the animals, then by waving their robes and arms, beating drums and shouting, the people would drive the herd into a bunch, whereupon they would gradually tighten the circle so that the entrapped animals could not maneuver effectively for lack of space. The menfolk would then shoot the animals in succession with arrows one after the other until all were killed. The entire population of a small herd would often be completely wiped out in such a manner, supplying the people with enough meat to last several months, along with material for the people's every need.

During winter when there was much snow on the ground, the animals singularly or in threes and fours, would be driven into the deep drifts by the women and children and whilst the animals were floundering, the men would rush up and kill them with arrows and spears. Even dogs were taught to assist in these hunts so that if an entrapped animal broke out of the surround, the dogs would bark and snap at its legs to drive it back into the circle.

Before the Cheyennes obtained horses, enough for their every need, the people owned many dogs; semi-domesticated and actually more wolf in manner and appearance than those kept in a later century. Upon the backs of these animals and upon small hide sledges which they pulled, the womenfolk packed all their camp baggage and equipment and after the big tribal hunts after the meat had been butchered, it was the chore of the dogs to drag home the heavy cuts of meat which were attached to long leather thongs tied to the necks of the dogs. It is said that upon reaching camp where they were relieved of their loads, the dogs would immediately race back to the scene of slaughter no matter how distant, and gorge upon the abandoned carcasses. Old informants used to relate how the bitches upon returning home, would regurgitate the meat from their stomachs for their puppies to feed on.

Buffalo, though, were not found in great abundance in the Coteau des Prairies year round, mainly because their having to cross the wide and treacherous Missouri River from the west. This river for most of the year was deep and fast flowing, and only occasionally were the herds likely to cross in any sizeable number. It was perhaps because of the sporadic scarcity of buffalo in the Coteau region and the Cheyenne's growing dependence upon them that certain rituals then evolved among the people, along with the emergence of Buffalo Priests who professed to having received special powers enabling them to bring forth the buffalo when needed.

It is known that during the latter decade of the seventeenth century and during the first decade of the eighteenth, the climate was such in the Coteau that corn-growing suddenly became a non-viable occupation owing to harsher weather conditions, particularly drought, which created a more acute dependence on hunting rather than raising crops. Thus with the unique powers now held by the Buffalo Priests, a crude form of buffalo drive was often employed when suitable occasions were presented. Such times occurred when a small herd of buffalo was observed grazing near a steep cut-bank or some other natural raised feature, such as a corridor of grassland on top of an elevated plateau, edged on one or both sides by brush or ridges, preventing the herd from turning left or right, and at one end a sudden drop in the guise of a cliff edge many meters above the prairie floor. Then the people from the village would go quickly to the scene, and after arranging themselves in two long lines, a number of chosen hunters would get behind the herd and drive it forward between the two rows of people. At the same time, the Buffalo Priest who had organized the whole affair directed the people in their tasks, and placing himself in front of the beasts while uttering sacred incantations along with the burning of a certain incense, he would entice the animals towards the edge of the height. In such a manner the whole herd would blunder over the edge and if not killed outright in the fall, the surviving animals would be finished off with arrows by a selected group of hunters waiting below.

Many other animals were also hunted both for food and clothing, and these ranged from small fur-bearing animals to large bears and ruminants. Communal deer hunts are particularly mentioned which were conducted in a similar fashion as were the buffalo surrounds noted earlier. Skunks were also killed and eaten. These were gathered in great number in communal hunts, and during which the whole band took part. After a successful hunt the skunks were placed in a pile, then divided equally among the people. At other times, small hunting parties would surreptitiously revisit their old hunting grounds in the lake country of central Minnesota, in order to collect bird eggs, feathers and wild fowl when in season.

Whilst roaming these rolling grasslands following the buffalo and antelope trails, the Cheyennes lived in small portable shelters usually fashioned from animal skins, stretched over a frame-work of bent willows and which, in some respects, resembled the oval shaped sweat-lodges of historic times. At a later date than that of which we are presently concerned, buffalo hide tepees were employed, but these were much smaller than those in use after the Cheyenne became nomadic horse-riding Indians of the Western Plains and were, in truth, only as large and heavy as could be packed on a dog, or transported on a crude form of travois.

Wood of any sort was sparse and stories are told of how the people in those far off days, used bundles of twisted grass for fuel in their lodges. These bundles if twisted tightly and lit at one end, burned very slow and bright, giving sufficient light to make living in a dark earth-lodge bearable. It was only later so it is said in tradition, that the people learned that buffalo droppings commonly known as "chips," burned for a long time, and could suit all their household needs, and these were gathered from the prairie in great quantity and used instead.

There were times when the weather proved particularly harsh with excessive rain and violent winds, which made the earth-lodges themselves too damp and cold to be of comfort, if indeed, they did not collapse completely and the earth of their construction simply wash away.

When such was the case, the occupants sought the protection of wooded areas in the region bordering the west side of the Red River. This the Moiseo remnant and Suhtaio regularly did when returning at intervals to the Lake district in northern Minnesota, although the Sheyenne River people usually joined the remnant band of Masikota in the timber land about the headwaters of the Minnesota further south. This was, of course, a dangerous choice, for again the people would be vulnerable to attack from enemies toting guns. But, it was thought, if the winter was sufficiently severe, it would likely deter enemy war-parties venturing abroad in the first place.

Other anecdotes referring to actual historical events are also recalled in tradition which relates to the time when Cheyennes and Suhtaio inhabited the Coteau country. Most if not all such anecdotes have hitherto, been associated with the Biesterfeldt village on Sheyenne River, but upon close inspection of the details, it becomes clear that there has been confusion in the interpretation of events described, and that certain episodes, at least, must pertain to one or another Cheyenne or Suhtaio band and their respective villages.

By 1720, each Cheyenne-speaking group in the Coteau along with their neighbours of foreign affiliation, were yet again being constantly raided by enemies from the north and northeast and were in daily terror of their enemy's deadly "Thunder-Sticks." Predominantly, these enemies were again Plains Cree and Assiniboine, who sometimes united their forces and raided all tribes of the Coteau in formidable well-armed parties. According to the Cheyennes themselves, however, the worst aggressors were the fearsome and much hated Assiniboine. On rare occasions when Cheyennes succeeded in killing an Assiniboine, it was cause for much excitement and rejoicing. Stories relating to this period of Cheyenne history tell of one particular episode during which, it is said, an old woman brought about the destruction of an entire Assiniboine war-party by her singular action. The tale has been told in several publications, but is worth repeating here.

It had happened one time that the occupants of a Cheyenne village including the men, women and children, had gone far into the Coteau on a communal hunt as they were then apt to do during certain seasons of the year. Only one old woman and her dog remained behind, pounding bones and boiling them in order to extract the grease, which she would then mix with corn to make a nourishing dish for winter use. It was dark, and to give herself light by which to work, she had thrust a cedar torch down the back of her dress, so that the light shone over her head as she bent at her task. Whilst busily engaged, the dog began to growl and a moment later, a group of fifty tall Assiniboine warriors quietly filed through the doorway and into the lodge. No words were spoken and the warriors, seeing the woman's helplessness, casually seated themselves on the dirt floor, whilst their leader gestured to the old woman in the sign language to feed them.

The Assiniboine were dressed and painted for war. Many carried flintlock muskets with powder horns attached to a leather thong slung over one shoulder, and a quilled or beaded leather pouch bag in a like manner slung over the other and in which were musket balls, gun flints and wadding. Some had an iron-bladed tomahawk stuck in their waist-belt and every face was bedaubed with hideous pigment markings in red, green or yellow. Their long hair was parted in the middle with the side locks bunched in roles above each ear, as was then the Assiniboine custom when going to war, and in all, they presented a terrifying picture which, initially, must have instilled terror into their reluctant host. The woman, however, composed herself and kept her wits about her. She proceeded to cook meat for her uninvited guests while at the same time, she was thinking how she could escape, knowing well that once the Assiniboine had sated their hunger, they would kill and scalp her; ransack the village and destroy it.

A large sheet of tallow was hanging from the lodge wall and this she took down; fixed it to a stick and started to heat it over the fire to supplement the meat already cooking. The woman was in a desperate situation. As the sheet of tallow became hot and dripping, she suddenly whirled it around above her head and so doing, splattered her guests with boiling globules of fat.

The Assiniboine were taken by surprise and put completely off guard. It was very dark inside the lodge and in the ensuing confusion, the woman ran through the doorway and out into the murky blackness of the night. With the burning cedar torch still thrust down the back of her dress, she ran as fast as she could towards a steep bluff overlooking a river below, and sought out a water trail leading down to the river's edge.

Meanwhile, having recovered from their shock, the Assiniboines rushed out of the lodge in pursuit of the old woman, whooping and screaming for her scalp as they ran. In the dark, they could plainly see the glow of the torch ahead of them, and they raced off in that direction not knowing exactly where they were going.

When reaching the water path, the woman took the burning brand from her dress and hurled it over the edge of the bluff, while she herself crouched in hiding just off from the trail. The pursuing Assiniboine, so sure of catching the woman and not being too careful where they were headed, continued towards where they had last seen the light, and in their haste they tumbled over the steep edge of the bluff and went crashing onto the rocks below. Most were killed outright in the fall, whilst the rest lay helpless, seriously injured with broken backs, arms and legs. When at last she thought it safe to move, the old woman fled the scene and sought out her people in their hunting camp on the open prairie.

At the camp she burst out the news of what had happened, and come daylight, the whole band returned as quickly as they could to the village, the warriors running ahead in order to count their coups on the bodies of their mortal foes. After reaching the village and gazing upon the scene of destruction at the foot of the bluff, they could hardly believe their eyes. Below them, fifty of their hated Assiniboine enemies were lying where they had fallen, all tangled up together. Those of the latter who were yet alive, but seriously injured, it is said, were still moaning and writhing in their agonies. The Cheyennes were jubilant. They slaughtered those of the enemy still breathing then cut the bodies into pieces. They collected all the weapons of the foe which included metal knives, hatchets and firearms, and this, say the Cheyennes, was the first time they acquired guns and ammunition in quantity.

The Cheyennes considered the event a great victory, but soon became alarmed, and after a short period of celebration, the chiefs agreed they should abandon the village at once and move far out on the prairie, lest some of the enemy had escaped and a formidable Assiniboine war-party would soon come against them for revenge. The very next morning, the tradition continues, this particular Cheyenne band left its village and moved away to wander as pedestrian nomads, living in small portable shelters transported on the backs of their women and on pole drags pulled by dogs, as at that time there were few, if indeed, any horses among them.

The Assiniboine yet have a story preserved in their own traditions, which tells of the time an old woman led an entire war-party to its death over the edge of a bluff or some other steep height, and in which event, eleven Assiniboine warriors were killed. It can reasonably be supposed that this recollection although brief in content, does refer to the same episode as recounted above. The number of eleven warriors killed in the Assiniboine account being, perhaps, a more realistic figure rather than fifty killed which, if true, would surely have instigated a grand punitive expedition being launched by the Assiniboine against the Cheyennes for revenge.

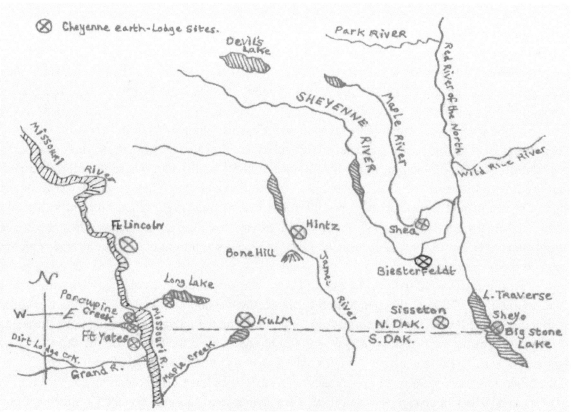

MAP OF THE COTEAU des PRAIRIES SHOWING CHEYENNE VILLAGE SITES,
[Author`s depiction]

It has hitherto been assumed by scholars, that the aforesaid massacre took place at the Biesterfeldt village on the Lower Sheyenne, but merely by the fact that the town on Sheyenne River has long been thought to be the only permanent village site definitely attributed to Cheyennes between the Missouri and Red River of the North, and further, that a water trail leading from the town to the river below is a feature of the Biesterfeldt site, which also stood on the summit of a steep bluff. There are particular reasons, though, which rule out the Sheyenne River village as being the actual site referred to in the story.

It is not inconceivable that there were other Cheyenne villages either along or near the course of the Lower Sheyenne, and it is also likely, as Cheyenne and other tribal traditions imply, that most Cheyenne villages were located adjacent to a river, and that after the people's abandonment of the Minnesota woodlands, such villages were invariably built on high ground as protection against enemy attack and floods.

In another version of the Assiniboine slaughter, albeit brief in content given by the Northern Cheyenne historian John Stands in Timber, we are told that it was mostly Suhtaio in the village at that time. Neither can we be certain that the Cheyennes [or Suhtaio] obtained their first supply of guns in the manner described, for other tribal informants stated emphatically that French or Mexican traders first brought firearms in quantity among them, prior to which only one or two such weapons had infiltrated their camps. One thing is obvious, without a regular supply of powder and ball along with even a cursory knowledge of their workings and repair, guns would soon have been rendered useless in their hands.

John Stands In Timber went on to state that the village in question had been a hunting camp; That the people had moved off except one old woman who stayed behind where the hunters had left a lot of animal bones, intending to boil them up to extract the grease and marrow. The Assiniboine then came into her lodge [i.e., tepee], and demanded food. The story then follows the same theme as recounted above, but instead of running down a water trail, the woman in John Stands In Timber`s version ran to a cut-bank and hid, whilst her pursuers went stumbling over the cliff to their deaths.

If one attempts to correlate the two accounts, then it must be assumed that the Cheyenne group in question had gone into the prairie not too far from the village, perhaps to a place where the people were accustomed to drive buffalo over a particular cliff or cut-bank. Having made their kill; butchered and packed the meat, they then returned to their earth-lodge village whilst one old woman, not being unduly concerned of staying alone on the prairie for a short period, remained behind to make grease from the discarded bones at the kill site. After the Assiniboine war-party appeared and the woman ran from the lodge, they followed her to the edge of the high bank where the buffalo drive had taken place, and over which they went tumbling to their deaths.

Of course, in later years after the story had become widely known among all Cheyenne and Suhtaio bands, each associated it as relating to one of their own old village sites when east of the Missouri, and thus we have the conflicting details in the above accounts, which in one case, it is a permanent village on top of a bluff with a water trail leading down to a river, and in the other, a hunting camp and a cut-bank on the open prairie.

All Cheyenne and Suhtaio informants agreed, however, that the massacre of the Assiniboine party by the old woman took place east of the Missouri, and at a time after the people had left the Minnesota country but before they had horses. The assertion from John Stands in Timber that it was mostly Suhtaio in camp, would rule out the Sheyenne River site [i.e. Biesterfeldt] as being the actual village in question. For later map references and journals designate the inhabitants of the Sheyenne River village specifically as Cheyenne, at a time when the Suhtaio were still regarded as a separate and distinct tribe known by the alternative names of *Chongaskiton* and *Shongashiton*. We know also from the results of excavations at the Biesterfeldt village that the inhabitants, long before abandoning the site as one of permanent occupation, owned both guns and horses, and furthermore, Cheyenne tradition is explicit in stating that the Suhtaio were met for the second time by Cheyennes when they [Cheyennes], were wandering as tepee-dwelling nomads over the Coteau in the eastern part of North Dakota *after* fleeing their village due to the Assiniboine massacre, and before settling along the Missouri`s west bank.

As regards the Suhtaio connection, it is probable that one or more old-time permanent village sites only recently discovered in the vicinity of James River near present-day Jamestown in eastern North Dakota, can be associated with Suhtaio occupation. One of these old village ruins designated as the "Hintz" site was, evidently, occupied during the 1750s and for a few decades thereafter, and thus is too late to have been contemporary with the traditional time of the Assiniboine slaughter. Niether is this site located on a bluff top, but stands at Lower level on the prairie floor.

Having said this, it is interesting to note that a very old man among the Suhtaio named Standing-All-Night who had actually been born an Arickara and died, it is said, in 1869 at the age of 140 years [but more probably 125 years, see pp. 407-409 this volume], recalled that when he was very young, circa, 1744 - 1750, his people were still in the habit of pounding down the bones of buffalo and other four-footed animals and then boiling them in order to extract the grease. Exactly what the old woman in the story of the Assiniboine massacre had supposedly been doing.

When the occupants of the Sheyenne River site did abandon their town as a permanent seat, the inhabitants were already mounted and likewise, as the Masikota had done earlier, they wandered over the Coteau for a number of years before crossing to the west side of the Missouri, and after residing for a short time adjacent to their Masikota cousins [then already entrenched for thirty years or more at the mouth of Porcupine Creek], they moved a short distance south and settled in a new earth-lodge village not far south from present-day Fort Yates. Sioux tradition concurs with this assertion, and the remains of both these sites have since been located by the Archaeologist.

Perhaps there was another earth-lodge village of either Cheyenne or Suhtaio affiliation on or in the vicinity of the Lower course of Sheyenne River, as the Priest-Chief, Flying-Thunder-Eagle asserted. But to date no other permanent village site along the Lower course of the Sheyenne which can be definitely attributed to Cheyenne occupation has since been identified.

Of several other sites recently discovered within the vicinity of the Lower Sheyenne, all supposedly have a dating which is too early to concern us here, although the river's altering course over the years may have undermined the site we should be looking for. However, at the risk of more sites being discovered in the region which might be associated with Cheyennes or Suhtaio during the mid-eighteenth century, the Masikota occupants at the head of Maple Creek near Kulm, appear to be the most likely candidates for the Cheyenne band responsible for the Assiniboine slaughter.

The assertion from the Sioux that it was the same Cheyenne group once inhabiting the Kulm village at the head of Maple Creek, which first settled in a position overlooking the mouth of the Porcupine on the west side of the Missouri, and the fact that the Sheyenne River group of Bowstring Cheyennes actually owned a good number of horses before they themselves moved across the Missouri, discredits George Bent's assertion that the first Cheyenne arrivals to settle permanently overlooking the Porcupine came from the town on the Lower bend of the Sheyenne. This is not to say that the people from this last mentioned site were not then in contact with the Masikota, and no doubt they were fully aware of the latter's movement across the Missouri at that time. The Omissis-Bowstrings would have congregated among the Masikota and Aorta when the ceremony of the Sacred Arrows required the coming together of all Cheyenne-speaking bands.

Most Cheyenne accounts state that not too long after the time of the Assiniboine massacre, the Cheyenne group occupying the village on the Lower Sheyenne adopted a semi-nomadic existence, and instead of residing year round at the Biesterfeldt site, they became more dependent for their subsistence upon what they could procure from the chase, although they did return to their old village seasonally to plant and harvest crops which they continued to cultivate.

There is extant a local legend well-known in Ransom County, North Dakota, which pertains to a time around 1740 and specifically, to the Cheyenne occupants of the Biesterfeldt village on the Lower Sheyenne. The legend states that about five miles southeast of the Biesterfeldt village within sight of, or close to a wind-swept eminence known as Horseshoe Hill, a great battle once took place between the Sioux and Cheyenne. In the event, the Cheyennes were sorely beaten due to the superior weaponry of the Sioux which included a number of guns, and as a result, the Cheyennes abandoned their village as a year-round permanent seat. The legend continues by saying that the Cheyennes then fled west deep into the heart of the Coteau des Prairies, and for several years lingered around Long Lake on the east side of the Missouri not far northeast of the Porcupine Creek site on the Missouri's west bank. If there is any truth in the legend, then, perhaps, it refers to when the people of the Biesterfeldt site for the first time, semi-abandoned their lodges, and would offer a sound reason why the Bowstring Cheyennes then adopted a semi- nomadic life-style around the same date, before returning as permanent residents of the Biesterfeldt site.

It is also indicative that at the later date of 1800, the English trader Alexander Henry the Younger noted in his diary for that year, that some sixty years earlier, i.e. 1740, Cheyennes had been obliged to abandon their village somewhere on Sheyenne River west of the Red River of the North. Certainly, from our previous analysis, the date of the Assiniboine massacre must have occurred sometime between circa, 1725 and 1735 owing to the lack of guns and other trade artefacts from the white man among Cheyennes at that time, and more importantly, the lack of horses among them as reported in the George Bent account. On the other hand, a second and final abandonment of the Biesterfeldt village by the Bowstrings as a year round seat of occupation, appears to have occurred much later around 1771, and thus both the Masikota at the Kulm site and Bowstrings at the Biesterfeldt site, albeit during widely separated periods in time, had both been obliged by hostile pressure to forsake their permanent villages in the Coteau.

It was then, no doubt, the Masikota, in company with the Aorta and after some thirty years of residence at their village near Kulm, vacated that site around 1725 due to the slaughter of the Assiniboine party by the old woman, along with the fact that the Kulm town itself by then, was probably already in a state of disrepair, and for ten years or so thereafter, the Aorta element among whom were the Sacred Arrows and their keeper, wandered over the Coteau as poor pedestrian nomads, as indeed, Bent asserted. Around the date 1735, however, the Masikota had a number of horses among them, and while the Aorta had settled in a new village in the vicinity of Long Lake on the east side of the Missouri, the main Masikota group in early 1743, actually crossed that river and established a new earth-lodge village overlooking the mouth of Porcupine Creek. The Bowstrings for their part, having also acquired horses in some quantity prior to 1743, and even though at times wandering the buffalo Plains west of the Missouri, they still regarded their town on the Lower Sheyenne as their permanent base. It was some thirty years later close to 1771, before they were obliged by enemy pressure to semi-abandon the village on the Sheyenne and take to a semi-nomadic existence, and during which time, they associated with the Aorta adjacent to Long Lake and with that Suhtaio group which having been obliged to vacate their own village at the Hintz site due to enemy harassment, was then also roaming in the Coteau country east of the Missouri.

There was, it seems, much tribal upheaval in the Coteau des Prairies and Coteau des Missouri between 1735 and 1771 attributed to enemies raiding from the north and northeast. By 1735 the Chippewa had advanced west from the western tip of Lake Superior, and begun raiding deep into central Minnesota and some distance west into the Coteau, perhaps as far as the Missouri.

As early as circa 1690, according to Arapahoe tradition, their tribe was roaming the south Saskatchewan Plains, but still indulging in a little agriculture in the Red River valley of northeastern North Dakota. They, along with the Siouan-speaking River Crow / Hidatsa practicing a similar culture, were also being beset by the Chippewa, Plains Cree and Assiniboine. These enemies first drove the Arapahoe northwest, whereupon, around 1720, the Arapahoe were then forced south by Blackfoot tribes into northeastern Montana and western North Dakota, and a few decades later around 1744, the River Crow / Hidatsa were also driven west across the Missouri.

Other groups in this part of Arapahoe tradition included a small group once known as "Wood-lodge People" and those later known as "Atsina." This last named group was a later offshoot from the Arapahoe parent band, while the Wood-lodge People had been a small independent Algonquian-speaking band that became closely confederated to the more populous Arapahoe and were absorbed by them. Also included must have been one band, at least, of Suhtaio, which, we are told in Cheyenne and Sioux tradition, roamed adjacent territory at that time.

It is certain from the evidence at hand, that since an early date and later, when in western North Dakota above the Missouri, the Arapahoe had more than a casual acquaintance with certain

Cheyenne-speaking groups, and this is indicated by the similarity of the Suhtaio dialect to that of the archaic dialect of the Arapahoe, which today is only used by Southern Arapahoe priests in certain religious ceremonies. A number of Arapahoe informants always declared that they had been closely associated with Cheyennes when resident in the valley of the Red River, and which must then refer to a time after the second Cheyenne - Suhtaio coming together in the Coteau des Prairies, rather than the latter's first meeting in northeastern Minnesota. It does appear that the Arapahoe, at first, were only in close and regular contact with the Moiseo and one Suhtaio band, although by 1740 there was some degree of contact also with both the Masikota and Bowstrings and other Suhtaio bands during the latter's excursions west of the Missouri, albeit not on a regular basis.

Now the old colonial term of *Kananivich* or it's like, meaning Bison-Path Indians, is said to have been applied specifically to the Arapahoe by the Chippewa and from whom the colonial French borrowed the name. This was also the case with the term `Fall` or `Rapid` Indians which was adopted by early English traders from an Assiniboine appellation, then applied jointly to the Arapahoe-Atsina and Hidatsa-Crow without distinction. This might serve to show that until the mid-1730s at the latest, the Arapahoe and Atsina - at that time still constituting one tribe – were still in contact with the Chippewa and Assiniboine who gave them their respective names. However, the Chippewa name of Bison-Path Indians was but a variant of Bison or Buffalo Indians, which; so we have noted in a previous chapter, was an early Chippewa term for the Suhtaio. A significant part of the Suhtaio had always been closely related to and associated with the Arapahoe, as far back as the time of the old Laurel people's expansion southeast from the Far North around the date A. D. 500, and during the later period of 1740, a part of the Suhtaio were then allied to the Arapahoe. Thus we have an explanation as to why the Arapahoe always declared that they were once closely aligned with Cheyenne-speaking peoples when in the Red River valley, and that their two tribes crossed the Missouri at the same time. The Cheyennes-proper, however, as opposed to the Suhtaio, adamantly asserted that they themselves crossed the Missouri on their own volition some years after the Arapahoe, although the Arapahoe statement would also explain why some Cheyenne informants late in the nineteenth century thought the Suhtaio a part of the Blackfoot, as at a later date, the Atsina became so closely aligned with the Blackfoot that both Indian and White observers often made no distinction between the two. The Arapahoe and their cognate groups, along with one or more Suhtaio band when earlier in adjacent areas of the northern Coteau, were then positioned some way north of the Masikota, and as a consequence, had long suffered the brunt of Assiniboine, Plains Cree and Chippewa attacks from the northeast. Thus the Arapahoe, River Crow / Hidatsa and a part of the Suhtaio had been the first peoples in the Coteau to vacate the Red River valley and the whole eastern part of North Dakota.

As a result of the eviction of the Arapahoe, those two Cheyennes groups which had moved west from Minnesota and established themselves at both the Kulm and Biesterfeldt villages, again found themselves fully exposed to the full intensity of aggression from the north and northeast. The result being that the Masikota and associated Aorta, not being in as good a protective position as were the Bowstrings on the Lower Sheyenne, were soon forced to abandon their town near Kulm as a permanent seat [perhaps due to the slaughter of the Assiniboine party by the old woman], and wander as nomads until; after ten years or so, they moved close to the Missouri, the Aorta at first to a point adjacent to what is known as Long Lake not far east of that river, while the main Masikota group moved across the Missouri to a bluff top overlooking the mouth of Porcupine Creek. The bulk of Suhtaio on the other hand, instead of moving northwest above the Missouri with the Arapahoe, remained in the Coteau des Prairies of eastern North Dakota.

Corroboration for this proposed date of Cheyenne and Suhtaio dispersal over the Coteau is to be found in Hidatsa-proper tradition, which states that their people were residing either on or near the headwaters of the Upper branches of Sheyenne River and in the Devil's Lake area of eastern North Dakota until about the date 1740, when they also were driven out by the Chippewa and others with their deadly Thunder-Sticks [i.e. Guns].

The Cree are included in the list of enemy tribes which came with their awesome weapons against all the tribes in the Coteau, to destroy, murder and enslave, and this is undoubtedly true regarding certain periods during the history of all tribes of the Eastern Dakotas. It does appear, though, particularly by what we learn from Cheyenne tradition, that between the years 1740 and 1790, the Cree were not then considered important foes. On the contrary, the Monsoni Cree division which resided immediately north and south of Rainy Lake and later around Lake of the Woods, were in some degree of friendly contact with the Moiseo Cheyenne faction and with the Suhtaio, if not with the Masikota and Bowstrings also, and hence, the Cheyenne statement that of old, the Monsoni had always been regarded as a friendly tribe. Perhaps it was this close friendship certainly between the Monsoni and Moiseo, which had persuaded other more belligerent Cree groups such as those known as Plains Cree to cease their hostility against the Suhtaio, and subsequently; for a while at least, with all other Cheyenne-speaking peoples.

The Monsoni Cree, evidently, were tolerant towards all Algonquian groups of the Red River country at this time [circa, 1740], and only their Plains Cree cousins had been deemed enemies to the Coteau tribes. But the Plains Cree by 1740, were then preoccupied in raiding towards the northwest against the Blackfoot, Arapahoe and the more remote Chipewyan tribes.

Nevertheless, it can be seen from the above that it was almost certainly due to enemy pressure, why certain bands of Suhtaio vacated the Minnesota country and moved deep into the Coteau des Prairies of eastern North Dakota, and where sometime between circa, 1740 and 1750, they confederated with the Aorta and Bowstring Cheyennes who, only recently, had semi-abandoned their permanent villages and were then wandering as nomads across the Coteau.

From here on, the Bowstrings were probably not troubled to any great extent by either Cree or Chippewa assaults until a much later date in the eighteenth century, a fact due in part that after the Bowstrings began returning sporadically to their old Sheyenne River town, they continued to raise an abundance of agricultural produce, the surplus of which - so Chippewa tradition informs us, - was then often traded to the Chippewa and at times, to the Cree.

What, though, of the Pipe-Stem-Men, who we left in the western part of the Coteau country?

CHAPTER 32.

ACROSS THE WIDE MISSOURI AND TROUBLE WITH THE MANDAN.

It has previously been noted how several decades before the migration of the Masikota from the Blue Earth district of Minnesota, the kindred Pipe-Stem-Men had already reached the Missouri and were occupying a permanent village on that river's east bank across from the mouth of White River, and roving further west, perhaps as far as the Black Hills of South Dakota.

To the white man endeavouring to carry his brand of civilization into the farthest reaches of the unknown, the Missouri was his highway; his route of exploration; his trade channel and base of operations. To the Indian, this same river was sometimes a war-road, but always a line of demarcation between the sedentary agriculturists along its course, and the buffalo-hunting wanderers of the open Plains.

For centuries past a number of tribal groups had resided in permanent villages along the Missouri, taking advantage of the rich bottom lands and flood-plains conducive to their horticultural pursuits. They also hunted various ruminants such as buffalo, antelope and deer found teeming in the vast expanse of short-grass prairie, stretching from the west bank of the river as far as the eye could see and beyond. Timber grew abundantly along the numerous streams flowing from the west into the great river itself, providing housing materials, firewood, domestic utensils and weaponry.

As early as circa, AD. 800, dome-shaped earth and timber lodges had topped the bluffs overlooking the Missouri at several points along its twisting confluence and overlooking the mouths of its many connecting streams. Certainly by 1450, clusters of such habitations were to be seen grouped according to tribe from the Niobrara River in the south, to Knife River in the north, and comprised those sedentary peoples known historically as Hidatsa, Mandan and Arickara.

As far as Indian values were concerned, these latter peoples were rich and comfortable with adequate supplies of corn, squash, beans, buffalo meat, venison and a variety of berries and tubers, along with fish from the river when needed. Their villages were many and well populated, yet their comfort had made them somewhat complacent and not so aggressive as other people further west who, in comparison, were not well-off materially or so sophisticated, being for the most part entirely nomadic.

Unfortunately, foreign peoples soon discovered the weakness of the River Tribes and by 1680, hostile war-bands from east and west of the Missouri were constantly raiding the river settlements in order to steal corn and other produce; kill the menfolk and kidnap women and children to trade in French and Spanish markets east and south.

Among these raiders Cheyennes were included, initially from Yellow Medicine River east of the Missouri. Pipe-Stem Men, in fact, in company with or at the instigation of their Omaha, Iowa and Oto allies. We might recall the Cheyenne historian Black-Moccasin's statement in 1880, that it was two-hundred and four winters before that date [1676] when Cheyennes first reached the Missouri, and the added information from Black-Pipe, that three years later, i.e. 1679, Cheyennes were at war with the Mandan living along that river`s banks. Elsewhere, Cheyenne accounts coupled with Sioux tradition declare that as early as 1683, some Cheyennes were already criss-crossing the Missouri back and forth on periodic hunting and raiding expeditions, and conducting occasional religious pilgrimages to "Navah-hous," the sacred mountain of Bear Butte north of the Black Hills in South Dakota.

These dates cannot be corroborated with any contemporary documentation, although as we have seen, events then taking place in adjoining territories involving Cheyennes and their allies against the River tribes do substantiate them. It is known that the Iowa and Oto were raiding the River Nations as early as 1679 if not before, for in that year they brought Pani captives to the French at LaSalle`s post east of the Mississippi to be sold as slaves. The Padouca scalp presented to LaSalle by an Oto warrior in 1682, showed that the latter were also raiding some distance beyond the Missouri, perhaps as far as the sand hills of western Nebraska where horse-riding Padouca-Apache groups were then entrenched. Undoubtedly, Cheyennes emulated their Siouan allies, if indeed, they had not commenced raiding west of the Missouri on their own volition, and as late as 1833 /`34, the Mandan could still recall stories of their early conflicts with Cheyennes, although not apparently, quite as far back as the initial period of hostilities.

Mandan traditions tell of a time when Cheyennes were attempting to settle permanently on the Missouri`s west bank in an area then claimed by the Mandan.

Even though Cheyennes had been crossing the Missouri as early as 1683, these had merely been brief excursions in order to obtain a few scalps, captives and horses from the Padouca and Panis, without the intention of residing permanently in the western country. Only later, having been forced to abandon the Coteau des Prairies, did some Cheyennes attempt permanent occupation on the west side of the Missouri, and only then did their conflict with the Mandan become a more serious affair.

The advent of Sioux infiltration into the Minnesota headwaters country and into the eastern part of the Coteau, was ever a threat to the Pipe-Stem-Men who, it will be recalled, were never too friendly with the Sioux and eventually, it set them upon another migration across the Missouri to the west bank where, it was hoped, the great river would act as a barrier between themselves and the Sioux. This event occurred soon after 1730, and traditional accounts from the Cheyennes say that when their people first migrated to the Missouri, they were made welcome by one of the resident River Tribes. However, as Cheyennes were then at war with all Mandans along the course of that river, it must have been the Arickara who welcomed them at that time.

Cheyenne informants of James Mooney [1907] stated that the first group of Cheyennes to reach the Missouri, settled in an earth-lodge village at a point on that river's east bank across from the mouth of White River. Soon after this they moved north to the mouth of the Little Cheyenne of South Dakota also on the Missouri`s east side, and sometime later, crossed the Missouri itself to the Big Cheyenne known as "Good River" to the Indians, and there built another earth-lodge village overlooking that river's mouth.

The Arickara, of course, had long been friends of the Pipe-Stem-Men since the intertribal peace council near the loop of the Big Sioux some fifty or more years earlier, and as will be seen below, all Cheyenne groups at a later date were much influenced by Arickara culture and, perhaps, none more so than the Pipe-Stem-Men. In the light of this, it would have been natural for the Pipe-Stem-Men to have gone straight to their good friends the Arickara, and engage in the same feuds and alliances in which their Arickara mentors were then involved.

The Arickara as a tribe was composed of members from numerous related groups, all of which belonged to the great Caddoan linguistic family and were very close relatives to those known historically as Skidi Pawnee. They then resided in several villages or towns clustered in the vicinity of the mouth of White River, this being the latter's most northern point of occupation along the Missouri at that time.

Before this, while both the Omaha and Cheyenne were residing on the Missouri's east side across from the mouth of White River, the Arickara according to Omaha tradition, had an abundance of corn, and invited six other tribes who were then without corn to spend the winter with them and share the Arickara's surplus stock.

This, the story goes, was how the Omaha first received corn and a specific sacred ceremony connected with it. On its own this assertion is contradicted by other Omaha statements which state emphatically, that their tribe was raising corn long before that time, even before their leaving the Ohio country in the east. There may, though, be some important elements of truth in the tradition and more likely, it applies to the tribe's acquisition of a specific type of Indian Maize raised by the Arickara. This was a hybrid strain which gave a twice yearly yield and was more abundant in quantity than that grown in the southern Minnesota and Iowa country from whence the Omaha had come.

It is apparent also that environmental conditions during the period in question had caused the crops to fail, and for a while, certain tribes such as the Omaha and their allies including the Pipe-Stem-Men Cheyennes, might had been forced to temporarily abandon agriculture in favor of the chase. Such a situation occurred at regular intervals among horticultural peoples both east and west of the Missouri, owing to either protracted drought or excessive precipitation, and it is known that between the years 1688 and 1707, the North Platte valley area did suffer prolonged periods of drought. This latter area includes the middle Missouri district which embraces the White River country, so that if this climatic condition extended further east as it most likely did, then those tribes east of the Missouri would have been unable to raise crops, especially corn of any quality or quantity for a significant period. It will be seen below how this particular condition did effect the Awigaxa Mandan group then living in the open Plains and along certain western tributaries of the Missouri close to the Black Hills of southwestern South Dakota, and forced them during the same period to move east to the Missouri to a point not far north of the mouth of White River. Thus when the Pipe-Stem-Men crossed the Missouri to its west bank, the newly arrived Awigaxa were their northern neighbours, and not long after this early period of contact, they were at war with each other on a grand scale.

The Awigaxa-Mandan according to their own traditions, initiated their corn ceremony around the date 1700, but which, in reality, represents their obtaining corn by either moving closer to the Missouri from the west to where they could raise corn on the productive flood plains of that river, or of obtaining the hybrid seeds from the Arickara which were superior to their own in hardiness and shorter ripening times. In typical Indian fashion, this event is explained by the mythical concept of the Awigaxa adopting the corn ceremony, the religious rites of which when properly performed, were thought to prevent their losing the corn again.

The six tribes said by the Omaha to have been invited by the Arickara to share their surplus corn, can be inferred from the tradition as including the allies of the latter, which were the same groups as participated in the grand peace council at the Loop of the Big Sioux of circa, 1685. These tribes must then have comprised the Omaha, Ponca, Iowa, Oto and Pipe-Stem-Men Cheyennes. The sixth tribe is not implied as being the Arickara themselves for they were the hosts, and probably the number was made up by the inclusion of some neighbouring group such as the Awigaxa Mandan perhaps. Furthermore, the Ponca - according to some Omaha informants - were at that time still a part of the Omaha tribe, and so it is probable that the Skidi Pawnee were also present to make up the number of six tribes said to have been involved. Certainly, so we are told in Skidi tradition, they [the Skidi] were then still allied to and in close contact with both the Omaha and Arickara during the period in question.

The actual corn ceremony introduced among the aforesaid tribes, thereafter became an important religious festival among them, although sometime during the course of their later wanderings and foreign relationships, the Cheyennes abandoned the ceremony, albeit that tribal informants late in the nineteenth century recalled that of old, the ceremony had once been considered important among them, and as late as 1876 a sacred ear of corn was still kept with reverence among the Northern Omissis Cheyennes, even though the rites connected with it had long since been abandoned.

We have seen in an earlier chapter how the corn ceremony as practiced among both the Arickara and Omaha, was also an integral part of the "Hako" rites earlier referred to, and thus we can infer that Cheyennes, or rather the Pipe-Stem-Men group who were off-shoots from the Omissis, did once observe the same corn ceremony and were greatly influenced by it.

It is indicative that the ceremony in question being a part of the `Hako` rites, was held during the advent of peace-making with other tribes and also involved the adoption of each other's children. Thus, the whole essence of Omaha tradition concerning their obtaining corn from the Arickara, most likely commemorates their own and the allied Pipe-Stem-Men`s migration to and across the Missouri, and of consolidating their pact with the Arickara, into whose hunting grounds they were then advancing.

We can be sure that a part of the Cheyenne-speaking Nation i.e., the Pipe-Stem-Men, were at the turn of the seventeenth century, already intimately associated with the Arickara and actually lived with or very near them for a number of years. Certainly Cheyennes and Arickara were constant friends and associates throughout the whole of the eighteenth century and for lengthy periods, not only did their two peoples reside in adjacent earth-lodge villages, but intermarried freely so that in later years, many Cheyennes could claim Arickara ancestry.

It was not long then, before these Cheyenne immigrants were influenced by the more secure situation and comparative affluence of their Arickara neighbours, and if they were to take up agriculture on a serious level, they would need a more permanent base and more durable lodges than previously employed.

No doubt it was for this reason that the Pipe-Stem-Men after first reaching the Missouri across from White River, moved north to the mouth of the Little Cheyenne, and a short while later, actually crossed the Missouri and built a new village on that river's west bank at the mouth of the Big Cheyenne, and where indeed, Cheyenne tradition locates another of their early permanent sites overlooking the Missouri. Such a position at the mouth of the Big Cheyenne was close enough to the Arickara to continue their harmonious relationship with that people, yet far enough away not to tread on each other's toes. If, however, the Awigaxa Mandan had been present at the Arickara corn-giving festival, it did not prevent hostilities breaking out between them and these new Cheyenne arrivals, who were now considered trespassers on Awigaxa land.

Not long prior to 1700, the Awigaxa had entrenched themselves in at least one large village very near the mouth of the Big Cheyenne, but by circa, 1725 they had retired above that point to the mouth of the Moreau also on the west side of the Missouri. Here they were often encamped, although they still considered the Big Cheyenne region as belonging to them. They therefore resented foreign encroachment into that district, let alone any permanent foreign settlement.

The Cheyennes say that their people's initial attempt to settle on the west bank of the Missouri was resisted violently by some "*enemy tribe,*" and there ensued a ferocious war between their peoples. For a time, it is said, this period of unrelenting warfare actually prevented those Cheyennes involved from establishing themselves in any permanent position along the west bank, and at first the enemy drove them back across the river from whence they came.

In corroboration of the above assertion, in the early nineteen-hundreds James Mooney obtained a story from Southern Cheyenne informants, which concerned the virtual extermination of an enemy tribe by Cheyennes. This event, Mooney was told, occurred soon after a part of the tribe first crossed the Missouri and attempted to settle permanently on its west bank. Unfortunately, the story does not specify if the Cheyenne group involved was Pipe-Stem-Men or Masikota, the last-named of whom around the later date of 1743, did settle at the mouth of Porcupine Creek on the west bank of the Missouri some distance north of where the Pipe-Stem-Men had earlier crossed. From an analysis of the given details, it seems, however, that after the Pipe-Stem-Men had been driven back across the Missouri by the aforementioned `enemy tribe;` the Masikota then became involved; perhaps with the inclusion of Bowstring Cheyennes from the Biesterfeldt site on the Lower bend of Sheyenne River and that together, they sought retribution from the enemy.

Cheyenne tradition recalls the enemy in question by the name "Owu`qeo" [singular Owuq], but the word has no meaning in the Cheyenne tongue. The Owuqeo, apparently, lived in tepees, at least part of the year, and at length, so vexed the Cheyennes that a winter expedition was launched against them with the intent of giving the Owuqeo a sound drubbing, if not to exterminate them all.

THE MIDDLE MISSOURI COUNTRY AND TRIBES THEREOF, CIRCA, 1735.
[Author's depiction]

The Cheyenne war-party was large and on foot. The warriors sought out the enemy and just before daybreak attacked them in their tepees, taking them by surprise. During the ensuing melee, the Owuqeo were driven to the river and onto the ice and the assault had been so sudden, that many of the foe had not time to arm themselves or even to put on moccasins. As a result, the ice peeled the skin from their feet and thus severely hampered, the Owuqeo were cut down by the vengeful Cheyennes who spared neither man, woman nor child, save one, a young attractive female who was taken captive by the Cheyenne chief and subsequently, became his wife. The remainder of the Owuqeo were practically exterminated, the few survivors fleeing in all directions to escape the slaughter, and never again did the Owuqeo reunite as a tribe.

It was also said by some informants that it was this same captive Owuqeo woman, who gave the Cheyennes the idea for originating their council of forty-four chiefs to govern their Nation, although as the same is said regarding other captive women from different tribes during various periods in Cheyenne history, we have no way of knowing whether this was or was not the case.

Who these Owuqeo people were has, hitherto, been deemed a mystery. Mooney suggested they may have been the same known as Awatixa, a tribe cognate with the Hidatsa, but this view is untenable as the Awatixa were in contact with Cheyennes for many years after the alleged time of the aforementioned massacre, and were always a large and important element within the Hidatsa Nation, which would not have been the case if they had been practically wiped out by Cheyennes. It has also been assumed that the Owuqeo were a Plains tribe, Comanche or Apache perhaps, which during the period in question were roaming the Plains to the west between the Black Hills and Missouri, and were the enemies of all the River Tribes and those immediately east of its course. It is, though, unlikely that Cheyennes would not then have recognized them as such, as around the same date and for several decades thereafter, Cheyenne groups were in contact with all tribes of the west and when at war with the Snakes, i.e. Shoshoni, Comanche and Plains Apache, they must have known if they were some of the same people who the Cheyennes had earlier destroyed. More likely it is, that the Owuqeo resided close to the Missouri, but at a point Lower down that river than Porcupine Creek, for the Cheyennes did not associate them with the Mandan-proper, with whom the Porcupine Creek people at a later date were in regular contact. Curiously, it is the Mandan traditions which actually solve the mystery of the Owuqeo, and add important details to this obscure yet relevant phase in Cheyenne history.

Now whilst Prince Maximilian Zu Wied was visiting among the Mandan late in 1833, an old man narrated a tradition recalling the first attempt of Cheyennes to settle permanently on the Missouri's west bank. The actual period appears to be rather free-floating in time, yet by comparing the story with other evidence, it actually correlates favorably with events occurring between 1725 and 1745, and concerns the same Mandan-speaking group of Awigaxa.

Around the date 1725, the Awigaxa occupied the southernmost Mandan town along the course of the Missouri at the mouth of Moreau River. Their Mandan-proper relatives then resided some distance north in the Heart River district, opposite where the city of Bismarck, North Dakota, now stands.

The Arickara were then further south below the Missouri's Great Bend on both sides of the river, and below them were the Omaha, Skidi, Ponca and Cheyennes of the Pipe-Stem-Men group.

Prior to 1725, all these last mentioned tribes including the Awigaxa, had tolerated each other and were generally on good terms. But only five years later [c. 1730], the situation had changed. Hostilities had broken out between the allied Arickara and Skidi on one side and the Omaha and Ponca on the other, and as a consequence, the Arickara were driven from their villages near the Missouri's Great Bend and forced north to a point just below the mouth of the Big Cheyenne. At first the Pipe-Stem-Men, then still on the east side of the Missouri and friends to both the Arickara and Omaha, remained aloof from these troubles. However, as an act of expediency because of their closer affinity with the Arickara and their wish to settle in a permanent village alongside them, they soon after moved north and during the early 1730s, occupied the country about the mouth of the Little Cheyenne on the Missouri's east side, and here Sioux tradition reports, an old-time Cheyenne village once stood. This same Cheyenne group, it is also said, then moved across the Missouri to the Big Cheyenne near where the Arickara had settled.

This is consistent with W. P. Clark's information obtained from Cheyenne sources, which states that the first Cheyenne-speaking group to build an earth-lodge town on the Missouri, lived for a while on that river's east side near the Little Cheyenne, then were ferried over the Missouri to the west bank, and near the mouth of the Big Cheyenne they built a new town.

This movement, of course, brought these same Cheyennes into closer proximity to the Awigaxa Mandan group positioned not far north on the Moreau and because of this, the Pipe-Stem-Men who were now interlopers in Awigaxa territory, understandably came into conflict with them. The Awigaxa would have seen these Cheyennes as a potential threat or, at least, resented their intrusion into their hunting grounds. War was inevitable, and we may take it that a period of small-scale feuding ensued before the situation reached a climax.

From circa 1730 onwards, the Awigaxa were also in enmity with the Arickara, while Mandan statements assert that prior to the great smallpox epidemic among all the tribes of the Missouri between 1781 and '82, both the Arickara and Cheyenne had been the Mandan's *"...natural and most virulent adversaries."* [1]

Prince Maximilian was additionally told, that the more serious conflicts between the Awigaxa and Cheyennes began in the following manner.

A woman had been busily engaged scraping hides near the Awigaxa town, when she was set upon by a small party of Cheyennes and killed. The enemy made good their escape, but the Awigaxa were so furious and eager for revenge, that soon after a war-party was assembled and started out on foot to chastise the culprits.

The war-party followed the enemy's trail and at length, came to a river upon the bank of which nestled the Cheyenne village. Perhaps the village was impressive by its size or defenses, for at this point, most of the Awigaxa lost heart and turned back for home. Only the husband and brother of the slain Awigaxa woman remained behind, and these two were determined to avenge their loss. They continued to loiter outside the Cheyenne village, merely waiting the opportunity to strike. Their chance finally came when a lone Cheyenne ventured out from the village unaware of the danger, and was immediately killed by the waiting avengers, who then cut off their victim's hair and sped back to their own country before the Cheyennes discovered the deed.

When the two reached their own village on the Moreau, the whole population came out to meet them and the women sang praise songs in their honour. It was at this time, so the old Mandan narrator declared, that the Mandan [Awigaxa?] first inaugurated their warrior societies.

The success of these two warriors against what the Awigaxa regarded as a *"new enemy,"* inspired their fellow tribesmen. They were not satisfied with a single Cheyenne scalp and were eager to attack the enemy in their own village. As a result, only a short while later another large war-party started forth from the Awigaxa town in order to engage the Cheyennes again.

The Cheyennes, though, must have seen them coming from afar, for as the Awigaxa neared their objective, the whole Cheyenne fighting force was already arrayed outside their village in battle order with their backs to the river bank, and appeared eager to join the impending confrontation.

The weather was very cold, but the Awigaxa who were wearing thick buffalo robes, did not hesitate to discard them as was their custom when going into battle to enable themselves to move more freely, and stacked them in a pile on the open prairie. The warriors then lined up facing the Cheyennes and the battle commenced.

The Awigaxa chief, it is said, was a man named "Robe-With-The-Beautiful-Hair." He wore a cap [cape?] of Lynx skins and cradled a medicine pipe in the crook of his left arm. At first he took no part in the fighting, but sat down to watch the proceedings as an avid spectator.

For the most part, the fighting consisted of two opposing lines protected behind large bull-hide shields, shooting arrows and hurling lances at each other amid torrents of abuse, in all inflicting little damage on either side. At intervals, respective champions would face one another in the no-man's land between the two lines, and battle it out to the death in a series of hand to hand single combats. It was only after several hours that all the Awigaxa warriors suddenly rose up in a body and charged the Cheyennes, who after a hard and bloody contest, were finally driven from the field and obliged to take refuge within their village. Nonetheless, the Cheyennes continued to present a stiff resistance and succeeded in repelling the Awigaxa onslaughts. But the latter remained undaunted and three or four times, they again threw themselves at the enemy only to be repulsed each time with heavy losses. And thus the battle raged on without respite with little advantage gained by either side.

Late in the day the Cheyennes managed to kill an Awigaxa holy man, which event set all the Awigaxa warriors into a frenzy, and their old Chief Robe-With-The-Beautiful-Hair was at last stirred into action. He bade his warriors to select a young poplar tree with large leaves from along the river bank and bring it to him. When this was done, the chief went forward into the no-man's land in front of his line of warriors and close to the Cheyenne village. He planted the tree upright in the ground beside him and confronted the enemy alone. He offered challenges to the Cheyennes, daring them to come out from behind their defenses and give him battle.

The Cheyennes could not be tempted. They only jeered at him and showered abuse upon his person. They answered that they would wait for the chief to attack them and instead, sent a barrage of arrows towards him. But the Awigaxa chief escaped injury save a few missiles merely grazing his arm and piercing his robe. Just at that time, however, a violent storm blew up and according to tradition, the poplar tree planted upright in the ground by the Awigaxa chief, started to grow until it reached a colossal size. A terrific gust of wind then lifted the tree bodily out of the ground and carried it high in the air over to the Cheyenne village, then hurled it down upon the occupants within, and many Cheyennes were crushed to death. By the end of the day the Cheyenne survivors had been forced to abandon their village, and were actually driven back across the Missouri by the triumphant Awigaxa. The tradition continues by saying that sometime after this singular victory, the Awigaxa left their position at the mouth of the Moreau, and went north to Heart River where other Mandan groups had long resided, and where some four years later, they met the Hidatsa proper, when that people themselves arrived on the Missouri.

Now the word "Owuqeo" as already mentioned, has no meaning in the Cheyenne tongue, indicating it having been adopted from a foreign term. If one omits the last syllable "eo," which denotes the plural of man or people in Cheyenne, then it can be seen at a glance that the term "Owuq" and "Awig" are in fact renderings of the same. The initial "O" in the Cheyenne case, is the old-time Algonquian idiom prefixed to several tribal names to show it as a proper noun, such as O-tawa [Ottawa], O-jibway [Chippewa] and O-Monsomi [Monsoni]. We might then conclude with a degree of confidence, that the massacre of the Owuqeo of Cheyenne tradition refers, in reality, to the destruction of the Mandan-speaking Awigaxa, which occurred as a result of that Cheyenne group near the mouth of the Big Cheyenne, having been defeated and driven back across the Missouri by the Awigaxa led by their chief, Robe-With-The-Beautiful-Hair.

That the Awigaxa as cited in the tradition told to Prince Maximilian, wore thick and heavy buffalo robes during their march to the Cheyenne village, suggests it was the winter season, and as the Cheyennes themselves declare that during this period of their history, they were without boats, then the Missouri river must have been frozen over to allow the defeated Cheyennes to flee across it.

It will be recalled that the Cheyenne attack upon the Owuqeo had also been conducted as a winter expedition, obviously in order that the Cheyennes could cross the Missouri on the ice and catch the enemy in its winter quarters. At a later date during the winter of 1742 / 43, two of LaVerendrye's sons accompanied an Indian crusade against the Snakes in the Western Plains who likewise, were expected to be surprised in their winter camp. Indeed, before horses became diffused profusely among the tribes, it was the custom to assault an enemy, if possible, during the snowy months, at which time the quarry was usually `snowed-in` and unable to maneuver effectively in the deep snow of the surrounding countryside. Of course, the fact that the Cheyennes in this instance are said to have been driven by the Awigaxa back across the Missouri, presupposes also, that the Cheyenne village had been sited on the west side of that river.

It is indicative that the Awigaxa tradition mentions the Cheyenne as a "new enemy," which statement implies that this Cheyenne group had only recently arrived at that point on the Missouri not far from the mouth of the Moreau.

This is important, for when the Sieur de LaVerendrye first contacted the Mandan late in 1738, he was told that the next group of people along the Missouri below the Mandan, were the

Panana i.e. Arickara, and below them were the Panini i.e. Skidi Pawnee. No mention was made by LaVerendrye regarding the Cheyenne and Hidatsa-proper, and it is apparent from several traditional sources that the Hidatsa- proper did not appear on the Missouri until after 1743, at which date two sons of LaVerendyre concluded their own expedition to that river, but who also did not mention the Hidatsa-proper as then being near the Mandan. Furthermore, we know from Sioux traditions, that the first Cheyenne-speaking band to settle permanently on the Missouri`s west bank was the Masikota group at the mouth of the Porcupine, but this was not before 1743 or 1744.

This being so, by ignoring the mythological embellishments to the above account as told to Maximillian, four important facts emerge.

[1]   The Cheyennes involved were entrenched in a reasonably strong position
          somewhere near the Moreau River adjacent to the Missouri.
[2]   It was a winter campaign undertaken by the Awigaxa.
[3]   That this particular Cheyenne group was without horses, and had not resided
          long in the area prior to the battle.
[4]   Most important, perhaps, is the similarity of the name Awigaxa with that in Cheyenne
          tradition of Owuqeo who were destroyed on the Missouri ice.
[5]   The Mandan have a similar story of their relatives the Awigaxa band, having been
          almost exterminated at around the same time when on the Missouri.

If the Masikota Porcupine Creek Cheyennes had been those involved in earlier hostilities with the Awigaxa, then it would have been most unlikely that they would then have chosen to site their village so near other Mandan foes located along Heart River only a short distance north of the Porcupine, and especially so after the Cheyenne had suffered such an ignominious defeat at the hands of the Awigaxa who, of course, were one of the Mandan`s kindred bands. Neither is it acceptable that the Awigaxa themselves soon after the event, according to their own account, would have left their position on the Moreau and moved north to a point even closer in proximity to the resident Masikota on Porcupine Creek, and who without doubt, would have been fully expected to retaliate in an attempt to even up the score.

It is a curious fact that Indians, generally speaking, had a propensity for conveniently forgetting disagreeable episodes in their history, particularly humiliating defeats and other details which they considered derogatory to their own tribal status. It should not be surprising then, that in later years the Cheyennes did not wish to recollect their enforced flight from the Awigaxa, and as regards the Awigaxa themselves, the account of their own people's movement north to Heart River was rendered as a voluntary movement, rather than an expulsion after the catastrophic defeat at the hands of the Cheyenne on the Missouri ice. It is most unlikely, if not inconceivable given the Indian philosophy of the period, that the Cheyennes having been at first expelled from their village on the Big Cheyenne by the Awigaxa, did not then seek the aid of other Cheyenne-speaking groups and their Arickara allies in an attempt to avenge their injury. This especially so, as the Awigaxa were a small tribe in comparison, and a long way from receiving immediate assistance from their Mandan relatives in the advent of a surprise attack. There would have been no practical reason why the Cheyennes should not have retaliated in kind, and this is likely what did happen, and which would then explain how the massacre of the Owuqeo occurred as a consequence to the Cheyenne's earlier defeat.

That Cheyenne informants of a later century should have had no idea as to who the Owuqeo were, is also understandable. The Awigaxa, even though later absorbed into the Mandan tribe proper, actually spoke a dialect peculiar to themselves and as noted in the tradition, they were then located some way south from other Mandan groups. These early Cheyennes on the Missouri probably did not at that time, associate the Awigaxa as being far-flung kinfolk of the Mandan, albeit Cheyennes had been raiding Mandan towns in the Heart River district since fifty years earlier.

During the late seventeenth century, the Awigaxa had likely been spared attack from Cheyenne war-parties coming from the Minnesota River in the east, owing to the Awigaxa's more western location from the Missouri banks which placed them away from the sphere of Cheyenne marauding at that time, and even after the Awigaxa had moved close to the Missouri because of their then initial friendship with the Arickara. Not until the Pipe-Stem Men from the east side of the Missouri crossed over that river to the mouth of the Big Cheyenne and attempted to settle permanently on the Missouri's west bank, did they and the Awigaxa come into inevitable hostile contact.

The date of the Awigaxa attack upon the Cheyennes, evidently, occurred sometime between 1735 and 1743, that is, after the Pipe-Stem Men had crossed the Missouri to the Big Cheyenne as a result of the outbreak of the Arickara-Omaha war, but before the Masikota Cheyennes first established themselves permanently overlooking the mouth of Porcupine Creek close to other Mandan towns.

The Cheyenne account asserts, that they had been fighting the Owuqeo for a number of years before they undertook their expedition which destroyed the Owuqeo as a contending power, and dispersed them once and for all from the country.

Thus it may be reasonably conjectured, that the first Awigaxa victory over the Cheyennes took place around the date 1735, and that the victory of Cheyennes over the Owuqeo [i.e. Awigaxa] occurred a few years later, perhaps around 1739/40, or at least, four years before the Hidatsa-proper appeared on the Missouri, as the Mandans told Maximillian, and which event is calculated circa, 1744.

It is unlikely that this Cheyenne - Arickara war with the Awigaxa began in earnest much earlier than 1735, for the Awigaxa being a comparatively small group, would not have been able to hold out too long on their own against such overwhelming odds as were the Arickara and Cheyennes combined.

However, the Cheyennes after their own eviction from the Big Cheyenne by the Awigaxa, did not again attempt to settle permanently along the Missouri until circa, 1743, and hence the reason why the explorer LaVerendyre was told in 1738, that the next tribe below the Mandan was the Arickara. LaVerendyre was also informed in that same year, that the Arickara had started a war with the Mandan four years earlier, i.e. 1734.

We now come to the question as to which Cheyenne-speaking group is referred to in both Awigaxa and Mandan tradition and by the Cheyennes themselves, concerning their war with the Owuqeo. *

Initially, it would appear that they belonged to the Pipe-Stem-Men Cheyenne group owing to the latter`s location at the appropriate time and place, and their close alliance with the Arickara, although it is probable that Bowstring Cheyennes from the village on Sheyenne River in the east were also very much involved. Certainly the story of the Owuqeo massacre was current among many Southern Cheyennes during a later century when James Mooney obtained his information, and it was among the Southern Cheyenne mixed Hevitainio and Suhtaio known as the Ridge Men band, that the descendants of the old Pipe-Stem-Men group could then be found. It was among the Southern Cheyennes also, that the Bowstring warrior society was extant, the term "Bowstrings," of course, being the name by which in olden times the main original Omissis group, i.e., the people of the Biesterfeldt Sheyenne River site were known. It will be recalled that in the Awigaxa account as given to Prince Maximilian, it is stated that after the lone Cheyenne was killed outside his village by the avenging duo, the Awigaxa after celebrating the news, inaugurated their own warrior societies. Regarding this point, it is interesting to note that one of the important Mandan warrior societies brought into being at that time, was called "Bowstrings," the personal insignia and customs of which were comparable if not almost identical with those of the same society among the Southern Cheyenne, indicating perhaps, that the Mandan had copied the idea for this particular society after observing first hand Cheyenne Bowstrings performing their Society dance, or simply, of the Awigaxa confronting Bowstring Society warriors on the field of battle during the above recounted conflict outside the Cheyenne town.

The Bowstrings, we know, had been frequenting the Missouri River at least as early as circa, 1735, at which times they traded with the Pipe-Stem-Men and also with the Arickara. There is evidence to suggest that the Bowstrings at regular intervals, actually stayed west of the Missouri for prolonged periods [of which we will speak later], when the Assiniboine and other enemy groups such as Eastern Sioux, made it too dangerous to remain at their permanent village on the Lower Sheyenne. Cheyennes of the Masikota and the associated Moiseo Kit-Fox element since known as the Aorta band, both with villages near Kulm, may also have been present during the first mentioned attack by the Awigaxa, although in that instance, the Pipe-Stem-Men would have been

* The number "four" was used among various Indian peoples merely as a symbolic number, having some sacred connotation in the same way as in the Buddhist religion and the phrases "seven years" and "forty years" are used in the Hebrew scriptures of the Bible. The term among the Mandan in this sense, could just as well mean "forty years" or indeed, any unspecified number, although in the above case, it is unlikely to refer to more than one generation.

the predominant Cheyenne faction involved. Later, during the concerted Cheyenne attack upon the Owuqeo, it was probably predominantly a Bowstring affair, partly to assist their kinfolk the Pipe-Stem-Men in obtaining revenge, and partly to remove the Awigaxa [i.e. Owuqeo] menace which had often obstructed both the Masikota and Bowstring`s passage to and fro across the Missouri, and as a consequence, had sometimes debarred them from reaching their trade markets west of that river. Subsequently, after the expulsion of the Awigaxa, the Masikota was actually the first Cheyenne band to take up permanent residence in an earth-lodge village on the Missouri`s west bank overlooking the mouth of Porcupine Creek.

This is why some Cheyenne informants today refer to the Masikota as "First named," being the first Cheyennes to settle permanently on the west bank of the Missouri, and who soon became affluent through their trading contacts both west and east of that river.

A few years after the arrival of the Masikota, the Pipe-Stem-Men did re-establish a permanent position on the west bank of the Missouri at the mouth of the Big Cheyenne, and from this base they thereafter hunted and roamed with impunity over the Western Plains before eventually drifting southwest, whereabouts they traded with and allied themselves to certain nomadic tribes including the Kiowa, Arapahoe and Gattacka [Kiowa-Apache].

For a while, perhaps, the Pipe-Stem Men had earlier occupied the old Awigaxa position overlooking the mouth of the Moreau, for here several tribal traditions also locate yet another old-time permanent Cheyenne village, long prior to the great smallpox scourge of 1781 / `82.

The Bowstring Cheyennes for their part, although in the habit of frequenting the Missouri and spending lengthy periods wandering the grasslands both east and west of that river, still sporadically returned to their own earth-lodge village on the Lower Sheyenne, and which continued to be recognized as their semi-permanent seat for several decades thereafter.

Not everything, though, was bliss for the Cheyennes after having dispersed the Owuqueo. Although friends and allies may be found west of the great river, there were still fierce and merciless enemies to contend with. During the 1740s, equestrian Padouca-Apaches, albeit having already been driven south and southwest from most of their villages in the north, were yet a danger to any wandering party if found too far south, and even more dire were other bands of horse Indians armed with Spanish sword blades and long-handled stone-headed war clubs, who came careering out of the western haze in order to destroy, enslave and kill. No wonder that their enemies called them "Snakes," and these murderous nomadic war-bands overnight, so to speak, became for a while the strongest and most feared power in the Central and Northern Plains. We know them historically as Shoshoni, Ute and Comanche.

- 0 - 0 - 0 - 0 - 0 - 0 - 0 - 0 - 0 - 0 - 0 - 0 - 0 - 0 - 0 – 0 -

CHAPTER. 33.

HORSEBACK RAIDERS FROM THE WESTERN PLAINS.

Since the early 1680s, horse-riding Snake and Padouca war-bands had constantly raided small camps of foreign peoples of the Rocky Mountain foothills and Western Plains; slaughtering menfolk and carrying off women and children to the Spanish markets of Mexico. It was the raids of these Snake and Padouca enemies that induced several tribal migrations east from the Mountains during the first decades of the eighteenth century. At a later date, so constant did such raids become, that there was founded a multi-tribal alliance among which Cheyennes were a predominant faction, in order to counteract the devastating Snake and Padouca inroads.

The Snakes and Padouca did not act as allies. They were at war with each other and prior to the mid-1720s, all the country north and south of the Black Hills, South Dakota, was being vigorously contested between Padouca-Apache groups on one side, and Snakes including the Shoshoni, Flathead and Kutenai on the other.

The Padouca had many villages or "Rancherias" as the Spaniards called them, scattered throughout the Smokey Hill River country of the Central Plains. They were assaulting the Missouri River tribes of Mandan, Hidatsa and Arickara, and also the Omaha and the latter's allies, among whom Cheyennes of the Pipe-Stem-Men were then included.

One Padouca group, however, although at war with most of the River Tribes and known in those early days as Gattacka of the Dismal River area in what is now northern Nebraska, remained at peace with the Arickara, with whom they traded and acted as allies when conducting joint ventures against mutual Snake enemies in the west.

The Gattacka, or Kiowa-Apache as they were later known, have no memory in their traditions of a homeland earlier than their people's residence in northwestern Nebraska, which suggests they had been in that part of the country many decades before the appearance of the Kiowa in the early 1720s and with whom they later amalgamated. Indeed, the Gattacka are mentioned by the Chevalier du LaSalle as early as 1682 as then living near the "Manhroats" west of the Missouri and near the "Panis." The name `Gattacka` as applied by LaSalle, was the Pani generic term for all Plains Apaches, while the term Pani in this case, was from a Sioux term, but used by the French for any Indian captives bought as slaves from the Western Tribes, even though such slaves were predominantly Arickara as opposed to Pawnee-proper peoples from further west. We know from both Arickara and Kiowa-Apache traditions that their two peoples had been friends for several years prior to 1720, and continued to keep in regular contact with each other until the second decade of the nineteenth century.

The "Manhroats," it must be admitted, remain a mystery, but as George Hyde postulated, they may have been an Oto group, some of which people were then already west of the Missouri in a similar location as noted by LaSalle during the mid-1680s, and the term, perhaps, is a corrupt rendering of "Waterroat" which was the Oto name for themselves. Certainly, LaSalle mentions the "Manhroats" as residing near the "Poncaras" who were the Ponca offshoots from the Omaha and kindred to the Oto and were positioned at that date just south of the Arickara, albeit on the east side of the Missouri, There is the alternative possibility that the "Manhroats" were Lipans, another Plains Apache group, which by 1725 had been driven south to the Lower course of the Arkansas River and into northern Texas, and who since an earlier date until as late as the 1820s, were also very closely associated with the Gattacka.

From at least 1682 the Omaha and their allies including Pipe-Stem-Men Cheyennes, had been at war with other Apache groups who they knew by the collective term Padonka, this being a variant of Padouca, but were at peace with the Gattacka and at a later date, played an important role with the aid of firearms and horses and Cheyenne allies, in finally evicting all other Padouca bands from the Central Plains and driving them south. These evicted Padouca groups; particularly those known later as Jicarilla and Mescalero, thereafter became known simply as Apache, and famous in late historic times as hardened guerilla fighters of the Arizona and New Mexico deserts.

That the "Gattacka" of LaSalle were synonymous with those later named Kiowa-Apache, is evidenced by the term's later use in various guises during the following century such as "Kataka," Cattackas" and "Kaskia," each of which terms were applied specifically to the Kiowa-Apache by one source and another. LaSalle had further noted that the "Gattacka" owned many horses, stolen, he supposed, from the frontier of New Spain which then embraced the Province of San Antonio in west Texas, and were trading such animals to the Panis [i.e. Arickara]. It is likely that at the time of LaSalle's writings [1681 / '83], the Gattacka were already trading horses and Spanish goods to the Pipe-Stem-Men Cheyennes and to the latter's Omaha and Oto allies, obtaining their stock not only from New Mexico, but from southern Padouca relatives such as the Lipan and others, who themselves were in regular contact with New Spain and also with French traders from settlements on the Lower Mississippi.

Corroborating the above is the account of Alonso de Posada, who in 1686, wrote of the great emphasis the Plains Apache put on their friendship with the Spaniards owing to their trading relations, and at a later date Posada further noted,

> "They [Plains Apache] are habitually bringing to the Pueblo Pecos, to trade for horses, young boys and girls carried off in attacks made in the land of the Quiviras…" [1]

Here the above term *Quiviras* applies to Caddoan-speaking peoples including the Witchita and Pawnee-proper tribes of the Arkansas, Red and Platte River regions, while the term Plains Apache refers to the more southern Padouca bands with whom the Gattacka of the north were in contact. In yet another place, the same chronicler mentioned that the Apaches were at war with other Nations, many of whom had been forced to retreat from their lands, and only the Yutas [Utes; a Shoshoni-speaking people and therefore Snakes], were able to match the Plains Apache on equal terms. Certainly by 1690 all the Padouca were mounted, and during the early years of the eighteenth century, they were the terror of their neighbours. However, with the later appearance of French firearms in Caddoan villages along the Red and Arkansas River, a tribal trading network began supplying Missouri River tribes below the Arickara with guns. As a result, just prior to 1719 when the French trader Bernard de LaHarpe ascended that same river as far as the mouth of the Platte, a grand allied offensive had already been undertaken by the Omaha, Ponca, Oto and Kansa [Kaw] against the southern Padouca, and this, coupled with a Snake drive from the northwest against the same enemy, suddenly turned the tide of fortune on the Padouca. It were they hereafter who suffered diabolical defeat and had to contend with disastrous attacks upon their camps. Padouca captives soon replaced those of the Panis in the slave markets of the French and Spanish colonies to the east and southwest, and in 1720, it was reported that 250 Padouca captives had recently been taken by the Ponca in their ongoing war with that people, and sold to the French.[2]

The Omaha and their allies including Pipe-Stem-Men Cheyennes while fighting the southern Padouca, were also at war with the Shoshoni or Snakes of the Western Plains, and, it seems that the term Padouca during the early years of its application, was applied by the Omaha and their allies to both Plains Apache and to Snake peoples regardless, and that the Omaha, Oto and Ponca, had adopted the name from their Arickara allies, albeit rendered in their own Siouan dialect as *Padonka*.

Another report by LaHarpe in 1723, tells us that the Padouca were then at war with the Ute and Comanche, but even before that date, Snake peoples had driven an invisible wedge into Padouca lands, so that although the Gattacka continued to hold out in South Dakota and northern Nebraska, they were separated from their Lipan and other Padouca kinfolk who had been forced south by intervening bands of hostile Snakes. Before 1720, most if not all Padouca camps are shown on French and Spanish maps as being west of the Missouri just below the Panis [i.e .Arickara], but after that date, notwithstanding a cluster of Padouca [Gattacka] camps northwest of the Panis, the rest are shown as having relocated much further south. Thus in 1724, when another Frenchman named Bourgmont travelled up the Missouri to the Kansa villages on the Mississippi above the mouth of the Arkansas, with the resolve of bringing the aforesaid warring tribes together in peace, it was the recently evicted Southern Padouca who were only too eager to accept the proffered olive branch. Bourgmont was successful in his enterprise, but it was the Padouca`s old enemies who actually derived most benefit from the truce. Hereafter, southern Caddoans closely related to the Arickara and Pawnee of the north, could obtain countless numbers of horses in trade from the southern Padouca, who themselves owned sizeable herds, while at the same time, the northern tribes could now visit French and Spanish settlements on the Lower Mississippi and on the New Mexican frontier without fear of being obstructed by enemies. Although once these northern tribes had secured enough horses and guns to satisfy their needs, their peace with the Padouca was thrown to the wind.

When the Kiowa appeared immediately north of the Black Hills around the date 1720, having migrated southeast from the mountain district of central Montana and northeastern

Wyoming, they were themselves at war with Snake groups in their rear. They thus formed an alliance with their old friends the Gattacka who were at war with the Shoshoni, Flathead and Kutenai, although with certain Comanche Snake bands in the Black Hills district, specifically the Kwahadi and Yamparika who were the most eastern Shoshoni-speaking people at that time, the Kiowa appear initially to have been at peace. It was this fact, no doubt, which help spare the Kiowa`s Gattacka Apache friends from also being driven out of the north country by the Snakes, as had been the fate of their more vulnerable now southern Padouca cousins, and it was these same Kwahadi and Yamparika bands who by trading with and raiding the Spaniards, were able to supply their Shoshoni Snake cousins in the north with Spanish weapons and horses. Thus ironically, the Kwahadi and Yamparika were trading horses and elk-horn bows got from the Snakes to the Kiowa and Arickara and inadvertently, to Pipe-Stem-Men Cheyennes, each of which at the same time, were still vigorously fighting all other Snake peoples. Something like this appears obvious, for between 1730 and 1750, all tribes of the eastern Plains and those along the middle Missouri were fighting both the Snakes and southern Padouca, and it is apparent that the French and Spanish journals also used the term "Padouca" as being interchangeable with that of "Snakes." *

A few decades after the majority of Padouca peoples had been evicted from the Central Plains, small pockets of Lipan Padouca did remain tentatively between the Platte River forks and the Arkansas, but by then they were no longer considered an enemy of importance, being regarded as a pathetic remnant of a once powerful Nation widely scattered and totally demoralized. They had been replaced as the dominant power in the eastern Plains by invading Siouan groups from the east, and by mounted Snakes from the west.

The last Lipan Padouca strongholds in the Central Plains, were in the area of the present-day Pine Ridge reservation of western South Dakota, but by 1730, those Comanche groups mentioned above, suddenly began assaulting the remaining Lipan camps from positions west of the Black Hills, whilst the Omaha, Ponca and Cheyenne, albeit at that date no longer as allies, continued their attacks from the east. Thus the last of the Lipans were finally evicted from their seats in western South Dakota, their old lands then occupied by the Comanche on the west, while the old Lipan lands on the east were then occupied by the Omaha, Ponca and Pipe-Stem-Men, so

*There have been various attempts to translate the term Padouca, but that given by Hyde appears the most sound. Hyde was of the opinion that the name is derived from the root form of the Pawnee word "Patu," meaning `blood,` which among the Pawnee is a synonym for `enemy.` Hence we have the abbreviated early French form of Pado. There was also the French trait of adding the term `White` or `Black` to tribal names as they did with the Pani, to distinguish those people with whom the French were in contact and therefore "White" as in "Pani Blanc," as opposed to those with whom the French were not in contact such as "Pani Noir" or "Black Pawnee." Thus we see on several charts of the early eighteenth century, the notations "Padouca Blanc" and "Padouca Noir."

that only the Gattacka still remained tentatively in the north. In a report on the then Provinces of New Spain penned by Jose Cortes in 1799, it is said of the Padouca, [termed Pados in the report and which most probably was meant to refer to the Gattacka alone],

"In times past the Pados were the most populous Nation in that area [west of the Missouri River], but that the wars that they have carried on with the others have decimated them, such that they have come to the extreme of consisting of no more than four small remnants whose structure saves them from the fury of the other Nations, which hate them intensely. Despite the persecution they suffer, they are thought to have more than 350 warriors who are very skilled with bow and arrow and fleet of foot." [2]

Certainly by 1725, the Snakes or more specifically, Shoshoni-proper, had advanced east from the mountain country of the Northwest from where earlier had come the Kiowa, and moved south and east from the Black Hills in order to be nearer the Spanish trading centers on one hand, and closer to the Missouri River towns on the other which they were regularly raiding in pursuit of plunder, captives and scalps. The Comanche and Ute at that date, were also included under the term Snake, and these, having acquired horses prior to their Shoshoni-proper relatives further north, had helped drive the Padouca-Apaches from the Central Plains. Snake peoples alone then claimed all the country to the immediate south and southwest of the Black Hills, and indeed, the same 1799 report of Jose Cortes further said of the Snakes, which people he referred to as Laytanes,

"The Laytanes or nomadic Apaches, live in the chain of mountains northeast of New Mexico and are held to be the best warriors of the Misoury [sic]. They dominate all neighbouring Nations, and although they are divided into several bands or small groups, they all live in unity and enduring friendship." [3]

The term *Laytanes* in the above passage derives from a Pawnee term for all Shoshoni-speaking peoples, and was also rendered as *Alitanes* and even *Naytanes* in several documents of the early eighteenth century, and by the above quote the Snakes were indeed then classified by the Spaniards as comprising one people with those also known as Apache, i.e. Padouca.

The Gattacka from their position in the sand hills of the Dismal River district and on the Upper Niobrara, then stood alone against their enemies, and had no adequate means of calling upon other Apache groups to assist them in their predicament. As a consequence, the Gattacka were obliged to ally themselves with the new invaders from the east such as the Omaha and Cheyennes in an expedient move to hold on to their tentative northern position. The fact that the Gattacka had long been in friendly contact with the Arickara, must have been a prime factor in making possible their subsequent alliance with the Cheyennes, and regarding the Omaha, notwithstanding their current enmity towards the Arickara, they continued fighting the Snakes as allies to the Gattacka.

Fortunately, the Lipan, Mescalero and Jicarilla Apache groups which had retreated south from the Central Plains into northwestern Texas, still had access to a little French trade carried on in the Caddoan villages along the Lower courses of the Red and Cimarron River of east Texas due to the aforementioned Bourgmont peace initiative, and added to this, they also had access to Spanish goods [minus firearms] at the trading fairs in San Antonio and at the Pueblo towns along the Rio Grande. By such means they managed to hold their own against continued inducement from the Snakes to retreat further south and southwest, and so continued to trade horses and both French and Spanish goods to their northern Gattacka cousins who after the rest of the Padouca had been driven from the Central Plains, remained in the Dismal River region which thus was known to the Omaha as *"Place where the Padonka build a fort."* [4]

The Gattacka continued in their friendship with the Kiowa and Arickara and with the latter's Cheyenne allies, and owing to their blood affiliation with the Lipans, they could still visit the Spanish possessions and *rancherias* of their Lipan kinfolk in the south with impunity. In such a way they continued to obtain horses in quantity and subsequently, the Gattacka became an integral and most important element in intertribal trade with northern peoples by supplying horses as the prime commodity. The Northern Nations wanted such animals above all else, and this was particularly true of the Arickara, who although claiming an extensive territory, horses were few among them because, so the aforesaid Cortes report tells us, *"... their land is arid and barren and does not produce the necessary pasturage."* [5]

Documents of the period invariably mention the Arickara as then being constantly at war with the Gattacka, but as this latter name was once given to all Apache speakers west of the Arickara, the statement should not have been applied to the Gattacka of Kiowa-Apache affiliation. On the contrary, even before the Bourgmont inspired peace of 1724, the Arickara had been friends and allies of the Gattacka, and had always welcomed each other among their lodges both as traders and as guests.

On the other hand, that the *Laytanes* of the early accounts were Shoshoni-speaking peoples allied to the Flathead and Kutenai, and not Plains Apache [i.e. Padouca], albeit that the terms Snake and Padouca were used interchangeably by their enemies, can further be deduced from Shoshoni tradition which recalls their residence on the Plains east of the Rocky Mountains at a time, they assert, when they [the Snakes] were a powerful Nation and feared by all. We also have both Blackfoot and Ponca traditions which actually describe the peculiar mode of warfare practiced by both the Shoshoni and Padouca before and during the mid-eighteenth century, and also recall the attire both the Snakes and Padouca wore at that time.

Blackfoot informants told the Hudson's Bay trader David Thompson in the 1780s, that initially, the Snakes or Shoshoni used to come against them on foot carrying large bull-hide shields behind which they would squat so as to be completely hidden from view, only showing themselves or a part of their body for an instant when they were apt to shoot off their arrows. A few years later, however, when again the Shoshoni came to attack, they appeared on horseback and wore a kind of body armour fashioned from tough hide several plies thick and stuck together with a mixture of sand and glue. Their horses likewise, were protected with the same kind of layered armour, and as the riders rode in amongst the terrified Blackfoot, they knocked them down with their horses and with long-handled stone war-clubs called "Pommegons" which they wielded with deadly effect. The first period referred to in this tradition is circa, 1720 / 30, and is comparable to the hostile Snake Indians with their big round shields who threatened the Chevalier LaVerendrye and his two companions somewhere in the Western Plains a number of years later in 1742.

Lewis and Clark when conducting their exploratory expedition between 1804 and 1806, saw such "Pommegons" while they were among the Lemhi Shoshoni more than fifty years later, and were informed by their hosts that within living memory of their oldest people, the Shoshoni had resided in the Northern and Central Plains east of the Rocky Mountains, but had been forced west by invading northern and eastern tribes which included Blackfoot, Cheyenne, Crow, Kiowa-Apache and others, each of whom had been armed with guns.

Ponca tradition agrees with that of the Blackfoot, in so much as they recall that the enemy with whom their tribe first came into contact after crossing the Missouri and termed Padonka [i.e. Padouca] in Ponca tradition, had strong bows made from elk-horn and arrows tipped with bone. But the weapon upon which the Padouca mostly depended, was a peculiar stone-headed battle axe [war-club] singularly employed by that people. It had a long handle fashioned from a sapling bound with rawhide, to which a grooved stone axe head - pointed at both ends - was attached. Such weapons, the Ponca said, made these Padouca foes terrifying and formidable fighters at close quarters, while the Padouca warriors protected their horses on the breast and flanks by covering the animals with thick leather, cut into round pieces and positioned so as to overlap one another in rows. On the surface of the leather, they applied sand held on with glue and so effective was it, the Ponca arrows would merely glance off without inflicting any noticeable damage. The Padouca protected their own bodies with large, round shields also made of rawhide, and some of the Padouca warriors wore leather breastplates fabricated in a like manner to that covering their horses.

There is yet extant a very old Indian painting on deerskin sent from Sonora, Mexico to Lucerne, Switzerland in 1759, and upon which is depicted an attack by mounted Indians on an enemy stronghold. The attackers and their horses are shown clad in leather armour very similar to that described in both Ponca and Blackfoot accounts cited above. The only difference between the Blackfoot and Ponca accounts is the identity of the particular enemy peoples concerned.

The term Padouca during the mid-eighteenth century, was applied by the Omaha, Ponca and their cognates primarily, to Apache peoples of the Plains, and the Snakes of Blackfoot tradition was applied specifically to Shoshoni speakers and their allies. Both these enemy groups were very numerous during the period in question. Some of their bands lived in semi-permanent villages or "forts," as the LaVerendrye journal calls them, while others wandered the Western Plains in temporary hide and brush shelters. Both were trading with and alternatively stealing from the Spanish possessions to the south, and both were fighting the Missouri River Tribes and the latter's allies which included Pipe-Stem-Men Cheyennes. Hence both the Padouca and Snakes had adopted the same style of leather attire which, one suspects, was the result of contact with Spaniards from whom they most likely copied the idea after observing the metal armour and similar quilted coverings of Spanish soldiers and their horses. The Blackfoot, though, were too far north to have been in regular contact with the Padouca-Apache, while the Ponca were in contact with both the Padouca and Shoshoni-speaking peoples, particularly Comanche bands. Thus as both the horse-riding Padouca and Snakes were raiding the Ponca and Omaha wielding Spanish sword blades and long-handled Pomegeons and wearing similar protective leather coverings, the Ponca tradition does not differentiate between the two. Indeed, to the Ponca and their cousins, all mounted foes coming from the Western Plains were regarded as Padouca, and later, after the Apaches had been driven southwest and their old hunting grounds occupied by Snake bands, the Ponca and Omaha among others, simply transferred the name Padouca knowingly or unknowingly, to Comanche Snake bands with whom they continued to be at war. At a later date the Comanche alone were known as Padouca, but which name had originally been applied to the Plains-Apache also.

Having said this, it was the Gattacka Padouca of the north who, from 1725 onwards, began supplying horses to other northern tribes and also to the sedentary earth-lodge village groups along the Missouri with whom they were still in friendly contact, as the Gattacka were the first of the so-called northern tribes to obtain such animals. Kiowa tradition concerning their own early history on the Plains are important here, as they add substance to the aforesaid analysis and conclusions.

In brief, the migration tradition of the Kiowa asserts that their people once lived in the mountain country of what is now the western part of the state of Montana. But owing to incessant warfare with neighbouring tribes, they moved south, then southeast until reaching the Black Hills, and in which country they remained for a number of years. They then migrated further south sometime late in the eighteenth century and at which time, they expediently allied themselves to their one-time Comanche enemies who had preceded them south. The Kiowa further assert that the Kiowa-Apaches accompanied them [the Kiowa] on their journey from the Northwest to the Black Hills; that they met the Crows and Arapahoe en route, and found Cheyennes to the east of those Hills.

This Kiowa account has generally been accepted by historians and certainly, we need not doubt that the Kiowa came originally into the Great Plains from the mountain country of the Northwest. However, the assertion that the Kiowa-Apache [Gattacka] were with them at that period and together, their two peoples migrated towards the Black Hills, I do not trust. All the evidence points to the assumption that the Kiowa-Apache under the name Gattacka, were already entrenched in the Plains west of the Missouri in South Dakota and the northern half of Nebraska, where they were noted by LaSalle in 1682 close to the Panis, i.e. Arickara, and to the Manroats. The Kiowa themselves at that time, were still in the western part of Montana and did not actually arrive near the Black Hills until just prior to 1720. The latter also recalled that they knew the Blackfoot when in the northwest, while the Arapahoe remember the Kiowa as inhabiting the headwaters country of the Three Forks district of the Upper Missouri when they, the Arapahoe, first arrived on the south side of the Missouri near the mouth of Milk River, and which event was close to the date 1720. Added to this is a current Crow tradition that the Kiowa and Crows once lived together in southern

Montana in the Three Forks region south of the Yellowstone, and even today, Crows point out a particular gap in the Big Horn Mountains over which the Kiowa passed in order to embark on their later-date migration south. Coupled to this, the Crows were not themselves in the Three Forks region much earlier than 1720.

Prior to their amalgamation with the Gattacka, the Kiowa tribe was made up of five bands which, during this early period of their history between 1700 and 1750, usually camped and roamed as separate units throughout most of the year, pursuing their own whims and fortunes. They seem to have only come together as a complete tribal entity during their annual religious festivals, held once a year in either mid or late summer, or at the time of peace-making with other tribes or when undertaking combined war-ventures against their enemies. Thus each of the five original Kiowa bands had probably migrated southeast from the Montana mountain districts as individual groups, each moving on its own volition and at slightly different periods in time. It is most likely that while some Kiowa bands had already arrived in the vicinity of the Black Hills, other bands were still in the vicinity of the Three Forks district of the Upper Missouri, where the Arapahoe assert, their tribe first encountered the Kiowa. Certainly the Blackfoot did not reach as far west as their historic seats in the northern part of Montana – in which territory they would have been noticed by the Kiowa, - until around the date 1710, having been pushed southwest from the northern Saskatchewan prairies by the Cree and Assiniboine with their English guns. In fact, the "*incessant warfare*" which, the Kiowa say, drove their people toward the southeast, was with the Snakes and the latter`s Flathead and Kutenai allies, who after acquiring horses from the Spanish and Pueblo tribes earlier that century, began vigorously raiding their pedestrian northern neighbours among whom were the Kiowa, for both plunder and captives, the latter of which were then sold in the Mexican Provinces as slaves. Indeed, a reliable Blackfoot tradition asserts, that their tribe obtained its first horses about the date 1730 during a raid on the Snakes with whom they were then at war.

So it was that when the Kiowa arrived north of the Black Hills [circa 1720], they were already in hostile contact with Shoshoni and Ute groups who the Kiowa also recognized as Snakes. So commenced a prolonged war of attrition between the three, although Initially, as previously noted, there must have been a period of tolerance between the Kiowa and one and another Comanche band, for Ten Bears, the great Yamparika Comanche chief of a later century, told the Kiowa in 1867 at the Medicine Lodge Treaty gathering with United States Government officials, that when the Kiowa first entered the Black Hills from the northwest, they, the Kiowa, were very poor, having only dogs and women to carry their loads. It was the Comanche, Ten Bears declared, who had taken pity on the Kiowa and had given that people their first horses. The Kiowa themselves did not dispute this claim, although it is certain that very soon after their arrival in the Black Hills, the Kiowa were at war with all Comanche bands and the Ute, and it was from raids upon the latter`s villages that the Kiowa obtained more horses which, coupled with other sources of supply including trading with the Gattacka of the Dismal River region, they greatly increased their herds.

In 1732 Kiowa were reported in a Spanish document as having visited New Mexico that year. These people the document states, were on foot, and it is obvious that they had risked the long and hazardous journey from the north all the way south to the Pueblo towns and New Mexican rancherias in their quest for horses, without which they were at the mercy of their more powerful mounted Snake enemies. Only three years later, however, Kiowa are again mentioned as appearing in New Mexico, but this time on horseback and it is evident that by then, they owned a sizeable number of such animals.

The Kiowa also had access to the Missouri River tribes, particularly the Arickara with whom the Kiowa were always on good terms. Soon the Arickara were supplying the Kiowa with small quantities of guns and ammunition obtained through an intertribal trade at the Arickara towns, and in sufficient quantity to enable the Kiowa to become not only a serious match for their once dreaded Snake enemies, but at a later date, enabled them with the aid of Arapahoe and Cheyenne allies, to turn the tables and drive the Comanche south into Texas, and the Utes southwest into the mountain districts of what are now the states of Colorado and Utah.

The Kiowa being good friends of the Gattacka since the time the former had resided in the Yellowstone region of western Montana, had naturally continued their friendship with them, and in truth, it was probably the Kiowa who around 1725, paved the way for the Gattacka to trade their surplus horses and Spanish artefacts to those allies of the Kiowa which included the Crow, Arickara and certain Cheyenne groups then roaming both west and east of the Missouri.

Thus by 1740 at the latest, the Pipe-Stem-Men Cheyennes through their friendship with the Gattacka also owned a sizable number of horses, and some such animals they then passed on to their Masikota and Bowstrings brethren in the Coteau country east of the Missouri.

Cheyenne tradition has a story which tells how horses first came into their possession. The story, though, is almost identical in content to tales told by several other Plains Tribes regarding their own acquisition of horses, and so is likely apocryphal. Whatever the case, the Cheyenne version as given to the present author by tribal informants, states that when their tribe's Culture Hero Sweet-Medicine returned from the Sacred Mountain after a four year absence, he told of a wonderful animal which his people had not seen before, but which would come among them during a future time and make their lives much easier. This new animal, he said, had four legs and a long hairy mane and tail; was very strong and could go a great distance before tiring. It could also carry and pull much heavier loads than the dogs which the people were accustomed to using, and could be ridden by humans when on the hunt or going to war, or when merely wishing to travel from one place to another.

Sweet-Medicine, of course, was prophesying the coming of horses. But, it is said, it was many years later before the Cheyennes actually got their first such animals which was a long time after Sweet-Medicine had died. When eventually the Cheyennes did get horses, it was when two young men went hunting towards the south. On their trip they discovered a trail of strange tracks on the ground, the likes of which the hunters had not seen before. Curious to know what or who had made the tracks, they followed the trail and at length, came upon a large, strange, four-legged beast with long hair on its neck and a long hairy tail. The hunters went back to their camp and told what they had seen. The chiefs of the village sat in council and discussed between them what the strange animal might be as described by the hunters, but could not make up their minds. They thus instructed the two men to go again to where they had seen the beast and try to capture it and bring it back so that the chiefs could see it for themselves. This the two men did. They made a pair of long lariats fashioned from buffalo hide and with these they managed to rope the animal and brought it back to camp. All the people looked with awe upon the animal, some comparing it to an elk and others to a large dog. They tied the animal to a stake hammered into the ground and left it alone, for the people were afraid that it might have strong *medicine* powers or be a holy creature in some way or another and they dare not go near it. Soon after this, the strange beast gave birth to a colt and later, after making a strange noise like a whinny, another animal of the same ilk came into the camp on its own accord and began grazing alongside the mare. This second animal was a stallion, but was quite tame, and soon the people lost their fear. They touched the stallion and ran their hands over its body. A number of young men then climbed upon the animal`s back taking turns to do so one after the other, and in this way, they soon learned to ride and how to get the animal to pull pole drags packed with camp belongings and tepee covers from one camping ground to another. The people then realized that these animals were what Sweet-Medicine had been talking about all those years before, and the people called the new animals *Mo`hoe`ohna*, meaning Elk-Dog, because such animals in some ways resembled an elk, and in other ways could be domesticated like a dog.

It was after this that some tribal members traveled a long way south on foot to where the Mexicans resided, and who had great numbers of both horses and mules. These Cheyennes, it is said, would visit the Pueblo towns of Picuris and Taos in what is now the northern part of New Mexico and southern Arizona, and from the Pueblo Indians they obtained more horses and also metal articles of Spanish manufacture. Indeed, early-date Spanish accounts often mention the appearance of buffalo hunting peoples of the Plains north of Mexico as visiting the Pueblo towns on trading expeditions. These northerners were accustomed to arrive on foot with dogs attached to pole drags carrying trade merchandise and all their domestic belongings. The Spanish chronicler Captain Juan de Ortega had reported as early as 1601,

> "The Pueblos obtain buffalo meat which they get in trade with the Vaqueros [buffalo hunters] in exchange for blankets and maize. The exchange is that the Vaqueros come from the Plains with the meat, fat, hides and tallow loaded on some dogs a little larger than water-dogs. They have them for that task and in order to carry their tents, which are mostly very white, although some are decorated with little black hands; and they place the tents at 300 or 400 paces from the said Pueblo and there the Indians go around and for the maize and blankets, the Vaqueros trade all the said things. On this occasion 400 or 500 came..." [6]

During the later period of the mid-1740s, with which we are now concerned, one or another band of Cheyennes in a similar manner to those described above, were by then visiting one or another Pueblo town such as Taos or Picuris. They were not, however, the people earlier referred to by the Spanish Governor DeVargas, when he wrote from Santa Fe in May 1696,

> "Some rancherias [bands] of Apaches [northerners] who live to the east and are called the Chipaines have arrived and they gave me information in the pueblo where they entered which is that of the Pecuries Nation, how some white and blond men have consumed a very large Nation of the Apache Conejeros which reside very far towards the interior from that of theirs and that they have returned." [7]

In an alternative translation of the same letter, it is said,

> "Certain Apaches from the east who are called Chiyenes, have recently come to Santa Fe." [8]

A number of scholars have supposed that the terms *Chipaines* and *Chiyenes* mentioned above, are but variant spellings of the name Cheyenne. But this is not so, as both terms apply to an Athapaskan-speaking Padouca-Apache group known as *Chihennes* and who, at a later date, were more commonly known as Warm Springs Apache. Having said this, it is true that by trading with and raiding the Pueblos and Spaniards, the Cheyennes, –at first only the Pipe-Stem-Men band - began to greatly increase their herds, and with horses in quantity among them their old-time lifeway was changed dramatically. Very soon after their acquisition of horses in sizable number, the Cheyennes became fierce equestrian buffalo-hunting nomads, roaming at will both east and west of the Missouri, and albeit at the slightly later date of 1742, they formed a league with other Plains Tribes against the Snakes and also against those southern Padouca-Apache groups recently evicted from the north.

In 1742 - `43 while the Snakes were still at the height of their power, two French brothers being the sons of the Siuer de LaVerendrye, undertook their own expedition into the Western Plains. The report which the brothers left for posterity gives us our first glimpse of horse-riding peoples of the Black Hills and the first eye-witness account of Cheyennes, albeit in obscure form, as equestrian tepee-dwellers of the Great Plains. The LaVerenderye journals have been published and analyzed many times, but not, I think, by any scholar who has carefully checked the journal`s content with all the relevant material at hand. For this reason, in order to determine that Cheyennes are indeed referred to in the LaVerendrye report, and to substantiate some assertions in the present study, a fresh appraisal must here be given.

- 0 - 0 - 0 - 0 - 0 - 0 - 0 - 0 - 0 - 0 - 0 - 0 - 0 - 0 - 0 - 0 -

PART 1V.

THE TIME OF HORSES.

SOUTHERN CHEYENNE CHIEF, THREE-FINGERS.
[Smithsonian Institution. Washington D. C.]

CHAPTER 34.

"PEOPLE OF THE BOW."

To discover a western passage across the North American Continent to the rich trading marts of Asia, had long obsessed several explorers of the colonial period. Not least was the Frenchman Pierre Gautier de Verennes du Sieur de LaVerendrye. By travelling northwest from Lake Superior, he hoped to find a practical route through the unchartered wilderness to a fabled "Western Sea," which, he believed, would open up access from the Atlantic seaboard to China and Japan. [1]

In the early seventeen-thirties, LaVerendrye had been told by Cree informants of a "white river" flowing west and that along its course, could be found walled cities and white men who used iron axes and knives; wore garments of cloth, but were without guns or firearms of any kind. Surely, thought LaVerendrye, this river must be the one he so eagerly sought.

Other Cree informants and some Assiniboine with whom he met, added that a tribe of Indians, the Mantannes [Mandan] who resided adjacent to the Missouri River, knew the way to the elusive "Western sea."

With this and other - though to prove - credulous information spurring him on, in October 1738, LaVerendrye set out from Fort LaReine on the Lower course of the Assiniboine River in what is now the Province of Manitoba, Canada, and with twenty French Canadian employees, a Cree interpreter who could speak the Mandan language, and an entire village of six-hundred Assiniboine who wished to visit the Missouri tribes to trade, he traveled south on foot over the one-hundred and fifty miles of open, almost treeless, rolling prairie separating the Assiniboine River from the Missouri, in order to make contact with the Mandan who, he hoped, would guide him to his long sought goal.

Their arrival among the Mandan lodges was an occasion for much rejoicing and ceremony; these being the first white men many of the villagers had seen. The Frenchmen were told by their hosts that this village was but one of six much larger towns, and the only one which did not actually overlook the Missouri River.

LaVerendrye was also told stories of mounted men to the south who wore beards and were clad in iron [armour]. These people sometimes crossed the Plains, he was told, but actually lived further south a whole summer's journey away. Arrows were useless against them the Mandans said, and one had first to shoot their horses after which the iron-clad riders could easily be run down and killed, being too encumbered on foot to effect a speedy escape. They [the people of the south] had bucklers [shields] of iron, very light in colour, and fought with lances and sabers in the use of which they were very skillful. The women of the south were never seen in the fields and their forts and houses were made of stone. Unfortunately the Mandans themselves were unable to visit the southern settlements, the chief said, because the way passed through Arickara country with which people his tribe were at war.

Perhaps LaVerendrye would have learned a great deal more, but once the Assiniboines finished their trade they soon wore out their welcome by making appreciable inroads into the food stocks of the Mandans. At length, after much persuasion and subtle ploys, the Mandans scared the Assiniboines into leaving by saying that a strong Sioux war-party was coming towards the town. The Assiniboines packed their belongings and departed for their own country in the north. With them alas, went LaVerendrye's Cree interpreter in pursuit of an Assiniboine maiden, and thus, the white men were left without satisfactory means of communication with their hosts.

As a result, a disappointed LaVerendrye who had originally intended to remain among the Mandans throughout the winter months, also took his leave and returned on foot with most of his men to Fort LaReine. Before leaving, however, he expediently took the precaution of delegating two Canadian employees to stay behind with the Mandans and learn their language, so that when he himself returned to the town the following summer, he would be able to follow up any further information concerning a route to the "Western Sea."

In September the following year 1739, the two French delegates returned to Fort LaReine with encouraging news. They had carried out their duties faithfully, and had been well-treated by the Mandan. Early the previous summer, they said, Horse Indians had come to trade at the town as they were apt to do every year at that time. From what his delegates told him, LaVerendrye reported as follows,

> "Every year at the beginning of June, there arrive at the great fort on the bank of the river of the Mandan. Several savage tribes which use horses and carry on trade with them....They bring dressed skins trimmed and ornamented with plumage and porcupine quills, painted in various colours, also white buffalo skins, and the Mandan give them in exchange maize and beans, of which they have an ample supply. Last summer two-hundred lodges came; sometimes even more; They are all of the same tribe but some are only allies; There was one tribe which said they came from the setting sun, where there are white men in towns and forts made of bricks and white stone.....They reported that to get to these white men the Indians had to detour to avoid the *Gens des Serpent* [i.e. Snakes], a numerous people, the greater part of whom live in forts, while the rest wander about, occupying a large extent of territory." [2]

The French delegates had added that the *Gens des Serpent* were also the enemies of the white people of the west [south?].

The following year LaVerendrye dispatched his eldest son Pierre and two other Frenchmen to go again to the Mandan towns, where they were to obtain guides from among the *"savage tribes"* when they came again to trade, and who, it was hoped, might lead them to the Western Sea.

Unfortunately, the 'savage tribes' did not go to the Mandan that year of 1740, at least not while the Frenchmen were there, and the intended guides could not be had. Reluctantly, Pierre and his two companions returned to Fort LaReine having accomplished nothing. This time, though, the

Frenchmen rode home on horses. They also brought home four porcelain mugs along with an embroidered cotton coverlet of Spanish manufacture, and by this we know that the Mandans along the Missouri were acquiring Spanish goods and horses at that time.

Notwithstanding his set-back, in the spring of 1742 Pierre LaVerendrye set out again heading for the Mandan towns, but this time accompanied by his younger brother the Chevalier de LaVerendrye and two Canadian employees.

The Frenchmen intended to await the arrival of the *"Gens des Chevaux,"* the "Horse Indians," who they had learned, usually traded at the town in early June, and then to accompany them to the "Western Sea."

By mid-July the Horse Indians had still not arrived and becoming impatient, the Frenchmen started out from the town on July 23d with two Mandan guides, in order to seek out the *Gens des Chevaux* in the latter's own country in the Western Plains. The two Frenchmen travelling horseback, followed a course west-southwest from the Mandan towns with the Black Hills on their left and the Little Missouri River on their right. En route they observed earths of different colours including red, black, green, blue, white and yellow which, evidently, is the region now known as the Bad Lands of the Little Missouri district, where a multitude of coloured earths and rocks are a prominent feature of the country.

For three weeks the party wandered over the open Plains travelling at a leisurely pace, until on August 11th, they reached the *"Mountain of the Gens des Cheveaux,"* which was recognized by other Indians as the country of the "Horse Indians." Here the small party encamped and built fires to attract attention to themselves while they awaited the Horse Indians to appear. Every day one or another among the white men went to the top of the high point and reconnoitered the surrounding country, searching for sign of their quarry. But not until the 14th of September were their signal fires answered by a distant thin column of smoke barely discernible on the far horizon.

In response, the Frenchmen and their Mandan guides mounted up and rode excitedly towards the smoke, and at last came face to face with an equestrian, buffalo hunting, nomadic Plains Tribe, far west of the Missouri River.

These people, though, were not the *Gens des Cheveaux* as first thought, but another group called in the journal, *"Gens des Beaux Hommes,"* i.e. "The Handsome Men." Apparently they were the enemies of the Mandan and so frightened LaVerendrye's guides, that the latter left the white men and fled precipitously back to their village on the Missouri.

Perhaps the *Beaux Hommes* could speak a little Mandan, or by that time the Frenchmen had picked up a smattering of sign talk, being the Plains Indian's ingenuous system of hand gestures practiced by all tribes west of the Mississippi as a common medium between them. Either way, the Frenchmen managed to make themselves understood, and requested the *Beaux Hommes* to help them in finding the "People of the Horse." The Indians said they would willingly supply the white men with guides until they met their first party of the *Gens des Cheveaux*.

For twenty-one days the brothers lingered in the camp of the *Beaux Hommes* and on October 9th, they bade farewell to their hosts, and with one *Beaux Hommes* guide continued their search for the "Horse Indians," this time travelling in a south by southwest direction.

After two days journey, during which they covered only a few miles, they were joined by another band of Indians which the journal calls, *"A village of the Nation des Petite Reynards,"* i.e. The Little Foxes, and having informed their chiefs that they were searching for the Horse Indians, the Petite Reynards agreed to take the white men to them. The two parties thus joined together and continued on, albeit now in a more southerly direction. Soon after this meeting, they met a second band of Little Foxes much larger than the first, and these, too, joined the cavalcade. Two days later, they came upon a village of "Pioya" Indians, and on the 17th, having altered course towards the southwest, they encountered a second, though much larger, "Pioya" band.

As a part of this now numerous company, the Frenchmen travelled on directly south, and at length, contacted the much sought after *"Gens des Chevaux."* Ostensibly, these were the same people originally met by LaVerendrye`s employees when the latter had spent the summer among the Mandan two years earlier.

Now, though, the *Gens des Chevaux* were in great distress. Their enemies the *"Gens des Serpent"* had recently destroyed all their camps - very few persons having escaped. The whole village resounded to the women-folk's hideous wailing's and doleful lamentations of those in mourning for loved ones lost. Only the year before, the Frenchmen were told, the same *"Gens des Serpent"* or "Snakes," had completely defeated seventeen of their villages, slaughtering the warriors, the old men and old women, and carrying off the young women and children into slavery, selling them on the sea coast for horses and other merchandise. The Chevalier was further told,

> "When making a raid upon the enemy, the Gens des Serpent are not satisfied with merely destroying one of their enemy's camps but, unlike most other tribes, will continue their raiding and killing from Springtime to Autumn. They are a numerous people, and woe to those who cross their path. They are not the friends of any other Nation." [3]

Indeed, at this date as they had been for several years previously, the "Snakes" were the terror of the Plains. They were the most hated foe of nearly every other tribe in all the country west of the Missouri River.

The "People of the Horse" had not themselves been to the "Western Sea," they said, because the route lay through hostile Snake lands. But they knew of a people who traded near it. These last were the *"Gens de L`Arc,"* the "People of the Bow." They alone did not fear the Snakes and had even given the Snakes cause to fear them by having at their head a great chief, whose wisdom and leadership surpassed any among the Snakes. The "Bows" themselves knew of a tribe with whom they alone, it seems, were on friendly terms and who had actually visited the "Great Sea" in question.

This statement most likely infers that the "Bow Indians" were in contact with a tribe which traded with the Spaniards and who, probably, were the same people referred to in the LaVerendrye journal of 1739, who then told the white men that when wishing to go south, they usually made a wide detour in order to avoid the *Gens des Serpent.*

The grand chief of the "Horse Indians" added that he personally would conduct the Frenchmen to the "People of the Bow." And so yet again the expedition set off across the Plains, this time with a great host of Indians composed of various tribes and bands.

Travelling south-west, the Frenchmen were first led to a large camp of people called in the journal *"Gens des Belle Riviere,"* The People of the Beautiful River." This name at an early date during French infiltration into the Western Plains, was applied to the Belle Fourche [North Fork as it is sometimes called] branch of the Big Cheyenne River of western South Dakota, and it was in this vicinity on November 21st, 1742, that the young LaVerendrye brothers and their French companions finally met for the first time, the "People of the Bow."

The "Bow" Indians were encamped in a great village; the largest seen so far by the Frenchmen. Their smoke-tanned buffalo-hide tepees dotted the prairie for a considerable distance, and the reception given the Frenchmen in this camp was ecstatic. The extent of jubilation and the courteous manners of the "Bows," far exceeded that received from the other bands with whom the white men had been travelling.

The great chief of the Bows, the Chevalier tells us, was at the head of a considerable number of people, and in the camp were many horses, asses and mules. The presence of mules was but one indication that the Bows were in regular contact with Spanish settlements, either trading or raiding, for the Spanish were the only suppliers of mules, which animals Indians were unable to raise in their own country.

The Frenchmen were taken under the wing of the Bow chief, who labored earnestly to teach his white guests his people's language. In a short time, the Chevalier tells us, he for one had picked up enough of the Bow language to enable him to discourse tolerably with his host. The Bow chief freely answered the Chevalier's enquiries with regard to those white men purported to be on the sea coast by saying,

> "We know them through what has been told us by prisoners from the Gens des Serpent, among whom we shall arrive shortly. Do not be surprised if you see many villages assembled with us. Word has been sent in all directions for them to join us. You hear war-songs every day; this is not without plan. We are going to march in direction of the great mountains by the sea, to hunt for the Gens des Serpent. Do not be afraid to come with us; you have nothing to fear. ....The French who are on the sea coast are numerous. They have a large number of slaves, whom they settle on their lands among each Nation. These have separate quarters, marry among themselves, and are not oppressed. The result is that they are happy, and do not try to run away. They raise a good many horses and other animals, which they use in working their land. They have many chiefs for the soldiers, and also many chiefs for prayer." [4]

The Bow chief then spoke a few words in the language of who, he supposed, were Frenchmen near the sea, but which the Chevalier recognized as Spanish. The chief further gave an account of a massacre by Indians of the Spanish expedition into the Central Plains led by Pedro

Villasur in 1720, and this confirmed the Chevalier's idea that the white men spoken of by the Bow chief were Spanish.

The large Indian camp was by now composed of many different bands of people, which, the chief said, had been drawn together from near and far in preparation for a combined war-venture against the Snakes, who were enemies to them all.

The chief of the Bows invited the Frenchmen to accompany the grand war-party saying,

"We will take you to the high mountains that are near the sea. From their summits, you will be able to look down upon it." [5]

The Frenchmen accepted the offer and early one morning after a period of much singing and dancing within the camp, the squaws took down their lodges, packed their belongings on pony drags, pack-mules and dogs, and the whole ensemble moved off at a leisurely, meandering pace across the grasslands against the Snakes.

The grand host travelled south-south-west, sometimes veering northwest, and were joined at various stages by more bands of mounted Indians. According to the journal, the Indians soon comprised some two-thousand warriors and these, including their families, constituted a grand conglomerate. Each night the warriors sang and danced and many came to *"weep upon our heads,"* the journal says,

"... to get us to accompany them to war." [6]

Finally on New Year's Day 1743, a distant snow-capped mountain came into view. [Evidently Pike`s Peak of the Rocky Mountain chain in what is now the state of Wyoming], and here the cavalcade halted and went into camp.

A council of war was then held to which the Frenchmen were duly invited.

Long speeches were made on behalf of each Nation present, the contents of which the Bow chief explained to the young Chevalier, which he in turn, recorded in his journal,

> "They (the speakers) all turned upon the measures to be taken for the protection of their women and children during their absence, and how best to approach the enemy. They then addressed us, begging us not to abandon them. I replied to the chief of the Gens de L`Arc, who then repeated it to all the assembly my reply that the great chief of the French, wished all his children to live peaceably and had ordered us to induce all the Nations to remain at peace, wishing to see all the country calm and peaceful; that knowing that their hearts were sick, and with good reason, I bowed my head, and we would accompany them, since they so ardently desired it, but only to aid them with our advice in case of necessity. They thanked us heartily, and held long ceremonies for us with the Calumet." [7]

It was decided among the assembled chiefs, to leave their women and children and old persons at this point on the prairie, while the warriors proceeded to the Snake country where, it was hoped, they would surprise the enemy in their winter camp. The young Chevalier with his two

French employees, thus prepared to join the warriors, while his brother Pierre would remain behind with the non-combatants.

Seven days later the grand war-party started forth, most of the warriors on horseback, but some evidently on foot and now the march was more orderly and disciplined. Scouts were out at all times on both flanks; to the rear and far ahead of the column, and utmost caution was observed lest the enemy discovered their approach. The pace, however, was again slow and meandering, and it was twelve days later before they reached the foothills of the mountains, whereabouts they expected to find the enemy camp. It was soon after this that scouts came in to report that they had found the Snake village, but to their dismay, it had already been abandoned and apparently, in great haste. Many of the lodges had been left standing, and personal belongings and camp paraphernalia lay strewn around.

Obviously the Snakes had become aware of their enemy's approach. They had not been prepared to face such a formidable host as was coming against them and expediently, had beat a rapid retreat. The People of the Bow and their allies did not think this the case. On the contrary, they suspected that the cunning Snakes had made a circuitous movement to their rear, and that even while the allies were listening to their scouts report, the Snakes were bearing down upon the unprotected allied camp, where the women and children had been left.

The warriors were suddenly seized with panic. The grand war-party at once broke up in terror and all the speech making of the chief of the "Bows," who alone exhorted the warriors to stay together and continue in their original objective, was lost in the tumult and confusion. Soon, all but a handful of warriors were racing their ponies back the way they had come in a frantic effort to reach their families. The war-party had been travelling for twelve days since setting out from their camp, yet in their frenzied flight, most of the warriors managed to reach the camp in only two days and nights.

In the meantime the three Frenchmen, in company with the chief of the "Bows" and a group of warriors, followed the retreat at a more leisurely pace, seemingly unperturbed. Whilst travelling, the Chevalier happened to look behind him and saw that his two French companions were missing. Fearing for their safety, he rode back along the trail until he eventually found them some distance in the rear feeding and resting their ponies. Hardly were the three reunited, when fifteen hostile Indians were discerned creeping towards them through the grass and semi-obscured behind large bull-hide shields. The Frenchmen did not wait to learn their intentions whether they be good or bad, but fired off a few shots from their muskets, whereupon the Indians made a precipitous retreat and disappeared from view.

The Frenchmen then attempted to catch up with the Bow chief and his entourage. But the ground was frozen and they had difficulty in finding the trail. As luck would have it, when thinking themselves lost, they suddenly came in sight of the non-combatant's camp where most of the allies had already arrived. The camp had not been attacked as feared, and the Frenchmen were glad of the security and warmth offered by friendly lodges in such a hostile environment.

The chief of the "Bows," meanwhile, having become anxious for his white friends, had previously gone looking for them fearing the worst, and it was five days later after the Chevalier and his companions had returned to the camp, that the chief and his followers themselves reappeared, *"more dead than alive,"* the journal says, having endured a fierce and blinding blizzard and below freezing temperatures on the open Plains. Notwithstanding his hardships, upon seeing his white friends alive and well, the "Bow" chief was overjoyed. He caressed the Frenchmen repeatedly and from thereon, gave them his constant and undivided attention.

So the grand crusade against the Snakes had actually come to naught. At length, the allied camp broke up into many small camps, as one by one the separate bands moved off, each in a different direction towards their respective hunting grounds. The four Frenchmen stayed with the *Gens de L`Arc* and travelled with them slowly and painfully through the deep snow, this time heading east by south-east.

Whilst en route, they met another band of Indians called in the journal *"Gens des Petite Cherries,"* i.e. People of the Little Cherry. This band was also moving east towards its winter quarters which proved to be an earth-lodge village overlooking the Missouri River. The Frenchmen resolved to join the *Gens des Petite Cherries,* and go with them to their town where they would remain throughout the duration of winter, and come spring, would start on their long return journey north to Fort LaReine.

Thus the white men bade farewell to the chief of the "Bows" who showed much emotion at their leaving, but who regained composure when Pierre told him that he would visit his people again, if they would site their village at a predetermined point along a certain stream.

The Frenchmen and the *Gens des Petite Cherries* then hastened on to the latter`s town on the Missouri, and here close by, the LaVerendrye`s buried in the side of a nearby hill an inscribed lead tablet with the name LaVerendrye and the date 1743 on one side, and the French coat of Arms on the other.

The brothers remained at the town throughout the rest of the winter, and in April 1743, set out on horseback heading north towards the Mandan villages. During this stage of their journey whilst following the twisting course of the Missouri on its west side, they passed a camp of twenty-five families of the *"Gens des Fleche Coleee,"* i.e. "People of the Stripped" or "Painted Arrows," and who the LaVerendrye`s also termed in the same journal, *"Sioux des Prairies."* The journal, however, noted only that they,

"...passed through squaws and camps stopping very little." [8]

When at last they reached the Mandan towns further north, they fell in with a trading party of Assiniboine which was about to take its leave, and in the company of these Indians, the Frenchmen returned to Fort LaReine and home.

So it was that the first expedition of white men into the Northern Plains, which was also the first time white men had met and actually lived among fully-fledged, equestrian, buffalo-hunting nomads west of the Missouri, finally came to an end.

In 1913, a young girl playing near the mouth of the Big Cheyenne on the Missouri`s west side opposite the present-day town of Pierre, South Dakota, discovered the LaVerendrye lead tablet still buried in the hillside in the vicinity of where an old Indian village once stood, and which has since been positively identified by archaeologists as a mid-eighteenth century Arickara earth-lodge town.

Information regarding the various Indian bands mentioned in the LaVerendrye journal is, to say the least, far from adequate. It might seem that it was the deliberate intention of the compilers to tease and confuse students of a later era, for tribal names as given, appear on the surface to have been peculiar to their singular imaginations. Indian groups appear and disappear like fleeting apparitions; there for a moment before vanishing into oblivion the next, leaving no discernible trace for future reference.

Such hitherto has been deemed the extent of the journal's ethno-historical value. Yet, in reality, most if indeed not all tribal names given in the journal, can be associated with well-known late-historic tribal groups, and in which case the account offers an important insight into the condition and relationships concerning Plains equestrian nomads west of the middle Missouri during the mid-eighteenth century. At the same time, it corroborates various tribal traditions which include those of our subjects, the Cheyenne.

The first group of Indians met by the LaVerendryes southwest of the Mandan towns, was most likely, an Arapahoe faction designated *"Beaux Hommes"* in the journal. However, several scholars since that time have invariably applied the name to the Crow tribe alone, although the Arapahoe were resident between the Little Missouri River and Black Hills during the time in question of 1742 / 43, and at which date they were friends of the Crows, but at war with the Mandan. Mandan, Hidatsa and Crow traditions indicate the Crows as then being friends of the Mandan and close to the Lower course of Powder River further west and on the North Platte. In the same year of 1742, the French Canadian trader Joseph LaFrance drew a map showing the *"Beaux Hommes"* as roaming somewhere southwest of Lake Winnipeg, and the Sieur de LaVerendrye material prior to 1739, as opposed to his son`s later-date journal, had placed the same *"Beaux Hommes"* northeast of the Missouri in what is now the southern part of Saskatchewan, Canada. On the other hand, the Bourgainville material of 1757 notes them southwest of the Missouri, perhaps in the general location when met by the LaVerendrye brothers in 1742.

Around the date 1680, a Crow-Hidatsa group moved north from eastern North Dakota due to serious Yanktonai Sioux attacks upon all tribes in the Red River valley and the northern part of the Coteau des prairies, and it is evident that for a number of decades following their enforced movement north, this Crow-Hidatsa group was then closely confederated with the Arapahoe, with whom they hunted and roamed along the Lower course of the Saskatchewan River southwest of Lake Winnipeg.

As explained in a previous chapter, around the same date of 1680, the Arapahoe, too, after being forced to abandon the Red River valley of North Dakota had, by their own admission, also fled north into southern Saskatchewan where they met and confederated with the Hidatsa-Crow. At a later date, however, the Arapahoe divided into two groups, one of which, the Atsina, remained in Saskatchewan, whilst the Arapahoe-proper moved southwest and by1720, had crossed the Missouri to its south side at a point opposite or just west of the mouth of the Little Missouri. Here the Arapahoe again met with Crows who earlier, had separated from them and had since moved south between Powder River in southeastern Montana and the Little Missouri of western North Dakota. The Arapahoe thence continued their alliance with the Crow from where they had left off, and at the same time, formed an alliance with the Kiowa and Gattacka and later, with those Cheyennes who by 1740, were themselves in the habit of frequenting the Black Hills region.

The Arapahoe did indeed have a faction among them known as the `Pleasant` or `Handsome Men,` and thus may well have been contacted by the LaVerendrye brothers in 1742 who translated the name as *"Beaux Hommes."* Certainly, the Arapahoe were still in the Little Missouri and Black Hills region for a number of decades after the LaVerendrye`s visit, as both Jean Baptiste Trudeau in 1794 / 95 and Lewis and Clark in 1805 / 06, reported the Arapahoe as residing in that area, and while there may have been Crows among the *Beaux Hommes* met by the LaVerendrye brothers as mentioned above, the Crows were not then enemies of the Mandan and resided further west at that time. The particular Crow group in alliance with the Arapahoe at that date would have been the Mountain Crow division, a part of which known as the Whistling Waters band, was then resident in the North Platte region of east-central Wyoming, before migrating north into the Lower Powder country where the rest of the Crows were entrenched.

During the 1740s, this last-named Crow band on the North Platte, was in regular and close contact with the Arapahoe, Kiowa and Gattacka [i.e. Kiowa-Apache], and likewise, were fighting the Snakes and the latter`s Flathead and Kutenais allies who were then in control of the Yellowstone and Bighorn country. The Arapahoe, Kiowa and Crow each declare that they obtained their first horses from certain Snake-Comanche bands, mostly by theft, but sometimes through trade, although, no doubt, they also acquired horses from the Gattacka with whom they were joined in an inter-tribal league which included Cheyennes, and together were conducting combined offensives against all other Snake peoples.

The Kiowa agree that they themselves met the Arapahoe in the vicinity of the Little Missouri about the date 1720 after the Kiowa arrived in the Black Hills, and from the first, the three tribes of Kiowa, Arapahoe and Crow were good friends and allies, probably owing to the fact that neither were then regarded as permanent residents of that country. Often these three groups roamed and hunted together so as to gain better protection against common "Snake" enemies from the West.

By the date of the LaVerendrye brothers visit in 1742, the Gattacka had an abundance of horses, while the latter`s Black Hills allies still had comparably few, even though their entire tribes were probably mounted. Thus the *"Gens des Cheveaux"* of the account with whom the Arapahoe, Kiowa, Crows, and by 1740 the Cheyennes, were allied, represent the Gattacka or Kiowa-Apache as they were later known, for the journal tells us that the *Gens des Chevaux* were then trading with New Mexico; had many horses, and were engaged in a violent war against the "Snakes," the same as would have been applicable to the Gattacka during that period in time.

If indeed, the *Gens des Chevaux* had lost seventeen villages destroyed by the Snakes in one year alone, as the journal states, then this ongoing war with the Snakes may well have had some bearing on the very small number of Kiowa-Apache that actually survived into the nineteenth century, and when coupled with several periods of severe contagions among them particularly of smallpox, is why they later amalgamated with and were eventually absorbed into the Kiowa tribe.

Of the five separate bands which comprised the Kiowa tribe during the late historic time, the name Little-Foxes was once conferred upon a particular Kiowa band by the Arickara, in whose language the name was rendered *"Tukiwaku,"* literally meaning `Fox Village` or `Fox People.` This name was in vogue as late as the early eighteen-hundreds in the guise of *"Tchiwak;"* *"Tokiwako"* and some other variants of the same, and all these names were applied to a Plains Indian group living in and around the Black Hills who were allied to the Arapahoe and Crows, and trading regularly with the Mandan, Arickara and Cheyennes on the Missouri. It is known also that as late as 1820, a part of the Kiowa known as Cold Men were still residing in the Black Hills region, so we might take it that the *"Gens des Petite Reynards"* refers to a Kiowa group. The second band of "Little Foxes," would obviously denote another Kiowa band, and the two "Pioya" groups - met next by the Frenchmen - most likely apply to the Kiowa proper who called themselves *"Gai-gwu."* It is possible that the initial `P` of LaVerendrye`s "Pioya," was, in truth, a slip of the pen, and should actually have been rendered as `K` or `G,` as both these consonants were normally of a silent nature in old French, and thus, an initial `P` may have been employed instead. The fifth Kiowa division or band was undoubtedly the *"Gens des Belle Riviere,"* which was an early name for the North Fork which flows east north of the Black Hills, before joining the Cheyenne River and entering the Missouri near present-day Pierre, South Dakota. Thus the Belle Fourche actually flowed through the same part of the Black Hills country as then claimed by the Kiowa.

So we see from the foregoing analysis, that the Kiowa appear to be compatible with those bands mentioned in the LaVerendrye journal as Little Foxes, Pioya and the *"Gens des Belle Riviere,"* as the Kiowa were then resident in the appropriate area at the appropriate time, and were at war with the Snakes, but allied to surrounding tribes.

We come now to the *"Gens de L`Arc"* the "People of the Bow."

We have seen that the various tribes of the Black Hills region had obtained horses in quantity by the mid-1730s. As a result, they opened a more regular trade in horses and items of Spanish manufacture with the sedentary Arickara, and from whom they received in return a small number of firearms and certain food produce grown by the river tribes. Among these trading groups we must include the Cheyenne-speaking bands of Masikota, Aorta, Pipe-Stem-Men and Bowstrings, each of whom, although not as yet residing permanently along the west bank of the Missouri, were apt to cross that river at intervals in order to roam the Western Buffalo Plains. There they formed an alliance with the Kiowa, Arapahoe, Crow and Gattacka against the Snakes, and attended intertribal trading fairs held annually in the Black Hills.

From the time of Arickara first contacts with the Gattacka, Crow and Kiowa, these tribes had been friends, and the Arickara were in the habit of going out as far as the Black Hills in order to visit and trade with the tribes thereof. It was, no doubt, owing to the very close relationship between Cheyennes and Arickara, which afforded Cheyenne groups the opportunity to meet with the same Black Hills tribes and become their allies.

Some Cheyenne today state that they got horses as gifts from either the Crow, Kiowa or Comanche, but they probably got a few horses from each of those peoples, and, of course, from the Gattacka who were the main suppliers of horses and mules to the northern tribes.

A current Cheyenne tradition asserts that when their people first began regularly criss-crossing the Missouri, they met both the Kiowa and one or another Comanche group in the Western Plains. The Comanche it was, the story goes, who taught the Cheyennes how to dress animal skins in one piece, and how to make fine robes from buffalo hides, whilst the Kiowa for their part, taught these same Cheyennes how to hunt antelope by the employment of a surround, more commonly known as an "Antelope Drive."

This adds substance to the assertion that one or more Comanche band was, initially, on good terms with the Kiowa and with some other tribes which included Cheyennes of the Pipe-Stem-Men, Masikota and Bowstring groups even prior to the LaVerendrye brother's visit in 1742. Indeed, Comanche factions known as "Kwahadi" and "Penateka" during the eighteenth century, were the most northern of all Comanche bands, and actually continued to be frequent visitors at the aforementioned trading fairs held in the vicinity of the Black Hills until some years into the second decade of the 1800s, long after Comanche kindred bands had been forced south out of the Northern Plains by the same allied tribes of the Black Hills region.

Of the Pipe-Stem-Men Cheyennes prior to 1730, although at times roaming the grasslands west of the Missouri, they still had as their base a permanent earth-lodge village at a point on the east side of that river near the mouth of the Little Cheyenne, and were in the habit of visiting one or another Pueblo town in what is now the state of New Mexico. This being so, then they, too, were returning with horses and mules which would have been their prime purpose in undertaking such long and hazardous treks in the first place. It is likely then, that they also were attending the same intertribal trading fairs as did their Masikota and Bowstring cousins.

Unlike most Missouri River Tribes, the Pipe-Stem Men did not reside for extensive periods in their earth-lodge village near the mouth of the Little Cheyenne, but spent most of the year roaming the prairie game lands to the west. They were in contact with the Gattacka at an early date, probably as invited members of an Arickara trading party, and it was in order to imitate the Gatacka that these Cheyennes had begun visiting the Spanish possessions themselves while also obtaining French goods from the east. They thus traded French goods to the Black Hills tribes which as early as 1740, included a few guns which the Pipe-Stem-Men acquired through trade with their own Bowstring cousins at the Biesterfeldt village on Sheyenne River, who in turn, had acquired such items when attending Sioux trading fairs at the head of the Minnesota.

The Pipe-Stem Men were quick to take advantage of such commerce and in a very short while, they themselves were supplying the Arickara and even the latter's Skidi Pawnee relatives with both horses and guns.

Most other Cheyennes, so we are told in their own traditions, had only a few horses before circa, 1730, and this is undoubtedly true regarding some segments of the Nation. The Pipe-Stem-Men in contrast, obviously owned enough horses for their every need, and the craving to increase their herds induced them at a later date, to abandon their permanent villages on the Missouri banks and take to a roving life in the Western Plains as fully-fledged nomadic equestrian hunters. Perhaps they did return to their old fields at intervals, but more likely thereafter, they obtained most of their agricultural supplies in trade with the Arickara, or from other Cheyennes east of the Missouri, and at a later date, from the kindred Masikota on Porcupine Creek, as did their new-found nomadic buffalo-hunting allies among the Black Hills Tribes.

As early as 1723 a Frenchman named Raundeire when describing the Nebraska country, noted that the Arickara had forty villages and were allied to the Omaha, and in the following year of 1724, the peacemaker Bourgmont recorded that whilst on the Missouri, he had observed the Arickara and Skidi as then residing near the mouth of White River, their several villages stretching north as far as the Missouri's Great Bend. He further mentioned that between them, they owned a number of horses and were adept horsemen, and this account coincides nicely with Skidi and also Mandan traditions, both of which state that they got their first horses from Cheyennes, and these latter had probably been members of the Pipe-Stem Men band.

Soon after Bourgmont's comments, however, certainly before the end of 1724, the Omaha and their cognate tribes the Ponca and Oto were attacking the Arickara, and drove them north to a point near the mouth of the Big Cheyenne. The Skidi Pawnee who were then also at war with the Omaha, thus became separated from their Arickara relatives and were forced west, first to the Elk Horn River and thence southwest to the North Fork of Loup River, Nebraska, at which time they made peace and confederated with their Pawnee-proper cousins.

It is apparent that this Arickara / Skidi war with the Omaha and Ponca had affected the Pipe-Stem-Men somewhat, in that this Cheyenne group then also moved north from their old position opposite the mouth of White River to the mouth of the Little Cheyenne still on the east side of the Missouri. Here they continued in a league with the Arickara and as explained in an earlier chapter, the Pipe-Stem Men soon after, actually crossed the Missouri and attempted to settle permanently along the Lower course of the Big Cheyenne, which they then claimed as their new hunting ground. As a consequence, they got into a war with the Mandan-speaking Awigaxa [i.e. the Owuqueo of Cheyenne tradition] who were then resident further north near the mouth of the Moreau, and at the same time, the Pipe-Stem-Men severed their once close ties with the Omaha, even though it did not as yet result in open war.

This northern movement of the Pipe-Stem-Men when east of the Missouri to the mouth of the Little Cheyenne, must have occurred no later than Bourgmont's visit in 1724, as the Omaha about that time, moved up the Missouri and occupied the district along the Lower course of White River, which, previously, had been regarded by the Arickara as their own tribal hunting grounds. At the later date of 1739 / '40, whilst in their new location on the Big Cheyenne on the west side of the Missouri and having defeated and evicted the opposing Owuqueo, the Pipe-Stem-Men continued to have regular contact with their kinsmen the Bowstrings further east, and to whom they traded horses along with Snake captives in exchange for guns and horticultural produce. By that time both the Bowstrings and Masikota were themselves already criss-crossing the Missouri and likewise, visiting intertribal fairs in the Black Hills and, according to a Cheyenne tradition collected by W. P. Clark in 1879, it was during their tribe's early days west of the Missouri, that Cheyennes or some of their bands, roamed as far west as *Navah-hous* or Bear Butte, this being the sacred mountain of the Cheyenne Nation north of the Black Hills in the vicinity of the Belle Fourche branch of the Big Cheyenne River. Bear Butte, though, was by then, already regarded as a sacred site by the Kiowa Apache who were known as Gattacka, and this is why the site was given the name *"Mountain of the Gens de Chaveaux"* in the LaVerendrye account.

There was around 1740, not a little regular intercourse between the Pipe-Stem Men, Bowstrings, Masikota and other Cheyenne-speaking bands including the Suhtaio, although the most populous group was that of the Bowstrings. As a consequence, the Cree and Assiniboine among others, began referring to all Cheyenne peoples by the collective name of "Bowstring Men," and as the LaVerendrye`s were told tribal names by their Cree and Assiniboine associates, they, too, naturally referred to Cheyennes collectively as *"Gens de L`Arc,"* or "People of the Bow."

It is indicative that in 1757, when Bourgainville penned his "memoir" relating to the position of tribal groups near the Missouri from information obtained from the LaVerendryes, he noted a particular tribal group by the name of *"Arcs"* or "Bows" as then residing in three villages opposite the "Panis" [Arickara]. Where precisely the *"Arcs"* were in relation to the Arickara, that is, whether on the east or west side of the Missouri, we are not told, although as the *"Arcs"* are said to have been opposite and not next to the Panis, it follows that Bourgainville was meaning the east side of the Missouri. The Bourgainville material further implies that the "Arcs" were, at the least, semi-sedentary village dwellers by his added comment when referring to peoples separate to those aforementioned,

> "For the rest, it is scarcely proper for me to use the term villages for all the Nations that inhabit the prairies; they form , like the Turks, wandering hordes, they follow the beasts by whose hunting they live, their dwellings are cabins of skins." [9]

The name *Gens de L`Arc*, most likely then, refers to the same tribal group or groups, generally known to the Assiniboine and Cree as `People of the Bowstrings or Bow,` a term no doubt, representing those comprising the Bowstrings, Masikota and Kit-Fox Moiseo [i.e. Aorta], and which bands prior to the early 1740s, according to the Cheyennes themselves, were then entrenched in permanent earth-lodge villages in the Coteau country on the east side of the Missouri across from the Arickara. They would, of course, have been in close contact with one another and able to bring their forces together when needed. Bourgainville also gave the Cree name for the *Gens L`Arc* which he rendered as *Atchapeivinioques*, and this is but a rendition of the Saskatchewan Cree term *Ahcapew- Piminahkwanis,* meaning "Bowstring." Thus some other tribes knew all the various Cheyenne bands in the Coteau country collectively as Bowstrings, or more simply, as "Bows."

If, of course, the "Bow" Indians were not Cheyennes, then are we to believe that no reference to that tribe was ever entered in the many documents relating to the region between the Missouri and the Black Hills during the period 1700 to 1794, whilst all the neighbouring tribes, most of whom were then allies of the Cheyenne, were consistently mentioned including some that had not actually been personally contacted by white men. George Grinnell tells us that a Frenchman had visited the Arickara in one of the latter's Missouri River villages prior to 1734, so that even if this man had not himself met with Cheyennes, he must certainly have heard of them by some name or other.

As regards the term *"Gens des la Fleche Colee"* in the LaVerendrye brother's account, it is similar to a common Mandan and Hidatsa name for the Cheyennes of "People of the Striped" or "Painted Arrows," and perhaps the LaVerendrye manuscript was intended to read, 'Couleur' meaning in French, 'coloured' or 'painted,' rather than 'colee,' meaning 'glued' or something of that ilk. It may have referred to the stripped turkey or sage hen feathers with which the Cheyennes are said to have fletched their arrows up until reservation days, and by which fact several other tribes in contact with them designated the Cheyenne Nation as "Striped Arrow People" or "Spotted Arrow Quills." It is also known that of old, according to the Cheyennes themselves, they often painted their arrows blue, perhaps, as some Cheyenne informants said, in recognition of the Blue Earth country in which area one or more of their important bands had once resided, but more likely, as other tribal members declared, as an act of religious symbolism for the "Sacred Blue Sky" which to the Cheyennes, personified Creation and the abode of the Supreme Being, Ma'heo itself.

Conversely, the Cheyennes were in the habit of attaching the feather flights to their arrows with a fish based glue, and as this was contrary to the custom of other tribes who either slotted or tied the flights to the shafts, it may have been a colloquial term used by some tribes, particularly the Arickara, in order to denote this peculiarity of their Cheyenne neighbours. In corroboration of this, White-Frog, an old Northern Suhtaio informant, once told George Bent that his people [here speaking of the Cheyenne Nation as a whole] were the only Indians among their neighbours who in olden times glued the flights to their arrows, and it will be recalled that the LaVerendryes had recently resided among the Arickara before meeting the *Gens de la Fleche Colee* and probably had Arickara guides accompanying them on their journey north to the Mandan towns. Thus the Arickara had likely given the LaVerendrye's the name which the Frenchmen translated as *Fleche de la Colee.* Contrary to this assumption, of course, the term may even have been a reference to the Cheyenne's Sacred Arrow talismans, and thus referring to the Aorta band specifically who had the said talismans in their care, and who previous to their crossing the Missouri and rejoining their Masikota brethren, seasonally occupied a permanent earth-lodge village near Long lake on the east side of that river.

The journal adds, however, that the *"Gens de la Fleche Colee"* were also known as "Sioux of the Prairies," and this name clinches the idea that the latter was a Cheyenne group, for the "Sioux of the Prairies" were also known as 'Mascoutens,' 'Maskoutecs' and 'Maskoutepoel,' each of which terms mean something in the way of "Prairie Warriors," "Prairie Men" or even "Prairie Eaters" and under which collective name Cheyennes were once included. Indeed, the collective Cheyenne term 'Masikota' meaning 'Prairie-eaters' and in the vernacular, 'Grasshoppers,' as deduced in an earlier chapter, is but a dialectical variant of the same, whilst a statement made by Father Aulneau who was with the elder LaVerenderye in 1736, reported as follows,

"The Assiniboine and Cree are warring on the Maskoutepoels or Sioux of the Prairies." [10]

Corroboration might be found in the fact that no Sioux band was then living along or near the Missouri River at the time the LaVerendrye brothers passed the camp of the *"Gens de la Fleche Colee" or "Prairie Sioux."* * Therefore, these latter must have been the same Cheyenne group referred to in Sioux tradition, which, after vacating its old village site at the head of Maple Creek near present-day Kulm in the Coteau des prairies, crossed the Missouri to that river's west bank, and settled in another permanent village at a point overlooking the mouth of Porcupine Creek.

A Sioux account gives the date of arrival of the Masikota on the west bank of the Missouri as around one-hundred years before "The Stars Fell," [i.e. 1833], [11] although the Masikota`s actual arrival at the mouth of the Porcupine would appear to have been closer to 1743. This assumption is corroborated by the elder LaVerendrye reports between 1738 and 1743, in which we are informed that in 1739, the Mandan told the elder LaVerendrye that the next tribes or groups of foreign people below them on or near the Missouri, were the Pananas [i.e. Arickara] and the Pananis [i.e., Skidi-Pawnee], both of whom, he was told, had horses. Four years later when the LaVerendrye brothers passed the *Gens de Fleche Colee*, these latter were the next people below the Mandan and above the Arickara and certainly, the LaVerendrye brother`s report implies that the *"Gens de la Fleche Colee"* had only then arrived on the west bank of the Missouri, at the time the brothers passed through their camps stopping very little. The fact that the latter then comprised only twenty-five families, suggests they were merely the vanguard, so to speak, of the larger Masikota band.

Returning to the Bowstrings, it becomes clear that prior to the middle years of the eighteenth century, they were not inclined to stay permanently in the prairie country west of the Missouri, but were moving back and forth across that river, sometimes hunting and raiding in the west, sometimes in the east. Occasionally, they visited their western allies to trade, and sometimes went east to the Sioux fairs at the head of the Minnesota. At other times they spent part of certain seasons in and adjacent to their earth-lodge town at the Biesterfeldt site on the Lower Sheyenne.

The Bowstrings were then a populous group; one of the largest Cheyenne-speaking divisions as is suggested by the size of the Biesterfeldt site, although it is unlikely that they alone ever constituted the two-thousand or more warriors as alleged in the LaVerendrye report. However, whilst Lieutenant W. P. Clark was collecting information for his book on Indian sign language between 1879 and 1880, he obtained a statement from an old Cheyenne named Black-Pipe, who told him that during his tribe's early years west of the Missouri, the whole Nation comprised between three-thousand and five-thousand lodges. This, he added, was prior to several diseases which in later years hit the tribe, carrying off large numbers of Cheyennes, and was before constant warfare with other tribes also took a heavy toll of their young men.

*Father Aulneau was killed that same year of 1736 along with another of LaVerendrye`s sons and a number of employees by the Sioux of the Prairies, on what has since become known as massacre Island in Lake of the Woods. In 1720, a Frenchman named Pachot, positioned these same Prairie Sioux near the headwaters of the Minnesota River, where, of course, one or more Cheyenne-speaking group including the remnants of the Masikota were then residing in close proximity to Teton Sioux bands.

If we are to assume that the lodges referred to by Black-Pipe were medium-sized earth and timber constructions, containing an average of at least ten persons per lodge, then four-thousand lodges would constitute some forty-thousand souls. This, of course, is a fantastic figure when we consider that the population of the great Sioux family or even of the larger Algonquian groups of Cree and Chippewa, never reached so high a number. Similarly, Black-Pipe's estimate could not have applied to the large buffalo-hide tepees in use at a later date, which housed an average of six persons per lodge, and certainly we know from official statistics recorded at various times throughout the nineteenth century, that the Cheyenne Nation then including the Suhtaio, never exceeded six-thousand souls at one time. Even allowing for a population decrease during times of disease, famine and warfare, forty-thousand persons is still far too high a figure at any period in their known history. Perhaps Black-Pipe's assertion was totally wrong, but if it applies to when the Cheyennes had only very few horses among them and for the better part of the year, were roaming the prairies with small portable skin shelters packed on the backs of dogs, as indeed tribal tradition states, then as these small lodges rarely sheltered more than three persons each and often less, it can be reasonably estimated that the whole Nation then comprised at a conservative guess, perhaps some ten-thousand persons in total.

The Mandan, Arickara and Pawnee Nation of the Missouri River and its tributaries, were very numerous during the early years of the eighteenth century, yet by the 1790s they had been drastically reduced through recurring disease [smallpox] and warfare. The Arickara who once boasted one-thousand lodges housing some twenty-thousand souls around the date 1740, could count only three-hundred lodges and some six-thousand souls less than thirty years later.

It is a fact that during the eighteenth century, many Indian Nations both east and west of the Missouri, lost half and in some cases two-thirds of their entire populations to disease, which even though introduced by the white man, actually ravaged many tribes before they themselves had had actual physical contact with them. Such contagions were spread from one tribe to another through the Indian's trading and war excursions, thus creating a chain reaction across the Plains.

That Cheyennes suffered from these deadly scourges is most probable, notwithstanding their traditional assertions obtained early in the 20th century, which adamantly declared that when west of the Mississippi, their people as a Nation escaped any serious decimation including the smallpox attack of 1781 / `82, and which particular event destroyed the power of many of their neighbours and allies. However, contagion's prior to the outbreak of 1781 were then, no doubt, too far back in time for Cheyennes to remember in detail, as was also the case with both the Mandan and Arickara accounts, and of whom it might be said, recalled virtually nothing of the disastrous epidemic of circa 1760 which, in its turn, had also swept away large numbers of their people.

That some Cheyenne bands were very closely confederated to and in regular contact with the Arickara and also with the Black Hills tribes, each of whom suffered from the same contagions, it cannot seriously be accepted that the Cheyenne alone remained immune, when they could not help but associate with other infected groups, and knew nothing concerning the transmission of germs from the source of contamination.

The truth of the matter is that by the latter decades of the eighteenth century, at which time all the various Cheyenne-speaking groups had become confederated into one Nation, their number had already dwindled through recurring disease, so that no Cheyennes before that time, probably knew the true number of their people`s then widely scattered population. It is highly likely then, that the LaVerendrye enumeration of two-thousand Bow warriors met in the Black Hills west of the Missouri, was meant to include the latter`s allies also, and would not then be so much of an exaggeration as it seems, as we have no way of knowing the population of the Pipe-Stem-Men faction. However, as the Bowstring village on Sheyenne River in eastern North Dakota contained around seventy large earth-lodges, representing between seven and eight hundred inhabitants, whilst the Masikota village at the mouth of the Porcupine on the Missouri contained at least seventy much larger lodges [often sixty feet in diameter], along with many smaller habitations of which no count was made, plus that an average of twenty persons dwelt together in each of the large lodges, then there must have been at least some two thousand persons resident in the Porcupine Creek village alone. If we add to this figure the Little Cheyenne River site on the east side of the Missouri which, archaeologists have determined, was also a large village comparable with that on the Porcupine, one can estimate a combined population of around five-thousand Cheyennes occupying these three sites alone, of which we have some knowledge.

If it is accepted that the *Gens L`Arc* were indeed Cheyennes, then it is interesting to note that the actual crusade against the Snakes in 1742 as recorded in the LaVerendrye journal, is very similar in detail to a supposed later-date allied tribal crusade against the same enemy, and of which expedition, Cheyennes were included as the predominant and most important force. This particular event, so the informant George Bent assumed, had taken place about the year 1817 and in which instance, the Cheyenne Sacred Arrows were carried against the foe to ensure the expedition`s success. In the event, the Snakes were not met and the allies broke up and dispersed, having slain only one of the enemy, and of two Snake women taken captive, they managed to escape in the night. It does appear that the dating of this episode as given by Bent, may have been wide of the mark, and should actually apply to the much earlier episode of 1742. Certainly such a grand crusade as indicated in the LaVerendrye report, may well have warranted the Cheyenne`s Sacred Arrow talismans being present, which would then account for the whole Cheyenne-speaking Nation along with its allies, being included on the expedition. Additionally, the status of the Head chief of the *Gens L`Arc* as indicated in the LaVerendrye report, does suggest that the chief himself may have been the Sweet Medicine Chief of the Cheyennes, and so would explain his importance among the allied force at that time.

Having said this, if the above be the case or not, all the evidence does point to the assumption that the *Gens L`Arc* of the LaVerendrye account were indeed Cheyennes, and so it can be inferred, that even then they were a prominent tribal group among their allies and neighbours. Thus it should not be surprising that the Bow chief himself was regarded as the great man and overall leader among the various tribes and bands of the aforementioned crusade against the *Gens de Serpent*, as the LaVerendrye report makes clear.

CHAPTER. 35.

ON PORCUPINE CREEK.

Today on the west bank of the Missouri, North Dakota, there are yet visible the remains of several earth-lodge village sites. One of these is situated on a promontory overlooking the south bank of Porcupine Creek where that stream enters the Missouri about five miles above present day Fort Yates. This site, so both Cheyenne and Sioux traditions tell us, was once occupied by Cheyennes, specifically that group which earlier had resided near the mouth of the Blue Earth in Minnesota, and thence, at the so-called Kulm site at the head of Maple Creek in the Coteau des Prairies. The inhabitants must, therefore, have been Cheyennes of the Masikota faction.

The Sioux account goes on to say that this village like that on the Lower bend of the Sheyenne, was known to the Sioux as *"Shien-woju,"* meaning "Cheyenne Plantings," and add that it was built about one-hundred years before "The Stars fell," which latter event, we know, occurred in November 1833. This, though, as previously mentioned, is only a rough calculation by the Sioux and more likely, the village in question was not actually built until sometime close to 1743. Having said this, these Cheyennes may initially have gone to a more southern point on the Missouri near the mouth of Grand River, where they would have met the Arickara before continuing north to the Porcupine. They may then, have been located on the west bank of the Missouri as early as the Sioux tradition asserts.

It has been noted in the previous chapter how in early 1743, the LaVerendyre brothers whilst travelling north from the Arickara villages along the west bank of the Missouri, encountered a newly-arrived Indian camp midway between the Arickara and Mandan. As no mention was then made of a permanent earth-lodge village, it can be inferred that the Indian camp in question had only very recently arrived at that place, and thus likely represents a Cheyenne group.

In reality, there are at least three permanent village sites along the west bank of the Missouri in the vicinity of Fort Yates. All three sites are attributed to Cheyenne occupation, although it is the most northern of these sites overlooking the mouth of the Porcupine which now warrants our attention.

Thanks largely to George Bird Grinnell, we have been left a brief description of the site which now, alas, has partly been obliterated by the undermining action of the Missouri River.

Grinnell`s account is as follows,

"The more northerly of the two (villages) is situated on a bluff above the Missouri River, on the south side of Porcupine Creek, less than five miles north of Fort Yates. This village has been partly destroyed by the Missouri River, which has undermined the bank and carried away some of the house rings, but many remain. A few are still seen as the raised borders of considerable earth-lodges, the rings about the central

393

hollow being from twelve to fifteen inches above the surrounding soil, and the hollows noticeably deep; usually however, the situation of the house is indicated merely by a slight hollow and by the particular character of the grass growing on the house site. The house rings nearest both Porcupine Creek and on the Missouri River, stand on the bank immediately above the water and some of those on the Porcupine, may also have been undermined and carried away by the stream when in flood.....This settlement must have been large. It stands on a flat top bluff which slopes slightly towards the river, and the houses were close together. Many of these were large, one at least being sixty feet in diameter. Besides the large houses there were many smaller ones, probably occupied by small families; by old people living alone, or perhaps used as menstrual lodges or even for dogs. We counted more than seventy large house sites, taking no account of the small ones. The houses extended several hundred yards back from the river that is toward the west, and one-hundred and fifty or two-hundred yards north and south. It is probable that once they were much more numerous, and they may even have extended a long way down the river.....On the gently rising land to the west of the Porcupine village, the Cheyennes are said to have planted their corn, as also on the flats on the north side of the Porcupine river.....The village site now stands (1923) on the farm of Yellow Lodge, a Yanktonai Sioux, who stated that he had always been told by the old people that this was a Cheyenne village, and that in ploughing, he had often turned up pottery from the ground. Most of this pottery was broken, but he had found some pots that were perfect. He had turned up glass beads, which he described as like the charms or beads which we know the Cheyennes used to manufacture - in later times perhaps - from pounded glass like those said to have been made by the Mandan." [1]

It is a pity that the unbroken Cheyenne pots found by Yellow Lodge cannot now be located, as then we would have something more definite with which to compare pottery shards found in other village sites both in the Dakotas and Minnesota, and thereby, perhaps, further corroborate the earlier locations of Cheyenne-speaking groups. This being so, we can construe from the above description, that this particular village at the mouth of the Porcupine housed a very large population. Calculating a conservative estimate of around twenty persons to a large lodge, then at least some two-thousand occupants must at one time have resided at the site, and which suggests that here was entrenched an entire Cheyenne division, and an important one at that.

Grinnell's description neglects to mention that the village had been fortified. Yet tribal tradition states that the village was thus protected, and when the Lewis and Clark expedition ascended the Missouri to that point in October 1804, during which time several long since abandoned earth-lodge sites were noted, the explorers were told by Arickara informants that they had once been occupied by Cheyennes and one of the sites, particularly that at the mouth of the Porcupine, had been fortified. Obviously then, as Grinnell did not observe the remains of a defensive ditch or earthwork, it must be assumed that the village had been protected by a timber stockade or picket fence, as indeed was a common feature of Mandan and Arickara towns, and excavation of the site perimeter, if undertaken, may have exposed a regular line of post-molds.

Cheyenne tradition recalls that this particular group's final crossing of the Missouri from east to west, was made in spring or early summer, and that either the Mandan or Arickara ferried them over in their round, skin-covered craft commonly called bull-boats. To the north of these Porcupine Creek Cheyennes were the Mandan, then residing in nine large towns nestling neatly along and adjacent to the Missouri about the mouth of Heart River across from where the city of Bismarck now stands. South of the Porcupine close to the mouth of the Big Cheyenne near present-day Pierre, were numerous Arickara towns, as many as twenty-three according to the Bourgainville report of 1757, while further south below the Platte stood villages of the Omaha, Ponca and Osage, and below these on the Arkansas River along its Lower course, were those of the Wichita and other Caddoan-speaking groups.

The position of the Porcupine Creek site in relation to the above-mentioned tribes, would at first suggest that those who assisted the Cheyennes in crossing the Missouri on this occasion were the Mandan, as they lived nearest the point of crossing. But as the Mandans were then at war with Cheyennes, and the Arickara were in the habit of wandering high up the Missouri as far as Grand River not far south of the present North / South Dakota state line, it is more likely that the Arickara were the hosts. At a later date, when other Cheyenne bands reached the same river from the east, there were indeed other points of crossing and on which occasions, the Mandan probably did supply their services.

Of course, since the sex-partite peace council at the Omaha village on the Big Sioux half a century earlier, Cheyennes and Arickara had been close friends and allies, while at the date 1743 Cheyennes were generally at loggerheads with the Mandan and engaged in open conflict with them. Often the Arickara and Mandan were themselves at each other's throats and during such times, it seems that Cheyennes aided the Arickara. In fact, the LaVerendrye material tells us that since four years prior to 1738, the Arickara had been at war with the Mandan. This statement adds substance to our assertion that it was the Arickara alone who ferried the Masikota across the Missouri, perhaps near the mouth of Grand River, before these Cheyennes actually went further north to Porcupine Creek, albeit while still openly hostile to the Mandan.

It was, however, say the Cheyennes, from both these river tribes that they learned how to build stronger, more comfortable lodges, and how to plant more effectively.

Whilst on the west bank of the Missouri, the Masikota Cheyennes collected fish from the river by the employment of long seines, as once they had done when inhabiting the cold lake country of the Northeast. They also fashioned strong dugout canoes by hollowing out tree trunks with fire. Old Cheyenne women would say that a whole family would be engaged in such work; keeping the fire going both day and night until the dugout was completed. Corn was planted on each side of Porcupine Creek along with squash, Pomme-blanche, Indian tobacco and some other crops which the Arickara and Mandan likewise, were in the habit of raising.

At planting time the Cheyennes in those days performed a corn ceremony, the rites of which have long since been forgotten, but one can guess that the ceremony had been adopted from the Arickara or Omaha and passed on to the Masikota along with other Cheyenne and Suhtaio groups through their Pipe-Stem Men kinfolk. It was also remembered by Cheyenne informants late in the nineteenth century, that they once had a sacred "corn dance" in which the females who planted the crop took the prominent role. But of this no further details were recalled. After planting time, the people packed up their belongings and took their hide-covered tepees out into the Plains transported on travois pulled by horses, as by that date the Cheyennes did own a number of such animals, although not enough to accommodate the whole band. Even so, the people could then follow the buffalo herds and thus, they wandered over the open Plains, sometimes far west of the Missouri where they spent most of the summer months hunting deer and buffalo for meat and hides. About the middle of autumn they would return to their earth-lodge village overlooking the Porcupine; harvest their crops and prepare them for winter use by caching them in deep storage pits both within and without the town. In mid-November they returned to the Plains for their late autumn hunt, when hides and robes were thick for winter use.

At about the same time as the Masikota first established themselves at the mouth of the Porcupine, another people also refugees from the Coteau des prairies, settled in the vicinity of Heart River close to the Mandan. This was a Siouan speaking group later known as Hidatsa, and was the parent band from which the River Crow evolved. Together with the cognate Awaxawi and Awaxtia, they comprised the Hidatsa Nation of historic times, but originally these three had been separate groups, albeit linguistically and culturally related.

At the later date of circa, 1780, Cheyennes were at peace with all the Missouri River tribes, excluding certain Siouan-speaking peoples such as the Kaw and Osage and some Caddoan bands farther south, and during times of sporadic feuding between the neighbouring Mandan, Hidatsa and Arickara, the Cheyennes generally remained neutral. As noted previously, though, the initial phase of contact between Cheyennes and Mandan was of a hostile nature, and for a few years at least, the Mandans had continued to fervently resist Cheyenne occupation on the Missouri's west bank.

Other than their attack on the Owuqueo, Cheyenne tradition recalls no specific details concerning this early phase of warfare with the Mandan, merely stating that their two peoples were then hostile towards each other. The Mandan, we have seen, recalled a little more and inferred that Cheyennes were the aggressors. They narrated to Prince Maximilian in 1833 another, albeit brief account of one of their many fights with Cheyennes during this early period of contact, which is given here as a supplement to the story previously related of the initial Awigaxa victory over the Pipe-Stem-Men Cheyennes.

This account applies, ostensibly, to a slightly later date than that concerning the Owuqueo, and pertains specifically to the Masikota group entrenched at the mouth of the Porcupine, at a time when the latter first settled permanently adjacent to that part of the Missouri.

Maximillian was told that four years after the Awigaxa [i.e. Owuqueo] Mandan group had fled north from the Moreau to Heart River, the Hidatsa-proper appeared on the Missouri's east bank directly across from Heart River and the Mandan towns. At that time the Hidatsa were without corn and after some verbal discourse to and fro between them, the Mandan shot corn cobs tied to their arrow shafts over the river to the Hidatsa and bewailed their misfortunes recently suffered at the hands of the Cheyenne. They declared that Cheyennes had slaughtered their womenfolk in the fields, and that the blood of their wounds had caused the corn to come up red. The Hidatsa took pity on the Mandans and next day, they crossed the Missouri en masse and united with them. It was

Site of the old Cheyenne earth-lodge village in background on left overlooking Porcupine Creek on its south side where it enters the Missouri. Looking east. *[Author's photograph]*

only a short time after this that a large Cheyenne war-party suddenly appeared and attacked the Mandan village, and fierce fighting ensued which lasted the whole day. At length, after many Cheyennes had been slain, the combined might of the Mandan and newly arrived Hidatsa managed to drive the enemy back, and they then pursued the Cheyennes to a small stream which flowed from the west and where, come sundown, the fighting finally ceased. The Maximillian account gives no further details, and we are posed with the question which particular Cheyenne-speaking group was involved, and at what date roughly did the event take place. There is, however, perhaps another account of the same affair related in the early 1920s by a Hidatsa chief named Bear's-Arm. [2]

In the Bear's-Arm account, it is said that a great battle was once fought between the Mandan and Cheyennes, at a time when the Cheyennes were attempting to hold their position on the west side of the Missouri overlooking a stream not far north from old Fort Yates. Bear's-Arm said that Cheyennes had only recently moved into the region and contested their right of occupancy with any who came against them. At one time a Mandan party, either on a hunting trip or as a war band, invaded the area and met the Cheyennes in battle on the slopes of a grassy eminence now known as Fire Heart Butte just north of the North-South Dakota state line. The battle was hard fought Bear's-Arm said, but at length the Mandan were the victors, having slain thirty-seven Cheyennes for the loss of only eleven Mandans.

No doubt the Mandans carried away their dead and wounded when they returned north to their villages on Heart River, and not long after, according to Bear`s-Arm, the Cheyennes returned to the butte where the battle had taken place to retrieve the corpses of their own slain comrades. These they transported to a nearby ravine leading from the butte, but some distance from their village, and laid the corpses in a row upon a stone shelf jutting out from one of the steep sides of the ravine. Bear`s-Arm further stated that Cheyennes thereafter, continued to visit the ravine in order to honour their dead, but the Mandans believed the site to be haunted by the ghosts of those who lay there, and would not go near for that reason. This place of burial was still visible in the early 1920s. It consisted of a narrow defile with steep sides lined with horizontal stratas of sandstone ledges. A quantity of human bones lay close to the overhanging ledges, having become exposed and scattered through the passage of time.

Bear`s-Arm was adamant that the fight had taken place long before the Sioux came into that part of the country, which was around 1760, and so the event had likely occurred near the time the Masikota first established their village overlooking the mouth of Porcupine Creek.

It would appear that a number of such fights as related above, would have taken place between the Mandan and the newly-arrived Masikota Cheyennes, and it is indicative that Porcupine Creek itself had earlier been known by its old Indian name of "Battle Creek."

As for dating the event, we do have a clue in the Mandan assertion that the Hidatsa had only just arrived on the Missouri at that time, and which event occurred close to 1744 or 1745. Indeed, the first meeting between the Mandan and Hidatsa is verified in part by another Hidatsa account of the same episode related by a woman of that tribe to one Gilbert Wilson in 1917. This version states that a Hidatsa war-party which had ventured to the Missouri, first met the Mandans who were lined up in battle array facing them across the river. Prior to their coming to blows with each other, some verbal discourse took place, the result being that both tribes decided not to fight and instead, the Mandan shot corn over to the Hidatsa across the river. However, even though the Hidatsa liked this *"new food,"* they could not persuade the rest of their people to accept it. In fact, only after several subsequent meetings with the Mandan, said Wilson's informant, did the Hidatsa finally accept the corn, and decide to move across the great river and settle near the Mandan.

Now we know that the Hidatsa were raising and gathering certain foodstuffs, such as potatoes and ground beans when in the Devils Lake country of the northeast long before they crossed the Missouri, so perhaps, the Hidatsa inference that they did not have corn at that time by the expression that corn was a *"new food,"* indicates that while in the northern Coteau, they had for some reason been prevented from raising their own. Such may have been due to drought or excessive precipitation in that part of the country and thus, the reason why the Hidatsa migrated en masse to the Missouri flood plains in the first place.

For the Cheyennes` part, the Masikota must - by elimination - be those referred to in the account, as their position on the Porcupine was closest to the Mandan towns at that date.

As regards the river to which the Cheyennes are said to have been driven by the allied Mandan and Hidatsa, it may have been the Cannonball lying between the Heart and the Porcupine. But the Cannonball was not a `small river` and as the Cheyennes according to the story apparently then held their ground, one suspects that somewhere along the river in question was the Cheyenne base, i.e. their stockade earth-lodge village on Porcupine Creek, and wherein they gained a refuge from their pursuers. Perhaps Masikota numbers had been augmented during their earlier attack on the Mandan town by members of the Bowstring group in the Coteau des Prairies along with Pipe-Stem-Men who still visited their old town on the east side of the Missouri near the mouth of the Little Cheyenne. Certainly the warrior strength from the Porcupine Creek village alone, would not have been anywhere near adequate to match the combined Mandan strength at that date with any hope of success. Conversely, it could be that the initial attack on the Mandan was solely a Masikota affair, and having first assaulted what they thought was one of the more isolated Mandan towns, they were surprised to find the Mandan force increased with additional ranks of recently arrived Hidatsa. As a result, the Cheyennes would have found themselves greatly outnumbered; forced on the defensive and obliged to fight hard and long, suffering many casualties before extricating themselves from imminent defeat if not annihilation. It must then have been more than just a lucky break for the Cheyennes when they reached the river during their retreat, at which point their foes gave up the fight, leaving the Cheyennes to lick their wounds. Surely, only a strong defensive position such as the stockade village on the south bank of the Porcupine is what saved the Masikota that time?

Of one thing we can be sure from the Mandan, Hidatsa and Cheyenne accounts, is that this period of hostile strife between the three groups was a war of intermittence; interspersed with truces of varying duration. For the aforesaid village on the Porcupine continued to be occupied for more than forty years, and during which time the warrior strength of the town was never on a par numerically with that of the Mandan, not to mention when the latter were united with the Hidatsa who, for many years thereafter, remained neighbours and allies to the Mandan. That Cheyennes were indeed residing in a permanent village at the mouth of the Porcupine at the date in question, albeit then still at war with the Mandan and Hidatsa, is further corroborated by the following.

The Awaxawi Siouan group, now extinct, but once consanguine with the Hidatsa, had already crossed the Missouri from the Northeast prior to 1743, and had settled just above the Mandan. This was before the migration of their Hidatsa-proper cousins who followed in their footsteps some years later.

The Awaxawi had a strong tradition which stated, that when they first arrived on the Missouri's west bank, they resided close to the Mandan near the mouth of Heart River, and were still in that location when their cousins the Hidatsa-proper arrived from the northeast. From this point on the Missouri the Hidatsa-proper, some years later, moved upriver to the Knife so to be near their Awaxita kinfolk who had long been entrenched in the Knife River area, and the Awaxawi followed suit soon after. The Hidatsa, though, then resented the latter`s presence and they and the Awaxawi went to war with each other which lasted a full three years. During this time, the Awaxawi moved back down the Missouri to a point near Porcupine Creek below the Mandan, *"...to live,"* the tradition says, *"near the friendlier Cheyennes."*

Here not far from the Cheyennes, the Awaxawi built another permanent earth-lodge village which they occupied for a number of years. According to the same account, this event occurred long prior to the first virulent smallpox epidemic which hit all the Missouri River tribes, and helps establish a rough date of initial occupancy of Cheyennes at Porcupine Creek.

Between 1801 and 1802 Smallpox ravaged the Mandan, Arickara and Hidatsa, then spread north and west where it destroyed two thirds of all the Indian populations in its path. Prior to this outbreak at least two similar contagions had already scourged the Upper Missouri tribes. The Lewis and Clark journals inform us, from Arickara sources, that one particular outbreak of any consequence among the River Tribes occurred around the year 1760, and at which time, many among the Arickara, Mandan and Hidatsa had been carried off in its wake.

Given that the most virulent of these periodic contagions appeared among the tribes during successive generations of every twenty years or so, it can be assumed that the first of the three attacks mentioned by the Arickara most likely occurred around 1761, and was followed by the outbreaks of 1781 and 1801, both of which are well documented in contemporary sources. This, when coupled with information given in the Awaxawi tradition noted above, the first outbreak of the early 1760s must be that referred to by the Awaxawi, and so the above recounted Mandan – Cheyenne fight had occurred long before that date. In some small way, this adds substance to the Sioux assertion which states that those Cheyennes from the Biesterfeldt Sheyenne River site, were not on the Missouri at the time of the 1760-`61 smallpox in any permanent village, and to the inference from the Awaxawi account that no other Cheyenne people were then on the Missouri near the Mandan, while according to the Cheyennes themselves, all Cheyenne bands escaped any serious smallpox attack until the outbreak of 1801-02, and which would then date the arrival of Cheyennes at Porcupine Creek long prior to the contagion of cica, 1760. *

The reason for this is that unlike the Mandan and Arickara who, incidentally, always seem to have suffered most during such visitations, the Cheyenne in common with most of the Hidatsa-proper, did not remain at their earth-lodge towns the year round, but after planting corn and other crops, they moved into the Plains far west of the middle Missouri in order to hunt. They only returned to their permanent villages in mid-autumn at harvest time, then disappeared again into the Plains of the west. As a consequence, they were probably not in contact with those River Tribes which actually contracted the disease, and could keep away until the scourge had burned itself out. Why the Awaxawi, though, should have been so friendly with Cheyennes and allowed to settle in such close proximity to them, at the same time as their Awatixa and Hidatsa relatives were then at war with Cheyennes, may be found in the fact that the Awaxawi and certain Cheyenne groups particularly the Masikota, had once been close neighbours and friends when in the Coteau country of the eastern Dakotas and, of course, by reason that as the Awaxawi were then at war with their own Hidatsa cousins, they found joint cause with the Cheyenne against a common enemy.

* The French Canadian trader Jean Baptist Trudeau, was told by the Arickara as early as 1795, that Smallpox had decimated their villages three times before he had come among them. Here Trudeau was referring to the outbreaks of 1781 and 1761 and another at some earlier date, probably between circa, 1741 and 1745.

ON PORCUPINE CREEK

As regards the economic situation of the Masikota while in residence on Porcupine Creek, the most important commodity and certainly, one of great advantage to their location, was the availability of horses. The acquisition of which afforded these Cheyennes much greater mobility and subsequently, a more comfortable existence than previously known when the only beasts of burden had been their dogs and women. With horses beneath them, hunting parties could go far afield in search of game and could follow the buffalo herds the year round. Enemies from the west could be sought out and matched on equal terms, whilst the tedium of village life could be alleviated by their being able to roam the prairies in a leisurely and comfortable manner. The effect of the horse on Cheyenne and for that matter, upon Indian culture and values in general, cannot be too strongly emphasized, and the obtaining of such animals soon became a prime objective in their day to day existence. It was the insatiable craving for horses, no doubt, which inspired the Masikota - as indeed it did other Cheyenne-speaking groups - to continue their migrations west and to woo the friendship of tribes already mounted, With horses; and at a later date with guns, the Cheyenne would prove themselves a match for any foe and become rich by the standards of Indian material culture at that time. This in turn caused the Cheyennes to strive in order to become arch traders in the intertribal commerce of the Plains.

The only practical way of obtaining horses whilst the Cheyenne were yet too weak to steal them in great number by force of arms, was through trade, and in order to do so, they needed access to certain commodities with which to barter to the horse-using tribes, and withal, they needed a regular supply on hand. Perhaps then, it was not by accident that the Masikota built their town at the mouth of the Porcupine, but by design. From such a position they could entice Indian traders from the Plains away from the Arickara and Mandan towns to their own village on the Porcupine, and for inducements could offer French and English trade goods coming from Sioux channels in the east, and which articles were far superior to those obtained from the Spanish markets with which the Plains Tribes had been accustomed. The Spaniards still had an embargo restricting the selling of firearms to Indians, whereas the French and English had no such scruples and actually encouraged the sale of guns by mass-producing short-barreled, smooth bore fusses, specifically for the Indian market.

It is true that the Mandan had regular contact with the Assiniboine and Plains Cree, and later, with Chippewa traders from the north and northeast who brought the Mandans guns, knives, brass kettles, awls and other iron implements got from the English on Hudson's Bay, and had probably been visiting the Mandan towns as early as the late seventeenth century. But both the Assiniboine and Cree were despised by the Mandan and at times fighting broke out between them. At best, they tolerated each other only as far as it was necessary to continue their mutual commerce.

Coupled to this, the Assiniboine and Plains Cree only traded their surplus European goods and such articles as were virtually worn out, whilst in exchange the Mandan offered tanned and ornamented robes of elk and buffalo; dyed porcupine quills, fine buckskins and feather-decorated accoutrements along with agricultural produce and home-grown tobacco, and more importantly, horses obtained by the Mandan from tribes of the Western Plains and Black Hills and also from the south. Hence, some Spanish sword blades and Mexican commodities were included in their merchandise, and thus; in a roundabout way, Spanish items eventually reached more distant peoples of the Upper Great Lakes far northeast of the Missouri, a long way indeed from the Spanish possessions of the Southwest.

During brief times when the Masikota were at peace with the Mandan and allowed to visit the latter's towns to trade, if the Assiniboine or Plains Cree were present, then the Cheyennes at first were obliged to tolerate them in accordance with tribal protocol, which gave sanctuary to any and all visitors who came in peace. This was due in part also because of the guns and ammunition which the Assiniboine and Plains Cree brought with them and which the Cheyennes, who did not themselves trade directly with the Assiniboine, afterwards purchased from the Mandan.

It is also apparent that French traders in order to carry on their commerce with Indian customers, had followed the Omaha, Iowa and Oto to the Missouri in 1691 after the latter had been forced west from the Minnesota and Iowa regions by the Sioux one year before, and when in 1743 the LaVerendrye sons visited the Arickara near the mouth of the Big Cheyenne, they were told that only three days journey south from the Arickara was another village, whereat resided a Frenchman.

The Arickara may have visited the Spanish and French trade centers themselves and also one or another Pueblo town in what are now the states of New Mexico and Arizona, and Cheyennes may well have gone with them. Certainly the Spanish authorities knew of the Arickara as early as 1717, for in that year they were mentioned in a Spanish document as residing in three villages and that, *"...They have seen the French and know them."*

It is evident then, that even during this period the Arickara were in communication with both Spanish and French traders, and twenty years later in 1737, it was reported that a Frenchman who had lived some years with the Pani-Maha [i.e. Skidi], had accompanied a band of the latter tribe on a visit to the *"Recaras,"* and it was this man, perhaps, of whom the LaVerendrye brothers were told in 1743.

Pawnee-proper bands were, by then, again peaceably associating with the Arickara and Skidi, having patched up their earlier quarrel with each other and together, were fighting Padouca Apaches of the Southern Plains, taking horses, scalps, equipment and captives as booty. These captives were then sold by the Arickara to the Spaniards and French, either directly or indirectly through Arickara trade channels with their Wichita relatives further south.

Early Spanish maps and reports between 1717 and 1740, variously mention *'40 villages des Carricara,* or *"40 villages des Panis,"* then located along both banks of the Missouri. It is, however, apparent that these estimates did not differentiate between those known historically as Arickara and of others known to the French as *"Pani Noir"* [Black Pawnee]. These latter being Caddoan-speaking groups known historically as Wichita and Caddo residing some way south of their Arickara and Skidi cousins.

By the early 1750s the Arickara were again at war with the Mandan, while the Pipe-Stem-Men Cheyennes at that time, remained aloof from becoming involved and by so doing, became overnight, as it were, intermediaries in the Mandan and Arickara trade with the Black Hills tribes.

It was then, because of their favorable position that the Masikota could procure both French and English goods which included guns obtained from the Sioux at the latter's own trading fairs at the head of the Minnesota, and at the same time, could acquire Spanish goods and horses from the Pipe-Stem-Men who attended the trading fairs of the Kiowa and Gattacka near the Black Hills. The Black Hills tribes for their part, also at times took their own merchandise to the Porcupine Creek village overlooking the Missouri, and in such a way through several links in an inter-tribal chain, Spanish and Pueblo goods reached the Bowstring Cheyennes east of the Missouri, and perhaps this is proved by the discovery of a Picuris Pueblo knife-blade found in the ruins of the Biesterfeldt site on the Lower bend of Sheyenne River.

.

That the Black Hills tribes were in close contact with Masikota Cheyennes even before the latter settled permanently on the west bank of the Missouri, is indicated perhaps by the earlier noted fact that the Kiowa always referred to the Cheyennes collectively as *Sakota,* and said to mean "Biters." The similarity of the word *Sakota* with that of the Cheyenne band name Masikota as explained in a previous chapter is striking, and we must remember that an early alternative interpretation of the term Masikota, refers to the grasshopper because of that insect's voracious appetite. This surely connects the two words, and suggests that *Sakota* which is actually pronounced *Sha-Kota*, is but a Kiowa corruption of the Cheyenne term Masikota. Thus we might take it that the Cheyenne-speaking Masikota certainly when at the mouth of the Porcupine if not earlier in the Coteau des Prairies, even then were in contact with tribes around the Black Hills among whom the Kiowa were included.

As a result of this inter-tribal trading network, there can be no doubt that all those involved were; by the early 1750s, being well supplied with horses and European artefacts, which last-named included iron-bladed weapons and a number of flintlock guns.

Thus by the latter date, there was no need for Cheyennes to continue humbling themselves before other tribes in order to keep their trading channels open. They themselves had much to offer; horses to one - guns to the other, and hence, within only a few years, Cheyennes became an important cog in the inter-tribal commerce of the Plains. They thereafter grew rich and astute and prominent among their neighbours and contacts, some of whom knew them collectively as "People of the Bow."

It was surely because of this new-found self-respect and importance that by circa 1750, the Cheyennes no longer felt obliged to tolerate the hated Assiniboine when met at the Mandan or Hidatsa towns, and thus the Cheyenne war with the "Ho-Hay" continued fierce and uninterrupted for another one-hundred years. Now the Cheyennes could not only match the fire power of the Assiniboine, but could out do them in ferocity, and with horses, which animals the Assiniboine themselves did not have in significant number, the Cheyennes always had the advantage when their two peoples met on the open grasslands north or south of the Missouri. From here on, few indeed were the times Cheyennes suffered defeat at the hands of the Assiniboine, while Cheyenne tradition informs us that after establishing themselves permanently along the Missouri, they [the Cheyenne] started to capture many guns from Assiniboine war-parties which they had put to rout, and in this way, they greatly increased their supply.

Such then was the condition of the Masikota / Aorta, Pipe-Stem-Men and Bowstrings at this period in their history, and which continued until 1756, when war having broken out between France and England in the colonies to the east, brought both French and English trade west of the Alleghenies to an abrupt halt. For the next seven years, French and English trade items became virtually non-existent among the Western Tribes. Guns and ammunition which had become necessary requirements in both war and hunting, and not least, as trade items in inter-tribal relations could not be replaced, and without a regular supply of powder and ball, such weapons as the Indians possessed soon became useless in their hands. As a consequence, the Cheyennes for a while, lost the impetus in their trading emporium, and for almost a decade, they retrogressed as did their erstwhile customers.

Be this as it may, from the early 1730s to the mid-1750s, Cheyennes including the Masikota, Aorta and Omissis; the *Gens de L`Arc* or People of the Bow, had reveled in their new-found affluence, having proved themselves the most adaptable and popular tribe among their allies, both east and west of the Missouri.

What, though, of the Suhtaio ?, who at this period were comparatively new-comers into the Coteau country west of Minnesota, and who were forging a strong alliance with the Bowstrings and Aorta Cheyennes then still roaming at will across the Coteau game lands east of the Missouri.

- 0 - 0 - 0 - 0 - 0 - 0 - 0 - 0 - 0 - 0 - 0 - 0 - 0 - 0 - 0 - 0 - 0 –

CHAPTER 36.

WANDERINGS OF THE SUHTAIO.

When the Bowstrings, Masikota and Aorta had first taken up residence in the Coteau country west of the Minnesota, the Suhtaio then known as *Songaskiton* and *Chongashiton*, had remained close to Mille Lacs in association with the Eastern Sioux of that region. By the mid-1740s, however, the Suhtaio were at war with the Assiniboine and Cree and with one or more Eastern Sioux band, and for the sake of expediency, they then followed in the footsteps of their Cheyenne-speaking cousins and relocated first near the headwaters of the Minnesota around one or another of the two large lakes which form a part of the Upper course of that river, thence further west into the Coteau des Prairies. It seems that whilst in the vicinity of one or other of the aforesaid lakes, one Suhtaio band at least, had occupied a permanent village and during their stay at that place, they discovered the Pipestone Quarries of southwestern Minnesota.

Long before this, the Pipe-Stem Men Cheyennes had known of the quarries, whence came the sacred red `catlinite` stone from which their ceremonial pipes and bowls were fashioned. They may not have visited the site themselves at that time, but merely traded the stone in its raw state from either Iowa or Oto allies who, we know from contemporary reports in the *"Jesuit Relations,"* were working the same quarries as early as the sixteen-fifties if not before, and which is substantiated by an entry in the journal of Pierre Radisson from personal observation in 1658, which states that red stone pipes were then in use among the Iowa. On the other hand early in the twentieth century, the Suhtaio claimed to have discovered the quarries themselves, and could yet recall the event in detail.

The northern Suhtai White-Frog related an account to George Bent in 1915 regarding the discovery of the quarries, White-Frog said he had heard the story from his father Red Water, also a Suhtai, who had died at an advanced age some few years earlier. The story had been told to Red Water by his father and by his father who in turn, had heard it from his father who had got it from his father before him. Thus by estimating a period of thirty years more or less as representing each of the six successive generations during which the story had been handed down [including that of White-Frog], the event had probably taken place sometime between 1735 and 1745.

The story according to White-Frog, tells of a war-party which had started out from a stockade earth-lodge village by a large lake near the head of the Minnesota with the intention of raiding enemies further west along the Missouri. The party was on foot and whilst crossing the open expanse of the Coteau west of the Minnesota, they came upon a solitary buffalo bull. The warriors brought down the beast with arrows and going up to their kill, saw that the animal was covered head to tail in a bright red dust in which it had evidently been wallowing. Being curious as to the source of the dust, the war-party gave up its original objective and decided to follow the bull's trail back from whence it came. At length, after travelling a long distance, they reached a stony place in the heart of a prairie and where, strewn around were red-coloured rocks, and the ground covered with what appeared to be a bright red soil. The warriors examined the rocks closely and could see in one place that a sprig of sagebrush, having been blown backwards and forwards by the wind, had worn a groove in the red stone surrounding it. It was because of this discovery, White-Frog said, that the warriors realized the stone's carving potential, whereupon, they each picked up several pieces of loose rock which they then took home to their village.

A variant version recorded by the Northern Cheyenne historian John Stands in Timber in the 1930s, obtained from two veterans of the buffalo days named Nelson Medicine Bird and Dan Old Bull, stated essentially the same as the above, but added some important details,

> "The first pipe stone which ever came into the possession of the Cheyenne tribe, was buried with Stump Horn, an Indian chief. The first pipe is still in the Sacred Hat Bundle where is also a flat piece of red pipe stone which came from the east. The first pipe stone was found by the Suktai (Suhtaio) tribe. Some old-time people led by a warrior named White Antelope. They were travelling with dogs for at this time, the people did not have any horses. An old man saw in the worn path of the buffalo, something red. It lay on the trail. It was next to a sagebrush. When the wind blew on the sage, it waved and a root or a branch rubbed the stone. In this way the red stone was grooved. The man thought maybe something could be done with this stone, so he dug it up. From this stone, the Suktai made the red stone plate and the two red stone pipes. The Suktai claimed territory to the east, that is in eastern Dakota and they came

from there and further east. They came from the Timber Mountains…..The red plate was taken first and made from a larger piece. It was made smaller and finished smooth on both sides. The man took a shank of deer bone and drilled holes to make the pipes from two other pieces at a later time….Tobacco was found before the White man came. They experimented. They got a plant and put it in a garden with corn. They got the tobacco plant from the Arickara Indians who planted it in their gardens too." [1]

This, say the Cheyennes, is how members of their tribe first discovered the catlinite stone quarries of south-western Minnesota, although the story actually relates to the Suhtaio specifically, rather than a Cheyenne-proper band. Even today, Indians from several tribes travel many miles in order to obtain the sacred red stone from this place for the production of pipe bowls. The site itself was once held in such reverence by most tribes that when enemies met on its ground, conflict was usually avoided. The exception to this rule were the Yanktonai Sioux who, apparently, had no such scruples and more than once, actually attacked and slaughtered foreign peoples they found digging there.

Most interesting is that according to John Stands in Timber, an original piece of stone obtained from the quarry was - many years later - in the possession of a Suhtaio chief named Stump-Horn and, subsequently, was buried with him. This suggests that the object in question had indeed been handed down among the Suhtaio over many generations, and as the Pipe-Stem-Men at a later date became associated with the Suhtaio to such a degree that they were later considered as one, it explains how Cheyenne-proper bands since that time, have repeated the same story as if it pertains to themselves, as opposed to the Suhtaio alone.

The Suhtaio claim to have once lived east of the Missouri near the place of "Red Rock" [i.e. Pipestone Quarries], not far west from the sacred Suhtaio site of "Timber Mountain" where, some informants stated, *Issiwun,* the Sacred Buffalo Hat of the Suhtaio had first been obtained. Certainly it was the Suhtaio who revered a small polished disc of red sand stone, said to be one of the original pieces of red rock brought home from the quarry, and which, thereafter, was always used as an integral element in the Suhtaio unique "Buffalo-calling" ceremony. It should be remembered that during the early years of their history, so it is said in tribal tradition, four individual bands constituted the Suhtaio tribe, and their supposed early habitat near the Pipestone Quarries after their obtaining the Sacred Buffalo Hat and ceremonial rites connected with it, actually applies to the different Suhtaio-speaking bands finally coming together as a united tribe, and of which event, the adoption of the ceremony and rites pertaining to *Issiwun* became representative of that fact. In addition, the Cheyenne Red-Shield warrior society of a more recent time, is said to have originated among the Suhtaio soon after the discovery of the quarries; the society's original concept having been inspired by the buffalo bull covered in red dust, and we know also from the writings of Johnathan Carver that as late as 1766 /`68, the *Chongouston* [i.e. Suhtaio], were still located west of the Headwaters of the Minnesota, not far perhaps, from where their stockade village had once been located at the time of their discovering the quarries.

The regalia attributed to the Red-Shields who were also known as `Bulls` or `Bull Soldiers,` included the wearing of a buffalo cap with tapered horns attached, while its members carried a large red painted bull-hide shield with that animal`s teat dangling from its Lower rim. A member of this society remained so for life, although when its number had dwindled to a significant degree through death in battle or old age, those remaining would retire en masse from active service, albeit still regarded as society members, and a younger body of warriors would take their place to continue the society`s existence.

When more specifically the event of the red dust covered buffalo Bull and the inauguration of the Red Shield Society took place, is perhaps indicated in the following analysis.

A Cheyenne informant named Big-Wolf, told George Bent that in 1869, there had died a very old man named Standing-All-Night, reputedly 146 years of age. Standing-All-Night had been born an Arickara, but when a young man had married a Cheyenne woman and lived among the Cheyennes from then on. At the time of his marriage, Standing-All-Night used to say, the Arickara were living in an earth lodge town adjacent to a large Cheyenne village also composed of earth lodges somewhere along the west bank of the Missouri in South Dakota. More importantly, the same Standing-All-Night often told of a time when in his younger days while living adjacent to the Missouri, he had accompanied the Red Shields to a French fort on the Big River, and which event, so Bent was told, had occurred some 160 years before 1917 when the statement was made The informant Big-Wolf added that the party of Red Shield warriors at that time, had put on a society dance inside the fort, but during the performance a violent wind blew the fort gates shut. The Red Shields, fearing some kind of trap set by the Frenchmen, stopped dancing and all at once scrambled over the picket stockade to escape. However, the Frenchmen managed to allay the warrior`s fears and persuaded them to go back inside the fort and finish their dance.. Soon after this, a Frenchman from the fort visited the Red Shields in their camp and brought many presents piled up in a wagon or some other kind of wheeled vehicle drawn by horses. The Red Shields had never before seen such a contraption and were much in awe of it and the Frenchman who was standing up driving his team. One among the Indians called excitedly to his fellows to come and watch this white man doing such a wonderful thing.

Now the term `Big River` among the Cheyennes and Suhtaio was their common name for the Mississippi, and it is known that no French fort was operational in the Upper Mississippi country after the conclusion of the French and Indian war in 1763. Big-Wolf`s assertion on the other hand, that the event had occurred 160 years prior to 1917, gives us a date of 1757 which does coincide with the existence of the French Garrison post known as Fort Beauharnois built in 1750 overlooking Lake Pepin`s east shore on the Mississippi about sixty miles below where the town of St. Paul now stands. This fort did have a picket stockade, but was abandoned in late 1757 or early 1758 after French troops stationed there, were ordered east to fight the English during the aforesaid war.

Other French forts both for trading and military purposes had been extant in earlier years in the Upper Mississippi region, but all these; including several predecessors to Fort Beauhanois, were far too early to be compatible with the life span of Standing-All-Night.

407

Having said this, we learn from French records of the period, that Indians representing the various tribes from what the French termed the "Sea of the West," did visit one and another French fort in 1757, even as far as Montreal on the Lower St. Lawrence, while a people referred to as `Chiens` were reported that same year as being in council with eastern Algonquians on the Lower Ohio discussing a proposed union with the French, but they, the *Chiens,* then being at war with the Algonquian Shawnee among others, refused to join the alliance. The term `Sea of the West` [as explained in an earlier chapter], was merely the French term for the vast unexplored lands west of the Upper Mississippi and Lake Winnipeg regions, and it is possible that the above mentioned *Chiens* did designate a people which at a later date, were included under the collective term of Cheyenne. However, Cheyenne tradition itself recalls that generally speaking, their forebears had been on good terms with the French who they knew as `Red White Men,` although as the Suhtaio - who were certainly known as *Chiens,* i.e. `Dogs`- were then hostile towards several eastern Algonquian tribes, it is likely that for a while at least, some Suhtaio as a consequence, were sporadically hostile towards the French who were allies to the Suhtaio`s Algonquian enemies. Certainly Suhtaio tradition as told by Bull-Thigh to Truman Michelson in 1915, stated that during the period in question, the Suhtaio were still roaming both east and west of the Mississippi, and in addition, it is known that the Algonquian Fox and Western or Teton Sioux who were then friends of the Suhtaio, were themselves at war with most other eastern Algonquians and with the French between 1755 and 1763.

This was the same period when the Eastern Sioux were at loggerheads with the more western Cheyenne-proper groups and as early as 1753, it was reported in a French missive that the Sioux of the rivers and lakes [i.e. Eastern Sioux or Dakota] were then at war with their relatives the Prairie or Western Sioux [i.e. the Tetons] and that the former were desirous of making peace with both the Cree and Chippewa in order to fight the Prairie Sioux together.

Thus as the Suhtaio by then were closely associated with Cheyennes who themselves, were then allied to the Teton, the Suhtaio were also regarded as enemies by the Cree, Chippewa and Eastern Sioux. Indeed, earlier in 1736, the Sieur LaVerendrye had reported that it was only the Monsoni Cree entrenched around his post Fort St. Pierre at the west end of Rainy Lake, which kept the Sioux of the Prairies in check, and among the latter, of course, were included the western Cheyenne-speaking bands which would then have included the Pipe-Stem Men, Masikota and Omissis [Bowstrings]. Such, though, would not necessarily have deterred members of the Suhtaio Red Shield Society from visiting the French fort as mentioned in tradition, perhaps in the company of Iowa allies who themselves, according to the Bourgainville and other contemporary reports of the day, were listed among French allies at that time. This would explain why the Red Shields, initially, had believed it a French trap when the fort gates had suddenly slammed shut.

As regards Standing-All-Night, it is highly unlikely that anyone even among Indians, could have reached such an advanced age of 146 years, although by analyzing the data, some reasonable conclusions can be made.

Assuming that Standing-All-Night was, more realistically, between 120 and 125 years old when he died in 1869, then he must have been born sometime between 1744 and 1749. It cannot then be accepted that as a young warrior of at least twenty years old he had accompanied the Red Shields to the aforesaid French fort, for such would then date the occurrence between 1764 and 1769, which would be contrary to historical fact, that no French controlled forts were then extant in the Upper Mississippi region after 1763 with the conclusion of the French and Indian war.

It would seem therefore, that Standing-All-Night had been younger than even he supposed at the time of the visit, and it is likely that he had been taken along in the capacity of a servant to the older warriors as indeed, often occurred with 12 to 17 year olds. If we accept that such was the case, then the date of the visit around 1757 would be a realistic scenario.

We are further informed from the George Bent material, that yet another old member of the Red Shields during the second half of the nineteenth century was a warrior named Bull-Could-Not-Rise. This man was well over one-hundred years of age when he died in 1865 and was so old, it is said, that for a long time he could not rise from his pallet and had to be carried from place to place while being fed only on liquids to keep him alive. He was also said to have been the last surviving member of the *original* Red Shields and in his younger days, he, too, had visited a French Fort on the Mississippi River. Certainly he had once lived east of the Missouri, for Grinnell obtained a story which told how Bull-Could-Not-Rise when a young man, had undertaken a lone journey from the east, across the Missouri and much further west, in order to retrieve the bones of a brother friend slain by the Crows.

Now if Bull-Could-Not-Rise had joined the Red Shields when between seventeen and twenty years old [as would have been the customary age to do so], and had died when around 125 years of age, then he had likely been born close to 1740 or a few years earlier. Bull-Could-Not-Rise therefore, could when in his late teens, have joined the original Red Shields as a later member of that society, and may well have been present when they visited the French Fort in 1757. But he would not himself have been one of the actual founding members of the Society.

As previously mentioned, the Red Shield society retained its members for life, and only incorporated new members when the old ones had mostly died off or, as more common a practice, after the oldest members had retired from active duty en masse. The society itself, so Cheyenne informants declare, became extinct in 1896 and that the last of the then retiring members had joined the society many years before when the previous intake of new members had occurred around 1826.

If we assume that the oldest surviving Red Shields were around 90 years old when finally they retired completely from office, and that the age of new members averaged twenty years of age, then perhaps the Red Shields changed members every seventy years or so. Seventy years prior to the transference of membership in 1826, gives us a date of 1756, and such was probably close to the time of the original inauguration of the society which had taken its inspiration from the red dust-covered buffalo bull and the discovery of the Pipestone quarries, and which event itself, ostensibly, had likely occurred several years earlier around 1740. Thus by employing this assumption as a rough basis, it can be calculated that Bull-Could-Not-Rise may indeed have accompanied the Red Shields in 1757, having been born around 1740, and which would make him close to 125 years of age when he died in 1865. Such, of course, would fit nicely with the informant

Big-Wolf's assertion that the Red Shields had actually visited the French fort 160 years before 1917, i.e. in 1757.

In an earlier chapter, mention has been made of the Suhtai Fire Wolf's account of how the Cheyenne-proper first met the Suhtaio in the lake and marsh country of northeastern Minnesota.

Model made in 1731 of the French Fort Beauhanois. *[French Historical Documents]*

Fire-Wolf's account further stated that the Cheyenne and Suhtaio thereafter, came together and separated another two times before finally amalgamating as one tribe.

George Bent also gave a version concerning a coming together of the Cheyenne and Suhtaio, but which applies to a later date than that of Fire Wolf's account pertaining to the first coming together of the two tribes. Bent stated that the particular meeting to which he was referring, had occurred sometime between the abandonment of the Biesterfeldt village on the Lower Sheyenne as a permanent base, and the period of Cheyennes roving the Coteau des Prairies as nomads before crossing the Missouri. He was unaware, apparently, of the existence of other Cheyenne village sites in the eastern Dakotas and so, in the light of Fire Wolf's statement, it must be taken that the Cheyenne - Suhtaio meeting of Bent`s account, actually refers to the second coming together of their peoples. Bent also stated that during the same time of roving in the Coteau country east of the Missouri, the Cheyennes also met the Mowisyu [i.e. Moiseo], who having previously suffered serious harassment from the Assiniboine and Cree, had left the Upper

Mississippi country in favor of the headwaters of the Minnesota and from there, again owing to enemy pressure, had moved further west into the rolling hill and prairie country beyond the Red River of the North.

These three wandering groups, Bent added, became confederates, and for a while hunted and moved their nomadic camps together. Ostensibly then, these three groups comprised the Bowstrings, Moiseo and Suhtaio and were the same later designated by the trader Trudeau in 1795 /`96 as Chaguiennes, Quissy and Chouta respectively.

The Moiseo had been closely associated with the Suhtaio from an early date, their dialects being more akin than with other Cheyenne-speaking groups. Their alliance, of course, had its origin in the period of occupation by the Moiseo in the Upper Mississippi district and the Suhtaio habitat in the same region, and as both groups were then being assaulted by enemies from the north and northeast armed with guns, they continued their close association during their migrations west into the Coteau. However, the particular Moiseo band referred to by Bent, must actually have been the breakaway Kit-Fox Moiseo faction, later known as the Aorta band and very closely associated with the main Masikota Cheyenne-proper group. This Aorta faction had the Sacred Arrows in their care and still had as a semi-permanent base, an earth-lodge village close to Long Lake a short distance east of the Missouri, and which was still in use after the main Masikota group had crossed that river and established their new earth-lodge village on Porcupine Creek. This is corroborated by what the Suhtaio informant Bull-Thigh told Truman Michelson in 1913, that when the Suhtaio first crossed the Missouri, they went north and met Cheyennes who were in the region of what is now Standing Rock, and so indicates the Masikota village at the mouth of Porcupine Creek, rather than that of the Bowstrings who at a later date, also settled on the west side of the Missouri in a village known archaeologically as the Farm School site, and of which we will speak later.

That Bourgainville in his report of 1757, saw no reason to update his earlier information regarding the *Gens de L`Arc* or People of the Bow from what the LaVerendryes or one or more of their associates had told him, suggests that after the Masikota relocated to the west side of the Missouri on Porcupine Creek, there were still three bands of so-called *Gens de L`Arc* east of the Missouri, and these would have included the Bowstrings and Aorta, but then confederated with the Suhtaio instead of the main Masikota group. Thus, there were still three Cheyenne-speaking groups in the Coteau region across from or opposite the Arickara, as noted in the Bourgainville account.

The Pipe-Stem-Men Cheyennes, it will be recalled, even though in the habit of returning east of the Missouri at intervals since the late 1740s, were often much further west in the buffalo Plains as a somewhat independent group, and so were not included in either the Bougainville or Bent enumerations.

As regards the remnant Moiseo band recently fled from the Mille Lacs region, it is said by the Cheyennes that after fleeing into the Coteau country and re-associating with their Aorta and Bowstring relatives, this remnant Moiseo band soon became homesick for the ducks and lakes of northern Minnesota, and were afraid to kill any more buffalo because, they said, the ghosts of those animals came into their lodges at night and haunted them with their big rolling eyes. As a result, the remnant Moiseo left the group, but at a later date returned, and thereafter, continued to roam

411

back and forth; sometimes living with the Cheyennes and Suhtaio on the west side of the Missouri, and sometimes east of that river. * During their periodic absences, this remnant Moiseo band sometimes went much further east than the Red River, notwithstanding the threat of enemy attack, and often visited their old friends the Monsoni Cree and also certain Eastern Sioux bands which included the Mdewancantons and Ouadabatons in the St. Croix region, and among whom some of their estranged remnant Moiseo relatives still resided.

The Suhtaio for their part, after establishing themselves along the Missouri some years later, did reside in one or more earth-lodge village both on the east and west side of that river, and it is reasonable to suppose they had earlier adopted the sedentary earth-lodge lifestyle from those Cheyenne-speaking groups met in the vicinity of Big Stone Lake and Lake Traverse, if not indeed, by their own innovation. The so-called Hintz village site near present-day Jamestown on the Upper course of James River between the Missouri and Red River of the North, shows by its archaeological findings to have been built during the 1750s. This village, apparently, was occupied for several decades thereafter, and would fit with the period of Suhtaio residence in that part of the Coteau country.

From its remains, the Hintz site was once an unfortified village about seventy-five miles as the crow flies southwest of the Biesterfeldt site on the Lower bend of Sheyenne River, and about one-hundred miles west of the main course of the Sheyenne, which, at that point, flows north to south parallel with the James. No definite tribal affiliation for the Hintz town has been ascertained to date, but pottery types and house floor plans along with the design plan of the village itself, show strong connections with that of Biesterfeldt. Indeed, other than a Cheyenne-speaking group, only the Hidatsa might be considered as having once been possible occupants, although as this site has yielded many European trade goods and was occupied between circa, 1750 and 1790, albeit sporadically during certain seasons, they must be eliminated, for no Hidatsa group was living so far east of the Missouri at that time.

There are, it is true, some peculiar differences which occur in Hintz site pottery when compared to what we know regarding the usual Cheyenne ware, yet the shards in question cannot be associated definitely with any other historic tribe, other than showing a degree of both Mandan and Hidatsa influence, which is also discernible in several examples of Cheyenne pottery of the same period, merely indicating a later contact between certain Cheyenne-speaking bands and Missouri River tribes. More important is that examples of Black Duck pottery which, we have earlier deduced, is a `type` representative of the Suhtaio, are also found scattered within the same site.

We might suspect that the Hintz site was once inhabited by a Suhtaio band, one or another

*This statement that the Moiseo were afraid of the buffalo, is here used as a metaphor [obviously misunderstood by George Bent] to explain in a poetic and enigmatic manner, how this remnant band of Moiseo would not accept the Sun-Dance ceremony or its ilk brought to them by the Suhtaio, while their Cheyenne relatives embraced it wholesale after establishing themselves permanently in the Buffalo Plains west of the Missouri.

of which so tribal tradition tells us, resided in a permanent earth-lodge village after leaving the lake and forest country of northeastern Minnesota.

It is indicative that late in the eighteenth century, a permanent Mandan village in which resided a large proportion of Suhtaio, stood on the east bank of the Missouri near Fort Lincoln, North Dakota opposite the mouth of Heart River [of which we will speak later], and thus in almost direct line due west from the Hintz site less than one-hundred miles east. This position opposite the mouth of Heart River, was close to where the Mandan had other villages from the mid-seventeenth century through to the latter years of the eighteenth, and it should be recalled that according to Cheyenne tradition, when one or another Cheyenne or Suhtaio band reached the Missouri during the second half of the eighteenth century, they were ferried over that river by the Mandan in the latter's bull-boats.

Many burial mounds of the round or conical variety, identical to those in other locations and said by the Sioux to have been built by Cheyennes, are found in close proximity to both the Biesterfeldt and Hintz sites on the Lower Sheyenne and Upper course of James River respectively, although this alone does not specifically denote that they represent either Cheyenne or Suhtaio origin.

More substantial, perhaps, is the promontory known as "Bone Hill" on the west side of James River not far south of the Hintz site, and only some fifty miles west from that of Biesterfeldt.

This hill is conical in shape and about thirty feet in height and on the sides of which, are several embedded rows of leg bones of buffalo placed end to end, with extensions called "walks" stretching several hundred feet from its base across the prairie floor. These bones have been carefully placed end to end and are two courses in width. The Sioux always called the hill *"Hu-Hu Pa-Pa,"* meaning "Bone Hill," and declared that in olden days, the Cheyenne had used it as a lookout point.

In view of the Cheyenne's constant expectation of attack from the Assiniboine, Plains Cree and Yanktonai, this Sioux statement would appear creditable, but why then was not a lookout post chosen further north or east, from which directions the enemy invariably came, instead of some distance south of the village, and if used by people of the Biesterfeldt site on the Lower Sheyenne, then by the time warning was given by runners some fifty miles away, it would probably have been too late to prepare adequately against attack. Smoke signals may have been used to give warning, but the success of this system was always dependent on the weather should the signal be seen or not. It is then more reasonable to associate Bone Hill with the Hintz site which stood only a few miles distant, although its function must have had some other purpose.

The informant George Bent suggested to George Hyde that Bone Hill may once have been a ritual site, where Buffalo Priests would perform their special ceremonies to aid them in "calling the buffalo." He himself, he said, had seen similar constructions during his days among the Cheyenne, and had actually witnessed the building of one such structure and the enactment of the ceremony connected with it as practiced by the Suhtaio.

This is important, for we know that it was the Suhtaio who were singularly recognized as having the supposed ability to "call the buffalo" to them. This fact must add substance to the above hypothesis that the Hintz site was once occupied by a Suhtaio-speaking group, and if this was so, some confusing statements regarding this period in Cheyenne history might be cleared up.

Regarding documentation for Cheyenne and Suhtaio groups in the Coteau country during the period in question, we see on a map drawn by the French-Canadian Joseph LaFrance in 1744 at the request of the Englishman Arthur Dobbs, but which refers to tribal positions as LaFrance remembered them between 1739 and 1742, there is a notation for the *Knaisitaras* [as near as the handwriting can be deciphered], as then being located west of a large lake, which is shown by LaFrance as being just west of another large lake on the Upper course of what he called the *Langue Riviere* [Long River]. This stream represents that known today as the Minnesota, and the lake at that river's head farthest west of the two as drawn by LaFrance, is obviously Big Stone Lake near which he also placed the *"L. of the Sioux Indians,"* which is the same *"Tinton Lac"* noted on the Franquelin map of !699. Thus the second lake east of that point along the `Langue Riviere` as shown on the LaFrance map, must represent present-day Granite Lake which also forms a part of the Upper course of the Minnesota. On an earlier chart drafted by the soldier / explorer Baron LaHontan in 1688/`89, there is likewise shown a *Langue Riviere,* and along which LaHontan placed the tribal group *Gnasitaries,* this being a variant spelling of *Knaisitaras,* while LaHontan`s *Langue Riviere* is also compatible with that of the Minnesota, which indicates that LaFrance had merely adopted LaHontan`s name for both the people so designated and for the river near which they resided.

Both terms of *Knaisitaras* and *Gnasitaries* are from the Algonquian tongue, but in a garbled French form, and have previously been thought to be connected with the Native term *Krinisteneaux* as applied to the Cree. However, these people on the LaFrance and LaHontan maps could not have been Cree owing to their location so far south and their being at war with the Sioux. The *Knaisitaras,* in fact, appear to be placed in a position where, traditionally, Cheyenne and Suhtaio groups then resided, either at the permanent earth-lodge village in the vicinity of Big-Stone Lake, or that located further west near the present-day town of Sisseton. Both these villages were still occupied during the time LaFrance was undertaking his travels, and continued to be so until a much later date. Coupled to the assumption that the *Knaisitaras* were of Algonquian stock in what was then a predominantly Western Sioux-speaking area, then here, perhaps, is evidence in documented form for the existence of one and another Cheyenne or Suhtaio group in the Coteau des Prairies during the middle part of the eighteenth century.

On the same LaFrance map, we also find some distance west of the *Knaisitaras*, a notation for another tribal group also earlier noted by LaHontan, and termed *Mozemleck*. The first part of *Mozemleck* has something to do with `grass` or `prairie,` and includes a corrupted Algonquian ending of *leck*, merely added to tribal names by the French in order to denote "People" or something similar. If the `z` in *"Mozem"* was meant to represent the sound `sh,` then LaFrance may have been referring to the Cheyenne group Masikota, once positioned along the Upper course of Maple Creek [where Sioux tradition locates them during the same period], if not actually indicating the territory roamed by the latter after abandoning their town near Kulm, but prior to their settling on Porcupine

Creek about the date 1743, and at which time as mentioned in an earlier chapter, the LaVerendrye brothers met the *Gens de Fleche Coolee* on the west side of the Missouri passing through *"Squaws and camps stopping very little."*

Yet another reference to Cheyenne and Suhtaio groups roaming the Coteau country and including the remnant Moiseo then still residing further east in the St. Croix region of the Upper Mississippi, can be found in the writings of the English military officer Johnathan Carver.

Between 1766 and 1768, Carver ascended the Upper course of the Mississippi and near the mouth of the St. Croix, he met with those he termed *"...the River bands of the Nawdowessie..."* i.e. Sioux. Carver reported as follows,

"This Nation is comprised at present of eleven bands. They were originally twelve, but the Assinipoils some years ago revolting, and separating themselves from the others, there remain only at this time eleven. Those I met here [mouth of the St. Croix] are termed the River Bands, because they chiefly dwell near the banks of the River. The other eight are generally distinguished by the title of the Naudowessies of the Plains, and inhabit a country that is more to the westward. The names of the former are the Nehogatawonaha, the Mawtawbauntowahs, and the Shahsweentowahs, and consist of about four hundred warriors...." [2]

Carver went on to state that the Sioux were then at war with the Chippewa, and later, after setting up his winter quarters among other Sioux bands far up the Minnesota River, he further recorded,

"...On the 7th of December [1767] ...I met with a large party of Naudowessies Indians, among whom I resided seven months. These constituted a part of the eight bands of Naudowessies of the Plains, and are termed the Wawpeentowahs, the Tintons, the Asracootans, the Mawhaws, and the Schians. The other three bands whose name are the Schianese, the Chongouseeton, and the Wadddapawjestin, dwell higher up to the west of the River St. Pierre, on the Plains that, according to their account, are unbounded..." [3]

In the first excerpt, Carver`s *Shahsweentowahs* likely included the small remnant of what remained of the Moiseo Cheyenne-proper band near the mouth of the St. Croix, and earlier noted on the Danial Coxe map of circa 1720 by the name *Schahas*. They had long resided in the St. Croix region in association with Eastern Sioux groups, but some among whom by the time of Carver`s visit were periodically, found much further west. It was, however, the two Eastern Sioux groups mentioned by Carver as associated with the *Shahsweentowahs,* with whom those of the more itinerant Moiseo when roaming back and forth between the Missouri and Mississippi, cohabitated during their trips back into the St. Croix region.

In the second excerpt, the *Schians* mentioned by Carver as then residing close to Western

Sioux bands of *Wahepaton* and *Tintons*, probably represent the remnant of Masikota also known as *Shiyo* or *Sheyo* then dwelling in the vicinity of Big Stone Lake, while the *Mahaws* represent the Ponca [Omaha offshoots] then recently aligned with the Brule who themselves, are likely Carver`s *Asracootans*. The so-called *Schianese, Chongouseeton* and *Waddapawhestin* represent respectively the Bowstring Cheyennes of the Biesterfeldt village on the Lower Sheyenne, the Suhtaio at the Hintz site on James River and the Masikota on Porcupine Creek which included the previously mentioned remnant band known also as Sheyo, then around Big Stone Lake and known alternatively as the *Waddapawhestin,* this being Carver`s corruption from the Sioux term *Watap* meaning `to eat with` and which more specifically was meant to imply `eaters with the Sioux.` Each of these bands were, however, semi-nomadic buffalo hunters in the western part of the Coteau close to and west of the Missouri. So we see that during the mid-1760s, having apparently patched up their earlier quarrels, the western Cheyenne bands were again in harmony with the Western or Teton Sioux, even though the Eastern Sioux were still regarded as potential enemies, not only to the Cheyennes and Suhtaio, but also towards their own Teton or Western Sioux cousins.

It has previously been noted that according to the George Bent material, after the abandonment of the village on the Lower bend of Sheyenne River, three associated bands of Cheyenne, Moiseo and Suhtaio then roamed back and forth across the Coteau country, and remained together east of the Missouri for several years. Bent further said that during that time of wandering, the Buffalo Hat Keeper of the Suhtaio and the Keeper of the Cheyenne's Sacred Arrows became great friends, to the extent that seldom were they not in each other`s company and together, they went to the Missouri several times before deciding to settle permanently on that river`s west bank. Bent further said that on their own volition, a part of the Moiseo returned to the old lake and marsh district of northern Minnesota.

Of the Bowstrings, Moiseo [Burnt-Aorta] and Suhtaio that remained in the west, a story is still told in Cheyenne tradition of how a division had occurred between these three groups while in the actual process of crossing the Missouri.

It had happened in late winter or early spring when the Missouri was still frozen over with ice, that a part of the Suhtaio including the Keeper of the Buffalo Hat and his clan, along with the Kit-Fox or Aorta band of Moiseo and a band of Cheyennes [Bowstrings], crossed over from the east bank and made camp on that river`s west side, while the rest of the Moiseo and Suhtaio had not yet crossed the river. During the night there was heard a loud rumbling noise and the people became frightened. A crier went around the camp telling the people to prepare themselves, as something terrible was about to happen. In fact, the ice was breaking up in the river. The rumbling noise became louder until suddenly, there was a tremendous crash and huge blocks of ice were thrown up before hurtling down upon the camps on both banks. The Cheyennes, Suhtaio and Moiseo on the west bank immediately fled the scene in great fear for their lives, whilst those of the Moiseo and Suhtaio still on the east bank likewise fled, and according to tradition, a part of the Suhtaio left on the east bank were never seen or heard of again. The Cheyennes add that they thought this missing band must have eventually gone northeast and joined the Cree, which might be correct in the light of the later existence of a Plains Cree band, still extant in Canada during the late nineteenth century, and known by the name of "Soto" and alternatively as "Dog People" which, we know, were old names for the Suhtaio who were once closely associated with the Monsoni Cree when residing in permanent birch-bark villages north and south of Rainy Lake.

Those Suhtaio remaining on the west bank of the Missouri with the Keeper of the Sacred Buffalo Hat, and which George Bent designated as the family of the keeper himself, must actually represent the Keeper's clan and, therefore, constituted another of the then four extant Suhtaio bands. Those left on the east bank would represent the third Suhtaio band which under the name *Chongouseeton* was noted by Johnathan Carver in 1766/'68 as then being west of the head of the Minnesota and thus, possible occupants of the Hintz site. The fourth Suhtaio band according to later-day tribal informants, fled northwest above the Missouri across from the mouth of the Yellowstone and allied themselves to the Arapahoe. This last-mentioned band became variously known during the first half of the nineteenth century as Squihitans or Kites, and also by the Sioux name Skutani, of which we will also speak later.

Again according to Bent, at that time both Cheyennes and Suhtaio had been very poor not having lodge poles or horses and only a few dogs with a little camp equipment, and when they did cross the Missouri, they built a village on the west bank overlooking Porcupine Creek not far above the present-day town of Fort Yates. Here, of course, Bent unknowingly, was referring to the Masikota group alone, but which had crossed the Missouri some thirty years earlier. The particular village established on the west bank of the Missouri by the old residents of the Sheyenne River site, actually applies to a much later date, and according to other Cheyenne accounts and Sioux tradition, this last-named village stood some few miles south from that on the Porcupine. Indeed as previously noted, Suhtaio tradition verifies this by stating that when they, the Suhtaio, first crossed the Missouri after the breakup of ice in that river, they met Cheyennes already long established on the west bank near Standing Rock, thus indicating the Masikota village at the mouth of the Porcupine.

In yet another traditional account relating to the same division on the ice, it is likewise asserted that those Moiseo who remained on the Missouri's east bank, drifted east, some of whom thereafter rejoined their estranged relatives much further east along the St. Croix. It does appear, however, that others amalgamated with Teton Sioux around Big Stone Lake and formed an independent band of their own. In the ilk of the remnant Masikota in the same region around Big Stone Lake, this second Moiseo remnant band continued to roam the country of eastern North Dakota, long after all other Cheyenne and Suhtaio bands had crossed the Missouri and were residing permanently in the Western Plains.

Having said this, as the breaking up of ice has been given by some other tribes as the reason for a division in their own Nation, such as the schism between the Arapahoe and Atsina and, as noted in an earlier chapter of this work, between the Westerners and other Algonquians in the Delaware migration tradition [See pp. 100-101], it may be assumed that this Cheyenne story of a separation in such a manner is apocryphal, and that the George Bent analogy of the specter of `buffalo with their big rolling eyes etc.;` is probably closer to the truth, as it relates to but one part of the Moiseo and suggests they acted on their own volition, rather than obliged to do so due to any

417

natural phenomena. Nevertheless, three important facts emerge; (1) Two groups; one Moiseo the other Suhtaio were, at a later date, still located in the prairies east of the Missouri, whilst other Cheyennes were entrenched in permanent villages west of that river. (2) The two Cheyenne bands of the three groups mentioned by Bent, refer specifically to the Moiseo Kit-Fox breakaways later known as Aorta and among whom the Sacred Arrows and their keeper were included, and to the Bowstrings-Omissis group from their semi-abandoned village on the Lower bend of Sheyenne River. (3) The division of the people while crossing the Missouri ice and subsequently settling on that river's west bank, must have occurred after the time of Carver's travels between 1765 and 1768, and refers to the Omissis-Bowstrings group from the Biesterfeldt site on the Lower Sheyenne, after which they occupied a new permanent earth-lodge village on the west side of the Missouri some distance south from their Masikota cousins on the Porcupine, and which event ostensibly, occurred close to 1771 as will be explained in the following chapter.

– 0 - 0 - 0 - 0 - 0 - 0 - 0 - 0 - 0 - 0 - 0 - 0 - 0 - 0 - 0 - 0 - 0 - 0 –

CHAPTER 37.

LAST DAYS AT THE SHEYENNE RIVER SETTLEMENT

Returning to the Bowstring village overlooking the Lower bend of Sheyenne River in eastern North Dakota, its occupants initially, had inadvertently placed themselves in direct line of attack by foreign war-parties, going to or coming from enemy villages both east and west.

The Red River of the North was used as a great war-road by several tribes whose painted warriors either paddled canoes along its course, or followed the river banks on foot in order to reach their quarry. Large war-parties of Yanktonai and Sisseton Sioux from the Upper stretches of the Minnesota and from that river's Elbow Bend, passed very near the Bowstring town when on their way west to war against the Arickara, and often traversed the Red River northwards to Lake Winnipeg when raiding the Assiniboine and Cree. It was only a short diversion if they decided to attack the Biesterfeldt site instead. On the other hand, the Assiniboine and Cree came south against the Sioux and crisscrossed the Coteau regions to raid the Missouri River tribes. The Assiniboine and Cree, of course, were the inveterate enemies of all Cheyenne peoples, and at times, directed their raids specifically against the Bowstring town on the Lower Sheyenne.

Cheyenne and Sioux traditions inform us that this particular earth-lodge village on the Lower Sheyenne was often assaulted, but being in a good defensive position on the summit of a bluff and defended fervently by its occupants, even though fierce battles raged about the town, the attackers were invariably driven off. Sometimes these Cree, Assiniboine, Sisseton and Yanktonai enemies in their separate escapades, attacked the inhabitants outside the walls of the town if only to vent their frustration at returning from an unsuccessful foray against other peoples to the west, south or north, although it does appear that most attacks had occurred during the early years of the settlement, and after a number of fruitless assaults which for the most part had ended in stalemate, the Sheyenne River settlement during its middle and later phase was, more often, left alone. During the town's early years, however, according to the Cheyennes themselves, the most persistent aggressors were the Assiniboine, who often came against the Biesterfeldt town with their Plains Cree allies, while at other times, the Assiniboine and Plains Cree came separately to terrorize the inhabitants with their fearsome "Thunder-sticks."

Some Cheyenne informants of Grinnell included the Chippewa among these enemies armed with guns and iron-bladed weapons, who came to kill and plunder the luckless Cheyennes and Suhtaio and enslave the latter's women and children when residing east of the Missouri. Other evidence, though, suggests that the Chippewa; after an initial period of hostility, generally avoided hostile contact with the town's folk, as long as the latter remained neutral in their dealings with other tribes. An added incentive was that the Cheyenne Bowstrings raised a certain amount of agricultural produce, including corn, beans, squash and a little tobacco of which the Chippewa were particularly fond, and which they could not grow themselves in their northern country. Expediently, the Bowstrings soon began trading their surplus food stuffs and tobacco to the Chippewa, who in return, left the villagers to themselves. Having said this, it is the Chippewa who must take full credit for the eventual destruction of the Bowstring town on the Lower bend of the Sheyenne.

The Assiniboine and Plains Cree for their part, showed no such tolerance toward the Cheyennes, if indeed, the Cheyennes themselves would ever have entertained them as guests, while memories of terror not long past, caused by cruel and decimating attacks from Plains Cree and Assiniboine still burned deep in Cheyenne and Suhtaio minds, and already, were enshrined in their traditions.

So it was that the Assiniboine and Plains Cree continued to assault the Sheyenne River people whenever the fancy took them, although due to the positioning of the Bowstrings; coupled with their determination to defend themselves with overt courage bordering on fanaticism, it became the habit of foes from the north to skulk around outside the town's perimeter and slaughter unsuspecting persons who happened to present themselves as easy prey. These unfortunates in the main, were lone hunters, or women out fetching water or brush for lodge fires. Even young children who strayed from the protective ditch and stockade surrounding the town, were either killed or carried into captivity by the same skulking foes.

As noted in an earlier chapter, several anecdotes are extant in Cheyenne and Suhtaio tradition relating to their period of occupation in the Coteau of eastern North Dakota, and hitherto, all such events have usually been associated with the Biesterfeldt site on the Lower Sheyenne.

It is known, however, that there were other Cheyenne-speaking groups residing in villages of permanent construction in the same country during the same period, particularly at the Hintz site, along with those located near the present-day town of Sisseton and adjacent to Big Stone Lake. Therefore, as some details of the aforementioned anecdotes do not fit with what we know of the topography and history of the Biesterfeldt town, they must, in truth, refer to other Cheyenne groups.

419

This being said, there are one or two episodes which cannot safely be associated with any specific Cheyenne or Suhtaio village, and we are merely told in tribal tradition, that these events had occurred whilst residing in the tall-grass prairies east of the Missouri River.

Such episodes typify the particular style of warfare both the Assiniboine and Plains Cree employed during this period, and it can be construed from the stories recounted, that Cheyennes were still being terrorized by, and at the mercy of guns. One such tale relates how a dog once saved the people from disaster.

It had happened one time that a man, his wife and grown son, were encamped in a hide tepee near a stream some distance from the main Cheyenne village, ostensibly that located on the Lower Sheyenne. One night the family dog came into the tepee and began whining over its pups and licking them fervently. The man of the lodge asked the dog why it was doing this thing.

"If you know something," the man said, *"tell us; we do not wish to die. If there is danger, help us, and we will save your pups."* [1]

As if in response the dog went out of the tepee, but after a short while returned and stood motionless, with eyes transfixed upon the door flap. The man's wife told her husband to gather up the puppies, and this he did, wrapping them in his robe which he then strapped in a bundle on his back. The woman meanwhile, built up the lodge fire so it would appear to anyone outside that people were still within, and then the man, his wife and son, followed the dog out through the door flap, and walked cautiously down to a nearby stream which they crossed to the other side.

They had not gone far before they heard short sharp cracks of musket fire, and knew that enemies were attacking the tepee they had just left.

Still following the dog, the family travelled on and at length, reached the village on the Lower Sheyenne where they burst out the news that the Ho-Hay were nearby and had already assaulted their lodge. The rest of the Cheyennes were alarmed. Almost immediately they moved away deep into the Coteau and when the Ho-Hay did reach the village, their kill-hungry warriors found no one to murder and little to carry off as booty. It was because of this dog, say the Cheyennes, that their village was not surprised and thus was averted a potential massacre of the people.

How much credence one can give this particular story as referring to an actual historical event, is determined by the fact that the Sioux have a very similar tale of how a dog once saved some of their own people from potential massacre. However, in the Sioux account as related to John G. Neirhardt by his Oglala Sioux informant Black-Elk during the early 1940s, there are varying details, although it might be that Black-Elk was repeating what had originally come from Cheyennes with whom; in Black-Elk`s day, the Oglala had been closely confederated and intermixed by blood. Interesting, though, is a story current among the Crow Indians of Montana. This story likewise involves a dog which, as in the Cheyenne tale, had warned the Crows that they were about to be attacked by an enemy force. The story is almost identical to that recounted above, but had first been told among the Chippewa and later adopted by the Crows. In the original version it is a Chippewa village which is saved from destruction, although as the Chippewa were close confederates of the Assiniboine and once enemies of the Cheyennes and Suhtaio, the Chippewa may have first heard it from the Assiniboine. The Cheyennes themselves when recounting episodes from this period in their people's history, often used the tribal names Assiniboine, Plains Cree and Chippewa as being interchangeable with one another, and referred to all three collectively by the term of "Ho-Hay."

Another Cheyenne tale which refers to Cheyenne and Suhtaio residence in the Coteau east of the Missouri, and which again has previously been associated with the Biesterfeldt village, tells how an Assiniboine war-party came against the town and escaped with a handsome Cheyenne girl.

It transpired that the Assiniboine warrior who had captured the girl, was the leader of the war-party and an important chief among his people. He already had a wife, but took the Cheyenne girl as his second woman. In the chief's lodge the first wife ill-treated the captive and after a while, the chief himself, realizing that the girl would never be tolerated by his first wife, began to pity her. One day, after giving the girl extra pairs of moccasins and some food, he told her to leave during the night and return to her people.

When it was dark and the camp occupants preoccupied in other amusements, the Cheyenne girl slipped out of the lodge and started on her long journey home. After a grueling and hazardous journey, she finally reached her own people and safety. She had been missing a whole year and her relatives had long given her up for dead or of ever seeing her again, so there was much rejoicing on her return. It was this girl, some Cheyenne and Suhtaio informants declared, who originally brought their tribe the idea of electing forty-four chiefs to govern their Nation, after she had explained the manner by which the Assiniboine then governed themselves.

This last part of the story might sound creditable, were it not that the Assiniboine system bears little, if indeed anything resembling the mode of government practiced by Cheyennes during their historic time. Also, a similar tradition was obtained by James Mooney in 1907 from Southern Cheyenne informants, who placed the event west of the Missouri and associated it with some other enemy tribe, namely the Owuqueo whose village Cheyennes destroyed after crossing the Missouri.

The truth of the matter is, that whilst resident in the Minnesota country and during the tribe's early years in the Coteau des Prairies, the Cheyennes often had one overall chief whose influence lasted only as long as his popularity held among the tribe. Soon after the people's entry into the Coteau and their organizing themselves into four specific bands or divisions, each band elected ten headmen to represent it as part of the Cheyenne Nation, and among each of these bands one additional Head chief was selected making four in total, to oversee the lesser chiefs and in order to have the last word in tribal decision-making if there was stalemate within the council itself, and such was compatible with the system among the Sioux.

It could be that the story of the captive Cheyenne girl does contain an element of truth, albeit that the enemy concerned were not Assiniboine, but Yanktonai Sioux [close kindred to the Assiniboine], or even some other Eastern Sioux group such as the Santee or Sisseton, who also were at war with Cheyennes in the western part of the Coteau during the same period in time.

There is yet a third variant of the above story, obtained by George Grinnell, and which supposedly, occurred at an even later date, and does have some definite historical basis which can be dated around 1786, and will be mentioned in a later chapter.

It was, however, whilst occupying the Sheyenne River town when attacks were constant and damaging, costing the Cheyennes many menfolk killed and women and children taken captive, that Cheyenne warriors themselves still found time to do their own raiding. Often their war-parties travelled on foot more than one-hundred and fifty miles west in order to harass the Mandan along the Missouri, and even crossed that river to raid the mounted Snakes and others as far as the Black Hills of western South Dakota. Such forays were nearly always conducted on foot even after the Cheyennes acquired horses, for their aim was to increase the size of their own herds from stock belonging to one or another of the Western Tribes. The Cheyennes did achieve a degree of success in these ventures, often getting away with Snake horses and one or two scalps thrown in for good measure, although captives were also considered valuable, as these were adopted into the tribe to compensate the loss of their own people taken by the Assiniboine and Cree.

Nevertheless, notwithstanding their numerous successes against several of the Missouri River Nations and the Snakes, which increased Cheyenne wealth in horses and provided them with artefacts of European manufacture from the Spanish trade, the Sheyenne River people could not sustain indefinitely the determined and constant assaults made upon them by northern enemies armed with guns, and who; subsequently, often wreaked havoc among the populace before eventually being driven off.

Unfortunately, no specific accounts of battles between Cheyennes of the Biesterfeldt site with their northern enemies including the eventual ruin of their town by the Chippewa, were, apparently, ever related by Cheyenne informants themselves. This is not surprising as Indians in general, certainly during the late nineteenth century when asked such things by white historians, always showed a reluctance to mention past defeats or events which they considered uncomplimentary to their prowess as a tribe. Other sources nevertheless, record two versions of the sacking of a Cheyenne village by the Chippewa, each of which, ostensibly, refers to the Biesterfeldt Sheyenne River site.

In the spring of 1798, the English trader David Thompson then of the North West Company, was at the trading house of Baptiste Cadotte on Red River not far north from the mouth of the Sheyenne. There he met a Chippewa chief named "Sheshkeput" or "Sugar," as the white men called him, and enquired the reason for his making war on the Cheyennes. The following was Sheshkeput`s reply,

"Our people and the Cheyennes for several years had been doubtful friends but as they had corn and other vegetables, which we had not and of which we were fond, and traded with them. We passed over and forgot many things we did not like; until lately; when we missed our men who went hunting, we always said, they have fallen by the hands of our enemies the Sioux Indians. But of late years we became persuaded the Cheyennes were the people, as some missing went to hunt where the Sioux never came; We were at a loss what to do when some of our people went to trade corn, and while there, saw a Cheyenne hunter bring in a fresh scalp, which they knew, they said nothing, but came directly to me. A council was called at which all the men who had never returned from hunting were spoken of by their relatives; And it was determined (that) the Cheyenne village must be destroyed; As the geese were now leaving us, and winter at hand, we deferred to make war on them until the next summer; and in the meantime we sent word to all the men of our tribe to be ready to meet us here when the berries are in flower. Thus the winter passed; and at the time appointed we counted about one hundred and fifty men; we required two hundred but some of the best hunters could not come. We made our war-tent, and our medicine men slept in it; their dreams forbade us to attack them until the Bulls were fat; The Cheyennes would then leave their village weak to hunt and make provisions, to which we agreed…The time soon came and we marched from one piece of woods to another, mostly in the night until we came to the last grove of timber that was near the village. Our scouts were six young men. Two of them went to a small grove near the village and were relieved every morning and evening by two others…We thus passed six days, our provisions were nearly done, and we did not dare to hunt. Some of our men dreamed we were discovered and left us. On the seventh morning as we were in council, one of the young men who were on the watch came to us, and gave us notice that the Cheyennes had collected their horses and brought them to the village. We immediately got ourselves ready and waited for the other young man who was on the watch; it was near midday when he came and informed us that a great many men, women and children had gone off a hunting, and very few remained in the village. We now marched leisurely to the small grove of oaks to give the hunting party time to proceed so far as to be beyond the sound of our guns. At this grove we ought to have remained all night and attack next morning; but our provisions were done, and if they found the bison near, part of them might return. From the grove to the village was about a mile of open prairie; as we ran over we were seen. There were several horses in the village which the young people got on and rode off. We entered the village and killed all but three Cheyenne women. Then we looted the village and fired it. After this we ran because we did not want to meet cavalry in the Plains." [2]

Thompson's host Cadotte then took up the story, and went on to say that only twelve Cheyenne men were in the village at that time, and whose heads the Chippewa cut off and carried with them to the woods abutting Rainy River near Rainy Lake where a grand victory dance was held.

One of the women captives had with her a baby boy about eight months old, and would not let the Chippewa take him from her.

During the victory dance, the Chippewa warriors formed a circle whilst the women and children formed an outer circle, and the Cheyenne captives were then placed in the center of the inner circle. Whilst the dance was going on, the Cheyenne woman with the baby several times picked up the severed head of her husband and kissed it repeatedly. Every time the Chippewa took the head from her, she would pick it up again and continue to caress it. After a while she drew forth a concealed knife and stabbing herself in the breast, fell dying across her husband's head.

The Chippewa chief, Sheshkeput, commented to Thompson,

"The great Spirit had made her a woman, but had given her the heart of a man." [3]

The baby boy survived the ordeal and later, was taken by the Chippewa to a trading house on Rainy River, where he was left to be brought up by the White men at that post.

Regrettably there is no way of knowing the exact years during which the trading post on Rainy River was operational. If known, we would have some idea regarding the date of the Chippewa attack. There is evidence to suggest that the French had occupied a post in the vicinity of Rainy Lake for a number of years prior to the conclusion in 1763 of the war between France and England, after which the British established a post named Rainy River House in the same region as a base for dealing with the Indians of the interior, and which may well have been operational as early as 1771. But when the Chippewa took their prisoner thither, we have no way of knowing.

That horses were mentioned by Sheshkeput and, evidently, many horses at that, must help date the event later than the mid seventeen-thirties, before which time all Cheyennes east of the Missouri, - unlike their relatives and allies west of that river - had very few if any horses among them, while the size of the attacking force implies, that the particular Cheyenne village referred to was deemed a formidable objective housing a large population and well-defended. Hence the reason why the Chippewa had planned to wait until the bulk of the inhabitants were absent on the hunt before launching their attack, and so also, why the Biesterfeldt site on the Lower Sheyenne is the village most likely indicated.

The second account which relates to the destruction of a Cheyenne village in the same region along the Sheyenne, and which also designates the Chippewa as being responsible, appears in the day by day journal of one Alexander Henry the younger under the year heading 1800. In that same year Henry built a small trading post near the mouth of Park River, a western tributary of the Red about thirty-five miles north of the mouth of the Sheyenne. At one time after having passed the mouth of Wild Rice River, Henry recorded in his journal,

> "Beyond this river about twelve leagues by land, is Shian (sic) river on the west. This derives its name from a formally numerous tribe of Indians who inhabited its Upper part. They were a neutral tribe between the Sioux and Saultaux (i.e. Chippewa) for many years, but the latter, who are of a jealous disposition, suspected they favored the Sioux. A very large party having been unsuccessful in discovering their enemies, on their return wreaked vengeance on these people, destroying their village and murdering most of them. This happened about sixty years ago. (i.e.1740) when the Saultaux were at war with their natural enemies the Sioux of the Plains who are the only inhabitants of the St. Peter's river (Minnesota). The Shians having been nearly exterminated, abandoned their old territories and fled southward across the Missouri where they are now a wandering tribe." [4]

424

This account does not indicate from whom Henry obtained his information, although he was well-acquainted with not only the Chippewa, but also with the Cree and Assiniboine, and in summer the following year of 1801, he met the son of the "Great Chief" of the Chippewa [as Henry called Sheshkeput], and later, actually met Sheshkeput himself whom he calls "Succiere" [Sugar], but by that time Henry had already penned the above account in his diary.

Now the first account as recorded by Thompson, implies by its wording, that the event had been of recent occurrence, that is to say, not long before 1798 when Thompson heard the story from Sheshkeput himself. Henry's account on the other hand, actually gives a date, and even though similar to Thompson's version, does contain some important differences.

In Thompson's account, the Chippewa attack seems to have been a premeditated organized affair, while that in Henry's version suggests an assault on the spur of the moment in which neither the presence of horses nor the burning of the town is mentioned. Either then, there was more than one Cheyenne permanent village situated along the Sheyenne, both of which were destroyed by the Chippewa at separate times, or that either Thompson or Henry erred in their chronology and somewhat misconstrued the true details. The problem has become more confused by the fact that both Cheyenne, Chippewa and Sioux traditions have invariably been taken to mean there was only one Cheyenne town in the area, and to date, only one permanent village site along the Sheyenne River at or near the point of its Lower bend, has yet been located by the archaeologist.

Henry stated that the village in question stood on the Upper course of the river, which would suggest a point some distance from the Biesterfeldt site on the southern bend, and if Henry's statement is correct, then perhaps there were indeed other Cheyenne towns along that river, and that its altering course over the years has undermined the site we should be looking for.

While it is true that evidence from the findings at Biesterfeldt coupled with tribal traditions and historical documentation, leave no doubt that Cheyenne peoples were once entrenched in an earth-lodge village overlooking the southern bend of the Sheyenne, these same sources also indicate the existence of other village sites extant at various periods during the same century between the Missouri and Red River of the North.

The assertion by Flying-Thunder-Eagle earlier referred to, that Cheyennes were living along Sheyenne River as early as circa, 1600, and that the last Cheyenne village along its course was finally abandoned late in the eighteenth century, also implies that there was more than one Cheyenne village in the valley of Red River on its west side. Perhaps the fact that the town on the Lower Sheyenne was said to have been occupied for the longest period, ostensibly between seventy and eighty years, caused both Sioux and Cheyenne informants of a later date, to recall only the Biesterfeldt town in their accounts. Generally speaking, an earth-lodge village lasted between 25 and 30 years before a new site was sought, owing to the lodges themselves by then being beyond repair and the adjacent crop-growing area having become barren due to over cultivation. Thus the inhabitants had likely moved to fresh sites along the same river, so in truth, there may have been several towns occupied successively by the same band.

The conflicting stories, however, regarding the destruction of a Cheyenne town, and the reason given by Cheyennes themselves for vacating a particular village due to the slaughter of the

Assiniboine war-party, make it tempting to suppose that each account as mentioned by Henry and Thompson, applies to separate Cheyenne villages in the Coteau country.

Having previously designated four Cheyenne groups as once occupying the Coteau region, these must have been the precursors of the four groups mentioned in Cheyenne and Sioux testimony which refer to four Cheyenne villages later established along the west bank of the Missouri between circa, 1743 and 1784, and when east in the Coteau had included, [1] the Bowstrings on the Lower Sheyenne at the Biesterfeldt site [2] the Pipe-Stem-Men, at a later date enjoined with a breakaway group from the Omissis-Bowstrings known as the Ridge Men Band near the mouth of the Little Cheyenne on the Missouri`s east side, [3] the Kit-Fox [Aorta] in the village adjacent to Long Lake [4] the Masikota from the town near Kulm who are said in tradition, to have been the first Cheyennes to relocate in a permanent earth-lodge village at the mouth of Porcupine Creek. In addition there was extant the Suhtaio group at the Hintz site on the west bank of James River.

The date 1740 given by Henry for the abandonment of a Cheyenne town, cannot apply to either the Hintz or Long Lake sites, as both were still occupied well into the second half of that century. Neither can Henry`s account be associated with the Assiniboine affair, for when the occupants of the aforementioned villages and that on the Lower bend of the Sheyenne did vacate their positions, they were already supplied with guns and had been semi-nomadic horse-using buffalo hunters for some years previous. Also, the village on the Lower bend would appear to be too far south from Henry`s Sheyenne River site of which he wrote.

It is possible that Henry`s assertion regarding the Chippewa assault had occurred *"...some sixty years ago,"* was a slip of the pen, so to speak, and that his account should actually have read, *"...some six years ago."* Such would then date the event as around 1794, and so fit with Thompson`s 1798 statement, *"...The Cheyennes who`s village was lately destroyed."* The term `lately` meaning in this case, three or four years prior to his time of writing, and thus, associating his and Henry`s account with the same Cheyenne village. Perhaps, though, Henry had been referring to another Cheyenne or Suhtaio group then roaming the same Coteau country, and in all fairness, it must be remembered that the occupants of each of the Cheyenne and Suhtaio towns in the Coteau and even when on the west side of the Missouri were semi-sedentary, so that if the Bowstrings had been forced by violent assault earlier in the same century to abandon the Biesterfeldt town as a year round place of residence, they likely returned at intervals to plant and harvest crops for several decades thereafter.

Such could be how both the Thompson and Henry accounts became confused, in so much as the town in question had earlier been abandoned as a permanent seat because of enemy assault, and later, during the 1790s, was assaulted again with more serious results which ruined the town once and for all. The Cheyennes thereafter, remaining west of the Missouri on a permanent basis, never to visit the Biesterfeldt village again.

When writing his account regarding the vacating of the Sheyenne River town, Henry may have misconstrued what he was told. He no doubt had heard from other tribal contacts that a group of Cheyennes had crossed the Missouri and built a new town near Porcupine Creek around the date 1743, and further, that the Cheyenne group from the Sheyenne River settlement had gone to the same Porcupine Creek when they themselves first relocated to the west bank of the Missouri. Both these Missouri River Cheyenne villages had long been abandoned by the time Henry came into that country, and he, – assuming that the Cheyennes had constituted one body during their migration west, he naturally supposed that the Sheyenne River town had been vacated around 1740, and at which same period albeit three years later, Cheyennes had arrived at Porcupine Creek. The fact that by 1800 most Cheyennes and Suhtaio were nomadic buffalo-hunters in the Western Plains, caused Henry to add in his journal entry for that year, *"...the Cheyennes are now a wandering tribe."* [5]

There are reasons for supposing that the initial semi-abandonment of the Sheyenne River town had occurred later than 1740 and a few decades before 1798. The first being from Sioux tradition, which mentions that the Sheyenne River people settled on the Missouri`s west bank between 25 and 30 years after the first Cheyenne group had already established itself at the mouth of Porcupine Creek, and therefore, suggests a date between 1770 and 1775. The second reason is that prior to the time of the LaVerendrye brother`s visit to the Western Plains in 1742, horses were not in sufficient number east of the Missouri for the Chippewa to *"...fear cavalry in the Plains,"* and in addition, the Chippewa did not resume their war with the Eastern and Western [Teton] Sioux until the latter part of the 1760s.

Before this, the Tetons when around Big Stone Lake, had been constantly beset by the Assiniboine and Cree, and as a consequence, were obliged to move from the headwaters of the Minnesota west into the eastern Coteau region. The Bowstrings Cheyennes along with the Suhtaio and those small Masikota and Moiseo remnants around Big Stone Lake, no doubt suffered accordingly from the same Assiniboine and Cree war-parties, and so had remained steadfast allies to the Tetons.

These Teton allies of the Bowstring Cheyennes and Suhtaio, were those known as Oglala and Brule Lakota Sioux. They then had very few horses among them, and were engaged in endemic warfare with most foreign tribes with whom they came in contact. The Cheyennes at this particular period were the exception, probably because they, too, were at war with the same enemies as were the Oglala and Brule, and that the latter having no ammunition for their guns owing to the cessation of French trade during the French and Indian war, these two Lakota bands were desirous of obtaining horses and metal weapons such as axes and sword blades from the Spanish trade, both of which accessories the Bowstring Cheyennes had continued to obtain on a regular basis from their kindred Masikota on Porcupine Creek, and from friends and allies among the Black Hills tribes.

After the conclusion of the French and Indian war in 1763, guns and other superior quality British goods appeared west of the Upper Great Lakes and, thereafter, the Tetons began holding annual trading fairs at the head of the Minnesota which were often attended by Cheyennes. The Cheyennes brought decorated hide shirts and leggings, eagle feathers and horses to barter with the Sioux for guns and ammunition, and thus, some Cheyennes, moreover the Bowstrings and Suhtaio, continued to occupy their town on the Lower bend of Sheyenne River and at the Hintz site on the James. By such means they kept up their friendly association with the Tetons, and so Cheyennes continued to be included under the collective term `Sioux of the Prairies,` and, as we have seen, were still regarded by the traveler Johnathan Carver in 1766-`68 as being a part of the Western Sioux.

In 1768 the Chippewa, who for some twelve years previously had been preoccupied as allies to the French and had been included in the so-called Pontiac rebellion which followed against English domination in the Upper Great Lakes region, suddenly regenerated their war with the Eastern Sioux who had been allies to the English, and as a result the Eastern Sioux soon after, were obliged to abandon their Mille Lacs positions and retire southwest to the head of the Minnesota. It was then that Eastern Sioux groups began attacking Cheyennes and Suhtaio and even their own Teton cousins in the Coteau region in order to gain a refuge from Chippewa enemies in their rear. Events, though, were changing rapidly and by1770, the Oglala and Brule, due to being themselves at war with the Chippewa, joined their Eastern Sioux cousins and they, too, soon after began raiding their erstwhile friends the Cheyennes and Suhtaio. It was this sudden escalation of hostility from an over-whelming combined Sioux force, which caused the Bowstrings and Suhtaio to initially vacate their permanent villages in the Coteau, the Bowstrings then seeking refuge on the west bank of the Missouri close to their Masikota and Aorta kinfolk, while one or another Suhtaio group wandered even further west, thereby, having the Missouri River as a barrier between themselves and the Sioux.

In 1829, Peter Buell Porter in his commissioned report as Secretary of War [the forerunner to the Indian Bureau], stated that the Cheyennes had been driven from the Red River country by the Sioux about the date 1770, and this coincides with the above mentioned occupation by hostile Eastern Sioux bands around the headwaters of the Minnesota and their subsequent alliance with the Tetons. These particular Eastern Sioux bands had actually begun attacking the western tribes two or three years earlier, but Porter`s dating does tally almost exactly with Dr. A. J. Comfort`s assertion gleaned from Eastern Sioux traditional accounts, which stated that the Cheyennes were dispossessed of the soil by the Dakotas [i.e. Eastern Sioux] about the date 1771. These latter dates are further corroborated by an entry in the Oglala Sioux winter-count of No-Ears, which records for the same year 1771, *"They burned the Mandan Village."* [6]

Now as it is not known that the Tetons themselves were at war with the Mandan at such an early date, and Mandan tradition itself, which usually details such events, makes no mention of such an occurrence around that date, it seems likely that as the Tetons were then at war with the earth-lodge dwelling Cheyennes and Suhtaio at the time in question, No-Ears was wrong in associating the burned town as belonging to the Mandan, simply because the latter were still earth-lodge dwellers during No-Ear`s day. The event, most likely, applies to either the Bowstring village on the Lower Sheyenne, or that of the Suhtaio at the Hintz site, and would have been cause for the Bowstrings and Suhtaio to abandon their towns and move across the Missouri to that river`s west bank, and where, between 25 and 30 years after the settlement of the main Masikota Cheyenne group at the mouth of Porcupine Creek according to Sioux tradition and referring therefore, to the early 1770s, the Bowstrings established a new permanent village now known as the Farm School site about fifteen miles below present-day Fort Yates.

The period of Chippewa – Sioux warfare referred to above, persisted until 1775, when the English negotiated a peace between the two, and as the Cheyenne were then no longer an obstacle to Sioux settlement in the Coteau, Sioux aggression towards them also abated, and the Bowstrings began returning again at intervals to their old abandoned village over-looking the Lower bend of the Sheyenne. Both Sioux and Chippewa then went as supplicants to the Bowstring Cheyennes, the Sioux to beg horses; the Chippewa to trade for corn and vegetables which the Bowstrings continued to cultivate in some quantity, even though, hereafter, they only visited the Sheyenne River town sporadically at planting and harvest times. The Bowstrings thus had two earth-lodge villages which they used alternatively, although that on the west bank of the Missouri below the Porcupine had since become their more permanent place of residence.

Such is apparent from the archaeology of the Biesterfeldt site, which shows that some of the earth-lodges have a good deal of Mandan and Arickara influence in their construction, and appear to have been built at a much later date than most other lodges in the village. There is also evidence that many of the occupants during the town's later decades, were more accustomed to camping in portable tepees outside the town rather than utilizing the earth-lodges themselves.

While the Chippewa were at peace with the Sioux, there was no reason for the Chippewa to regard the Cheyennes as potential foes because of their being allies to the Sioux, and it will be recalled that the Chippewa Chief Sheshkeput had said, that at the time the Sheyenne River village was destroyed, his people were at war with the Sioux, and so must refer to the later-date regeneration of Chippewa – Sioux warfare which began in 1784.

In 1798 Thompson estimated that Chief Sheshkeput was then around sixty years of age, although still agile and wielding much influence over his band. Having said this, Sheshkeput would only have been around two years old if the Chippewa attack on the Cheyenne town had occurred in 1740, as the Henry account asserted, so the final destruction of the Biesterfeldt site must have occurred sometime later, ostensibly during the second period of Chippewa – Sioux conflict which broke out in 1784, and was still going on when Thompson met Sheshkeput in 1798.

Substantiating the above analysis, are passages from the James Mckay journal which relates to late 1786 and early 1787 during his sojourn among the Mandan on the Missouri. McKay stated that the Cheyennes at that time had already gone from the Sheyenne River to the Missouri, and thus, the first time abandonment of the Sheyenne River village as a permanent year round residence, must have occurred some years prior to 1787 when McKay made his observation.

Cheyenne informants when talking to Grinnell and others late in the nineteenth century denied all this, saying instead that they were not "driven out" of the Coteau country by any tribe, but moved west across the Missouri on their own volition in search of new hunting grounds. The tradition, however, concerning the massacre of the Assiniboine war-party by the old woman previously referred to, contradicts this view, and even if the Cheyennes were not obliged by some catastrophe to migrate west, then the situation as existed in eastern North Dakota during the same period, certainly made it expedient to do so. The discovery of unfinished house pickets at the Biesterfeldt site certainly indicate sudden abandonment, although as previously averred, a part of the Bowstrings group continued to frequent the site sporadically, even after the bulk of their people had relocated to the west bank of the Missouri and established a second town, but certainly, the attack led by Sheshkeput a few years before 1798 and to which event Thompson was referring, must have finally destroyed the town on Sheyenne River completely, and likely, ruined the adjacent fields to such extent, that Cheyennes no longer took the trouble to visit the site again.

If this was the case, then the last sporadic visit to the Biesterfeldt site was probably no later than 1794, as by then, French, English and Spanish traders had ascended the Missouri as far north as the Arickara and Mandan towns, and only the great Sioux trading fairs since moved to James River in the heart of the Coteau, could induce Cheyennes to go again that far east. Once entrenched on the west side of the Missouri, the Cheyennes as semi-nomadic residents had virtually all they needed at their fingertips, so to speak, including guns obtained from the Tetons in exchange for Cheyennes horses, which animals the Sioux still lacked in any sizable number in their eastern country.

-0-0-0-0-0-0-0-0-0-0-0-0-0-0-0-0-0-0-

CHAPTER 38.

CHEYENNE VILLAGES ADJACENT TO AND WEST OF THE MISSOURI.

Certainly, by the early 1770s, all Cheyenne and Suhtaio bands, - apart from a small remnant of mixed Moiseo and Masikota associated with Miniconjou Sioux around Big Stone Lake, - had established themselves in several earth-lodge villages on both banks of the Missouri, between the Mandan to the north, and Arickara to the south.

When the Bowstring Cheyennes first crossed the Missouri with a view to permanent settlement on that river`s west bank, they are said in tradition to have settled in an earth-lodge village near their Masikota cousins at the mouth of the Porcupine, but after only a few years the Bowstrings moved south, to a place since known archaeologically as the Farm School Site about fifteen miles below present-day Fort Yates also on the Missouri`s west bank. There they built a new earth-lodge village where they remained for many years.

The first occupational site of the Bowstrings adjacent to the Masikota, is said by the Sioux to have stood about two miles below the village on the Porcupine. At a much late date, a group of Standing Rock Sioux built a number of log houses on the same site, the foundations of which virtually obliterated the remains of the old-time Cheyenne house rings. During this later time of Sioux occupation, the site was known derisively as "Slobtown," for reasons to be imagined. It is, however, probable that the original Cheyenne village on this site had been built as an annex to that on the Porcupine, as the continuance of house rings in that direction suggests. Unfortunately, since before the early years of the twentieth century, the Missouri had already carried away much of the River`s west bank, so that if there were intervening lodges joining both sites, their remains, too, have long since been obliterated. In 1956 and again in `57, the so-called "Slobtown" site was investigated by archaeologists, although neither exploration unearthed enough artefacts to prove exclusive Cheyenne occupation. Of the few pottery fragments found, none can be associated definitely with Cheyenne manufacture, and moreover, they appear to be indicative of one or more older occupations of either Mandan or Hidatsa affiliation.

More feasible is that the "Slob Town" site was not originally a Cheyenne village at all, but had been built by the Awaxawi Hidatsa who, as noted in an earlier chapter, had a short time prior to the early 1770s fled from their Hidatsa relatives on Knife River, and moved some distance down the Missouri where they built a new village near, *"... the friendlier Cheyennes,"* [i. e., on Porcupine Creek ?]. The Awaxawi it is said in that people`s own traditions, remained in this new position for three years before returning to the mouth of Knife River, and thus, as the Bowstrings crossed the Missouri soon after the Awaxawi returned to the Knife, the Bowstrings may have utilized the abandoned Awaxawi lodges for a few years as temporary accommodation, before moving south to their second and more permanent location at the Farm School site.

It would appear that the Bowstrings when at the Slobtown site, had been undecided where exactly they should establish themselves along the Missouri, and although probably taking advantage of the old Awaxawi farming grounds adjacent to the town, they likely; for the most part, resided in portable tepee-like shelters and did not build earth-lodges themselves in that particular locality. Indeed, without a sensible reason for abandoning the site only a few years after their arrival, it is inconceivable that the people should have exerted themselves so laboriously in building such a large concentration of earth and timber lodges, only to abandon them within a few short years, in order to merely repeat the procedure a little distance downstream.

It is true that any one of a number of virulent epidemics along the Missouri did induce the River Tribes to make sudden moves to new locations, but as the Farm School site was much closer to the Arickara, who usually suffered most during such contagions, it is unlikely that if the Bowstrings had moved suddenly in order to escape such a malady, they would have moved nearer the Arickara, where any contagion would have been severe.

Concerning the Farm School village occupied by Cheyennes after leaving the Slobtown site, as late as 1957 the remains of old house rings were still visible before the Ohae reservoir inundated the area. Fortunately in 1918, George Bird Grinnell in the company of a Reverend Dr. Beede had previously investigated the old village site and described it as follows,

"The farm school is just over the boundary line between North Dakota and South Dakota, perhaps three miles south of the mouth of Blackfoot Creek and a mile below what I suppose to be Eagle Feather Creek, and seems to have been established in the very center of this old Indian village. It is east and a little north of the Cheyenne Hills. Just above Blackfoot Creek and on the state boundary line is an old village site with three mounds and many house sites said by the Sioux to have been Mandan. To the south and southeast of the school are a dozen or twenty house rings, and to the north, close along the river, are other house rings. Within the boundaries of the farm school are three Lower mounds. One of these has been excavated to make a root cellar, and by one of the men who had helped dig the cellar I was told that a considerable amount of pottery fragments had been thrown out. On another mound stands the Roman Catholic chapel; and a Lower mound almost within the school enclosure is partly occupied by one of the office buildings of the school. To the south of the school buildings and on or among the old house rings, are a number of places where modern Indian houses have stood, and small tracts which have been cultivated as gardens within recent years, and are still more or less overgrown with weeds…..This village was once of considerable size, and the way in which the houses at its border were placed suggests also that attacks by enemies were not anticipated. The cultivation of the soil, the erection of the school buildings, and the westward movement of the Missouri River, which continually undermines the high bank and causes it to drop into the river, have greatly reduced the area of the village….." [1]

Grinnell also found a few pottery shards during his inspection, which after showing them to an old Northern Cheyenne woman, she declared, *"…her grandmother had made dishes like that."* [2]

Testimony from present-day Hunkpapa Sioux on the Standing Rock Reservation, South Dakota, states that from the early 1770s onwards if not before, grand intertribal trading rendezvous were being held at two places on the west bank of the Missouri, one of which was near the present-day town of Morbridge, South Dakota not far north of Pierre, and which most likely, applies to the Arickara who then lived close by. The second important trading point, however, was further north near the now abandoned town of Kennel on the Missouri`s west bank not far south of the North / South Dakota state line. This last-named point must then, allude to the old Farm School permanent Omissis-Bowstrings Cheyenne village once occupied in the same vicinity, and indicates the town as being a center for intertribal trade from both east and west of the river. This same Sioux account further states that the original occupants of the site near Kennel finally moved west, and at a much later date, became those known as Northern Cheyenne [therefore referring specifically to the Omissis-Bowstrings group], and further states that after the Cheyennes had left, the site was re-occupied first by the Mandan, then the Arickara and after them by a band of Sioux, as the site`s location was still regarded ideal for trading purposes when accommodating tribes both east and west of the Missouri.

Additionally, according to a Yankton Sioux historian named Blue-Thunder, the same old-time Farm School village, was first occupied about thirty years after Cheyennes had already established themselves on Porcupine Creek, and that the Farm School site itself was occupied twenty-five years or so before finally being abandoned in 1795, at which time the Cheyenne inhabitants, Blue-Thunder said, moved west along Grand River as far as a tributary known as Dirt-Lodge Creek, and where, – as the name suggests – they built and resided for a time in yet another permanent earth-lodge village.

Accepting then, that the Bowstrings had first stayed adjacent to their Masikota cousins for a few years, the Bowstring`s arrival on the west bank of the Missouri as permanent residents must have occurred during the early 1770s, and which is consistent with the proposed date of 1771 [as mentioned in the previous chapter] when the Bowstring village on the Lower bend of the Sheyenne had first been vacated as a year-round habitation. However, Blue-Thunder`s assertion that the Farm School village as a year round seat of residence was abandoned in 1795 appears far too late, as white traders were among Cheyennes in that year and had been since 1791 if not earlier. Some of these men left documents showing they were familiar with Cheyennes and their locations, but do not mention, or indeed imply, that any Cheyenne group was then permanently residing along the west bank of the Missouri. Cheyenne tradition itself is also adamant that none of their people were still permanent residents on the Missouri by the early 1780s, and qualify this statement by saying that their people did not contract the virulent smallpox epidemic of 1781/ `82, which swept away large numbers among all the Missouri River tribes. The Cheyennes state emphatically that they themselves entirely escaped that particular visitation, which would not have been the case if Cheyennes were then entrenched year round adjacent to the Missouri.

This is not to say that all Cheyenne and Suhtaio Missouri River towns had been completely abandoned by that date. Rather, the occupants were no longer permanent residents, only visiting the towns for short periods twice a year in order to plant and harvest a small amount of food stuffs. Such a practice was continued by some Cheyennes well into the nineteenth century, and Blue-Thunder`s date of 1795 therefore, must be taken as referring to the last time the Cheyenne village at the Farm School site had been visited, albeit only on a seasonal basis.

Having said this, the Cheyenne declaration that none of their people were on the Missouri during the great smallpox epidemic between 1781 and 1782 must mean, in reality, that most Cheyennes and Suhtaio had then remained in buffalo-hide tepees in the Plains and Black Hills country west of the Missouri where they were isolated from the infected tribes. Only after the disease had burned itself out did some Cheyennes and Suhtaio patch up their old quarrels with the Mandan and Hidatsa and return to the Missouri, although due to the event of a great flood which engulfed much of the middle course of that river in 1784, the Masikota Cheyennes finally abandoned their town at the mouth of the Porcupine once and for all, and moved west along the north side of Grand River where they built a new town some 20 miles west of that river`s mouth, and at the same time, they renewed their war with the Mandan.

Such is evident from the report of the French trader Jacques D`Eglise who, in late 1791, ascended the Missouri on behalf of his Spanish benefactors in order to visit the Missouri River Nations and assess the extent of English infiltration in that region. Thus D`Eglise was among the Mandans throughout the winter of 1791 /`92 and at which time he had dealings with the `*Tayenes*` [i.e. Cheyennes]. His journal of the expedition makes no mention of any Cheyenne or Suhtaio group occupying a permanent village on the Missouri`s west bank. On the contrary, D`Eglise stated,

"The Tayenes are a wandering people roaming a country as yet unknown by white men." [3]

This is important, for the country immediately west and southwest of the Mandan towns and along the Lower courses of the Missouri`s western tributaries was, by then, already known to both French and Spanish traders since the early 1780s if not a decade earlier. In another passage from the same journal, D`Eglise further stated that he had first to bring the *Tayenes* and *Mandanes* together and effect a truce between them, before the *Tayenes* could be induced to come to the Missouri with their furs.

Evidently this initiative from D`Eglise had the desired effect, as both Cheyenne and Mandan traditions declare that their tribes did make peace at the time Cheyennes returned to the Missouri for a second time, and remained at peace with one another apart from a few minor dissensions for a number of years thereafter. It was during this particular time according to the Mandan themselves, that they, the Mandan, first received horses in some quantity by trading with the then *"...friendly Cheyennes."*

The following year of 1793, after being granted a trading license from the Spanish authorities, D`Eglise returned to the Upper Missouri with a French Canadian named Joseph Garreau, and began trading with both the Mandan and Cheyennes. Garreau remained among the Cheyennes throughout the winter of 1793 /`94 after D`Eglise himself had returned to St. Louis, and the trader Jean Baptiste Trudeau when on the Missouri met this same Garreau in the summer of 1795. Trudeau in his later writings pertaining to that year, also mentioned that the Cheyennes were a wandering Nation and for the previous two winters Garreau had been living among them. So it appears that Cheyennes had not been permanent village-dwellers on the Missouri since before the time of the first visit of D`Eglise in late 1791, but for most of the year were roaming the Western Plains and Black Hills country and only sporadically, revisited their new village site on Grand River during the planting and harvest seasons.

It had not been long after the Masikota moved from Porcupine Creek to their new site on the Grand, that the Bowstring Cheyennes [Omissis] of the Farm-School site, also abandoned their town for the last time, and likewise, moved out along Grand River, but to its northern tributary of Dirt-Lodge Creek some distance west of their Masikota cousins, although concerning this particular village, there is little if any significant information to be had.

Thus by the mid-1780s, the two largest component groups of Cheyenne, i.e. Masikota and Omissis, were no longer permanently in situ along the Missouri. Instead, their new places of residence on Grand River, Dirt-Lodge Creek and in the adjacent region between the Grand and Big Cheyenne, had become their center of occupancy in the Plains immediately west of the Missouri.

The Masikota earth-lodge village on the north side of the Grand twenty miles from that river`s mouth, became a well-known land mark, and a century later was still recalled in both Cheyenne and Sioux traditions.

The aforementioned George Grinnell also did a cursory inspection of the Grand River site, and noted that some of the old lodge remains measured forty feet in diameter, while Sioux informants stated that some of the earth lodges in this village were so large, that the occupants took their horses into them at night as protection against thieves. A number of Grinnell`s old female Cheyenne informants further told him that these earth-lodge Cheyennes were then in the habit of making clay pots and wove baskets from a certain kind of reed. Certainly, both the Cheyennes and Suhtaio continued to mould clay pots and other domestic utensils after leaving the Missouri; so Michellson`s informants told him, and only ceased to do so about ten years before the fight at Dry Creek [i.e. Sand Creek, 1864]. Their people, they said, would roll a ball of clay into the required size of the pot, then simply hollow out the inside.

In addition, a Sioux Indian named Red-Hail [born 1833], told Dr. Beede that when he, Red-Hail, was a young boy; seven or eight years old, he had several times visited this site on the Grand,

and remembered eating the green corn which was then still being sporadically cultivated in the adjacent fields. Grinnell's inspection also noticed several large cache pits both within and outside the said village, some of which were very deep and would have stored a great quantity of corn.

Perhaps this particular village mentioned by Red-Hail, although by then long abandoned as a permanent seat of residence, was actually still being temporarily visited by Cheyennes when the traders Alexander Henry the Younger and Charles McKenzie with a Hidatsa peace party, visited a large Cheyenne camp in the summer of 1806. The McKenzie journal records that the peace party after leaving the Hidatsa villages on Knife River, crossed the Clearwater, Heart and Cannonball rivers, before arriving at a large camp of Cheyennes comprising 220 lodges [the Henry account says 120 lodges].

The site of this village so Henry recorded,

"…is situated in a delightful spot on a level, elevated Plains in the rear, on the S. runs a rivulet, beyond which the river is bounded by high, barren hills, partly covered with large round stones. On the front or N. side runs the rivulet we crossed, and there the view extends no further than the hill we passed over. On the W., within about one-quarter of a mile, a range of high hills run N. and S. on the E. the Plains is more level for about five miles, when the view is terminated by high hills, covered with large round stones; and indeed the level Plains are nearly covered in the same manner. " [4]

The same account continues,

"The Schians having made their winter's hunt, move northward. They sometimes dispose of their skins to the Pawnees [Arickara] and Sioux; or if they find any traders from the Islenois [Illinois River], they deal with them. They [Cheyennes] are of a roving disposition, and seldom remain long in any one spot." [5]

The first of these Henry descriptions does suggest that the river he was referring to close by the Cheyenne camp on its south side, was, in fact, south of the Cannonball, which river received its name owing to the profusion of large ball-like rocks in its vicinity. No mention is made of earth-lodges, but rather, a large tepee encampment indicating a sporadic visit to the site by Cheyennes at that time. Henry went on to state that some of the Cheyenne women were engaged in *"...working robes with straw and porcupine quills."* [6] and which statement indicates that corn fields were then nearby for the said women to have access to straw, and Henry also noted that the Hidatsa could not dispose of all the corn they had carried with them to trade to the Cheyennes, which suggests that the latter then had enough of their own corn not to need any more from their visitors.

The next large river south of the Cannonball is Grand River, and we have seen from the D'Eglise report of some ten years earlier, Cheyennes even then were residing permanently further west in the Black Hills region. However, as late as 1811, the adventurer William Price Hunt when west of the Missouri as a member of John Jacob Astor's "Astoria" expedition to the Pacific coast, also stopped at a Cheyenne camp on what Hunt termed, "The Big River," but was actually that known today as the Grand, and there his party obtained a number of horses from the camp's

Cheyenne occupants. As the Hunt account also does not mention earth-lodges, but rather, a large encampment of skin tepees, the Cheyennes were likely only temporarily in situ at that place whilst planting or harvesting crops near one or another of their old abandoned towns, either on Dirt-Lodge Creek, Grand River or the Cannonball.

Indeed, a Suhtai informant of Grinnell named Elk-River, stated that during their early days west of the Missouri, some Cheyennes were apt to camp on the River of Rocks, i.e. the Cannonball, and sometimes on Ree River, this last being the Cheyenne name for what is now known as the Grand.

We must not forget also, the two abandoned Cheyenne village sites noted by Lewis and Clark in 1804, the remains of which were then still visible on the west bank of the Missouri just below the mouth of the Big Cheyenne, and close to a village site of the Arickara which had been abandoned not many years before the explorers made their observation.

In late summer of 1812, a small camp of Cheyennes visited Manuel Lisa`a short-lived trading post on the west bank of the Missouri about twenty miles above the mouth of Grand River, and traded fifty bushels of corn to the white men. These Cheyennes informed the post trader that three large bands of their people were then encamped on the Missouri some distance above the fort. Likely then, the three large bands which these visitors were referring to, had originally come from some place further west and by having such a quantity of surplus corn among them, even then they were probably still taking advantage of their old fields adjacent to the long-since abandoned earth-lodge villages near the mouth of the Cheyenne, or indeed, from one or another old village site further west.

According to other tribal informants, yet another permanent Cheyenne or Suhtaio village once stood on the Little Missouri River [Antelope Pit River to the Cheyennes] west of Knife River and north of the Black Hills [where Henry placed the *Shians* after their winter hunt], and the fields adjacent to this last named site according to Cheyenne testimony, were still being utilized in 1833 and perhaps, much later. However, from the mid-1780s onward, there were still other Cheyenne and Suhtaio earth-lodge villages adjacent to the Missouri, albeit on the east side of that river.

It appears from Cheyenne accounts that one or two years after the great Missouri flood of 1784, whereupon the Mandans had moved upriver close to their Hidatsa allies, a number of Cheyenne and Suhtaio did return to the Missouri from the Western Plains, and re-occupied at least one of their old village sites on the east side of that river.

One of these east side villages stood overlooking the Missouri directly across from the Farm School site, and may originally have housed the Moiseo Kit-Fox band when in the vicinity of Long Lake after having left the Kulm site in the Coteau region of the east, and among whom were the Nation`s Sacred Arrow talismans and their Keeper. This same band was then known as "Smokey Lodges" [no doubt in reference to the smoke-filled earth houses in which they lived as opposed to their kindred Cheyenne bands which then dwelt in buffalo hide tepees], but at a later date they were known as the "Burnt Aorta band." These are said to have sometimes resided on the east side of the Missouri and sometimes on its west side and on a seasonal basis, continued to visit their adjacent fields on the Missouri as late as the early 1830s.

A second Cheyenne village of earth-lodges is also said in both Cheyenne and Sioux traditions, to have stood on the east side of the Missouri near the mouth of the Little Cheyenne River. This old village stood further south than that opposite the Farm-School site and close to the later-day hamlet known as Forrest City, South Dakota, across from a point somewhere between the mouths of the Morreau and Big Cheyenne. Sioux informants of Grinnell early in the twentieth century often mentioned this old village on the Little Cheyenne. They said it had been occupied many years and that the Cheyennes who once lived there, built fences of sticks set up crisscross in the ground and filled with brush in order to enclose their corn fields, a statement later elaborated upon by the Northern Cheyenne historian John Stands-in-Timber when he wrote,

> "They protected their corn gardens by making looped fences. One end was set in the ground and then the stick was bent over and the top stuck in, making a wicket. These fences were put up to keep buffalo out of their gardens. They kept out other animals [also]." [7]

Most likely, this village on the Little Cheyenne had originally been occupied by the Cheyenne Pipe Stem-Men group, as according to the Sioux who knew the site also by the term *Shaiena wojubi,* i.e. "Cheyenne Plantings," the occupants; when finally abandoning the village, went south; or more specifically, southwest, and having amalgamated with the Cheyenne-proper group later known as Ridge Men, they resided in an earth-lodge village along a stream known as Cherry Creek not far from where it enters the Big Cheyenne, and from there, moved to a point along the Niobrara River at a place subsequently known to the Cheyennes as Pipe-Stem River in present-day Nebraska.

Yet a third permanent earth-lodge village attributed to Cheyennes on the east side of the Missouri, and occupied from the mid-1780s until between 1814 and 1816, stood near present-day Fort Lincoln across from the mouth of Little Heart River on the west side of the Missouri below Heart River. It is likely that this east side site was occupied by a combined Moiseo Kit-Fox and Suhtaio group among whom again, were the Sacred Arrows and their Keeper in association with that band of Suhtaio among which resided the Sacred Buffalo Hat and its keeper. According to testimony given by Suhtaio members themselves, the actual population of this village included a number of Mandan, and it appears from the archeological inventory to have originally been built as a Mandan village, but among its population – certainly during its later phase of circa, 1800, – there then resided a significant number of Moiseo and Suhtaio.

Regarding this last-named site, Grinnell tells us,

> "In the year 1877 Little Chief's band of Cheyenne while being taken south, was for some time detained at Fort Lincoln, N D., and among them were the mother of old Elk-River and part of her family. During their stay at Fort Lincoln, this old woman took her daughter and granddaughter about to various points not far from the post, and with laughter and tears showed them the well-known places where as a girl, she had played and worked. She said that at the time of which she then told, her group of

437

Cheyenne lived in a permanent village on the east bank of the Missouri River and planted there. In the large houses of this village, the grandmother said, there were often a considerable number of people, two or three or four families. She explained that the small house sites in the permanent villages were menstrual lodges, or those occupied by old women who lived alone, as often they did when they were old, and believed that they had not long to live." [8]

The aforementioned informant Elk-River was himself a Suhtai, born sometime between 1810 and 1814. His mother must then have been Suhtai, as among the Cheyennes and Suhtaio, clan descent is passed through the female line. Elk-River's mother, we are also told, was born in 1786, so the village she referred to must still have been occupied for a number of years after her birth, and as late as 1804, it was recorded in the journal of the Lewis and Clark expedition,

"The Cheyennes are divided into two groups, the Shaha or People on the other side, and the Wheeskeeu, or people on this side…" [9]

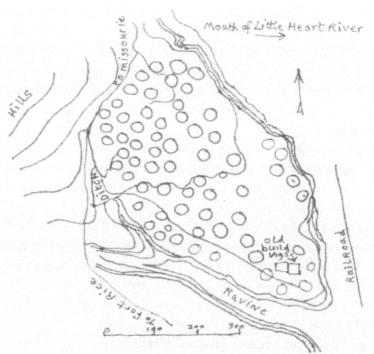

PLAN OF THE FORT LINCOLN VILLAGE SITE

Lewis and Clark were then on the west side of the Missouri, so the *Shahas* are implied as being on the east side of that river, and indeed, the actual term *Shahas* as explained earlier in this study, pertains to both the Suhtaio and the Moiseo Kit-Fox element later known as the Burnt Aorta band. The term *Wheeskeeu* on the other hand, pertains to the Omissis [i.e. Bowstrings] Cheyenne-speaking group, and the expression as recorded by Lewis and Clark was actually an Indian metaphor to designate the two component groups of Moiseo and Omissis as having separate origins.

Another of Grinnell's Cheyenne informants stated that an old warrior named Doll-Man [over eighty years old when he died in 1871], always said that along with his particular Cheyenne-speaking band, he, too, in his younger days, had lived in an earth-lodge village on the east side of the Missouri with or close to the Mandan, and had married a Mandan woman. Doll-Man was thus referring to a time prior to and after the date 1800 and he himself belonged to the Moiseo or Burnt Aorta clan. It was because of this connection and close association between the Moiseo and Suhtaio, that the later-date famous Holy man Grey-Thunder [also known as White-Thunder] although born a Suhtai, joined the Burnt Aorta band and actually became the Keeper of the Nation's Sacred Arrows, notwithstanding that he was not considered as belonging to the Cheyenne proper, which failing should have debarred him from such a position, as indeed, had previously been, and was subsequently the case, regarding all other holders of that office. Additional information regarding this site may be gleaned from the writings of the archaeologist George Will, who reported in 1941 from what Cheyenne informants told him,

> "The Sioux in their westward progress again came up with the Cheyennes. As they tell it, at first there were only a few Sioux, poor people begging for meat and horses, which the Cheyennes had acquired after reaching the Missouri. Then they came in ever increasing numbers and became threatening. At this time, according to one Cheyenne narrator, both the Arickara and Cheyennes became frightened and fled to the Mandan villages; where the three tribes lived together for some time. They [Cheyennes] soon returned to their own villages, however; but the old, peaceful life was gone....The Sious [sic] continually plundered their fields and threatened the village. The people, tired of working the soil for the benefit of others, began to leave in small parties for the Black Hills country where game was exceedingly abundant. Finally the last remnants forsook the old village and the tribe was reunited near the Black Hills, no longer a sedentary agricultural people; but a nomadic host, flitting here and there, living in skin tepees, and subsisting on the fruits of the chase and such vegetable food as they might obtain in trading horses to their old neighbours, the Arickara and Mandans." [10]

The above extract mentions only one Cheyenne or Suhtaio village, and thus likely refers to the Fort Lincoln site on the east side of the Missouri, as the aforementioned Will went on to say; again from Cheyenne testimony,

> "Some few families felt so strongly the ties of the old village life that they refused to abandon it. We are told that some Cheyennes joined the Arickara and some the Mandans, into which tribes they were gradually fused." [11]

There are other contemporary references to one or more Cheyenne or Suhtaio group when still adjacent to the Missouri in the guise of several map notations of the late eighteenth century. On one of these charts, drawn up by the Hudson`s Bay Company trader Donald Mackay and relating to his trip to the Mandan and other tribes on the Missouri in early 1781, we find the *Flying Big-Bellies* [Hidatsa], *Shew* [Awaxawi], *Mandane* [Mandan] and *Shevitoons* as residing from north to south along the Missouri on that river`s east side, and includes the additional notation,

"…These 4 tribes live on the islands being afraid of the Snakes and hunts [sic] on the east side of the river." [12]

The map gives no indication regarding earth-lodges or temporary camps of hide tepees, and Mackay`s observation was made before the smallpox visitation in late 1781, and thus some years prior to the Missouri flood of 1784, which would have swept away most such islands in that river.

The actual term *Shevitoons* is repeated on a number of later-date maps of the middle Missouri and western regions, but by various spellings such as *Shevitaun, Chionitones* and, more importantly, *Shiwitoons.*

Mackay had with him a French interpreter, and so the tribal name as Mackay heard it would have been its French equivalent. Both French and Spanish had difficulty with the consonant `w` so that `v` may well have been used instead [as in the Spanish term Jivaro for that people`s proper name of Shawa or Shuar].The name *Shevitoon* would then, more properly, have been rendered *Shewitoon*, which when detached from the tribal suffix `toon,` gives a variation of the more common terms of *Shawa, Showay, Shaha* and *Shahaway*, each of which were once applied specifically to the Suhtaio and Moiseo Cheyennes combined. An alternative hypothesis is that the `v` in *Shevitoon* is from the old Suhtaio dialect where `v` is used as a dialectical alternative to the Cheyenne-proper sound of `w.` Of course, neither is the sound `h` pronounced in French or Spanish, and so `v` may also have been used in *Shevitoon* in place of `h` to create the suffix `vitoon` as being a corruption of `hitan` which was the Suhtaio dialect word meaning `men` or `people.` From the alternative spellings such as *Shevitaun* and *Chevitoons*, it appears that the prefixes `She` and `Che` were; at a later date, sometimes also pronounced both as `Stai` and `Squi, `and are compatible with *Staihitan* and *Squihitan*, which, likewise, were names once applied to the Suhtaio. There is no `qui` sound in the Sioux language, being represented by `k` or `ku` and hence, the Sioux term for *Squihitan* of *Skutani,* which was a Sioux term used specifically to designate the Suhtaio. The Northern Suhtai informant John Stands-in-Timber in his written manuscripts incidentally, always typed the name *Skutai* and sometimes *Suktai* instead of Suhtai, although whether this was key-board error on his part or deliberate, is open to debate.

In 1787, six years after Donald Mackay`s trip up the Missouri, a James Mackay of the Northwest Company also visited the Mandan and other tribes along that river, and later recorded in a memoir relating to his expedition,

"The Indian Nations that reside as well on the borders of the Missouri as in the Environs of this River are the Attotactoes or Ottoes, the Mahas, the Poncas, Sioux of the Grand Detour or Great Bend, Sioux of the Plains, Shevitauns and Corbeaus. There are other Nations who reside at the foot of the Rocky Mountains of whom I could not procure any information." [13]

Corroboration can be had in associating the various spellings of *Shevitoons* with the Suhtaio, when one consults the later-date Soulard map of 1795. This chart was specifically prepared to aid yet another expedition intending to ascend the Missouri late that same year [1795] and led by the same James Mackay, but now in the company of a Welshman named John Evans. Both were then in the employ of the Spanish authorities in St. Louis, and on this map, which had probably been drawn up from information obtained during MacKay's first and subsequent expeditions of 1787 and 1792, there is the notation *N. Chivitoune o` Chaguines* just below four dots which, on most other charts, usually denote villages. This notation is inserted west of the Missouri between the Niobrara River [northern Nebraska] and Knife River [South Dakota], and leaves no doubt that the term represents a Cheyenne-speaking group. The four villages would, of course, be compatible with the four then extant Cheyenne groups of Masikota, Aorta, Bowstrings and the Pipe-Stem-Men / Ridge-Men Band, while overall, the notation is consistent with the assertion from several Cheyenne informants, that their people had all left the Missouri's west bank as permanent residents by the time of the Missouri flood of 1784, having moved west along the Cannonball and Grand River and along one and another stream such as the Moreau and that of Cherry Creek, the Lower courses of which embrace the same general region where the *N. Chivitoune o` Chaguines* are positioned on the Soulard chart. It does appear though, that at least one Cheyenne-speaking band later returned to the Missouri, for in a missive sent by the same James Mackay to his Spanish superiors in 1796, he requested a number of medals for,

"...the 5 Mandane villages [evidently including the Hidatsa], 2 villages of Rees [Arickara] and 1 for the Chaguinne village and the Sioux who live with them." [14]

The one Cheyenne village referred to and *"...the Sioux who live with them,"* although not shown on Soulard's map, must have applied to the combined Suhtaio–Moiseo group then ensconced among the Mandans at the Fort Lincoln site and also, to Miniconjou Sioux who's name actually translates as *"They plant by the water."* We are told in both Cheyenne and Sioux traditions that a part of the Miniconjou known in early documents as the *TaCorpa* band, were then friendly to and often camped with Cheyenne-speaking peoples during the same period in question.

Further evidence that the *Shevitoons* included the Suhtaio, can be gleaned from the fact that after John Evans returned to St. Louis in 1797, he compiled his own map of the Upper Missouri and its environs, but showed the *Shevitoon* as then located much further west on the north side of the Missouri across from the mouth of the Yellowstone. This location is compatible with both Cheyenne and Suhtaio traditions, which state that when their two peoples came together for a third time after a long period of separation, the Cheyennes were in the Black Hills of South Dakota and adjacent to the Little Missouri River of North Dakota, while the Suhtaio [at least one of their bands], were on the north side of the Missouri across from the mouth of the Yellowstone, and thus must have been those also known as *Staihitan, Squihitan* and *Kites,* albeit then including Arapahoe and Atsina tribal members among their number. It would appear then, that the tribal name *Shevitoon* in one guise and another, did actually apply to the Suhtaio and also, to the mixed Suhtaio and Cheyenne-proper Moiseo band as existed at that time.

The Grinnell material which includes comments from several old-time tribal informants, does suggest there had been several other, albeit smaller permanent villages once occupied by Cheyennes and Suhtaio in the region embracing the Grand and Cannonball river and along one or more lesser streams flowing east into the Missouri, such as that known today as the Morreau River earlier known to the Cheyennes as Owl River. Thus we also find on a map drafted by Victor Collett in 1796, from information likely obtained from the French Canadian trader Jean Baptiste Trudeau [domiciled among the Arickara at that date], that yet another permanent Cheyenne village was located on Cherry Creek near its junction with the Big Cheyenne, and of which Collett wrote,

> *"The Chaguene Nation is settled a little above the fork and cultivate Indian corn and tobacco. They are divided into three hordes, the Chaguenes, Vouisy and Chouta."* [15]

Of the Western allies of the *Chaguenes,* Collett listed as follows;

> *Pitapahata;* .... *on the northern branch of the Cherry Creek River.*
> *Tokiwako;* .... *on the southern branch of the Cherry Creek River.*
> *Kayoha;* .... *on the southern branch of the Cherry Creek River.*
> *Tokaninambich;.. on the southwestern branch of the Cheyenne River.* [16]

In corroboration, we have Trudeau`s own account of his travels between 1795 and 1796, in which he mentions Cheyennes who he met at the Arickara villages,

> "Two leagues above the dwelling of the Rees issues forth the river of the Cheyennes which some hunters have named the Fork....About thirty leagues from its mouth, upon one of its tributaries, called the River of the Bunch of Cherries, the Cheyennes built there some permanent huts, around which they cultivated little fields of maize and tobacco; but furthermore, this Nation which is divided into three bands, or hordes, of which the largest bears the name of Chaguienes, the second is called, Ouissy, the third Chousa, wanders without cessation the length of this river and crosses in search of wild cows, even many chains of hills that separate, by several ranges these vast prairies... Several savage wandering peoples scour this country, such as are the Kiowa, Tocaninanbiche, the Tokiouako, the Pitapahato, all allies of the Cheyenne but speaking different languages. The Chaguennes know very well how to hunt the beaver, the skins of which they barter with the Sioux for merchandise.... [17]

Indicatively, the Trudeau account [from which Collett evidently obtained much of his information], does infer that Cheyennes by then, had already abandoned the Cherry Creek site as a permanent residence, as Trudeau mentions the town in its past tense.

Of the *"three hordes"* so designated by both Collett and Trudeau, they undoubtedly represent the Omissis-Bowstrings, Masikota-Moiseo [Aorta] and the Suhtaio in that order, and here Trudeau was also referring to the same village mentioned by Collett near the mouth of Cherry Creek, which flows into the Big Cheyenne at a point some fifty miles west of the Missouri.

Certainly whilst roaming as nomads across the Western Plains, the Cheyennes and Suhtaio continued to raise small patches of corn, and did so as late as 1851 when; according to Grinnell's Northern Cheyenne informant Hankering-Wolf, just before attending the Horse Creek Treaty gathering that year on a branch of the Laramie River, one Cheyenne or Suhtaio group had first planted its corn on the North Platte River before moving down to the treaty ground itself. In addition, the Suhtaio informant of Michellson named White-Bull, stated that as late as 1833 when *"Stars fell from the sky,"* Cheyennes were still in the habit of camping on the west bank of the Missouri, although they did not then reside in earth lodges.

This last mentioned group in 1833, included a mixed Cheyenne and Suhtaio band in company with a band of Sioux, and among whom the Sweet Medicine Chief, High-Backed-Wolf [originally a Suhtai], was then residing. This man was met and painted by the artist George Catlin in 1832 at the mouth of Teton River on the Missouri, and thus, not long before the said chief was slain during a drunken brawl by one of his own tribesmen the following year.

The Collett map previously referred to, depicts the Cheyenne village on Cherry Creek straddled between the *Pitapahatoe* [Kiowa-Apache] to the immediate west, and the *Tokaninambich* [Arapahoe] to the immediate southwest. The Cheyenne village itself is shown as a cluster of permanent lodges enclosed by some kind of protective perimeter, and may have been built many years earlier to house that breakaway group of Ridge-Men from the Omissis-Bowstrings, and among whom the old Pipe-Stem-Men group was eventually absorbed. Thus at one time they were likely included under the term *Gens L`Arc,* and at a much later date, were also included under the name Hevitanio which denoted those bands constituting the tribal division referred to collectively as `Southern Cheyennes.` Such would be consistent with the LaVerendrye brother`s request in 1742, that the chief of the *"Gens L`Arc"* or "Bows," who`s village was then located at the Biesterfeldt site on the Lower bend of Sheyenne River east of the Missouri, site a new village, ostensibly along the same Cherry Creek, this being a more convenient place for Frenchmen to visit in the future [See Chapter 34.]. The Cherry Creek Cheyenne village may indeed, have been the same permanent Cheyenne village mentioned in 1767 by the English explorer Jonathan Carver, when he wrote,

"A little west of the Mahahs is a tribe called the Shyans who are scarcely known by any. Some war parties from the Naudowessie [Sioux] say they have been among them and report they live in a village and raise corn. They, [the Sioux] say they have horses on which they fight. When these people overtake any parties of enemies on the Plains they are sure of destroying them. [18]

Since the LaVerendrye brother`s sojourn with the *"Gens L`Arc"* in 1742, no other white men; niether English, French or Spanish as far is known, returned to make contact with Cheyennes until 1781, when the previously mentioned Donald McKay visited the Missouri tribes early that year. The *Mahahs* in the above extract, represent those known at a later date as Omaha, and who; at the time of Carver`s writing, were then on the west side of the Missouri somewhere between the mouths of the Big Cheyenne and the Platte. The Collett map designates only the *Chaguienes* as located on Cherry Creek, and so must denote those once known as *Chaiena* and *Chaienaton*, and who, as earlier deduced in this study, were the same as the Omissis-Bowstrings Cheyenne-speaking group, but who at the time of Collett`s observation had separated into two groups, one of which known as the Ridge-Men Band had since joined with the Pipe-Stem-Men, and were those specifically entrenched on Cherry Creek. That both the *Vouisy* [Ouissy, i.e. Masikota on Grand River and the associated Aorta since moved to Morreau River], and *Chouta* [i.e. Suhtaio] are not shown on the Collett map, suggests that the exact locations of these groups were not known to him at that time, or alternatively, they were regarded as merely sub-bands of the predominant Cheyenne-speaking group referred to as *Chaguiennes* and earlier known as the *Gens d L`Arc,* both of which terms once served as collective names for the Cheyenne-speaking Nation as a whole.

Yet another map drawn by James Pitot in 1802 which depicts the country and inhabitants west of the Missouri at that time, shows the *Terres des Cheyens* between the Cannonball and Big Cheyenne, and must then, be applicable to those Cheyennes who, at that date [1802] and albeit then living in portable tepees, were still visiting their gardens at one and another of their old abandoned earth-lodge villages either on Dirt-Lodge Creek, Grand River, the Cannonball, the Morreau, or Cherry Creek.

On an even later-date map attributed to the Lewis and Clark expedition of 1803 – 1806, but obviously a copy of Soulard`s original 1795 map with additional notations by Lewis and Clark, the insert *Chaguienne Indians* is clearly shown between two rivers which the explorers call Little Missouri and the Platte, and southwest of the *Chaguiennes* are placed both the *Blue Bead Indians* and the *Red Bead Indians* The river named Little Missouri was, however, but an early colonial name for that known later as the Big Cheyenne, while *Blue Bead Indians* was an old name sometimes applied to the Arapahoe and at other times to a part of the Crow, and even to the Arapahoe and Crow combined, while the *Red Bead Indians* likely refer to another Crow group later known specifically as the River Crow. Certainly the Lewis and Clark positioning of the Blue Bead Indians is consistent with the same location earlier noted on the Collett map of 1796 for that of the *Tokaninambick Nation* and who, undoubtedly, were Arapahoe.

This being said, it does appear that during the time of the Lewis and Clark expedition, there were still Moiseo and Suhtaio peoples on the east side of the Missouri [ostensibly at the Fort Lincoln site] and probably remained so as late as circa, 1816, when due to a severe climatic shift to a colder, non-productive environment because of fall-out from the great volcanic eruption of Mount Tamora in faraway Indonesia, there came a decisive end to Moiseo and Suhtaio permanent village life in both North and South Dakota, an event which is known historically as *"The year without summer."* [21] This corresponds with the informant George Bent`s assertion that the Moiseo finally joined the rest of the Cheyennes as nomadic buffalo hunters sometime around the date 1814.

However, even after the latter date, small bands of Cheyennes and Suhtaio did occasionally return to the fields adjacent to their old village sites when on friendly trips to the Mandan and Arickara, or when visiting the white man's trading posts actually on the Missouri.

So it was that from the mid-1780s onward, the new and recognized heartland then claimed by the four original Cheyenne groups of Masikota, Omissis, Aorta and the mixed Pipe-Stem-Men / Ridge-Men band, embraced the region between the Cannonball in the north and Big Cheyenne in the south, although each group was apt to spend much time roaming west as far as the Black Hills and beyond. It was then, most likely, that the two Cheyenne-speaking groups which the aforesaid Trudeau referred to in an account of his travels in 1795 when he wrote, "...*the most important men from both Chaguenne villages...*" [22] must have applied to those comprising specifically the combined Masikota-Moiseo band and the Omissis, and of whom Trudeau additionally made clear, were then in close contact with, and allied to the Black Hills Tribes. The Suhtaio for their part appear to have been in two groups. One of which remained in close association with Cheyenne-proper bands in the vicinity of the Lower part of Cheyenne River, the other known alternatively as *Staitans, Squitans, Skutani* and *Kites* or *Flyers*, located higher up the Missouri on both sides of that river near the mouth of the Yellowstone. These last were closely associated with the Arapahoe and Atsina, and also were allies to the Black Hill's Tribes.

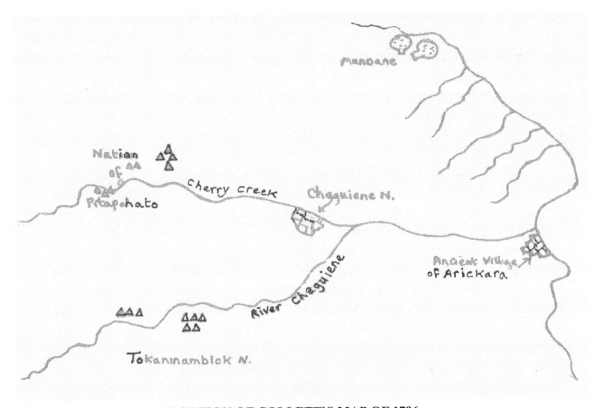

PORTION OF COLLETT'S MAP OF 1796.

CHAPTER 39.

INTO THE BLACK HILLS and the COMING OF THE TETONS.

From their position between Grand River and the Big Cheyenne, the two main Cheyenne groups of Masikota and Omissis [Bowstrings], became frequent visitors to the intertribal trading fairs in the Black Hills. As a consequence, they continued their alliances with tribes thereof, which included the Kiowa, Crow, Gattacka [Kiowa Apache] and Arapahoe, the same who at an earlier date along with the *Gens d L'Arc*, had been met by the LaVerendrye brothers in 1742, and since then, had been in contact with Pueblo and Spanish settlements along the Rio Grande, and still at war with the Snakes.

To these fairs in the Black Hills, the Arapahoe, Kiowa and Gattacka brought Spanish artefacts and horses from the south, while the Cheyennes brought agricultural produce and guns obtained in the east. The Black Hills tribes themselves were already well-supplied with horses, and with the addition of firearms, they all at once turned the tables on the Snakes, who for generations past, had been the terror of all the Black Hills and River Tribes.

Cheyennes from the mid-1740s onwards became particularly active against the Snakes and with the assistance of Kiowa and Arapahoe allies, even before the turn of the century they had evicted all Shoshoni-speaking peoples from the Western Plains. Cheyenne parties thereafter, wandered far afield, south to the Pueblo towns and Spanish haciendas and west across the Rockies, and even southwest across the Sierra Mountains into the desert scrublands of Nevada. Indeed, the Trudeau material tells of a time in 1793 when a combined Cheyenne and Kiowa war-party travelled far southwest, in order to pursue their aggression against Shoshoni-speaking peoples. Trudeau reported,

"…When I had dealings with the Cheyenne people in the course of the summer of 1795, where I spoke to many chiefs and leading men of the Tocaninanbiche and Kiowa Nations…They told me that two years before the Cheyennes and Kiowa, their allies, had formed a considerable war-party in which the great chief of the Cheyennes took part, who himself reported to me this fact for certain;- that having crossed the mountains, they had come after many days journey to the banks of a wide and deep river, well timbered, the waters of which appeared to go in the direction of the winter sunset. That along this river which they had followed in descending, they had discovered seven huts of unknown savages; having attacked them and defeated them, they found in their booty none of the small effects coming from the white men, all of their utensils being of their own invention. Their huts were made of rush matting and of long straw. The large animals of the skins of which the savages are accustomed to make their tents are absolutely wanting in this country. Their garments, their shoes and even the saddlecloths were of skins of beaver, of otter, of kid and deer, of wolf, of fox, of hare and so forth. They have as of all others, the use of the bow and arrow, the armour of which is of stone or bone. A little bag full of Indian corn which they found among their baggage, gave them occasion to inquire of some women prisoners if their Nation cultivated the plant. They answered no; but that in the Lower part of this river there was a large village of savages who sowed and reaped a great quantity of it. These women had hung around their neck and ears some shells of various kind and shapes, pierced and threaded on little strings of leather. They asked them where they obtained this kind of glass bead. They answered that at the mouth of this river appeared a large body of water, the other bank of which was not visible; that the waters rose and fell considerably at certain times of day and night; that the savages that had their homes about there, attached to the end of a long line large pieces of meat which they threw into the water when deep and drew out when it ebbed; that a quantity of these shells were found adhering to those pieces of meat; and that having detached them, they pierced them and hung them thus around the neck and ears for ornament. [1]

It would appear that the people referred to in the above account were, most likely, Paiutes who were of Shoshoni stock, and the river mentioned is that known as the Colorado, which flows southwest through the old Paiute country of the Sierra Nevada, and into the Gulf of California.

Another memorable episode pertaining to Cheyenne hostility with the Snakes, was recorded by the French traveler Perin Du Lac from information supplied by the aforementioned Trudeau who Du Lac met on the Missouri in 1802. The event recorded had obviously taken place some few years earlier than Du Lac's recital, and the tribal name *Halitanes,* used to designate the enemy involved, was merely a variant form of *Halisanes* and also of *Alitanes, Laytanes* and *Naytanes,* each of which terms were alternatively applied to those later known as Shoshoni-proper [Snakes] and to the latter's Comanche kinfolk.

Apparently, a war-party of Cheyennes comprising some eighty warriors attacked a small *Halitanes* [Snake] camp of eight or ten lodges, the occupants of which were easily and completely over-whelmed. Some of the *Halitanes* managed to escape and took word of the disaster to another much larger *Halitanes* village not far away. At once a strong party of *Halitanes* warriors mounted their ponies and after starting out towards the vanquished village, they arrived while the victorious Cheyennes were still in the process of looting the lodges. The *Halitanes* attacked at once and succeeded in killing at least sixty Cheyennes before the remaining twenty survivors; on foot and led by their chief, extricated themselves from the scene and took refuge in a nearby ravine,

"...*where horses could not penetrate.*" [2]

The Cheyenne chief told his comrades to place their muskets at his side, as only he would shoot at the enemy to be sure of hitting his mark while the others should reload each piece after it had been discharged. By so doing, they would keep a constant stream of leaden balls being fired at the foe. When the *Halitanes* came up, every time the Cheyenne chief fired an enemy fell either dead or wounded, and the *Halitanes* were obliged to retreat in order to seek cover from the deadly missiles. The *Halitanes* then cut a number of bushes which they held before them as they crawled

447

along the ground towards the Cheyenne position, supposing that the bushes would obscure them from view. In response, the Cheyenne chief now handed back the guns to each of his comrades, and commanded that only half their number should fire at one time, so that when the enemy charged after the first volley had been fired, expecting to catch the Cheyennes reloading with ram rods half way down the barrels, a second volley from the remaining Cheyenne guns would stop them in their tracks. This is what happened and many more *Halitanes* were killed and wounded before retiring again to a safe distance.

The affair was a stale-mate. The *Halitanes* would not disperse, and the Cheyennes could not be budged.

At length, the *Halitanes* chief wishing to regain lost prestige, challenged the Cheyenne chief to a one against one contest on the open space between their opposing forces, and to this the Cheyenne chief agreed. Thus the lone Cheyenne stepped out from the ravine and stood with gun in hand facing his lone adversary, who with shield and raised lance, suddenly ran headlong at his opponent. The Cheyenne chief remained calm and impassive. Slowly he raised his musket to one shoulder, took careful aim and fired, and the oncoming *Halitanes* chief went stumbling to the ground, mortally wounded with a leaden ball in his chest.

Seeing the demise of their chief, the rest of the *Halitanes* lost heart to continue the fight, and in a demoralized bunch departed the scene, leaving the surviving Cheyennes to escape with their lives, and eventually the Cheyennes reached their home camp without further miss-hap.

Corroborating the superiority achieved by Cheyennes and their Black Hills allies over the Snakes and those consanguine with them, is found in a report by the Spanish Governor of Santé Fe penned in November, 1805, wherein it is mentioned that the Yamparika Comanche who had formerly lived in the north, were now to be found on the Rio Colorado near the Conchos, and it was further stated by the Governor that the Yamparika had been driven south by the enmity of the Kiowa and *"Flecha Rayada"* or "Striped Arrows," which was then a Spanish term for Cheyennes adopted from the Comanche name for that people.

In addition, a Sioux informant of Rufus B. Sage in 1844, told of a time past when the Cheyennes or "Scarred-Arms" as the narrator called them had with their allies, expelled the Snakes and all other Shoshoni-speaking peoples from the Black Hills, and as a result, the Shoshoni-proper fled west across the Rocky Mountains, whilst their Comanche cousins retreated south to and below the Arkansas River.

On the other hand, Kiowa tradition states it were they, the Kiowa alone, who drove the Shoshoni-speaking Comanche south from the Black Hills and Platte River district, and that half the Kiowa tribe then followed the retreating Comanche south, while the other half remained in the north and thereafter, were known as "Cold Men." These northern Kiowa by remaining allies to the Gattacka, Suhtaio, Cheyennes, Crows and Arapahoe, were allowed to continue trading freely at the Mandan and Arickara towns. In truth, the `Cold Men`s` continued alliance with the aforementioned tribes was crucial to northern Kiowa survival as it was for the rest of the Black Hill`s Tribes, for without each other`s support, none alone would have been able to resist Snake war-parties in the field and certainly, could not have traded regularly on the Missouri without the risk of dire consequences from skulking war bands of Sioux.

Cheyenne testimony on the contrary, states adamantly that their people allied to the Arapahoe, was the force which harried the Comanche south, and then pushed the Kiowa south from the same Black Hills country immediately after.

That this is what happened to most Comanche bands in the north, according to both Kiowa and Cheyenne tradition, there can be little doubt, as we know that the Kiowa and Cheyennes were at war with that people before the close of the eighteenth century. But the inclusion of Kiowa among the list of Cheyenne enemies at that time, cannot be trusted. Disagreements may have occurred between the two during their early years of contact, but not to the extent that full-scale warfare ensued, which would have been sufficiently severe to induce the expulsion of the Kiowa. The fact previously noted, that Cheyennes were allied to the Kiowa in 1793 and remained so as late as circa; 1820 according to contemporary documents, confound such an assumption.

If indeed Cheyennes had been at war with the Kiowa during the earlier period in question, then why did they allow half that tribe to remain in and around the Black Hills while they, the Cheyenne, supossedly evicted the rest of that people from the same country?

Prior to the Kiowa movement south, their tribe was one body and did not divide into two separate divisions until not long before the date 1790. One should also note that the Kiowa who had slightly better memories of their early history than did most other tribes, could not recall any serious trouble with Cheyennes before circa, 1826, at which time war in the proper sense of the term, finally broke out between the two.

On the other hand, the Kiowa were ever at war with the Snakes, i.e. Shoshoni of the west, and the fact that before the opening of the nineteenth century, the Comanche had little to distinguish them from their Shoshoni cousins make it likely that Kiowa tradition is partly correct, in that they were at war with the Comanche, but was not the primary reason why a part of the Kiowa vacated the Black Hills and moved south merely to carry on their war with the retreating Comanche.

A more logical circumstance is that while the Kiowa had been engaged in driving the Comanche south, the Sioux became a predominant force above the Platte between the Missouri and the Black Hills, and the Kiowa found it increasingly difficult to visit the Missouri River tribes, particularly the Arickara, with whom they had traded for generations past. The Kiowa could not then obtain supplies of guns and ammunition along with corn and other food stuffs to which they had grown accustomed, and this lack of intertribal commerce caused the Kiowa to quickly lose their advantage over the more populous Comanche. The result was that around the date 1791, albeit while still at war with the Shoshoni, the Kiowa made a lasting peace with the Comanche which has never since been broken. Thus an important factor for their moving south was that the Kiowa needed access to the Spanish trade south of Comanche lands, for without trade of any sort, they could not have hoped to stand against their northern foes.

The Kiowa along with the Cheyennes, always called the Kwahadi and Yamparika Comanche bands "Snakes," although after the Kiowa-Comanche peace had been confirmed, it was the Yamparika according to Comanche tradition, which returned to the North Country where they remained for several decades more, long after other kindred bands had moved permanently south.

That Cheyennes initially, also played a leading role in the earlier eviction of Comanche bands from the Black Hills and surrounding country, is substantiated by tribal tradition and some documented sources. The Cheyennes must then have been in a league with the Kiowa, and not against them. Yet why the Cheyennes did not then follow the Kiowa south and thereby, escape future hostile inroads from the Sioux is a mystery. And especially so, as the Cheyennes were losing a strong ally against the Snakes. However, trade goods including guns, were of better quality and more easily obtained from their position along the Big Cheyenne River, and this habitat, called "Good River" by the Cheyennes, was the finest country in the region.

As regards additional friends and enemies of Cheyenne-speaking groups during their early years of crisscrossing the Plains west of the middle Missouri, it has previously been noted that Cheyennes for a third time came together with the Suhtaio, who by then were already associated with the Black Hills Tribes. This particular meeting is said, traditionally, to have occurred when Cheyennes were wandering the region embracing the Little Missouri River on the Missouri`s south side, and the Suhtaio roaming north of the Missouri across from the mouth of the Yellowstone.

The Suhtaio location, however, across from the mouth of the Yellowstone, had placed them in direct contact with the Crow whose country it was, and inevitably, there soon arose conflict between the two.

The Suhtaio, of course, had long known the Crows and the latter`s Hidatsa confederates when resident in the Minnesota and Coteau des Prairie regions of the east. But since then, the Crows, having earlier been driven from that country by gun-toting Cree, Chippewa and Assiniboine who later forced the Cheyennes and Suhtaio from the same country, had retreated first to the Missouri and thence further west between the Little Missouri River and the Yellowstone. There they befriended the Kiowa, Arapahoe-Atsina and Gattacka, and by the mid-1770s, were fully mounted and armed with a few guns, obtained from Atsina contacts who traded with Hudson`s Bay Company posts in Canada. Thus the Crows no longer felt obliged to tolerate foreign interlopers in their hunting grounds, and with the event of the Suhtaio encroaching south from north of the Missouri into the same Yellowstone country then claimed by the Crows, friction between the two was brought to a head. The famous Mountain Crow, Chief Long-Hair, was born around 1765, and whilst a very young boy, so Crow tradition asserts, his parents were slain by Cheyennes [but who were probably Suhtaio] when the latter surprised and routed a Crow camp. This war must then have already been extant at that date, and certainly by 1780, the Suhtaio were engaged in constant enmity with the Crow.

So it was that although Cheyenne-proper bands during their early period west of the Missouri, had been in friendly contact with Crows when visiting allies and trading fairs in the Black Hills, war between their Suhtaio cousins and Crows, eventually; not long prior to 1800, brought the Cheyennes themselves into the conflict, and was the beginning of Cheyenne - Crow warfare which, but for brief interruptions, lasted another ninety-eight years.

Such a state of affairs did not at first seriously effect Cheyenne and Suhtaio relationships with the Kiowa, Arapahoe and Gattacka who remained friends and allies to the Crows, and freedom of movement throughout the Black Hills region by Cheyennes and Suhtaio, continued for more than forty years thereafter.

It was say the Cheyennes whilst roaming the intervening country between the Black Hills and Missouri between the mid-1770s and early `80s, that small parties of itinerant Teton Sioux first began appearing on a regular basis west of the great river, sometimes when raiding enemies further west, or simply to beg horses from their Cheyenne friends. Initially these Sioux were small in number and on foot, but as time progressed more Sioux appeared, and was the precursor of a great migration of Teton Sioux groups en masse across the Missouri and into the Western Plains. Indeed, Cheyenne oral history contains several anecdotes pertaining to the early appearance of these horse-begging Sioux, such as that told to John Stands-in-Timber by his grandfather Wolf-Tooth which states,

> "One day a strange Indian walked into a Cheyenne camp. He had taken his war-cloths off. He was asked who he was and he answered he was Sioux. He was taken to the Sacred Tepee and an agreement of friendship was made. He was sent back to where his clothes were and given the first horses the Sioux ever received. The Sioux looked at the horses and stood around until they should fill up eating. They [Sioux] decided to return to the Cheyenne camp and see if what the first man had said was true. Some went back and spent the night in the Sacred Tepee and got more horses and gifts." [3]

The above account as narrated by Stands-in-Timber, does suggest that previous to the time indicated, the Sioux had been considered at the least, potential enemies, and that the said meeting initiated a subsequent period of peace between Cheyenne-proper bands and one and another band of Teton Sioux.

On the other hand, the Sioux Chief American-Horse recorded in his winter-count for 1775, that an Oglala Teton in that year travelled west as far as the Black Hills, and brought back a pine tree bough to show his people, who at that time, still resided in the Coteau district east of the Missouri. This event may date the same period when the Sioux first began their horse-begging trips to the Cheyenne.

A variant story, however, told by Cheyennes, also recalls a time when a small band of Sioux said to have been poor and on foot, was discovered in the prairies west of the Missouri. At first the Cheyennes were undecided whether to attack the strangers, as such were often thought as being synonymous with enemies, but as the strangers drew near, it was seen that one among them was carrying a buffalo skull – the symbol of food. So instead, it was agreed among the Cheyennes that they should invite the strangers to their camp. The Sioux accordingly were made welcome and remained among the Cheyennes several months. When finally the Sioux were about to depart, the Cheyennes presented them with two colts and these, the story goes, were the first horses the Sioux ever owned. Two or three years after this the Sioux returned with a larger party. Again the Cheyennes made them welcome and when the visitors were about to leave, the Cheyennes gave them more horses.[4] From that time on, the Sioux came in ever increasing number in order to visit their "good friends" the Cheyennes, and always the visitors acquired more horses as tokens of Cheyenne goodwill.

Yet another account, this time from the Suhtaio informant White-Frog [born circa 1840], stated that in the prairies west of the Missouri, a party of Suhtaio came face to face with a party of Sioux. Each side was suspicious of the other and neither would come close through fear of mutual hostility. They therefore conversed in signs from a distance, after which they shot arrows over to each other in order that the arrows could be taken back to their respective villages as proof of the encounter.[5] From this meeting, it is said, the strong and lasting friendship which subsequently has endured between the Cheyennes and Sioux was first confirmed, although as the Suhtaio were later at war with the Oglala and Brule Sioux, and that just such a story is current also among both the Hidatsa and Mandan regarding the first meeting of their two peoples, this Suhtaio version may have been adopted from the latter when the Suhtaio along with a band of Moiseo, were living among the Mandan at the Fort Lincoln village site.

Whatever the case, friendship with the Teton Sioux brought benefits to the Cheyennes. Hereafter, they could obtain firearms in some quantity from Sioux trading fairs in the east, and initially, gained a strong ally in the Cheyenne's ongoing wars with the Snakes and Crows. But such a congenial situation was not to last. The Oglala Black-Elk recalled that one time, when a party of Sioux visited Cheyennes to trade for horses, a fight broke out between them and for a while their two peoples were at war. Certainly by the mid-1780s the Suhtaio; who by then were regarded by the Sioux as being a part of those known as Cheyenne, were at war with certain bands of Teton Sioux. History has left few details of this war, yet in its entirety it typifies Plains Indian relationships during this early period, and offers an example of how historical fact can sometimes become distorted.

In truth this particular Sioux-Cheyenne conflict was brief and lacked decisive consequences, and it has therefore been suggested by no less an authority than George Grinnell among others, that a state of war was unlikely to ever have been extant between the two. For reasons to be elucidated later, Grinnell might be excused for his assumption, but several scholars since his time have followed his claim blindly, when a close study of the available contemporary material shows conclusive evidence of such a conflict. Grinnell; an eminent Historian and Ethnologist, to whom all praise should be given for his recording from first-hand information a great deal of what we know concerning the Cheyennes, took his informants at their word when they declared, that as far as they knew their tribe had never taken up the hatchet against the Sioux. Many times they had fought with the Sioux-speaking Assiniboine, they said, and had actually been evicted from their early homes by that people, but with the Western Sioux, i.e. The Teton and Saoni, the Cheyennes had always been at peace. In order to substantiate their claim, Grinnell's informants added that before their people and the Sioux became allies, they would meet with each other in the western prairies when the Sioux in small number came to Cheyenne camps to beg for horses.

In the eighteen-nineties when Grinnell started collecting his data, memories of the then oldest living Cheyennes recalled their people as having been constantly at peace with the Sioux during their lifetimes, even allies against mutual foes. Grinnell, notwithstanding the documented evidence of Sioux - Cheyenne warfare, specifically that of Rufus Sage [1844] and official reports between 1835 and 1836, concluded that in his opinion if the Cheyennes ever fought the Sioux, then it was with the Assiniboine branch of that family who the Cheyennes recognized by their speech and dress as Yankton Sioux offshoots.

Not a few reports contemporary with the time of Sioux - Cheyenne hostility between circa, 1783 and the end of that century, alternatively speak of the two Nations being at war and peace almost in the same breath, as it were, and are so confusing and often contradictory in content that Grinnell should be excused for succumbing to information gleaned from the Cheyennes themselves who, though sometimes credulous in their historical knowledge, were consistent and exact in what they said. Since Grinnell`s time, however, much more information in the form of early journals and manuscripts have come to light; items which Grinnell had no way of consulting when writing his classic accounts of the Cheyenne. Nevertheless, it is not sufficient simply to dismiss his assumption upon this later evidence alone, neither is it advisable to accept random corroboration for the existence of Sioux - Cheyenne hostility without first analyzing the evidence on hand. In all fairness to Grinnell, and in order that readers might draw their own conclusion, a brief run-down both for and against the case in question will be given.

A contemporary of Grinnell, A. R. Odsell, stated in 1899 that those Cheyennes once occupying the Sheyenne River town in the Coteau Des Prairies east of the Missouri, had many battles with the Assiniboine Sioux, and the Rev. T. S. Williamson declared when writing about the Cheyenne settlement on the Yellow Medicine in Minnesota,

> "The Sioux who expelled the Iowas, a kindred race, made a league with the Cheyennes, who `though of a different origin, have ever been counted a part of the Dakota Nation." [6]

In addition, in his annotations to the James Mackay journal of the trip to the Missouri River Nations between 1786 and `87, John Hay wrote in 1803,

> "The Cheyenne or Shayen who formally lived on a tributary of the Red River of that name, were so harassed by the Assiniboine and Siouxs [sic] that they, (the Cheyennes) had to leave their village and go to the Missouri river." [7]

Grinnell quotes these sources in order to add validity to his assertion, and goes on to refer to Carver [1766], Trudeau [1795-96] and Henry [1806], each of whom speak of the friendship then in vogue between Cheyennes and Sioux to bare out his claim.

Probably Grinnell`s most authoritative companion in thought was George Bent, the educated half-breed who lived among the Cheyenne for more than fifty years until his death in

1918. His knowledge and integrity when relating Cheyenne history has been invaluable, yet even he declared that although Sioux traditions tell of attacks upon the Cheyenne,

"The attacks must have been petty ones for our people have no recollection of ever having been at war with the Sioux." [8]

That these Cheyenne informants of both Grinnell and Bent had no recollection of a Sioux - Cheyenne war is undoubtedly true, but not true of the whole tribe if we are to believe W .P .Clark`s assertion in 1885, that his Cheyenne informant Black-Pipe told him,

"Many years ago we (the Cheyenne) were at war with the Sioux, particularly the Wycheayelas, (all those of the `D` and `N` dialect)." [9] [These are Siouan speakers commonly known as the Dakota also called Santee, and the Yanktonai respectively].

Now we know that as early as 1770, these last named Eastern Sioux groups were ardently raiding the Missouri River Nations and all other tribes in the area both east and west of that river, and were still fighting the Suhtaio as late as 1804, when the Lewis and Clark expedition heard that Yankton had recently wiped out a war-party of "Kite" [Suhtaio] Indians in the Black Hills. The Tetons conversely, albeit continuing their encroachment west of the Missouri and remaining in close harmony with the Santee and Yanktonai from whom they obtained guns and ammunition at the head of the Minnesota, had themselves by circa, 1800, finally made peace with the Suhtaio, and the informant Black-Pipe, incidentally, had been a Suhtaio band member.

The French trader Pierre Antoine Tabeau was on the Upper Missouri among the Arickara between 1803 and 1805, and in his report penned a short time later, he asserted,

"This Nation (Cheyennes) was for a few years established on the Missouri, but having neither the patience nor the weakness of the Ricaras (sic) to endure the insults and vexations of the Sioux, it had to resort to open war. The Sioux always wandering, left little for capture to the enemy, who often knew not where to find them, and the Cheyennes settled there, were every day exposed, in spite of their superior courage, to some particular catastrophe. To lessen this disparity more, they abandoned agriculture and their hearths, and became a nomadic people. In a short time they reduced the warlike ardour of the Sioux, who willingly consented to a peace, which still exists. But since it is only the fruit of necessity, the truce is not very sincere and these two Nations live in mutual fear of treachery and always potentially in a state of war." [10]

More recent contradictions to both Grinnell and Bent`s informants can be had in the Sioux Chief Red Cloud`s autobiography [1997], the Black Elk interviews with Nierherdt [1984], the Casper Collins Letters [1965], the letters of A. P. Chouteau [1834/`35], the Charles LeRaye journal for 1801-`03 [1810], the Belden memoirs [1877] and the George Bushotter texts [unpublished], but translated in part from the Sioux by A. J. Dorsey and which in story 110 of the last named,

Cheyennes are referred to as enemies of the Lower Brule near the date 1835, when the Sioux were also fighting the Utes.

Of prime importance among these confirmatory sources, is a story contained in the traditional folklore of the Oglala and Brule Sioux, as opposed to the more chronologically precise winter-counts of those bands. In fact, these traditional tales often supplement some of the `count` entries or are the basis for them. The story has been alluded to in an earlier chapter, but is relevant at this point, and thus warrants more detailed inspection.

Two printed versions have appeared in print in somewhat varied form, but agreeing in all essential details. It is a story still recited by some older persons on one and more Lakota reservations today.

The first of these printed accounts was obtained by a Lieutenant Casper Collins whilst stationed at Fort Laramie on the North Platte in 1865, and was told him by a member of the Loafer band of Teton Sioux which itself, comprised a conglomerate of Oglala and Brule members, so-called because they spent most of their time "loafing" around in the vicinity of the aforesaid fort, begging handouts from the soldiers garrisoned there and from passing wagon trains of white emigrants. The tradition itself attempts to explain in a quazi-historical manner how the Teton Sioux became divided into so many different bands. It is not necessary to repeat the whole of the account, but only that part relevant to our study,

"In the first place the Sioux were a single Nation. They were then on the Missouri, near its junction with the Mississippi. When the Whites began to settle that country, they moved up towards the head of the latter, and there began making war against the Cheyennes. The latter, being small in numbers, were driven westward to the head of the Missouri on Powder River and the North Platte. In the meantime they had to fight the Crow, Kiowa, Arapahoe, Pawnee and Comanche, and by that means got horses…The Sioux and Cheyennes took many prisoners, one from another, and by that means they learned the languages of one another. The Sioux and Cheyennes both used dogs at that time and had no horses. Some of the Sioux prisoners, getting away, bore news to their people that the Cheyennes were willing to make peace. The Sioux sent emissaries that they were willing to make peace on certain grounds, which the Cheyennes agreed to…The first peace was made on Powder River or, as it is sometimes called, Cheyenne River. At that time the Sioux were governed by one chief, whose will was law. During the deliberations the children of the Sioux, playing about, made so much noise that they disturbed the chief. He ordered all of them away until the deliberations were over - some ten or fifteen miles.........After their parents had taken them and returned, it was nightfall. One of the Sioux young men ran off with a Cheyenne woman, the wife of one of the tribe. That broke up the council, the Cheyenne making a great outcry and demanding his wife back. The Sioux resisted and the chief, to prevent bloodshed, ordered the lodges to be taken down and the village to move. The Cheyenne chief did the same. They moved a long distance in contrary directions, each fearing an attack from the other. The children that were left, finding the time long, started for the camp. Those that reached the camp and found it was moved were frightened and told the others; then they started on the trail to overtake them. They mistook the trail and followed the Cheyennes. They did not find out their mistake until they were nearly on the camp, when they got frightened and returned. In the meantime the old people returned for them and found them gone. After searching diligently for them, they concluded that the Cheyennes had wiped them out and gave up the search in despair." [11]

The story goes on to recount how the " Lost children " managed to survive; how they grew up and by inter-marrying among themselves, became a small band in their own right. Finally, after fifteen years of wandering, they rediscovered their relatives who were still under the rule of the chief who had sent the children away in the first place. His name was Yellow Horse because he always rode a horse of that colour. In a fight which followed the meeting of the two bands, Yellow Horse was slain, and as no one chief could be decided upon to take his place, the two bands after having come together in friendship, divided into a number of smaller entities each led by a chief of their individual choosing, and in such a way, supposedly, the Teton Sioux became split into their seven component bands. The Collins account then continues by saying,

"The whole country was open to them, (i.e. the different bands.) All the old inhabitants having been driven away. The tribe called the Minnekorhues were the first to meet with the Cheyennes and intermarried with them." [12]

The second of these printed versions appears in the *"Autobiography of Red Cloud, War leader of the Oglala"* [1997]. The original manuscript was penned by Charles W. Allen in 1893 from information acquired from Sam Deon a friend of Red Cloud, and who in turn, had personally interviewed the old chief and obtained his stories through the medium of verbal conversation with Red Cloud himself. The result, therefore, especially concerning this version of "The Lost Children" is perhaps, third hand, if not actually fifth hand through the influence of later editors, and which might account for some glaring discrepancies when compared to the Collins` account quoted above. According to this Red Cloud version, the story in essence runs as follows,

"Many winters ago when I was a little boy, I often heard my grandfather, who was then a very old man, say that he had heard his father tell how the old men of the village would talk of the time long ago, when the Sioux lived far towards the east and were in one large village and under one chief. They had enemies to the south and Southwest of them who gave them great annoyance. It was necessary to keep detachments from their village posted on the outskirts of their territory, in that direction to fight these enemies back. From time to time these guardsmen and their families were regularly relieved and would return to the village. The bands taking their places would begin fresh onslaughts upon their enemies, who were gradually driven further away, until the Sioux following them finally established themselves in the country they occupied and returned not to the present band. But their absence decreased the strength of their village very little as it was a powerful one and under the leadership of a great chief by the name of Yellow Horse...On the west of the village was another strong tribe who called themselves "The Cut Fingers" but who were called by the Sioux, then and since the Cheyennes. The relation between these people and ours had been that of a watchful, suspicious peace which finally ended in war, in which our people were the victors. Having put the Cheyennes to route, they kept following them up. Every year they would fight them and drive them further west until finally, they had driven them across the Missouri River.It was not a war of extermination. They would take prisoners back and forth, and they seemed to have been fighting each other only for the reason that they had no other enemies to fight. But when they (The Sioux) crossed the Missouri river, they soon discovered that there were powerful tribes of Indians both to the north and west of them. The Sioux following the advice of their chief, The Yellow Horse, decided to quit fighting the Cheyennes and to make allies of them if possible. Accordingly messengers were sent to the Cheyenne village, among whom were fifteen of the fifty or more Cheyennes that the Sioux had long held as prisoners. After travelling four days they came to the Cheyenne village. The Sioux remaining at a distance, the Cheyenne prisoners went into the village and made known the object of their visit. They were received cordially. The Sioux were escorted in and feasted and entertained in a hospitable manner until the following day, when a council was held at which the Sioux stated that they had been sent by their chief, The Yellow horse, to ask the Cheyennes to move their village to a certain point midway between the two villages where they would be met by the Sioux village for the purpose of holding a great council that would have for its object the establishment of peace between the two tribes. The Cheyennes accepted the proposition and sent an escort of Sioux prisoners back with the messengers as an earnest indication of their intentions. At the appointed time and designated place the tribes met and set up their villages close to each other. The next day the great council lodge of the Sioux having been chosen as the place to deliberate, the council began with the Sioux chief, The yellow Horse and the Cheyenne chief, Long Bow, as the leading spirits. The first half of the day was spent in making speeches, The Yellow Horse telling the Cheyennes that they had been fighting so long that they had become well acquainted and that they were neighbours and that during their wars each side had taken so many prisoners that they were now not only neighbours but relations and that they were in a new country where their rights were liable to be disputed by powerful tribes and it would be better for them to remain near to each other and to fight together in the future. He was followed by Chief Long Bow and others, all of whom favored the idea, and it was soon decided that such arrangements should be effected." [13]

In reality, the story relates to the Oglala and Brule Sioux alone, and not to the Tetons as a whole, whose later band divisions broke away from the parent group during later and varying periods in time one from the other. The name "Long Bow" on the other hand, given in the above version, most probably refers to a type of Bow-Lance which the Cheyenne chief carried as the insignia of a particular warrior society, and perhaps, this was the same Cheyenne chief met by Trudeau in 1795 who he referred to as "The Lance." If so, it would indicate a rough working date for the peace council mentioned in the Red-Cloud version, which may then have occurred around the date 1800, when a lasting peace was indeed, effected between the Oglala and Brule on one side and Cheyenne-speaking peoples on the other.

By mentioning the separation of a part of the Sioux which then went southwest to occupy lands vacated by their Cut-Finger foes, the account agrees with what is known regarding the separation of the Brule [then a part of the Oglala] from the parent Santee Sioux.

The story as recited by Red-Cloud actually begins at a time when the Teton resided in the Mills Lac district of the Upper Mississippi where they were contacted by Louis Hennepin in 1680. By circa, 1700, however, when the trader LeSueur reached the Great Bend of the Minnesota at the mouth of Blue Earth River, a large Teton group was already entrenched around the headwaters of the Minnesota and Big Stone Lake, which because of its inhabitants, LeSueur named *Lac des Tintons* [sic]. The Sioux accounts would have us believe that this Teton movement southwest from the Upper Mississippi was a voluntary move, although, in truth, it was an expulsion, they having been evicted from the north by their old enemies the Cree and Chippewa at times aided by the Assiniboine.

Now for these Teton refugees to have occupied the Upper Minnesota country, they had first to expel resident peoples to the immediate south and southwest, and which then included the Iowa and Omaha and that Cheyenne-speaking group known as Pipe-Stem-Men then south of the Minnesota on the Yellow Medicine. This event is that referred to in the Red-Cloud story of fighting enemies towards the south and southwest, and of taking over that part of the country once the resident peoples had been evicted, an event which can be dated with some precision.

As explained in an earlier chapter, when residing adjacent to the Upper Minnesota, the Teton group from which later evolved the Brule and Oglala, allied themselves to their Yanktonai cousins and together, drove the Iowa from that river and the Omaha from the Loop of the Big Sioux. This was during the second half of the 1680s and thereafter in 1690, the same Tetons followed their retreating enemies, forcing them further southwest into the Lake Andes area and thence, Lower down the Big Sioux as far as that river's junction with the Missouri. As allies to the Omaha, the Pipe-Stem-Men Cheyennes were driven from the Yellow Medicine and likewise forced west, and finally reached the Missouri across from the mouth of White River at a point slightly north of the Omaha.

Ironically, these same Teton Sioux aggressors some years later, were themselves pushed out of the Minnesota country by their own relatives the Santee and Sisseton, and as a result they, too, fled southwest to the Lake Andes region, but which by then had already been vacated by the Omaha and their allies. This Teton occupation of the Lake Andes region began around the date

1725, and by 1750 these same Teton refugees had moved north along the east bank of the Missouri as far as the mouth of James River. From that point around the mid-1770s, they began crossing the Missouri, at first in small number when on hunting excursions and when raiding foreign tribes in the Western Plains.

This then is the period referred to in Cheyenne tradition, when small parties of Sioux on foot and as supplicants, came west of the Missouri at intervals to beg horses from the Cheyennes. Not until after the great Smallpox epidemic of 1781 /`82, did these same Teton Sioux now on horseback and armed with guns, attempt permanent occupation on that river`s west side.

The fact that the story of "The Lost Children" mentions that those Sioux groups at war with Cheyennes were mounted and residing permanently west of the Missouri, cannot then date the event earlier than 1782, if indeed, not a few years later.

From the evidence at hand, it thus appears that the actual Cheyenne-speaking people at war with the Sioux during the last quarter of the 1700s were Suhtaio and Pipe-Stem Men, and were the only Cheyenne-speaking peoples involved.

The Suhtaio once known as *Chongaskitons* or Dog People, were also known as Cut-Arms and Cut-Fingers due to their singular custom of amputating either the arm or fingers of their slain enemies, and had, at a much earlier date, resided in close proximity with both Cheyenne-proper bands and with Sioux groups in the Upper Mississippi country. At that time all tribes of the region were suffering diabolically from Cree, Assiniboine and Chippewa attacks with their deadly Thunder sticks, and eventually, the Suhtaio had been forced to abandon their hearths completely and flee towards the west. At a later date, hostile pressure from the same gun-toting enemies also obliged the Sioux to move from the region, whereupon some bands thereafter, crossed the Red River of the North and moved deep into the eastern Coteau country, and this at a time when the Changaskitons, i.e. Suhtaio, were still located in that same region, according to the Jonathan Carver report of 1768.

It was around the same date of 1768, however, that the Sisseton and Santee Eastern Sioux aided by the Yanktonai, suddenly also advanced west from the Upper Minnesota and after crossing Red River began harassing all the resident tribes in the Coteau country among whom were their erstwhile neighbours the Suhtaio. Soon after this, the Oglala and Brule Teton bands who, initially, had also been on the receiving end of Santee and Yanktonai aggression, made peace with the latter, and thereafter joined their Eastern Sioux cousins in raiding the Suhtaio. Conversely, the Cheyenne-proper bands of Masikota, Aorta and Omissis then along and west of the Missouri, were immune from this spate of Teton hostility, although they did suffer at times from the latter`s Santee, Sisseton and Yanktonai allies.

As a result, the Suhtaio themselves were forced to flee further west following the north bank of the Missouri in order to escape the Sioux, and it is this movement which was alluded to in 1829, when the then Secretary of War, Peter Porter, previously cited, reported that Cheyennes [Omissis and evidently including the Suhtaio], had been driven west from Red River by the Sioux in 1771.

Coupled to this is the assertion from no less an authority than the Santee born Reverend Charles Eastman, who for many years lived and worked among various Dakota or Eastern Sioux bands, that it was the Sioux who drove the Cheyennes west to and across the Missouri.

The Cheyennes and Suhtaio, of course, deny all this, and like the Sioux describe the abandonment of their old homes in the east and their relocation west of the Missouri as a voluntary exodus, when in reality, it was an expulsion in every sense of the term.

Once the Suhtaio crossed the Missouri, the Tetons abated their hostility somewhat, until that is, the Tetons themselves crossed that river with a view to permanent occupation in the Western prairies, and when their number had increased sufficiently, they regenerated their war with the Suhtaio in order to secure their foothold. Predominantly then, this new outbreak of hostilities with the Sioux which began, ostensibly, around the date 1783, was a Suhtaio affair, although during the feud, it is likely that some Cheyennes such as the Pipe-Stem Men could not but help becoming involved, if only sporadically due to their recent re-confederation with the Suhtaio.

The "Lost Children" account does offer clues which allow us to roughly date this later period of Sioux-Cheyenne warfare west of the Missouri by the assertions that, [1] horses are mentioned and inferred as then being in some quantity among the Sioux bands involved, [2] the reference to the use of guns, [3] the Sioux in question were permanent residents west of the Missouri at a time, we might add, when the Brule Sioux according to their own testimony, had not long before broken away from the parent Oglala band.

Now according to the Baptiste Good Brule Sioux Winter-Count, the term *"Sichangu"* or Burned Thighs, to give the full name, did not come into use until 1765 or thereabouts, owing to a great prairie fire in that year which had burned the legs of their people, and prior to which they had been one group with the Oglala. The current traditional story of the Brule` receiving their name is relevant at this point, as it, too, indicates at least an intermittent hostile relationship between Cheyennes and Teton Sioux during that period of time.

The story goes that a war-party of Oglala probably allied to the Yanktonai Sioux, had attacked a Cheyenne village and in the event, the Cheyennes set light to the prairie grass and the Sioux were obliged to flee from the fast moving flames which the wind fanned in their direction. The flames, however, rapidly overtook the Sioux who were on foot, and many among them suffered severe burns to their legs. Upon reaching Long Lake they jumped into the waters at that place and thereby escaped the flames. This event must have occurred on the east side of the Missouri not far from Long Lake in the tall-grass prairies of the Coteau, and the Cheyenne village referred to would have been that occupied by Cheyennes later known as the Aorta band, who`s village then stood near Long Lake on the east side of the Missouri, across from where the town of Fort Yates now stands.

By 1768, however, the Brule had finalized their split from the Oglala and after taking the name Burned Thighs which their French contacts rendered as Brule, they aligned themselves with a Ponca band which must have been the *Mawhaws* [i.e. Omaha offshoots] met by Carver in the vicinity of Big Stone Lake in 1767. By what name the Oglala were then documented is undetermined, but perhaps, they were the "Ojestpoitens" earlier noted by LeSueur as residing in the vicinity of the Upper Minnesota in 1700. More important, however, is at a later date one band of Brule had the name "Orphans," dubbed upon it by other Brule bands after the destruction of their chief, Little-Thunder's village and his people, by American troops in 1855. My own informant Bear-Comes-Running, a Miniconjou Sioux, believes the term `Orphans` was originally a band name among the Brule of a much earlier time owing to their separation from the Oglala parent band, but which had fell into disuse until restored after the calamity attending Little-Thunder's people. Possibly then, the original band of `Orphans` had been composed of the "Lost Children" of tradition or their descendants, and who, so the story asserts, became a band in their own right. This, of course, is conjecture, but Red-Cloud's father was a Brule, and his story was associated moreover with the Brule Sioux, rather than the Oglala or any other Teton band, albeit that these other bands at a later date, also had sub-bands among themselves known as `Orphans,` but for various other and diverse reasons.

All this serves to show that the people referred to as Cheyennes and Cut-Fingers in the two accounts are indeed, our subjects the Cheyenne, or more specifically, the Suhtaio and Pipe-Stem Men, and further, that there can be no doubt that a new period of warfare did exist between these two Cheyenne-speaking groups and the Teton Sioux during the last quarter of the eighteenth century.

Of the early English, French and Spanish-speaking traders on the Upper Missouri who were in contact with both Cheyennes and Sioux, none were in any doubt as to the people they were referring to in their letters and journals regarding this particular period of warfare between the two, and being on the ground, so to speak, they could comment from their own experience and firsthand knowledge of contemporary events.

Thus in 1795 whilst residing among the Arickara on the Upper Missouri, the French Canadian trader Jean Baptist Trudeau implied that war was then in progress between the Cheyennes and Sioux, and American Horse, an Oglala, confirmed this period of friction which evidently continued throughout 1795-96 to 1798-99 in his winter-count entries for those years.

Added to this, are comments in the Charles LeRaye journal of his `supposed` travels in the Upper Missouri country between 1801 and 1803, perhaps derived from information relating to a slightly earlier date and supplied by other white traders and trappers in the country at that time, but which states,

"...*The Chien or Dog Indians are at war with the Sioux.*" [14]

Here LeRaye must have been referring to the Suhtaio as shown by the alternative name of `Dog Indians,` while in a latter passage, he mentions that the Sioux and Dog Indians were then camped together at one of the Arickara villages near the mouth of Cheyenne River and from there, LeRaye and the Indians moved north to what is now Beaver Creek. Again this must refer to the Suhtaio, but then in harmony with that Saoni Sioux group of combined Miniconjou and Two-Kettle Saoni and some Cheyennes, these last being the remnant band of Masikota once resident around Big Stone Lake, as will be explained in the following chapter. Suffice to say, those particular Cheyennes comprising the Masikota, Omissis and Aorta-Moiseo remained at peace with the

Tetons, even while the Oglala and Brule continued to war with the Suhtaio and Pipe-Stem Men Cheyenne-speaking groups.

There are indeed several additional contemporary reports which mention, or at least, allude to this period of hostility between Cheyenne-speaking peoples and the Sioux, such as that penned by the traveler Perin Du Lac who, in 1802, wrote that the Sioux,

"… Who are deceitful and cruel, often plunder the Ricaras and Chaguiennes of clothes and horses, and the Mandan of maize and tobacco." [1]

Suffice to say, probably our most conclusive evidence pertaining to Cheyenne–Sioux warfare are the various Teton Sioux "Winter-Counts," wherein are contained a number of references to this particular spate of conflict during the late 1700s. That these "counts" are historically correct and for the most part, accurately dated, is apparent when cross-checked with actual contemporary documented data and thus, by taking these recorded incidents to form a basis, a satisfactory resume of Teton Sioux hostilities against Cheyenne-speaking peoples during the period in question can be deduced.

It must be concluded nevertheless, that this war; even though certainly extant, was interrupted by truces of varying duration and was, in its early phase, rarely conducted to the extent that the complete destruction of the enemy was contemplated, and that most episodes regarding these hostilities which have come down to us are, seemingly, petty incidents as George Bent himself asserted. Be this as it may, at least two episodes of the war do indicate it being slightly more than just a past-time as the Red Cloud narrative appears to suggest. One should therefore, take such episodes not to convey the triviality of the conflict by what incidents we know, but its growing escalation by taking them as characteristic of many other such episodes, the details of which are not known, but which undoubtedly took place.

If indeed more evidence is needed, in 1913 the popular author S. M .Barret published the life story of a Southern Cheyenne woman named ` Hoistah.` According to the published account, this woman had died about 1875 having been born in the year 1800, although an analysis of content suggests her birth occurred a few years earlier about 1795 or`96. It is said, however, that Hoistah was born at the time a Cheyenne war party was out against the Sioux. In fact, Hoistah had received her name which means "bright light," in commemoration of the signal fires which the victorious Cheyenne war-party had lit to advertise its return to camp. There appears no reason to doubt this part of Barrett`s narrative, even though some other episodes therein are inserted incorrectly in their chronological order, and others are perhaps tainted with poetic license. The important thing here, is that the Sioux and not Assiniboine are indicated as having been the specific enemy in question. The dating of the event fits nicely with that given by American Horse for this same period of Sioux - Cheyenne warfare, which is also substantiated by Sioux oral tradition and documentation relating to the Upper Missouri country at that time.

It is true that the Sioux often also used the term "Shi-e-ena" to designate all foreign peoples and more especially, enemies, whose proper tribal appellation was unknown, but the statement by

Red-Cloud that the enemy he was specifically referring to were also known as "Cut-Fingers," was a name conferred at a later date by the Sioux upon the Cheyennes, although in earlier years had been used to designate the Suhtaio alone. The fact is then, that while some bands of Teton Sioux were at war with the Suhtaio and Pipe-Stem Men, the Tetons; generally speaking, remained tentatively at peace with all other Cheyenne-speaking bands.

Such is apparent when one recalls that Cheyennes had long been associated with certain Saoni Teton groups and, as explained in a previous chapter, were evidently those who Jonathan Carver mentioned as located west of the Upper Minnesota and who he termed *Shian, Shianese, Chongaskiton* and *Waddapawjestin.* So friendly and intimate were the latter with Sioux bands at that time, that Carver considered them members of the Sioux Nation. Certainly from an earlier date and until the turn of the eighteenth century, the Cheyennes were fully engaged in a determined war against the Assiniboine, while at the same time, they were in a league with the Miniconjou and Two Kettle Teton Sioux bands who then were fighting the same enemy. Thus these Sioux and Cheyennes having a common interest, had often hunted and roamed together when inhabiting the eastern Coteau country. However, continuing pressure from the north, coupled with a sudden spate of aggression from the Santee, Sisseton and Yanktonai, had finally obliged these particular Cheyenne and Saoni bands to vacate that country altogether as a permanent habitat, and seek refuge west of the Missouri. The *Chongaskitons,* i.e. Suhtaio, for their part, after crossing the river later moved out along the Missouri on its north side and eventually, established themselves across from the mouth of the Yellowstone. From this location the Suhtaio now allied to the Pipe-Stem Men, began foraying against the Crows and Snakes in competition for the rich hunting lands embracing the Lower Powder and the Yellowstone, but with the Black Hills Tribes the Suhtaio were at peace and became staunch allies to both the Kiowa and Arapahoe, who being themselves at war with the Sioux, naturally brought the Suhtaio and Pipe-Stem Men into the same conflict. With the Hidatsa and Mandan the Suhtaio were intermittingly at peace or at war, depending how they felt at any given time, but at the same time, both the Suhtaio and Pipe-Stem Men grew somewhat aloof from all other Cheyenne-speaking bands between Grand River and the Big Cheyenne.

- 0 - 0 - 0 - 0 - 0 - 0 - 0 - 0 - 0 - 0 - 0 - 0 - 0 - 0 - 0 - 0 - 0 -

CHAPTER 40.

HOME AT LAST, and WAR AND PEACE WITH THE TETONS.

The acquisition of guns and ammunition obtained at Eastern Sioux Trading Fairs on the Upper Minnesota, coupled with a comparatively small loss of population during the smallpox of 1781 / `82, had given the Teton Sioux a profound advantage over their western enemies. This resulted in a further Teton migration en masse from the Coteau district and across the Missouri into the short-grass buffalo country, then claimed by the River Tribes and the Cheyenne and Suhtaio.

In previous years, certain bands among the Tetons, particularly those known as Oglala and Brule, had crossed the Missouri at intervals in order to hunt and raid enemies, but until now there had been no serious attempt to take up permanent residence in the west. All the while, that is, the River Tribes of Mandan, Arickara and Omaha had remained strong enough to oppose them and controlled as they did, the few river crossings available. However, all the River Tribes and particularly the Mandan and Arickara whose Earth-Lodge villages stood in direct line of the Teton advance, had suffered diabolically in the recent contagion, perhaps two-thirds of their entire populations having been carried away. Thus numerically weak and demoralized, rather than oppose this new influx of foreign peoples into their hunting grounds, they endeavoured to accommodate them. At first both the Mandan and Arickara occasionally ferried the migrants across the Missouri in their bull-boats, while at other times, the Teton Sioux came to their towns as pedestrian supplicants, crossing the river on the ice before the spring thaw in order to trade their metal artefacts from the east in exchange for horses, corn, tobacco and garden produce. All too often these visits, although initially welcomed by the townspeople, culminated in friction usually at the instigation of the Sioux, who, after finishing their trade and having feasted to excess on the larders of their hosts, all at once shed their veil of complacency and lording their sense of superiority, became arrogant and aggressive and attempt to take whatever else they wanted by force of arms. Bloody battles were sometimes fought outside the towns before the Sioux finally moved off into the short-grass prairies to spend the summer and autumn months hunting game and raiding enemies further west. They then returned east to James River and the headwaters of the Minnesota, where they customarily spent the winter months with their Santee and Sisseton relatives, and seeking protection from the inclement season in the thick timber country of that region.

Whatever the endeavours of the River Tribes, either with battle-axe or Calumet of peace, they alone could not hope to stem the inroads of the Sioux and by 1785, the Tetons were flooding across the Missouri at three points.

At two points between the mouths of the Moreau and Big Cheyenne north of the Arickara towns, two separate Teton groups advanced, generally known as Saoni Sioux during these early years. The more northern of these Saoni then including those later known as Sans Arc and Siasapa [Blackfoot] Sioux, crossed the Missouri unopposed and moved in a north-westerly direction along the Cannonball, whilst below them the second Saoni group comprising Miniconjou and Two Kettle bands advanced due west along the Big Cheyenne. At the same time a third more southerly Teton-proper group advanced west below the Arickara, and comprised the Oglala and Brule who had crossed the Missouri at a place now called Sioux crossing near the mouth of Crow Creek below the Missouri's Great Bend. Once established on the Missouri's west side, they went their separate ways and encroached further west, the Oglala following the course of Bad [Teton] River upstream, while those of the Brule moved out along the White.

The northernmost Saoni bands which finally settled along both sides of the Cannonball and Grand River southeast of the Mandan towns, apparently incurred little resentment from the inhabitants of the prairie country they were encroaching into, for we have no record in tribal traditions of serious trouble with those Masikota, Aorta and Omissis Cheyennes who were then roaming as far west as the headwaters country of the Little Missouri, and seasonally visited their fields adjacent to the old earth-lodge villages on Dirt Lodge Creek and the Grand.

This seems to have been the case also regarding that Saoni group comprised of Miniconjou and Two Kettle, who being west of the Arickara, occupied country along the Lower course of the Big Cheyenne, albeit still claimed by one or more Cheyenne-speaking band whose people continued to frequent their town on Cherry Creek and also, albeit sporadically, the two old villages at the mouth of Cheyenne River. Certainly by the turn of the eighteenth century, these particular Cheyenne groups were actually allied to the Miniconjou and Two Kettle Sioux in joint offensives against the Crows and Snakes.

The Oglala and Brule on the other hand, certainly the wildest and most belligerent of all these migrant Sioux were, from the start, engaged in constant warfare with the Arickara and intermittingly with the Mandan and Hidatsa higher up the Missouri. At the same time these two Sioux groups were in enmity with all the Black Hills Tribes including the Suhtaio, which was a situation peculiar to this southern sphere of Teton infiltration. The reason for this was simple. The Oglala and Brule had known the Suhtaio for many generations. At least as far back as when the Suhtaio had lived in the vicinity of Big Stone Lake and even earlier, when resident in the Upper Mississippi district. Generally speaking, during their many years of contact they had been on good terms with each other, even though periods of warfare had from time to time erupted between the two. Here, however, were these same Suhtaio hunting and fighting alongside the Black Hills Tribes which included the Arapahoe and Kiowa among others, who were sworn enemies of the Sioux. The Suhtaio were also regularly visiting the Arickara towns to trade horses, iron weapons and furs to the very people who, in years past, had come regularly on horseback carrying heavy Buffalo-lances tipped with Spanish sword blades in order to terrorize Sioux peoples east of the Missouri. Mercilessly they had slaughtered Sioux menfolk and carried off their women and children into captivity. The Oglala and Brule had long memories and did not easily forgive.

It is also apparent that at this period in their history, the Suhtaio were going through a character change. They now possessed a plentiful supply of horses; could acquire all the metal blades and domestic artefacts of European manufacture for which they had need from allies who traded with Spanish merchants in the south, and also corn and other horticultural foodstuffs from the Missouri River Tribes. Perhaps, more importantly, not having lost their manpower in the smallpox scourge of `81-`82, they held a prominent position in the balance of power in and around the Black Hills, so that no longer were they the timid folk, harassed from one hunting ground to another.

Indeed, the Suhtaio now held the Upper hand in their conflicts with the once dreaded Assiniboine, and declare that the last woman taken captive from them by those people had occurred in 1786, she being the wife of a then young Suhtai warrior known as Cinemo or Tobacco who at a later-date, became a famous chief among his people. Thus each autumn the Suhtaio, often in company with their Arapahoe and Kiowa confederates, went brazenly and unafraid to the Arickara and Mandan villages, sauntering leisurely back and forth over the grasslands between the Black Hills and Missouri, defying any foe to match them. The Sioux must have sensed this new-found arrogance of their erstwhile neighbours, and realized that if they were to face serious resentment from the Western Tribes, it was the Cheyenne-speaking Suhtaio who were likely to promote it. Tension there undoubtedly was, and a struggle for power imminent.

The Sioux, of course, were no less arrogant, and since the decimation by smallpox of the Arickara and Mandan, there remained no barrier to Teton expansion across the Missouri. The River Nations, once powerful adversaries, could now only hold their own when fighting from within the protection of their palisade towns. Indeed, the Oglala and Brule and even those Saoni groups to the north after taking up permanent residence west of the Missouri, soon found it easier and far more profitable to simply rob the River Nations of their produce rather than barter for it. But still these Sioux invaders could not obtain all the horses they required from the Arickara and Mandan alone. At such times when the latter's towns were attacked, their horses were herded inside the palisades, and at night ushered into the very lodges of their owners. When the Sioux "Came down" they could merely storm the palisades with futile charges; ransack the fields and show their spite by burning everything they could not carry away.

It is conceivable that Suhtaio in large or small number had been present at one or another River Town during one of their many trading excursions when the Sioux attacked, and possibly, had suffered casualties along with their hosts. Likewise, Suhtaio may have been with Kiowa, Gattacka or Arapahoe when Sioux raiders assaulted the Black Hills Tribes and would, therefore, offer good reason for an outbreak of hostilities between the Suhtaio and Sioux at this time. The fact, however, that these Plains-dwelling Suhtaio owned large numbers of horses was, in truth, probably all the incentive the Sioux needed to aggravate the situation. Why should the Sioux with their guns and new found prowess, humble themselves to beg horses as once they had been obliged to do when now they could take them by force? It was not expedient for the Sioux to trade, when their only exchange articles of value as far as the Suhtaio were concerned, were guns and ammunition, for to supply the Suhtaio with such items was risking the chance of directly or indirectly arming Sioux enemies in the Black Hills, or even the River Tribes with whom the Suhtaio were then on friendly terms.

What the inaugurating incident was which plunged this age-old Suhtaio -Sioux relationship into open hostility with each other, we cannot know, neither can it be determined if Suhtaio first attacked Sioux or Sioux first attacked the Suhtaio. But this is not important. It is obvious from the above analysis that a number of circumstances common to both parties exacerbated the situation into an inevitable climax, which to the Indian mind could only be resolved through war.

So it was as regards the southern Teton group comprised of Oglala and Brule, whose habitat now embraced the Bad and White River south of the Arickara, that their old-time friendship with the Suhtaio evaporated, while the Suhtaio themselves saw these Sioux peoples as interlopers and antagonists. It should also be noted that as the Suhtaio were now too far west to be bothered much by the Assiniboine and Cree; who were still largely pedestrian, they did not need Sioux allies to assist them on that front.

It was a similar situation regarding the Pipe-Stem Men Cheyennes then roaming the Niobrara River country in northern Nebraska. The Pipe-Stem Men were regular visitors to their friends in the Black Hills among whom were the Suhtaio, and to the trading fairs held in that region. As noted in earlier chapters of this study, the Pipe-Stem Men had long been enemies of the Sioux and thus because of their alliance with the Suhtaio and others among the Hill Tribes, and more especially, their continuing friendship with the Omaha and Oto of the eastern Nebraska Plains, it is not surprising that they, too, became fully engaged in warring against the Oglala and Brule who were now carrying their aggression deep into the western country.

As regards the Cheyenne-proper bands between the Big Cheyenne and the Black Hills, it was a reverse situation. When the Oglala and Brule began spreading out along the Bad and White River, they again met their old-time friends the Masikota, Aorta and Omissis from who these Sioux had earlier received their first horses as gifts. As the latter were then still ardently fighting the Assiniboine they and the Sioux made common cause which, thereby, allowed these Cheyennes to continue obtaining guns and metal weapons from the Oglala and Brule who were regularly visiting their eastern Yankton and Sisseton kinsmen at the latter`s own trading fairs, by then re-located on James River closer to the Missouri.

The fact then, as explained in the previous chapter, is that while some bands of Sioux were at war with Cheyenne-speaking peoples, i.e., the Suhtaio and Pipe-Stem Men, all other Cheyenne-bands remained at peace.

Thus the aforementioned assertions by George Grinnell and T. S. Williamson that the Siouan-speaking enemies fighting Cheyennes at this time were the Assiniboine alone, is true when referring to the Masikota, Aorta and Omissis Cheyennes between the Cannonball and Grand River and in the Little Missouri region, but which statements should not be used to include the Suhtaio and Pipe-Stem Men. The eventual integration of all the scattered Cheyenne and Suhtaio bands into one united cohesive entity and, as a consequence, the amalgamation of each bands` individual history and traditions, is what has since confused the issue, i.e., that as war with the Teton Sioux involved only those Cheyennes predominantly of Suhtaio and Pipe-Stem Men affiliation, memory of such a conflict soon became clouded over by that of the longer-lasting peaceful relationship between the Tetons and all other Cheyenne-speaking bands.

Regarding events of the war, it is recorded in the Oglala winter-count of Left-Heron for the year 1782, that Cheyennes slaughtered each other`s horses owing to a spate of anger or jealousy between them. The fact that the Sioux chose to record the event, suggests they were present in the Cheyenne camp on that occasion, and previously at peace with the Cheyennes. It may have been, though, that the said altercation was between the Sioux and Cheyennes, thereby triggering the slaughter of animals either belonging to, or recently given as gifts or traded to the Sioux, and had been the inaugurating incident culminating in the outbreak of the Cheyenne–Sioux war at this period. It seems, in fact, to be a reference to the same episode referred to by the Oglala Black-Elk [previously cited, see page 452], who stated that war first broke out between the Cheyennes and Sioux after a disagreement during an event of trading horses.

It must also be remembered that in the above and following references in the winter-counts relating to this war, the enemy are designated by the collective name `Cheyenne` when, in reality, the enemy in question were either Suhtaio or Pipe-Stem Men. Having said this, for convenience sake the term `Cheyenne` will be used in the following so to render the Sioux accounts in their verbatim form. Thus the same Left-Heron `count `quoted above, further tells us that in the following year of 1783, there was a big battle between Cheyennes and Sioux [Oglala] and in the event, a Cheyenne warrior or chief draped in a scarlet blanket was killed by the Sioux. [2]

The next important conflict between Sioux and Cheyennes according to the winter-counts, occurred around 1785, and was recorded in the `count` of the Brule Sioux Baptist Good also known as Brown-Hat, under the heading for that year, "Shadow`s Father Killed." This man "Shadow" had been an important warrior among the Teton Sioux, perhaps a chief and, apparently, had received his name because of a white man`s umbrella which he carried, in all likelihood the first of such items to come among his band. The circumstances leading to Shadow`s father`s untimely demise and what action was taken as a result, is not determined, and the event must merely be taken as it stands, that Cheyennes slew him.

Again according to the Left-Heron `count,` we are further informed that two years later in 1787, an Oglala Sioux chief by the name of Blue-Blanket was killed by Cheyennes, albeit east of the Missouri River in what is now Walworth County, South Dakota, near a stream ever since known as "Blue-Blanket Creek."

It is likely that a truce was effected not long after this event, as the `counts` are silent regarding any further hostilities between the two peoples in question for the rest of that decade. That truces were not infrequently made during these years of Cheyenne–Sioux warfare, is substantiated by W. P. Clark`s Suhtaio informant Black-Pipe who stated,

> "Peace would be made, they [Sioux] would hold out the pipe to us and smilingly and apparently with sincere intentions say, "let us be friends." But time and again treacherously broke their promise." [3]

Baptist Good`s Winter-count,

"Shadow`s father killed," 1785/`86.

The arrow touching the umbrella
Indicates "attacked" and the three
vertical strokes convey the Cheyenne
tribe, symbolizing "striped" or "Cut-Arms."
The arrow connecting with the figure`s
abdomen with a splash of red at the point
of entry, tells us that the man was killed.

Indeed, in order to pursue offensives against other enemies, the Tetons needed guns and ammunition which gave them the advantage over the bow and arrow using Black Hills Tribes, and the only articles of commerce acceptable to white traders from whom the Sioux obtained such weapons, were slaves and furs, moreover, beaver pelts, an abundance of which could then be found in Cheyenne country along the Big Cheyenne and its tributaries and in the Black Hills region. Because the Brule and Oglala were not then strong enough west of the Missouri to take possession of Cheyenne hunting grounds by force of arms; peace was a necessity, all the while that is, the Teton were obliged to rely upon the ever-dwindling stock of game and fur-bearing animals east of the Missouri. Only through trade could these Sioux obtain the required pelts and so, it might be assumed, the Suhtaio along with the Pipe-Stem Men themselves had actually been the instigators of regenerating, or at the least of intensifying the war with the Sioux at this time. The Suhtaio and Pipe-Stem Men had little to lose, while the Sioux without an adequate supply of guns and horses, would have lost the impetus and with it their advantage over their numerous western foes.

Such a situation, however, was not to last. As Teton numbers and prowess continued to increase, they themselves were willing to risk further aggression in order to control the Black Hills, and if there had been a hiatus in hostilities, then certainly by 1790, Sioux warfare with the Suhtaio and Pipe-Stem Men was, once again, being conducted in earnest.

According again to the aforementioned Left-Heron winter-count, it was the year 1790 when there occurred another battle between Cheyennes and Sioux, and during which one among the Cheyennes whilst he and his comrades were in retreat, accidently stubbed his toe and fell to the ground. The pursuing Sioux came up and killed him before he could rise to his feet, although if he had not stubbed his toe, say the Sioux, he could have escaped along with the rest of his comrades.

In that same year also, an Oglala named Picket-Pin went on a raid against Cheyennes and brought home many horses. The Oglala Cloud-Shield gave the chronology for this episode in his `count` for the winter of 1790 -`91. His reason for recording the event may have been due to the great number of horses captured and therefore, worthy of mention, or because such animals were then still comparatively few among the Sioux. It could, though, just as well be that Picket-Pin`s raid was the inaugurating incident which sparked a new period of conflict with Cheyennes and thus memorable, it being unusual to raid Cheyennes at that time. [4]

This man Picket-Pin had been a brave warrior and had killed enemies as shown by his face paint, a black band covering his Lower face and neck. Again we have no further information concerning this man or of the raid and its consequences, if any, and are left with a gap in the war`s continuity of four years before the next episode to mention `Cheyennes` is recorded.

Throughout these `counts` as regards the military aspect, only raids in which important persons had been killed, important battles fought or when large numbers of horses had been stolen are usually recorded, unless the event itself had been considered unique, such as the first mule seen, the first white man met, or the first fight with an enemy tribe.

As it was, the opening of the decade 1790 saw the beginnings of a great upheaval of tribes in the Plains west of the Missouri, and there can be no doubt that Teton Sioux were the instigators as their offensives began reaching out like tentacles over the western country; northwest as far as the Little Missouri and southwest to the Niobrara and the Black Hills and beyond. Sioux influence soon became apparent to peoples far removed from their sphere of wandering and most particularly, to the Snakes, Crows, Utes and Comanche. Teton war-parties both mounted and on foot, began rampaging over a wide area, attacking virtually anyone they met. So consistent and aggressive did the Sioux become towards all the Black Hills Tribes, that the Yamparika Comanche recall that an

Cloud-Shield's Winter-count,

"Picket-pin went against Cheyennes." 1790 / '91.

A picket pin is attached by a line to the figure indicating the warrior's name, and also, that it was he who stole the horses on this occasion. In this case vertical lines to denote the Cheyenne tribe are absent, but the cross symbol serves the same purpose.

entire camp of their people was wiped out by Sioux during this period in time, and we are further told in reliable Kiowa tradition, that a whole band of Kiowa namely that of the Kuato, was likewise around this date, totally destroyed by the Sioux. As a result around the date 1790 the Kiowa divided into two groups, the southern Kiowa moving south of the Platte in the wake of the retreating Comanche, and the Northern Kiowa or `Cold Men` remaining tentatively in and around the Black Hills. It was because of the disaster befalling the Kuato and to Sioux aggression in general, which had actually accelerated half the Kiowa tribe in vacating their lands and migrating south to escape the Sioux, rather than following their Comanche enemies merely to continue their harassment of them.

A serious affair involving Cheyennes seems to have taken place during this same period, and was recorded by Rufus B. Sage in an account of his travels published in 1855.

When among the Brule Sioux some years earlier in 1842, Sage was told by an old Brule chief that more than a generation past, his people had then been at war with the Scarred-Arms and with whom they fought with varied success for many years. The old chief went on to say that at one time a Brule war-party went west on a raid against the Cheyenne, but on its return journey, the party was ambushed by Cheyennes and almost wiped out. Only six Brule managed to escape and eventually took refuge in a cave in the side of a mountain close by the headwaters of Old Woman Creek in what is now Niobrara County, Wyoming. Here the fugitives remained for some time until the pursuing Cheyennes gave up their search, after which the survivors set out for their home camp which they safely reached in due course. Not long after this, a large Brule force went against the Cheyennes for revenge. The Sioux came upon the Cheyennes encamped at the base of the same mountain in which was the cave wherein the original vanquished Brule survivors had previously used as a refuge. The Sioux attacked the Cheyennes at that place and were victorious, taking thirty-five Cheyenne scalps in the process.

The next serious event in this Cheyenne-Teton war appears to have occurred in the Sioux calendar year of 1795 /`96 as recorded in the American-Horse winter-count. In this event, it is said that a Brule war-party led by a brave and popular warrior named Owner-of-Flute, started out against the Black Hill`s Tribes, although for what reason and against which specific tribe we are not told. Somewhere on the open Plains the party was surprised by a large body of Cheyennes and as a result, Owner-of-Flute was killed and his followers almost annihilated.

In response, the Brule carried word of the disaster to their kinfolk the Oglala, and a grand crusade was organized by the combined bands to go against the Cheyennes and avenge Owner-of-Flute. At the same time of the aforesaid crusade, a band of Cheyennes [Suhtaio?] was encamped just south of the Black Hills near a place since known as Rawhide Butte. The camp itself comprised some fifty-eight lodges, the occupants of which had recently conducted a successful buffalo hunt. All around were buffalo hides staked out on the ground ready for fleshing, while the lodges themselves were full of prime robes and skins of various other animals. In their busy state, the people had no inclination of the grand enemy host coming against them.

The Oglala and Brule had no difficulty locating the camp, and as their own force grossly outnumbered that of the Cheyennes, they surrounded the camp and took it by surprise. It must have been a bloody battle that ensued, for hardly any Cheyennes escaped the musket balls and tomahawks of the vengeful Sioux. Men, women and children were cut down and slaughtered indiscriminately, their bodies then stripped, scalped and mutilated in a most fiendish manner. Of the Cheyenne non-combatants escaping death, they were taken into captivity along with many captured ponies, while the lodges themselves were looted of everything of value and then set ablaze.

American-Horse Winter-Count,

"Owner-of-Flute Was Killed." 1795/`96.

The red patch on the head signifies the man was scalped, and the bow extending from the crown, that he had been slain by an arrow, although the tee-like mark below the shoulder also denotes a gun shot wound. The flute has sound waves issuing from its end and is connected to the figure by a line to convey that it belonged to him, and if the four markings on it are not flute holes, then it bears the symbolic markings denoting `Cheyennes.`

Among the Cheyenne warriors who had fallen during the fight, one was particularly noticeable by having his hair bound up in two large deer-hide sacks one on each side of his head, and which when opened, exposed a great profusion of hair wound around in coils and of which, the Sioux say, when unwound measured the length of a lodge pole. The victorious Sioux scalped this man and proudly displayed the long tresses attached to the end of a willow wand. This unusual

American-Horse Winter-Count.

[1796 / '97]

"A Long-haired enemy was killed."

The flowing scalp represents the long hair of the enemy killed, and although no stripe marks or crosses are included to indicate the man killed had belonged to the Cheyennes, the figure holding the willow-wand with scalp attached, is depicted in being specifically Sioux.

Baptist Good`s Winter-count.
1793 – 1794.
"Killed a long-haired man at Rawhide Butte."

Cloud-Shield's Winter-count.
1786 – 1787.
"Long-Hair was killed."

discovery gave its name to the event in the winter-counts of several Teton bands, albeit that their own warriors had not been part of the attacking force on that occasion. In addition, the vast quantity of buffalo robes and other skins taken as booty by the Sioux, inspired the latter to name a nearby eminence at the base of which had stood the camp, as Rawhide Butte, and by which name it is known today. The site stands not far south of the present-day town of Lusk in north-eastern Wyoming.

We are not informed if any Cheyennes escaped to carry news of the disaster to their kin-folk, as the `counts` and tribal traditions are silent regarding the aftermath of the event, and it may be that the whole affair is but a variant account of the previously mentioned episode as related to Rufus Sage in 1842. In later years, however, when a defeat on such a scale as inflicted at Rawhide Butte occurred, it usually resulted in the vanquished band or tribe then fleeing the area, for it was considered bad luck to remain where so many ghosts might linger. Probably then, the Suhtaio did just that, and for a while licked their wounds far from the reach of further Sioux harassment. Several winter-counts record the affair under the heading, *"Winter when Long-Hair was Killed,"* [5]

These different `counts` are at variance to one another regarding their respective dating of the event, and only the `count` of American-Horse reports the death of Owner-of-Flute which had instigated the crusade in the first place. The fight at Rawhide Butte had been an important episode by the standards of the time, and only a disaster such as befell Owner-of-Flute`s party, was likely to have been considered severe enough to promote an expedition of the size and resolve as subsequently undertaken by the Sioux in revenge.

The Miniconjou, Chief Joseph White-Bull, recorded in his winter-count that it was during the period 1794 / 1795 when Long-Hair was slain, but gave no details, and Cloud-Shield an Oglala, but of a different band to American-Horse, records the same event, albeit for the period 1786 /1787. Reference to the event in the American-Horse `count,` was originally inserted by a member of the actual Teton band involved and who himself was probably in the battle, and where documented evidence exists for other events recorded in the American-House `count,` it often corroborates the entries both in detail and dating. There are discrepancies, as for example although the American-Horse chronology frequently coincides with events occurring in the first part of the `winter` depicted, that is, during the first year date given, this is not always the case, and some events have been shown to belong to the second inserted date. Having said this, Owner-of-Flute`s death likely does refer to1795, as in the previous year of 1794, the trader Trudeau was on the Upper Missouri and reported that the Teton were then in harmony with Cheyennes including the Suhtaio [i.e. Chousa, as Trudeau called them], and who together were then visiting the Arickara towns. Thus the killing of the Long-haired Cheyenne must have occurred in 1796 following the death of Owner-of-Flute in 1795.

Another Sioux-Cheyenne fight is said, traditionally, to have also taken place during the mid-1790s in the vicinity of Hot Springs in the Black Hills, South Dakota, and during which event a bunch of Cheyennes fortified themselves on the top of a butte since known as `Battle Mountain" some short distance east of the springs. The Sioux are said to have besieged the position and after winning the contest, laid claim to that part of the country. There is, however, some debate whether this Sioux fight was with Cheyennes, or against one or another Black Hill`s tribe such as either the Kiowa or Arapahoe. But whatever the case, while the Suhtaio and Pipe-Stem-Men continued at war with the Sioux, the Masikota, Omissis and Aorta Cheyennes persisted in their precarious roles as intermediaries between the warring tribes at that time.

Earlier, in September 1794, Trudeau in the employ of the Spanish Government in St. Louis and whilst traveling up the Missouri to open trade with the Arickara, was stopped at that river`s Great Bend below the Arickara by a band of Sioux who forced the party to land at the mouth of Crow Creek.

It appears then, that while the Cheyennes were occupied in raiding Snake and Padouca enemies to the west, the Sioux were concentrating their aggression along the Missouri banks. It has been noted that for several years previously, the Sioux had held the advantage over the River Tribes owing to their regular acquisition of guns on the Minnesota and James River, but now, indeed since 1787, French and Spanish traders had forged up the Missouri and were supplying the Arickara with firearms. The Brule, Northern Saoni and Yankton Sioux, were fully aware of the potential change in the balance of power if their enemies were able to meet them on equal terms, and in an endeavour to counteract such a shift, these same Sioux groups now straddled themselves across the Missouri below the Arickara in order to block the white man`s trade route north.

The Sioux who stopped Trudeau at the mouth of Crow Creek were Tetons, but with three Yankton families among them from the east. They told Trudeau that twenty-two lodges of their people were living in the west on White River and that the `Northern Indians,` their name for the Saoni, were higher up the Missouri. These Teton on White River were evidently Brule Sioux, the bulk of which still lived east of the Missouri and traded regularly with their Yanktonai and Sisseton cousins. The Sioux further said they were at war with the Arickara and that same summer had driven them from their towns, some of whom fled north to the Mandan, and the rest southwest to Skidi Pawnee kinfolk on the Loop Fork of the Platte. Upon learning of Trudeau`s intention to trade with the Arickara, the Sioux became angry and openly showed their dissent at the prospect of their enemies receiving firearms. They requested Trudeau to trade with them first, and when he refused, they forced him to do so upon pain of incurring their wrath. In such a way they were able to lighten his load of goods to a considerable extent, the bargaining of which, Trudeau said, was so one-sided that he received only a few furs in return.

This for the time being seemed to satisfy the Sioux and Trudeau was allowed to resume his journey up river. However, what the Sioux had told him proved true, for when the white men reached the Arickara towns they found them deserted. Trudeau returned downriver where he sat out the winter, and waited for spring when he would again try to contact the Arickara who by then, hopefully, would have returned to their towns. It was not, though, until June, 1795, before Trudeau again visited the Arickara, who he then found located on the west bank of the Missouri about three miles below the mouth of the Big Cheyenne.

The Arickara had only re-occupied one of their towns, their population being much reduced in number due to a smallpox epidemic the previous year, along with two of their bands which having fled the Sioux assault in the summer of `94, still refused to return. Evidence of the attack was still very much apparent. Many lodges were in a ruined state with the roofs caved in, while others consisted merely of charred shells and the whole in general, presented a dilapidated scene. The Arickara, Chief Crazy-Bear, invited Trudeau to abide in his lodge and from there, the Frenchman began soliciting for Arickara, Mandan and Hidatsa trade, along with a view of contacting the Western Tribes for the same purpose.

Messages were thus sent by moccasin telegraph across the Plains, informing those tribes of the Black Hills that emissaries of the Spanish Government were eager to meet their chiefs in order to confirm Spanish goodwill and harmony with their Red Brethren, and to bring the warring Nations together in peace. Trudeau further recorded that he also summoned the most important men from *"both Cheyenne villages"* to announce to them the words of their Spanish Father, and to deliver a medal, flag and letter patent along with presents which their Father had sent them. Here Trudeau was likely referring to the two Cheyenne earth-lodge villages then sporadically re-occupied at intervals for short periods at the mouth of the Big Cheyenne River some three miles above the Arickara. Whatever the case, the Cheyennes complied with the request and did visit Trudeau who then suggested they,

> *"...choose one among them to accept the medal and be made the great chief of their Nation."* [6]

A young brave named The-Lance was accordingly selected. This man was already a famous warrior who had earned considerable respect and success in recent military escapades, although such a position was oft-times short-lived, either terminating in death at the hands of enemies, or the tribe suffering reverses under his leadership which would occasion his removal from office. The successful expedition previously recounted of the combined Kiowa and Cheyenne party against peoples to the southwest in 1793, had likely been the episode which had elevated The Lance to his present standing, and it might be conjectured that it had been The-Lance who had carried the pipe on that occasion, or at least, had been most prominent during that conflict.

Indeed, this man was then the pride of all the Cheyennes present. He graciously accepted the medal, flag and letter patent, and promised to abide by the recommendations set forth by his, *"Father, the chief of the White men."* [7]

Trudeau had met Cheyennes before this visit to the Arickara, at which time he had traded a few furs from them. He also knew the trader Garreau who had lived among Cheyennes since 1792. The particular Cheyenne band among which Garreau resided consisted of no less the 150 lodges, which were reported in 1795 to be located near the Pawnee-Hoca [an Arickara sub-band which had fled their town after the Sioux attack], and thus was probably the same Cheyenne band led by The-Lance who now met Trudeau at the Arickara town.

Whilst still among the Arickara a war-party came in, proudly displaying an *Ysanti* [Santee Sioux] scalp taken in revenge for three Arickara slain earlier by that people. There was much jubilation in the town, until two members of the *TaCoropa* Sioux [a Minniconjou band friendly towards the Arickara], arrived with news that a big war-party of *Ysanti* comprising some five-hundred warriors from three bands, was preparing to attack the town. In response, many among the

Arickara were seized with panic. Some among them began hurriedly erecting a protective palisade, although others immediately fled again to the Mandan and to the Skidi Pawnee, as they had the previous year, and few persons actually remained at the town.

Soon after this scare, on June 6,[th] three Cheyennes arrived in compliance with Trudeau's earlier invitation sent to the Black Hill's Tribes. They came from a village named *Quisy* [i.e. Omissis], and Trudeau reported,

> "The Cayoguas, the Caminanbichesm the Pitapahatoes…had drawn near and were camped just beyond them, that on the reports they had received concerning the arrival and residence of White men among the Arickara, they wished to form an alliance with these last in order to obtain from them ammunition and knives, of which they were so much in need, but the dread they felt, either of the Sioux or Riccararas who often killed them without provocation, prevented their approaching." [8]

The first two of the three Nations so mentioned, denote those tribes later known as Kiowa and Arapahoe, while the third, *Pitapahatoes,* seems to have been a rendering of the Suhtaio name *"Vitapatiu,"* used by the Suhtaio to designate the Kiowa-Apache [i.e. Gattacka] specifically.

It also appears that the Black Hill's Tribes had been humouring the Arickara somewhat by portraying such humility, for other than the occasional squabble, no serious breaches of friendship between them and the Arickara had occurred, and it would be credulous to suppose that the Black Hill's Tribes when united, as they undoubtedly were at this time, would have had much to worry about if in hostile confrontation with the townsfolk, whose number and prowess had been nullified by three successive smallpox epidemics during recent years. The Sioux on the other hand, did pose a real threat to the western tribes. The Sioux were numerous and well-armed with a regular supply of ammunition, and withal, were aggressive and determined foes to contend with. It was then, surely because of the Sioux, and they alone, why the three Nations were reluctant to come close to the Missouri without first knowing Sioux intentions and the whereabouts of the latter's war bands.

The Cheyennes for their part, were able to keep at peace with the Tetons with whom some of their people were inter-married, and so could act as intermediaries between the Sioux and the Black Hill's Tribes. Hence the arrival of the three Cheyennes among the Arickara at this time, appearing on behalf of the western allies to pave the way ahead.

Strange to say that even with the threat of a Sioux assault looming, the Arickara young men were bold enough to contemplate a raid upon the approaching Black Hill's allies in order to steal their horses. Only Trudeau's intervention delayed the war-parties departure, although it was left to Chief Crazy-Bear to discourage them further. In the words of Trudeau,

> "Crazy-Bear told his young men to go and make war and so drive back the White men to their own villages with all their powder and other merchandise, while he and his family would withdraw to the Cheyennes." [9]

The intentions of the war-party were thus staid, and Trudeau then proposed that he and his companions would go themselves to the western allies with the pipe of peace from the Arickara, and to this the chiefs agreed. The three visiting Cheyennes had told the chiefs where exactly the allies were encamped, but the chiefs regarded it too far a distance for them to start out at once. Instead, they sent tobacco via the Cheyenne emissaries as a token of their intent to form an alliance with the western tribes.

After receiving the Arickara tobacco offering and each having been given by Trudeau himself, a knife, vermillion and extra tobacco for personal use, the Cheyennes departed for the allied encampment.

Having distributed such a quantity of trade goods in order to appease several hostile situations during his stay, Trudeau felt obliged to excuse himself to his Company bosses in a missive stating,

> "After so many losses and expenses due to unfortunate events. ...by which the Company finds itself much aggrieved, and those which I have made since my arrival here, whether to maintain peace with the Cheyennes and the village of Sioux settled here, who are at variance with one another, and whom it is necessary to keep on friendly terms..." [10]

On July 18th ten Cheyennes arrived at the Arickara town with word that their entire band was approaching, travelling in slow stages, being too heavily laden to move faster. They had dispatched messengers with the tobacco to the *Cayogues, Caminanbiches* and *Pitapahatoes,* they said, but the messengers had not yet returned, and they also told Trudeau of a singular event which had recently occurred among them.

This event concerned The-Lance, the Cheyenne warrior upon whom Trudeau had earlier bestowed the title "Chief." Apparently, after being elevated to his high status position by Trudeau, The-Lance had begun treating strangers and even his own people badly. Instead of making peace with the Mandan and Hidatsa, he had their horses stolen, and had even murdered a Sioux man along with the latter's wife and three children who were then living among the Cheyennes. For such actions, the Indians believed, the Great Spirit itself had become angry. Three of the chief's own children had subsequently died, and lighting had struck the lodge of his brother who with his wives, children, dogs and even horses tied at the door flap of his tepee, had all been reduced to ashes. Apparently the chief's actions did not incite war with the Sioux, probably because both bands needed each other's support against possible Arickara treachery, and for the Cheyennes it was just as well. The following day a band of eighty lodges of *TaCoropa* arrived at the town, and went into camp alongside the Sioux already there who belonged to a band designated by Trudeau as *Oconomas.* The *TaCoropa* informed their hosts that yet another band of Saoni Sioux and a Teton-proper band would be arriving soon. However, before the last-named bands came in, word was also brought that the aforementioned Eastern Sioux war-band of some five-hundred warriors comprised of Wahepeton, Sisseton and Isanti, was now actually en route in order to attack the town.

Word of the impending invasion soon reached the western allies who by then, were already moving downstream along the Big Cheyenne towards the Arickara town. Such news halted them in their tracks, and they went instead to the Mandan villages higher up the Missouri so as to keep their distance from the Sioux.

Certainly from the above excerpts, there can be little doubt that the Sioux were then the terror of both the Western Plains and Missouri peoples, and that only the Masikota, Omissis and Aorta Cheyennes were able to arbitrate between them and the Black Hill`s Tribes. So it was that the Black Hill`s Tribes along with their allies the Suhtaio and Pipe-Stem Men, continued their war with the Sioux in all its fury.

Thus we are informed in the American-Horse winter-count for 1798 /`99, that yet another Sioux-Cheyenne conflict took place, during which a famous Oglala named Owns-the-Pole went to war and came home victorious bringing many Cheyenne scalps. No further details are given, but it can be deduced that the Sioux war-party on that occasion had been formidable, able to overcome the Cheyennes in battle and escape with many scalps.

Following this, however, as recorded in the Oglala Left-Heron`s `count` for the same period of 1799, during another conflict with Cheyennes, a Holy woman among the enemy was captured by the Sioux, but owing to her sacred status was released and returned to her people unharmed. This same event is confirmed in the Oglala No-Ear`s `count` also commemorating the year 1799, in which it is stated, *"They took a good woman with them."* [11]

Importantly, this is the final entry in all the Teton winter-counts recording hostile confrontations during this particular period of Cheyenne–Sioux warfare, and from later testimony given by Left-Heron himself, soon after the episode relating to the Holy woman being released, an *"everlasting peace"* was made between the Sioux and Cheyennes at the mouth of Cheyenne River on the Missouri. [12]

American-Horse Winter-Count.

[1798 /`99]

"Own`s-the-Pole takes many scalps."

A single scalp waves from the end of a willow-wand. One scalp being deemed sufficient to convey `many.` In this case the symbol of a cross indicates that the enemy again were Cheyennes.

Not only are there no further winter-count entries for a continuation of Sioux – Cheyenne warfare from hereon and for another thirty years, but in 1801 according to the American-Horse `count` and which is corroborated by Crow tribal tradition, both Sioux and Cheyennes in a combined force conducted a large-scale hostile crusade against the Crows. It must be then, that the peace alluded to by Left-Heron was close to the date 1800, and may actually have resulted from the Holy woman having been released by her Oglala captors, and which led to peaceful overtures being made by one side or the other.

It was, Left-Heron said, at this same time of peace-making that the Sacred Arrow Keeper among the Cheyennes, and the Keeper of the Sacred Buffalo-Calf Pipe among the Sans Arc Sioux came together, and conducted a special ceremony to cement the` everlasting` peace between their peoples. This same account additionally states that the peace-making event was close to the occurrence of a smallpox epidemic which struck the people, and has since been assumed by some recent scholars to refer to the smallpox outbreak of 1781/`82. But this assumption cannot be correct and Left-Heron`s statement must, in reality, refer to a later date. Also it is likely that it was not the Cheyenne Sacred Arrows Keeper as stated by Left-Heron, but rather, the Suhtaio Keeper of the Sacred Buffalo Hat or *Issiwun,* and that the Holy woman referred to as having been captured and released by the Sioux, had probably been the wife or Sacred Woman of the Suhtaio Hat keeper himself. Left-Heron was specific in stating that the peace then effected was a *"lasting"* one, whereas only a few years after the `81/`82 smallpox, the Sioux – Cheyenne war was still being conducted in earnest as the previously depicted winter-count entries attest. There was, however, a smallpox outbreak of significant severity among all the Missouri tribes both east and west of that river during the period 1801 /`02, and thus soon after the event of the Cheyenne Holy woman being spared. It is also said in present day Lakota Sioux oral history, that a quantity of red pipestone [Catlinite] was given by one side or the other during the peace-making at the mouth of the Cheyenne, and this likely pertains to one or more pieces of red pipe-stone held in reverence by the Suhtaio [See pp. 370-372, this volume], and being presented to the Keeper of the Sacred Calf Pipe of the Tetons as a symbol of the "lasting peace" referred to by Left-Heron.

Sioux tradition also states that the Oglala Sioux sub-band named *Ku-hinyan*; which name translates from the Sioux as *"Gives the Rock,"* i. e. the red Catlinite stone, [13] and who are said to have been originally a Cheyenne-speaking group, actually joined the Oglala around the same time of the aforesaid peace-making at the mouth of the Cheyenne. Now as the Masikota, Omissis and Aorta Cheyenne groups had not been included in the Sioux – Cheyenne war, then the *Ku-hinyan* band which made their pact with the Sioux and gave away pieces of red rock at this time, must have been Suhtaio or, perhaps, Pipe-Stem Men. George E. Hyde the old-time expert on the Tetons, thought the term *Ku-hinyan* meant something like `stand offish` because they often chose to camp on their own away from the main group, although it is further said by the Sioux that *Ku-hinyan* was the name of the Head chief of the band at that time, and with the more proper meaning of, `bad-tempered,` `brutal,` `ferocious` or something of that ilk. Certainly, a chief by the name *Ku-hinyan* was prominent among the Sioux during the period 1790 to 1810 and appears to have been the same or a contemporary of the Oglala chief at that time known as Mad or Crazy-Dog. The band itself at a later date was known among the Sioux as the `Gopher` band [*Tacnaitca*] and was a part of the larger and more important *Kiyuksa* band of Oglala. The informant Left-Heron was surely correct regarding the *Ku-hinyan*, as his mother was a Ku-hinyan living among the Oglala, and his father a Miniconjou. On the other hand, the shorter Lakota term *Kinyan*, actually translates as `Flyers,` which, of course, was an old-time alternative name for the Suhtaio specifically [See p. 445].

Another, albeit tentative piece of evidence substantiating this proposed date of peace-making with the Suhtaio, is the Oglala winter-count of No-Ears, previously referred to, where it is noted that in 1800 /`01 a man known as Eats-No-Heart died. The interesting thing here is that this man was recognized as a Buffalo Priest who had the supposed ability to "call" the buffalo to him. This we know was a priestly position and attribute specifically associated with the Suhtaio, so perhaps, the man designated may actually have been a member of the Suhtaio, which having previously made their peace with the Sioux, were afterwards in harmonious and close contact with the Oglala, as indeed was the case of the *Ku-hinyan* band noted above.

The advantages of effecting an everlasting peace with the Tetons were manifold. As allies and confederates the Cheyennes and Tetons together, became overnight, as it were, the predominant force in the Western Plains, Thereafter, they frequently intermarried and to an extent, amalgamated their bands to include an admixture of Cheyenne and Sioux. Consistently they united in future dealings with enemy tribes and against Government troops when, at a later date, they were at war with the white men. However, still the Cheyennes and Suhtaio retained their own religious concepts and language, even though in most other things they and the Sioux were inseparable in their common practices and mentality.

Indeed, it was close to the date 1805, when 165 Cheyenne lodges then joined the Hunkpapa Tetons, the Hunkpapa before that time, having been part of the Oglala and thus, would have been included in the earlier peace gathering at the mouth of the Cheyenne. These 165 Cheyenne lodges comprised the remnant Masikota and Moiseo groups lately from Big Stone Lake at the head of the Minnesota, and who by then, were already a conglomerate of Cheyenne and Sioux owing to their previous long-term association in that region. In 1768 they had been noted by Jonathan Carver as the *Waddapawjestin*, which he referred to as a band of Sioux, this being Carver`s rendition of the Sioux word `watap` meaning `to eat with,` a term used by the Tetons to designate this particular Cheyenne-speaking group as, "Eaters with the Sioux." The Sioux themselves also referred to them by the more common collective term of *Shiyo* or *Sheo,* which, as explained in an earlier chapter, translates from the Sioux as `Sharp-tailed grouse,` but has the additional connotation of `legs flexed` or `legs drawn up,` which were synonyms for the Cheyenne band of Masikota.

Regarding the time period for this Cheyenne [*Shiyo*]-Hunkpapa association, it is told in Teton oral history that the event occurred just after the Hunkpapa themselves, led by a chief named Black-Moon, split from the Oglala as a result of in-fighting due to the distribution of spoils after a memorable victory over the Omaha. The Hunkpapa then went their separate way and were afterwards joined by the 165 lodges of Cheyenne. These Cheyennes intermarried frequently with the Hunkpapa and with whom they remained in close contact for half a century thereafter. Among the Hunkpapa they later comprised what became known as the *Taku-hkpaye* band, which again has a connection with the Cheyenne term Masikota, by translating as `something pertaining to a corpse` as in the Cheyenne connotation of `a corpse on a scaffold,` this being yet another synonym for the term Masikota [See Capter 16, p.171]. Earlier, these same Cheyennes had been associated with a part of the Miniconjou, noted by the trader Trudeau during the mid-1790s as the *TaCoropa* band, and then on the Missouri in company with other Cheyennes and the Arickara. Eventually, some among the aforementioned Cheyenne group of 165 lodges became dispersed and completely absorbed among the Hunkpapa, Oglala, Brule and Miniconjou Sioux bands, although the larger part rejoined the Cheyenne camp circle and were later known as the Watapio band, i.e. "Eaters with Sioux." They were, of course, of Masikota and Moiseo extraction, and should not be confused with the Omissis Cheyenne group, whose name also in the Cheyenne vernacular means `Eaters.`

The actual Hunkpapa break from the parent Oglala is said to have occurred around the same time as the Sioux – Cheyenne [Suhtaio] peace council at the mouth of the Cheyenne, and thus not during the earlier time of the 1750s as some present-day scholars have assumed, due to a passage from Lieutenant G. K. Warren`s journal of his expeditions between 1855 - `57. Warren was then told by a Sioux informant that the Hunkpapa break from the Oglala had taken place *"a life time"* earlier, and which either his Indian informant or Warren himself supposed, represented some one-hundred years more or less prior to 1855. However, the expression `a life time` more probably meant only fifty years or so prior to the comments of Warren`s informant, and which would then place the event of the Cheyenne – Hunkpapa coming together as around 1804 or 1805. Such would coincide with a great victory the Sioux did achieve over their Omaha enemies in late July of 1804, an event noted in several Teton winter-counts, and also mentioned in the day by day journals of the Lewis and Clark expedition at that time.

There is no evidence of any `large-scale` conflicts between the Sioux and Omaha during the second half of the eighteenth century, not in fact until 1804, when the Oglala took between sixty-five and seventy-five Omaha scalps and twenty-five women captive in one fight alone. Prior to this event, the entries in the several Teton winter-counts pertaining to fights with the Omaha in the eighteenth century are of trivial episodes in comparison. It is indicative also that in the following year of 1805, the Omaha sued for peace in order to get their captured women returned, and according to the account of John Ordway then with the Lewis and Clark expedition, the Sioux promised Captain Lewis they would send the women captives back to their people and make peace with the Omaha.

This is important, as along with the Suhtaio, the Pipe-Stem-Men Cheyennes should also be included in peace-making with the Sioux around this time, as the informant Left-Heron went on to say that not long after the gathering at the mouth of the Cheyenne, another peace council was held with Cheyennes on the Niobrara River. This last was where the Pipe-Stem-Men were then entrenched along what has since been known as Pipestem River, and were then in a league with their old-time friends the Omaha and Oto. In all likelihood then, the Pipe-Stem-Men were included in this second event of peace-making, having themselves been at war with the Sioux and hence, why the Maha, i. e. Omaha and their Ponca kinsmen, were sometimes mentioned by old traders as among the Black Hills Tribes at the latter`s trading fairs, because they were then allied to the Pipe-

Stem Men and the Black Hill`s Tribes who were then also at war with the Sioux. It was indeed, so Cheyenne tradition asserts, around this same time that the Pipe-Stem-Men reunited with other Cheyenne bands, and after dropping their old name of Pipe-Stem-Men, amalgamated with those later known as the Ridge Men Band in the Cheyenne camp circle.

Perhaps we do have other references to this Sioux peace-making with the Omaha and Pipe-Stem-Men on the Niobrara, such as in several Teton winter-counts, particularly those of Lone-Dog and Baptist-Good, where it is recorded that during the period 1804 to 1805, the *"Hunka"* or `Calumet` ceremony was introduced among the Tetons for the first time. This ceremony, we know, was specifically practiced by the Omaha and, more important to our theme, by the Pipe-Stem-Men and by which fact, the Pipe-Stem-Men had originally earned their name. The ceremony was, moreover, an adoption and peace-making ritual which hereafter, was adopted by the Teton Sioux themselves. This event would not have occurred too long after the first grand peace-gathering at the mouth of the Cheyenne, and prior to which pact, even the main Cheyenne bands of Masikota, Omissis and Aorta, albeit already at peace with the Tetons, had always been wary of the latter`s intentions, often viewing them as potential foes. Such apparently was still the case, even after the peace-making at the mouth of the Cheyenne of circa, 1800, for the Charles LeRaye journal pertaining to 1803, mentions an uncertain peace as then existing between Cheyennes and Sioux because, he states, of treachery on the part of the Sioux.

Peace, however, between the Suhtaio and Tetons actually forged a stronger association between the Suhtaio and all other Cheyenne-speaking bands, albeit since the early 1740s, so the informant Bill Tall-Bull asserted, the Suhtaio had already become allied and to and in some degree, confederated with the majority of Cheyenne bands as a collective entity. It had been during that period of cohesion not long prior to the mid eighteenth century, that the Suhtaio actually transferred their sacred site of Timber Mountain in the east, to that of the Cheyenne`s own sacred site of Bear Butte in western South Dakota. [14] It was also at that time, Bill Tall-Bull added, that the Cheyennes inaugurated their Warrior Societies, having adopted the concept from innovations originating among their new-found Suhtaio confederates, [15] as indeed, Suhtaio testimony itself as given to Truman Michellson in 1907, likewise asserted.

During the mid-1830s, at least one Suhtaio band along with a few members belonging to their Cheyenne-proper associates, were once again engaged in intermittent hostility with one and another Teton Sioux band, due to the Oglala and Brule taking up permanent residence in the North Platte and Powder River regions close to the newly established trading post Fort John on the Laramie Fork of the Platte. Not until 1840 did these Suhtaio and Cheyennes led by the Suhtaio Chief Red-Arm, make peace with the aforementioned Sioux under a Minniconjou chief named Lone-Horn, and thereafter, Cheyennes and Sioux again became staunch allies both in warfare against mutual enemies and on a political level.

All being said, as allies and confederates to the Sioux; these being the most populous people on the Western Plains, and among whom the Cheyennes inter-married freely and amalgamated, the Cheyenne and Suhtaio could then match any enemy confronted, and hold the land which, they believed, had been given them by the Great Ma`heo itself.

Around the date 1832, the Masikota, Watapio, Hevietanio and Pipe-Stem / Ridge Men bands along with a small part of the Omissis, moved permanently south from the Black Hills country to a point between the South Platte and the Arkansas, and soon after, one of the three then still extant Suhtaio bands led by a chief named Black-Shin, followed suit and also moved south on a permanent basis. Thereafter, these particular bands became known among themselves collectively as the *Hevietanio,* i. e. "Hair-rope Men," and later, at the Horse Creek Treaty signing in 1851, they were recognised officially by the American Government as the `Southern Cheyenne.`

A second Suhtaio band known alternatively as *Staihitan, Kites* and *Skutani,* and among whom were members of Atsina [Gros Ventre] and Arapahoe affiliation, had its camp destroyed by Crows near Big Timbers on the Arkansas in 1833 and its occupants dispersed. The third and largest Suhtaio band remained in the north, where they amalgamated with the majority of Omissis who had also stayed in the north and together, became known among themselves collectively as the Omissis, i. e. "Eaters," and after the 1851 treaty above referred to, became officially known as `Northern Cheyenne.`

Notwithstanding, however, their separate locations and designations, both Northern and Southern divisions continued to regard themselves as one Nation, and persisted in visiting each other to hold religious ceremonies together and to assist each other in both their intertribal wars and later conflicts with United States government forces. Even today, although politically separate, tribal members travel back and forth; north to south and south to north in order to socialise and act together as a singular tribal entity, and which forever will be Cheyenne.

Thus we have traced the history of the Cheyenne and Suhtaio from their origins in the dark days of the Prehistoric era. Then down through the centuries, following their circuitous wanderings and survival during times of extreme hardship and privation and potential extermination from numerous foes. We have followed the people as they evolved into a Nation in their own right, and their finally claiming the Black Hills and Western Plains as their tribal domain, where *Navah-hous,* – the sacred hill of Bear Butte, – stands at the center of their Universe. Truly, at last, the Cheyennes and Suhtaio had become "Keepers of the Game," having proved themselves the rightful heirs of "Ma`heo`s Children."

- 0 - 0 - 0 - 0 - 0 - 0 - 0 - 0 - 0 - 0 - 0 - 0 - 0 - 0 - 0 - 0 –

Northern Cheyenne, Little-Chief. Photographed by Bogardus, New York. 1879.

APPENDIX A.

Re; Chapter 6.

It may appear from the Cheyenne creation tradition, wherein mention is made of an ancient southern movement from the `Beautiful Country` of the north, that this corroborates a recent hypothesis put forward by Karl H. Schlesier, who stated that around the date 250 BC. Proto-Cheyennes, having been forced from the north owing to a colder climate which allowed the tundra to extend much further south, finally reached the High Plains region of the United States and for a prolonged period, roamed the open grasslands and Black Hills district in what are now the states of North and South Dakota.

During this time, Schlesier asserts, the tribe obtained its Sacred Arrow talismans, subsequently allowing them to become a singular people in their own right. Schlesier further added that around AD. 600 the weather became warmer, whereupon the Cheyennes, now a complete unified tribe both physically and spiritually, returned to the north in pursuit of big-game herds which were moving in that direction as the tundra receded, and as a consequence, the grasslands expanded northward.

This assertion of an ancient Cheyenne residence both south and west of the Missouri River, much earlier than has previously been imagined, and which Schlesier associates with what the archaeologists term the `Eastern Besant` culture phase of the Great Plains, is not as yet supported by either the archaeological or climatic evidence, although Schlesier`s hypothesis may indeed be feasible with regard to some early Algonquian bands. Unfortunately, though, the Cheyennes at that time would not have been `Cheyenne` in any sense of the term. No more, that is, than any other Algonquian-speaking group. This is not to say that Schlesier`s statement does not correspond with Cheyenne tradition previously cited, which speaks of moving south from the `Beautiful Country` of the north, before moving back at a later date when the same `Northland` had become cold and barren. But this event must have occurred long before the tribe obtained its Sacred Arrow talismans. While it is true that our subjects did not become a separate entity until after their organization into a discernible cohesive political unit, of which the coming of the Sacred Arrows and the inauguration of rituals connected with them not only formed a basis for the people's unification, but are symbolic and representative of that fact, it has been seen throughout the course of our study that the Sacred Arrows - traditionally acquired by the TsisTsisTsas culture hero Sweet Medicine at `Novha`hous` [Bear Butte] northeast of the Black Hills, South Dakota, - are unlikely to be much more than four-hundred and fifty years old at the most, and also that the people later known as Cheyenne were - before circa, AD.1200, - an inseparable part of a much larger Cree population. So that if we were to accept Schlesier`s assertion of such an early date for Cheyenne residence in the Western Plains, cal; circa, 250 BC., then we must obviously think of them as Cree, who themselves would then have been incorporated among a host of other closely related Algonquian groups, which in more recent time, have become known independently as Chippewa, Delaware, Sauk, Fox and others.

I believe that Schlesier`s account of an early Cheyenne association with the Black Hills, should actually refer to a much later period in Cheyenne history, after the Cheyennes had become a distinct tribal body separate from the Cree, and after their having reached the Mississippi headwaters country around AD.1500. If indeed the `Holy Mountain` of Bear Butte had been recognized as a sacred site of such importance between 250 B.C. and AD 600 [this being the time span Schlesier suggests for early Cheyenne residence in the South Dakota Black Hills region], why then did not the Cree themselves, if not other Algic peoples revere that butte also, or that in later years they did not have some recollection or make some reference to it in their own traditions and religious observances? For the people we now know as Cheyennes would, at that time, have been one and the same as the Cree and indistinguishable from them.

APPENDIX B

In relation to the `Besant phase` of the Dakota Plains, as far as our present knowledge is concerned, its cultural traits including tools and pottery fragments, might just as well relate to any other Algonquian-speaking group or groups [moreover of the proto-Arapahoe type], or for that matter, to any Athapaskan-speaking people once belonging to one or more of the various Plains Apache bands, which in early times, occupied the same area for a prolonged period and practiced a similar culture and lifestyle as indicated by archaeological findings associated with the `Besant people,` whoever they might have been. Consequently, Schlesier`s hypothesis does not hold water. Neither is it particularly important here, as we have been involved primarily, with the ancestral Cheyennes as being a component part of a much larger conglomerate of Algonquian-speaking bands which - as has been made clear through the course of this study - were closely associated in habitat and confederated with, Cree-speaking peoples.

APPENDIX B.

Re; Chapter 7.

The trouble with Heckewelder`s rendition is, I believe, that he had taken the premise that an earlier part of this Delaware tradition [not included in this account], referred to as he thought, that people's ancient residence in the far western part of North America, and by travelling west to east, they must therefore, have reached the Mississippi River, and having supposedly moved down that stream, he assumed that they next settled for a prolonged period on that river's west side some distance above the mouth of the Ohio. His interpretation was conditioned by this view, even though the tradition itself was not intended to refer to any earlier seat of occupation than that of the far North Country and which, we have previously deduced, was the boreal forest and tundra area of Keewatin northwest of Hudson's Bay.

Actually the term `Namaessisipu` means "Fish River," which was the universal Algonquian name specifically applied to the St. Lawrence. Certainly, the great river now known as Mississippi, was generally called "Big River" by all Indians who were familiar with its course, and further, that this stream was never regarded among the indigenous populations living along and adjacent to its banks, as a more favorable fishing area compared to, that is, other numerous fish-filled lakes and streams found elsewhere in the country along that river's length, especially north from the mouth of the Ohio or indeed, in any of the districts through which the Mississippi flows. The St. Lawrence conversely, was renowned among all Northern and Eastern Algonquians and also among the various Iroquois tribes, for its seemingly unlimited fish stocks of countless different varieties, so that of old, many bands were in the habit of trekking great distances in order to take advantage of this fact.

Heckewelder appears to have assumed that the term `Namaessissipu` was synonymous with that of the great river Mississippi, which was the only sizeable stream with a similar sounding name in both Canada and the United States then known to Heckewelder and his associates. Added to this, there is no great expanse of spruce pine in the area designated in the Heckewelder account, so it cannot be the land next entered by the Delaware host, according to the main Delaware version.

This becomes evident when we read further in Heckewelder`s account, that the Delaware followed the river's course *[Namaessippiu]* until they came within one hundred miles above the Ohio where it falls into the same. Of course we know that the Ohio does not flow into the St. Lawrence, but if the proper meaning here is that the Delaware merely came within a certain distance of the Ohio, then this would be compatible with other evidence already discussed, which places the Delaware along the southern shores of Lake Ontario and Lake Erie close the Headwaters of three separate streams flowing into the Ohio from the northeast which the Indians did not differentiate with separate names, but applied the name *"Allegwi-Sipu,"* i.e. "The River of the Allegwi" to all three.

By Heckewelder's own admission, the Delaware at this point were some way distant from the Ohio, and the Delaware account goes on to say that whilst reconnoitering to the east, they met the 'Mengue' who had come in more to the north and were about settling in the vicinity of large lakes in that direction. Now the term *'Menque,'* we know, definitely refers to Iroquoian peoples, and in this instance, specifically to the various Huron, Neutral, Petun and Erie groups as opposed to the five confederated Iroquois-proper tribes, and upon whom at a later date, the Delaware also applied the name. Even later, the colonial English adopted the same name from the Delaware, which they in turn corrupted to *"Mingo."*

- 0 - 0 - 0 - 0 - 0 - 0 - 0 - 0 - 0 - 0 - 0 - 0 - 0 - 0 - 0 -

NOTES AND SOURCES.

The previous study has been the result of the present Author`s personal analysis of documented data, along with information supplied in one to one interviews with Cheyenne and Suhtaio tribal members, which have included James King, Bill Tall-Bull, Wayne Medicine-Elk and Clarence `Bisco` Spotted-Wolf among many others over a twenty-two year period of contact.. Documented data consists of a plethora of scholarly works listed in the accompanying bibliography, albeit too extensive to itemise separately regarding each individual chapter of this work. This being the case, only references to direct quotes within the work are entered below.

PART I.

CHAPTER 1.

1.　Athapaskan-speakers that include the Apache, Navaho, Sarsi and Chipewyan among others, show very close linguistic connections with Siberian peoples, and when on the North American Continent, they appear to have radiated out from a collective position in the McKenzie Delta region of north-western Canada. [Bishop, Charles A. *"Handbook of the North American Indian, Vol.6. pp. 161-162. "Sub-Arctic."* Smithsonian Institution, Washington DC. 1981]. Shoshonian peoples on the other hand, that include the Shoshoni, Ute and Comanche, speak dialects related to the Uto-Aztecan linguistic family, which predominates the North American Southwest and Mexico regions and who likewise, share a Siberian connection, albeit having originally migrated from Siberia in an eastern direction to Alaska; thence south along the Alaskan coast and further south through the states of Washington and California.[Swanton, John R. *"The Indian Tribes of North America."* [See under; *Shoshoni*].Smithsonian Institution, Bureau of Ethnology. Bulletin 145.1952. Siouan-speaking peoples conversely, such as the Dakota, Crow and Mandan, show ancient linguistic connections to Asiatic Indo-European proto-types. There are several examples of this to warrant a more in-depth study of comparisons in mythology and linguistics. The Dakota, for their part, use a system of expression which is very closely compatible with that of the Asiatic Mongols, and one can also find numerous and unique comparisons in the mythologies and theologies of both the Siouan and Mongol concepts, which further attests to a likely connection during both people`s prehistoric past.

CHAPTER 2.

1.　Stands-in-Timber, John In; *"Cheyenne Memories."* Edited by Margot Liberty.　Pp.13-15. Yale University Press. 1967.

CHAPTER 3.

1.　Grinnell, George. *"The Cheyenne Indians."* Vol. 1. P.15. Yale University Press. 1923.

CHAPTER 4.

1.　Mooney, James. *"The Cheyenne Indians."* P.404. memoirs of the American Anthropological Association. 1907.

2.　Father Allouez *"Journal."* In; *Early Narratives of the Northwest* [Edited by Louise P. Kellogg. New York. 1917.

CHAPTER 5.

NOTES AND SOURCES

1.   Morgan, Lewis H. *"The Indian Journals, 185- 62"* University of Michigan Press. Ann Arbor. 1959.

CHAPTER 6.

1.   Daniel G. Brinton. *The Lene Lenape and their Legends,"* Part 1.*The Library of Aboriginal American Literature*. Vol. 5. 1882 – 85.

2.   Stands-in-Timber, John In; *"Cheyenne Memories."* Edited by Margot Liberty. Pp.13-15. Loc; cited.. 1967.

3.   Daniel G. Brinton. *The Lene Lenape and their Legends,"* Part 1. *Loc; cited.*

CHAPTER 7.

1.   For an analytical discussion on the validity of the Wallum Ollum, see; Daniel G. Brinton. *The Lene Lenape and their Legends,"* Part 1.*The Library of Aboriginal American Literature*. Vol. 5. 1882 - 85.

2.   *Ibid.*

3.   *Ibid.*

4.   *Ibid.*

5.   *Ibid.*

6.   *Ibid.*

7.   Blair, Emma H. *"The Indian Tribes of the Upper Mississippi Valley and Region of the Great Lakes."* Vol. 1. Cleveland. 1911. [This monumental work in two volumes, contains the Major Marston material and also the writings of Nicolas Perrot].

8.   Daniel G. Brinton. *The Lene Lenape and their Legends,"* Part 1.*The Library of Aboriginal American Literature*. Vol. 5. 1882 – 85.

9.   *Ibid.*

10.   Blair, Emma H. *"The Indian Tribes of the Upper Mississippi Valley and Region of the Great Lakes."*

11.   Brinton, Daniel G. Loc; cited.

12.   *Ibid.*

13.   *Ibid.*

14.   *Ibid.*

CHAPTER 8.

1.   Heckwelder, John. *"Account of the History, manners and Customs of the Indian Nations."* Pp. 17-56. Philadelphia, 1881.

2.   Brinton, Daniel G. *"The Lenape and their Legends."* Part 1v. 1882-`85.

3.   Heckwelder, John. *"Account of the History, manners and Customs of the Indian Nations."*1881.

4.   Clark, W. P. *"The Indian Sign Language."* P.102. Uni; Nebraska Press. 1982 [Reprint].

5.   Mooney, James. *"The Cheyenne Indians."* P.404. Loc; cited.

6.   Grinnell, George Bird. *"Some Early Cheyenne Tales."* Journal of American Folklore. 20; 78. 1908.

CHAPTER 9.

1.   Heckwelder, John. *"Account of the History, manners and Customs of the Indian Nations."* Loc; cited.

2.   *Ibid.*

3.   Brinton, Daniel G. *"The Lenape and their Legends."* Part 1 vol. 5. 1882-`85. *Loc; cited*

4-   *Ibid.*

5.   *Ibid.*

CHAPTER 10.

1.   This chapter includes data from Dorsey, George A. *"The Cheyenne. Part 2. Myths."* Pp.34ff. [Reprint]; Ye Galleon Press. Fairfield Washington 1975 and, Warren, William. *"A History of the Ojibway Indians."* P.180. Minnesota Historical Society Press. 1984.

CHAPTER .11.

1.   Dusenbury, Verne. *"The   Horn in the Ice."* in *"The Red Man`s West."* Pp. 11-12. Hasting House Publishers, New York. 1965.

2.   Dorsey, George A. *"The Cheyenne. Part 2. Myths."* Pp.34ff. [Reprint]; Ye Galleon Press. Fairfield Washington 1975.

3.   *Ibid.*

CHAPTER 12.

1.   Raudot, Antoine D. *"Memoir concerning the different Indian Nations of North America."* Letter 39. 1710.

CHAPTER 13.

1.   James King [Northern Cheyenne informant] to Author. Summer [Aug;] 1994. Note book 2. P.2. See also; Grinnell, George Bird. *"The Cheyenne Indians."* Vol. 1. P.3. footnote 2. New Haven, Yale University Press. 1923, and Hyde, George E. *"Life of Bent."* P.4. University of Oklahoma Press. 1967.

2.   Radisson, Pierre Espirit. *"Journals."* Pp.131-132. Ross and Haines. Minneapolis, Minnesota. 1961.

3.   *Ibid.*

4.   O`Meara, Walter. *"The Last Portage."* The story of John Tanner`s captivity among the Indians. P. 131. Houghton and Miffin Company. Boston. 1962. Grinnell, George Bird. *"Some Early Cheyenne Tales."* Journal of American Folklore. 20; 78. 1908. See also; Tall-Bull, Henry and Weist, Tom. *"The Rolling Head."* Montana Indian Publications. 1971.

5.   Isham, James. *"Notes and Observations on the Dobbs Galley of 1749 to Hudson`s Bay."* Pp. 225-226. [Edited by E.E. Rich 1949].

6.   James King [Northern Cheyenne informant] to Author. Summer [Aug;] 1994. Note book 2. P.2.

PART II.

CHAPTER 14.

1.   Bill Tall Bull, [Northern Cheyenne informant] l to Author. 1994. Note pad 2. Page 2.

2.   *Ibid.*

3.   Schoolcraft, Henry R. *"Journal of Travels."* P. 243 ff. 1820.

4.   *Ibid.*

5.   Stands-in-Timber, John In; *"Cheyenne Memories."* Edited by Margot Liberty. Pp.13-15. Loc; cited, 1967.

6.   Schukies, Renate [Editor]. *"Red hat, Blue Sky maker and Keeper of the Sacred Arrows."* P. 64. University of Hamburg, Germany. 1993.

7.   Radisson, Pierre Espirit. *"Journals."* Pp.131-132. Ross and Haines. Minneapolis, Minnesota. 1961.

8. Thompson, David. *"Narrative of his explorations in Western America, 1784-1812."* [Edited by J. B. Tyrrell.] Publ. Champlain Society. No 12. Toronto.

9. Warren, William. *"History of the Ojibway Indians."* Minnesota Historical Society press. 1984.

10. *Ibid.*

CHAPTER 15.

1. This chapter is comprised of data from, Dorsey, Grinnell, Stands-in-Timber and Mooney among others, and added information from Cheyenne informants James King and Bill Tall Bull.

2. Dorsey, George A. *"The Cheyenne. Part 2. Myths."* Pp.34ff. [Reprint]; Ye Galleon Press. Fairfield Washington 1975.

3. George Bent also stated that the expedition against the Shoshoni in 1817, was the first remembered move of the `Sacred Arrows` against an enemy, and that the second move was against the Crows in 1820. However, if Bent had been told that the move against the Shoshoni had occurred four years prior to that against the Crows, then, perhaps, he misconstrued the real meaning of the Cheyenne statement. In so much as the expression "four years" in the Cheyenne idiom, merely represented an unspecified period in time Thus, if two extra Sacred Arrows were added to the bundle around the date 1740, in order to represent the four groups of Aorta-Masikota, Omissis, Pipe-Stem Men and Suhtaio coming together at Bear Butte as a confederated body, it would have followed that the power of the *new* expanded `Arrow` bundle was, soon after, tested against the enemy. The `move` therefore against the `Snakes`[i.e. Shoshoni] as recorded in the LaVerendrye journal of 1742, would have been recalled among the Cheyennes themselves, as the first move of the `Arrows` in their expanded number, and such, incidentally, would have coincided with the four original warrior societies being inaugurated and adopted among the newly united Cheyenne and Suhtaio bands.

CHAPTER 16.

1. Hennepin, Louis. *"Discovery of a Vast Country in America."* P.225. Collins Publishing Co. Toronto.1974. [Reprint from the 1698 edition]. The map shown is derived from a copy of Hennepin`s data but described as "Law`s Louisiana" in Justin Winsor`s, *"The Mississippi Basin."* P.107. Reprint published by Heritage Classics 2003.

CHAPTER 17.

1. This chapter comprises data from the works of Grinnell, John Stands in Timber, Father Peter Powell and the Pierre Radisson journals, all previously cited. .

CHAPTER 18.

1. Allouez, Father, *"Journal."* In; *"Early Narratives of the Northwest."* New York. 1917.

2. *Ibid.*

3. Clark, W. P. *"The Indian Sign Language."* P.102. Uni; Nebraska Press. 1982 [Reprint].

CHAPTER 19.

1. De Baurain, M. de Chevalier. *"La Harpe, Bernard De. "Journal of New France and Louisiana."* Historical Collections of Louisiana. New York, 1851.

2. Thompson, David. *"Narrative of his explorations in Western America, 1784-1812."* [Edited by J. B. Tyrrell.] Publ. Champlain Society. No 12. Toronto.

3. Thwaites, Rueben Gold [Editor], *"The Jesuit Relations."* Vols. 16 and 17. *"The Charles L`Allemant Relation."* Cleveland, Ohio. 1896-1901.

4. Radisson, Pierre Espirit. *"Journals."* Pp.131-132. Ross and Haines. Minneapolis, Minnesota. 1961.

5. *Ibid.*

6. *Ibid.*

7. James King [Northern Cheyenne informant] to Author. Summer [Aug;] 1994. Note book 2. P.2.

8. Grinnell, George Bird. *"The Cheyenne Indians."* Vol. 1. P.3. footnote 2. New Haven, Yale University Press. 1923, and Hyde, George E. *"Life of Bent."* P.4. University of Oklahoma Press.

CHAPTER 20.

1. Coleman, Winfield, *"Field Notes."* In; *"People of the Buffalo."* Vol 2. P244. Tatanka Press, 2005.

2. Petter, Rudolph, *"Sketch of Cheyenne Grammar."* P. 464. American Anthropological Association. Kraus Reprint, 1976.

CHAPTER 21.

1. Hennepin, Louis. *"Discovery of a Vast Country in America."* P.225. Collins Publishing Co. Toronto.1974. [Reprint from the 1698 edition]. The map shown is derived from a copy of Hennepin`s data but described as "Law`s Louisiana" in Justin Winsor`s, *"The Mississippi Basin."* P.107. Reprint published by Heritage Classics 2003.

2. Father Allouez *"Journal."* In; *Early Narratives of the Northwest* [Edited by Louise P. Kellogg. New York. 1917.

3. Trudeau, Jean Baptiste. *"Journals."* *South Dakota Historical Society Collections.* Vol.   111.

CHAPTER 22.

1. Fire-Wolf, Cheyenne informant. In, Powell, Peter, *"Issiwun."* Lame Deer, Montana [No date].

CHAPTER 23.

1. Grinnell, George. *"Papers and Note books."* Braun Research Library. Los Angeles California.

2. Stands in Timber, John. *"Papers."* Dull knife College, Lame Deer, Montana.

3. Radisson, Pierre. *"Journals."* Pp.131-132. Ross and Haines. Minneapolis, Minnesota. 1961.

4. *Ibid.*

CHAPTER 24.

1. DuLuth, *"Memoir"* In; Louise P. Kellog`s *"Early Narratives of the Northwest."* Pp. 329-332

PART III

CHAPTER 25.

1. Sangrain, Pere and Pierre Prault. *"Dictionaire Universel de la France, Ancienne et Moderne, et Nouvelle France."* Paris 1723.

2. LeSueur, Charles, *"Manuscript."*

3. Sangrain, Pere and Pierre Prault. *"Dictionaire Universel de la France,"* Loc; cited.

4. LaHontan, Baron. *"New Voyages to North America."* Vols 1 and 2. English translation published 1703.

5.   Sangrain, Pere and Pierre Prault. *"Dictionaire Universel de la France,* Loc; cited.

6.   Cornelli, Vincent. "Map" The Newbery Library. Chicago.

7.   Blair, Emma H. *"The Indian Tribes of the Upper Mississippi Valley and Region of the Great Lakes."* Vol. 1. Cleveland. 1911. [Contains the writings of Nicolas Perrot].

CHAPTER 26.

1.   LaSalle, Chevalier Du, In, Margry, Pierre. *"Discoveries."* Vol. 11. P. 54. See also; Weddle, Robert S. *"LaSalle, the Mississippi and the Gulf; Three Primary Documents."* College Station: Texas A & M University Press. 1987.

2.   *Ibid.*

3.   Michelson, Truman, *Field Notes and Pape*rs; 1910. MS. 222684.

4.   Grinnell, George Bird. *"The Cheyenne Indians."* Vol. 1. P.3. footnote 2. New Haven, Yale University Press. 1923,

5.   Williamson, T. S. Minnesota Historical Society Collections, Vol. 1. P. 242, and Vol. 111. P. 284. See also; Comfort, Dr. W. Smithsonian Report for 1871. P. 402. Washington. 1873.

CHAPTER 27.

1.   The descriptions of Cheyenne pottery styles are from several Archaeological journals, both published and unpublished.

CHAPTER 28.

1.   Comfort, Dr. W. Smithsonian Report for 1871. P. 402. Washington. 1873.

2.   Williamson, T. S. Minnesota Historical Society Collections, Vol. 1. P. 242, and Vol. 111. P. 284.

3.   Riggs, Stephen R *"Dakota Grammar, Texts and Ethnography."* Vol. 1X, P.193. Contributions to North American Ethnology. 1894.

4.   *Ibid.*

CHAPTER 29.

1.   LaSalle, Chevalier Du, In, Margry, Pierre. *"Discoveries."* Vol. 11. P. 54.

CHAPTER 30.

1.   Strong, William. *"North Dakota Historical Quarterly"* 1940.

CHAPTER 31.

1.   Clark, W. P. *"The Indian Sign Language [Cheyenne]"* P. 39. University of Nebraska Press. [Reprint] 1982.

2.   Coquart, Father Claude Godfroy, *"Letter to Gov; Charles de Marquis de Beauharnois,"* July, 1742.

CHAPTER 32.

1.   Maximillian, Prince Zu Wied, *"Travels through North America."*1844. Most of the data pertaining to this chapter is from Maximillian and the works of Alfred Bowers and George Will.

2.   Maximillian, Prince Zu Wied, *"Travels in North America."* London, 1844.

CHAPTER 33.

NOTES AND SOURCES

1.   Posada, Alonso de, In, Forbes, Jack D. *"Apache, Navaho and Spaniard."* P. 99. University of Oklahoma Press. 1960.

2.   Cortes, Jose. *"Report on the Provinces of New Spain."* Pp. 98-99. University of Oklahoma Press. 1989.

3.   *Ibid.*

4.   Flecther, Alice. *"The Omaha Tribe."* Vol. 2. Pp.47.ff. University of Nebraska Press 1972.

5.   Cortes, Jose. *"Report on the Provinces of New Spain."* Pp. 98-99. University of Oklahoma Press. 1989.

6.   Ortega, Captain. In, Forbes, Jack D. *"Apache, Navaho and Spaniard."* P. 99. University of Oklahoma Press. 1960.

7.   DeVargas, Governor. *"Letters."* In, Twitchell, New Mexican Archives, Vol. 1. P. 265. See also; Forbes, Jack D. *"Apache, Navaho and Spaniard."* P.262. University of Oklahoma Press. 1960.

8.   *Ibid.*

PART IV.

CHAPTER 34.

1.   Smith, G. Hubert, *"The Explorations of the LaVerendryes in the Northern Plains."* University of Nebraska Press. Pp. 104-115. 1980. See also; Burpee, Lawrence, *"Journals and Letters of the LaVerendryes."* Toronto. The Champlain Society, 1927.

2.   *Ibid.*

3.   *Ibid.*

4.   *Ibid.*

5.   *Ibid.*

6.   *Ibid.*

7.   *Ibid.*

8.   *Ibid.*

9.   Bourgainville, Louis. *"Memoir."* Wisconsin Historical Collections. P. 189. 1908.

10. Jones, Father Arthur, *"The Aulneau Collection."* S. J. Montreal. St. Mary`s College. 1893.

11. Grinnell, George Bird. *"The Cheyenne Indians."* Vol. 1, p. 23. Yale University Press. 1923.

CHAPTER 35.

1.   Grinnell, George Bird. *"The Cheyenne Indians."* Vol. 1 and 2. Loc; cited. 1923.

2.   Welch, Colonel A. B. Dakota Papers.com [Indian Histories].

CHAPTER 36.

1.   Stands-in-Timber, John. *"Papers."* No.-123-062. Wooden Leg College and Library Archives. Lame Deer, Montana.

2.   Carver, Jonathan. *"Travels through the Interior Parts of North America."* Ross and Haines. Minneapolis, Minnesota. 1956.

3.   *Ibid.*

CHAPTER 37.

1.   Grinnell, George Bird. *The Fighting Cheyennes*. University of Oklahoma Press. 1956.

2.   Thompson, David. *"Narrative of his explorations in Western America, 1784 -181"* [Edited by J. B.Tyrrell.] Publ. Champlain Society. No 12. Toronto

3.   *Ibid.*

4.   Henry, Alexander the Younger. *"Journals."* [See; August, 1801 entries]. Manitoba Historical Society. Manitoba, Canada. See also; Mallery, Garrick. *"Pictographs of the North American Indians."* Winter-Counts. Fourth Annual Report of the Bureau of American Ethnology. Washington D. C. 1886.

5.   *Ibid.*

CHAPTER 38.

!.   Grinnell, George Bird. *"The Cheyenne Indians."* Vol. 1 and 2. New Haven, Yale University Press. 1923.

2.   *Ibid.*

3.   Deglise, Jacques. In; A. P. Nasatir`s *"Before Lewis and Clark."* Vol. 1. University of Nebraska Press. 1991.

4.   Henry, Alexander the Younger. *"Journals."* [See; 1806 entries]. Manitoba Historical Society. Manitoba, Canada.

5.   *Ibid.*

6.   *Ibid.*

7.   Stands-in-Timber, John. *"Papers."* No.-123-062. Wooden Leg College and Library Archives. Lame Deer, Montana.

8.   Grinnell, George Bird. *"The Cheyenne Indians."* Vol. 1 and 2. New Haven, Yale University Press. 1923.

9.   Coues, Elliott. *"History of the Lewis and Clark Expedition."* 1893. [Reprint; Dover Publications].

10.   Will, George, F. *The Cheyenne Indians in North Dakota.* Proceedings of the Mississippi Valley Historical Association. 1913-14. Vol. V11. Cedar Rapids, 1914.

11.   *Ibid.*

12.   Mackay, Donald. *"Journal and papers of Donald MacKay."*

13.   Mackay, James. *"Journal."* Proceedings State Historical Society, Wisconsin. 1915.

14.   *Ibid.*

15.   Collett, Victor. *"A Journey in North America."* Vol. 2. Firenge, O, Lange, 1924.

16.   *Ibid.*

17.   Trudeau, Jean Baptiste. *"Trudeau`s Journals."* South Dakota Historical Collections. Vol. II,.1912-1913, and *"Trudeau among the Arickara Indians."* Missouri Historical Society Collections. Vol. 1V. 1914.

18.   Carver, Jonathan. *"Travels through the Interior Parts of North America."* Ross and Haines. Minneapolis, Minnesota. 1956.

CHAPTER 39.

1.   Trudeau, Jean Baptiste. *"Trudeau`s Journals."* South Dakota Historical Collections. Vol. II,.1912-1913, and *"Trudeau among the Arickara Indians."* Missouri Historical Society Collections. Vol. 1V. 1914.

2.   Du Lac, Perin. *"Travels Through Two Louisianas and among the Savage Nations of the Missouri."* London. 1807. Pp. 62-82.

3.   Stands-in-Timber, John. *"Papers."* No.-123-062. Wooden Leg College and Library Archives. Lame Deer, Montana. See also. Stands-in-Timber, John, In; *"Cheyenne Memories."* Edited by Margot Liberty. Pp. 119-120. Loc; cited, 1967.

4.   King, James, [Northern Cheyenne informant] to Author. Lame Deer. August 1994.

5.   Grinnell, George Bird. *"The Cheyenne Indians."* Vol. 2. P. 32. Yale University Press. 1923.

6.   Williamson, T. S. *"Minnesota Historical Society Collections."* Vol. 1. P. 242, and Vol. 111. P. 284.

7.   Mackay, James. *"Journal."* Proceedings State Historical Society, Wisconsin. 1915.

8.   Bent, George. See; Hyde, George E. *"Life of Bent."* 1967. The University of Oklahoma Press. 1968.

9.   Clark, W. P. *"The Indian Sign Language [Cheyenne]"* P. 39. University of Nebraska Press. [Reprint] 1982.

10.   Abel, Annie Heloise. *"Tabeau`s Narrative of Loisel`s Expedition to the Upper Missouri."* University of Oklahoma Press, Pp. 151-158. 1968.

11.   Service, Alex. *"The Life and Letters of Casper W. Collins."* Wyoming, City of Casper. 2000.

12.   *Ibid.*

13.   Allen, Charles Wesley. *"Autobiography of Red Cloud."* Montana Historical Society Press, 1997. Pp. 165-176.

14.   LaReye, Charles. *"The Journal of Charles LaReye,"* South Dakota Historical Society, 1V. 1908.

CHAPTER 40.

1.   Du Lac, Perin. *"Travels Through Two Louisianas and among the Savage Nations of the Missouri."* London. 1807.

2.   Left-Heron`s winter count. In; Waggoner, Josephine. *"Witness."* University of Nebraska Press. Pp. 530-548. 2013.

3.   Clark, W. P. *"The Indian Sign Language [Cheyenne]"* P. 39. University of Nebraska Press. [Reprint] 1982.

4.   Mallery, Garrick. *"Pictographs of the North American Indians."* Winter-Counts. Fourth Annual Report of the Bureau of American Ethnology. Washington D. C. 1886.

5.   *Ibid.*

6.   Trudeau, Jean Baptiste. *"Trudeau`s Journals."* South Dakota Historical Collections. Vol. II,.1912-1913, and *"Trudeau among the Arickara Indians."* Missouri Historical Society Collections. Vol. 1V. 1914.

7.   *Ibid.*

8.   *Ibid.*

9.   *Ibid.*

10.   *Ibid.*

11.   Waggoner, Josephine. *"Witness."* University of Nebraska Press. Pp. 530-548. 2013.

12.   *Ibid.*

13.   Mekeel, H. Scudder, *"Field Notes, Pine Ridge Reservation. [Interviews with Left-Heron],"* 1931. Archives of American Anthropology, American Museum of Natural History. New York.

14.   Tall-Bull, William, Interview with Author. Lame Deer, Montana. Sep; 1994. Author`s collection Note book 1. P. 2.

15.   *Ibid.*

BIBLIOGRAPHY

UNPUBLISHED SOURCES.

Smithsonian Institution, National Anthropological Archives, Washington DC.

Clark, Benjamin. *Cheyenne Ethnography and Local Names*. 1887. MS. 3449.
Michelson, Truman, *Field Notes and Papers*; 1910. MS. 222684.
Mooney, James. *Cheyenne Clan Names*, MS. 3203, pt.23. Note Books: *Cheyenne*. MS. 2531.

Southwest Museum. Los Angeles. California.

Grinnell, George Bird. *Papers and note books.*

Denver, Colorado.

George Bent – George E. Hyde correspondence. 1904-1906. Colorado Historical Society.
George Bent – George E. Hyde correspondence. 1904-1918. Denver Pub: Lib: Western History Collections.

Archives, American Museum of Natural History, New York.

Mekeel, H. Scudder, *"Field Notes."* Pine Ridge Reservation. [Interviews with Left-Heron]. 1931.

Internet explorer.

Bray, Kingsley. In; American Tribes.co.uk.
Welch, Colonel A. B. Dakota Papers.com [Indian Histories].

Author`s Collection.

Medicine Crow, Joe *[Crow Indian informant]* to Author. Lodge Grass. Montana. Through the years 1992 to 2009. Note pads and audio tapes.
James King, Et al; *Northern Cheyenne informants*. Note pad 1 and 2. 1992.
Wayne Medicine Elk. *Southern Cheyenne informant*. Note pad. 1. 1994.
Bill Tall Bull. *Northern Cheyenne informant*. Note pad. 1. 1994.
`Bisco` Spotted Wolf. *Northern Cheyenne informant*. Note pad 1. 1994.

PUBLISHED WORKS.

Abel, Annie Heloise.
    "Tabeau`s Narrative of Loisel`s Expedition to the Upper Missouri." University of Oklahoma Press, Pp. 151-158. 1968.
Adams, Richard C.
    "Legends of the Delaware Indians and Picture-writing" Washington DC. 1905.
Alencaster, Governor.
    In; *"Pedro Vial and the Road to Santa Fe."* Noel Loomis and Abraham P. Nasitir. 1967.
Allen, Charles Wesley.
    "Autobiography of Red Cloud. "Montana Historical Society Press, 1997.
Aubin, George F.

"*A Proto-Algonquian Dictionary.*" National Museum of Man, Canadian Ethnology Service Paper no. 29. National Museum of Canada. 1975.

Berthrong, Donald J.
"*The Southern Cheyennes.*" University of Oklahoma Press, Norman, 1963.

Blair, Emma H.
The Indian Tribes of the Upper Mississippi Valley and Region of the Great Lakes. 2 vols. Cleveland. 1911. [this monumental work contains the Major Marston material and also the writings of Nicolas Perrot].

Bowers, Alfred W.
"*Hidatsa Social and Ceremonial Organization.*" University of Nebraska Press.1992.

Brinton, Daniel G.
"*The Lene Lenape and their Legends. The Wallum Ollum.*" parts 2 and 3. The Library of Aboriginal American Literature. Vol. 5. 1882 -85.

Brose, David S.
"*Late Prehistory of the Upper Great Lakes Area.*" In: *Handbook of North American Indians* [Northeast] Vol. 15. Smithsonian Institution. Washington D.C. 1978.

Browman, David L.
"*Early Native Americans.*" Moulton Publishers. 1980.

Burpee, Lawrence,
"*Journals and Letters of the LaVerendryes.*" Toronto. The Champlain Society, 1927.

Carver, Jonathan.
"*Travels through the Interior Parts of North America.*" Ross and Haines. Minneapolis, Minnesota. 1956.

Champlain, Samuel D.
"*The Works of Samuel Champlain.*" 6. Vols. The Champlain Society. Toronto. 1922-36.

Clark, Peter Dooyentate.
"*Origin and History of the Wyandots*". Toronto; Hunter, Rose and Company. 1870.

Clark, William P.
"*The Indian Sign language.*" University of Nebraska Press. [Reprint] 1982.

Connelley, William Elsey.
"*Wyandot Folklore.*" Pp.17-24. Crane and Company, Topeka, Kansas. 1899.

Cleland, Charles E.
"*The Prehistoric animal and Ethnozoology of the Upper Great Lakes Region.*" University of Michigan; Museum of Anthropology, Anthropological papers 29. Ann Arbor. 1996.

Collett, Victor.
"*A Journey in North America.*" Vol. 2. Firenge, O, Lange, 1924.

Connelley, William Elsey.
"*Wyandot Folklore.*" Crane and Company, Topeka, Kansas. 1899.

Cortes, Jose.
"*Report on the Provinces of New Spain.*" University of Oklahoma Press. 1989.

Coxe, Daniel.
"*A Description of the English Province of Carolina.*" London. 1722.

Curtis, Edward S.
"*The North American Indian.*" 20 Vols. 1907-1930

DeVargas, Governor.
"*Letters.*" In, Twitchell, New Mexican Archives, Vol. 1. P. 265.

Dorsey, George A.
[a] *The Cheyenne: Ceremonial Organization.* Field Columbian Museum Publication No. 99. Anthropological Series Vol.1X, No. 1. Chicago, March, 1905.
[b] *The Cheyenne: The Sun Dance.* Field Columbian Museum Publication No. 103. Anthropological Series Vol.1X, No. 2. Chicago, May, 1905.

BIBLIOGRAPHY

Du Lac, Perin.
      "Travels Through Two Louisianas and among the Savage Nations of the Missouri." London. 1807.

Dunn, J.P.
      "Massacres of the Mountains." London; Eyre and Spottiswoode 1963.

Dusenberry, Vern.
      "The Northern Cheyenne." In: *"Montana."* The Magazine of Western History. 5, no. 1 [Winter 1955].

Eggan, Fred.
      "Cheyenne and Arapahoe Kinship System." In: *Social Anthropology of North American Tribes.*
      University of Chicago Press. Chicago. 1955.

Ewers, John C.
      "The Blackfeet: Raiders on the Northwestern Plains." University of Oklahoma Press. Norman.
      1958.

Fagan, Brian M.
      "Men of the Earth." Little Brown and Company. Boston. 1974.

Fitting, James E.
      "Regional Cultural Development, 300 B.C. to A.D. 1000. In: Handbook of North American
      Indians." [Northeast] Vol. 15. Smithsonian Institution. Washington D.C. 1978.

Fletcher, Alice C.
      "The Omaha Tribe." Vol. 2. Pp.47.ff. University of Nebraska Press. 1972.

Forbes, Jack D.
      "Apache, Navaho and Spaniard." University of Oklahoma Press. 1960.

Goddard, Ives.
      [a] *"Eastern Algonquian languages."* In; *Handbook of American Indians* [Edited by Bruce E. Trigger]
      Smithsonian Institution, Vol. 15, 1978.
      [b] *"The Suhtaio dialect of Cheyenne."* Papers of the Ninth Algonquian Conference. Pp. 68-80. Ottawa.
      Carleton University. 1978.

Gough, Barry M. [Editor].
      "The Journal of Alexander the Younger, 1799-1814." The Champlain Society. Toronto. 1992.

Grinnell, George Bird.
      [a] *The Cheyenne Indians* Vol. I and II. Yale University Press.1923.
      [b] *The Fighting Cheyennes.* University of Oklahoma Press. 1956.

Hanson, James Austin [Editor], "Little Chief's Gatherings." The Smithsonian Institution's G. K. Warren 1855-1857
      Expeditions Journals. The Fur Press. 1996.

Harp, Elmer Jr.
      "Pioneer cultures of the Sub-Arctic and the Arctic." Ancient Native Americans. San Francisco, W. H.
      Freeman.

Heckewelder, John.
      "An Account of the History, Manners and Customs of the Indian Nations." [Ms.] Philadelphia, 1881.

Hennepin, Louis.
      "A New Discovery of a Vast Country in America." London. 1698.

Henry, Alexander.
      "Journals." [See; August, 1801 entries]. Manitoba Historical Society. Manitoba, Canada.

Hester, James J.
      "Pleistocene Extinctions," Yale University Press. 1967.

Hodge, Frederick W.
      "Handbook of American Indians North of Mexico." Bureau of American Ethnology. Bulletin No. 30. 2 Vols.
      Smithsonian Institution, Washington DC.

Hoebel, E. Adamson.
      "The Cheyennes: Indians of the Great Plains." New York. 1963.

And, Karl N. Llewellyn. *The Cheyenne Way*. University of Oklahoma Press. 1941.

Hunt, George T.
   "The Wars of the Iroquois." University of Wisconsin Press. 1940.

Hunter, John D.
   "Memoirs of Captivity among Indians of North America." London. 1823.

Hyde, George E.
   [a] *Life of Bent*. 1967. The University of Oklahoma Press. 1968.
   [b] *Indians of the Woodlands*. 1962. The University of Oklahoma Press
   [c] *Indians of the High Plains*. 1959. The University of Oklahoma Press. 1959.
   [d] *Corn among the Indians of the Upper Missouri*. University of Nebraska Press. n.d.

Isham, James.
   "Notes and observations on the Dobbs Galley of 1749 to Hudson`s Bay." [Edited by E.E. Rich 1949].

Jackson, Donald. [Editor]
   "Black Hawk, an Autobiography." University of Illinois Press. [reprint] 1964.

Jennings, Jesse D. and Norbeck, Edward [Editors].
   "Prehistoric Man in the New World." University of Chicago Press. 1964.

Jones, Gwyn.
   "The Norse Atlantic Saga." Oxford University Press. 1986.

Keane, A.H.
   "Man Past and Present." Cambridge University Press. England. 1900.

Keim, De. B. Rudolph,
   "Sheridan`s Trooper on the Borders." University of Nebraska Press. 1995.

Kennedy, Michael Stephen.
   "The Assiniboine." Norman, University of Oklahoma Press. 1961.

Lacombe, Albert.
   "Dictionnaire et Grammaire de la Langue des Cris." Montreal. 1894-1901.

LaHontan, Baron.
   "New Voyages to North America." Vols 1 and 2. English translation published 1703.

LaReye, Charles.
   "The Journal of Charles LeRaye," South Dakota Historical Society, 1V. 1908

LaSalle, Chevalier Du,
   In, Margry, Pierre. *"Discoveries."* Vol. 11. P. 54.

LeSueur. Charles,
   "Narrative of LeSueur" In; *Pierre Margery, Decouvertes et etablissements des Francais dans l`oust et dans le sud de l`Amerique Septentrionale. 1614-1754*. Paris. 1875- 86.

Lissner, Ivar.
   "Man, God and Magic." Jonathan Cape. London, England. 1961

Long, Major Stephen.
   "From Pittsburgh to the Rocky Mountains, 1819-1820." Fulcrum ino. Golden, Colorado. 1988.

Mackay, Donald.
   "Journal and papers of Donald MacKay." Hudson`s Bay Archives. Provincial Archives of Manitoba, Winnipeg. Catalogue. E. 223/1.

Mackay, James,
   "Journal." Proceedings State Historical Society, Wisconsin. 1915.

Mallery, Garrick. *"Pictographs of the North American Indians."* Winter-Counts. Fourth Annual Report of the Bureau of American Ethnology. Washington D. C. 1886.

Marshall, Ingerborg.
   "A History and Ethnography of the Beothuk." McGill-Queen`s University Press..[No date].

Medicine Crow, Joe.

"From the Heart of the Crow Country." The Library of the American Indian. New York. 1992.

Mooney, James,

[a] *The Cheyenne Indians*. Memoirs of the American Anthropological Association, 1. Lancaster, Pa. 1905-1907.

[b] *The Ghost Dance Religion*. Fourteenth Annual Report. Bureau of American Ethnology. Washington. 1896.

Moore, John,

[a] *"The Cheyenne Nation."* University of Nebraska Press. 1987.

[b] *The Cheyenne*. Blackwell Publishers, Massachusetts. 1996.

[c] *Cheyenne Names and Cosmology*. American Ethnologist 11, 2: 1984.

Morgan, Lewis H.

"The Indian Journals, 1859 – 62" University of Michigan Press. Ann Arbor. 1959.

Mourant, A.E.

"The Distribution of the Human Blood Groups." Oxford, Blackwell. 1954.

Nasitir, Abraham P.

[a] "Before Lewis and Clark." University of Oklahoma. 1952.

[b] "Pedro Vial and the Road to Santa Fe." University of Oklahoma Press. 1967.

O`Meara, Walter.

"The Last Portage." The story of John Tanner`s captivity among the Indians. Houghton and Miffin Company. Boston. 1962.

Ossenberg, Nancy.

"Origins and relationships of Woodland People.". In *"Aspects of Upper Great Lakes Anthropology."* [Editor; Eldon Johnson] St. Paul. Minnesota Historical   Society. 1974.

Petter, Rudolph.

[a] *Cheyenne-English Dictionary*. Kettle Falls, Washington.1913-15.

[b] *Cheyenne Grammar*. Memoirs of the American Anthropological Association. 1907.

Pitot, James.

"Observations on the Colony of Louisiana from 1796 -1802." Boston Rouge. 1979.

Powell, Father Peter.

[a] *Sweet Medicine*. 2. Vols. University of Oklahoma Press. 1969.

[b] *People of the Sacred Mountain*. 2. Vols. Harper & Row. San Francisco, California. 1981.

[c] *Issiwun*. Montana Indian Publications. [No date].

Radisson, Pierre E.

"The Explorations of Radisson." Ross and Haines Ltd. 1961.

Rafinesque, Constantine.

"The American Nations." Philadelphia.1886.

Randolph, Richard W.

"Sweet Medicine." Caldwell, Idaho. Caxton Printers. 1937.

Raudot, Antoine D.

"Memoir concerning the different Indian Nations of North America." 1710.

Rhodes, Richard A. and Evelyn M. Todd.

"Sub-Arctic Algonquian languages," In; *Handbook of American Indians* [Edited by Bruce E. Trigger] Smithsonian Institution, Vol. 6, 1981.

Riggs, Stephen R.

"Dakota Grammar, texts and Ethnography. " Contributions to North American Ethnology, Vol. 9. Washington DC. Government Printing Office. 1893.

Ritchie, William A.

"Cultural Influences etc. "American Antiquity, Vol. 2. No.3. Smithsonian Institution Misc; Colls; 1940.

Robinson, Doane.

"*The History of the Dakota or Sioux Indians.*" Ross and Haines [Reprint]. 1967.

Roe, F.G.

"*The North American Buffalo.*" University of Toronto Press. 1970.

Sage, Rufus B. "*Scenes in the Rocky Mountains.*" Philadelphia. G. D. Miller. 1855.

Schukies, Renate [editor].

"*Red Hat; Blue Sky maker and Keeper of the Sacred Arrows*" University of Hamburg. Germany. 1993.

Schlesier, Karl H.

[a] *The Wolves of Heaven.* University of Oklahoma Press.1987.

[b] *Plains Indians; AD. 500 – 1500.* University of Oklahoma Press. 2001.

Schoolcraft, Henry R.

"*Journal of Travels.*" 1820.

Seger, John H.

"*Traditions of the Cheyenne Indians.*" Arapahoe, Oklahoma. 1905.

Service, Alex.

"*The Life and Letters of Casper W. Collins.*" Wyoming, City of Casper. 2000.

Siebert, Frank T.

"*The Original Home of the Proto-Algonquian People.*" National Museum of Canada, Bulletin no. 214. Anthropological Series no. 78. National Museum of Canada. 1967.

Smith, G. Hubert.

"*Explorations of the LaVerendryes in the Northern Plains.*" University of Nebraska Press. 1980.

Snow, Dean R.

"*Late Prehistory of the East Coast.*" In; *Handbook of American Indians* [Edited by Bruce E. Trigger] Smithsonian Institution, Vol. 15, 1978.

Speck, Frank G.

"*Montagnais-Naskapi Bands etc.;*" Proceedings of the American Philosophical Society. Vol. 85. No 2. 1942.

Stands In Timber, John. Margot Liberty [Editor].

[a] *Cheyenne Memories.* University of Oklahoma |Press. 1967.

[b] *John Stands In Timber Papers.* Wooden Leg College Archives. Lame Deer, Montana.

Swanton, John R.

"*The Indian Tribes of North America.*" Bureau of American Ethnology, Bulletin 145. Washington DC. 1952.

Tall Bull, Henry and Weist, Tom.

"*The Rolling Head.*" Montana Indian Publications 1971.

Tanner, John.

"*Narrative of Captivity and Adventures during Thirty Years Residence among the Indians of North America.* " New York. 1830.

Taylor, Colin.

"*Warriors of the Plains.*" The Hamlyn Publishing Group. 1975.

Taylor, Joseph H.

"*Sketches of Frontier Life.*" Washburn, North Dakota. 1895.

Thomas, David H.

"*Ancient Encounters; Kennewick Man etc.*" Basic Books ltd. 2000.

Thompson, David.

"*Narrative of his explorations in Western America, 1784 -181*" [Edited by J. B. Tyrrell.] Publ. Champlain Society. No 12. Toronto

Thwaites, Reuben G.

[a] *Jesuit Relations and Related Documents.* 73 vols. 1896 to 1901.

[b] *Lewis and Clark Journals.* Vol. 1.New York. 1904.

Tooker, Elisabeth.

An Ethnography of the Huron Indians. Syracuse University Press. 1991.

502

BIBLIOGRAPHY

Trigger, Bruce.

    [a] *Handbook of North American Indians*. Vol.6 Sub-Arctic. Smithsonian Institution. Washington DC. 1978.

    [b] *Handbook of North American Indians*. Vol. 15 Northeast. Smithsonian Institution, Washington DC. 1981.

    [c] *The Children of Aataentsic, a History of the Huron people to 1660*. 2Volls.McGills
        Queens University Press. Montreal. 1976.

    [d] Trigger, Bruce, and James F. Pendergast [Editors]. *"Hochelga; History and Ethnohistory."*
    Pp. 1-107 *in Cartier`s Hochelelga and the Dawson Site."* Montreal.
    McGills Queen`s University Press.

Trudeau, Jean Baptiste.

    "Trudeau`s Journals." South Dakota Historical Collections. Vol. II,.1912-1913, and *"Trudeau
    Among the Arickara Indians."* Missouri Historical Society Collections. Vol. 1V. 1914.

Trudeau, Pierre,

    "Journals." American Historical Review. Vol. X1X. No.2. January 1914 and   Missouri Historical
    Society Collections. Vol. 1V. St. Louis 1915.

Tuck, James A.

    "Regional Culture and Development." In; *Handbook of American Indians* [Edited by Bruce E.
    Trigger] Smithsonian Institution, Vol. 15, PP.28-43. 1978.

Umfreville, Edward.

    "The Present State of Hudson`s Bay." Charles Stalker. London. 1790.

Voegelin and Voegelin

    1946. Pp. 181-182.

Waggoner, Josephine.

    "Witness." Left-Heron`s Winter-Count. University of Nebraska Press. 2013.

Warren, William.

    "History of the Ojibway Indians." Minnesota Historical Society Press. 1984.

Weddle, Robert S.

    "LaSalle, the Mississippi and the Gulf; Three Primary Documents." College Station: Texas A & M University
    Press. 1987.

Wedel, Waldo R.

    "Prehistoric Man on the Great Plains. " University of Oklahoma Press. 1961.

Wied, Prince Maximillian Zu,

    "Travels in North America." London, 1844.

Weist, Tom.

    "A History of the Cheyenne People." Montana Council for Indian Education. Billings. Montana. 1977.

Weslager, C. A.

    "The Delaware Indians." Rutgers University Press.1989.

Wheat, Carl I.

    "Mapping the Trans Mississippi West." Institute of Cartography. San Francisco. 1957.

Will, George F. and George E. Hyde.

    [a] *Corn Among the Indians of the Upper Missouri*. Lincoln, Nebraska. n.d.

    [b] *The Cheyenne Indians in North Dakota*. Proceedings of the Mississippi Valley Historical Association.
    1913-14, 7 1914.

Winsor, Justin.

    "The Mississippi Basin." Boston Mass; 1895.

Wissler, Clark and Duvall, D.C.

    "Mythology of the Blackfoot Indians." University of Nebraska Press. 1995.

Wissler, Clark.

    [a] *The American Indian*. Published by Peter Smith. 1957.

    [b] *Indians of the United States*. The American Museum of Natural History. 1940.

BIBLIOGRAPHY

Wood, W. Raymond.

    [a] *"Biesterfeldt, a Post contact Coalescent Site of the Northern Plains."* Smithsonian Contributions to Anthropology no. 15. Washington DC. Smithsonian Institution Press. 1971.

    [b] *"The Explorations of the LaVerendryes in the Northern Plains."* University of Nebraska Press. 1980.

    [c] *"Prologue to Lewis and Clark; The MacKay and Evan`s Expedition."* University of Oklahoma Press. 2003.

Wright, James V.

    [a] *The Shield Archaic.* National Museum of Canada. Publications in Archaeology, no. 3 Ottawa. 1972.

    [b] *Prehistory of the Canadian Shield.* In; *Handbook of American Indians* Vol. 6.[Sub-Arctic]. [Edited by Bruce E. Trigger] Smithsonian Institution, Vol. 15, 1981.

ARTICLES.

Allouez, Francis.

    "Journals." Wisconsin Historical Society Collections. Bloomberg et al. 1964.

Bock, Philip K.

    *Micmac.*In *"Handbook of the North American Indian."* Vol.15. [The Northeast] Smithsonian Institution. Washington DC. 1978.

Cooper, John M.

    The Shaking Tent Rite among Plains and Forest Algonquians. Primitive Man, Vol. XV11, Nos. 3 and 4. [July and October, 1944].

Dorsey, George A.

    How the Pawnees Captured the Cheyenne Medicine Arrows. American Anthropologist, N.S. Vol. V, No. 4 [October – December, 1903].

Dusenberry, Verne.

    The Horn in the Ice, a Cheyenne Story. Montana State Historical Society Press. n.d.

Grinnell, George Bird.

    [a] *The Cheyenne Medicine Lodge.* American Anthropologist, N.S., Vol.XV1, No. 2. [April – June. 1914].

    [b] *A Cheyenne obstacle Myth.* Journal of American Folklore, Vol. XV1, No. XL [Jan – March. 1903].

    [c] *Cheyenne Stream Names.* American Anthropologist, N.S., Vol.V111, No. 1. [Jan – March. 1906].

    [d] *Early Cheyenne Villages.* American Anthropologist, N.S. Vol. XX, No. 4. [Oct: - Dec: 1918].

    [e] *The Great Mysteries of the Cheyenne.* American Anthropologist, N.S., ol.X11, No. 4. [Oct: - Dec: 1910].

    [f] *Some Early Cheyenne Tales.* Journal of American Folklore, Vol. XX, and XX1.Nos. 78 and 82. [July– September 1907 and Oct: Dec: 1908].

Kroeber, A.L.

    Cheyenne Tales. Journal of American Folklore, Vol. X111, No. 50 [July– Sep. 1900].

Petersen, Karen D.

    Cheyenne Soldier Societies. Plains Anthropologist, Vol. 1X, No. 25 [August, 1964].

Powell, Father Peter.

    Issiwun: Sacred Buffalo Hat of the Northern Cheyenne. *"Montana."* The Magazine of American History, Vol. X, No. 1 [Winter 1960].

Rhodes, Richard A. and Evelyn M. Todd.

    Sub-Arctic Algonquian languages. In, Handbook of American Indians [Edited by Bruce E. Trigger] Smithsonian Institution, Vol. 6, 1981.

    Silvy 1974 and Fabvre 1970

    Segar, John H. *"Traditions of the Cheyenne Indians."* Chronicles of Oklahoma, Vol. 6 no. 3. 1928.

Snow, Dean R.

Late Prehistory of the East Coast." In, Handbook of American Indians [Edited by Bruce E. Trigger] Smithsonian Institution, Vol. 15, 1978.

Strong, William Duncan.
From History to Pre-History in the Northern Great Plains. Smithsonian Miscellaneous   Collections, Vol. C. Washington D.C. 1940.

Swanton, John R.
Some Neglected Data Bearing on Cheyenne, Chippewa and Dakota History. American   Anthropologist, N.S., Vol.XXX11, No. 1. [Jan: - March: 1930].

Vasilevich, G.M.
Early concepts about the Universe among Evenks. In*; Studies in Siberian Shamanism.* University of Toronto Press. 1963.

Will, George F.
The Cheyenne Indians in North Dakota. Proceedings of the Mississippi Valley Historical Association. 1913-14. Vol. V11. Cedar Rapids, 1914.

Wood, W. Raymond.
[a] *"The John Evan`s 1796-1797 map of the Missouyri River."* Great Plains Quarterly. 1. [1]. 1981.
[b] *"Earliest Map of the Mandan Heartland, the Jarvis and Mackay 1791 Map."*.Plains Anthropologist. Vol. 55. No. 216, 2010.

Abenaki [tribe], v, 1, 46.

Above World, xvii, 6, 150, 158, 242.

Agatomitou, [tribe] 219, 267.

Ainu, 4, 5, 10, 12, 17, 18, 52.

Alaska,, 2, 4.

Algonkin-proper, 33, 34, 37, 77, 90, 97, 174, 223.

Algonquian linguistic family, viii, xx, 1, 5, 134.

Alimouspigioa [tribe]*k*, 219, 248.

Allouez, Father, 37, 191, 200, 223, 224, 252, 256, 489, 491.

Altai Mountains, 1, 5.

Altamira, 9.

American-Horse, vii, viii, 162, 163, 165, 451, 470, 473, 478.

Amur River, 4.

Ancient Time, xix, 13, 50, 52, 73, 74, 75, 92, 94, 95, 101, 102, 115, 118, 170, 223.

Anglo Saxons, 1.

Aorta [Cheyennes], xvi, 21, 30, 36, 76, 79, 163, 166, 174, 177, 180, 236, 237, 238, 284, 298, 299, 333, 334, 343, 344, 345, 346, 359, 385, 388, 389, 404, 411, 416, 417, 426, 428, 436, 438, 439, 441, 442, 444, 459, 460, 464, 466, 479, 482.

Apache [tribe], 25, 151, 155, 160, 348, 353, 360, 361, 362, 364, 365, 366, 367, 368, 372, 384, 388, 443, 446, 488.

Arapahoe [tribe], 1, 23, 24, 25, 26, 30, 82, 97, 101, 118, 125, 129, 135, 136, 138, 139, 140, 148, 149, 160, 184, 185, 186, 190, 196, 197, 201, 208, 209, 210, 211, 226, 239, 243, 281, 330, 338, 344, 345, 346, 349, 360, 368, 369, 370, 383, 384, 385, 417, 443, 444, 446, 448, 449, 450, 455, 462, 465, 473, 486, 488, 498, 502.

Arctic seas, 5.

Argenson, Pierre de Voyer Viscount d, 251.

Arickara [tribe], 175, 293, 301, 309, 310, 311, 312, 313, 314, 315, 316, 317, 318, 320, 325, 330, 347, 348, 349, 350, 351, 353, 354, 357, 358, 359, 361, 362, 363, 364, 365, 366, 368, 370, 375, 382, 384, 385, 386, 387, 388, 389, 390, 391, 393, 394, 395, 396, 400, 401, 402,406, 407, 411, 418, 429, 430, 431, 432, 435, 436, 439, 441, 442, 444, 448, 449, 454, 461, 463, 464, 465, 466, 473, 481.

Arkansas River, 30.

Arrow Keeper, 160.

Arvilla complex, 56, 148, 149, 211.

Assiniboine River, 59.

Assiniboine [tribe], 19, 20, 59, 145, 186, 187, 191, 192, 193, 195, 196, 197, 203, 204, 206, 228, 231, 238, 247, 256, 261, 262, 269, 274, 275, 276, 278, 279, 280, 281, 282, 291, 296, 297, 298, 310, 315, 318, 319, 330, 332, 333, 338, 339, 340, 341, 342, 343, 344, 345, 346, 359, 369, 375, 376, 382, 388, 389, 401, 402, 403, 404, 411, 413, 418, 419, 420, 421, 422, 424, 425, 426, 427, 429, 450, 452, 453, 458, 459, 462, 465, 466.

Assinipoulak [tribe], 145.

Astor, John Jacob, 435.

Athapaskan, 4, 51, 486, 488.

atlatl, vii, 6.

Atsina [tribe], 23, 25, 101, 135, 201, 262, 281, 383.

Attigamiques [tribe], 37.

Aulneau, Father, 389, 390.

Awatixa [tribe], 152.

Awaxawi [tribe], 146, 396, 399, 400, 431, 439.

Awigaxa [tribe], 349, 350, 351, 353, 354, 355, 356, 357, 358, 359, 360, 387, 396.

Balder [Norse god], 8.

Baptist Good, 467.

Baring Straits, 4.

Barret, S. M .461.

Bear Butte, 151, 154, 155, 156, 242, 244, 348, 388, 482, 485.

Bear Hills, 63.

Bear-Comes-Running, 460.

Bear-in-the-Water, 293.

Bear Spirit warriors, 9.

Beauharnois, Marquis de, 407, 492.

Beautiful Country, 13.

Beaux Hommes [tribe], 377, 383, 384.

Beccancouer River, 90, 97.

Beede, Reverend Dr. 431.

Bell, Captain, 214.

Bellin, 278, 279.

Below World, xvii,6, 7, 20, 150, 158, 242.

Bent, George, 27, 36, 175, 235, 344, 392, 407, 410, 411, 416, 417, 454, 490, 491.

Beothuk [tribe], 55, 56.

Beringia, 1, 4.

Berserkers, .

Besant culture, 485.

Biesterfeldt village site, 274, 291, 292, 296, 321, 322, 323, 324, 325, 326, 327, 328, 332, 335, 338, 340, 341, 343, 345, 351, 359, 386, 390, 400, 403, 410, 412, 413, 416, 418, 419, 421, 422, 424, 425, 426, 429, 443.

Big Cheyenne River, 317, 349, 351, 354, 356, 357, 358, 360, 379, 382, 387, 395, 402, 434, 436, 437, 442, 443, 444, 446, 450, 462, 463, 464, 466, 468

Big Sioux River, 305, 308, 309.

Big Stone Lake, 20, 181, 234, 269, 270, 274, 289, 304, 314, 315, 316, 317, 328, 331, 333, 334, 335, 412, 414, 415, 417, 419, 427, 430, 458, 460, 461, 464, 480.

Big-Wolf, 407, 410.

Black-Duck Culture, vii, viii, 53, 56, 82, 121, 128, 136, 138, 147, 148, 149, 209, 210, 211, 246, 291.

Black-Elk, 420, 452, 454, 467.

Blackfoot [tribe], xii, 1, 8, 22, 23, 25, 26, 43, 56, 57, 97, 118, 125, 135, 136, 139, 140, 184, 185, 186, 190, 197, 201, 208, 209, 220, 226, 262, 270, 278, 281, 344, 345, 346, 366, 367, 368, 369, 431, 464, 503.

Black Hills, vi, xx, 23, 24, 76, 94, 151, 154, 214, 243, 309, 317, 347, 348, 349, 353, 361, 363, 364, 365,

368, 369, 372, 377, 383, 384, 385, 386, 387, 388, 391, 392, 402, 403, 422, 427, 433, 434, 435, 436, 439, 441, 445, 446, 448, 449, 450, 451, 454, 462, 464, 465, 466, 468, 469, 471, 473, 481, 485.

Black Hills Tribes, 445, 450, 462, 464, 465, 468, 469, 481.

Black-Kettle, 241.

Black Moccasin, 25.

Black-Moon, 480.

Black Mountain, 211, 244.

Black-Pipe, 73, 75, 92, 95, 309, 348, 390, 454, 468.

Black-Shin, 241, 483.

Blood-Clot Boy, 25.

Blue Bead Indians [tribe], 444.

Blue Earth Country, 15.

Blue Earth River, 182, 286, 299.

Blue Sky, 6, 7, 8, 49, 389.

Blue-Blanket, 468.

Blue-Thunder, 331, 432, 433.

Bone Hill, 413.

Bourgainville, General Louis, 383, 388, 395, 408, 411.

Bourgmont, 363, 366, 387.

Bowstring Lake, 142, 152, 163, 165, 183, 226, 259.

Bowstring River, 152, 163, 183, 226, 259.

Bowstrings [Cheyennes], xvii, 162, 163, 164, 165, 166, 167, 168, 175, 177, 178, 181, 183, 184, 207, 208, 224, 226, 237, 238, 258, 261, 262, 267, 269, 273, 274, 282, 291, 297, 298, 302, 307, 317, 318, 319, 324, 328, 332, 333, 334, 335, 343, 344, 345, 346, 359, 370, 385, 387, 388, 390, 404, 408, 411, 416, 418, 419, 426, 427, 428, 429, 430, 431, 432, 438, 441, 442, 443, 444.

Bradley, Bruce, 2.

Brendan, Saint, 11.

Brule [tribe], 270, 332, 415, 427, 428, 452, 454, 455, 457, 458, 459, 460, 461, 463, 464, 465, 466, 467, 468, 470, 471, 481.

Bubonic Plague, 106.

Buddhism, 17.

Buffalo, 76.

Buffalo Hat Keeper, 416.

Buffalo Priest, 337, 480.

Bull or Buffalo Soldiers, xvii, 407.

Bull-Could-Not-Rise, 409.

Bull-Thigh, 36, 165, 309, 408, 411.

Burnt Aorta [Cheyenne band], xvi, 438.

Bush Cree [tribe], 29, 63.

Bushotter, George 454.

Caddoan [tribe], 303, 308, 312, 313, 330, 349, 362, 363, 366, 395, 396, 402.

Cahokia, 105, 106.

Calumet Ceremony, 183, 252 ,305, 308, 311, 380, 464, 482.

Cambrian Culture, 147, 294.

Canada, 2, 4.

Cannibalism, 125.

Cannonball River, 293, 398, 435, 436, 441, 442, 444, 464, 466.

Caribou,4, 13.

Cartier, Jacques, 40.

Carver, Jonathan, 43, 333, 406, 415, 417, 427

Cass Lake, 258

Caucasians, 1 ,2, 9.

Cave Bear, 6.

Cedar-Tree, 24.

Celestial Bear, 10, 17, 31, 42.

Celtic, 1, 2, 8, 10, 11, 21, 154, 159.

Central Algonquian, 30, 63, 113, 133, 182, 183, 209, 220, 224, 244, 249, 251, 254, 260.

Chaa, 41.

Chaguiennes [tribe], 411, 444.

Chaiena, [tribe] 255, 267.

Chaienaton [tribe], 267, 268, 269, 272, 273, 274, 275, 276, 281, 284, 297, 443.

Champlain, Samuel, 86, 89, 188, 198, 199, 490, 491, 493, 497, 502.

Chang Tung [tribe], 17.

Changaskiton Lac, 220.

Charlevoix, [Jesuit Priest], 97.

Chauvet caves, 9.

Chequamegon Bay, 231.

Cherokee [tribe], 70.

Cherry Creek, 437, 441, 442, 443, 444, 464.

Chesapeake Bay, 2.

Cheyenne dialect, xi, 23, 43, 59, 173, 213, 247.

Cheyennes and Suhtaio unite. 237-238, 482.

Cheyenne River, viii, 379, 385, 387, 392, 436, 442, 450, 455, 461, 478.

Chief Little-Man, 160.

Chief Long-Hair, 450.

Chief Masco, 50.

Chief Masqua, 197, 198, 199, 200.

Chief Snowbird, 75.

Chief Soldiers, xvii.

Chiens [tribe], 25, 408.

Chionitones [tribe], 440.

Chipewayans [tribe], 191.

Chippewa [tribe], xii, 1, 5, 24, 26, 30, 33, 34, 37, 38, 40, 42, 44, 45, 48, 50, 51, 57, 58, 59, 60, 63, 64, 68, 69, 72, 82, 84, 85, 86, 87, 88, 90, 91, 92, 95, 96, 97, 98, 99, 102, 103, 104, 105, 107, 108, 110, 111, 113, 114, 118, 119, 120, 122, 125, 126, 127, 133, 145, 146, 147, 148, 149, 166, 172, 173, 174, 186, 187, 190, 192, 193, 194, 195, 196, 197, 198, 199, 200, 202, 204, 207, 208, 210, 211, 213, 214, 216, 219, 220, 222, 223, 225, 228 passim.

Chiwere [tribe], 292.

Chongaskiton [tribe], 222, 223, 238, 256, 269, 284, 333, 342, 462.

Chongouseeton, [tribe] 415, 417.

Chouta [tribe], 411, 442, 444.

Chouteau, A. P. 454.

Christeneaux [tribe], 29.

Cinemo [Cheyenne], 465.

Clans, 30, 36, 42, 63, 92, 96,119, 138, 152, 180, 192, 212, 416, 417, 437, 438.

Clark, Ben, 172, 214.

Clark, W. P., 13, 73, 92, 307, 354, 387, 390, 454, 468.

Closed-Man, 312, 313.

Cloud-Shield, vii, 469, 473.

Clovis point culture, 2, 12, 17, 18, 20.

Cold-Wind, 147.

Collett, Victor, viii, 442, 443, 444.

Collins, Casper 454, 455.

Colorado, 24.

Comanche [tribe], 30, 160, 353, 360, 363, 364, 365, 368, 369, 370, 384, 385, 386, 447, 448, 449, 455, 469, 488.

Comfort, Dr. 300, 428.

Contraries, xvii.

Coquart, Father Claude Godfroy, 492.

Corn, 76.

Coronado, Francisco, 161.

Cortes, Juan, 66.

Coteau des Missouri, 329.

Coteau des Prairies, 24, 135, 152, 204, 208, 238, 239, 262, 274, 284, 298, 318, 324, 328, 329, 331, 332, 333, 335, 336, 343, 344, 345, 346, 348, 393, 399, 403, 404, 410, 414, 421.

Coxe, Daniel, 225, 270, 282-287, 415.

Crazy-Dog [Sioux Chief], 479.

Crazy-Dogs [Cheyenne Society], xvii.

Cree [tribe], v, xii, 1, 8, 15, 19, 20, 21, 22, 23, 25, 26, 27, 29, 30, 31, 32, 33, 34, 36, 37, 38, 39, 40, 41, 43, 44, 45, 47, 52, 54, 60, 61, 63, 74, 79, 82, 88, 89, 90, 92, 97, 101, 107, 108, 112, 113, 114, 118, 119, 126, 127, 128, 133, 135, 138, 139, 144, 147, 148, 152, 158, 163, 164, 165, 168, 172, 173, 174, 175, 178, 186, 187, 189, 191, 192, 193, 194, 195, 196, 197, 198, 199, 200, 201, 202, 203, 204, 206, 207, 208, 209, 210, 211, 213 *passim.*

Creux, Father, 216, 219, 220, 224, 256, 37, 191, 223, 224, 225, 504.

Cro-Magnon, 1, 9.

Crooked-Lances [Cheyenne Society], vii, xvii.

Crow [tribe], iv, xii, xiii, 25, 30, 145, 147, 168, 186, 191, 262, 267, 272, 275, 278, 281, 282, 291, 298, 304, 326, 330, 344, 345, 367, 369, 370, 383, 384, 385, 396, 420, 444, 446, 450, 455, 464, 478, 488, 490.

Crow Creek massacre, 186.

Crow Wing, 146.

Cut-Arms [tribe], 315, 459.

Cut-Fingers [tribe], 459, 461, 457, 462.

D'Eglise, Jaques, 433, 434, 435.

Dakota Sioux [tribe], 9, 19, 107, 121, 149, 171, 197, 210, 222, 250, 255, 269, 270, 271, 273, 284, 290, 294, 300, 314, 324, 332, 334.

Danube, [River], 62.

De Vargas, Governor, 25.

DeIsle, Guilliam, 268.

Delaware [tribe], xii, 1, 9, 10, 11, 31, 40, 43, 44, 45, 46, 47, 48, 49, 50, 51, 52, 53, 54, 55, 56, 57, 58, 59, 60, 61, 62, 63, 64, 67, 68, 69, 70, 71, 72, 73,

75, 80, 81, 82, 84, 85, 87, 88, 90, 96, 103, 104, 105, 107, 108, 110, 111, 136, 138, 148, 190, 210, 485, 486, 487, 489, 497, 503.

Denig, Edwin T., 228.

Denisovans, 1, 17.

Des Moines River, 305.

Desert Men, 177.

DeSoto, Hernando, 161.

Dirt-Lodge Creek, 432, 434, 436, 444

DNA technology, 1, 2

Dog Lake, 225.

Dog or Dog Rope Soldiers, vii, xvii, 226.

Doll-Man, 439.

Dorsey, George A. 13, 14, 92, 104, 223, 225.

Duck Bay culture, 56, 211.

Du Lac, Perin, 447.

Duluth, Daniel Greysolon Sieur, 222, 260-262, 270, 284, 288.

Dutch, 190.

E`hyoph`sta, 9.

Eagle`s-Nest, 156.

Early Woodland culture, 136.

Earth Renewal ceremonies, xvii.

East Asia, 2.

East Cree [tribe], 23, 25, 33, 37, 38.

Eastern Algonquians [tribe], 408.

Eastern Sioux [tribe], 21, 231, 250, 251, 254, 255, 260, 261, 262, 271, 292, 294, 297, 298, 306, 310, 314, 318, 332, 333, 359, 404, 408, 412, 415, 416, 421, 428, 454, 459, 463.

Eastern United States, xii.

Eastman, Reverend Charles, 459.

Eats-No-Heart, 480.

El Salvador, 56.

Elk, 4.

Elk Horn River, 387.

Elk warrior society, vii, xvii, 242.

Elk-River, 436, 437, 438.

English, 190.

Erect-Horns, xv, 235.

Eskimo, 13, 47, 50, 52, 58, 106, 191.

Eurasian, xii.

Europid-Asiatic, 4.

Evenk, [Tungas], 5, 10, 48.

Evans, John, 441.

Falls of St. Anthony, 142, 194, 224, 249, 254, 271, 275, 282, 284, 289, 301, 305.

Farm School village, 428, 430-436.

Fathers of the White Eagle [tribe], 61.

Fine-Day, 227.

Fire Heart Butte, 397.

Fire-Wolf, vii, 176, 179, 233, 234, 410.

Flathead [tribe], 361, 364, 366, 369, 384.

Flint Band [Cheyennes], 30.

Flyers [tribe], 214, 445, 480.

Flying Big-Bellies [tribe], 439.

Flying-Thunder-Eagle, 324, 327, 328, 342, 425.

Folsom point culture, 17, 18, 20.

Fort Beauharnois, vii, 407.

Fort Crevecoeur, 41, 285, 292.

Fort Larned, ix.

Fort Lincoln, 211, 413, 437, 439, 441, 444, 452

Fox [tribe], xvii, 1, 22, 25, 26, 32, 37, 38, 40, 44, 46, 47, 50, 61, 63, 71, 79, 87, 88, 89, 90, 91, 95, 96, 97, 98, 107, 108, 110, 111, 112, 113, 119, 120, 136, 163, 164, 165, 166, 167, 175, 177, 178, 180, 190, 193, 220, 225, 226, 231, 237, 238, 243, 244, 246, 249,251, 252, 254, 260, 262, 269, 274, 275, 284, 288, 297, 298, 299, 310, 332, 335, 359, 385, 388, 408, 411, 416, 417, 426, 436, 437, 438, 485.

Franquelin, Louis Baptiste, viii, 36, 256, 262, 267, 268, 269, 270, 271, 272, 274, 275, 276, 277, 278, 279, 280, 281, 282, 284, 286, 290, 313, 414.

French, 40, 309.

Gaelic, 2.

Garreau, Joseph, 434, 475.

Gattacka [tribe], 312, 360, 361, 362, 363, 364, 365, 366, 368, 369, 370, 383, 384, 385, 386, 388, 403, 446, 448, 450, 465.

Gens de L`Arc [tribe], 163, 380, 382, 385, 388, 404, 411.

Gens de la Fleche Colee [tribe], 389, 390, 414.

Gens des Cheveaux [tribe], 377, 378, 384.

Gentle-Horse, 241.

Georgian Bay, 52, 111, 114.

Germanic, 2, 8, 10, 154.

Giant beaver, 17.

Giant buffalo, 17.

Giant caribou, 4.

Giant elk, 17.

Giant moose, 17.

Giant sloth, 17.

Giant Stag-Moose,, 49.

Giant Turtle, 13, 48.

Gilyak [tribe], 4, 12, 48.

Glooskap, 8.

Goddard, Ives, 28, 136, 209, 498.

Good River, 349, 450.

Goths, 62.

Grand River, 393, 395, 432, 433, 434, 435, 436, 441, 444, 446, 462, 464, 466.

Grasshoppers [tribe], 169, 170, 173, 175, 176, 177, 178, 179, 180, 181, 184.

Great Elbow Bend, 144, 168, 183, 184.

Great Hollow Well, 63.

Great Ice-Age, 4.

Great Medicine, 13.

Great White Father, ix.

Greeks, 1.

Green Bay, 190.

Greenland, 4, 9, 17, 52, 58, 106.

Grey-Thunder, 160, 439.

Grinnell, George Bird,, xiii, 13, 15, 25, 202, 211, 239, 302, 324, 393, 431.

Gros Ventre [tribe], 23.

Grossillers, Des, 145.

Gulf of the St. Lawrence, 40, 60, 106

Hair-Rope-Men, xvi, 30, 483.

Hairy People, 14, 15, 17, 18, 38, 52.

Hako, 183, 303, 305, 307, 308, 311, 312, 350

Half Sioux / Half Heviatanio, xvi.

Halitanes [tribe], 447, 448.

Hankering-Wolf, 443.

Heckewelder, John D. 69, 71, 80, 81, 84, 486, 487, 489, 499

Hennepin, Father Louis, viii, 220, 222, 223, 224, 225, 256, 258, 312, 491, 499

Henry, Alexander the younger, 58, 59, 100, 142, 214, 277, 327, 328, 343, 424, 425, 426, 429, 435, 436, 453, 490.

Heviatanio [Cheyennes], xvi.

Heviqsnipahis [Cheyennes], xvi.

Hi-mo`weyuhks [Cheyennes], xvii.

Hidatsa [tribe], 22, 23, 25, 98, 139, 144, 145, 146, 147, 148, 149, 151, 152, 154, 155, 156, 160, 185, 186, 191, 193, 195, 196, 197, 208, 210, 212, 232, 262, 278, 281, 291, 293, 296, 320, 326, 327, 328, 330, 344, 345, 346, 347, 353, 356, 357, 358, 361, 383, 389, 396, 397, 398, 399, 400, 403, 412, 430, 431, 433, 435, 436, 439, 441, 450, 452, 462, 464, 497.

High Plains., 15.

High-Backed-Wolf, iv, vii, 160, 241, 335, 443.

Hill Men [Cheyennes], 184.

Himatanohis [Cheyennes], xvii.

Hintz village site, 211, 342, 344, 412, 413, 414, 416, 417, 419, 426, 427, 428.

Hodge, Frederick, 29.

Hofnowa [Cheyennes], xvi.

Ho-Hay [tribe], v, 186, 195, 202, 203, 204, 205, 206, 207, 231, 249, 274, 332, 403, 420, 421.

Hohnuhk`e [Cheyennes], xvii.

Hoistah, 461.

Holocene period, 15.

Hota`mita`niu [Cheyennes], xvii.

Hotami`-Massau [Cheyennes], xvii.

Houebatons, [tribe] 260.

Hudson`s Bay Company, 146, 196, 439, 450

Hudson's Bay, 9, 44, 51, 53, 56, 60, 61, 81, 116, 146, 191, 192, 196, 247, 257, 259, 275, 277, 278, 280, 281, 366, 401, 422, 486.

Hunka Ceremony, 252, 482.

Hunkpapa [tribe], 270, 432, 480, 481.

Hunt, William Price, 435.

Huron [tribe], 33, 41, 44, 51, 57, 64, 67, 69, 70, 71, 72, 73, 74, 75, 79, 80, 81, 84, 85, 86, 87, 88, 89, 95, 96, 99, 107, 108, 110, 111, 112, 113, 114, 115, 119, 157, 219, 229, 230, 250, 251, 487, 502, 503.

Hyde, George E., xiii, 171, 257, 479, 496, 503.;Iceland, 4.

Illini [tribe], 104, 172, 181, 190, 249, 251, 254, 288.

Illinois, 41, 104, 106, 113, 182, 193, 210, 225, 249, 254, 262.

Illinois River, 276, 283, 285, 289, 312, 435

Indian People, 13, 14.
Inuit [Eskimo], 13.
Iowa [tribe], 207, 282, 283, 285, 286, 287, 288, 290, 291, 292, 294, 297, 298, 301, 303, 304, 305, 306, 307, 308, 309, 310, 311, 312, 313, 314, 315, 317, 329, 331, 332, 347, 348, 349, 350, 402, 405, 408, 458.
Iroquoian, 88.
Iroquois [tribe], 37, 64, 69, 72, 108.
Isantiton [tribe], 270.
Island of Montreal., 72.
Issiometanui [Cheyennes], xvi.
Issiwun, v, 236, 241, 406.
James Bay, 54, 57, 61.
Jicarilla [tribe], 362, 366.
Joliet, Louis, viii, 36, 183, 217, 219, 220, 223, 224, 229, 233, 255, 256, 257, 258, 259, 267-269, 272.
Kamchatka, 4, 5, 9, 17, 48, 52, 158.
Kansa [tribe], 190, 292.
Kayoha [tribe], 442.
Keepers of the flame, 5, 30, 36.
Keewatin, 9, 12, 46, 47, 50, 52, 53, 54, 55, 56, 57, 59, 60, 104, 111, 135, 138, 486.
Keim, De B.Randolph, 20.
Kelsey, Henry, 277.
Kennewick Man, 17.
Kentucky, 70.
Keronki Reserve, 9.
Kickapoo [tribe], 50, 63, 79, 87, 90, 96, 97, 107, 108, 110, 119, 120, 249, 252.
Kilistinouc [tribe], 37.
King, James [Jim], vii, xv, 29, 184, 185, 197, 203, 219, 251, 252, 259, 260, 490, 491, 496.
Kiowa [tribe], 30, 50, 98, 151, 155, 160, 175, 330, 360, 361, 362, 363, 365, 366, 367, 368, 369, 370, 383, 384, 385, 386, 388, 403, 442, 443, 446, 448, 449, 450, 455, 462, 464, 465, 470, 473
Kites [tribe], 214, 417, 445, 483.
Kit-Fox [Cheyennes], vii, xvii, 32, 39, 164, 166, 178, 180, 226, 237, 238, 242, 298.
Kit-Fox Warrior Society, xvii, 164, 269.
Kiyuksa [tribe], 479.
Knaisitaras, [tribe] 414.
Knife River, 146, 147, 152, 156, 262, 347, 399, 431, 435, 436, 441.
Koryak [tribe], 2.
Krakatoa, 55.
Kuato [tribe], 470.
Kinyan [tribe], 480.
Ku-hinyan, [tribe] 479, 480.
Kulm, 274, 291, 304 *passim.*
Kutenais [tribe], 384.
Kwahadi [tribe], 364.
L`Allemant, Father Charles, 198.
L`Anse aux Meadows, 108.
LaHontan, Baron, 414.
La Petite Nacion, 33, 37.
La Point, 85.

Labrador, 52, 59.
Lac des Assenipoils, 279.
Lac des Tintons, 458.
Lac Qui Parl, 290, 304.
LaFrance, Joseph., viii, 36, 261, 275, 383, 414.
Lakdah, 17.
Lake Taureau, 105.
Lake *Alimibeg*, 145.
Lake Andes, 297, 314, 316, 458.
Lake Erie, 41, 71.
Lake Forest Archaic, 51.
Lake Huron, 87, 114, 115.
Lake lac Qui Parle, 183.
Lake Llopango, 56.
Lake Michigan, 67, 111, 121, 182, 189, 247.
Lake Nipigon, 129, 191, 192, 210, 214, 216, 219, 222, 223, 225, 229, 231, 256, 261.
Lake Nipissing, 108, 115.
Lake of the Woods, 187, 276.
Lake Ontario, 41.
Lake Pepin, 285, 292.
Lake St. Clair, 72.
Lake Superior, 37, 40, 41, 44, 45, 54, 81, 82, 86, 112, 114, 115, 116, 118, 119, 120, 121, 122, 128, 129, 134, 139, 141, 187, 189, 192, 193, 196, 197, 200, 202, 207, 209, 210, 213, 219, 220, 222, 223, 224, 225, 230, 231, 246, 247, 249, 250, 257, 258, 260, 261.
Lake Taureau, 74, 75, 76, 80, 92, 119, 127.
Lake Traverse, 20, 236, 262, 276, 304, 310, 314, 316, 317, 328, 331, 334, 412.
Lake Winnibegoshish, 142, 258.
Lake Winnibigosis, 136.
Lake Winnipeg, 44, 53, 54, 60, 136, 139, 201, 257, 262, 277.
Lakota [tribe], 9, 20, 212, 270, 427, 455, 479.
Laramie River, 443.
LaSalle, Chavalier du, 41, 287.
Last Great Ice Age, 4.
Late Pleistocene, 2.
Late Point Peninsular., 53.
Late Woodland culture, 74, 291.
Laurel culture, viii, 47, 51, 53, 81, 82, 127, 128, 135, 136, 138, 170, 208, 209.
LaVerendrye, 43, 277, 278, 279, 281, 357, 367, 372, 375, 376, 377, 378, 379, 382, 383, 384, 385, 386, 388, 389, 390, 392, 395, 402, 408, 414, 427, 443, 446.
Leech Lake, 142, 147, 210, 213, 219, 225, 229, 233, 250, 256, 257, 258, 259.
Left-Heron, 467-469, 478, 479, 481.
Lery, Baron de, 161.
Les Pouls ou Assenipoils, 280.
LeRaye, Charles, 454, 461, 482.
LeSueur, Pierre Charles, 197, 267, 268, 269, 270, 271, 281, 289, 315, 331, 332, 458, 460.
Lewis and Clark, 34, 36, 77, 214, 257, 258, 367, 384, 394, 400, 436, 438, 444, 454, 481, 502.

Light-skinned Hairy People, 13, 17.
Lipan [tribe], 362, 363, 364, 366.
Little-Bird, James, 247.
Little Cheyenne River, 348, 351, 354, 386, 387, 392, 399, 426, 436, 437.
Little-Chief, 437.
Little Coyote, Henry, 213.
Little Foxes [tribe], 378, 385.
Little Ice Age, 120.
Little-Man, [chief], 160.
Little Missouri, 94, 377, 383, 384, 436, 441, 444, 450, 464, 466, 469.
Little-Thunder, 461, 484.
Little-Wolf, 242.
Llano culture, 2.
Loki, 8.
Lone-Dog, 482.
Long Bow, 457.
Long Lake, 274, 343, 344, 346, 411, 426, 436, 460.
Long Lance, Buffalo Child, 197.
Long, Major Stephen, 214.
Long-haired Cheyenne, 473.
Long-heads., 13.
Lost Children, 315, 456, 458, 460.
Louis XIV, 251.
Lower Brule [tribe], 454.
Lower Great Lakes, 43, 52, 54, 57, 59, 63, 68, 70, 72, 74, 75, 79, 81, 84, 87, 103, 108, 110, 187, 230.
Lower Red Lake, 142, 144, 145, 147, 149, 152, 163, 165, 167, 168, 169, 172, 175, 176, 183, 184, 187, 191, 192, 193, 194, 195, 197, 204, 206, 210, 231, 233.
Lusson, Sieur de St. 251, 252.
Ma`heo, xvii, 5, 8, 13, 14, 17, 150, 155, 158, 243.
Mackay, Donald 439, 440.
Mackay, James, 440, 441, 453.
Maha [tribe], 312.
Mahabozo, 5, 8.
Mahohe`was, xvii.
Malecite [tribe], 59.
Maliseet [tribe], 46.
Mammoth, 4, 17.
Mandan [tribe], 151, 154, 155, 224, 293, 296, 301, 307, 308, 309, 317, 320, 325, 347, 348, 349, 350, 351, 353, 354, 355, 356, 357, 358, 359, 361, 375, 376, 377, 378, 382, 383, 384, 385, 387, 389, 390, 391, 393, 394, 395, 396, 397, 398, 399, 400, 401, 402, 403, 412, 413,422, 428, 429, 430, 431, 432, 433, 434, 437, 439, 440, 444, 448, 452, 462, 463, 464, 465, 488.
Manhroats [tribe], 361.
Manitoba, 12, 23, 25, 26, 44, 45, 47, 51, 53, 56, 81, 102, 127, 128, 135, 136, 138, 139, 140, 193, 196, 201, 208, 211, 257, 262, 493, 494, 499.
Manitoulin Island, 107, 114.
Many Flies [tribe], 29, 174.
Maple Creek, 274, 291, 301, 304, 325, 334, 335, 342, 343, 390, 393, 414.

Maple River, vii, 325.
Marquette, Father Jacques, 255, 256.
Marston, Major, 50.
Maryland, 2.
Mascoutecs [tribe], 182.
Mascoutens [tribe], 181-182, 252, 389.
Masikota, xvi, 32, 162, 163, 164, 165, 167, 168, 170, 171, 173, 175, 176, 177, 178, 181, 184, 207, 208, 216, 236, 237, 247, 248, 257, 258, 259, 261, 267, 268, 269, 273, 274, 275, 276, 282, 284, 285, 288, 289, 291, 297, 298, 299 *passim.*
Maskoutecs [tribe], 389.
Maskouten [tribe],, 220.
Maskoutepoel [tribe], 389.
Massachusetts, [Tribe], 54, 59.
Massaum, xvii, 19, 38, 158, 159, 166, 488.
*M*mastodon, 17.
Matabele [tribe], 230.
Matawin River, 74, 75.
McKenzie, Charles, 435.
Mdewancanton [tribe], 412.
Medicine Arrows, [Mahuts], xvi.
Medicine Lodge or Willow Dance,, xvii.
Medicine Bird, Nelson 405.
Medicine-Crow, Joe [informant], xii, 147.
Medicine-Elk, Wayne [informant], xii.
Mega-fauna, 4, 5, 17, 19.
Menominee [tribe], 1, 30, 50, 63, 121, 210, 220, 249, 252, 254, 260.
Menque [Mengwe], 80.
Mero complex, 82, 136, 138, 148, 149, 209, 210, 211.
Mescalero [tribe], 362, 366.
Miami [tribe], 1, 47, 50, 67, 136, 181, 182, 210, 220.
Michabo, 5.
Michelson, Truman,, xiii, 13, 24, 29, 36, 39, 159, 165, 216, 227, 261, 270, 309, 408, 411.
Michigan, 87.
Micmac [tribe], 46, 55, 56.
Middle Laurel culture, 47, 128, 209.
Middle Woodland culture, 51.
Mill Creek culture, 307.
Mille Lacs, 207, 220, 222, 250, 254, 255, 258, 260, 291.
Mini Ha-Ha Falls, 73, 282.
Minnesota state, v, 22, 23, 58.
Minnesota River, 20, 94, 142, 144, 147, 152, 167, 168, 169, 170, 177, 181, 182, 183, 194, 203, 206, 207, 231, 262.
Minnesota., v, 23.
Minniconjou [tribe], 270, 274, 335, 430, 441, 461, 462, 473, 480.
Mississippi headwaters, 27, 38, 39, 147, 151, 152, 156, 159, 162, 165, 169, 175, 181, 193, 194, 195, 207, 213, 220, 235, 256, 485.
Missouri River, xx, 15, 22, 23, 32, 34, 36, 41, 76, 96, 98, 101, 135, 156, 175, 186, 211, 212, 226, 227, 236, 239, 240, 257, 292, 485.
Mohawk [tribe], 63, 68.

Moiseo [Cheyennes], xvi, xx, 21, 29, 30, 31, 32, 34, 36, 37, 38, 39, 41, 43, 45, 46, 50, 52, 54, 57, 58, 61, 63, 69, 71, 72, 74, 75, 76, 77, 79, 80, 82, 85, 87, 88, 89, 90, 91, 92, 95, 96, 97, 98, 99, 100, 102, 103, 105, 107, 108, 110, 112, 113, 114, 115, 118, 119, 120, 121, 122, 127, 128, 133, 134, 135, 136, 138, 139, 140, 148, 149, 157, 158, 162 *passim.*

Mongol, 1, 2, 4, 8, 11,12, 18, 48, 50, 94,487.

Monsoni [tribe], 1, 29, 31, 32, 33, 34, 36, 37, 38, 39, 40, 43, 44, 45, 46, 47, 54, 57, 61, 63, 71, 73, 74, 79, 82, 87, 88, 89, 90, 91, 92, 95, 98, 100, 105, 107, 108, 110, 112, 116, 118, 119, 120, 128, 133, 134, 135, 139, 148, 152, 164, 166, 175, 187, 191, 192, 193, 197, 200, 213, 214, 216, 217, 219, 223, 228, 229, 230, 234, 238, 247, 248, 249, 250, 252, 254, 255, 256, 257, 258, 260, 262, 275, 346, 356, 408, 412, 416, 489.

Monsoni / Plains Cree [tribe], 61.

Montagnais [tribe], 1, 13, 25, 29, 31, 33, 34, 36, 37, 38, 40, 41, 43, 44, 45, 46, 47, 48, 50, 51, 52, 57, 59, 60, 61, 63, 71, 74, 82, 84, 87, 88, 89, 90, 91, 96, 100, 102, 107, 108, 110, 120, 133, 134, 148, 161, 166, 168, 208, 209, 489, 502.

Montagnais-Naskapi dialect, 25.

Montreal, 40, 44, 45, 50, 60, 62, 64, 68, 72, 73, 74, 79, 81, 84, 85, 86, 89, 90, 92, 99, 110, 111, 114, 157, 197, 199, 259, 267, 272, 286, 287, 408.

Montreal Island, 74, 86.

Mooney, James., xiii, 13, 25, 29, 73, 94, 121, 167, 175, 348, 351, 359, 421, 488.

Moore, John H., 121, 500.

Moose people [tribe], 61.

Moreau River, 351, 353, 354, 355, 356, 357, 360, 387, 396, 441, 463.

Morgan, Lewis H., 39.

Morgana, 8.

Moses, 154.

Mosquitoes [tribe], 174.

Motsonitanio, 32, 36, 39, 177, 226.

Mount Tamora, 444.

Mourant, A. E., 1.

Mowissiyu [Cheyennes], 29, 32, 36.

Mundua [tribe], 91, 92, 95, 96, 97, 99, 102, 105, 107, 111, 120, 193.

Munsey [tribe], 31.

Muskegon Cree [tribe], 29, 61, 63, 88, 89, 90, 128, 135, 139, 192, 193, 197, 200, 228, 256.

Musk-ox, 4.

Nacion du chien, [tribe] 220, 223.

Nadouechiouek [tribe], 145.

Nadourononons [tribe], 199.

Nakomis Complex, 51, 54.

Narraganset [tribe], 57.

Naskapi [tribe], 13.

Natick [tribe], 43.

Navahos [tribe], 242.

Navah-hous [Bear Butte], 243, 348, 388, 483.

Neanderthal, 1, 9, 17.

Neutrals, 79.

Neutral [Hurons], 72, 79, 271.

New Brunswick, 54, 59.

New York State, 64.

Newfoundland, 11, 52, 55, 108.

Nez Perce [tribe], 102.

Niagara Falls, 73.

Nicolet, Jean 197, 250, 254

Niobrara River, 347, 437, 441, 466, 481.

Nipissings [tribe], 85, 252.

No-Ear`s winter count, 428, 480.

Norse, 8, 10, 11, 105.

North Arvilla culture, 148.

North Atlantic Ocean., xii, 2.

North Atlantic seaboard, 46.

North Platte, 349, 383, 384, 443, 455.

Northern Asiatic, 1, 4, 6, 9, 11, 12, 18, 47, 51, 127, 487.

Northern Cheyenne, xv.

Northern Europe, 4.

Northern Hemisphere, 4, 19.

northern Minnesota, 20, 56, 59, 88, 112, 126, 127, 128, 129, 133, 138, 140, 144, 146, 147, 148, 149, 151, 154, 156, 158, 163, 165, 168, 174, 176, 183, 185, 186, 187, 189, 190, 192, 193, 195, 197, 200, 202, 203, 204, 206, 207, 208, 209, 224, 225, 226, 228, 229, 232, 238, 239, 243, 248, 249, 251, 255, 256, 261

Northern Plains, 50, 52.

Notsawaga Bay, 72.

Nova Scotia Island, 54, 59.

Odsell, A. R. 453.

Oglala [tribe], 187, 270, 315, 332, 420, 427, 428, 451, 452, 454, 455, 456, 457, 458, 459, 460, 461, 463, 464, 465, 466, 467, 468, 469, 471, 473, 478, 479, 480, 481.

Ohio, 81.

Ohio River, 487.

Oivimana [Cheyennes], xvi.

Ohk`tsin Lance, vii, 93, 94, 95, 158, 159.

Oki, 8.

Oktouna [Cheyennes], xvi.

Old Bull, Dan, 405.

Old Woman Creek, 470.

Old Woman Phase, 56, 136.

Omaha [tribe], 189, 190, 207, 282, 287, 288, 289, 290, 291, 292, 297, 298, 301, 303, 304, 305, 306, 307, 308, 309, 310, 311, 312, 313, 314, 315, 316, 317, 323, 328, 331, 332, 347, 349, 350, 353, 358, 361, 362, 363, 364, 365, 366, 367, 387, 395, 402, 415, 443, 458, 460,463, 466, 480, 481, 482, 498.

Omissis [Cheyennes], xvi, xx, 36, 76, 77, 79, 80, 98, 101, 105, 107, 108, 119, 121, 122, 127, 162, 163, 165, 167, 175, 178, 183, 184, 208, 236, 237, 238, 250, 254, 257, 258, 259, 261, 262, 267, 269, 273, 274, 282, 285, 287, 289, 297, 298, 302, 306, 307, 317, 318, 343, 350, 359, 404, 408, 418, 426, 432,

434, 438, 442, 443, 444, 446, 459, 464, 466, 479, 481, 482.

Oneota, 285, 287, 290, 291, 292, 293, 294, 296, 297, 298, 299, 325, 328.

Ontario, viii, 31, 41, 45, 46, 47, 50, 51, 53, 54, 57, 62, 65, 67, 68, 69, 73, 76, 79, 80, 81, 82, 85, 87, 112, 119, 122, 126, 127, 128, 129, 133, 134, 135, 136, 138, 139, 140, 141, 145, 148, 149, 152, 156, 157, 166, 167, 168, 170, 174, 184, 185, 186, 189, 192, 201, 202, 208, 209, 210, 211, 256, 258, 262, 487

Oppelzer, 322.

Ordway, John, 481.

Orphans, v, 94, 102, 460.

Osage [tribe], 182, 183, 190.

Oto [tribe], 181, 182, 190, 194, 203, 207, 232, 282, 283, 285, 286, 287, 288, 289, 290, 291, 292, 294, 297, 298, 301, 303, 304, 305, 306, 307, 308, 310, 311, 312, 313, 314, 315, 316, 317, 323, 328, 332, 348, 350, 361, 362, 363, 387, 402, 405, 466, 481.

Ottawa [tribe], 1, 33, 50, 51, 52, 54, 57, 62, 63, 64, 68, 69, 81, 84, 85, 87, 102, 108, 110, 113, 114, 124, 188, 189, 190, 192, 193, 198, 223, 225, 230, 231, 246, 251, 498, 504.

Ottawa River, 52, 110.

Ouadabatons [tribe], 412.

Ouiss [tribe]i, 183.

Own`s-the-Pole, 478.

Owner-of-Flute, 471, 473.

Owuqeo [tribe], 352, 353, 356, 357, 358, 359, 360.

Ox`zem lance, vii.

Pachot, 390.

Padouca [tribe], 307, 308, 309, 310, 311, 312, 313, 316, 317, 348, 360, 361, 362, 363, 364, 365, 366, 367, 372, 402.

Pakistan, 17.

Palaeo-Asiatic, 4, 11.

Palaeo-European, 12.

Palaeolithic,, xx.

Palaeo-Siberian, 1.

Paleolithic Algonquian, 13.

Pana [tribe], 307-308.

Pana-Maha [tribe] 311-313.

Pani Blanc [tribe], 308, 364, 402.

Pani-Noir [tribe], 308, 364, 402.

Panis [tribe], 307, 308, 348, 361, 362, 363, 368, 388, 402.

Passamaquoddy [tribe], 54, 59.

Pawnee [tribe], xii, 39, 301, 303, 308, 309, 311, 312, 313, 317, 320, 349, 350, 357, 361, 362, 363, 364, 365, 386, 387, 390, 391, 402, 455.

People of the Bow [tribe], 163, 259, 324, 378, 379, 381, 385, 388, 403, 404, 411.

People of the White Wolf [tribe], 61.

Pequot [tribe], 57.

Perrot, Nicholas, 64, 183.

Petter, Rudolph, 29, 171, 173, 212, 225.

Petun Huron [tribe], 71, 72, 79.

Piapot, 197.

Picket-Pin, 469.

Picuris [tribe], 371, 372, 403.

Pigeon River, 276, 278.

Pipe-Stem-Men [Cheyennes], 127, 165, 168, 169, 207, 267, 274, 275, 282, 298, 299, 302, 303, 304, 305, 306, 307, 308, 309, 310, 312, 313, 314, 315, 316, 317, 318, 328, 331, 332, 333, 334, 346, 347, 348, 349, 350, 351, 353, 354, 358, 359, 360, 361, 362, 363, 364, 367, 370, 372, 385, 386, 387, 388, 392, 396, 399, 402, 403, 404, 406, 426, 441, 443, 444, 458, 481.

Pipe-Stone Quarries, 176, 177, 211, 233.

Pitapahata [tribe], 442.

Plains Apache [tribe], 316, 353, 362, 363, 366, 486.

Plains Cree [tribe], 26, 29, 33, 37, 38, 44, 61, 128, 139, 172, 192, 193, 197, 201, 213, 227, 228, 229, 278, 281, 282, 319, 338, 344, 345, 346, 401, 402, 413, 416, 419, 420.

Platte River, 362, 364, 443, 448.

Pleistocene period, 15.

Plenty-Hoops, Winona [Crow informant], xii.

Point Peninsular culture, 81.

Poison Blancs [tribe], 37.

Ponca [tribe], 307, 311, 314, 316, 350, 353, 362, 363, 364, 366, 367, 387, 395, 415, 460.

Porcupine Creek, vi, vii, 274, 334, 335, 342, 343, 344, 346, 351, 353, 357, 358, 360, 386, 390, 392, 393, 395, 397, 398, 399, 400, 401, 403, 411, 414, 416, 417, 426, 427, 431, 432, 434.

Porter, Peter 459.

Portugal, 2.

Potawatomi [tribe], 1, 30, 50, 63, 84, 85, 110, 119, 172, 181, 182, 189, 190, 230, 249.

Poualaks [tribe], 145.

Powell, Father Peter, 213, 241, 244.

Powhatan confederacy [tribe], 54.

Prairie Men [tribe], xvi, 170, 173, 176, 179, 222, 273.

Proto-Algonquians, 4, 5, 8, 9, 17, 26, 29, *Passim.*

Proto-Arapahoe, 82, 129, 136, 138, 148, 210, 485.

Proto-Cheyenne, xx, 15, 18, 20, *Passim.*

Proto-Iroquians, 4.

Proto-Siouans, 4.

Pueblo [tribe], 362, 366, 369, 370, 371, 372, 386, 402, 403, 446.

Pyrenees, 9.

Qu`Appelle, 211.

Quafsi [tribe] 183.

Quapaw [tribe], 190.

Quassis [tribe[, 275.

Quebec, 39, 40, 53, 102.

Quebec Province., 74.

Quissicouseton [tribe], 183.

Quissiloua [tribe], 183, 219, 267.

Quissy, [tribe] 183, 257, 289, 411.

Radisson, Pierre 61, 124, 145, 182, 196, 199, 200, 246, 254.

Rafinesque, C. S., 45.

Rainy Lake, 73, 75, 127, 142, 144, 187, 191, 196, 222, 229, 249, 256, 276, 277, 278, 279, 281, 346, 408, 423, 424.
Rainy River, 73.
Raudot, Antoine D., 116.
Rawhide Butte, 471, 472, 473.
Red-Arm, 482.
Red Bead Indians [tribe], 444.
Red-Cloud, 315, 316, 457, 458, 460, 462.

Red-Hat, Edward, xii, 145, 163, 165.
Red Lake, v, 146, 147, 152, 160, 165, 168, 178, 187, 206, 207, 231.
Red Lakes, 147, 148, 154, 164, 194, 195, 197, 202, 206.
Red-Paint, 236.
Red River of the North, 23, 24, 26, 135, 136, 138, 142, 146, 147, 148, 191, 193, 202, 204, 206, 208, 210, 214, 228, 231, 235, 236, 238, 239, 261, 262, 268, 269, 273, 274, 275, 276, 277, 278, 281, 282, 284, 291, 292, 304, 310, 312, 318, 319, 321, 324, 326, 329, 332, 333, 334, 337, 340, 343, 344, 345, 346, 383, 411, 412, 418, 422, 425, 428, 453, 459.
Red River valley, 23, 24.
Red Shields, xvii, 165, 237, 407, 408, 409.
Red-Tassels, 236.
Red Water, 405.
Red White Men, 408.
Ridge Men [Cheyennes], xvi, 165, 307, 318, 359, 426, 437, 481.
Riggs, Stephen R. 300, 493, 501.
River of Turtles, 73.
River Tribes, 293, 347, 367, 386, 400, 431, 446, 463, 465.
Riviere des Assinibouels, 275, 276, 278.
Rocky Mountains, 214.
Rolling Head, 25, 125, 490, 502.
Roman-Nose, 241.
Round-heads, 13.
Rum River, 222, 254, 283.
Rustling-Corn-Leaf, 156.
Saber-Tooth Tiger, 6.
Sacred Arrows, 32, 36, 39, 94, 98, 134, 145, 149, 150, 151, 152, 159, 160, 163, 164, 175, 177, 236, 239, 269, 389, 392, 436, 479, 485.
Sacred Buffalo Hat ["Issiwun"], vii, xvi, 38.
Sacred Buffalo Head [Hat], 236.
Sacred Buffalo-Calf Pipe, 479.
Sacred Mountain, 155.
Sacred Red Score, 11.
Sacred Red Stone, 406.
Sage, Rufus B, 448, 470.
Saginaw Bay, 87, 110, 111, 119.
Saguenay River, 79, 223.
Sakhalin Island, 4.
SaKota [tribe], 175.
Sami reindeer herders, 12.
Sand Hill People, 177.

Sandy Lake, 145, 291.
Sans Arc [tribe], 270, 463, 479.
Santee [tribe], 220, 250, 260, 270, 281, 297, 319, 332, 333, 421, 454, 457, 458, 459, 462, 463.
Sarsi [tribe], 102, 488.
Saskatchewan, 23, 24, 44, 56, 135, 136, 139, 196, 208, 211, 227, 228, 262, 278, 329, 344, 369, 383, 388.
Sauk [tribe], 1, 38, 40, 44, 46, 47, 50, 61, 62, 63, 71, 79, 87, 90, 95, 96, 107, 108, 110, 111, 113, 119, 120, 136, 190, 209, 220, 231, 243, 244, 246, 249, 251, 252, 254, 485.
Sault St. Marie, 40, 71, 82, 86, 111, 112, 113, 114, 115, 118, 119, 120, 121, 122, 129, 134, 136, 139, 167, 192, 197, 199, 210, 213, 216, 219, 220, 228, 229, 230, 246, 251, 260.
Saulteaux [tribe], 33, 59.
Scandinavian, 2, 8, 11, 12, 50, 52, 105, 106, 108.
Scarred-Arms [tribe], 448, 470.
Schahas [tribe], 283, 284.
Schianese [tribe], 415.
Schians, [tribe] 415, 435.
Schlesier, Karl H., xii, 215, 485, 486, 501 485.
Schoolcraft, Henry, 142.
Scioto River, 81.
Sea of the West, 286, 408.
Selkirk culture phase, vii, 61, 119, 128, 148, 209, 211.
Seneca [tribe], 63, 85.
Shahsweentowahs [tribe], 415.
Shawa [tribe], 440.
Shawanigan Falls,, 74, 79.
Shawnee [tribe], 1, 47, 50, 61, 63, 65, 113, 127, 408.
Shea [village site]eyo, 325, 326, 327, 328.
Sheridan, General Phil., ix.
Sheshkeput, 422, 423, 424, 425, 429.
Shevitaun [tribe], 440.
Shevitoons, [tribe] 439, 440, 441.
Shew [tribe], 439.
Sheyenne River, vi, vii, 147, 202, 208, 268, 269, 274, 281, 291, 292, 293, 294, 296, 301, 317, 319, 322, 323, 324, 325, 326, 327, 330, 332, 337, 338, 340, 341, 342, 343, 346, 351, 359, 386, 392, 400, 403, 412, 416, 417, 418, 419, 422, 425, 426, 427, 429, 443, 453.
Sheyenne River village, 341, 342, 429.
Sheyo [tribe], 234, 237,335, 416.
Shield Archaic culture, 12, 46, 47.
Shiyo [tribe], 416, 480.
Shiwitoons [tribe], 440.
Shonaskitons [tribe], 222, 238, 285.
Shongashiton [tribe], 224, 270, 342.
Shoshoni [tribe], 4, 59, 353, 360, 361, 362, 363, 364, 365, 366, 367, 369, 446, 447, 448, 449, 488.
Shota-winniwug [tribe], 213, 225, 229.
Shuar [tribe], 440.
Siberia, xii, 1, 2, 4, 8, 9, 10, 12, 17, 48, 49, 51, 488
Siberian Peoples, viii.
Siebert, Frank, 52.

Siouan, 19, 20, 22, 105, 112, 127, 128, 134, 145, 170, 171, 182, 189, 190, 194, 209, 229, 250, 251, 267, 270, 282, 283, 284, 285, 287, 290, 291, 292, 293, 294, 296, 297, 304, 305, 306, 308, 309, 312, 314, 344, 346, 348, 363, 364, 396, 399, 452, 454, 466, 488.

Sioux [tribe], xii, xvi, xix, 19, 20, 21, 22, 32, 36, 38, 43, 50, 58, 98, 121, 139, 142, 145, 164, 165, 169, 171, 175, 176, 178, 181, 182, 183, 185, 186, 187, 190, 191, 193, 194, 196, 197, 199, 200, 202, 204, 207, 219, 220, 222, 223, 224, 225, 228, 229, 231, 232, 233, 238, 239, 243, 247, 248, 249, 250, 251, 252, 254, 255, 256, 257, 258, 259, 260, 261, 262, 316, 488, 501.

Sioux of the Prairies, 332, 333, 382, 389, 390, 408, 427.

Sisseton [tribe], 21, 190, 191, 207, 222, 250, 297, 304, 319, 332, 333, 414, 418, 419, 421, 458, 459, 462, 463, 466.

Skidi [tribe], 301, 309, 311, 312, 313, 315, 349, 350, 353, 357, 386, 387, 390, 402.

Skutani [tribe], 212, 270, 417, 440, 445, 483.

Slaves, 94, 192, 193, 198, 202, 252, 260, 264, 307-311, 332, 348, 361, 363, 369, 379m, 468..

Smallpox, 37, 106, 157, 354, 360, 384, 391, 400, 433, 440, 466, 479.

Snakes [tribe], 58, 59, 60, 61, 62, 63, 64, 67, 68, 71, 82, 84, 353, 356, 360, 361, 362, 363, 364, 365, 366, 367, 369, 372, 376, 378, 380, 381, 382, 384, 385, 392, 422, 440, 446, 447, 448, 449, 450, 452, 462, 464, 469.

Solutrean Culture, 2.

Songaskitons [tribe], 225, 260.

Soulard, 441, 444.

South Arvilla culture, 136, 148.

South Asia peoples, xii.

South Dakota, xx, 24.

Southern Cheyenne, xv.

Southern Chippewa, 118.

Southern France, 2.

Southern Ontario, 45.

South-western Europe, 2.

Spain, 2.

Spanish, 25, 75, 161, 308, 310, 312, 347, 360, 361, 362, 363, 364, 365, 366, 367, 368, 369, 370, 371, 372, 377, 379, 385, 386, 401, 402, 403, 422, 427, 430, 433, 434, 440, 441, 443, 446, 448, 449, 461, 464.

Spirit Being, 7.

Spotted-Wolf, Clarence `Bisco`, xii.

Squihitans [tribe],270, 417, 440, 442.

St. Croix River, 73, 121, 190, 249, 262, 276, 282, 283, 284, 285, 286, 289, 297, 412, 415, 417.

St. Francis, 283.

St. Lawrence Algonquians, 96.

St. Lawrence River, 37, 39, 40, 43, 44, 50, 57, 60, 62, 75, 81, 95, 119, 120, 138, 198.

St. Lusson, Sieur de, 251.

St. Maurice River, 33, 37, 41, 45, 74, 75, 80, 88, 89, 92, 96, 97, 102, 105, 108, 223.

Staihitans [tribe], 270, 440, 442, 483.

Standing-All-Night, 239, 240, 342, 407, 408, 409.

Standing-Sweet-Grass, 156.

Stands in Timber, John, vii, 19, 144, 169, 170, 176, 177, 181, 244,341, 437, 440, 451, 490, 491

Stanford, Dennis, 2.

Stone Hammer Mountain, 244.

Stone Medicine Wheels, 6

Stone-Calf, ix.

Strong, William, 319, 324, 493, 505.

Stump-Horn, 405, 406.

Sub-Arctic, 13.

Sub-Arctic Cree [tribe], 29.

Suhtaio [tribe], ii, iv, v, vi, xii, xvi, 22, 24, 27, 38, 56, 119, 121, 129, 134, 136, 138, 149, 162, 163, 165, 169, 170, 176, 177, 178, 208, Sun Dance, xvii, 38, 158, 238, 488, 498 *passim.*

Sun`s-Road, 241.

Susquehanna River, 69.

Swampy Cree [tribe], 29.

Swazi [tribe], 230.

Sweet-Medicine, xv, 149, 150, 151, 154, 155, 156, 159, 160, 161, 162, 163, 164, 165, 166, 226, 305, 485.

Sweet-Medicine-Chief, 166.

Sweet-Root-Standing, 156.

Swift Hawks, xvii.

Tacoropa [Lakota band], 475, 477, 481.

Tadoussac, 33, 37, 54, 57, 73, 79,90, 97, 193,198, 223

Tall-Bull, Bill [Informant], xii, 482.

Tallegwi [tribe], 69, 70, 84.

Talon, Jean Baptiste, 251.

Tanner, John, 125.

Taos [tribe], 372.

Tashota, [tribe] 214.

Tayenes, [tribe] 433.

Teton River, 443.

Teton Sioux [tribe], 21, 22, 36, 102, 181, 187, 207, 223, 262, 271, 275, 282, 299, 307, 310, 311, 315, 334, 335, 390, 408, 416, 417, 451, 452, 455, 456, 458, 460, 461, 462, 463, 466, 467, 468, 469, 482.

The Great Hare, 5, 8.

The Great Race, 17.

The Lance, 457.

The Wolf, 24.

Thompson, David, 146, 196, 366, 422, 423, 425, 426, 429, 490, 491.

Thule Eskimo, 58.

Tibet, 17.

Timber Mountain, 155, 211, 406, 482.

Time of Buffalo, xix, 13.

Time of Dogs, xix, 13, 145.

Time of Horses, xix, 13.

Tintons [tribe], 270, 315, 415, 458.

Tobacco, 75.

Tokaninambich [tribe] 442, 443.

Tokiwako [tribe], 385, 442.

Totoimana, [Cheyennes] 212.

Trading fairs, 79.

Trois Rivieres, 54, 71, 74, 79, 96, 97.

Trudeau, Jean Baptiste, 13, 41, 257, 384, 400, 411, 434, 442, 445, 446, 447, 453, 457, 461, 473, 474, 475, 480, 491.

TsisTsisTsas, xii, xv, xvi, xvii, 5, 24, 25, 29-31, 76, 77, 94, 127, 129, 133, 164, 169, 170, 176-178, 180, 214, 236, 242, 243-246, 302, 484.

Tungus [tribe], 2.

Tunguska River, 6.

Two Kettle [tribe], 270.

Underworld, the, 9.

Upper Great Lakes, v, 22, 43, 44, 50, 51, 54, 56, 64, 71, 84, 105, 110, 111, 113, 114, 118, 120, 124, 128, 135, 136, 191, 192, 193, 198, 203, 213, 216, 219, 222, 225, 228, 238, 239, 243, 244, 246, 248, 250, 254, 256, 259, 263, 497.

Upper Minnesota River, 20.

Upper Mississippi, viii, 20, 25, 27, 39, 41, 74, 75, 120, 121, 129, 133, 134, 140, 142, 146, 148, 149, 152, 162, 164, 167, 168, 170, 173, 175, 176, 178, 179, 182, 183, 185, 186, 187, 190, 191, 194, 197, 202, 204, 206, 207, 208 passim.

Upper Mississippi Forks, 187.

Upper Missouri, 146, 147, 499, 503.

Upper St. Lawrence, 72.

Upper St. Maurice, 37.

Ursa Major, 7.

Utes [tribe], 362, 370, 454, 469.

Vikings, 11, 52, 59.

Waddapawjestin [tribe], 415, 462, 480.

Wahepaton [tribe], 415.

Wallum Ollum, 11, 45, 46, 47, 50, 51, 52, 53, 58, 59, 60, 61, 63, 64, 67, 68, 69, 70, 71, 73, 75, 80, 82, 84, 85, 88, 97, 99, 104, 105, 486, 489, 497.

Wan-Wan ceremony, 183.

Warren, Lieutenant G. K. 481.

Warren, William, 86, 146 .

Warrior Societies, xvi, xvii, 32, 151, 159, 162-166, 180, 226, 227, 237-239, 355, 360, 482, 490, 504.

Watapio [Cheyennes], xvi, 165, 181, 271, 481.

Waters, Michael R., 2.

Wazikute [tribe], 186, 270.

Welch, Colonel A. B. 293.

Weslager, C. A., 49, 80, 489.

West Main or Swampy Cree [tribe], 29.

Western Cree [tribe], 33, 38.

Western Europe, 2.

Western Men [tribes], 88.

Western or Plains Cree [tribe], 26.

Western Plains, 95, 485.

Western Cree tribes], 29.

Wheel-Lance, 93, 94, 95, 158, 159.

Wheskerinni [tribe], 1, 33, 34, 36-38, 40, 41, 45-47, 63, 71, 74, 79, 87-91, 95-98, 100, 102, 107, 108, 110, 120, 133, 134, 164, 166, 168, 174, 223.

Whiiu`Nutkiu [Cheyennes], xvii.

White Buffalo Woman, 10.

White Bull, 216, 225, 227, 234, 235, 236, 261.

White-Bull, vii, 219, 234, 241, 270, 443, 473

White-Bull, Joseph 473.

White Dirt, 234, 235.

White Earth, 145, 147.

White-Frog, 389, 405, 452.

White River, 309, 314-17, 347-49, 351, 387, 458, 466.

White-Tail, Ralph, 160.

White-Thunder, 439.

Whkesh`hetaniu [Cheyennes], xvii.

Whoksihitanio [Cheyennes], 226.

Wied, Prince Maximilian Zu 353.

Wilipawi [tribe], 63.

Will, George, 439.

Williamson, Rev. T. S. 300, 453.

Wilson, Gilbert, 398.

Winnebago [tribe], 190, 251.

Winter Man, 6.

Winter-Counts, xix.

Wisconsin, 57, 71.

Wise-Buffalo, 234.

Wolf-Chief, 236.

Wolf Soldiers,, xvii.

Woods [Cree] [tribe], 29.

Woolly mammoth, 4.

World Below, 6, 7.

Wrapped Hairs [tribe], 241.

Wright, James V. xii, 504.

Wyandot [tribe], 70, 72.

Wynkoop, Edward [Agent], ix.

Wyoming, 24.

Yakut [tribe], 2.

Yamparika [tribe], 364, 369, 448, 449, 469.

Yankton [tribe], 21, 190, 194, 231, 255, 256, 262, 269, 270, 271, 281, 289, 292, 296, 297, 298, 299, 301, 308, 310, 311, 313, 314, 315, 316, 318, 319, 332, 333, 383, 394, 406, 413, 418, 421, 454, 458, 459, 460, 462.

Yanktonais [tribe], 20, 21, 22, 25, 98, 186, 187, 190, 191` 192, 193, 194, 195, 196, 197, 231, 254, 262

Yellow Haired Maiden, 8, 9, 20, 76, 79, 99, 244.

Yellow Medicine River, vi, 9, 168, 183, 285, 287, 288, 290, 299, 300, 301, 302, 303, 304, 305, 306, 307, 309, 310, 311, 312, 314, 315, 316, 317, 318, 331, 333, 347, 453, 458.

Young Dogs, 228.

Younger Dryas Period, 4, 17.

Zulu [tribe], 230.

Lightning Source UK Ltd.
Milton Keynes UK
UKHW030447230620
365403UK00005B/547